Southern Living.

1988 ANNUAL RECIPES

Southern Living
1988 ANNUAL RECIPES

Oxmoor House ®

Library of Congress Catalog Number: 79-88364
ISBN: 0-8487-0733-8
ISSN: 0272-2003

Manufactured in the United States of America
First printing 1988

Southern Living®
    Foods Editor: Jean Wickstrom Liles
    Associate Foods Editors: Deborah G. Lowery,
        Susan Payne
    Assistant Foods Editors: Phyllis Young Cordell,
        Helen Anne Dorrough, Susan Dosier
    Editorial Assistants: Karen Brechin, Cathy Dunklin,
        Catherine Garrison
    Test Kitchens Director: Kaye Adams
    Assistant Test Kitchens Director: Patty Vann
    Test Kitchens Staff: Jane Cairns, Judy Feagin, Diane Hogan,
        Peggy Smith
    Photo Stylist: Beverly Morrow
    Senior Foods Photographer: Charles E. Walton IV
        Additional photography by *Southern Living* photog-
        raphers: Sylvia Martin, viii, ix, x, xi upper left and lower
        right, 70; Howard L. Puckett, xi lower left, 105.
    Production Manager: Clay Nordan
    Assistant Production Manager: Wanda Butler

Oxmoor House, Inc.
    Executive Editor: Ann H. Harvey
    Production Manager: Jerry Higdon
    Associate Production Manager: Rick Litton
    Art Director: Bob Nance
    Production Assistant: Theresa Beste

Southern Living® *1988 Annual Recipes*

    Editor: Olivia Kindig Wells
    Copy Editor: Mary Ann Laurens
    Editorial Assistant: Pam Beasley Bullock

    Designer: Carol Middleton
    Illustrator: Barbara Ball

Cover: *(From front) Caramel-Filled Butter Pecan Cake, Baked
Christmas Pudding With Brandy Sauce, and Carolina Dream Cake
(Recipes begin on page 278).*

Page i: *Christmas Salad (page 249).*

Pages ii and iii: *Shrimp Bayou, Cucumber-Stuffed Cherry Tomatoes,
Marinated Flank Steak, and (in back) Eggplant Caviar (pages 261-262).*

Page v: *Seasoned Fried Quail (page 220).*

Page xii: *Cajun-Style Catfish Stew (page 12).*

Back cover: *Pumpkin Chiffon (page 260).*

To find out how you can receive *Southern Living* magazine, write to
Southern Living®, P.O. Box C-119, Birmingham, AL 35283.

Table of Contents

French-Style Potato Salad (page 171)

Green Pepper Soup (page 250)

Right: *Associate Foods Editors Deborah Lowery (left) and Susan Payne analyze favorite foods photos from past years while previewing upcoming food photos.*

Below: *Assistant Foods Editors Susan Dosier (left) and Helen Anne Dorrough research story ideas they are developing.*

Below right: *Editorial Assistant Catherine Garrison (left) and Assistant Foods Editor Phyllis Young Cordell discuss the thousands of recipes submitted each month by our readers.*

Foods Editor Jean Wickstrom Liles handles hundreds of telephone and mail inquiries each month.

Our Year At Southern Living®

Have you ever wondered how the *Southern Living* foods staff selects recipes, or how we test them? Most of our recipes come from cooks who are well known for the delicious food they serve family and friends. The recipes we publish are usually treasures that have been perfected in the contributor's home and then tested in one of our three test kitchens.

As recipes go through our precise testing procedure, they are evaluated on taste, appearance, practicality, and ease of preparation by our discriminating panel of six foods editors, six test kitchens home economists, and *Southern Living* Editor Gary McCalla. On a typical day we taste test 20 to 25 dishes. Once the evaluation is completed, we give an in-house rating to each passing recipe, so that when a reader requests our best chocolate cake recipe, we can actually send our very best.

In addition to recipe testing, our test kitchens home economists artistically prepare dishes for photography. Effective photography also depends upon the skills and talents of our photographer and our photo stylist.

Our foods editors select recipes and plan and write about 300 foods stories each year. Whether the story is a holiday dinner in Texas, a North Carolina pork barbecue, or a low-cholesterol menu, this group of home economists makes *Southern Living* special.

Because we receive thousands of recipes each month from our readers across the South, our files bulge with wonderful recipes. Maintaining these files, typing recipes, and handling daily mail and calls require the skills of our three editorial assistants.

Our 17-member foods staff (the majority married, with children) collectively represents over 122 years of *Southern Living* experience. It's apparent that this dedicated staff likes to cook and eat, is curious about food, and works together as a team. We think you'll agree that this teamwork has produced exciting pages in this *1988 Annual Recipes*.

Jean Wickstrom Liles

Right: *Assistant Test Kitchens Director Patty Vann (left) helps Test Kitchens Director Kaye Adams label pickles and relishes tested in our kitchens.*

Right: *Senior Foods Photographer Charles Walton IV and Senior Photo Stylist Beverly Morrow put finishing touches on setting up a food photo in the studio.*

Left: *Editorial Assistant Karen Brechin (left) sorts incoming recipes while Editorial Assistant Cathy Dunklin unwraps a new assortment of photo props.*

Below left: *Marketing Manager Peggy Smith (left) is assisted by Test Kitchens Home Economist Jane Cairns in purchasing groceries for testing approximately 3500 recipes this year.*

Below: *Test Kitchens Home Economists Diane Hogan (left) and Judy Feagin prepare to taste and evaluate a pasta salad.*

JANUARY

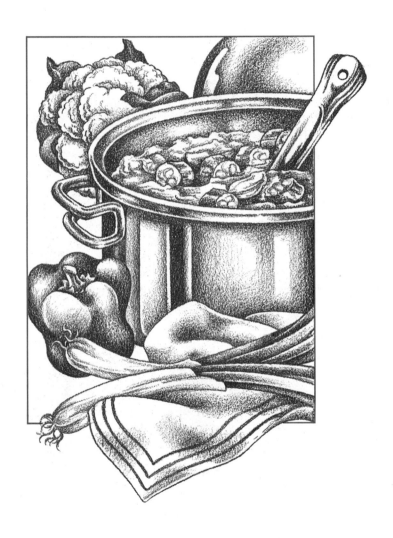

A Party For Good Luck

You may have a hard time keeping up with Ellen McCarn of Birmingham, Alabama. She is an international businesswoman, yet she takes time out to do some creative cooking.

Take her menu for a black-eyed pea party, for instance. It includes a basic recipe, Best Ever Plain Ole Peas, that she stretches into four other colorful and varied dishes. For dessert, Ellen offers her smashing new recipe, Chocolate-Amaretto Heavenly Tarts, saying she counts on serving at least two tarts per guest, and more to the real chocolate lovers in the group.

Spiced Fruit Punch
Layered Seafood Appetizer
Best Ever Plain Ole Peas
Chinese Peas
Cajun Peas
Sweet-and-Sour Peas
Mexi-Peas
Beef Tenderloin
With Mushroom Sauce
Sour Cream-Horseradish Sauce
Marinated Vegetables
Commercial rolls
Chocolate-Amaretto
Heavenly Tarts

SPICED FRUIT PUNCH

10 whole cloves
2 medium-size oranges, cut into ½-inch slices
1 lemon, cut into ½-inch slices
1 (46-ounce) can pineapple juice
1 (32-ounce) bottle apple juice
Juice of 1 lemon
1 (3-inch) stick cinnamon
¼ cup honey
¼ teaspoon ground cinnamon
¼ teaspoon ground allspice
¼ teaspoon ground nutmeg
1 (33.8-ounce) bottle ginger ale

Insert cloves into fruit slices. Combine fruit slices and next 8 ingredients in a Dutch oven; simmer, uncovered, 30 minutes. Remove cinnamon stick. Add ginger ale; heat and serve hot, or add ice and serve cold. Yield: about 3 quarts.

Note: Add 1 (25.4-ounce) bottle white wine or champagne, if desired. Yield: about 4½ quarts.

LAYERED SEAFOOD APPETIZER

2½ cups water
¾ pound unpeeled medium-size fresh shrimp
1 (8-ounce) package cream cheese, softened
½ cup commercial sour cream
¼ teaspoon onion salt
Dash of ground red pepper
¼ cup plus 2 tablespoons chili sauce
1½ teaspoons Worcestershire sauce
¾ teaspoon lemon juice
½ teaspoon prepared horseradish
¼ teaspoon dried whole tarragon (optional)
Parsley sprigs (optional)
Lemon slices (optional)

Bring water to a boil; add shrimp, and cook 3 to 5 minutes. Drain well; rinse with cold water. Peel and devein shrimp. Chop two-thirds of shrimp, and set aside the remaining shrimp for garnish. Chill.

Beat cream cheese at medium speed of an electric mixer until light and fluffy. Add sour cream, onion salt, and a dash of red pepper; beat until mixture is smooth. Spread mixture onto a serving platter, shaping into a 5-inch circle 1 inch thick. Cover platter, and chill cream cheese round at least 30 minutes.

Combine chili sauce, Worcestershire sauce, lemon juice, and horseradish in a small bowl; stir well. Spread mixture over cream cheese round. Sprinkle with chopped shrimp. Top with whole shrimp. If desired, sprinkle with tarragon, and garnish with parsley sprigs and lemon slices. Cover and chill at least 30 minutes. Serve with assorted crackers. Yield: about 3 cups.

Note: One-half pound of lump crabmeat can be substituted for shrimp.

BEST EVER PLAIN OLE PEAS

1 (16-ounce) package dried black-eyed peas
6 cups water
4 slices hickory-smoked bacon
1 tablespoon salt
1 tablespoon sugar
1 tablespoon white wine vinegar
¼ teaspoon pepper
¼ teaspoon garlic salt

Sort and wash peas; place in a large Dutch oven. Cover with water 2 inches above peas; let soak 8 hours. Drain. Add 6 cups water and remaining ingredients. Bring to a boil; cover, reduce heat, and simmer 1½ hours. Yield: 6 cups.

Note: Check the amount of peas used in the ingredient listing of the recipes following to determine how many recipes of Best Ever Plain Ole Peas to make.

Tip: *To freshen air throughout the house, boil 1 tablespoon of whole cloves in a pan of water.*

CHINESE PEAS

1 bunch green onions, sliced
1 teaspoon butter or margarine, melted
1 (8-ounce) can sliced water chestnuts, drained
1 (8-ounce) can bamboo shoots, drained
½ teaspoon chicken-flavored bouillon granules
1 teaspoon teriyaki sauce
1 teaspoon soy sauce
4 cups Best Ever Plain Ole Peas
Salt and pepper to taste
1 bunch green onions, cut into strips
1 teaspoon butter or margarine, melted

Sauté 1 bunch sliced green onions in 1 teaspoon butter in a large skillet until crisp-tender. Add water chestnuts and next 4 ingredients, stirring until blended. Add peas, salt, and pepper. Stir gently until mixed.

Sauté remaining green onions in 1 teaspoon butter.

Transfer peas to serving bowl. Sprinkle onions around edges of bowl. Yield: 8 to 10 servings.

CAJUN PEAS

3 cups cooked long-grain rice
1 (8-ounce) carton commercial sour cream
1 teaspoon poultry seasoning
1 (16-ounce) can red beans, drained
2 cups Best Ever Plain Ole Peas
½ cup diced hickory smoked sausage
½ cup (2 ounces) shredded Monterey Jack cheese

Place rice in a lightly greased 2-quart baking dish. Combine sour cream and poultry seasoning; spread over rice. Combine red beans and peas, and spoon over sour cream mixture. Bake at 350° for 30 minutes. Sprinkle with sausage and cheese; bake an additional 5 minutes. Yield: 8 to 10 servings.

SWEET-AND-SOUR PEAS

8 cups Best Ever Plain Ole Peas
1½ cups commercial sweet-and-sour sauce
1 (8-ounce) can crushed pineapple, drained
2 teaspoons commercial sweet-and-sour sauce
⅓ cup chopped green onions

Combine peas and 1½ cups sweet-and-sour sauce; spoon into a greased 2-quart baking dish. Combine pineapple and 2 teaspoons sweet-and-sour sauce; spoon on top of peas. Sprinkle with green onions. Bake at 350° for 30 minutes. Yield: 8 to 10 servings.

MEXI-PEAS

⅔ cup chopped onion
1 tablespoon butter or margarine, melted
⅔ cup chopped green pepper
1 tomato, peeled and chopped
2 teaspoons chopped jalapeño pepper
½ cup mild taco sauce, divided
4 cups Best Ever Plain Ole Peas
1 (15½-ounce) can Mexican-style chili beans, undrained
1 cup (4 ounces) shredded Cheddar cheese (optional)

Sauté onion in butter in a skillet until crisp-tender. Add green pepper, tomato, jalapeño peppers, and ¼ cup taco sauce, stirring well. Set aside.

Combine peas, chili beans, and ¼ cup taco sauce, stirring well. Spoon into a 2-quart baking dish. Top with vegetable mixture. Bake at 375° for 25 minutes. Sprinkle with cheese, if desired; bake an additional 5 minutes. Yield: 8 to 10 servings.

BEEF TENDERLOIN WITH MUSHROOM SAUCE

1 cup bourbon
1 cup water
Juice of 1 lemon
2 teaspoons Worcestershire sauce
2 teaspoons Pickapeppa sauce
1 teaspoon onion salt
1 teaspoon lemon-pepper seasoning
1 teaspoon paprika
1 (5-pound) beef tenderloin, trimmed
2 slices bacon
½ pound fresh mushrooms, sliced
1 cup water
1½ teaspoons chicken-flavored bouillon granules
1½ teaspoons beef-flavored bouillon granules
2 teaspoons browning-and-seasoning sauce
2 tablespoons cornstarch
¼ cup water
Lettuce (optional)
Tomato rose (optional)

Combine first 8 ingredients; stir well. Spear tenderloin in several places. Place tenderloin and marinade in a zip top heavy-duty plastic bag; seal tightly. Refrigerate 8 hours.

Drain and reserve marinade. Place tenderloin on rack of broiler pan; place bacon lengthwise over tenderloin. Insert meat thermometer, making sure it does not touch fat. Bake at 425° for 45 to 60 minutes or until thermometer registers 140° (rare) or 150° (medium). Baste occasionally with marinade while baking. Remove to a serving platter. Reserve remaining marinade.

Pour remaining marinade in a saucepan; cook over medium heat until reduced to ½ cup. Add mushrooms, 1 cup water, bouillon granules, and browning-and-seasoning sauce; cook until mushrooms are tender. Combine cornstarch and ¼ cup water; stir into mushroom mixture. Bring mixture to a boil; cook 1 minute or until thickened and bubbly, stirring constantly. Brush tenderloin with mushroom sauce. Slice tenderloin, and serve with sauce. If desired, garnish with lettuce and tomato rose. Yield: 12 servings.

SOUR CREAM-HORSERADISH SAUCE

1 (8-ounce) carton commercial sour cream
2 to 3 teaspoons prepared horseradish
1 teaspoon Worcestershire sauce
½ teaspoon onion salt
Dash of ground red pepper

Combine all ingredients; stir well. Cover and chill 1 to 2 hours. Serve with rolls. Yield: about 1 cup.

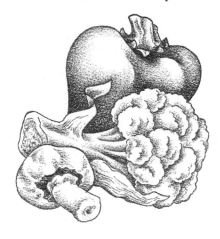

MARINATED VEGETABLES

1 cup olive oil
1½ cups white vinegar
¼ cup sugar
2 teaspoons salt
¾ teaspoon freshly ground pepper
1 clove garlic, minced
12 pearl onions
1 cup water
1 small cauliflower, cut into flowerets
½ pound small fresh mushrooms
2 green peppers, cut into ½-inch strips
18 ripe olives

Combine first 6 ingredients in a saucepan; bring to a boil, stirring constantly. Cool 5 minutes.

Combine onions and water in a saucepan; bring to a boil. Cover, reduce heat, and simmer 2 minutes or until tender; drain.

Combine onions and remaining ingredients in a large bowl; pour marinade over vegetables. Toss gently. Refrigerate 8 hours, stirring occasionally. Yield: 10 to 12 servings.

CHOCOLATE-AMARETTO HEAVENLY TARTS

1 (1-ounce) square unsweetened chocolate
½ cup butter, softened
2 cups powdered sugar
1 tablespoon vanilla extract
Dash of salt
4 egg yolks
3 tablespoons amaretto
1½ cups whipping cream
1½ tablespoons amaretto
Tart shells (recipe follows)
Sliced almonds, toasted (optional)

Melt chocolate in a heavy saucepan over low heat; set aside.

Cream butter; gradually add powdered sugar, beating at medium speed of an electric mixer until smooth. Add chocolate, mixing until blended. Add vanilla and salt; mix until blended. Add egg yolks, one at a time, beating after each addition. Add 3 tablespoons amaretto, 1 tablespoon at a time, beating well after each addition.

Beat whipping cream until soft peaks form. Gradually add 1½ tablespoons amaretto; mix until blended. Fold 1 cup whipped cream mixture into chocolate mixture. Reserve remaining whipped cream for garnishing tarts at serving time.

Fill cooled tart shells with chocolate filling. Chill 3 to 4 hours or until firm. Pipe or dollop with reserved whipped cream. Garnish tarts with toasted almond slices, if desired. Yield: 5 dozen tarts.

Tart Shells

66 vanilla wafers, divided
2 cups flaked coconut, divided
1 cup pecan pieces, divided
1 cup butter or margarine, melted

Crumble 33 vanilla wafers in container of a food processor; add 1 cup coconut, and process 5 seconds. Add ½ cup pecans; process 5 seconds. Transfer wafer crumb mixture to a large mixing bowl. Repeat process with remaining vanilla wafers, coconut, and pecans.

Pour melted butter over crumb mixture; toss lightly until well mixed. Spoon 1 tablespoon crumb mixture into miniature muffin pans. Press on bottom and sides to form crust.

Bake at 375° for 8 to 10 minutes. Cool. Loosen tarts, and fill them in pan. Refrigerate if not served immediately. Yield: 5 dozen tart shells.

From Our Kitchen To Yours

Mention dried peas and beans to a Southerner, and a simmering pot of savory black-eyed peas comes to mind. There are, however, many varieties of dried peas and beans, all of which are flavorful and economical. Served in a bowl of soup, as a bean-based entrée, or in a mixed-bean salad, this food is a source of protein, B vitamins, calcium, iron, complex carbohydrates, and fiber.

At the Market

Buy dried peas and beans in clear packages; examine them for color, size uniformity, and visible defects. Loss of color indicates long storage, which influences cooking time; however, taste and nutritive value are not affected. Mixed sizes cause uneven cooking. Cracked seed coats, foreign materials, and pinholes inflicted by insect damage are signs of a low-quality product.

Storing

Dried peas and beans keep indefinitely in unopened packages or in tightly covered containers. Store in a cool, dry place—not in the refrigerator. After opening a package, do not mix the contents with others because peas and beans stored for greater lengths of time require longer cooking times.

Refrigerate cooked peas and beans in covered containers up to five days, or freeze up to six months.

Soaking

Dried beans require soaking to rehydrate. Dried peas do not require soaking to soften; however, our tests indicate more water is necessary when cooking unsoaked peas.

For quick soaking, add 6 to 8 cups water to 1 pound dried beans. Bring to a boil; cover and cook two minutes. Remove from heat, and let stand for one hour.

For overnight soaking, add 6 cups water to 1 pound dried beans. Let stand eight hours at room temperature. (Beans tend to sour if they are placed in too warm a place.) Beans soaked using this method retain their shape and cook faster.

Cooking

Cooking time varies depending on age of peas and beans, and hardness of cooking water. Generally they cook in 1 to 2½ hours. Split peas and lentils cook in approximately 45 to 55 minutes. Simmer gently to prevent skins from bursting, and stir occasionally to prevent sticking. The longer beans are soaked and the slower they are cooked, the easier they are to digest.

Perk Up Foods With Citrus

Juicy oranges, sunny lemons, blushing grapefruits, and cool, green limes—each fruit imparts its own individual goodness to a host of foods and can be enjoyed year-round.

The beauty of citrus is that the entire fruit can be used. Even the colorful outer rind has tiny oil sacs that are full of intense flavor. When the rind is grated and added to recipes, you get a fresh-as-fruit aroma and rich citrus flavor.

Oranges are a natural for salads. Rather than sectioning oranges, we slice them crosswise into thin slices called cartwheels. This way, less juice is lost and the nutrient-rich membrane can be eaten.

Lemons are a cook's best friend. Just a few drops of their tart juice enhance the natural flavors of other foods, both savory and sweet. It may be added to stews, meatballs, meat loaves, or spaghetti sauce, as well as cakes and breads.

Avocados, mangoes, papayas, and kiwifruit all have richer flavors when they are drenched with lime juice. Limes may be substituted in just about any recipe that calls for lemons, but lemons will rarely do when a recipe calls for limes.

GRAPEFRUIT-AND-SHRIMP SALAD

4½ cups water
1½ pounds unpeeled small fresh shrimp
4 pink grapefruits
Bibb lettuce
4 hard-cooked eggs, chopped
½ cup mayonnaise
¼ cup catsup
1 tablespoon plus 1 teaspoon pickle relish
⅛ teaspoon white pepper

Bring water to a boil; add shrimp, and cook 3 to 5 minutes. Drain well, and rinse with cold water. Peel and devein shrimp.

To make grapefruit shells, use 1 grapefruit for each bowl. Cut a thin slice from stem end of each grapefruit to level the base. Score rind, using a sharp knife to make a shell with 4 petals, starting about 2 inches from top of grapefruit and ending within 2 inches of base. Then cut just through the rind along scoring. Carefully pull each petal from fruit, using a grapefruit knife to separate pulp from rind. Remove grapefruit pulp intact, using thumb to dislodge pulp; set shell aside. Remove white membrane from pulp. Section grapefruit, reserving half of sections for other uses. Repeat entire procedure for all grapefruits.

Line grapefruit shells with lettuce; spoon grapefruit sections into shell. Combine eggs, mayonnaise, catsup, pickle relish, and pepper; spoon egg mixture over grapefruit. Top with shrimp. Yield: 4 servings.

Mrs. W. C. Gibbs
Gadsden, Alabama

FRUIT SALAD WITH CITRUS DRESSING

½ teaspoon grated orange rind
⅔ cup orange juice
½ teaspoon grated lemon rind
⅓ cup lemon juice
⅓ cup firmly packed brown sugar
1 (3-inch) stick cinnamon
½ teaspoon cornstarch
4 oranges, peeled and sliced
2 kiwifruit, peeled and sliced
2 cups fresh pineapple chunks
1 cup seedless red grapes
2 cups fresh strawberries, sliced
3 bananas, sliced

Combine first 7 ingredients in a small saucepan; bring to a boil, stirring constantly. Boil 1 minute. Cool.

Combine oranges, kiwifruit, pineapple chunks, and grapes. Pour dressing over fruit; cover and chill. Add strawberries and bananas; toss gently. Serve immediately. Yield: 6 to 8 servings.
Dorothy Martin
Woodburn, Kentucky

CHICKEN-AND-CELERY SKILLET

4 chicken breast halves
½ teaspoon salt
1½ cups orange juice
1 tablespoon plus 1 teaspoon cornstarch
1 teaspoon salt
¾ teaspoon ground ginger
¾ teaspoon grated orange rind
1½ tablespoons dry sherry
2 cups diagonally sliced celery
¾ cup red pepper strips
¾ cup green pepper strips
2 tablespoons vegetable oil
Hot cooked rice
Toasted slivered almonds
Orange slices (optional)

Combine chicken and ½ teaspoon salt in a large saucepan; cover with water. Bring to a boil; cover, reduce heat, and simmer 30 minutes or until tender. Remove chicken, and let cool. (Reserve broth for other uses.)

Remove skin; bone chicken, and cut into ¼-inch julienne strips. Set aside.

Combine orange juice and next 5 ingredients in a small bowl; stir until cornstarch dissolves. Set aside.

Sauté celery and pepper strips in oil in a large skillet until crisp-tender. Add juice mixture and chicken; bring to a boil. Boil 1 minute, stirring constantly. Serve over rice. Sprinkle with almonds. Garnish with orange slices, if desired. Yield: 4 servings.
Barbara E. Bach
Clearwater, Florida

LIME-PINEAPPLE TART

1 (8-ounce) can crushed pineapple, undrained
2 (8-ounce) packages cream cheese
¼ cup butter or margarine, softened
⅔ cup sugar
1 egg, beaten
¼ cup whipping cream
2 teaspoons grated lime rind
Spicy Cookie Crust
½ cup sugar
2 tablespoons cornstarch
Dash of salt
½ cup lime juice
1 tablespoon rum
2 teaspoons grated lime rind
3 tablespoons butter or margarine
Sweetened whipped cream (optional)
Lime rind (optional)

Drain pineapple, reserving 2 tablespoons juice. Set aside.

Combine cream cheese, ¼ cup butter, and ⅔ cup sugar; beat until fluffy. Add egg, ¼ cup whipping cream, and reserved pineapple juice; blend well. Stir in 2 teaspoons grated lime rind and pineapple. Pour into prepared crust. Bake at 350° for 40 minutes; cool.

Combine ½ cup sugar, cornstarch, and salt in a small saucepan. Stir in lime juice, rum, and 2 teaspoons lime rind. Bring to a boil, and cook 1 minute, stirring constantly. Remove from heat. Add 3 tablespoons butter, stirring until melted; cool. Spread mixture over cream cheese filling. Chill 8 hours. If desired, garnish with whipped cream and lime rind. Yield: one 10-inch tart.

Spicy Cookie Crust

1½ cups all-purpose flour
½ teaspoon baking powder
Dash of salt
¼ cup sugar
¼ teaspoon ground mace
⅛ teaspoon ground nutmeg
½ cup butter or margarine, softened
⅓ cup chopped almonds, toasted
2 egg yolks
2 tablespoons whipping cream
1 teaspoon grated lime rind

Combine flour, baking powder, salt, sugar, mace, and nutmeg; cut in butter with pastry blender until mixture resembles coarse meal. Stir in almonds. Add egg yolks, 2 tablespoons whipping cream, and 1 teaspoon lime rind; stir with a fork until all ingredients are moistened. Shape into a ball, and chill 30 minutes.

Press pastry into bottom and up sides of a 10-inch round tart pan. Bake at 350° for 15 minutes. Yield: crust for one 10-inch tart.

Nancy Bone
Gadsden, Alabama

Tip: *When squeezing fresh lemons, limes, or oranges for juice, first grate the rind by rubbing the washed fruit against surface of grater, taking care to remove only the outer colored portion of the rind. Wrap the rind in plastic in teaspoon portions, and freeze for future use.*

■ Tart Lemon-Cheese Cake, an old-fashioned layer cake, contains no cheese but was justly named for its rich, creamy cheeselike filling.

TART LEMON-CHEESE CAKE

1 cup butter, softened
2 cups sugar
¾ cup water
¼ cup milk
3¼ cups sifted cake flour
2¾ teaspoons baking powder
½ teaspoon salt
½ teaspoon rum flavoring or 1 teaspoon vanilla extract
6 egg whites
Lemon-Cheese Filling
Lemony White Frosting
Lemon slices (optional)
Orange leaves (optional)

Cream butter; gradually add sugar, beating well.

Combine water and milk in a small bowl; set aside.

Combine flour, baking powder, and salt; add to creamed mixture alternately with milk mixture, beginning and ending with flour mixture. Stir in rum flavoring.

Beat egg whites (at room temperature) until stiff peaks form; fold into batter. Pour batter into three greased and floured 9-inch round cakepans. Bake at 350° for 20 to 25 minutes or until a wooden pick inserted in center comes out clean. Cool layers in pans 10 minutes; remove layers from pans, and let cool completely.

Spread Lemon-Cheese Filling between layers and on top of cake. Spread Lemony White Frosting on sides. If desired, garnish with lemon slices and orange leaves. Yield: one 3-layer cake.

Lemon-Cheese Filling

1 cup sugar
3 tablespoons cornstarch
⅛ teaspoon salt
2 tablespoons grated lemon rind
1 cup lemon juice
6 egg yolks, beaten
⅓ cup butter or margarine

Combine sugar, cornstarch, and salt in a heavy saucepan; stir. Add lemon rind and juice; cook over medium heat, stirring constantly, until mixture thickens and comes to a boil. Boil 1 minute, stirring constantly.

Gradually stir half of hot mixture into egg yolks; add to remaining hot mixture, stirring constantly. Cook, stirring constantly, about 1 minute or until mixture is thoroughly heated. Remove from heat. Add butter, stirring until butter melts; cool completely. Yield: 2 cups.

Lemony White Frosting

1 cup sugar
⅓ cup water
2 tablespoons light corn syrup
2 egg whites
¼ cup sifted powdered sugar
½ teaspoon lemon extract

Combine 1 cup sugar, water, and corn syrup in a heavy saucepan. Cook over medium heat, stirring constantly, until clear. Cook, without stirring, until candy thermometer reaches 232°.

Beat egg whites (at room temperature) until soft peaks form; continue to beat, slowly adding syrup mixture. Add powdered sugar and lemon extract to mixture; continue beating until stiff peaks form and frosting is thick enough to spread. Yield: about 3 cups.

Elsie Young
Montgomery, Alabama

Appetizers Made Easy

Whether you're planning for a large group or small, you can rely on your microwave oven to make the food preparation easier. Each of these recipes may be served as an appetizer before a meal or as part of a larger party spread.

To shorten preparation time, the appetizer recipes below use some of the microwave tips featured in the sidebar on this page.

CHIPPED BEEF DIP

2 (8-ounce) packages cream
  cheese
¼ cup milk
1 (8-ounce) carton commercial
  sour cream
¼ cup dried minced onion
¼ teaspoon garlic powder
½ teaspoon pepper
½ cup chopped green pepper
1 (2½-ounce) jar sliced dried
  beef, chopped
1 tablespoon butter or margarine
½ cup chopped pecans

Place cream cheese in a 1-quart casserole; microwave at HIGH 1 minute, stirring after 30 seconds. Stir until cream cheese is smooth and creamy. Stir in milk, sour cream, onion, garlic powder, pepper, chopped green pepper, and chopped dried beef, mixing well.

Spread mixture evenly in a 9-inch pieplate; set aside.

Place butter in a 1-cup glass measure; microwave at HIGH 30 seconds or until melted. Toss pecans with butter; sprinkle evenly over cream cheese mixture. Microwave at MEDIUM (50% power) 7 to 8 minutes, giving dish a quarter-turn after 4 minutes. Let stand 5 minutes. Serve with unsalted crackers. Yield: 4 cups.

BIT-OF-BRIE APPETIZER

¾ cup finely chopped pecans
¼ cup Kahlúa or other
  coffee-flavored liqueur
3 tablespoons brown sugar
1 (14-ounce) mini Brie

Spread pecans in a 9-inch pieplate; microwave at HIGH 4 to 6 minutes, stirring every 2 minutes until toasted. Add Kahlúa and brown sugar, stirring well.

Remove rind from top of Brie and discard. Place Brie on a microwave-safe serving plate.

Spoon pecan-Kahlúa mixture evenly over top of Brie. Microwave, uncovered, at HIGH 1½ to 2 minutes or until Brie softens to desired consistency, giving dish a half-turn after 1 minute.

Serve appetizer with melba toast or assorted crackers. Yield: 12 appetizer servings.

CHICKEN SALAD PARTY SPREAD

2 chicken breast halves, skinned
2 tablespoons chopped onion
2 tablespoons water
4 slices bacon
¼ cup plus 2 tablespoons
  mayonnaise
2 tablespoons commercial
  barbecue sauce
1 tablespoon lemon juice
½ teaspoon pepper

Arrange chicken in a 9-inch pieplate, placing meatier portions to outside of dish; sprinkle with onion. Pour water over chicken. Cover with heavy-duty plastic wrap; microwave at HIGH 3 minutes. Give dish a half-turn, and microwave at HIGH 3 to 3½ minutes or until chicken is no longer pink and juices run clear. Drain well; remove chicken from the bone, and finely chop meat.

Place bacon slices on a rack in a 12- x 8- x 2-inch baking dish; cover with paper towels. Microwave at HIGH 3½ to 4 minutes or until bacon

is crisp. Drain bacon; crumble and set aside.

Combine mayonnaise and remaining ingredients in a medium bowl. Add chicken and bacon, tossing until well mixed. Spread on party bread or crackers. Yield: 1½ cups.

Appetizer Shortcuts With the Microwave

■ Soften cream cheese in the microwave. Place in a microwave-safe bowl. One 8-ounce package of cream cheese will soften on HIGH for 30 seconds. Stir cream cheese until soft and smooth. Then follow the recipe.

■ Use the microwave to cook meats for salads and spreads. Two chicken breast halves, cooked with the bone in, will yield 1 to 1½ cups chopped chicken. Place in a 9-inch microwave-safe pieplate. Cover and microwave at HIGH 5½ to 6 minutes, giving dish a half-turn after 2½ minutes. Remove bone, and chop chicken.

■ Melt chocolate morsels to dip pretzels or cookies. Place morsels in a microwave-safe bowl. One 6-ounce package melts in 2 to 3 minutes at MEDIUM (50% power); a 12-ounce package melts in 3 to 4 minutes at MEDIUM. Stir to distribute heat. Dip pretzels or cookies in melted chocolate, and refrigerate. Serve after coating hardens.

■ Soften Brie in the microwave. You'll notice a difference in the cooking time if the Brie is very ripe—a longer aging period makes the Brie softer and decreases the required cooking time for recipes.

Muffins That Can't Be Beat

For tender, moist muffins, follow these simple tips. Stir ingredients together just until moistened. After baking, be sure to remove muffins from the pans so that the bottoms of the muffins won't get soggy.

CHUNKY PECAN MUFFINS

1½ cups all-purpose flour
2 teaspoons baking powder
¼ teaspoon salt
½ cup firmly packed brown sugar
Pinch of allspice
1 egg, slightly beaten
⅓ cup milk
¼ cup maple-flavored syrup
½ cup butter or margarine, melted
1 cup coarsely chopped pecans
1 teaspoon vanilla extract
¼ cup sugar
¼ teaspoon ground cinnamon
¼ cup butter or margarine, melted

Combine first 5 ingredients in a medium bowl; make a well in center of mixture.

Combine egg, milk, syrup, and ½ cup butter; add to dry ingredients, stirring just until moistened. Stir in pecans and vanilla. Fill paper-lined muffin pans two-thirds full. Bake at 400° for 15 to 20 minutes.

Combine sugar and cinnamon. Dip tops of warm muffins in remaining ¼ cup butter, then sugar mixture. Yield: 1 dozen.   *Linda Magers*
Clemmons, North Carolina

RAISIN-PECAN GINGER MUFFINS

2 cups all-purpose flour
1½ teaspoons baking soda
¼ teaspoon salt
1½ teaspoons ground ginger
⅓ cup butter or margarine
1 cup molasses
½ cup buttermilk
1 egg, slightly beaten
½ cup chopped pecans
½ cup raisins

Combine first 4 ingredients in a medium bowl; set aside.

Combine butter and molasses in a small saucepan; cook over medium heat until the butter melts. Remove from heat.

Make a well in center of flour mixture. Add molasses mixture, buttermilk, and egg, stirring just until ingredients are moistened. Stir in chopped pecans and raisins.

Spoon mixture into greased muffin pans, filling three-fourths full. Bake at 325° for 18 minutes or until done. Yield: 1½ dozen.   *Joel Allard*
San Antonio, Texas

CARROT-WHEAT MUFFINS

¾ cup whole wheat flour
2 teaspoons baking powder
½ teaspoon baking soda
1 teaspoon pumpkin pie spice
2 tablespoons wheat germ, toasted
1 cup grated carrots
½ cup raisins
1 egg, slightly beaten
1 cup milk
¼ cup honey
¼ cup vegetable oil
1½ cups morsels of wheat bran cereal

Combine flour, baking powder, soda, pie spice, wheat germ, grated carrots, and raisins in a medium bowl; set mixture aside.

Combine egg and remaining ingredients in a small bowl; stir well, and let stand 3 minutes.

Make a well in center of flour mixture. Add cereal mixture to dry ingredients, stirring just until moistened.

Spoon wheat mixture into greased muffin pans, filling three-fourths full. Bake at 400° for 18 to 20 minutes. Yield: 1 dozen.   *Gloria Pedersen*
Brandon, Mississippi

Use A Cornbread Mix

Corn-Cheese Spoonbread comes hot and steaming from the oven. Reminiscent of the spoonbread you may remember Grandma making, this one is much easier. Cornbread mix and canned corn make it a snap.

CORN-CHEESE SPOONBREAD

4 eggs, beaten
2 (17-ounce) cans cream-style corn
½ cup butter or margarine, melted
1 (6-ounce) package Mexican cornbread mix
1 teaspoon baking powder
1 cup (4 ounces) shredded Cheddar cheese

Combine eggs, corn, butter, cornbread mix, and baking powder in a large bowl. Pour mixture into a lightly greased 2-quart casserole. Bake at 400° for 30 minutes.

Sprinkle top of casserole evenly with 1 cup shredded cheddar cheese, and bake an additional 5 minutes or until cheese melts. Yield: 8 servings.   *Azine G. Rush*
Monroe, Louisiana

Tip: *Unless otherwise specified, always preheat the oven at least 20 minutes before baking.*

SPINACH-CHEESE BAKE

1 (6-ounce) package corn muffin mix
2 eggs, beaten
1 (8-ounce) carton commercial sour cream
1 (10½-ounce) can French onion soup, undiluted
1 (10-ounce) package frozen chopped spinach, thawed and drained
½ cup butter or margarine, melted
½ cup (2 ounces) shredded Cheddar cheese

Combine first 6 ingredients; stir until blended. Spoon into a greased 12- x 8- x 2-inch baking dish. Bake at 350° for 25 minutes; top with cheese, and bake 5 minutes. Yield: 8 servings.

Pamela F. Collins
Marietta, Georgia

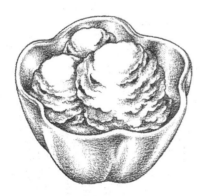

Scoop Snow For Ice Cream

When you wake up to find a blanket of snow, try making Snow Ice Cream. You can prepare the recipe indoors or outdoors. Prepare the sweetened milk mixture in advance so that you can add the snow as soon as you bring it into the house. Or take the milk mixture outdoors, and stir it into snow that has been measured into a large bowl.

Although the recipe calls for 1 gallon of snow, it yields only 3 quarts. The snow compresses a little as you add the milk mixture. Stir gently to minimize volume loss.

SNOW ICE CREAM

1 egg, beaten
¾ cup sugar
1 cup evaporated milk
2 teaspoons vanilla extract
1 gallon clean, fresh snow

Combine egg and sugar; stir well with a wire whisk. Add milk and vanilla, stirring well.

Place snow in a large bowl. Gradually add milk mixture to snow, gently stirring with a wooden spoon until blended. Yield: about 3 quarts.

Brenda Little
Greenville, North Carolina

Fruit Flavors These Cakes

When you bake your next cake, depend on fruit to flavor it. The juice and rind of oranges add just the right spark to Orange Streusel Cake, while pineapple provides the flavor for classic Pineapple Upside-Down Cake.

PINEAPPLE UPSIDE-DOWN CAKE

3 tablespoons butter or margarine
½ cup firmly packed brown sugar
1 (8-ounce) can sliced pineapple, drained
12 maraschino cherries
⅔ cup chopped pecans
¼ cup shortening
1 cup sugar
2 eggs
1½ cups all-purpose flour
2 teaspoons baking powder
½ teaspoon salt
½ cup milk
1 teaspoon vanilla extract

Melt butter in a 10-inch cast-iron skillet. Spread brown sugar evenly over butter. Arrange pineapple and cherries on sugar. Top with pecans.

Combine shortening and 1 cup sugar; beat well at medium speed of an electric mixer. Add eggs, one at a time; beat after each addition.

Combine flour, baking powder, and salt; add to creamed mixture alternately with milk, beginning and ending with flour mixture. Stir in vanilla. Spoon batter evenly over pineapple slices. Bake at 350° for 45 to 50 minutes or until cake tests done. Cool cake 5 minutes; invert onto plate. Yield: one 10-inch cake.

Georgia C. Lindler
Little Mountain, South Carolina

ORANGE STREUSEL CAKE

2 cups all-purpose flour
2 teaspoons baking powder
⅛ teaspoon salt
½ cup sugar
1 tablespoon grated orange rind
1 egg, beaten
½ cup skim milk
½ cup orange juice
⅓ cup vegetable oil
½ teaspoon cornstarch
⅓ cup orange juice
¼ cup gingersnap cookie crumbs

Line a greased 9-inch round cakepan with wax paper; grease and lightly dust wax paper with flour. Set aside.

Combine flour, baking powder, salt, sugar, and grated orange rind in a large bowl; make a well in center. Combine egg, milk, ½ cup orange juice, and oil; add to dry ingredients, stirring just until moistened.

Pour batter into prepared pan. Bake at 350° for 22 to 25 minutes. Cool in pan 10 minutes. Remove from pan, and cool completely on a wire rack.

Combine cornstarch and ⅓ cup juice in a saucepan. Cook over medium heat until mixture has thickened; stir constantly. Boil 1 minute. Spread over cake; cool. Sprinkle cookie crumbs over cake. Yield: 6 to 8 servings.

Julia Kalman
Kingwood, Texas

Spectacular Soufflé

You'll be the talk of the town when you serve Cream Cheese Soufflé sent to us by Eileen MaCutchan of Largo, Florida.

CREAM CHEESE SOUFFLÉ

2 (3-ounce) packages cream cheese, softened
1 cup commercial sour cream
1 tablespoon honey
2 egg yolks, beaten
4 egg whites
2 tablespoons sugar
¼ cup currant jelly
1 (10-ounce) package frozen strawberries or raspberries, thawed
1½ teaspoons cornstarch
1 tablespoon water

Combine first 4 ingredients; beat at medium speed of an electric mixer until smooth. Set aside.

Beat egg whites (at room temperature) until soft peaks form; gradually add sugar, beating until stiff peaks form. Fold egg whites into creamed mixture. Pour into a 1½-quart soufflé dish. Bake at 325° for 45 minutes.

While soufflé is baking, heat currant jelly in a medium saucepan; add fruit. Combine cornstarch and water; add to fruit mixture. Bring to a boil over medium heat, stirring constantly. Boil 1 minute. Serve warm with soufflé. Yield: 6 servings.

Sample Feta Cheese

Turn a macaroni-and-beef casserole into Pastitsio, a popular Greek casserole, by adding feta cheese. Pastitsio is best prepared in advance because when it cools, you can cut it into squares and reheat portions.

PASTITSIO

1½ pounds ground beef
1 cup chopped onion
1 (16-ounce) can tomatoes, undrained and chopped
1 (6-ounce) can tomato paste
¼ teaspoon dried whole thyme
1¾ teaspoons salt, divided
1 (8-ounce) package elbow macaroni
½ cup crumbled feta cheese
4 egg whites, slightly beaten
½ cup butter or margarine
½ cup all-purpose flour
¼ teaspoon ground cinnamon
1 quart milk
4 egg yolks, slightly beaten
Paprika (optional)

Combine ground beef and chopped onion in a large skillet. Cook over medium heat until beef browns, stirring to crumble beef; drain well. Stir in tomatoes, tomato paste, thyme, and ¾ teaspoon salt; bring to a boil. Cover and reduce heat; cook mixture 30 minutes, stirring often.

Cook macaroni according to package directions, adding ¼ teaspoon salt; drain. Stir in feta cheese and egg whites.

Add feta cheese-macaroni mixture to beef mixture; stir well. Spoon mixture into a lightly greased 13- x 9- x 2-inch baking dish; set aside.

Melt butter in a heavy saucepan over low heat; add flour and cinnamon, stirring until smooth. Cook 1 minute, stirring constantly. Gradually add milk; cook over medium heat, stirring constantly, until mixture is thickened and bubbly. Stir in ¾ teaspoon salt. Gradually stir about one-fourth of hot mixture into yolks; add to remaining hot mixture, stirring constantly.

Cook 1 minute, stirring constantly. Pour sauce over beef mixture; bake at 350° for 35 to 40 minutes or until thoroughly heated.

Remove from oven; let stand 10 minutes before serving. Sprinkle casserole with paprika in rows, if desired. Yield: 8 servings.

Mrs. P. J. Davis
Drexel, North Carolina

Low-Sodium Soups And Stews

If you're watching the sodium in your diet, you may be avoiding homemade soup and stew, which are traditionally high in sodium. But with the following recipes, you'll discover that you can enjoy soup and cut down on sodium at the same time.

SPICY VEGETABLE-BEEF SOUP

1 pound ground chuck
2 cloves garlic, minced
1 (46-ounce) can no-salt-added tomato juice
⅔ cup water
2 cups shredded cabbage
1½ cups cubed potatoes
½ cup chopped celery
½ cup chopped green pepper
2 teaspoons dried Italian seasoning
¾ teaspoon salt
¾ teaspoon crushed red pepper
½ teaspoon dried whole oregano
½ teaspoon pepper
1 (16-ounce) package frozen mixed vegetables

Combine beef and garlic in a Dutch oven; cook over medium heat until browned, stirring to crumble meat. Drain meat in a colander, and pat dry with a paper towel. Wipe pan drippings from skillet with a paper towel.

Return meat to Dutch oven; add tomato juice, water, and next 9 ingredients. Bring to a boil. Cover, reduce heat, and simmer 40 minutes, stirring occasionally. Stir in mixed vegetables. Cover and cook mixture 25 minutes. Yield: 10 cups (177 calories per 1-cup serving).

□ *11.8 grams protein, 6.6 grams fat, 18.7 grams carbohydrate, 27 milligrams cholesterol, 241 milligrams sodium, and 38 milligrams calcium.*

CHUNKY MUSHROOM SOUP

Vegetable cooking spray
½ pound fresh mushrooms, sliced
¾ cup thinly sliced green onions
1 tablespoon vegetable oil
1 tablespoon all-purpose flour
2 cups skim milk
1 teaspoon chicken-flavored
   bouillon granules
½ cup water
1 tablespoon minced fresh parsley
⅛ teaspoon garlic powder
1 bay leaf

Coat a Dutch oven with cooking spray. Place over medium-high heat until hot. Add mushrooms and green onions; sauté until tender.

Add oil, stirring until heated. Add flour; cook over medium heat 1 minute, stirring constantly. Gradually add milk, stirring until blended. Stir in bouillon granules and remaining ingredients; cook 10 minutes or until bubbly and slightly thickened. Remove bay leaf. Yield: 3 cups (103 calories per ¾-cup serving).

☐ 6 grams protein, 4.3 grams fat, 11.2 grams carbohydrate, 2 milligrams cholesterol, 272 milligrams sodium, and 166 milligrams calcium.

CHUNKY CHICKEN-NOODLE SOUP

1 (3-pound) broiler-fryer, skinned
4 cups water
3 fresh celery leaves
¾ teaspoon poultry seasoning
¼ teaspoon dried whole thyme
⅓ cup sliced green onions
½ cup sliced celery
½ cup sliced carrot
2 tablespoons minced fresh
   parsley
¼ teaspoon coarsely ground
   pepper
2 cups water
1 teaspoon chicken-flavored
   bouillon granules
1 cup uncooked egg noodles
1 bay leaf
Coarsely ground pepper (optional)

Combine chicken, 4 cups water, celery leaves, poultry seasoning, and thyme in a Dutch oven; bring to a boil. Cover, reduce heat, and simmer 45 minutes. Remove chicken from broth, and let cool.

Strain chicken broth; discard celery leaves and fat. Return broth to Dutch oven; add green onions and remaining ingredients. Cover and simmer for 20 minutes.

Bone and coarsely chop chicken; add to broth mixture, and cook an additional 5 minutes. Remove bay leaf. Yield: 6 cups (201 calories per 1-cup serving).

☐ 25.3 grams protein, 6.5 grams fat, 8.8 grams carbohydrate, 82 milligrams cholesterol, 220 milligrams sodium, and 30 milligrams calcium.

CAJUN-STYLE CATFISH STEW
(pictured on page xii)

Vegetable cooking spray
½ cup chopped onion
½ cup chopped green pepper
1 clove garlic, minced
2½ cups peeled, coarsely chopped
   tomatoes
1 bay leaf
½ teaspoon ground cumin
½ teaspoon dried whole thyme
½ teaspoon dried whole oregano
¾ teaspoon hot sauce
¼ teaspoon salt
¼ teaspoon pepper
4 cups water
1 pound unpeeled small fresh
   shrimp
½ cup uncooked long-grain rice
1 pound catfish fillets, cut into
   1-inch pieces
1 (10-ounce) package frozen cut
   okra, thawed
Filé gumbo (optional)

Coat a Dutch oven with cooking spray. Place over medium-high heat until hot. Add onion, green pepper, and garlic; sauté until tender.

Add tomatoes and next 8 ingredients. Cover, reduce heat, and simmer 20 minutes, stirring often.

Peel and devein shrimp; set aside. Add rice and catfish to mixture in Dutch oven; stir well. Cover, reduce heat, and simmer 15 minutes. Stir in okra; cook 5 minutes. Stir in shrimp, and return mixture to a boil; remove from heat. Remove bay leaf. Serve stew with filé gumbo, if desired. Yield: 10 cups (138 calories per 1-cup serving).

☐ 16.1 grams protein, 2 grams fat, 13.5 grams carbohydrate, 77 milligrams cholesterol, 140 milligrams sodium, and 70 milligrams calcium.

CREAM OF CAULIFLOWER SOUP

5 cups cauliflower flowerets
½ cup chopped onion
1 clove garlic, minced
2 teaspoons chicken-flavored
   bouillon granules
½ teaspoon dried whole thyme
2½ cups water
1 tablespoon vegetable oil
1 tablespoon all-purpose flour
2 cups skim milk
Freshly ground pepper (optional)

Combine first 6 ingredients in a Dutch oven; bring to a boil. Cover, reduce heat, and simmer 20 minutes or until cauliflower is tender.

Spoon half of cauliflower mixture into container of an electric blender; blend until smooth. Repeat procedure with remaining mixture. Set aside.

Heat vegetable oil in a 2-quart heavy saucepan over medium-low heat. Add flour, stirring well. Cook 1 minute, stirring constantly. Gradually add milk; cook over medium heat, stirring constantly, until thickened and bubbly.

Add cauliflower mixture to milk mixture. Add pepper, if desired. Cook over low heat until thoroughly heated, stirring often. Yield: 6 cups (82 calories per 1-cup serving).

☐ 4.9 grams protein, 3 grams fat, 10.4 grams carbohydrate, 2 milligrams cholesterol, 328 milligrams sodium, and 131 milligrams calcium.

FEBRUARY

Our Best Home Cookin'

Envision golden fried chicken with cream gravy, potato salad and baked ham, crunchy corn sticks and fist-size biscuits slathered with butter and honey. Add meat loaf and mashed potatoes, old-fashioned chicken and dumplings to the feast. For dessert, bite into fried peach pie or pound cake, and sample banana pudding with mile-high meringue.

Southerners have always taken their food seriously. But recently folks outside the South have caught on to our down-home cookin', and Southern-style foods are now appearing in fancy restaurants from New York to California. Food writers who don't hail from our region refer to these specialties as "comfort foods."

For over 20 years, *Southern Living* has published as many different versions of these home-style foods as there are good cooks in the South. After being asked over and over which of these recipes were really the best, the foods staff decided to assemble "the best" into a grand, inclusive cookbook.

After two years of developing new recipes, retesting and updating our published ones (often reducing sugar, sodium, and fat), combining two or more recipes to make good dishes even better, and adding microwave conversions, we have our collection, *The Southern Living Cookbook*. This complete guide to cooking is packed with over 1,400 delectable recipes.

Recipes reprinted from *The Southern Living Cookbook,* ©1987 by Oxmoor House, Inc. Reproduced with permission.

DIXIE FRIED CHICKEN

1 (2½- to 3-pound) broiler-fryer, cut up
½ teaspoon salt
⅛ teaspoon pepper
2 cups all-purpose flour
1 teaspoon red pepper
1 egg, slightly beaten
½ cup milk
Vegetable oil
Cream Gravy (recipe on page 15)
Watercress (optional)

Season chicken with salt and pepper. Combine flour and red pepper; set aside. Combine egg and milk; dip chicken in egg mixture, and dredge in flour mixture, coating well.

Heat 1 inch of vegetable oil in a skillet (350°); place chicken in skillet. Cover and cook over medium heat 20 to 25 minutes or until golden brown; turn occasionally. Drain chicken on paper towels. Serve chicken with Cream Gravy, and garnish with watercress, if desired. Yield: approximately 4 servings.

COMPANY POT ROAST

½ cup chopped onion
¼ cup butter or margarine, melted
1 (3½- to 4-pound) chuck roast
1 bay leaf, quartered
2 tablespoons grated orange rind
¼ teaspoon ground allspice
⅛ teaspoon pepper
1 (10½-ounce) can consommé, diluted

Sauté onion in butter in a large Dutch oven until tender; add meat, and brown on both sides.

Combine bay leaf, orange rind, allspice, pepper, and diluted consommé; pour over meat. Cover and simmer 2½ hours. Remove bay leaf. Yield: 6 to 8 servings.

Microwave Directions: Combine chopped onion and melted butter; set aside. Place chuck roast in a roasting bag in a 12- x 8- x 2-inch baking dish; pour onion and butter over roast. Sprinkle seasonings over roast. Add diluted consommé. Tie bag loosely with string or a ½-inch-wide strip cut from open end of bag (do not use twist tie).

Microwave at MEDIUM LOW (30% power) for 33 to 37 minutes per pound or to desired degree of doneness, turning bag over and rotating dish every 30 minutes. Let stand 10 to 15 minutes in bag before serving. Remove bay leaf.

BASIC MEAT LOAF

1½ pounds ground beef
2 (8-ounce) cans tomato sauce, divided
1 cup soft breadcrumbs
2 eggs, slightly beaten
2 tablespoons dried minced onion flakes
¾ teaspoon salt
¼ teaspoon pepper
2 teaspoons dried parsley flakes
1 teaspoon Worcestershire sauce

Combine ground beef, ½ cup tomato sauce, and next 5 ingredients; mix well. Shape meat mixture into a loaf. Place on rack of a lightly greased broiler pan. Bake at 350° for 1 hour.

Combine remaining tomato sauce and last 2 ingredients; stir well. Pour over meat loaf, and bake an additional 5 minutes. Yield: 6 servings.

Microwave Directions: Combine ground beef, ½ cup tomato sauce, and next 5 ingredients; mix well. Shape mixture into a 7-inch round loaf. Place loaf on a microwave-safe rack in a 12- x 8- x 2-inch baking dish. Cover with wax paper. Microwave at HIGH for 14 to 16 minutes or until almost firm to the touch, turning dish after 8 minutes.

Combine remaining tomato sauce and last 2 ingredients; stir well. Pour over meat loaf, and microwave at HIGH for 1 to 2 minutes. Let stand 5 minutes before serving.

Hurry-Up Meat Loaves: Shape meat mixture into 6 individual loaves; place on rack of a lightly greased broiler pan. Bake at 450° for 25 minutes or to desired degree of doneness. Add topping as directed for whole meat loaf.

SWEET-AND-SOUR GLAZED HAM

2 cups apple jelly
2 tablespoons prepared mustard
2 tablespoons lemon juice
½ teaspoon ground cloves
1 (5- to 7-pound) smoked, fully cooked ham half
Whole cloves
Fresh parsley sprigs (optional)
Apple slices (optional)

Combine jelly, mustard, lemon juice, and ground cloves in a saucepan; bring to a boil over medium heat, stirring occasionally. Set aside.

Slice away skin from ham. Score fat on ham in a diamond design, and stud with whole cloves. Place ham, fat side up, on rack in a shallow roasting pan. Insert meat thermometer, making sure it does not touch fat or bone. Bake, uncovered, at 325° for 1½ to 2 hours or until thermometer registers 140° (18 to 24 minutes per pound); baste every 15 to 20 minutes with sauce. Heat remaining sauce, and serve with ham. If desired, garnish with parsley and apple slices. Yield: 10 to 14 servings.

Microwave Directions: Combine jelly, mustard, lemon juice, and ground cloves in a 4-cup glass measure. Microwave at HIGH for 1 to 2 minutes or until thoroughly heated, stirring after 1 minute. Set aside.

Slice away skin from ham. Score fat on ham in a diamond design, and stud with whole cloves. Place ham, fat side up, on rack in a 12- x 8- x 2-inch baking dish. Insert microwave-safe meat thermometer, making sure it does not touch fat or bone. Shield upper cut edge of ham with a 1½-inch wide strip of aluminum foil. Cover entire dish with heavy-duty plastic wrap.

Microwave at MEDIUM (50% power) for 8 to 10 minutes per pound or until thermometer registers 140°, basting 4 times during cooking. Turn ham over after half the cooking time has elapsed. (Rearrange foil strip when ham is turned.) Let stand 10 minutes before serving. If desired, garnish ham with parsley sprigs and apple slices.

CREAM GRAVY

¼ cup pan drippings
¼ cup all-purpose flour
2½ to 3 cups hot milk
½ teaspoon salt
⅛ to ¼ teaspoon pepper

Pour off all except ¼ cup drippings from skillet in which chicken or other meat was fried; place skillet over medium heat. Add flour, and stir until browned. Gradually add hot milk; cook, stirring constantly, until thickened and bubbly. Stir in salt and pepper. Serve hot. Yield: 2¾ cups.

QUICK BUTTERMILK BISCUITS

½ cup butter or margarine
2 cups self-rising flour
¾ cup buttermilk
Butter or margarine, melted

Cut ½ cup butter into flour with a pastry blender until mixture resembles coarse meal. Add buttermilk, stirring until dry ingredients are moistened. Turn dough out onto a lightly floured surface, and knead lightly 3 or 4 times.

Roll dough to ¾-inch thickness; cut with a 2-inch biscuit cutter. Place on a lightly greased baking sheet. Bake at 425° for 13 to 15 minutes. Brush biscuits with melted butter. Yield: 1 dozen.

QUICK CORN STICKS

1¼ cups cornmeal
¾ cup all-purpose flour
1 tablespoon plus 1 teaspoon baking powder
¾ teaspoon salt
1 tablespoon sugar
2 eggs, lightly beaten
1 cup milk
¼ cup vegetable oil

Combine first 5 ingredients, mixing well. Combine eggs, milk, and oil; add to dry ingredients, stirring just until moistened.

Place a well-greased cast-iron corn stick pan in a 425° oven for 3 minutes or until hot. Remove pan from oven; spoon batter into pan, filling two-thirds full. Bake at 425° for 12 minutes or until lightly browned. Yield: 1½ dozen.

Quick Corn Muffins: Season muffin pans as for corn sticks. Spoon batter into pans, filling two-thirds full. Bake muffins as for corn sticks. Yield: 15 corn muffins.

CONFETTI POTATO SALAD

6 medium potatoes
4 green onions, thinly sliced
½ cup finely chopped green
  pepper
1 stalk celery, thinly sliced
1 small carrot, shredded
2 to 3 pimiento-stuffed olives,
  thinly sliced
3 hard-cooked eggs, chopped
½ cup commercial coleslaw
  dressing
3 tablespoons commercial sour
  cream
1 tablespoon lemon juice
Lettuce leaves (optional)
Paprika

Cook potatoes in boiling salted water to cover 30 minutes or until tender. Drain and cool slightly. Peel and dice potatoes. Combine potatoes and next 6 ingredients in a large bowl.

Combine dressing, sour cream, and lemon juice; stir well. Add to potato mixture, tossing gently. Serve on lettuce, if desired; sprinkle with paprika. Yield: 5 to 6 servings.

COUNTRY CLUB SQUASH

2 pounds yellow squash, sliced
½ cup chopped onion
½ cup water
1 (8-ounce) carton commercial
  sour cream
½ teaspoon salt
¼ teaspoon pepper
¼ teaspoon dried whole basil
1 cup soft breadcrumbs
½ cup (2 ounces) shredded
  medium Cheddar cheese
⅓ cup butter or margarine,
  melted
½ teaspoon paprika
8 slices bacon, cooked and
  crumbled

Cook squash and onion in ½ cup boiling water until tender; drain and mash. Combine squash, sour cream, salt, pepper, and basil; pour into a greased 2-quart casserole. Combine breadcrumbs, cheese, butter, and paprika; sprinkle over squash mixture. Top with bacon. Bake at 300° for 20 minutes. Yield: 6 servings.

Microwave Directions: Combine first 3 ingredients in a 12- x 8- x 2-inch baking dish; cover with heavy-duty plastic wrap. Microwave at HIGH for 11 to 13 minutes or until tender, stirring once; drain and mash. Combine squash, sour cream, salt, pepper, and basil; pour into a greased 2-quart casserole. Combine breadcrumbs and next 3 ingredients; sprinkle over mixture. Microwave at MEDIUM HIGH (70% power) for 10 minutes. Top with bacon.

OLD-FASHIONED BUTTERMILK POUND CAKE

½ cup butter or margarine,
  softened
½ cup shortening
2 cups sugar
4 eggs
½ teaspoon baking soda
1 cup buttermilk
3 cups all-purpose flour
⅛ teaspoon salt
2 teaspoons lemon extract
1 teaspoon almond extract

Cream butter and shortening; gradually add sugar, beating well at medium speed of an electric mixer. Add eggs, one at a time, beating after each addition.

Dissolve soda in buttermilk. Combine flour and salt; add to creamed mixture alternately with buttermilk, beginning and ending with flour mixture. Mix just until blended after each addition. Stir in flavorings.

Pour batter into a greased and floured 10-inch tube pan. Bake at 350° for 1 hour and 5 to 10 minutes or until a wooden pick inserted in center comes out clean. Cool in pan 10 to 15 minutes; remove from pan, and let cool completely on a wire rack. Yield: one 10-inch cake.

Note: Cake may also be baked in two 9- x 5- x 3-inch loafpans. Bake at 350° for 45 to 50 minutes.

Chocolate Marble Pound Cake: Melt 1 tablespoon shortening and 1 (1-ounce) square unsweetened chocolate in a small saucepan, stirring until smooth. Set aside.

Prepare batter for Old-Fashioned Buttermilk Pound Cake, using vanilla extract in place of lemon extract. Remove 2 cups of batter, and add chocolate mixture, stirring until blended. Spoon one-third of remaining plain batter into a greased and floured 10-inch tube pan; top with half of chocolate batter. Repeat layers, ending with plain batter. Gently swirl batter with a knife to create marble effect. Bake as directed above.

BANANA PUDDING

3½ tablespoons all-purpose flour
1⅓ cups sugar
Dash of salt
3 eggs, separated
3 cups milk
1 teaspoon vanilla extract
1 (12-ounce) package vanilla
  wafers
6 medium bananas
¼ cup plus 2 tablespoons sugar
1 teaspoon vanilla extract

Combine flour, 1⅓ cups sugar, and salt in a heavy saucepan. Beat egg yolks; combine egg yolks and milk, mixing well. Stir into dry ingredients; cook over medium heat, stirring constantly, until mixture is smooth and thickened. Remove from heat; stir in 1 teaspoon vanilla.

Layer one-third of wafers in a 3-quart baking dish. Slice 2 bananas, and layer over wafers. Pour one-third of custard over bananas. Repeat layers twice.

Beat egg whites (at room temperature) until foamy. Gradually add ¼ cup plus 2 tablespoons sugar, 1 tablespoon at a time, beating until stiff peaks form. Add 1 teaspoon vanilla, and beat until blended. Spread meringue over custard, sealing to edge of dish. Bake at 425° for 10 to 12 minutes or until golden brown. Yield: 8 to 10 servings.

COOKING Light

Make Eating A Healthy Habit

To be healthier and trimmer, plan to make positive changes in your lifestyle so that cooking and eating light will become habits.

First, keep a record of everything you eat for a period of several days, noting the time of day, place, your emotions, and hunger level. You can pinpoint when, where, and why you are most likely to overeat.

It's easy, for instance, to consume numerous calories while watching television without ever remembering doing so. Instead, turn off the television and sit at the table whenever you eat or snack.

If you taste foods while cooking or eat leftovers while scraping the pots and pans, you're taking in calories that add up quickly.

Plan menus a week ahead and make your grocery list accordingly. Go to the supermarket after you've eaten—it's a well-known fact that people buy more groceries when they're hungry. Shop alone so that you won't be tempted by others to buy items that you'd rather avoid.

When you're thirsty, drink water or low-calorie beverages. The calories in soft drinks, alcoholic beverages, sweetened tea, and even fruit juice can be substantial.

If you want to cut back on the salt, sugar, or butter you add at the table, remove these items and put them in a less-accessible place.

Instead of going on a diet, make a permanent change by eating more fiber, fruits, vegetables, leaner meats, and low-fat dairy products.

Eat Well, And Save Money, Too

Practicing low-calorie, healthy eating habits doesn't require expensive foods. In fact, many basic foods are inexpensive sources of nutrients (see chart on page 19).

In Rice-and-Lentil Pilaf, one cup of chicken is stretched to feed a crowd. It provides enough high-quality protein for six main-dish servings. Brown rice supplies magnesium, vitamin B-6, niacin, and thiamine.

Chicken-Vegetable Soup starts with a whole chicken, which is less expensive than chicken parts. The chicken and its nutritious, defatted broth are the basis of the soup. Lima beans add enough protein to make it a main-dish soup. Nutrients supplied in chicken include protein, niacin, vitamin B-6, and pantothenic acid.

Spicy Bean Enchiladas rely on dried pinto beans, part-skim milk cheese, and corn tortillas for the high protein combination in this meatless main dish. Inexpensive dried beans are a good source of fiber, zinc, iron, magnesium, calcium, and phosphorus, in addition to protein.

The high-fiber, whole-grain goodness of oats is further enhanced by unpeeled apple and raisins in Fruited Oatmeal. Count on oats as an economical source of magnesium, thiamine, pantothenic acid, and zinc.

RICE-AND-LENTIL PILAF

⅓ cup chopped onion
1 tablespoon vegetable oil
1 cup uncooked brown rice
3 cups water
¼ teaspoon ground cinnamon
2 teaspoons vegetable bouillon granules
1 tablespoon tomato paste
¼ cup dried lentils, uncooked
1 cup chopped cooked chicken breast
½ cup shredded carrot
½ cup unsalted sunflower seeds
½ cup raisins

Sauté onion in vegetable oil in a skillet until tender. Add rice, and stir until lightly browned. Add water and next 4 ingredients; stir well. Cover, bring to a boil, reduce heat, and simmer 30 minutes. Stir in chicken, shredded carrot, sunflower seeds, and raisins. Cover and cook 20 minutes. Yield: 6 main-dish servings (304 calories per 1-cup serving).

☐ *13.5 grams protein, 9.8 grams fat, 42.5 grams carbohydrate, 17 milligrams cholesterol, 189 milligrams sodium, and 47 milligrams calcium.*

Carol Schulz
Crossville, Tennessee

CHICKEN-VEGETABLE SOUP

1 (3-pound) broiler-fryer
6 cups water
1 cup sliced celery
1 cup chopped onion
2 teaspoons garlic salt
½ teaspoon pepper
1 (10-ounce) package frozen cut okra
1 (10-ounce) package frozen baby lima beans
1 (10-ounce) package frozen mixed vegetables
2 (14½-ounce) cans no-salt-added tomatoes, undrained and chopped

Combine first 6 ingredients in a large Dutch oven; bring to a boil. Cover, reduce heat, and simmer 30 minutes. Remove chicken and vegetables from broth; let cool separately. Skin and bone chicken. Discard skin and bones; cut chicken into small pieces. Set aside.

Pour chicken broth through a gravy skimmer, reserving 5 cups fat-free broth. Combine broth, vegetables cooked with chicken, chicken, okra, lima beans, and mixed vegetables. Bring to a boil; cover, reduce heat, and simmer 30 minutes. Add tomatoes; cook an additional 15 minutes. Yield: 12 main-dish servings (142 calories per 1-cup serving).

□ *13.5 grams protein, 2.8 grams fat, 15.8 grams carbohydrate, 24 milligrams cholesterol, 415.5 milligrams sodium, and 76 milligrams calcium.*
Rachael Laird
Savannah, Georgia

Tip: *Look for non-traditional ways to include a variety of foods in your diet. If you don't care for milk as a beverage, you may enjoy a milk-based soup as part of your milk allowance for the day.*

ORANGE-SPICED CARROTS

3 cups sliced carrots
¼ cup water
¼ cup unsweetened orange juice
1 teaspoon grated orange rind
1 tablespoon reduced-calorie margarine
¼ teaspoon ground nutmeg
½ teaspoon vanilla extract
2 teaspoons chopped fresh parsley

Combine carrots, water, and orange juice in a small saucepan. Cover and simmer 5 to 7 minutes or until carrots are crisp-tender. Add orange rind and next 3 ingredients; stir well. Garnish with parsley. Yield: 5 servings (46 calories per ½-cup serving).

□ *0.8 gram protein, 1.3 grams fat, 8.4 grams carbohydrate, 0 milligrams cholesterol, 51 milligrams sodium, and 21 milligrams calcium.*
Miriam Maddox
Chatsworth, Georgia

STUFFED CABBAGE ROLLS

12 large cabbage leaves
2 pounds raw frozen ground turkey, thawed
1 cup chopped onion
2 cups cooked brown rice (cooked without salt or fat)
2 teaspoons Italian seasoning
¼ teaspoon garlic powder
¼ teaspoon salt
¼ teaspoon pepper
2 (8-ounce) cans no-salt-added tomato sauce
1 cup water
1 teaspoon Italian seasoning
¼ teaspoon garlic powder
½ teaspoon salt
½ teaspoon pepper

Cook cabbage leaves in boiling water 5 to 8 minutes; drain.

Combine turkey and next 6 ingredients; stir well. Place ½ cup meat mixture in center of each cabbage leaf; fold ends over, and roll up. Place cabbage rolls, seam side down, in a 13- x 9- x 2-inch baking dish. Combine tomato sauce and remaining ingredients; stir well. Pour over cabbage rolls; bake, uncovered, at 350° for 1 hour, basting occasionally with sauce. Yield: 12 cabbage rolls (190 calories per roll).

□ *11.4 grams protein, 9.8 grams fat, 15.3 grams carbohydrate, 40 milligrams cholesterol, 193.8 milligrams sodium, and 64.7 milligrams calcium.*
Alice Fatch
Naples, Florida

SPICY BEAN ENCHILADAS

¾ pound dried pinto beans
8 cups water
2 cloves garlic, minced
1 bay leaf
¾ teaspoon salt
Spicy Tomato Sauce
½ teaspoon chili powder
¼ teaspoon pepper
8 (6-inch) corn tortillas
Vegetable cooking spray
1 cup (4 ounces) shredded 40% less fat Cheddar cheese
½ cup plain low-fat yogurt
2 tablespoons chopped green onions
Shredded lettuce (optional)

Sort and wash beans. Cover with water 2 inches above top of beans, and let stand 8 hours. Drain.

Combine beans, 8 cups water, garlic, bay leaf, and salt in a Dutch oven; bring to a boil. Cover, reduce heat to medium, and cook 1½ hours or until tender. Drain beans, and discard bay leaf. Mash beans; add ½ cup Spicy Tomato Sauce, ½ teaspoon chili powder, and ¼ teaspoon pepper, stirring well.

Spread ½ cup bean mixture over each tortilla. Roll up; place seam side

Inexpensive Sources of Nutrients

Vitamin A	Liver, fresh carrots, sweet potatoes, margarine, instant nonfat dry milk powder, eggs, frozen leafy vegetables
Vitamin C	Frozen concentrated orange or grapefruit juice
Thiamine	Whole grains and products made with whole grains, dried beans, liver, frozen leafy vegetables
Riboflavin	Instant nonfat dry milk powder, eggs, liver, whole grains, products made with whole grains, frozen leafy vegetables
Niacin and Folic acid	Liver, whole grains, products made with whole grains, dried beans
Calcium	Instant nonfat dry milk powder, sardines (with bones), frozen leafy vegetables
Iron and Zinc	Liver, whole grains, products made with whole grains, lean red meat, dried beans

down in a 13- x 9- x 2-inch baking dish coated with cooking spray. Spoon remaining Spicy Tomato Sauce over tortillas; cover and bake at 350° for 20 minutes. Top with cheese, and bake, uncovered, an additional 5 minutes or until cheese melts. Serve with a dollop of yogurt, and sprinkle with green onions. Garnish with lettuce, if desired. Yield: 8 servings (294 calories per enchilada).

☐ *17.5 grams protein, 4.7 grams fat, 47.6 grams carbohydrate, 14.9 milligrams cholesterol, 424 milligrams sodium, and 259 milligrams calcium.*

Spicy Tomato Sauce

2 (8-ounce) cans no-salt-added tomato sauce
1 (4-ounce) can chopped green chiles, undrained
1 clove garlic, minced
¾ cup chopped green onions
2 teaspoons chili powder
1 teaspoon ground cumin
¼ teaspoon dried whole oregano

Combine all ingredients in a saucepan; simmer, uncovered, 5 minutes. Yield: 2 cups plus 2 tablespoons.

Note: If tortillas crack or are hard to roll up, soften them by steaming. To steam, place 2 or 3 tortillas at a time in a strainer, and place over boiling water. Cover and steam 2 to 3 minutes or until tortillas are softened and pliable.

FRUITED OATMEAL

2 cups water
⅓ cup raisins
1 tablespoon frozen orange juice concentrate, thawed
⅔ cup regular oats
¼ teaspoon ground cinnamon
1 cup chopped unpeeled apple
⅛ teaspoon maple flavoring

Combine water and raisins in a medium saucepan; bring to a boil. Add orange juice concentrate, oats, and cinnamon. Cover, reduce heat, and simmer 8 to 10 minutes; let mixture stand 5 minutes. Stir in chopped apple and maple flavoring. Serve hot. Yield: 5 servings (87 calories per ½-cup serving).

☐ *1.9 grams protein, 0.9 gram fat, 19 grams carbohydrate, 0 milligrams cholesterol, 3 milligrams sodium, and 16 milligrams calcium.*

Desserts Full Of Fruit

Plain, unadorned fruit—whether fresh, frozen, or canned—is always a good dessert. But when the occasion calls for something more, turn to these recipes.

MELTING APPLES

Vegetable cooking spray
4 cups peeled and thinly sliced apples (about 4 medium)
½ teaspoon ground allspice
1 teaspoon vanilla butter-and-nut flavoring
8 large marshmallows, halved

Coat a 10- x 6- x 2-inch baking dish with cooking spray. Arrange apple slices in baking dish; sprinkle with allspice and flavoring. Top with marshmallow halves. Cover and bake at 350° for 30 to 35 minutes. Serve warm. Yield: 6 servings (71 calories per ½-cup serving).

☐ *0.4 gram protein, 0.4 gram fat, 18 grams carbohydrate, 0 milligrams cholesterol, 5 milligrams sodium, and 7 milligrams calcium.*

Emma Prillhart
Kingsport, Tennessee

BANANAS FOSTER

¾ cup unsweetened apple juice
2 dashes apple pie spice
3 medium-size, ripe, firm
  bananas, peeled
2 teaspoons cornstarch
2 tablespoons rum
⅛ teaspoon maple flavoring
⅛ teaspoon butter flavoring
3 cups vanilla ice milk

Combine apple juice and apple pie spice in a large skillet. Cut each banana in half crosswise, and slice in half lengthwise. Add bananas to juice mixture; cook over medium heat just until bananas are heated, basting often with juice.

Combine cornstarch, rum, and maple and butter flavorings; add to banana mixture. Bring to a boil. Boil 1 minute, stirring constantly. Serve hot over vanilla ice milk. Yield: 6 servings (165 calories per banana half, ½ cup ice milk, and 2½ tablespoons sauce).

☐ *3.2 grams protein, 3.1 grams fat, 32.9 grams carbohydrate, 9 milligrams cholesterol, 54 milligrams sodium, and 94 milligrams calcium.*

Tip: *Burned food can be removed from an enamel saucepan by using the following procedure: Fill the pan with cold water containing 2 to 3 tablespoons salt, and let stand overnight. The next day, cover the pan, and bring water to a boil.*

KIWIFRUIT-PEACH TART

1 cup part-skim ricotta cheese
2 tablespoons sugar
2 tablespoons frozen orange juice
  concentrate, thawed and
  undiluted
¼ teaspoon grated orange rind
Tart shell (recipe follows)
1 (16-ounce) can sliced peaches
  in light syrup, drained
1 kiwifruit, peeled and sliced
3 tablespoons reduced-calorie
  orange marmalade

Combine ricotta cheese, sugar, orange juice concentrate, and grated orange rind; beat at medium speed of an electric mixer until smooth.

Spread mixture into prepared tart shell. Arrange peaches and kiwifruit in a circle on top of filling.

Heat orange marmalade over low heat until melted, stirring often. Spoon warm preserves evenly over fruit. Yield: 8 servings (179 calories per slice).

☐ *5.4 grams protein, 6 grams fat, 26 grams carbohydrate, 10 milligrams cholesterol, 141 milligrams sodium, and 91 milligrams calcium.*

Tart Shell

1 cup all-purpose flour
½ teaspoon ground ginger
Pinch of salt
¼ cup plus 1 tablespoon
  reduced-calorie margarine,
  chilled
½ teaspoon almond extract
4 to 5 tablespoons cold water

Combine flour, ginger, and salt in a medium bowl; cut in margarine with pastry blender until mixture resembles coarse meal. Sprinkle almond extract and cold water, 1 tablespoon at a time, evenly over surface; stir with a fork just until dry ingredients are moistened. Shape dough into a ball; chill.

Roll dough to ⅛-inch thickness on wax paper. Transfer to a 9-inch tart pan. Prick bottom and sides of tart shell with a fork.

Bake at 350° for 30 minutes or until pastry is lightly browned. Let cool completely on a wire rack. Yield: one 9-inch tart shell.

POACHED PEARS IN CUSTARD

3 medium pears
1 quart water
2 tablespoons lemon juice
Vegetable cooking spray
2 cups skim milk
¼ cup sugar
1 teaspoon vanilla extract
3 eggs
Ground nutmeg
Zest of 1 orange (optional)

Peel, core, and cut pears in half. Combine water and lemon juice in a large saucepan; bring to a boil. Add pears; return to a boil. Cover, reduce heat, and simmer 15 to 20 minutes. Cool. Arrange pears cut side down in a 9½-inch deep-dish pieplate coated with cooking spray.

Place milk in a saucepan; bring to a boil. Remove from heat. Add sugar and vanilla; stir until sugar dissolves.

Slowly add milk mixture to eggs, beating at medium speed of an electric mixer. Pour over pear halves; sprinkle nutmeg on top. Place pieplate in a 15- x 10- x 1-inch jellyroll pan; pour hot water around pieplate.

Bake at 350° for 35 minutes or until set. Cool. Garnish with orange zest, if desired. Yield: 6 servings (154 calories per serving).

□ 6.2 grams protein, 3.4 grams fat, 25.8 grams carbohydrate, 139 milligrams cholesterol, 77 milligrams sodium, and 124 milligrams calcium.
Marion Bogart
Baltimore, Maryland

FRESH FRUIT WITH LEMON CURD

1 cup water, divided
⅓ cup sugar
2 tablespoons grated lemon rind
2 tablespoons plus 2 teaspoons lemon juice
Pinch of salt
1 tablespoon cornstarch
1 teaspoon reduced-calorie margarine
2 eggs
Fresh strawberry (optional)
Assorted fresh fruit

Combine ¾ cup water, sugar, lemon rind, lemon juice, and salt in a saucepan; bring to a boil.

Dissolve cornstarch in remaining ¼ cup water; add to lemon mixture, stirring constantly. Add margarine; cook over medium heat, stirring constantly, until smooth.

Beat eggs well. Gradually stir about one-fourth of hot mixture into eggs; add to remaining hot mixture, stirring constantly. Bring to a boil over medium heat; boil 1 minute, stirring constantly.

Cool completely. Cover and chill. Garnish with a fresh strawberry, if desired. Serve with assorted fresh fruit. Yield: 1⅓ cups (17 calories per tablespoon).

□ 0.5 gram protein, 0.5 gram fat, 2.9 grams carbohydrate, 20 milligrams cholesterol, 7 milligrams sodium, and 3 milligrams calcium.
Margaret Ellen Holmes
Jackson, Tennessee

Leave The Peel On

You've probably heard that dietary fiber is important to good health. It is thought to help protect against colon and rectal cancer. Another benefit is that fiber may also lower the level of cholesterol in the blood. Bran, whole wheat breads and cereals, fresh fruits, and fresh vegetables are all good sources.

Much of the fiber in fresh fruits and vegetables is in the peel, and these recipes show you the healthy habit of leaving the peel on.

LEMON POTATO WEDGES

Vegetable cooking spray
1 tablespoon reduced-calorie margarine, melted
¾ teaspoon grated lemon rind
1 tablespoon lemon juice
¾ teaspoon dried whole dillweed
3 medium-size unpeeled baking potatoes (1¼ pounds)
2 tablespoons grated Parmesan cheese

Line a baking sheet with aluminum foil; coat with cooking spray. Set baking sheet aside.

Combine margarine, grated lemon rind, lemon juice, and dillweed in a small bowl; set aside.

Cut each unpeeled potato into 4 wedges. Brush cut edges of potatoes with margarine mixture; dredge in Parmesan cheese. Place wedges, cut side up, on prepared baking sheet. Bake at 425° for 25 minutes or until potatoes are tender. Yield: 6 servings (44 calories per wedge).

□ 1.4 grams protein, 0.9 gram fat, 8 grams carbohydrate, 1 milligram cholesterol, 31 milligrams sodium, and 19 milligrams calcium.
Judi Grigoraci
Charleston, West Virginia

SESAME-APPLE TOSS

1 cup unpeeled, chopped red apple
1 cup seedless green grape halves
1 cup sliced celery
⅓ cup orange low-fat yogurt
4 lettuce leaves
2 teaspoons sesame seeds, toasted

Combine first 4 ingredients; toss gently. Spoon over lettuce leaves; sprinkle with sesame seeds. Serve immediately. Yield: 4 servings (77 calories per ¾-cup serving).

□ 1.8 grams protein, 1.4 grams fat, 16 grams carbohydrate, 1 milligram cholesterol, 40 milligrams sodium, and 62.3 milligrams calcium.
Anne M. Grimes
Lexington, Kentucky

February 21

POACHED PEAR FANS WITH RASPBERRY-ORANGE SAUCE

2 firm medium-size pears, unpeeled
1½ cups water
2 tablespoons frozen orange juice concentrate, thawed and undiluted
1 (2-inch) stick cinnamon
Raspberry-Orange Sauce
Fresh mint sprigs

Cut pears in half lengthwise, leaving stem end of pear intact; core. Place cut side down in a Dutch oven. Combine water and orange juice concentrate; stir well. Pour over pears; add cinnamon stick. Bring to a boil over medium heat. Cover, reduce heat, and simmer 10 minutes or until pears are tender but firm. Remove from heat; let cool in cooking liquid.

Remove pears from liquid; place each pear half, cut side down, on a cutting surface. Slice lengthwise into ¼-inch strips, leaving stem end of pear intact.

Spoon ¼ cup Raspberry-Orange Sauce onto each of 4 dessert plates. Place a pear half on each of the plates, fanning out the slices. Garnish with fresh mint. Yield: 4 servings (63 calories per pear half plus 85 calories per ¼-cup sauce).

Raspberry-Orange Sauce

1 (10-ounce) package raspberries in light syrup, thawed
1 tablespoon frozen orange juice concentrate, thawed and undiluted
2 teaspoons cornstarch
⅛ teaspoon grated orange rind

Place raspberries in container of an electric blender; process until smooth. Strain raspberries, and discard seeds.

Combine remaining ingredients in a small saucepan; add raspberry puree, and stir well. Cook over medium heat, stirring constantly, until mixture comes to a boil. Cook 1 minute, stirring constantly. Remove from heat. Place in a bowl. Cover and chill. Yield: 1 cup (85 calories per ¼-cup sauce).

□ *0.5 gram protein, 0.3 gram fat, 15.8 grams carbohydrate, 0 milligrams cholesterol, 0 milligrams sodium, and 12 milligrams calcium per pear half plus 0.6 gram protein, 0.1 gram fat, 21.4 grams carbohydrate, 0 milligrams cholesterol, 1 milligram sodium, and 12 milligrams calcium per ¼ cup sauce.*

Mint Freshens The Flavor

Fresh mint is a part of our Southern heritage. When warm weather arrives, it springs up from dormancy with sweet, pungent aroma. The delicate, green leaves have awakened taste buds for generations, adorning tall glasses of iced tea and highlighting a number of dishes.

You can store mint sprigs in the refrigerator for several days. Wrap the stems in a moistened paper towel, and seal in a plastic bag.

Growing Mint at Home

Mint, a perennial, grows and spreads rapidly by means of stems that creep above and just below soil surface. It should be planted where it will get plenty of moisture. It prefers full sun or partial shade and fertile soil.

You can propagate mint by several methods. Using seed is not recommended. Instead, start with young plants that you buy at a nursery, or you can root stem cuttings or dig plants from a friend's patch. Mint propagates itself by runners. As these runners creep along and form a mat, they root and send up new plants. After the last spring frost, move new plants to your garden. Leave at least 1 foot between plants of the same type and 4 feet between different types. Plant mint where it can spread without hindering other plants.

Text is from *Southern Living Growing Vegetables & Herbs,* © 1984, Oxmoor House, Inc. Reprinted by permission.

LEMON-MINT BEANS

1 cup water
1 (9-ounce) package frozen cut green beans
1 (16-ounce) can golden cut wax beans, drained
½ teaspoon grated lemon rind
3 tablespoons lemon juice
1 tablespoon minced fresh mint

Bring water to a boil in a medium saucepan. Add green beans; cover and simmer 8 minutes. Add wax beans, and simmer 2 minutes; drain. Place in a serving bowl. Add remaining ingredients; toss gently. Serve

hot or cold. Yield: 5 servings (29 calories per ½-cup serving).

☐ *1.4 grams protein, 0.2 gram fat, 6.9 grams carbohydrate, 0 milligrams cholesterol, 157 milligrams sodium, and 42 milligrams calcium.*
Agnes Brandt
Arlington, Texas

MINTED VEGETABLE SALAD

2⅔ cups diced unpeeled tomatoes
¾ cup diced sweet red pepper
2 cups diced unpeeled cucumber
¾ cup sliced green onions
1 cup minced fresh parsley
⅓ cup minced fresh mint
½ cup diced radishes
10 pitted ripe olives, sliced
1 clove garlic, crushed
2 tablespoons olive oil
¼ cup lemon juice
½ teaspoon pepper
Lettuce leaves
¼ cup crumbled feta cheese

Combine first 12 ingredients in a large bowl; toss gently. Cover and chill at least 1 hour.

Spoon chilled vegetable mixture into a lettuce-lined serving bowl. Sprinkle crumbled feta cheese over vegetable salad. Yield 12 servings (55 calories per ½-cup serving).

☐ *1.5 grams protein, 3.9 grams fat, 4.8 grams carbohydrate, 3 milligrams cholesterol, 73 milligrams sodium, and 43 milligrams calcium.*
Catherine Spradling
Muskogee, Oklahoma

Tip: *Crush dried herbs gently with a mortar and pestle to enhance their flavor. Slightly bruising fresh plants will increase their effectiveness.*

FRESH MINT SHERBET

¼ cup sugar
½ teaspoon cornstarch
1½ cups skim milk
1 cup chopped fresh mint
¼ cup light corn syrup
2 cups skim milk
1 teaspoon lemon juice
1 (8-ounce) can unsweetened crushed pineapple, undrained
Green food coloring (optional)

Combine sugar, cornstarch, and 1½ cups milk in a small saucepan; bring to a boil over medium heat, stirring constantly. Boil 1 minute. Pour hot mixture over mint; let stand 30 minutes. Strain milk mixture; discard mint. Add corn syrup and remaining ingredients; stir well. Pour into freezer trays; freeze.

Spoon frozen mixture into a bowl, and beat at medium speed of an electric mixer until smooth. Pour into tray, and freeze. Yield: 10 servings (87 calories per ½-cup serving).

☐ *3 grams protein, 0.2 gram fat, 19 grams carbohydrate, 2 milligrams cholesterol, 50.5 milligrams sodium, and 112.5 milligrams calcium.*
Martha Camp
San Antonio, Texas

Feature Fish In A Low-Sodium Menu

You won't be needing the salt shaker when you dine on this menu, even though it's low in sodium. That's because it takes full advantage of garlic, wine vinegar, orange rind, and a variety of herbs and spices. These seasonings help create a pleasing meal that's under 500 calories and 300 milligrams sodium per serving.

Orangy Snapper
Yogurt-Stuffed Potatoes
Zucchini With Baby Carrots
Salad greens
With Basil Dressing
Chocolate-Almond Pudding
Tea   Coffee

ORANGY SNAPPER

6 (4-ounce) red snapper or other lean white fish fillets
Vegetable cooking spray
3 tablespoons water
2 tablespoons frozen orange juice concentrate, thawed and undiluted
2 teaspoons olive oil
½ teaspoon grated orange rind
Dash of freshly ground pepper
Ground nutmeg
Orange wedges (optional)
Parsley sprigs (optional)

Place fish fillets in a 12- x 8- x 2-inch baking dish coated with vegetable cooking spray.

Combine water, undiluted orange juice, olive oil, and grated orange rind in a small bowl; stir well. Pour mixture over fillets. Sprinkle with pepper and nutmeg. Bake, uncovered, at 350° for 20 to 25 minutes or until fish flakes easily when tested with a fork. If desired, garnish with orange wedges and parsley sprigs. Yield: 6 servings (129 calories per 3 ounces fish).

☐ *22.6 grams protein, 2.6 grams fat, 2.3 grams carbohydrate, 62 milligrams cholesterol, 76 milligrams sodium, and 21 milligrams calcium per 3 ounces fish.*
Mary C. Lear
Live Oak, Florida

YOGURT-STUFFED POTATOES

3 medium baking potatoes (1½ pounds)
¾ cup plain low-fat yogurt
⅛ teaspoon salt
¼ teaspoon coarsely ground black pepper
Vegetable cooking spray
¼ cup thinly sliced green onions
¼ cup (1 ounce) shredded Swiss cheese
1 tablespoon chopped chives
Paprika

Wash potatoes; prick with a fork. Bake at 400° for 1 hour or until done. Let cool slightly. Cut potatoes in half lengthwise. Scoop out pulp, leaving a ¼-inch shell. Set shells aside. Combine potato pulp, yogurt, salt, and pepper in a medium bowl; mash until light and fluffy. Set aside.

Coat a small skillet with cooking spray; place over medium-high heat until hot. Add green onions; sauté until tender. Remove from heat.

Add green onions, cheese, and chives to potato mixture; stir well. Spoon potato mixture into shells. Place potatoes on an ungreased baking sheet. Bake, uncovered, at 350° for 10 minutes or until thoroughly heated. Sprinkle with paprika. Yield: 6 servings (122 calories per stuffed potato half).

☐ *5.4 grams protein, 2 grams fat, 21.3 grams carbohydrate, 6 milligrams cholesterol, 91 milligrams sodium, and 116 milligrams calcium.*

Tip: *Baked stuffed potatoes can be prepared ahead of time. Simply bake the potatoes, scoop out the pulp, mix the filling, stuff the potato, top with cheese, and wrap for freezing. Unwrap the potatoes before heating.*

ZUCCHINI WITH BABY CARROTS

¾ pound baby carrots, scraped
¼ teaspoon dried Italian seasoning
¼ teaspoon coarsely ground black pepper
¼ teaspoon chicken-flavored bouillon granules
⅛ teaspoon garlic powder
⅓ cup water
2 medium zucchini, cut diagonally into ½-inch slices

Combine all ingredients except zucchini in a skillet. Cover and cook 5 minutes, stirring occasionally. Add zucchini; cover and cook 3 minutes or until vegetables are crisp-tender. Add additional water, 1 tablespoon at a time, if necessary, to prevent sticking. Yield: 6 servings (31 calories per ½-cup serving).

☐ *1.1 grams protein, 0.2 gram fat, 7.2 grams carbohydrate, 0 milligrams cholesterol, 56 milligrams sodium, and 24 milligrams calcium.*

BASIL DRESSING

¼ cup tarragon-flavored wine vinegar
¼ cup vegetable juice
2 tablespoons vegetable oil
1 clove garlic, minced
1 tablespoon chopped fresh basil or 1 teaspoon dried whole basil
½ teaspoon paprika
¼ teaspoon salt-free herb-and-spice blend
⅛ teaspoon freshly ground pepper

Combine all ingredients in a jar. Cover jar tightly, and shake vigorously. Chill. Shake well before serving dressing over salad greens. Yield: ½ cup plus 1 tablespoon (31 calories per tablespoon).

☐ *0.2 gram protein, 3.1 grams fat, 1.2 grams carbohydrate, 0 milligrams cholesterol, 25 milligrams sodium, and 10 milligrams calcium.*

*Eileen R. MaCutchan
Largo, Florida*

CHOCOLATE-ALMOND PUDDING

2 tablespoons cornstarch
2 cups skim milk, divided
1 (4-ounce) package sweet baking chocolate, coarsely chopped
¾ teaspoon almond extract
18 almond slices

Combine cornstarch and ½ cup milk in a heavy saucepan; stir until blended. Add remaining milk and chocolate. Cook over medium heat, stirring constantly with a wire whisk, until chocolate melts. Bring mixture to a boil, stirring constantly. Boil 1 minute; remove from heat. Stir in almond extract. Spoon into individual serving dishes. Cover and chill 1 to 2 hours. Garnish each serving with 3 almond slices. Yield: 6 servings (141 calories per ⅓-cup serving).

☐ *3.7 grams protein, 7 grams fat, 18 grams carbohydrate, 2 milligrams cholesterol, 43 milligrams sodium, and 109 milligrams calcium.*

Offer A Tasty New Entrée

If you are ready for some menu variation, you may want to try these colorful entrées. They're all tasty and nutritious without being laden with extra calories.

BEEF BURGUNDY

1 pound lean boneless sirloin
   steak
Vegetable cooking spray
1 medium onion, sliced and
   separated into rings
1 teaspoon chicken-flavored
   bouillon granules
¼ teaspoon dried whole
   oregano
¼ teaspoon dried whole thyme
¼ teaspoon pepper
1 bay leaf
½ cup Burgundy or other dry
   red wine
½ cup water
1 cup sliced fresh mushrooms
2 teaspoons cornstarch
¼ cup water
¼ teaspoon browning-and-
   seasoning sauce
2 cups hot cooked rice (cooked
   without salt or fat)

Trim fat from steak; slice thinly into
bite-size strips.

Coat a Dutch oven with cooking
spray; place over medium heat until
hot. Add half of meat, and brown on
each side. Remove meat, and repeat
with remaining meat.

Combine meat, onion, and next 7
ingredients in a Dutch oven. Cover,
reduce heat, and simmer 20 minutes.
Add sliced mushrooms; cover and
simmer 5 minutes.

Combine cornstarch, ¼ cup water,
and browning-and-seasoning sauce;
stir until smooth. Add to meat, stirring constantly. Bring to a boil; boil 1
minute, stirring constantly. Remove
bay leaf. Serve over rice. Yield: 4
servings (208 calories per ½ cup plus
2 tablespoons meat mixture plus 103
calories per ½ cup rice).

□ *26.8 grams protein, 8 grams fat,
6.1 grams carbohydrate, 76 milligrams cholesterol, 264 milligrams sodium, and 25.3 milligrams calcium
per ½ cup plus 2 tablespoons meat
mixture and 1.9 grams protein, 0.1*

*gram fat, 22.7 grams carbohydrate, 0
milligrams cholesterol, 1 milligram sodium, and 6.8 milligrams calcium per
½ cup rice.* Marie A. Davis
Morgantown, North Carolina

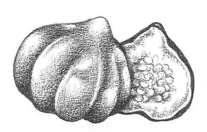

PORK CHOP DINNER

1 (8-ounce) can unsweetened,
   sliced pineapple
Vegetable cooking spray
4 (4-ounce) lean centercut,
   boneless pork loin chops,
   trimmed
1 medium-size sweet potato,
   peeled and cut into 4 slices
   (about ⅓ pound)
1 small acorn squash, cut
   crosswise into 4 slices
   (about 1 pound)
1 tablespoon brown sugar
2 teaspoons browning-and-
   seasoning sauce
2 tablespoons raisins
½ cup unsweetened apple juice
1 unpeeled cooking apple, cored
   and cut into 4 slices

Drain pineapple, reserving juice; set
aside. Coat a nonstick skillet with
cooking spray; place over medium-
high heat until hot. Add pork chops;
brown on each side. Layer sweet potato, squash, and pineapple slices
over pork chops.

Combine reserved pineapple juice,
brown sugar, and next 3 ingredients;
stir well, and pour over pineapple.
Cover, reduce heat, and simmer 30
minutes. Add apple slices; cover and
cook an additional 5 minutes. Yield: 4
servings (384 calories per pork chop
with fruit and vegetables).

□ *26.2 grams protein, 11.8 grams
fat, 45 grams carbohydrate, 77 milligrams cholesterol, 70 milligrams sodium, and 66 milligrams calcium.*
Dorothy Jean Evans
Russellville, Arkansas

DANTE'S CHICKEN

½ teaspoon ground ginger
½ teaspoon curry powder
⅛ teaspoon red pepper
4 (4-ounce) boned and skinned
   chicken breast halves
Vegetable cooking spray
2 cloves garlic, minced
3 tablespoons minced shallots
¼ cup sliced celery
½ cup sweet red pepper strips
½ cup canned chicken broth
½ cup Chablis or other dry
   white wine
¼ teaspoon ground ginger
Celery leaves (optional)

Combine first 3 ingredients; rub
spice mixture on chicken. Set aside.

Coat a large nonstick skillet with
cooking spray; place over medium-
high heat until hot. Add garlic, shallots, celery, and red pepper strips;
sauté 1 minute, stirring constantly.
Remove from skillet. Place chicken in
skillet; cook until lightly browned,
turning once. Return vegetables to
skillet. Combine broth, Chablis, and
¼ teaspoon ginger; stir well. Pour
over chicken. Cover, reduce heat,
and simmer 15 minutes. Arrange
chicken and vegetables on a platter;
garnish with celery leaves, if desired.
Yield: 4 servings (166 calories per
chicken breast half with vegetables).

□ *27.5 grams protein, 3.5 grams fat,
4.4 grams carbohydrate, 72 milligrams cholesterol, 170 milligrams sodium, and 27 milligrams calcium.*
Mae Certain
Tulsa, Oklahoma

COOKING Light

SPICY TURKEY CUTLETS WITH PEPPER SALSA

1 egg, slightly beaten
2 tablespoons water
2 cloves garlic, minced
1½ teaspoons ground cumin
½ teaspoon ground coriander
¼ teaspoon ground cinnamon
1 pound turkey cutlets
1 cup crushed tortilla chips
Vegetable cooking spray
Green onion fans (optional)
Pepper Salsa

Combine first 6 ingredients; stir well. Dip turkey cutlets into egg mixture; dredge in crushed tortilla chips.

Coat a large nonstick skillet with cooking spray; place over medium-high heat until hot. Add cutlets; cook 3 to 4 minutes on each side. Place on a serving platter; garnish with green onion fans, if desired. Serve with Pepper Salsa. Yield: 4 servings (280 calories per 3 ounces turkey serving plus 4 calories per tablespoon salsa).

Pepper Salsa

¼ cup sliced green onions
½ cup diced sweet red pepper
1 (4-ounce) can chopped green chiles, undrained
⅛ teaspoon hot sauce
3 tablespoons lime juice

Combine all ingredients in a small bowl; stir well. Cover and chill thoroughly. Serve salsa with turkey cutlets. Yield: 1 cup (4 calories per tablespoon).

☐ *29.4 grams protein, 9.5 grams fat, 17.4 grams carbohydrate, 139 milligrams cholesterol, 181 milligrams sodium, and 71 milligrams calcium per 3 ounces turkey serving plus 0.1 gram protein, 0 grams fat, 0.8 gram carbohydrate, 0 milligrams cholesterol, 8 milligrams sodium, and 1 milligram calcium per tablespoon salsa.*
Edith Askins
Greenville, Texas

Tofu–It's Good And Good For You

Have you noticed a mysterious white food that resembles cream cheese in the produce section of the grocery store? It's tofu, made from curding the liquid from cooked soybeans.

Tofu is high in protein and low in calories, sodium, and fat. Equally important, tofu contains no cholesterol.

You can fry, steam, toast, bake, cube, slice, blend, or freeze tofu. When it is blended, it can be substituted for yogurt, sour cream, cottage cheese, or ricotta cheese as a base in many sauce and salad dressing recipes.

Two things make tofu so versatile: its mild flavor, which tends to pick up the flavor of other foods used in the same recipe, and its different textures. Soft tofu has a custardlike texture that makes it a good choice for dips, spreads, and sauces. Medium-firm (also called Japanese or regular) tofu works well in casseroles, soups, or salads because of its cheeselike texture. Firm or Chinese tofu is the best choice for crumbling, coating cutlets, or deep-frying.

TOFRUITTI BREAKFAST DRINK

½ cup (¼ pound) soft tofu
1 cup skim milk
1½ cups apricot nectar, chilled
1 cup unsweetened pineapple juice, chilled

Combine tofu and milk in container of an electric blender; process 1 minute. Add remaining ingredients, and pulse 2 or 3 times to blend. Chill well. Yield: 9 servings (57 calories per ½-cup serving).

☐ *2.2 grams protein, 0.6 gram fat, 11.4 grams carbohydrate, 1 milligram cholesterol, 17 milligrams sodium, and 57 milligrams calcium.*
Mrs. Robert Burriss
Alexandria, Virginia

SPANISH RICE WITH TOFU

⅓ cup chopped onion
⅔ cup chopped green pepper
⅔ cup chopped celery
2 cloves garlic, minced
3 tablespoons water
2 cups (12 ounces) firm tofu, drained and crumbled
½ teaspoon dried whole thyme
1 teaspoon chili powder
2 teaspoons chicken-flavored bouillon granules
1 (16-ounce) can whole tomatoes, undrained and chopped
3 cups cooked brown rice (cooked without salt or fat)
¾ cup (3 ounces) shredded 40% less fat Cheddar cheese
2 tablespoons sliced ripe olives

Combine first 5 ingredients in a large skillet; cover and cook until vegetables are tender. Add tofu, thyme, chili powder, bouillon granules, tomatoes, and rice; simmer, uncovered, 15 minutes or until liquid is absorbed.

Sprinkle rice mixture with ¾ cup shredded cheese; cover and continue to cook until cheese melts. Garnish with olive slices. Yield: 7 main-dish servings (223 calories per 1-cup serving).

☐ *14 grams protein, 8 grams fat, 26.6 grams carbohydrate, 12 milligrams cholesterol, 445 milligrams sodium, and 234 milligrams calcium.*
Clarine Spetzler
Salem, Virginia

TOFU SALAD

8 ounces firm tofu, drained and
   cut into ½-inch cubes
2 cloves garlic, minced
1 tablespoon vegetable oil
1 cup thinly sliced cucumber
1 cup chopped tomato
1 cup sliced fresh mushrooms
½ cup sliced green onions
¼ cup chopped walnuts
5 lettuce leaves
Yogurt dressing
   (recipe follows)

Sauté tofu and garlic in oil in a non-stick skillet 5 minutes or until tofu is lightly browned; drain well on paper towels. Combine tofu mixture, cucumber, and next 4 ingredients; chill 2 hours.

Spoon salad onto lettuce-lined plates, and top with yogurt dressing. Yield: 5 servings (116 calories per ½-cup serving plus 9 calories per tablespoon dressing).

Yogurt Dressing

½ cup plain low-fat yogurt
1 tablespoon plus 1 teaspoon
   dried whole coriander leaves
2 tablespoons lemon juice
¼ teaspoon ground ginger
¼ teaspoon salt
¼ teaspoon pepper

Combine all ingredients in a small bowl; stir well. Chill thoroughly. Yield: ½ cup plus 2 tablespoons (9 calories per tablespoon).

□ *5.6 grams protein, 8.6 grams fat, 6.6 grams carbohydrate, 0 milligrams cholesterol, 10 milligrams sodium, and 81 milligrams calcium per ½-cup serving plus 9 calories, 0.7 gram protein, 0.2 gram fat, 1.3 grams carbohydrate, 1 milligram cholesterol, 67 milligrams sodium, and 25 milligrams calcium.*
Noel Todd McLaughlin
Chapel Hill, North Carolina

Staying Comfortable While Exercising

Southern exercise enthusiasts have learned to take precautions in weather extremes.

In the Cold

■ Wear several layers of lightweight clothing. For extra warmth, wear exercise tights under sweatpants; as you warm up, remove the top layers.

■ Always wear a hat because most body heat is lost through the head. To protect the ears and mouth, wear a scarf or ski mask.

■ Exercising in cold weather may give you chest pains. While cold air can make the back of the throat or the lungs hurt, chest pains signal something more serious. If you experience them, see your physician.

■ Walkers who are breathless at the top of a hill with their hearts pounding should slow down. Before starting an exercise program, discuss with your physician or exercise specialist what your optimum heart rate should be; then check your heart rate often to gauge how fast to walk up and down hills.

In the Heat

■ Wear loose-fitting, light-colored clothing. Cotton is best because it "breathes." To help stay cool, you can also tie a wet bandanna or handkerchief around your neck. Wrap a few ice cubes in the bandana and let them melt as you work out.

■ Never wear plastic or rubberized clothing or belts. These are extremely dangerous, especially in hot weather. Your body cools itself through the evaporation of perspiration. When a plastic or rubber suit traps that perspiration inside, it cannot evaporate and thus cool the body. As the body keeps perspiring, you lose more and more water and become dehydrated, increasing the chances of heat stroke.

■ Exercise indoors; stationary cycling, indoor swimming, and walking in a cool mall or gym with good air circulation are all possibilities.

■ At a pool, you can do calisthenics, walk or run against the water's resistance, or enjoy water games, such as volleyball or polo. The water helps carry your body weight and causes less strain on your joints.

■ Wear a cap or visor to keep the sun off your face. You can even wet the hat to make it cooler.

■ Heat makes your heart rate increase faster, so it's not necessary to exercise as hard. Exercise in intervals—do 5 to 10 minutes of exercise alternated with a few minutes of walking and a water break. Check your pulse often.

■ Drink plenty of water. Your brain's thirst center is content with just a bit, but your body is not. Drink fluids—preferably water—before, during, and several hours after exercise. Other fluids take longer to be digested, and some, such as those containing sugar, caffeine, or alcohol, can dehydrate you.

■ Take extra time to cool down. Walk or exercise at a slow pace until your heart rate returns to near normal and your breathing is regular.

A final note: If you experience any of the following symptoms while exercising, stop immediately, drink water, and call for help. These are signs of heat exhaustion and heat stroke: a chilled feeling even though it's hot; arm hair "standing up"; nausea or vomiting; pale skin; or dry, hot, red skin.

Sprinkle On An Herb Blend

Whether you're cooking poultry, meat, fish, or vegetables, a few shakes of the right seasoning blend will win you praise every time.

Designed mainly to help you cook without a recipe, these herb blends complement foods no matter what cooking method you use. Try the seasoning mixtures in our few simple recipes to help familiarize yourself with their uses. Then experiment to come up with some of your own tasty concoctions.

Two teaspoons of seasoning blend per pound of meat or vegetables is a good guide. Our herb blends have so much flavor, you probably won't need to add any salt to the foods that you prepare with them.

You can use either commercially dried herbs or your own home-dried herbs to make these blends. Label them, and store in airtight containers in a cool, dry place. Use the herbs loose if you want them to remain in the food, or tie the mixture in a cheesecloth bag if you prefer to remove the herbs after cooking.

■ Our Fish-and-Seafood Seasoning Blend boasts the flavors of dill and lemon, which are commonly chosen to complement foods of this type.

FISH-AND-SEAFOOD SEASONING BLEND

¼ cup plus 2 tablespoons dried whole parsley
3 tablespoons dried whole dillweed
3 tablespoons lemon-pepper seasoning
4 bay leaves, crumbled, or ½ teaspoon ground bay leaves

Combine all ingredients, stirring well. Store in an airtight container in a cool, dry place. Yield: ½ cup.

BROILED FLOUNDER

2 tablespoons butter or margarine, melted
4 (4- to 6-ounce) flounder fillets
2 teaspoons Fish-and-Seafood Seasoning Blend
Lemon wedges

Line a shallow baking pan with aluminum foil; lightly brush foil with a small amount of butter. Arrange fillets in prepared pan. Brush fillets with remaining butter, and sprinkle with Fish-and-Seafood Seasoning Blend. Broil 5 inches from heat 10 minutes or until fish flakes easily when tested with a fork. Garnish flounder fillets with lemon wedges. Yield: 4 servings.

SCALLOP SAUTÉ
(pictured on page 35)

1 pound fresh scallops, drained
3 tablespoons butter or margarine, melted
1 cup sliced fresh mushrooms
1 small onion, sliced and separated into rings
¼ cup dry white wine
2 teaspoons Fish-and-Seafood Seasoning Blend
1 tomato, diced

Sauté scallops in butter in a large skillet about 5 minutes or until tender; drain and set aside, reserving drippings in skillet.

Sauté mushrooms and onion in drippings in skillet 4 minutes or until tender; drain and set aside, reserving drippings in skillet.

Add wine and Fish-and-Seafood Seasoning Blend to drippings in skillet; cook over high heat until mixture is reduced by about half. Add scallops, mushrooms, onion, and tomato to drippings in skillet. Cook over high heat 1 minute or until heated. Serve immediately. Yield: 3 to 4 servings.

■ Composed of a mixture of eight herbs and seasonings, our Poultry Seasoning Blend will flavor both domestic and wild birds. When roasting whole birds, generously sprinkle the cavity and exterior with the mixture.

POULTRY SEASONING BLEND

1½ tablespoons rubbed sage
1½ tablespoons onion powder
1½ tablespoons pepper
1½ tablespoons celery seeds
1½ tablespoons dried whole thyme
1½ tablespoons dried marjoram leaves
2¼ teaspoons dried rosemary leaves
2¼ teaspoons garlic powder

Combine all ingredients, stirring well. Store in an airtight container in a cool, dry place. Yield: ½ cup.

HERBED CHICKEN PICCATA

6 chicken breast halves, skinned and boned
⅓ cup all-purpose flour
1½ teaspoons Poultry Seasoning Blend
¼ cup plus 2 tablespoons butter or margarine, divided
¼ cup lemon juice
1 lemon, thinly sliced

Place each piece of chicken between 2 sheets of wax paper, and flatten to ¼-inch thickness, using a meat mallet or rolling pin. Combine flour and Poultry Seasoning Blend; dredge chicken in flour mixture.

Melt ¼ cup butter in a large skillet over medium heat. Add chicken, and cook 3 to 4 minutes on each side or until golden brown. (Add additional butter, 1 tablespoon at a time, if needed.) Remove chicken, and drain on paper towels. Place on serving platter; keep warm. Add lemon juice and lemon slices to pan drippings in skillet; cook until thoroughly heated. Pour lemon mixture over chicken. Yield: 6 servings.

HERB-ROASTED CORNISH HENS
(pictured on page 35)

2 (1- to 1¼-pound) Cornish hens
1 tablespoon plus 1 teaspoon
  Poultry Seasoning Blend,
  divided
¼ cup butter or margarine,
  softened
¼ teaspoon hot sauce
Red grapes (optional)
Dried sprigs of rosemary
  (optional)

Remove giblets from hens, and reserve for other uses. Rinse hens with cold water, and pat dry. Lift wingtips up and over back so that they are tucked under hen. Sprinkle cavities with 2 teaspoons Poultry Seasoning Blend. Close cavities, and tie leg ends together with string; set hens aside.

Combine butter, remaining 2 teaspoons seasoning blend, and hot sauce; spread on hens. Place hens, breast side up, in a shallow roasting pan. Insert meat thermometer in breast so that thermometer doesn't touch bone or fat.

Bake at 350° for 1 hour and 15 minutes or until meat thermometer registers 185°, basting often with pan drippings. Transfer to platter; if desired, garnish with grapes and rosemary. Yield: 2 servings.

■ Thyme, onion powder, and cumin add the bulk of the flavor to our Meat Seasoning Blend. Use this flavorful combination for all types of beef, pork, veal, and lamb, as well as meaty soups and stews.

MEAT SEASONING BLEND

3 tablespoons dried whole thyme
2 tablespoons onion powder
1½ tablespoons cumin seeds or
  1½ teaspoons ground cumin
1 tablespoon pepper
1 teaspoon ground cloves
1 teaspoon garlic powder
3 small bay leaves, crumbled, or
  ¼ teaspoon plus ⅛ teaspoon
  ground bay leaves

Combine all ingredients, stirring well. Store in an airtight container in a cool, dry place. Yield: about ½ cup.

SPICY BEEF TENDERLOIN
(pictured on page 35)

1 cup port wine
1 cup soy sauce
½ cup olive oil
3 tablespoons Meat Seasoning
  Blend
1 (5- to 6-pound) beef tenderloin,
  trimmed
Fresh watercress

Combine wine, soy sauce, oil, and Meat Seasoning Blend, and mix well.

Place tenderloin in a large shallow dish; pour wine mixture over top, and cover tightly. Refrigerate 8 hours, turning occasionally.

Uncover tenderloin; drain and reserve marinade. Place tenderloin on a rack in a roasting pan; insert meat thermometer, making sure it does not touch fat. Bake at 425° for 45 to 60 minutes or until thermometer registers 140° (rare), basting occasionally with marinade. (Bake until thermometer registers 150° for medium-rare or 160° for medium.) Transfer tenderloin to a serving platter, and garnish with watercress. Yield: 10 to 12 servings.

POT ROAST WITH HERBED RED SAUCE

1 (2½- to 3-pound) boneless
  chuck roast
1 tablespoon vegetable oil
3 (8-ounce) cans tomato sauce
2 tablespoons vinegar
1½ tablespoons Meat Seasoning
  Blend
Hot cooked spaghetti

Brown roast on all sides in hot oil in a Dutch oven.

Combine tomato sauce, vinegar, and Meat Seasoning Blend; pour over roast. Cover and simmer over low heat 2½ hours or until tender. Remove roast to serving platter, and

keep warm. Cook sauce over medium heat 3 to 5 minutes or until reduced to about 2½ cups. Skim off fat. Cut roast into serving-size pieces, and serve with spaghetti and red sauce. Yield: 4 to 6 servings.

■ Parsley, basil, oregano, and savory team up in our Vegetable Seasoning Blend to flavor all types of vegetables. You can also add it to an oil-and-vinegar dressing.

VEGETABLE SEASONING BLEND

3 tablespoons dried parsley flakes
2 tablespoons dried basil leaves
2 tablespoons dried whole
  oregano
1 tablespoon dried whole savory
  or 1 teaspoon ground savory

Combine all ingredients, stirring well. Store in an airtight container in a cool, dry place. Yield: about ½ cup.

HERBED SALAD DRESSING

⅓ cup white wine vinegar
¼ cup vegetable oil
¼ cup olive oil
2 tablespoons water
1 tablespoon Vegetable Seasoning
  Blend

Combine all ingredients in a jar; cover tightly, and shake vigorously. Serve dressing over salad greens. Yield: ¾ cup.

TOMATOES ITALIANO

4 medium tomatoes, sliced
3 tablespoons olive oil
1 tablespoon Vegetable Seasoning
  Blend
2 to 3 tablespoons lemon juice

Place tomatoes in a shallow dish. Combine remaining ingredients; stir well, and pour over tomatoes. Cover and chill 2 hours, tossing gently after 1 hour. Yield: 6 to 8 servings.

Soups With A Mexican Flavor

If you like the earthy, robust flavor of Mexican food, then you'll love the soups and stews we feature here. They're not fancy but just hearty samplings of the great flavor adopted by Southerners near the border.

For a real meal-in-one, Guadalajara Soup offers a tasty vegetable-and-pork medley. If you're cautious about hot, spicy food, you'll be pleased to find this chunky soup mild in flavor. In fact, many Mexican-style soups and stews feature a mild flavor to make them compatible with such traditional accompaniments as fresh hot peppers or fiery homemade salsa. Peppers are eaten with soup as you would eat crackers, and salsa is stirred into individual servings of soup, as desired.

Tortilla Soup sports bite-size pieces of corn tortillas in a savory broth—sort of a Southwest version of noodle soup. It is one way to use up dry, stale tortillas no longer suitable for use in enchiladas or other recipes. For an updated touch to this old favorite, deep-fry a few of the tortilla pieces and sprinkle atop each serving of soup.

For the spicy flavor of the Southwest, try Mexican Pollo en Pipián. This hot, robust stew is tamed by side dishes of rice and tortillas (and, if you like, guacamole). If the spice is still too hot for you, stir in a little lime juice.

You'll have a complete meal with any of these favorites.

GUADALAJARA SOUP

1¼ cups dried pinto beans
3½ to 4 pounds country-style pork ribs
¼ cup vegetable oil
1 cup finely chopped onion
2 cloves garlic, minced
2 (14½-ounce) cans beef broth, undiluted
4 cups water
2 teaspoons chili powder
1 teaspoon dried whole oregano
1 teaspoon ground cumin seeds
½ teaspoon salt
¼ teaspoon pepper
4 cups thinly sliced carrots
1 (7-ounce) jar baby corn on the cob
Cherry tomatoes, halved (optional)
Fresh cilantro, chopped (optional)
Sour cream (optional)
Jalapeño salsa (optional)

Sort and wash beans; place in a large Dutch oven. Cover with water 2 inches above beans, and bring to a boil; cook 2 minutes. Remove beans from heat. Cover and let soak 1 hour; drain.

Brown pork ribs in oil in a large Dutch oven. Remove ribs from Dutch oven; set aside. Add onion and garlic to Dutch oven; sauté until tender. Add beans, ribs, broth, and next 6 ingredients; cover and simmer 1½ hours or until meat is tender. Remove ribs; cool and remove meat from bone. Return meat to broth. Chill broth until fat rises to the surface and hardens; remove fat.

Bring mixture to a boil. Add carrots and corn; cover and simmer 30 minutes. Additional broth may be added. If desired, serve with cherry tomato halves, chopped cilantro, sour cream, and jalapeño salsa. Yield: 2 quarts.
Jana Dominguez
Navasota, Texas

BLACK BEAN SOUP

1 pound dried black beans
6 cups chicken broth
2 cups water
2 small ham hocks (about 8 ounces)
¼ pound salt pork
1 bay leaf
1 cup chopped onion
½ cup chopped celery with leaves
1½ cups chopped green pepper
1 large tomato, peeled and chopped
1 clove garlic, minced
6 serrano peppers, seeded and chopped
1 (6-ounce) can tomato paste
¼ teaspoon pepper
¼ teaspoon hot sauce
2 tablespoons Worcestershire sauce
Lemon slices (optional)

Sort and wash beans; place in a large Dutch oven. Cover with water 2 inches above beans; let soak at least

8 hours. Drain well. Add chicken broth, 2 cups water, ham hocks, salt pork, and bay leaf to beans; bring mixture to a boil. Cover, reduce heat, and simmer 1½ hours.

Remove ham hocks and salt pork. Discard bone and fat; return ham to soup mixture. Add onion and remaining ingredients, except lemon slices; cover and simmer 2 hours. Remove bay leaf. Partially mash beans with a potato masher. Garnish each bowl of soup with lemon slices, if desired. Yield: 3 quarts.   *Carol Barclay*
Portland, Texas

LIME SOUP

1 (3- to 3½-pound) broiler-fryer, cut up
6 cups water
1 medium onion, quartered
1 stalk celery
3 fresh cilantro or parsley sprigs
6 whole peppercorns
2 teaspoons salt
½ teaspoon dried whole thyme
1 medium-size green pepper, chopped
1 medium onion, chopped
2 tablespoons vegetable oil
2 large tomatoes, peeled and chopped
1½ teaspoons grated lime rind
Juice of 2 limes
3 tablespoons chopped fresh cilantro or parsley
¼ teaspoon salt
¼ teaspoon pepper
8 corn tortillas
Vegetable oil
Lime slices (optional)
Fresh cilantro (optional)

Place first 8 ingredients in a large Dutch oven; bring to a boil. Cover, reduce heat, and simmer 1 hour. Remove chicken, reserving broth; let chicken cool. Bone and chop chicken; set aside. Strain chicken broth to remove vegetables; set broth aside, and discard vegetables.

Sauté green pepper and chopped onion in 2 tablespoons oil in Dutch oven. Stir in tomatoes; cook 5 minutes. Add reserved broth, lime rind, lime juice, and 3 tablespoons chopped cilantro. Bring mixture to a boil; reduce heat, and simmer, uncovered, 20 minutes. Stir in chicken, ¼ teaspoon salt, and pepper; simmer, uncovered, 10 minutes.

Cut each tortilla into 8 wedges; fry in hot oil until crisp. Drain. To serve, place 8 tortilla wedges in each soup bowl; add soup, and if desired, garnish with lime slices and cilantro. Yield: 8 cups.   *Mrs. John R. Allen*
Dallas, Texas

TORTILLA SOUP
(pictured on page 34)

1 dried ancho chile
¼ cup olive oil
4 corn tortillas, cut into 1-inch pieces
1 large onion, coarsely chopped
1 medium-size green pepper, chopped
3 cloves garlic, minced
4 cups chicken broth
½ teaspoon ground cumin
½ teaspoon freshly ground black pepper
2 tomatoes, unpeeled and chopped
2 tablespoons chopped fresh cilantro
1 tablespoon chopped fresh parsley

Remove stem and seeds from chile; sauté chile in hot oil in a Dutch oven until soft. Remove chile, and chop, reserving drippings in Dutch oven.

Fry tortilla pieces in drippings until brown. Remove tortillas, and drain, reserving drippings in Dutch oven.

Sauté onion, green pepper, and garlic in drippings until tender. Add broth, cumin, and pepper. Bring to a boil; cover, reduce heat, and simmer

20 minutes. Stir in reserved chile and tomatoes; simmer 10 minutes. Before serving, stir in chopped cilantro and chopped parsley.

To serve, place fried tortilla pieces in individual soup bowls, reserving one-fourth of chips; add soup. Top with reserved chips. Yield: 6 cups.
Bertha Y. Ivaldi
Brownsville, Texas

MEXICAN POLLO EN PIPIÁN

6 dried ancho chiles
½ cup hot water
1 (4-pound) broiler-fryer, cut up
2 medium onions, quartered
½ green pepper, cut into strips
2 carrots, cut into 4 pieces
1 teaspoon dried whole coriander seeds
1 (10¾-ounce) can chicken broth
3½ cups water
¼ cup peanut butter
½ teaspoon salt
¼ teaspoon ground cinnamon
¼ teaspoon dried whole thyme
⅛ teaspoon ground cloves
Hot cooked rice
Tortillas

Remove stems and seeds from chiles. Chop chiles, and combine with ½ cup hot water in a small bowl; cover and set aside 1 hour. Drain.

Combine chicken and next 6 ingredients in a large Dutch oven; bring to a boil. Cover, reduce heat, and simmer 1 hour. Remove chicken and vegetables from broth; set aside. Strain broth; reserve 1 cup broth, and return 2 cups remaining broth to Dutch oven. Bone and chop chicken; return chicken and vegetables to Dutch oven.

Combine chiles and reserved 1 cup chicken broth in container of an electric blender; process until smooth. Add peanut butter; process until smooth. Add to chicken mixture; stir well. Add salt, cinnamon, thyme, and cloves; stir well. Cover and simmer 30 minutes. Serve with rice and tortillas. Yield: 6½ cups.
Zelma Estelle Standridge
Russellville, Arkansas

Puddings—Still A Family Favorite

You may not find pudding listed on menus at the fanciest restaurants, but a peek inside the homes of Southerners reveals it's still a family favorite after all these years.

OLD-FASHIONED BREAD PUDDING WITH RUM SAUCE

3 eggs, slightly beaten
3 cups milk
3 cups crumbled day-old biscuits
½ cup sugar
½ cup raisins
¼ cup butter or margarine, melted
¼ teaspoon salt
1 tablespoon grated lemon rind
¼ teaspoon ground nutmeg
Rum Sauce

Combine eggs and milk; stir well. Add crumbled biscuits and next 5 ingredients; stir gently. Spoon mixture into a greased 2-quart baking dish, and sprinkle with nutmeg. Place dish in a larger shallow pan; add water to depth of 1 inch. Bake at 350° for 50 minutes or until knife inserted in center comes out clean. Serve pudding warm with Rum Sauce. Yield: 6 to 8 servings.

Rum Sauce

¾ cup sugar
1 tablespoon cornstarch
⅔ cup water
⅓ cup rum
½ teaspoon lemon juice
1 tablespoon butter or margarine

Combine first 4 ingredients in a small saucepan; bring to a boil over medium heat. Cook 1 minute, stirring constantly. Add lemon juice and butter; stir until butter melts. Serve warm. Yield: 1½ cups.
Mrs. Bob Nester
Charleston, West Virginia

BANANA PUDDING
(pictured on facing page)

⅔ cup sugar
3 tablespoons cornstarch
¼ cup water
2 eggs, separated
1½ cups milk
1 teaspoon vanilla extract
18 to 24 vanilla wafers
2 medium bananas, sliced
⅛ teaspoon cream of tartar
2 tablespoons sugar

Combine ⅔ cup sugar and cornstarch in a heavy saucepan; mix well. Stir in water; mix well.

Beat egg yolks; add milk, mixing well. Gradually add milk mixture to cornstarch mixture. Cook over medium heat, stirring constantly, until mixture boils. Boil 1 minute, stirring constantly, until thickened. Remove from heat; stir in vanilla. Cool slightly.

Arrange half of vanilla wafers in the bottom of a 1½-quart baking dish; spread with half of pudding. Top with banana slices. Arrange remaining wafers around the outside edge of dish. Spread with remaining pudding.

Combine egg whites (at room temperature) and cream of tartar; beat at high speed of an electric mixer until foamy. Gradually add 2 tablespoons sugar, beating until stiff peaks form. Spread meringue over pudding, sealing to edge of dish. Bake at 400° for 8 to 10 minutes or until golden brown. Serve warm or at room temperature. Yield: 6 servings.
Joyce Dean Garrison
Charlotte, North Carolina

VANILLA PUDDING
(pictured on facing page)

2 eggs
¼ cup plus 2 tablespoons sugar
¼ cup all-purpose flour
3 cups milk
1 tablespoon plus 1 teaspoon butter or margarine
2 teaspoons vanilla extract
Mandarin orange slices

Beat eggs at medium speed of an electric mixer until foamy. Add sugar and flour, beating until blended.

Heat milk in a heavy saucepan. Gradually stir about one-fourth of hot milk into egg mixture; add to remaining milk, stirring constantly. Cook over medium heat, stirring constantly, until thickened (about 8 minutes). Remove from heat, and stir in butter and vanilla. Spoon into individual compotes. Cover and chill. Top with mandarin orange slices. Yield: 6 servings.
June Bostick
Greenwood, Delaware

PEANUT BUTTER PUDDING
(pictured on facing page)

⅓ cup sugar
2 tablespoons cornstarch
2 cups milk
¼ cup creamy peanut butter
1 teaspoon vanilla extract
2 egg whites
¼ teaspoon salt
2 tablespoons sugar
Whipped cream
Chopped peanuts

Combine ⅓ cup sugar and cornstarch in heavy saucepan; stir until blended. Slowly stir in milk; bring to a boil. Cook, stirring constantly, 1 minute or until thickened. Remove from heat; stir in peanut butter and vanilla.

Combine egg whites (at room temperature) and salt; beat until foamy. Gradually add 2 tablespoons sugar, beating until stiff but not dry. Do not overbeat. Fold egg whites into peanut butter mixture. Spoon into compotes. Cover and chill. Garnish with whipped cream and peanuts. Yield: 6 servings.
Mrs. C. Gibson
Brooksville, Florida

Right: (Clockwise from left) Banana Pudding, Peanut Butter Pudding, and Vanilla Pudding are family desserts most folks grew up enjoying. (All recipes are on this page.)

Above: *Our herb mixtures add extra flavor to all types of foods: (from front) Herb-Roasted Cornish Hens, Scallop Sauté, and Spicy Beef Tenderloin. (Recipes begin on page 28.)*

Left: *You can make a complete meal with Tortilla Soup (page 31) or any other of these robust Mexican soups and stews. Tortillas, salads, peppers, sour cream, green onions, and cheese can be served with them.*

Step 1: *After slicing top and bottom of cake, cut vertically around and through cake ¾ inch from edge. Remove outer shell; set on bottom slice. Slice two (½-inch) layers from center. Use remaining portion to plug center holes in layers.*

Step 2: *Place cake shell in center of a 15- to 16-inch serving tray. Plug hole in center of cake bottom, and spoon ½ cup commercial strawberry glaze on bottom, spreading glaze across bottom and to sides of cake shell.*

Step 3: *Arrange half of sliced strawberries over glaze; top with one layer of cake, and plug hole in center. Repeat layers of glaze, sliced strawberries, and cake (with hole plugged). Spread ½ cup glaze on cake, spreading to sides.*

Step 4: *Invert whole strawberries, and arrange on top of glaze. Brush strawberries lightly with small amount of glaze. Spoon remaining glaze onto serving tray and spread with a pastry brush. Pipe whipped cream according to recipe instructions.*

For an easy dessert with a sophisticated look, try Elegant Strawberry Shortcake. (The recipe is on facing page.)

Strawberry Shortcake Takes Center Stage

The flavor remains just as wonderful as you remember—pound cake drenched with juicy fresh strawberries and sweetened whipped cream. But the look is a little more contemporary, and it dresses this traditional dessert for special occasions.

The design of Elegant Strawberry Shortcake looks challenging, but don't be fooled—there's not even any cooking involved. Our recipe uses a commercial pound cake, two jars of strawberry glaze, strawberries, and whipped cream.

About half of the strawberries for this shortcake are used on top, so before slicing the berries to be used between the layers, set aside the prettiest, most uniform ones.

When entertaining, you can partially assemble the cake up to 24 hours before you plan to serve it. (The recipe gives complete directions.) Insert several wooden picks in the top of the cake, and cover loosely with plastic wrap; then chill. The wooden picks hold the wrap away from the cake so that it won't stick to the berries. Wait until just before serving to add the whipped cream and glaze. If you have the decorating bags of whipped cream ready ahead of time, it shouldn't take more than 5 to 10 minutes to pipe the cream and make the linear design at the base of the cake.

For piping the design, be sure cream is whipped just until slightly thickened. For a quick substitute to the linear design, pipe swirls of the lightly whipped cream freehand, creating a different look.

ELEGANT STRAWBERRY SHORTCAKE
(pictured on facing page)

1 (9- to 10-inch diameter) commercial pound cake
2 (16-ounce) jars commercial strawberry glaze
4 cups small whole strawberries, divided
2 cups whipping cream
¼ cup sifted powdered sugar

Using a long serrated knife, slice off top of pound cake to level cake. Slice ½ inch from bottom of cake, and set aside; reserve top for other uses.

Using a gentle, sawing motion, cut vertically all the way around and through bottom of remaining portion of cake ¾ inch from edge. Gently remove outer shell of cake, and set on bottom slice of cake. Slice center portion of cake horizontally to make 2 (½-inch) layers. From remaining portion of cake, cut 3 (½-inch-thick) rounds (the size of hole in center of cake) to plug holes.

Place cake shell in center of a 15- to 16-inch serving tray that has a small lip around the edge. Plug hole in center of cake, using one of cake rounds. Spoon ½ cup strawberry glaze on bottom of cake shell, and spread to sides.

Wash, hull, and slice 2 cups strawberries. Arrange half of sliced strawberries over glaze. Top with 1 slice of cake cut from center portion. Plug hole in center of cake, using another cake round. Spoon ½ cup glaze on cake layer, and spread to sides. Arrange remaining sliced strawberries over glaze. Top with remaining slice of cake, and plug hole with remaining cake round. Spread ½ cup glaze on cake layer, and spread to sides.

Wash and hull remaining strawberries. Invert strawberries, and arrange on top of glaze. Brush strawberries lightly with a small amount of glaze. (At this stage, cake may be covered and chilled up to 24 hours before finishing and serving, if desired.)

Spoon remaining strawberry glaze onto serving tray around base of cake, and spread with a pastry brush; set aside.

Beat whipping cream at high speed of an electric mixer until foamy. Gradually add powdered sugar, beating until slightly thickened. Set aside ½ cup of thickened cream. Continue beating remaining cream until firm peaks form. Spoon firmly beaten cream into a decorating bag fitted with metal tip No. 2110. Pipe vertical zigzag strips along sides and top edge of cake, starting at base of cake and piping upward.

Spoon lightly whipped cream into a decorating bag fitted with metal tip No. 3. For linear design, pipe 3 parallel lines about ½ inch apart around glaze at base of cake. Gently pull a wooden pick back and forth perpendicular to lines to make decorative border. (For a quicker design, pipe swirls of lightly whipped cream freehand.) Serve immediately. Yield: one 9- to 10-inch cake.

Chicken And Rice In Just One Dish

In plain or fancy recipes, chicken and rice make a natural pair. The two ingredients are compatible with a wide range of seasonings and flavors.

If you're looking for something quick, then try Chicken Cashew. Another dish, Rice-Stuffed Roasted Chicken, is elegant enough for company, but easy enough to prepare for an everyday meal. (For more on chicken, see "From Our Kitchen to Yours" on the next page.)

CHICKEN CASHEW

2½ cups water
½ teaspoon salt
1 cup uncooked long-grain rice
4 chicken breast halves, skinned and boned
1 tablespoon vegetable oil
2 cups sliced fresh mushrooms
½ cup sliced green onions
1 small green pepper, cut into 1-inch pieces
1 (8-ounce) can sliced water chestnuts, drained
2 teaspoons chicken-flavored bouillon granules
1¼ cups boiling water
2 tablespoons soy sauce
1 tablespoon cornstarch
2 teaspoons light brown sugar
½ teaspoon ground ginger
½ cup cashews

Bring 2½ cups water and salt to a boil in a medium saucepan; add rice. Cover, reduce heat, and simmer 20 minutes or until rice is tender and water is absorbed. Keep warm.

Cut chicken into 1-inch pieces. Heat oil in a large skillet. Add chicken, and cook until browned, stirring often. Remove chicken from skillet. Add mushrooms and next 3 ingredients to skillet; sauté 5 minutes or until tender.

Dissolve bouillon in 1¼ cups boiling water. Combine soy sauce, cornstarch, sugar, and ginger; stir into bouillon mixture. Add chicken to vegetables. Stir in bouillon mixture; cook over low heat, stirring constantly, 1 minute or until thickened. Stir in cashews. Serve over hot cooked rice. Yield: 4 servings.

Dorothy L. Akers
Vinton, Virginia

RICE-STUFFED ROASTED CHICKEN

2½ cups cooked brown rice
1 cup chopped apple
½ cup chopped dried prunes
½ cup chopped dried apricots
¼ cup chopped celery
¼ teaspoon garlic powder
½ teaspoon grated lemon rind
1 teaspoon ground ginger
¼ teaspoon salt
¼ cup butter or margarine, melted
1 (2½- to 3-pound) broiler-fryer
2 tablespoons butter or margarine, melted
¼ teaspoon paprika

Combine first 10 ingredients in a large bowl; mix well.

Place chicken, breast side up, on a rack in a shallow roasting pan. Stuff lightly with brown rice mixture. Truss the chicken. Combine 2 tablespoons melted butter and paprika; brush over chicken. Bake at 375° for 1½ hours or until done.

Spoon remaining rice mixture into a lightly greased 1-quart casserole; bake at 375° the last 15 to 20 minutes of baking time. Transfer chicken to serving platter, and spoon rice around it. Yield: 4 servings.

Louise Ellis
Baker, Florida

QUICK CHICKEN-AND-RICE CACCIATORE

4 chicken breast halves, skinned and boned
½ cup chopped onion
2 tablespoons vegetable oil
1 green pepper, cut into strips
½ teaspoon dried whole oregano
½ teaspoon dried whole basil
1 (16-ounce) jar spaghetti sauce
1¼ cups water
1½ cups uncooked instant rice
1 (8-ounce) can whole water chestnuts, drained and diced

Cut chicken into 1-inch pieces. Sauté chicken and chopped onion in oil in a large skillet until lightly browned, stirring often. Add green pepper and next 4 ingredients, stirring well.

Bring mixture to a boil; stir in rice and water chestnuts. Cover, remove from heat, and let stand 5 to 10 minutes or until liquid is absorbed and rice is tender. Yield: 4 servings.

Mrs. J. David Stearns
Mobile, Alabama

CHICKEN ROLLUPS

1 (6-ounce) package wild rice-and-mushroom stuffing mix
6 large chicken breast halves, skinned and boned
Pepper
2 tablespoons butter or margarine, melted
2 tablespoons Dijon mustard
1¼ cups ground pecans
3 tablespoons vegetable oil
¾ cup chicken broth
¾ cup commercial sour cream

Prepare wild rice-and-mushroom stuffing mix according to package directions. Set aside.

Place each chicken breast between 2 sheets of wax paper. Flatten to ¼-inch thickness, using a meat mallet or rolling pin.

Divide stuffing mixture evenly, and place on top of each chicken breast; fold sides of chicken breast over stuffing, roll up, and secure with wooden picks. Sprinkle with pepper.

Combine butter and mustard in a small bowl; stir well. Brush mustard mixture over chicken, completely coating all sides; roll in pecans.

Brown chicken on all sides in hot oil in skillet; drain and discard pan drippings. Add chicken broth to skillet; cover, reduce heat, and simmer 20 minutes. Transfer chicken to serving dish; keep warm. Stir sour cream into broth in skillet; cook over low heat, stirring constantly, until heated. Spoon over chicken. Yield: 6 servings.   *Connie H. Woodruff*
Charlottesville, Virginia

COUNTRYSIDE CHICKEN BAKE

1 cup uncooked long-grain rice
1 cup sliced celery
¾ cup chopped onion
2 tablespoons butter or
**   margarine, melted**
2 teaspoons dried parsley flakes
¼ teaspoon salt
⅛ teaspoon pepper
6 chicken breast halves
1 (10¾-ounce) can cream of
**   mushroom soup, undiluted**
⅔ cup mayonnaise or salad
**   dressing**
¼ cup milk
1 (16-ounce) can baby carrots,
**   drained**
Paprika

Cook rice according to package directions. Combine rice and next 6 ingredients; mix well. Spoon into a lightly greased 13- x 9- x 2-inch baking dish; top with chicken breasts.

Combine soup, mayonnaise, and milk; spoon mixture over chicken breasts. Bake, uncovered, at 350° for 45 minutes. Remove from oven; add carrots, and sprinkle top with paprika. Bake an additional 15 minutes. Yield: 6 servings.
Imogene Narmore
Russellville, Alabama

Tip: *Keep all dry foods in their original containers or airtight ones.*

From Our Kitchen To Yours

Delicate flavor plus high-protein and low-fat content ensure chicken as a Southern favorite. From quick family meals to festive company fare, chicken can be teamed with almost any seasoning, vegetable, or fruit.

Chicken is packaged in a variety of ways. The commonly used broiler-fryer is packaged whole, cut up, or as parts. If your family prefers white meat, it's more convenient and possibly more economical to purchase only chicken breasts.

Boneless breasts are called for in many recipes. For economy, buy bone-in breasts, and debone them yourself. All you'll need is a boning knife or other thin sharp knife.

To bone a chicken breast, pull the skin from the chicken, and discard. Split the breast in half lengthwise, if it's not already split. Place chicken breast half on work surface, bone side down. Starting at the breastbone side of the chicken, slice meat away from the bone, cutting as close as possible to the bone.

Microwave Chicken

When microwaving a 3- to 3½-pound broiler-fryer, place chicken, breast side down, on a microwave roasting rack in a 12- x 8- x 2-inch baking dish. Season to taste. Microwave at HIGH 3 minutes. Microwave at MEDIUM (50% power) 20 minutes. Turn chicken, breast side up, and brush with butter. Microwave at MEDIUM 25 to 30 minutes or until drumsticks are easy to move.

To microwave chicken pieces, arrange meatier portions around the outside of the dish. Rearranging the pieces halfway through microwaving helps promote even cooking. The general rule for cooking chicken pieces in the microwave is to allow 6 minutes per pound on HIGH.

For a browned appearance, brush chicken with melted butter, soy sauce, browning-and-seasoning sauce, or teriyaki sauce before or during cooking.

Tips on Chicken

■ A 3-pound broiler-fryer yields four servings or 2½ to 3 cups cooked meat.
■ Turn chicken with tongs when broiling or frying; forks pierce the meat, causing loss of flavorful juices.
■ Whole broiler-fryers can be cooked conveniently in oven cooking bags. The chicken will not be crisp, but the meat will be moist and tender without basting. Follow the directions on the cooking bag package for microwave or conventional cooking.

After-Work Entrées

What's for dinner? These main-dish recipes will make the answer easy and your dinner delicious. Once the entrée begins cooking, you can tend to the rest of the meal and be serving it in no time at all.

HORSERADISH STEAK

1¼ pounds boneless round steak
½ cup all-purpose flour
½ teaspoon salt
½ teaspoon pepper
¼ cup vegetable oil
1 cup water
¼ cup prepared horseradish

Trim excess fat from steak; cut into serving-size pieces. Combine flour, salt, and pepper. Dredge steak in flour mixture. Brown in hot oil; add water. Top each piece of steak with horseradish; cover, reduce heat, and simmer 45 minutes or until tender. Yield: 4 servings.   *Chris Deitch*
San Antonio, Texas

QUICK PEPPERONI SPAGHETTI

1 large onion, chopped
1 green pepper, chopped
1 pound ground beef
1 (3-ounce) package sliced
 pepperoni, chopped
1 (32-ounce) jar commercial
 spaghetti sauce with
 mushrooms
1 (12-ounce) package spaghetti
1 cup (4 ounces) shredded
 mozzarella cheese
1 tablespoon grated Parmesan
 cheese

Combine onion, green pepper, ground beef, and pepperoni in a large skillet. Cook over medium heat until beef browns, stirring to crumble. Remove from heat; drain. Return beef mixture to skillet. Add spaghetti sauce, and bring to a boil. Cover, reduce heat, and simmer 20 minutes, stirring occasionally.

Cook spaghetti according to package directions, omitting salt. Drain. Arrange on an ovenproof platter; spoon meat sauce on top. Sprinkle mozzarella cheese over sauce; bake at 400° for 3 to 5 minutes. Remove from oven; top with Parmesan cheese. Serve immediately. Yield: 6 servings.
Vivian Epperson
Crossville, Tennessee

SHERRY-APPLE PORK CHOPS

6 (1-inch-thick) pork chops
2 tablespoons vegetable oil
2 cooking apples, peeled
 and chopped
1 medium onion, chopped
¾ cup dry sherry
½ cup orange juice
2 tablespoons brown
 sugar
2 tablespoons soy sauce
½ teaspoon garlic powder
2 tablespoons cornstarch
¼ cup water

Brown pork chops in vegetable oil in a large skillet; drain pan drippings. Place chopped apples and onion on top of pork chops.

Combine sherry and next 4 ingredients; pour over chops. Cover, reduce heat, and simmer 1 hour or until chops are tender. Transfer chops to serving plate, reserving pan drippings.

Combine cornstarch and water, stirring until smooth; stir into pan drippings. Bring to a boil, and cook 1 minute or until thickened, stirring constantly. Serve with chops. Yield: 6 servings.
Madeline Gibbons
Little Rock, Arkansas

CITRUS-AND-SPICE HAM

2 (½-inch-thick) ham slices
 (about ¾ pound each)
4 slices pineapple, drained and
 divided
½ cup firmly packed brown
 sugar
¼ teaspoon mace
¼ teaspoon allspice
¼ teaspoon paprika
½ cup orange juice

Place 1 ham slice in a lightly greased 12- x 8- x 2-inch baking dish. Arrange 2 pineapple slices on ham. Set aside remaining ham and pineapple.

Combine brown sugar, mace, allspice, and paprika in a small bowl; sprinkle half of mixture on ham and pineapple. Top with second slice of ham. Arrange 2 pineapple slices on ham; sprinkle with remaining brown sugar mixture. Pour orange juice over ham; cover and bake at 425° for 35 minutes or until ham is tender. Yield: 4 servings.
Mrs. L. Mayer
Richmond, Virginia

ONION-CRUSTED CHICKEN

4 chicken breast halves, skinned
 and boned
¼ teaspoon salt
¼ teaspoon pepper
½ cup butter or margarine,
 melted
1 tablespoon Worcestershire
 sauce
1 teaspoon dry mustard
1 (2.5-ounce) can fried onion
 rings, crushed

Place each piece of chicken between 2 sheets of wax paper, and flatten to ¼-inch thickness, using a meat mallet or rolling pin. Sprinkle with salt and pepper.

Combine butter, Worcestershire sauce, and mustard; stir well. Dredge chicken in butter mixture, then in crushed onion rings. Arrange chicken in a 13- x 9- x 2-inch pan; top with remaining onion rings. Drizzle with remaining butter. Bake at 350° for 30 minutes. Yield: 4 servings.
Geri J. Oberer
Dunedin, Florida

Simple, Savory Vegetables

These savory recipes highlight the natural flavor of vegetables, while adding just enough zip to make the dishes fresh and interesting. They're easy to prepare, too.

TANGY BRUSSELS SPROUTS

½ cup water
1 chicken-flavored bouillon
 cube
1 (10-ounce) package frozen
 brussels sprouts
½ cup chopped onion
2 tablespoons tarragon
 vinegar

Place water in a medium saucepan; bring to a boil. Add bouillon cube, stirring until dissolved. Add brussels sprouts; return to a boil. Cover, reduce heat, and simmer 5 to 6 minutes or until brussels sprouts are tender. Drain.

Add chopped onion and tarragon vinegar to brussels sprouts; stir gently. Cover brussels sprouts, and chill 3 to 4 hours, stirring occasionally. Yield: 4 servings.

Dorothy Nieman
Dunnellon, Florida

ITALIAN-STYLE BROCCOLI

1½ pounds fresh broccoli
¼ cup olive oil
2 cloves garlic, minced
2 tablespoons lemon juice
¼ teaspoon grated lemon rind
Lemon slices (optional)

Trim off large leaves of broccoli. Remove tough ends of lower stalks, and wash broccoli thoroughly. Cut broccoli into flowerets.

Cook broccoli in a large skillet, covered, in a small amount of boiling water 5 minutes or until crisp-tender; drain in colander.

Pour oil into skillet; add garlic, and cook over medium high heat, stirring constantly, until bubbly. Add broccoli and lemon juice; toss gently. Cover and cook 1 minute. Remove from heat, and arrange broccoli on a serving platter. Sprinkle with lemon rind. Garnish with lemon slices, if desired. Serve immediately. Yield: 6 servings.

Joy L. Garcia
Bartlett, Tennessee

CREAMY POTATO BAKE

½ (6½-ounce) package instant
   mashed potatoes
½ cup whipped cream cheese
1 tablespoon butter or margarine
1 egg, beaten
2 tablespoons finely chopped
   green onions
1 tablespoon finely chopped
   parsley
Paprika

Prepare potatoes according to package directions, omitting butter. Add cream cheese and 1 tablespoon butter, stirring until combined. Stir in egg, green onions, and parsley. Spoon potatoes into a greased 1-quart baking dish. Sprinkle with paprika. Bake at 400° for 25 minutes or until thoroughly heated. Yield: 4 servings.

Elizabeth A. Kvist
Baltimore, Maryland

MARINATED ARTICHOKES

1 (9-ounce) package frozen
   artichokes
1 cup vegetable oil
3 tablespoons red wine vinegar
1 tablespoon lemon juice
3 cloves garlic, minced
½ teaspoon salt
½ teaspoon pepper
¼ teaspoon red pepper
¼ teaspoon dry mustard
Dash of hot sauce

Cook artichokes according to package directions, omitting salt; drain. Place artichokes in a shallow dish.

Combine oil and remaining ingredients in a jar. Cover tightly, and shake vigorously. Pour mixture over artichokes. Cover and marinate 8 hours. Drain artichokes before serving. Yield: 4 servings.

Lib Alford
Lynchburg, Virginia

LIMA BEANS IN SOUR CREAM

2 (10-ounce) packages frozen lima
   beans
2 tablespoons chopped onion
2 tablespoons diced pimiento,
   drained
2 tablespoons butter or
   margarine, melted
1 cup commercial sour cream
⅛ teaspoon white pepper

Cook beans according to package directions; drain and set aside.

Sauté onion and pimiento in butter until onion is tender; remove from heat, and add sour cream and pepper, stirring well. Add sour cream mixture to lima beans; stir until blended.

Cook over low heat until thoroughly heated. Serve immediately. Yield: about 6 servings.

Libby Winstead
Nashville, Tennessee

Pasta Makes The Perfect Salad

Vermicelli and rotini—even if you're not fluent in Italian, you can enjoy the variety and versatility of these pastas. Some of our readers have incorporated them into several tasty recipes for salads.

RAMEN NOODLE SALAD

2 cups water
1 (3-ounce) package chicken-
   flavored Ramen noodles
1 teaspoon butter
¼ cup finely chopped celery
¼ cup shredded carrots
¼ cup thinly sliced green onions
1 tablespoon finely chopped green
   pepper
1 teaspoon lemon juice
1 teaspoon soy sauce
2 tablespoons mayonnaise

Bring water to a boil. Crumble noodles, and add to water; stir in seasoning packet. Return to a boil, and cook 2 minutes, stirring often. Drain.

Combine noodles and butter, stirring until butter melts. Add celery and remaining ingredients, stirring gently to coat. Cover and chill 3 to 4 hours. Yield: 2 servings.

Kathy Simms
Montezuma, Georgia

ROTINI SALAD

2½ cups rotini
1 cup sliced fresh mushrooms
½ large green pepper, cut into strips
½ large sweet red pepper, cut into strips
¼ cup sliced green onions
½ cup freshly grated Parmesan cheese
½ cup oil-free Italian salad dressing
2 tablespoons capers
¼ teaspoon coarsely ground pepper
8 slices bacon, cooked and crumbled

Cook rotini according to package directions, omitting salt; drain. Rinse rotini with cold water; drain.

Combine rotini and remaining ingredients except bacon; toss gently. Cover and chill at least 1 hour. Add bacon; toss gently, and serve. Yield: 6 to 8 servings.   *Patricia Pashby*
Memphis, Tennessee

COLD PASTA PLATTER

1 (3-pound) broiler-fryer
¼ cup wine vinegar
2 teaspoons Dijon mustard
2 teaspoons chopped garlic
½ teaspoon salt
½ teaspoon freshly ground black pepper
2 tablespoons olive oil
2 tablespoons vegetable oil
½ pound vermicelli
½ cup mayonnaise
Leaf lettuce
2 tablespoons chopped parsley (optional)
Pickled beets
Marinated mushrooms
Marinated artichokes
Cherry tomatoes
Parsley sprigs (optional)

Place chicken in a Dutch oven, and add water to cover. Bring to a boil; cover, reduce heat, and simmer 45 minutes or until tender. Remove chicken, and let cool. Bone chicken,

and chop meat into ½-inch pieces; set aside.

Combine vinegar and next 4 ingredients, mixing well. Gradually add olive oil and vegetable oil; whisk mixture until blended.

Cook vermicelli according to package directions, omitting salt; drain.

Combine pasta and dressing, tossing well. Add chicken and mayonnaise, mixing well; chill mixture at least 1 hour.

Spoon mixture into center of a lettuce-lined platter. Sprinkle with chopped parsley, if desired. Arrange beets, mushrooms, artichokes, and tomatoes around pasta. Garnish with parsley sprigs, if desired. Yield: about 6 servings.   *Celeste Pittman*
Rocky Mount, North Carolina

Dinner For Two

Chicken, rice, and green beans are classic dinner companions, and our readers use simple techniques to dress them up. Together, these recipes make a fine menu.

Chicken in Scotch Cream
Rice Pilaf
Oriental Green Beans
Orange-and-Beet Salad
Quick Lemon Sauce Soufflés

CHICKEN IN SCOTCH CREAM

2 chicken breast halves, boned and skinned
2 tablespoons all-purpose flour
1 tablespoon butter or margarine
1 tablespoon olive oil
½ cup scotch
Pinch of dried whole marjoram leaves
Pinch of dried whole tarragon leaves
½ cup chicken broth
¼ cup half-and-half

Dredge chicken in flour; shake off excess. Heat butter and oil in a small skillet; add chicken, and sauté about 4 minutes on each side or until lightly browned. Remove chicken, reserving drippings in skillet.

Add scotch and herbs to skillet; cook on high heat, stirring constantly, until liquid is reduced to 2 tablespoons. Add chicken broth; return chicken to skillet. Cover, reduce heat, and simmer 15 minutes. Transfer chicken to dinner plates; keep warm. Strain liquid, and return to skillet. Add half-and-half; cook over medium heat until sauce thickens. Pour sauce over chicken. Yield: 2 servings.   *Eugenia Bell*
Louisville, Kentucky

RICE PILAF

1⅓ cups chicken broth
½ cup uncooked long-grain rice
1 tablespoon vegetable oil
¼ cup sliced green onions
¼ cup thinly sliced mushrooms
¼ cup chopped fresh parsley

Bring chicken broth to a boil in a medium saucepan. Stir in rice; cover, reduce heat, and simmer 20 to 25 minutes or until liquid is absorbed. Remove from heat.

Heat oil in a small skillet; sauté green onions and mushrooms until crisp-tender. Toss onions, mushrooms, and parsley with rice. Serve immediately. Yield: 2 servings.
Marian Dils
Altamonte Springs, Florida

ORIENTAL GREEN BEANS

½ pound fresh green beans
1 tablespoon vegetable oil
¼ to ½ teaspoon ground ginger
⅓ cup water
1 teaspoon soy sauce

Wash and trim beans; cut in half.

Heat oil in a large skillet over medium high heat; add beans. Cook 4 minutes, stirring constantly. Combine ginger and water; pour over beans. Cover, reduce heat, and simmer 15 minutes or until beans are crisptender. Toss with soy sauce. Yield: 2 servings.
Marge Killmon
Annandale, Virginia

ORANGE-AND-BEET SALAD

1 orange, peeled and sectioned
1 (8¼-ounce) can whole beets, drained and quartered
Bibb lettuce
1 small purple onion, thinly sliced
¼ cup commercial creamy Italian dressing

Arrange orange sections and beets on Bibb lettuce. Top with sliced onion. Serve with dressing. Yield: 2 servings.
Louise Bodnar
Beaumont, Texas

QUICK LEMON SAUCE SOUFFLÉS

1 egg, separated
⅓ cup milk
2 tablespoons lemon juice
1 tablespoon butter or margarine, melted
⅓ cup sugar
2 teaspoons all-purpose flour
Dash of salt

Beat egg yolk until light and lemon colored; add remaining ingredients, except egg white, mixing well.

Beat egg white (at room temperature) until stiff peaks form; fold into egg yolk mixture. Pour into 2 greased 6-ounce ramekins or custard

cups. Place in a pan of warm water. Bake at 350° for 25 minutes or until a knife inserted in center comes out clean. Serve warm. Yield: 2 servings.
Mrs. William H. Smith
Lynchburg, Virginia

Stuff A Pita With Flavor

If you're ready for a sandwich that's different, try serving it on something besides buns or whole grain breads. Split a pita bread round to create a pocket sandwich. We borrowed our readers' best salad and sandwich ideas to come up with the pita sandwiches featured here.

TURKEY SALAD PITA SANDWICHES

2 tablespoons vinegar
2 teaspoons water
½ teaspoon salt
¼ teaspoon sugar
¾ pound cooked turkey, cut into julienne strips
2 hard-cooked eggs, chopped
½ cup chopped celery
½ cup seedless red grapes, halved
½ cup mayonnaise
3 (6-inch) pita bread rounds, cut in half
Lettuce leaves
½ cup pimiento-stuffed olives, sliced

Combine first 4 ingredients; stir well. Pour over turkey; toss lightly. Cover and chill 2 hours. Drain.

Combine turkey, eggs, celery, grapes, and mayonnaise; toss gently to coat. Line each pita bread half with lettuce, and fill with turkey mixture. Sprinkle with olives. Yield: 3 servings.
Sarah Watson
Knoxville, Tennessee

SPINACH-WALNUT PITAS

4 cups torn spinach, lightly packed
1 cup chopped iceberg lettuce
1 small zucchini, thinly sliced
1 (6-ounce) jar marinated artichoke hearts, drained and chopped
2 green onions, sliced
1 avocado, coarsely chopped
¼ cup toasted chopped walnuts
2 tablespoons toasted sesame seeds
Piquant French Dressing
4 (6-inch) pita bread rounds, cut in half

Combine first 8 ingredients in a large bowl. Toss with Piquant French Dressing. Spoon mixture into pita bread halves. Serve immediately. Yield: 4 servings.

Piquant French Dressing

2 tablespoons sugar
½ teaspoon salt
½ teaspoon paprika
½ teaspoon dry mustard
⅛ teaspoon pepper
½ teaspoon celery seeds
½ teaspoon grated onion
2 tablespoons lemon juice
¼ cup plus 2 tablespoons vegetable oil
1 clove garlic, cut crosswise

Combine first 8 ingredients; beat at medium speed of an electric mixer until blended. Add oil slowly while mixer is running. Continue beating until mixture thickens. Add garlic, and refrigerate dressing mixture at least 1 hour. Remove garlic. Stir dressing well before serving. Yield: ½ cup.
Anita Cox
Fort Worth, Texas

HAM-AND-CHEESE PITA SANDWICHES

1 cup chopped cooked ham
½ cup (2 ounces) shredded Swiss cheese
½ cup (2 ounces) shredded Cheddar cheese
¼ cup chopped onion
2 tomatoes, chopped
½ cup torn lettuce leaves
Salt and pepper to taste
3 to 4 tablespoons mayonnaise
3 (6-inch) pita bread rounds, cut in half
Lettuce leaves (optional)

Combine first 8 ingredients; toss gently. Line pita bread halves with lettuce, if desired; fill with ham mixture. Yield: 3 servings.

Jaquie Waller
Oklahoma City, Oklahoma

Combine first 5 ingredients in a large mixing bowl. Combine eggs and milk; add to dry ingredients, stirring well.

Peel, core, and slice each apple into ¼-inch-thick rings. Dip apple slices in batter, and fry in deep, hot oil (375°). Cook only a few at a time, turning once. Fry 2 to 3 minutes or until golden brown. Drain well on paper towels. Sprinkle with powdered sugar. Serve immediately. Yield: 12 to 14 slices.

Thelma Peedin
Newport News, Virginia

CHEESY ZUCCHINI FRITTERS

1½ cups all-purpose flour
2 teaspoons baking powder
½ teaspoon salt
1 cup chopped zucchini
½ cup (2 ounces) shredded Cheddar cheese
¼ cup finely chopped onion
1 egg, beaten
1 cup milk
Vegetable oil

Combine flour, baking powder, and salt in a large bowl. Stir in zucchini, cheese, and onion; set aside.

Combine egg and milk; add to flour mixture, stirring just until moistened. Carefully drop batter by rounded tablespoonfuls into 1-inch hot oil (375°). Cook only a few at a time, turning once. Fry 2 to 3 minutes or until golden brown. Drain on paper towels. Yield: about 2 dozen.

Jill Rorex
Dallas, Texas

Fry Some Old-Fashioned Fritters

The flavor of old-fashioned fritters has long been popular in the South, and it remains a favorite today.

For the best tasting fritters, make sure the oil is hot enough (at least 375°) before adding the batter. Hot oil helps to crisp the outside quickly while leaving the inside moist.

APPLE FRITTER RINGS

2 cups all-purpose flour
2 teaspoons baking powder
½ teaspoon salt
¼ cup sugar
½ teaspoon ground nutmeg
2 eggs, slightly beaten
1 cup milk
2 large cooking apples
Vegetable oil
Sifted powdered sugar

SWEET POTATO FRITTERS

1 cup plus 2 tablespoons all-purpose flour
1 teaspoon baking powder
⅔ cup milk
2 eggs, beaten
2 tablespoons butter or margarine, melted
4 slices bacon, cooked and crumbled
2 cups shredded uncooked sweet potato
Vegetable oil
Maple syrup

Combine flour and baking powder; stir well. Add milk, eggs, and butter; stir until smooth. Add bacon and sweet potato, stirring well.

Heat 3 to 4 inches oil to 375° in a Dutch oven. Carefully drop batter by rounded tablespoonfuls into hot oil. Cook only a few at a time, turning once. Fry 2 minutes or until fritters are golden brown. Drain well on paper towels. Serve warm with maple syrup. Yield: about 3 dozen.

Edith Askins
Greenville, Texas

MICROWAVE COOKERY

Fast Chocolate Desserts

Chocolate desserts and special occasions go hand in hand, and here are some quick chocolate recipes to help you celebrate those occasions. With these recipes you'll get an idea of how to use different types of chocolate in microwave cookery. For melting chocolate squares or semisweet morsels in your microwave, use MEDIUM (50% power) to keep from overcooking the chocolate.

Remember that morsels will appear to hold their shape even after melting; when the chocolate becomes soft and shiny, stir to mix. When you melt chocolate squares, stir after half the time has elapsed.

BEST-EVER CHOCOLATE PIE

¾ cup sugar
3 tablespoons all-purpose flour
¼ teaspoon salt
1 (12-ounce) can evaporated milk
1 (5.5-ounce) can chocolate syrup
3 egg yolks, beaten
¼ cup butter or margarine
1 tablespoon vanilla extract
Graham cracker crust (recipe
　follows)
1 cup whipping cream
¼ cup sifted powdered sugar
Cocoa (optional)

Combine ¾ sugar, flour, and salt in a microwave-safe mixing bowl; stir in milk, chocolate syrup, and egg yolks. Microwave at MEDIUM (50% power) 8 to 10 minutes or until thick, stirring every 2 minutes with a wire whisk. Add butter and vanilla; stir until butter melts. Pour chocolate mixture into prepared graham cracker crust; chill thoroughly.

Before serving, beat whipping cream until foamy; gradually add powdered sugar, beating until soft peaks form. Pipe or dollop whipped cream onto pie; sprinkle with cocoa, if desired. Yield: one 9-inch pie.

Graham Cracker Crust

1 cup graham cracker crumbs
2 tablespoons sugar
3 tablespoons butter or
　margarine, melted

Combine all ingredients; mix well, and press into a 9-inch pieplate. Microwave at HIGH 1½ minutes or until firm, giving dish a half-turn after 1 minute. Cool. Yield: one 9-inch graham cracker crust. *Mary Andrew Winston-Salem, North Carolina*

MOCHA POTS DE CRÈME

1 (6-ounce) package semisweet
　chocolate morsels
3 tablespoons sugar
1⅓ cups half-and-half
1½ tablespoons Kahlúa or other
　coffee-flavored liqueur
½ teaspoon instant coffee
　granules
3 egg yolks
1 teaspoon vanilla extract
Sweetened whipped cream
　(optional)
Semisweet chocolate triangles
　(optional)

Place chocolate morsels in a 1-quart glass mixing bowl. Microwave at MEDIUM (50% power) 2 to 3 minutes or until chocolate appears soft and shiny. Stir until melted and smooth. Add sugar, stirring until dissolved. Using a wire whisk, gradually stir in half-and-half. Microwave at HIGH 3½ to 4 minutes, stirring at 1-minute intervals.

Combine Kahlúa and coffee granules, stirring to dissolve coffee. Add to chocolate mixture; stir well.

Beat yolks with a wire whisk. Gradually stir about one-fourth of hot chocolate mixture into yolks; quickly add to remaining chocolate mixture, stirring constantly. Stir in vanilla. Pour into stemmed glasses or custard cups. Chill 3 to 4 hours. If desired, garnish with sweetened whipped cream and chocolate triangles. Yield: 4 servings.

CHOCOLATE-ALMOND SURPRISE COOKIES

¼ cup butter or margarine
2 (1-ounce) squares unsweetened
　chocolate
1 cup sugar
2 eggs, beaten
2 teaspoons baking powder
½ teaspoon salt
½ teaspoon almond extract
2 cups all-purpose flour
¼ cup finely chopped almonds
About 48 whole unblanched
　almonds
Sifted powdered sugar

Combine butter and chocolate in a 2-cup glass measure. Microwave at MEDIUM (50% power) 2 to 3 minutes or until melted; mix well. Combine chocolate mixture, 1 cup sugar, and next 4 ingredients. Stir in flour and chopped almonds. Cover and refrigerate dough at least 8 hours.

Shape dough around each whole almond to make 1-inch balls. Roll each ball in powdered sugar. Line a pieplate with wax paper. Arrange 6 to 8 balls of dough around outside edge of pieplate; place 1 ball of dough in center. Microwave at MEDIUM (50% power) 1½ to 2½ minutes or until tops of cookies feel dry to touch, giving pieplate a quarter-turn every 30 seconds. Remove wax paper with cookies from pieplate, and place directly on countertop to cool. Repeat procedure with remaining dough. Yield: about 4 dozen.

Chocolate Melting Chart

Place chocolate in a microwave-safe measure, custard cup, or bowl, and microwave at MEDIUM (50% power) for the recommended time.

Chocolate	Microwave Time
6 ounces semisweet morsels	2 to 3 minutes
12 ounces semisweet morsels	3 to 4 minutes
1 or 2 (1-ounce) squares chocolate	1½ to 2 minutes
3 (1-ounce) squares chocolate	2 minutes
4 or 5 (1-ounce) squares chocolate	2 to 2½ minutes
6 (1-ounce) squares chocolate	2½ minutes

Simple, Yummy Pancake Topping

Spruce up hot pancakes or waffles with this simple topping. Just keep the topping and a pancake mix on hand for a quick breakfast. (Or for an easy dessert, try topping ice cream with this crunchy sauce.)

CINNAMON-PECAN-HONEY PANCAKE SAUCE

2 cups maple syrup
½ cup mild-flavored honey
¾ cup coarsely chopped pecans
½ teaspoon ground cinnamon

Combine all ingredients; stir well. Pour mixture into an airtight container. Store at room temperature. Serve over waffles, pancakes, or ice cream. Yield: 3 cups.

Add Fennel To Your Next Recipe

Best known for its role as an Italian seasoning or in a blend of spices, fennel can stand gracefully on its own, as well.

Although fennel tastes similar to licorice, it's much like celery in appearance and usage. The base can be used fresh in salads or on vegetable trays, marinated, or even braised.

At this time of year, you can usually find fresh, whole fennel in a large grocery store. If you can't buy it fresh, fennel seeds are a delicious alternative. Most of the time, you can substitute about 1 teaspoon seeds for 1 tablespoon fresh leaves.

CREAM OF CARROT SOUP

1 small onion, chopped
2 tablespoons butter or margarine, melted
2½ cups water
2 cups sliced carrots
1 (10¾-ounce) can chicken broth, undiluted
1 tablespoon sugar
1 teaspoon salt
¼ to ½ teaspoon freshly ground pepper
¼ teaspoon fennel seeds
⅛ teaspoon ground mace
1 cup milk
Sour cream (optional)
Parsley sprigs (optional)

Sauté onion in butter in a Dutch oven until tender; add 2½ cups water and next 7 ingredients. Bring to a boil; cover, reduce heat, and simmer 20 minutes or until carrots are tender.

Pour mixture into container of an electric blender; process until smooth. Return to Dutch oven; add milk and simmer 10 to 12 minutes. If desired, add sour cream and parsley for garnish. Yield: 5 cups.

Georgie O'Neill
Welaka, Florida

FENNEL MEAT LOAF

2 eggs
¼ cup catsup
2 teaspoons Worcestershire sauce
½ teaspoon fennel seeds
½ cup soft breadcrumbs
1½ pounds ground beef
1 medium onion, chopped
½ cup shredded carrot
  (1 medium)
2 large cloves garlic, pressed
1 teaspoon salt
½ teaspoon dried whole thyme
¼ teaspoon ground nutmeg
¼ teaspoon pepper

Combine eggs, catsup, Worcestershire sauce, and fennel, mixing well. Stir in breadcrumbs. Let stand 10 minutes. Add ground beef and remaining ingredients, mixing well. Place in an 8½- x 4½- x 2½-inch loafpan; bake at 350° for 1 hour and 10 minutes or until done.

Remove meat loaf from pan; let stand 5 minutes before slicing. Yield: 6 servings.

Reba Wilson
Jasper, Alabama

ITALIAN SAUSAGE SOUP WITH TORTELLINI

1 pound hot or mild Italian sausage
1 clove garlic, minced
1 large onion, chopped
4 (14.5-ounce) cans tomatoes, undrained and chopped
2 cups water
1 tablespoon chopped fresh fennel or 1 teaspoon fennel seeds
½ teaspoon salt
½ teaspoon coarsely ground pepper
1 (9-ounce) package tortellini

Remove sausage casing; crumble sausage in a large Dutch oven. Add garlic and onion; cook until meat is browned. Drain meat; pour off pan drippings. Add tomatoes and next 4 ingredients; cover and simmer 15 minutes.

Cook tortellini according to package directions; drain and add to soup. Cover and simmer 10 minutes. Yield: 11 cups.

Carol Savage
Charleston, South Carolina

BRAISED FENNEL

2 cloves garlic, minced
2 teaspoons vegetable oil
3 cups thinly sliced fresh fennel
½ cup water
1 (0.14-ounce) envelope low-sodium beef-flavored instant broth and seasoning
¾ teaspoon minced fresh basil
¼ teaspoon pepper

Sauté garlic in oil in a large skillet over medium heat about 1 minute, stirring occasionally. Add fennel; cook about 3 minutes, stirring occasionally. Add water and remaining ingredients; cover, reduce heat, and simmer about 15 minutes or until tender. Yield: 4 to 6 servings.

Sandra Hensley
San Antonio, Texas

MARCH

Spring-Fresh Salads

Crisp fresh salads on the menu bring on the long-awaited taste of the season's best vegetables. With the recipes we offer, you'll enjoy these delightful flavors of spring.

The fresher the salad ingredients, the sweeter tasting they will be. For extra-crisp lettuce leaves, place washed and drained leaves in a plastic bag and chill in the freezer a few minutes. Immediately mix with the other ingredients, and serve.

Be sure to store salad greens in the crisper section of the refrigerator. Spinach keeps better when it is stored unwashed.

SPRING VEGETABLE SALAD

1 pound fresh asparagus spears
1 (16½-ounce) jar pickled whole beets, drained
Bibb lettuce leaves
4 hard-cooked eggs, sliced
½ cup commercial Caesar-style salad dressing
4 radish roses

Snap off tough ends of asparagus. Remove scales with a knife or vegetable peeler, if desired. Cook asparagus, covered, in a small amount of boiling water 6 to 8 minutes or until crisp-tender; drain well. Let asparagus chill thoroughly.

Cut beets into wedges; drain. Line serving plate with lettuce leaves. Arrange asparagus, beets, and eggs over lettuce. Drizzle with dressing, and garnish with radish roses. Yield: 6 servings.

Mrs. Paul Raper
Burgaw, North Carolina

LETTUCE WITH SOUR CREAM DRESSING DELUXE

1 cup commercial sour cream
½ cup mayonnaise
2 teaspoons vinegar
1 teaspoon sugar
1 teaspoon salt
¼ cup minced green onions
¼ cup minced radishes
¼ cup minced cucumber
¼ cup minced green pepper
1 small clove garlic, minced
1 head iceberg lettuce, cut into 8 wedges

Combine sour cream, mayonnaise, vinegar, sugar, and salt, stirring well. Add green onions, radishes, cucumber, green pepper, and garlic, mixing well. Chill several hours.

Spoon dressing over lettuce wedges on individual salad plates. Serve immediately. Yield: 8 servings.

Erma L. Morris
Lubbock, Texas

BLUE CHEESE SALAD

8 cups torn mixed salad greens
2½ to 3 cups chopped cooked ham
2 cups chopped tomatoes
1 cup shredded carrots
½ cup chopped green pepper
1 (8-ounce) package cream cheese, softened
¾ cup (3 ounces) crumbled blue cheese
½ cup plus 2 tablespoons milk
¼ cup mayonnaise
1 tablespoon chopped fresh chives
2 teaspoons lemon juice
1 cup croutons

Layer half of first 5 ingredients in order listed in a large salad bowl. Set remaining half of ingredients aside.

Combine cream cheese, blue cheese, milk, mayonnaise, chives, and lemon juice, mixing well; spread half of dressing mixture over salad. Repeat layering of first 5 ingredients, and spread remaining dressing mixture over top of salad. Cover salad tightly, and chill. Sprinkle salad with 1 cup croutons just before serving. Yield: 8 to 10 servings.

Velma McGregor
Gretna, Virginia

CHINESE GREEN SALAD

¾ cup zesty Italian salad dressing
1 tablespoon grated fresh gingerroot
1 medium Chinese cabbage (about 1½ pounds) thinly sliced
3 cups broccoli flowerets
3 ounces fresh snow pea pods, trimmed
3 green onions, sliced
Additional Chinese cabbage leaves

Combine salad dressing and gingerroot in a small bowl; stir well. Cover and let stand 30 minutes.

Combine sliced cabbage and next 3 ingredients; toss gently. Pour dressing mixture over salad; toss gently. Line container with cabbage leaves; spoon salad over leaves. Yield: 6 to 8 servings.

Mildred Bickley
Bristol, Virginia

GREEN SALAD WITH SHRIMP

1½ cups water
½ pound unpeeled small fresh
    shrimp
1 head romaine lettuce, torn
4 stalks celery, sliced
2 carrots, grated
1 tomato, cut into wedges
½ cup shredded red cabbage
1 hard-cooked egg, sliced
Dash of grated Parmesan cheese
Croutons
Commercial salad dressing

Bring water to a boil; add unpeeled
shrimp, and cook 3 to 5 minutes.
Drain well; rinse with cold water.
Chill. Peel and devein shrimp.
  Combine lettuce, celery, carrots,
tomato, and red cabbage in a large
bowl. Top with shrimp, egg slices,
cheese, and croutons. Serve with
dressing. Yield: 6 to 8 servings.
Louise Osborne
Lexington, Kentucky

Entrées Filled With Flavor

Top-notch Southern cooks are turning to stuffed entrées when they
want to serve a special dinner.
Whether it's for a formal dinner party
or a casual supper, these selections
lend elegance to any meal.

MARYLAND STUFFED COUNTRY HAM

1 (16-pound) uncooked country
    ham
6 cups chopped cabbage
1 (12-ounce) bag frozen chopped
    onions
2 (10-ounce) packages frozen
    chopped kale or spinach,
    thawed
1½ tablespoons whole mustard
    seeds
2 tablespoons crushed red pepper
¼ teaspoon pepper

Place ham in a large container, cover
with water, and soak 24 hours. Pour
off water. Scrub ham with a stiff
brush, and rinse well.
  Combine vegetables in a large
Dutch oven. Simmer over low heat
15 minutes or until vegetables are
tender. Add mustard seeds and remaining ingredients, and mix well.
  Score ham in a diamond pattern
making 2-inch-deep slits, 2 inches
apart. Press vegetable mixture into
the slits.
  Place ham on a large square of
cheesecloth; fold ends over tightly,
and tie securely. Place ham in a large
cooking container, and cover with
water. Cover and simmer about 4
hours or until meat thermometer
registers 142° (about 15 minutes per
pound). Remove ham from water,
and refrigerate 8 hours. Remove
cheesecloth. Slice ham, and serve
cold. Yield: about 42 servings.
Peggy Aud
Lexington Park, Maryland

CROWN ROAST OF PORK WITH CRANBERRY-SAUSAGE STUFFING

1 (16-rib) crown roast of pork
    (about 10 pounds)
⅛ teaspoon salt
½ teaspoon pepper
½ pound bulk pork sausage
1 (8-ounce) package
    herb-seasoned stuffing mix
1 (16-ounce) can whole-berry
    cranberry sauce
1½ cups chopped cooking apple
¼ cup butter or margarine,
    melted

Season roast with salt and pepper;
place roast, bone ends up, on rack in
a shallow roasting pan. Insert meat
thermometer, making sure it does
not touch fat or bone.
  Cook sausage in a skillet until
browned, stirring to crumble; drain.
Combine sausage and remaining ingredients, mixing well. Spoon mixture into center of roast. Cover

stuffing and ends of ribs with aluminum foil. Bake at 325° for 4 hours or
until meat thermometer registers
160°. Yield: 10 to 12 servings.
Lorraine Brownell
Salisbury, North Carolina

EASY CABBAGE-AND-BEEF ROLLS

1 large cabbage
1 (15-ounce) can tomato sauce,
    divided
1 pound ground beef
1 (4-ounce) can mushroom stems
    and pieces, undrained
½ cup uncooked instant rice
½ cup chopped onion
¼ teaspoon salt
⅛ teaspoon pepper
⅛ teaspoon garlic powder
1 teaspoon sugar
½ teaspoon lemon juice
1 tablespoon cornstarch
1 tablespoon water

Remove 10 outer leaves of cabbage.
Cover leaves with boiling water;
cover and let stand 10 minutes.
Drain well.
  Combine ½ cup tomato sauce and
next 7 ingredients, mixing well. Place
⅓ cup meat mixture in center of
each cabbage leaf. Fold 2 opposite
ends over, and place rolls, seam side
down, in a lightly greased 8-inch baking dish. Combine remaining tomato
sauce, sugar, and lemon juice; pour
over cabbage rolls. Cover and bake
at 350° for 1 hour.
  Remove cabbage rolls to a serving
platter; drain tomato sauce mixture
into a saucepan. Combine cornstarch
and water, stirring until smooth; stir
into tomato sauce mixture. Bring to a
boil over medium heat, stirring constantly. Boil 1 minute. Pour over
cabbage rolls. Yield: 10 rolls (4 to 5
servings).
DeLea Lonadier
Montgomery, Louisiana

Tip: *Count on 4 servings per pound
when serving ground beef.*

STUFFED TENDERLOIN
(pictured on page 69)

½ pound chicken livers
2 tablespoons butter or margarine, melted
½ cup chopped onion
4 ounces mushrooms, sliced
1 tablespoon butter or margarine, melted
¼ teaspoon salt
½ teaspoon pepper
1 (6- to 8-pound) whole beef tenderloin
2 teaspoons lemon-pepper seasoning
4 slices bacon
Watercress (optional)
Tomato roses (optional)
Sculptured mushrooms (optional)

Sauté chicken livers in 2 tablespoons butter until livers are done; drain.

Sauté onion and sliced mushrooms in 1 tablespoon butter.

Spoon livers into container of an electric blender or food processor fitted with a steel blade; process 1 minute, scraping sides of container occasionally. Stir in salt, pepper, and sautéed onion and mushrooms.

Trim excess fat from tenderloin. Cut tenderloin lengthwise to within ½ inch of outer edge, leaving one long side connected. Rub whole tenderloin with lemon-pepper seasoning.

Spoon chicken liver mixture into opening of tenderloin. Fold top side over stuffing. Tie tenderloin securely with heavy string at 2- to 3-inch intervals. Place stuffed tenderloin on a rack in a roasting pan.

Bake at 425° for 20 minutes. Place bacon strips on tenderloin, and continue baking 25 minutes or until a meat thermometer registers 140° (rare) or 160° (medium). If desired, garnish with watercress, tomato roses, and mushrooms. Yield: 12 to 14 servings.   *Richard A. Duenkel*
Atlanta, Georgia

Tip: *Always use a meat thermometer when roasting to prevent overcooking. Get in the habit of using a minute timer for precise cooking.*

SPECIAL MANICOTTI

½ pound link Italian sausage
1 pound ground chuck
2 medium onions, chopped
5 cloves garlic, minced
2 (15-ounce) cans tomato sauce
1 (16-ounce) can tomatoes, chopped and undrained
1 (12-ounce) can tomato paste
1½ teaspoons dried whole oregano
1¼ teaspoons dried whole basil
1 teaspoon sugar
½ teaspoon salt
½ teaspoon pepper
½ teaspoon dried whole thyme
½ teaspoon dried whole rosemary
¼ teaspoon dried whole marjoram
⅛ teaspoon red pepper
16 manicotti shells
1 (8-ounce) package cream cheese, softened
1 (3-ounce) package cream cheese with chives, softened
4 cloves garlic, crushed
½ teaspoon pepper
½ teaspoon dried whole thyme
½ teaspoon dried whole oregano
1 (16-ounce) container ricotta cheese
4 cups (16 ounces) shredded mozzarella cheese
½ cup grated Parmesan cheese

Remove sausage from casing; crumble. Combine sausage, beef, onions, and minced garlic in a large Dutch oven. Cook over medium heat until beef is browned, stirring to crumble; drain well. Add tomato sauce and next 11 ingredients; bring to a boil. Cover, reduce heat, and simmer 2½ hours, stirring occasionally.

Cook manicotti shells according to package directions. Combine cream cheeses and next 7 ingredients in a large bowl; stuff mixture into shells.

Spoon half of sauce into a lightly greased 14- x 11½- x 2¼-inch baking dish or 2 lightly greased 2½-quart shallow casseroles. Arrange stuffed shells over sauce. Spoon remaining sauce over shells. Bake at 350° for 30 to 40 minutes or until heated. Let manicotti stand 5 minutes before serving. Yield: 8 servings.

Mary I. Newsom
Etowah, North Carolina

STUFFED CHICKEN BREASTS

1½ cups water
½ pound unpeeled medium-size fresh shrimp
⅔ cup chopped celery
⅔ cup chopped green onions
¼ cup butter or margarine, melted
½ cup mayonnaise
½ cup chicken broth
1 tablespoon lemon juice
Dash of hot sauce
¾ cup Italian-seasoned breadcrumbs
⅓ cup (1.3 ounces) shredded Swiss cheese
2 tablespoons minced fresh parsley
½ teaspoon seasoned salt
¼ teaspoon dried whole basil
¼ teaspoon pepper
8 chicken breast halves, skinned and boned
⅓ cup all-purpose flour
¼ cup butter or margarine, melted
1 (10¾-ounce) can cream of shrimp soup, undiluted
Paprika

Bring water to a boil; add shrimp, and cook 3 to 5 minutes. Drain well; rinse with cold water. Chill. Peel, devein, and chop shrimp.

Sauté celery and green onions in ¼ cup butter in a skillet over medium heat until vegetables are tender. Add mayonnaise, broth, lemon juice, and hot sauce, stirring well. Add chopped shrimp, breadcrumbs, Swiss cheese, parsley, seasoned salt, basil, and pepper, stirring well; set aside.

Place each chicken breast between 2 sheets of wax paper; flatten to ¼-inch thickness, using a meat mallet or rolling pin. Place stuffing mixture evenly on center of each chicken breast. Fold long sides of chicken over stuffing mixture; fold ends over, and secure with wooden picks. Roll chicken in flour, and dip in ¼ cup melted butter.

Place stuffed chicken in a lightly greased 12- x 8- x 2-inch baking dish. Spoon undiluted soup evenly over chicken. Cover chicken and bake at 375° for 30 minutes. Uncover and bake an additional 30 minutes. Remove stuffed chicken to a serving platter, and sprinkle top evenly with paprika before serving. Yield: 8 servings.

Gladys Murphy
Palacios, Texas

FLOUNDER STUFFED WITH SHRIMP

1½ cups water
½ pound unpeeled medium-size fresh shrimp
½ cup butter or margarine, softened
1 (3-ounce) package cream cheese, softened
1 to 2 ounces crumbled blue cheese
1 tablespoon lemon juice
1 tablespoon minced onion
1½ teaspoons chopped fresh parsley
¼ teaspoon hot sauce
⅛ teaspoon pepper
4 (6-ounce) flounder fillets
Whole cooked shrimp, peeled and deveined (optional)
Fresh parsley (optional)
Lemon twists (optional)

Bring water to a boil in a large saucepan; add shrimp, and cook 3 to 5 minutes. Drain well; rinse with cold water. Peel, devein, and chop shrimp.

Combine chopped shrimp, butter, and next 7 ingredients, mixing well. Place about ¼ cup shrimp mixture in center of each fillet; roll up fillets, and place, seam side down, in a lightly greased 12- x 8- x 2-inch baking dish. Bake at 375° for 15 to 20 minutes or until fish flakes easily when tested with a fork.

If desired, spoon pan drippings over fillets, and garnish each with whole cooked shrimp, parsley, and lemon twists. Yield: 4 servings.

Barbara Ruth
Kingsport, Tennessee

Spice Up Your Meals With Sausage

You'll find sausage served in many more ways than pan-fried patties. Inventive cooks have found that well-seasoned sausage can spice up all types of food served any time of day.

HOMINY-SAUSAGE BAKE

1 pound bulk pork sausage
¾ cup chopped onion
¾ cup chopped celery
2 (8-ounce) cans tomato sauce
¼ teaspoon dried whole oregano
1 (15½-ounce) can golden hominy, drained
2 cups (8 ounces) shredded Monterey Jack cheese

Combine sausage, onion, and celery in a skillet; cook over medium heat until sausage is browned, stirring to crumble. Drain between paper towels. Return sausage mixture to skillet; stir in tomato sauce and oregano. Cook mixture over medium heat 5 minutes.

Layer half each of hominy, sausage mixture, and cheese in a lightly greased shallow 2-quart baking dish. Repeat layers with remaining hominy and sausage mixture. Bake at 350° for 20 minutes; sprinkle with remaining cheese, and bake an additional 5 minutes. Yield: 6 servings.

Angie McIntosh
Flag Pond, Tennessee

SAUSAGE-BACON ROLLUPS

12 slices bacon, halved crosswise
½ pound bulk pork sausage
1 (8-ounce) package cream cheese, softened
12 slices white bread

Cook bacon until transparent; drain well on paper towels, and set aside.

Cook sausage over medium heat until browned, stirring to crumble; drain. Combine sausage and cream cheese; stir well, and set aside.

Trim crust from bread; cut slices in half. Spread cream cheese mixture over bread. Starting with short end, roll up each slice of bread, jellyroll fashion. Wrap each with bacon, and secure with a wooden pick.

Place rollups on an ungreased baking sheet. Bake at 350° for 15 minutes. Yield: 2 dozen.

Note: Rollups may be frozen before adding bacon. Remove from freezer (do not thaw); wrap with bacon, and secure with wooden picks. Bake as directed.

Mrs. Harry Herrmann
Jacksonville, Florida

SAUSAGE 'N' CHEESE TARTS

½ pound bulk pork sausage
1¼ cups biscuit mix
¼ cup butter or margarine, melted
2 tablespoons boiling water
1 egg, slightly beaten
½ cup half-and-half
2 tablespoons thinly sliced green onions
½ cup (2 ounces) shredded Cheddar or Swiss cheese
Cherry tomato rose (optional)
Fresh parsley sprigs (optional)

Cook sausage over medium heat until browned, stirring to crumble; drain and set aside. Combine biscuit mix, butter, and boiling water; stir well. Press about 1 tablespoon of dough into bottom and up sides of well-greased and floured muffin cups. Spoon sausage evenly into cups.

Combine egg, half-and-half, and green onions in a small bowl; stir well. Spoon about 1 tablespoon egg mixture into each cup.

Bake at 375° for 20 minutes. Sprinkle cheese over tarts; bake an additional 5 minutes. If desired, garnish with cherry tomato rose and parsley. Yield: 1 dozen.

Pat Whitehead
Norcross, Georgia

SAUSAGE MUFFINS

½ pound bulk pork sausage
Butter or margarine, melted
2 cups all-purpose flour
1 tablespoon baking powder
¼ teaspoon salt
2 tablespoons sugar
1 egg, slightly beaten
1 cup milk
½ cup (2 ounces) shredded
   Cheddar cheese

Cook sausage over medium heat until browned, stirring to crumble; drain well, and reserve drippings. Add butter to drippings to measure ¼ cup. Set sausage and drippings aside.

Combine flour and next 3 ingredients in a medium bowl; make a well in center of mixture. Combine egg, milk, and ¼ cup reserved drippings; stir well. Add liquid mixture to dry ingredients, stirring just until moistened. Stir in cheese and sausage.

Spoon batter into greased muffin pans, filling three-fourths full. Bake at 375° for 18 to 20 minutes. Remove muffins from pans immediately. Yield: 1 dozen.	*Pauline Carroll*
Brandon, Mississippi

SAUSAGE-CHILE RELLENOS CASSEROLE

1 pound bulk pork sausage
3 (4-ounce) cans whole green
   chiles, drained and cut in half
   lengthwise
4 cups (16 ounces) shredded
   Colby cheese
4 cups (16 ounces) shredded
   Monterey Jack cheese
6 eggs, beaten
1 (5-ounce) can evaporated milk
2 tablespoons all-purpose flour

Cook sausage in a large skillet over medium heat until browned, stirring to crumble; drain well.

Layer chiles in a lightly greased 13- x 9- x 2-inch baking dish. Sprinkle with sausage and cheeses. Combine eggs, milk, and flour, mixing well. Pour over sausage and cheese. Bake, uncovered, at 325° for 45 minutes. Serve with picante sauce, flour tortillas, or refried beans, if desired. Yield: 10 servings.	*Jamie Hutson*
Midland, Texas

MICROWAVE COOKERY

It's Quicker With Convenience Products

Grocery stores are overflowing with new products to make microwave cooking even faster and easier. Convenience foods, such as pre-chopped frozen vegetable combinations, seasoning mixes, and soups, can save preparation time.

CHICKEN-AND-VEGETABLE PLATTER

1 (16-ounce) package frozen
   broccoli, cauliflower, and
   carrots
1 tablespoon lemon juice
½ teaspoon salt, divided
¼ teaspoon pepper, divided
½ teaspoon dried whole basil,
   divided
4 chicken breast halves, skinned
   and boned
¼ cup chopped green onions
1 (0.9-ounce) package hollandaise
   sauce mix

Arrange frozen vegetables on a microwave-safe round 12-inch platter; cover tightly with heavy-duty plastic wrap. Vent and microwave at HIGH 4 minutes. Sprinkle lemon juice, ¼ teaspoon salt, ⅛ teaspoon pepper,

and ¼ teaspoon basil over vegetables, stirring gently. Push vegetables to center, leaving a 3-inch border.

Sprinkle chicken with remaining salt, pepper, and basil; arrange chicken around vegetables with thickest portion to outside. Sprinkle with green onions. Cover tightly with heavy-duty plastic wrap; microwave at HIGH 8 to 9 minutes or until chicken is tender, giving platter a half-turn after 4 minutes. Let stand 3 minutes. Drain liquid from platter.

Prepare hollandaise sauce according to package directions. Serve over chicken. Yield: 4 servings.

MARINATED POT ROAST WITH VEGETABLES

1 (3- to 4-pound) boneless chuck
   roast
1 teaspoon pepper
½ cup zesty Italian dressing
½ cup red wine vinegar
½ teaspoon browning-and-
   seasoning sauce
1 (10-ounce) package frozen
   whole baby carrots
1 (8-ounce) package frozen whole
   mushrooms
1 (6-ounce) can tomato paste

Pierce roast with a fork in several places; sprinkle with pepper. Combine dressing, vinegar, and browning-and-seasoning sauce in a 4-quart casserole with lid. Add roast, and turn to coat. Cover and refrigerate 6 to 8 hours, turning twice.

Cover tightly, and microwave at HIGH 15 minutes. Reduce temperature to MEDIUM (50% power), and microwave 30 minutes; turn roast over. Cover and microwave at MEDIUM 25 minutes. Add carrots and mushrooms; cover and microwave at MEDIUM 10 minutes. Let roast and vegetables stand, covered, 10 minutes. Transfer meat and vegetables to a serving platter. Add tomato paste to drippings, stirring well, and microwave at HIGH 2 minutes. Yield: 6 to 8 servings.

CREAMY HAM CHOWDER

1 (8-ounce) package frozen mixed
  vegetables, mixed vegetables
  with onion sauce, or green
  peas in onion sauce
1 (18¾-ounce) can creamy
  chunky mushroom soup,
  undiluted
1 cup milk
¼ teaspoon dillweed
⅛ teaspoon coarsely ground black
  pepper
1 (6¾-ounce) can chunk ham,
  drained and broken into chunks
¼ cup (1 ounce) shredded Swiss
  cheese
¼ to ½ cup plain croutons

Place vegetables in a 2-quart casserole. Cover and microwave at HIGH 7 to 9 minutes or until vegetables are crisp-tender. Stir in soup; gradually add milk, stirring until blended. Add dillweed and pepper. Microwave at HIGH 3 minutes; stir. Add ham, and microwave at HIGH 2 to 3 minutes or until thoroughly heated. Let stand 2 minutes. Sprinkle each serving with shredded cheese and croutons. Yield: 4½ cups.

Classic Hollandaise Step-by-Step

The flavor of hollandaise sauce is unmatched by other sauces. The classic sauce, thickened only with egg yolks, is a delicacy that must be served immediately and can't be stored.

Because it's associated with some elegant recipes, hollandaise has a reputation for being difficult to make. Actually, the preparation is quite simple. It does curdle easily, but you can avoid this by stirring constantly and adding ingredients gradually.

It's important to use a double boiler to prevent the egg yolks from heating too quickly. If you don't have a double boiler, place a small rack inside a medium-size saucepan, add water, and set a mixing bowl inside the saucepan.

The thickening of the sauce occurs when butter is beaten into the egg yolks, so be sure to stir constantly during this step. It's also important to beat in each portion of butter before adding the next one.

Hollandaise sauce is best served immediately. If you must keep it warm for a short time before serving, place the container of sauce in a bowl of warm (not hot) water.

If you're concerned about the steps necessary for making it the conventional way, use the blender for an easier version that's just as tasty, but a little thinner in consistency. It will also be a little lighter yellow than the conventionally made sauce.

CLASSIC HOLLANDAISE SAUCE

3 egg yolks
⅛ teaspoon salt
Dash of red pepper
2 tablespoons lemon juice
½ cup butter or margarine

Beat egg yolks, salt, and red pepper in top of a double boiler; gradually add lemon juice, stirring constantly. Add about one-third of butter to egg mixture; cook over hot, not boiling, water, stirring constantly, until butter melts.

Add another third of butter, stirring constantly. As sauce thickens, stir in remaining butter. Cook until thickened. Yield: about ¾ cup.

Blender variation: Use the same ingredients and amounts as for Classic Hollandaise Sauce.

Place egg yolks, salt, red pepper, and lemon juice in container of an electric blender. Cover and blend at high speed about 5 seconds.

Melt butter in a small saucepan. With blender on high, gradually add melted butter to egg mixture in a slow steady stream. Blend about 30 seconds or until sauce is thickened. Yield: about ¾ cup.

COOKING LIGHT®

Low-Calorie Ideas For Plain Yogurt

To cut calories and fat, substitute plain low-fat yogurt for sour cream. Yogurt is nutritious, containing protein, calcium, phosphorus, riboflavin, and potassium. The plain low-fat variety has only about 150 calories per cup, compared to 490 calories per cup of sour cream.

TURKEY WALDORF SALAD WITH YOGURT DRESSING

1 cup cooked, cubed turkey
½ cup diced, unpeeled apple
¼ cup diced celery
2 tablespoons chopped walnuts
1 tablespoon raisins
½ cup plain low-fat yogurt
1 tablespoon honey
1 teaspoon grated orange rind
2 lettuce leaves

Combine first 5 ingredients in a medium bowl; toss mixture gently, and set aside.

Combine yogurt, honey, and orange rind; stir well. Pour dressing over turkey mixture; toss gently. Spoon onto lettuce leaves; serve immediately. Yield: 2 servings (263 calories per ¾-cup serving).

☐ *31 grams protein, 6.1 grams fat, 22 grams carbohydrate, 74 milligrams cholesterol, 100 milligrams sodium, and 134 milligrams calcium.*
                          Elaine Gentry
                   Ransom Canyon, Texas

Cooking with Yogurt

Cooking with yogurt is different from cooking with sour cream, but these hints will help:

■ To add yogurt to hot foods, make sure it is at room temperature. Blend a little of the hot food into the yogurt first to prevent curdling.

■ For baking, it should be at room temperature. Generally, you will need only ½ teaspoon baking soda per cup yogurt.

■ When cooking, keep temperature low and heating time short to prevent separating.

■ Combine yogurt with a small amount of cornstarch or flour before adding to other ingredients to prevent separation. (If yogurt does separate, it will not change the flavor, only the appearance.)

■ Yogurt thins more than sour cream when cooked.

■ Fold, rather than stir, yogurt into other ingredients. Stirring tends to thin it.

STUFFED TOMATO WITH TUNA PASTA

1 cup uncooked medium-size whole wheat shell macaroni
1 (6½-ounce) can water-packed tuna, drained and chilled
¾ cup thinly sliced carrots
½ cup frozen green peas, thawed
¼ cup chopped celery
¼ cup chopped, unpeeled cucumber
¼ cup thinly sliced radishes
1 tablespoon minced onion
½ cup plain low-fat yogurt
2 tablespoons Dijon mustard
1 tablespoon reduced-calorie mayonnaise
1 tablespoon vinegar
⅛ teaspoon pepper
5 medium-size tomatoes
5 lettuce leaves
Carrot curls (optional)
Parsley sprigs (optional)

Cook macaroni according to package directions, omitting salt; drain. Rinse with cold water; drain well.

Combine macaroni, tuna, and next 6 ingredients; toss gently. Set aside.

Combine yogurt, mustard, mayonnaise, vinegar, and pepper in a small bowl; stir well. Fold yogurt mixture into tuna mixture; toss gently to mix.

Core tomatoes; cut each into 6 wedges, cutting to, but not through, base of tomato. Spread wedges slightly apart, and place on lettuce-lined serving plates. Spoon tuna mixture into tomatoes. If desired, garnish with carrot curls and parsley sprigs. Yield: 5 servings (175 calories per ¾ cup salad with tomato).

□ *13.1 grams protein, 3 grams fat, 25.5 grams carbohydrate, 18 milligrams cholesterol, 477 milligrams sodium, and 79 milligrams calcium.*
Louise Jones
Lithia Springs, Georgia

CHICKEN WITH ARTICHOKE HEARTS

¼ teaspoon pepper
¼ teaspoon paprika
4 (4-ounce) boned and skinned chicken breast halves
Vegetable cooking spray
1 clove garlic, minced
1 cup onion, chopped
1 large tomato, chopped
½ teaspoon dried whole rosemary
½ teaspoon dried whole thyme
¼ teaspoon salt
¼ teaspoon pepper
¼ cup Chablis or other dry white wine
1 (14-ounce) can artichoke hearts, drained and halved
½ cup plain low-fat yogurt
1 tablespoon cornstarch

Combine pepper and paprika; sprinkle on chicken. Coat a nonstick skillet with cooking spray; place over medium heat until hot. Cook chicken 5 minutes, turning once.

Combine garlic and next 7 ingredients; stir well, and pour over chicken. Cover and simmer 10 minutes. Add artichokes; cover and simmer an additional 5 minutes.

Remove chicken to serving platter; keep warm. Combine yogurt (at room temperature) and cornstarch in a small bowl; stir gently. Spoon a small amount of hot vegetable mixture into yogurt mixture; stir gently. Slowly add yogurt mixture to skillet, stirring constantly. Do not let mixture boil. Pour vegetable sauce over chicken breasts. Yield: 4 servings (217 calories per serving).

□ *30.1 grams protein, 2.8 grams fat, 15.4 grams carbohydrate, 67 milligrams cholesterol, 288 milligrams sodium, and 112 milligrams calcium.*
Betty Wise
Duncanville, Texas

LEMON-YOGURT SLAW OR SALAD DRESSING

1 (8-ounce) carton plain low-fat yogurt
3 tablespoons reduced-calorie mayonnaise
2 tablespoons lemon juice
1 tablespoon plus 1 teaspoon Dijon mustard
⅛ teaspoon garlic powder
⅛ teaspoon white pepper

Combine all ingredients in a small bowl; stir well. Cover and chill. Yield: 1 cup plus 3 tablespoons (16 calories per tablespoon).

□ *0.6 gram protein, 0.9 gram fat, 1.2 grams carbohydrate, 2 milligrams cholesterol, 53 milligrams sodium, and 22 milligrams calcium.*
Lori Adams
Ellaville, Georgia

BROCCAMOLI CURRY SPREAD

1 (10-ounce) package frozen
    chopped broccoli, cooked and
    drained
¼ cup plain low-fat yogurt
1 tablespoon reduced-calorie
    mayonnaise
¼ teaspoon curry powder
⅛ teaspoon garlic powder
⅛ teaspoon salt
½ teaspoon lemon juice
2 tablespoons diced onion

Combine all ingredients in container
of an electric blender; process at medium speed until smooth. Serve
spread with carrot sticks or melba
toast. Yield: 1¼ cups (8 calories per
tablespoon).

☐ 0.6 gram protein, 0.3 gram fat,
1.1 grams carbohydrate, 0 milligrams
cholesterol, 24 milligrams sodium,
and 13 milligrams calcium.
Irlene Kincaid
San Antonio, Texas

YOGURT-CHEESE TOPPING

½ cup low-fat cottage cheese
¼ cup (1 ounce) crumbled blue
    cheese
1 tablespoon sliced green onions
⅛ teaspoon garlic powder
¼ teaspoon Worcestershire
    sauce
1½ teaspoons lemon juice
¼ cup plain low-fat yogurt

Combine cottage cheese and blue
cheese; stir well. Add green onions,
garlic powder, Worcestershire sauce,
and lemon juice; stir well. Fold in
yogurt; cover and chill.

    The topping may be served on
baked potatoes or as a spread or dip.
Yield: about 1 cup (15 calories per
tablespoon).

☐ 1.5 grams protein, 0.7 gram fat,
0.6 gram carbohydrate, 2 milligrams
cholesterol, 57 milligrams sodium,
and 21 milligrams calcium.
Frank H. Fogg
Tulsa, Oklahoma

YOGURT SNACK

1 (8-ounce) carton plain low-fat
    yogurt
⅓ cup orange juice
2 teaspoons honey
¼ teaspoon almond extract
1 cup sliced banana, frozen

Combine first 4 ingredients in container of an electric blender; process
until smooth. Gradually add banana
slices; process until mixture is
smooth. Yield: 2¼ cups (121 calories
per ¾-cup serving).

☐ 4.7 grams protein, 1.4 grams fat,
23.9 grams carbohydrate, 5 milligrams cholesterol, 54 milligrams sodium, and 144 milligrams calcium.
Barbara G. Oneto
Lafayette, Louisiana

YOGURT MUFFINS

1 cup whole wheat flour
½ cup all-purpose flour
1 teaspoon baking powder
1 teaspoon baking soda
⅓ cup sugar
⅓ cup chopped pecans
1 egg, slightly beaten
1 (8-ounce) carton plain low-fat
    yogurt
¼ cup plus 1 tablespoon
    reduced-calorie margarine,
    melted
Vegetable cooking spray

Combine first 6 ingredients in a large
bowl; make a well in center of mixture. Combine egg, yogurt, and margarine in a small bowl; stir well. Add
to dry ingredients; stir just until
moistened.

    Coat bottom of muffin cups with
cooking spray; spoon batter into
cups, filling three-fourths full. Bake
at 350° for 18 to 20 minutes or until
lightly browned. Yield: 1 dozen (149
calories per muffin).

☐ 3.6 grams protein, 6.8 grams fat,
18.4 grams carbohydrate, 24 milligrams cholesterol, 143 milligrams sodium, and 73 milligrams calcium.
Clara L. Cannistra
Alexandria, Virginia

LIGHT-AND-EASY
CHEESECAKE

1 (16-ounce) carton part-skim
    ricotta cheese
1 (8-ounce) carton plain low-fat
    yogurt, drained
1 cup sugar
2½ tablespoons all-purpose flour
1 tablespoon lemon rind
2 tablespoons lemon juice
1 (8-ounce) carton light process
    cream cheese product, softened
2 eggs
2 egg whites
2½ teaspoons vanilla extract
Graham cracker crust (recipe
    follows)
Lemon slices (optional)
Mint sprigs (optional)

Combine ricotta cheese, yogurt,
sugar, flour, lemon rind, and juice in
container of an electric blender; process until smooth, and set aside.

    Beat cream cheese at medium
speed of an electric mixer until
smooth. Add eggs, egg whites, and
vanilla; beat until smooth. Gradually
add ricotta cheese mixture, and beat
until smooth. (Mixture will be thin.)

    Pour into graham cracker crust;
bake at 325° for 1½ hours. Remove
from oven; cool on wire rack. Cover
with plastic wrap; chill 8 hours.

    If desired, garnish with lemon
slices and mint sprigs. Yield: one 9-
inch cheesecake or 16 servings (173
calories per serving).

☐ 7 grams protein, 6.7 grams fat,
22.1 grams carbohydrate, 44 milligrams cholesterol, 170 milligrams sodium, and 131 milligrams calcium.

Graham Cracker Crust

⅔ cup graham cracker crumbs
1½ tablespoons reduced-calorie
    margarine, melted
1 tablespoon sifted powdered
    sugar
⅛ teaspoon grated lemon rind

Combine all ingredients; stir well.
Press into bottom of a 9-inch springform pan. Bake at 350° for 8 minutes; cool. Yield: one 9-inch graham
cracker crust. *Mrs. C. Gibson*
Brooksville, Florida

Build Your Menu Around These Vegetables

When planning meals for families, many cooks rely on frozen vegetables to keep menus bright, colorful, and nutritious. Try one of these tasty frozen-vegetable recipes.

SPINACH PIE

1 (10-ounce) package frozen chopped spinach
3 eggs
½ cup half-and-half
½ cup milk
¼ cup minced fresh mushrooms
½ cup minced onion
½ teaspoon salt
Dash of pepper
⅛ to ¼ teaspoon ground nutmeg
Cheese Pastry

Cook spinach according to package directions. Drain very well, pressing out additional moisture with paper towels; set aside.

Beat eggs in a large bowl; set aside. Combine half-and-half and next 5 ingredients in a small saucepan; simmer over low heat 1 minute. Slowly add hot mixture to eggs. Stir in nutmeg; add spinach. Pour spinach mixture into Cheese Pastry. Bake at 400° for 15 minutes. Reduce heat to 325°, and bake 20 to 25 minutes. Yield: one 9-inch pie.

Cheese Pastry

¾ cup all-purpose flour
½ teaspoon salt
½ teaspoon dry mustard
1 cup (4 ounces) shredded Cheddar cheese
¼ cup butter or margarine, melted

Combine all ingredients, mixing well. Press mixture in bottom and up sides of a 9-inch pieplate. Yield: one 9-inch pastry shell.   *Mrs. E. W. Hanley*
Palm Harbor, Florida

ASPARAGUS SALAD VINAIGRETTE

1 (10-ounce) package frozen asparagus spears
¼ cup vegetable oil
3 tablespoons vinegar
1 tablespoon minced parsley
1 tablespoon minced dill pickle
1 teaspoon minced onion
¼ teaspoon salt
⅛ teaspoon pepper
Pinch of dried whole tarragon
Lettuce leaves
Pimiento strips

Cook asparagus according to package directions. Drain well. Place in a 10- x 6- x 2-inch baking dish.

Combine oil, vinegar, parsley, pickle, onion, salt, pepper, and tarragon; mix well. Pour over asparagus. Cover and chill at least 1 hour.

Arrange lettuce on salad plates. Place asparagus on lettuce; garnish with pimiento strips. Yield: about 4 servings.   *Mrs. H. F. Mosher*
Huntsville, Alabama

HEARTY VEGETABLE CHOWDER

1 (10¾-ounce) can chicken broth, undiluted
⅔ cup water
4 cups frozen mixed vegetables
¼ cup minced onion
¼ cup minced green pepper
3 tablespoons butter or margarine, melted
¼ cup all-purpose flour
½ teaspoon paprika
½ teaspoon dry mustard
2 cups milk
⅛ teaspoon pepper
2 cups (8 ounces) shredded Cheddar cheese
Carrot curls (optional)
Parsley sprigs (optional)

Combine chicken broth and water in a saucepan; bring to a boil. Add mixed vegetables, and cook 15 minutes or until tender. Sauté onion and green pepper in butter in a Dutch oven until tender. Blend in flour, paprika, and mustard. Gradually add milk, vegetables, and broth; cook over medium heat, stirring constantly, until mixture comes to a boil. Remove from heat; add pepper and cheese, and stir until cheese melts. If desired, garnish each serving with a carrot curl and parsley. Yield: 7 cups.   *Mrs. Clayton J. Turner*
De Funiak Springs, Florida

CREAM-OF-BROCCOLI SOUP

2 cups water
1 (16-ounce) package frozen broccoli cuts
½ cup chopped onion
½ cup butter or margarine, melted
½ cup all-purpose flour
6 cups milk
4 chicken-flavored bouillon cubes
1 teaspoon white pepper

Bring water to a boil in a medium saucepan; add broccoli. Cover, reduce heat, and simmer 5 minutes. Remove from heat, and set aside.

Sauté onion in butter in a Dutch oven over low heat about 10 minutes or until tender. Add flour, stirring until smooth; cook 1 minute, stirring constantly. Gradually add milk and bouillon cubes; cook over medium heat, stirring constantly, until mixture is thickened. Add broccoli, cooking water, and pepper. Simmer 20 to 30 minutes, stirring occasionally. Yield: 9 cups.   *Deborah Beckes*
Dunwoody, Georgia

THREE-BEAN CASSEROLE

1 (10-ounce) package frozen French-cut green beans
1 (10-ounce) package frozen English peas
1 (10-ounce) package frozen lima beans
1½ cups mayonnaise
4 hard-cooked eggs, grated and divided
1 small onion, grated
1 tablespoon prepared mustard
1 teaspoon Worcestershire sauce
½ cup chopped fresh parsley

Cook vegetables separately according to package directions. Drain and toss together; set aside.

Combine mayonnaise, 2 grated eggs, onion, mustard, and Worcestershire sauce; mix well.

Layer half of vegetables and half of sauce in a greased 2-quart casserole. Repeat layers. Cover and bake at 350° for 15 minutes or until thoroughly heated. Garnish with remaining egg and parsley. Yield: 8 servings. *Mrs. Charles L. Poteet*
Little Rock, Arkansas

GREEN BEANS WITH BLUE CHEESE

½ cup water
¼ teaspoon salt
1 (9-ounce) package frozen French-cut green beans
1½ tablespoons butter or margarine, divided
2 tablespoons crumbled blue cheese
⅛ teaspoon pepper
½ cup soft breadcrumbs

Combine water and salt in a medium saucepan; bring to a boil, and add beans. Cover and cook 6 to 8 minutes or until beans are crisp-tender; drain. Toss beans with 1 tablespoon butter, blue cheese, and pepper. Spoon into a lightly greased 1-quart casserole, and set aside.

Melt reserved ½ tablespoon butter in a small skillet; add breadcrumbs and toast, stirring often, until golden brown. Sprinkle breadcrumbs over beans. Bake, uncovered, at 350° for 15 minutes. Yield: 4 servings.

Connie Burgess
Knoxville, Tennessee

Layer Breakfast Into A Casserole

Layered breakfast casseroles originated with a simple version of sandwich bread, sausage, milk, and eggs, but the idea has taken on a new dimension. Here the recipes retain the make-ahead quality of the original casserole, but sport new ingredients.

ITALIAN SAUSAGE BRUNCH

12 slices white bread, crust removed
1 pound Italian sausage, cut in ¼-inch slices
½ pound fresh mushrooms, sliced
1 medium onion, chopped
¼ cup butter or margarine, melted
4 cups (16 ounces) shredded Cheddar cheese
5 eggs, beaten
2¼ cups milk
1 tablespoon Dijon mustard
1 teaspoon dry mustard
1 teaspoon ground nutmeg
½ teaspoon salt
¼ teaspoon pepper
2 tablespoons minced fresh parsley

Place 6 slices bread in a lightly greased 13- x 9- x 2-inch baking dish. Set aside.

Cook sausage, mushrooms, onion, and butter in a large skillet over medium heat until sausage is browned; drain well. Spoon half of sausage mixture over bread; sprinkle half of cheese over sausage. Layer remaining 6 slices of bread, sausage mixture, and cheese.

Combine eggs and next 6 ingredients; pour over cheese. Cover and refrigerate 8 hours.

Remove from refrigerator, and let stand at room temperature 30 minutes. Sprinkle with parsley. Bake, uncovered, at 350° for 50 minutes. Yield: 8 to 10 servings. *Diane Jenc*
Springfield, Virginia

CHILE 'N' CHEESE BREAKFAST CASSEROLE

3 English muffins, split
2 tablespoons butter or margarine, softened
1 pound bulk pork sausage
1 (4-ounce) can chopped green chiles, drained
3 cups (12 ounces) shredded Cheddar cheese
1½ cups commercial sour cream
12 eggs, beaten

Spread cut side of each muffin with 1 teaspoon butter, and place, buttered side down, in a lightly greased 13- x 9- x 2-inch baking dish.

Cook sausage in a skillet until browned, stirring to crumble; drain. Layer half each of sausage, chiles, and cheese over muffins. Combine sour cream and eggs; pour over casserole. Repeat layers with remaining sausage, chiles, and cheese; cover and refrigerate 8 hours.

Remove from refrigerator, and let stand at room temperature 30 minutes. Bake, uncovered, at 350° for 35 to 40 minutes. Yield: 8 to 10 servings. *Linda Schooler*
Amarillo, Texas

BRUNCH FOR A BUNCH

1 pound hot bulk pork sausage
3 cups frozen hash brown potatoes, thawed
½ teaspoon salt
3 cups (12 ounces) shredded Cheddar cheese
½ cup chopped green pepper
12 eggs, beaten
2 cups milk

Cook sausage in a skillet until browned, stirring to crumble; drain.

Place hash browns in a lightly greased 13- x 9- x 2-inch baking dish; sprinkle with salt. Layer sausage, cheese, and green pepper.

Combine eggs and milk, stirring well; pour over green pepper. Bake at 350° for about 50 minutes. Yield: 8 to 10 servings. *Joanne Winn*
Fredonia, Kentucky

CREOLE SAUSAGE-AND-RICE BAKE

1 pound bulk pork sausage
3 cups cooked rice
2 cups (8 ounces) shredded sharp
  Cheddar cheese, divided
3 eggs, beaten
1 (10¾-ounce) can cream of
  mushroom soup, undiluted
½ cup milk
1 (4-ounce) can sliced
  mushrooms, drained
2 teaspoons Creole mustard
¼ teaspoon onion powder

Cook sausage in a skillet until browned, stirring to crumble; drain and set aside.

Combine rice and 1½ cups cheese. Spread mixture into a lightly greased 12- x 8- x 2-inch baking dish. Sprinkle with sausage.

Combine eggs and next 5 ingredients; mix well. Pour over sausage. Bake at 350° for 35 minutes. Sprinkle with remaining ½ cup cheese, and bake an additional 5 minutes. Yield: 8 servings.   *Azine G. Rush*
Monroe, Louisiana

SAUSAGE-CHEESE BAKE

1 pound bulk pork sausage
1 (8-ounce) can refrigerator
  crescent rolls
2 cups (8 ounces) shredded
  Monterey Jack cheese
2 tablespoons chopped green
  pepper
4 eggs, beaten
¾ cup milk
½ teaspoon dried whole oregano,
  crushed
⅛ teaspoon pepper

Cook sausage in a skillet until browned, stirring to crumble. Drain and set aside.

Unroll each half of crescent roll dough, making a rectangle. Line bottom and ½ inch up sides of a lightly greased 13- x 9- x 2-inch baking dish with rectangles, pressing seams securely to seal. Sprinkle sausage over

dough; top with shredded cheese and green pepper.

Combine eggs and remaining ingredients, and pour over casserole. Bake at 400° for 18 to 20 minutes. Yield: 8 servings.   *Pat Lubas*
Tulsa, Oklahoma

Lamb Flavor Is Better Than Ever

Lamb is more available in meat markets today than it has been in years. In fact, you may have seen some surprising cuts packaged—such as chops, ground lamb, kabob pieces, or ribs—alongside more traditional lamb shanks or a whole leg of lamb.

In the past, a leg of lamb was more likely to be reserved for company, but as you will see in the recipes here, lamb fits into everyday family meals as well as more formal menus for entertaining. Lamb Chops With Shrimp, for example, is an elegant entrée for family or guests.

For more information on lamb, please see "From Our Kitchen to Yours," on the next page.

LAMB CHOPS WITH SHRIMP

8 (1-inch-thick) lamb loin chops
½ teaspoon salt
½ teaspoon white pepper
1 teaspoon dried whole marjoram
1 large tomato
Hollandaise sauce (recipe follows)
16 medium-size fresh shrimp,
  unpeeled
2 tablespoons butter or
  margarine, melted
Curly endive (optional)

Sprinkle chops with salt, pepper, and marjoram; grill over medium-hot coals 30 minutes, turning once. Arrange lamb chops on serving platter; keep warm.

Cut top third from tomato; discard top, and scoop out pulp from bottom, leaving shell intact. Drain well. Pour hollandaise sauce into tomato cup; place in center of serving platter.

Peel and devein shrimp, leaving tails intact. To butterfly, make a deep slit down back of each shrimp, cutting almost through it. Sauté in butter 3 to 5 minutes, stirring frequently. Place 2 shrimp on each lamb chop. Garnish with endive, if desired, and serve with hollandaise sauce. Yield: 4 servings.

Hollandaise Sauce

3 egg yolks
⅛ teaspoon salt
Dash of red pepper
2 tablespoons lemon juice
½ cup butter or margarine

Place first 4 ingredients in container of an electric blender. Cover and blend at high speed about 5 seconds. Melt butter; with blender on high, gradually add melted butter in a slow steady stream. Blend about 30 seconds or until sauce is thickened. Yield: about ¾ cup.

LAMB STEW

Juice of 2 lemons
3 pounds boneless lamb shoulder,
  cubed
6 cups cold water
4 medium potatoes, peeled and
  quartered
3 medium onions, sliced
3 to 4 cloves garlic, chopped
2 chicken-flavored bouillon
  cubes
½ teaspoon salt
½ teaspoon freshly ground
  pepper
6 cups water
8 small boiling onions, sliced
8 small new potatoes, peeled and
  quartered
8 baby carrots, scraped and cut
  in half
1½ teaspoons fresh thyme or ½
  teaspoon dried whole thyme

Drizzle lemon juice over lamb, and let stand 10 minutes. Place in a large

Dutch oven; add 6 cups cold water. Bring to a boil, and simmer 5 minutes; drain and discard liquid. Rinse lamb and Dutch oven in cold water.

Return lamb to Dutch oven; add 4 potatoes, 3 onions, and next 5 ingredients. Bring to a boil; reduce heat, and simmer, uncovered, 1½ hours. Remove potatoes and onions; place in container of a blender or food processor. Add ¼ cup cooking liquid, and process until smooth; stir into lamb mixture. Add 8 onions, 8 potatoes, carrots, and thyme; cover and simmer for 30 minutes. Yield: 3½ quarts.
Sue Sims
San Angelo, Texas

MESQUITE-GRILLED LAMB BURGERS

Mesquite chips
1 large tomato, chopped
½ cup chopped onion
1 small jalapeño pepper, chopped
1 pound ground lamb
2 tablespoons butter or margarine, softened
4 hamburger buns

Soak mesquite chips in water at least 30 minutes. Set aside.

Combine tomato, onion, and jalapeño in a small bowl, mixing well. Set sauce aside.

Shape lamb into 4 patties. Place soaked mesquite chips over medium-hot coals. Grill lamb patties 15 minutes or to desired degree of doneness, turning once.

Spread butter on inside of buns; toast until golden brown. Serve burgers with sauce on buns. Yield: 4 servings.
Marilyn Mertz
San Angelo, Texas

Tip: *When using your grill, never allow the coals to flame during cooking, as flames may either burn the food or cause it to dry out. Just remember to keep a container of water nearby so that you can douse flames as they appear.*

From Our Kitchen To Yours

Broaden your food horizons with lamb. Nutritious and low in calories, it can be prepared in many ways.

Lamb comes from animals less than a year old. It provides tender, flavorful meat containing very little marbling (internal fat). To make the meat leaner, you can trim the majority of fat found on the edges.

One 4-ounce serving of lean cooked lamb cut from the loin is about 212 calories and contains protein, iron, zinc, and B vitamins.

Selecting and Purchasing

According to the American Lamb Council, new cutting procedures are creating additional serving possibilities. American lamb cuts are now larger with a higher meat-to-bone ratio than imported lamb.

Allow, per person, ¼ to ⅓ pound boneless meat or ½ pound with bone in. Select fine-textured, bright pink lamb with pink bones. High-quality lamb has a smooth covering of pinkish white firm fat over most of the exterior. This exterior fat is covered with a thin skin called fell.

Storing

Store lamb in the coldest part of your refrigerator up to three days. Refrigerate ground lamb up to two days, and cooked lamb two to three days. Fresh lamb, with the exception of ground lamb, can be frozen six to nine months. Store ground lamb and cooked lamb in the freezer three to four months.

Cooking

Because most lamb cuts are tender, you can cook them by dry-heat methods. Roast, grill, broil, or panbroil the rack, loin, shoulder, and leg cuts. When broiling or panbroiling, cook lamb approximately 10 minutes per side for each inch of thickness. Braising or cooking in liquid, which are moist-heat methods, are necessary when preparing less-tender shank cuts.

Lamb is best cooked at the recommended temperature of 325°. If cooked at higher temperatures, fat burns due to its low melting point.

Avoid overcooking lamb; the internal temperature should register 140° for rare, 150° to 155° for medium, 160° for medium well, 170° for well done. Although lamb tastes best rare, the preferred internal temperature is usually medium. Because it continues to cook after removal from oven, the meat thermometer should register 5° lower than the desired degree of doneness. For easier carving, let lamb stand 20 minutes.

To cook roasts, leave the fell on to retain shape and to hold in natural juices. Remove fell from steaks to prevent shrinking and curling.

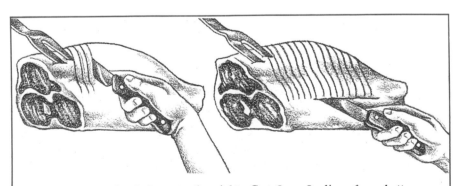

(Left) *Place shank bone to the right. Cut 2 or 3 slices from bottom, parallel to leg bone. Turn leg over so that it rests on cut side. Steady leg with carving fork, and make vertical slices down to leg bone.*
(Right) *Cut horizontally along the leg bone to release slices.*

Southerners Win With Beef

When ballots were counted at The National Beef Cookoff, 5 of the 11 winners hailed from the South. We were thrilled with the results and even recognized the names of some of the winners from our list of recipe contributors. We thought you'd enjoy preparing these recipes for your family and friends.

PEPPERCORN LONDON BROIL

1 (3½-pound) top sirloin steak, cut 2½ inches thick
1 cup dry red wine
¾ cup chopped fresh parsley, divided
¼ cup olive oil
3 cloves garlic, minced
3 green onions, minced
1 teaspoon green peppercorns
1 teaspoon dry mustard
½ teaspoon ground thyme
1 bay leaf
1 tablespoon coarsely ground black pepper
Green Peppercorn Butter, divided
1 pound fresh broccoli, cut into flowerets
1 tablespoon vegetable oil
1 large green pepper, cut into ¼-inch strips
1 large sweet red pepper, cut into ¼-inch strips
1 large yellow pepper, cut into ¼-inch strips
2 cups cherry tomatoes

Trim excess fat from steak; pierce both sides with a fork. Place steak in a large shallow dish. Set aside.

Combine wine, ½ cup parsley, and next 7 ingredients. Pour over steak; cover and marinate in refrigerator 4 hours, turning occasionally.

Drain steak; pat dry with paper towels. Press pepper onto both sides of steak.

Preheat broiler pan 10 minutes. Place steak on preheated broiler pan. Broil 4 to 6 inches from heat 15 minutes; turn and broil an additional 10 minutes or to desired degree of doneness. Brush both sides of steak with ⅓ cup Green Peppercorn Butter. Let stand 15 minutes.

Cook broccoli, covered, in a small amount of boiling water 8 minutes or until crisp-tender. Drain broccoli, and set aside.

Heat vegetable oil in a large skillet over medium heat; add peppers, and sauté 2 to 3 minutes. Remove from heat. Add cherry tomatoes and remaining ¼ cup parsley; toss lightly.

Cut steak diagonally across the grain into thin slices. Arrange steak and vegetables on platter. Serve with remaining Green Peppercorn Butter. Yield: 8 to 10 servings.

Green Peppercorn Butter

½ cup butter, softened
½ cup chopped fresh parsley
2 tablespoons green peppercorns
2 teaspoons lemon juice
2 teaspoons Worcestershire sauce
1 teaspoon Dijon mustard

Position knife blade in food processor bowl; combine all ingredients in bowl. Top with cover; process 1 minute or until smooth. Yield: ⅔ cup.
Gloria Norton
Jacksonville, Florida

CURRIED BEEF STEAK

1 (3- to 3½-pound) boneless sirloin steak, 1½ inches thick
⅓ cup vegetable oil
2 tablespoons lemon juice
2 tablespoons white wine vinegar
2 teaspoons curry powder
2 teaspoons Worcestershire sauce
2 cloves garlic, crushed
1 teaspoon salt
½ teaspoon pepper
3 dashes of aromatic bitters
Fresh parsley sprigs
Cherry tomatoes

Place steak in a large shallow dish. Combine vegetable oil and next 8 ingredients. Pour over steak; cover and refrigerate 6 to 8 hours, turning steak occasionally.

Remove steak from marinade, reserving marinade. Grill steak over medium-hot coals 10 to 12 minutes on each side or to desired degree of doneness, basting occasionally with reserved marinade.

Cut steak into thin slices. Garnish with parsley and cherry tomatoes. Yield: 6 to 8 servings. *Ann Whelan*
Catonsville, Maryland

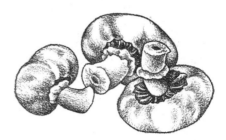

PEKING BEEF SALAD

1 ounce fresh snow pea pods
2 pounds top round steak (¾-inch thick)
3 tablespoons vegetable oil
Dressing (recipe follows), divided
1 teaspoon browning-and-seasoning sauce
¾ to 1 pound fresh spinach
2 cups thinly sliced Chinese cabbage
¼ pound fresh mushrooms, sliced
1 small red onion, sliced and separated into rings
3 hard-cooked eggs, quartered
12 cherry tomatoes
5 slices beef bacon, cooked and crumbled
2 tablespoons sesame seeds, toasted

Blanch snow peas in boiling water 3 minutes; drain and chill.

Partially freeze steak; slice diagonally across grain into ¼-inch strips.

Heat oil in a large skillet. Add half of steak; stir-fry until no longer pink. Transfer to a bowl. Repeat procedure. Add 1 cup dressing and browning-and-seasoning sauce. Cover and chill 1½ hours, stirring once.

Remove stems from spinach; wash leaves, pat dry, and tear into bite-size pieces. Combine spinach, next 3 ingredients, and snow peas; place on a platter. Arrange steak in center of salad mixture; garnish with eggs and tomatoes. Sprinkle with bacon and sesame seeds. Serve with remaining dressing. Yield: 6 to 8 servings.

Dressing

1 cup vegetable oil
¾ cup chili sauce
¾ cup red wine vinegar
½ cup sugar
1 tablespoon soy sauce

Combine all ingredients in a jar. Cover tightly, and shake vigorously. Yield: 2⅔ cups.   *Diane Lentz*
Nicholasville, Kentucky

GINGERED BEEF SALAD

1 small onion
3 whole cloves
1 (2½-pound) boneless beef brisket
4 cups water
1 cup dry red wine
1 large clove garlic, halved
1 (6-ounce) package long-grain and wild rice
1 cup cooked English peas
½ cup sliced celery
½ cup sliced green onions
⅓ cup diced sweet red pepper
½ cup sliced almonds, toasted
¼ cup chopped fresh parsley
Ginger Dressing
Curly endive
Sweet red pepper rings (optional)

Stud onion with cloves; set aside.

Trim excess fat from brisket. Place brisket in a Dutch oven; add onion, water, wine, and garlic. Bring mixture to a boil; cover, reduce heat, and simmer 2½ hours or until brisket is tender. Remove brisket; cover and chill. Cut brisket into ¾-inch cubes; set aside.

Prepare rice according to package directions. Combine rice, beef, peas, celery, green onions, diced red pepper, almonds, and parsley. Add Ginger Dressing; toss lightly. Spoon salad onto serving dish lined with endive. Garnish with red pepper rings, if desired. Serve warm or at room temperature. Yield: 8 servings.

Ginger Dressing

¼ cup vegetable oil
2 tablespoons red wine vinegar
1½ teaspoons grated fresh ginger
1 teaspoon Dijon mustard
½ teaspoon freshly ground pepper
¼ teaspoon salt

Combine all ingredients in a jar. Cover tightly, and shake vigorously. Chill several hours. Shake again before serving. Yield: ⅓ cup.
Frances Andrews
Wilson, North Carolina

HERBED SIRLOIN TIP ROAST WITH MUSTARD CREAM SAUCE

1 tablespoon dried whole thyme
1 teaspoon dried whole rosemary, crushed
1 teaspoon rubbed sage
1 teaspoon garlic salt
1 teaspoon coarsely ground pepper
1 (3-pound) beef tip roast
Mustard Cream Sauce
Capers
Fresh parsley sprigs

Preheat oven to 500°. Combine thyme, rosemary, sage, garlic salt, and pepper in a small bowl; rub onto surface of roast. Place roast, fat side up, on rack in a shallow roasting pan; insert meat thermometer into thickest part of roast.

Reduce oven temperature to 325°. Bake roast, uncovered, for 1 hour and 45 minutes or until meat thermometer registers 140° for rare or 160° for medium. Let stand 20 minutes before carving.

Drizzle a small amount of Mustard Cream Sauce over roast; sprinkle with capers, and garnish with parsley. Serve roast with remaining sauce. Yield: 8 to 10 servings.

Mustard Cream Sauce

2 tablespoons butter
2 tablespoons all-purpose flour
1 cup half-and-half
¼ cup dry white wine
¼ cup Dijon mustard
2 tablespoons butter
1 tablespoon capers

Melt 2 tablespoons butter in a heavy saucepan over low heat; add flour, stirring until smooth. Cook 1 minute, stirring constantly. Gradually add half-and-half; cook over medium heat, stirring constantly, until mixture is thickened and bubbly. Stir in wine, mustard, and 2 tablespoons butter; cool slightly. Fold in capers. Yield: 1⅔ cups.   *Elaine Fronczek*
Knoxville, Tennessee

Almonds Any Time

Almonds add zip to breads, salads, vegetables, fish, chicken, and more.

Almond paste, a mixture of ground almonds and sugar, has become available in some grocery stores and in stores which sell candymaking supplies. When you use chopped, slivered, sliced, or whole almonds, you'll find them more flavorful if the nuts are roasted or toasted. (If you want them chopped or sliced, do so before roasting.)

ALMOND FRENCH TOAST

8 slices white bread
1 (3-ounce) package cream cheese, softened
3 tablespoons almond paste
3 eggs, beaten
1 cup milk
½ teaspoon vanilla extract
¼ cup butter or margarine
2 tablespoons vegetable oil

Trim crust from bread; set bread slices aside. Process crust in a blender or food processor until finely crumbled. Set crumbs aside.

Combine cream cheese and almond paste; beat at medium speed of an electric mixer until smooth. Spread the mixture evenly on 4 bread slices; top with the remaining bread slices. Slice each sandwich diagonally to form 4 triangles.

Combine eggs, milk, and vanilla. Dip each bread triangle into egg mixture, coat with crumbs, and dip again in egg mixture.

Melt butter in a large skillet; add oil. Cook triangles over medium heat 4 minutes on each side or until browned. Serve immediately. Yield: 4 servings.
Marie T. Horbaly
Springfield, Virginia

ALMOND-BROCCOLI CASSEROLE

1 pound fresh broccoli
⅓ cup slivered almonds, toasted
2 tablespoons butter or margarine, melted
2 egg whites
½ cup mayonnaise
⅓ cup grated Parmesan cheese
1 tablespoon grated onion

Trim off large leaves of broccoli, and remove tough ends of lower stalks. Wash broccoli thoroughly, and cut into spears. Cook in a small amount of boiling water 8 minutes; drain.

Arrange broccoli in a lightly greased 8-inch square baking dish with flowerets placed toward outside edges of dish. Sprinkle with almonds; drizzle with melted butter.

Beat egg whites (at room temperature) in a small bowl at high speed of an electric mixer until soft peaks form; fold in mayonnaise, cheese, and onion. Spoon over center of broccoli-almond mixture, leaving the edges of the broccoli exposed.

Bake at 450° for 5 minutes or until meringue is puffy and lightly browned. Serve immediately. Yield: 6 servings.
Marie H. Webb
Roanoke, Virginia

BANANA-HONEY-NUT MUFFINS

1¾ cups all-purpose flour
2½ teaspoons baking powder
¾ teaspoon salt
⅓ cup sugar
⅔ cup chopped almonds, toasted
1 egg, beaten
¾ cup mashed banana (about 2 small)
½ cup plus 1 tablespoon milk
⅓ cup vegetable oil
¼ cup honey
2 tablespoons butter or margarine, melted
⅓ cup chopped almonds, toasted

Combine first 5 ingredients in a large bowl; make a well in center of mixture. Combine egg, banana, milk, and oil; add to dry mixture, stirring just until moistened.

Spoon batter into greased and floured muffin pans, filling three-fourths full. Bake at 400° for 15 minutes or until golden brown. Remove from pans immediately.

Combine honey and butter, mixing well. Dip top of muffins in honey mixture, and sprinkle with ⅓ cup almonds. Yield: 14 muffins.
Naomi Reed
Knoxville, Tennessee

Roasting and Toasting Almonds

Use the following directions for bringing out the best flavor:

■ **Roasting:** Spread almonds in a shallow pan lightly coated with butter or vegetable oil. Bake at 350° for 10 minutes or until light golden brown; stir occasionally. (Nuts will continue to brown after they are removed from oven.)
■ **Microwave roasting:** Toss almonds with either vegetable oil or melted butter. Spread in a single layer on a microwave-safe plate. Microwave at HIGH 2 minutes. Stir and let stand 1 minute. Microwave at HIGH an additional 2 minutes. Drain and cool.
■ **Toasting:** Follow the directions for roasting, using an ungreased pan. This method makes almonds crisper.
■ **Microwave toasting:** Spread the almonds in a single layer on a microwave-safe plate. Microwave at HIGH 1½ minutes. Stir and let stand 1 minute. Microwave at HIGH 1½ minutes.

Tip: *If you grease more muffin cups than you need, fill the empty cups with water to keep grease from baking on the cups.*

Healthier Baking With Whole Wheat Flour

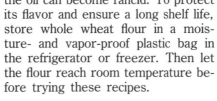

Along with a rich, nutty taste, whole wheat flour recipes offer special hidden bonuses. They have an abundance of vitamins and minerals, and add fiber to the diet.

All types of flour should be stored in airtight containers, but whole wheat flour needs special attention because of the oil-rich wheat germ; the oil can become rancid. To protect its flavor and ensure a long shelf life, store whole wheat flour in a moisture- and vapor-proof plastic bag in the refrigerator or freezer. Then let the flour reach room temperature before trying these recipes.

WHOLE WHEAT FRENCH BREAD

2 packages dry yeast
1 teaspoon sugar
3¼ cups warm water (105° to 115°)
2 tablespoons sugar
2½ teaspoons salt
3 cups whole wheat flour
4 to 4¼ cups all-purpose flour, divided
About ¼ cup cornmeal

Dissolve yeast and 1 teaspoon sugar in warm water in a large mixing bowl; let stand 5 minutes.

Add 2 tablespoons sugar, salt, whole wheat flour, and 2 cups all-purpose flour to yeast mixture. Beat at medium speed of an electric mixer until mixture is smooth. Gradually stir in enough all-purpose flour to make a soft dough.

Turn dough out onto a floured surface, and knead until smooth and elastic (about 5 minutes). Place dough in a well-greased bowl, turning to grease top of dough. Cover and let rise in a warm place (85°), free from drafts, 45 minutes or until dough is doubled in bulk.

Grease 4 French bread loafpans; sprinkle each pan with cornmeal, and set aside.

Punch dough down; divide into 4 portions. On a lightly floured surface, flatten each portion into an oval. Fold dough over lengthwise, and flatten with open hand. Fold it again, and roll with palms of hand to a 15- x 2-inch rope; place ropes of dough in prepared pans.

Cover pans tightly with plastic wrap, and let rise in a warm place (85°), free from drafts, 30 minutes or until doubled in bulk.

Gently cut ¼-inch-deep slits crosswise at intervals on loaves with a razor blade or sharp knife.

Place loaves in oven; spray loaves with water. Bake at 400° for 15 minutes, spraying every 3 minutes without removing loaves from oven. Bake an additional 10 to 15 minutes or until loaves are golden and sound hollow when tapped. Yield: 4 loaves.

Geraldine A. Murphy
Louisville, Kentucky

BROWN BREAD

1 cup whole wheat flour
1 cup rye flour
¾ teaspoon baking soda
½ teaspoon salt
1 cup yellow cornmeal
1¾ cups buttermilk
¾ cup dark molasses
1 cup raisins

Combine first 5 ingredients in a large mixing bowl; set aside.

Combine buttermilk and molasses, mixing well. Add buttermilk mixture to dry ingredients, stirring well. Stir in 1 cup raisins.

Pour batter into 3 well-greased 1-pound coffee cans. Cover the cans with a double thickness of aluminum foil; tie securely with string.

Place cans on a shallow rack in a large deep kettle; add water to a depth of 1 inch. Cover kettle; steam bread 3 hours in continuously boiling water. (Replace water as needed.) Remove bread from cans; let cool 10 minutes on wire racks. Yield: 3 loaves.

Carolyne M. Carnevale
Ormond Beach, Florida

SPICY RAISIN COFFEE CAKE

½ cup butter or margarine, softened
1 cup sugar
2 eggs
1 teaspoon vanilla extract
1 cup commercial sour cream
2 cups whole wheat flour
1½ teaspoons baking powder
½ teaspoon baking soda
¼ teaspoon salt
1 cup chopped walnuts
⅓ cup firmly packed brown sugar
1 teaspoon ground cinnamon
½ cup raisins

Cream butter in a large mixing bowl; gradually add sugar, mixing well. Add eggs and vanilla, mixing well. Add sour cream, mixing until blended, and set aside.

Combine whole wheat flour and next 3 ingredients. Add to creamed mixture, beating until blended.

Spread half of batter in a greased 9-inch square pan. Combine walnuts, brown sugar, and cinnamon; sprinkle half of mixture over batter. Sprinkle raisins over walnut mixture. Top with remaining batter. Sprinkle remaining walnut mixture on top. Bake at 350° for 35 minutes or until a wooden pick inserted in center comes out clean. Yield: one 9-inch coffee cake.

Ruth Sigg
Fairfax, Virginia

Munch On These Snacks

Next time you get the munchies, prepare one of these recipes. Both are easy to make, and they use ingredients you may have on hand.

CARAMEL CORN

Vegetable cooking spray
6 quarts popped corn
1½ cups pecan halves
1½ cups firmly packed brown sugar
¾ cup butter or margarine
¾ cup light corn syrup
1½ cups raw peanuts
½ teaspoon baking soda
1 teaspoon vanilla extract

Coat 2 large roasting pans with cooking spray. Combine popcorn and pecans in pans; set aside.

Combine sugar, butter, corn syrup, and peanuts in a large saucepan; bring to a boil, and boil 5 minutes. Remove from heat; stir in soda and vanilla.

Pour mixture evenly over popcorn mixture. Stir with a lightly greased long-handled spoon until popcorn is well coated. Bake at 250° for 1 hour, stirring every 20 minutes. Remove from oven, and immediately pour onto wax paper, breaking it apart as it cools. Store in airtight containers. Yield: 6½ quarts.   *Carolyn Webb*
Jackson, Mississippi

CHILE-HAM TURNOVERS

1 (4-ounce) can chopped green chiles, well drained
1 (2⅛-ounce) can deviled ham
½ cup (2 ounces) shredded Monterey Jack cheese
1 (10-ounce) can refrigerated flaky biscuits
1 egg white, beaten

Combine first 3 ingredients, stirring well; set aside.

Cut each biscuit in half; on a lightly floured surface, roll each half to a 3-inch circle. Place 1 teaspoon ham mixture in center of each circle; moisten edges of circles with egg white. Fold circles in half, and press edges together with a fork. Prick tops with a fork.

Place on an ungreased baking sheet; bake at 400° for 12 minutes or until lightly browned. Yield: 20 appetizer servings.   *Mrs. John Rucker*
Louisville, Kentucky

Attention, Peanut Butter Fans

While children for the most part love peanut butter, it is fast becoming a favorite of adults, too. According to recent statistics, adults eat half the peanut butter sold in this country.

PEANUT BUTTER BREAD

2 tablespoons butter or margarine, melted
¼ cup firmly packed brown sugar
¼ cup chopped roasted peanuts
1 tablespoon water
1 egg
1 cup firmly packed brown sugar
2 tablespoons peanut butter
2 tablespoons butter or margarine, melted
1 cup buttermilk
2 cups all-purpose flour
1 teaspoon baking powder
½ teaspoon baking soda
½ teaspoon salt

Grease bottom and sides of an 8½- x 4½- x 2½-inch loafpan. Pour 2 tablespoons butter in pan. Sprinkle ¼ cup sugar and peanuts evenly over bottom of pan. Sprinkle 1 tablespoon water over mixture.

Beat egg at medium speed of an electric mixer. Add 1 cup sugar, and beat well. Add peanut butter and 2 tablespoons butter, mixing well. Add buttermilk, mixing until blended. Combine flour and remaining ingredients; add to creamed mixture, mixing well. Spoon into prepared pan. Bake at 350° for 50 minutes or until a wooden pick inserted in center comes out clean. Cool in pan 10 minutes; remove from pan, and let cool on a wire rack. Yield: 1 loaf.
Mary McCoy Hamilton
LaFayette, Alabama

PEANUT BUTTER ICE CREAM

1 envelope unflavored gelatin
¼ cup cold water
1 (14-ounce) can sweetened condensed milk
1 (12-ounce) can evaporated milk
1 (12-ounce) jar crunchy peanut butter
1 cup sugar
6 eggs
1 tablespoon vanilla extract
1 quart half-and-half

Sprinkle gelatin over cold water in a small saucepan; let stand 5 minutes. Heat gelatin mixture over low heat, stirring constantly, until dissolved; set aside.

Combine sweetened condensed milk, evaporated milk, peanut butter, sugar, eggs, vanilla, and gelatin mixture in a mixing bowl; beat at medium speed of an electric mixer until blended. Pour mixture into freezer can of a 1-gallon hand-turned or electric freezer; add half-and-half. Freeze according to manufacturer's instructions. Let ice cream ripen at least 1 hour. Yield: 2 quarts.

Carole May
Shawmut, Alabama

Tip: *Freshen dry, crusty rolls or French bread by sprinkling with a few drops of water, wrapping in aluminum foil, and reheating at 350° for about 10 minutes.*

CRISP PEANUTTIEST COOKIES

½ cup butter or margarine, softened
½ cup crunchy peanut butter
1½ cups firmly packed brown sugar
¾ cup sugar
2 eggs
2½ cups all-purpose flour
1 teaspoon baking soda
½ cup flaked coconut
¾ cup Spanish peanuts

Cream butter and peanut butter; gradually add sugars, beating well at medium speed of an electric mixer. Add eggs, mixing well.

Combine flour and soda; add to creamed mixture, mixing well. Stir in coconut and peanuts. Shape dough into 1-inch balls. Place on ungreased cookie sheets; bake at 350° for 12 to 15 minutes or until lightly browned. Cool on wire racks. Yield: 6 dozen.
Mrs. John W. Stevens
Lexington, Kentucky

PEANUT BUTTER CREAM PIE

2 cups milk, divided
½ cup peanut butter
¼ cup plus 2 tablespoons light corn syrup
⅓ cup sugar
3 tablespoons cornstarch
¼ teaspoon salt
3 eggs, separated
1 tablespoon butter or margarine
1 teaspoon vanilla extract
1 baked 9-inch pastry shell
⅛ teaspoon cream of tartar
3 tablespoons sugar

Scald 1 cup milk in a heavy saucepan; add peanut butter and corn syrup, stirring well.

Combine ⅓ cup sugar, cornstarch, and salt; gradually add remaining 1 cup milk, mixing well. Add to scalded milk mixture, stirring until blended.

Cook over medium heat, stirring constantly, until mixture thickens and comes to a boil. Boil 1 minute, stirring constantly. Remove from heat.

Beat egg yolks until thick and lemon colored. Gradually stir about one-fourth of hot mixture into yolks. Add to remaining hot mixture, stirring constantly. Cook over medium heat 1 minute, stirring constantly. Remove from heat; stir in butter and vanilla. Spoon into pastry shell.

Beat egg whites (at room temperature) and cream of tartar at high speed of an electric mixer until soft peaks form. Gradually add 3 tablespoons sugar, beating until stiff peaks form and sugar dissolves. Spread meringue over hot filling, sealing to edge. Bake at 400° for 5 minutes or until browned. Yield: one 9-inch pie.
Mrs. H. D. Baxter
Charleston, West Virginia

MARBLED PEANUT BUTTER FUDGE

4 cups sugar
1 (12-ounce) can evaporated milk
1 cup butter or margarine
1 (7-ounce) jar marshmallow cream
3 (6-ounce) packages semisweet chocolate morsels
1 tablespoon vanilla extract
1 cup peanut butter

Combine first 3 ingredients in a heavy saucepan; bring to a boil, and cook 8 minutes, stirring constantly. Add marshmallow cream, chocolate morsels, and vanilla; stir until blended. Pour half of mixture into a buttered 13- x 9- x 2-inch pan; dollop with peanut butter. Spoon remaining chocolate mixture over peanut butter; gently swirl mixture with a knife to create a marble effect. Chill until set. Cut into 1-inch pieces. Store in an airtight container in refrigerator. Yield: 5 pounds.
Velma Bryant
Johnson City, Tennessee

Highlight Chocolate With Mint .

Southerners appreciate mint for more than just mint juleps and iced tea. It lends a refreshing flavor to desserts, especially combined with chocolate. Fresh mint, extracts, liqueurs, and even ice cream and cookies offer mint flavor in these recipes.

CHOCOLATE-PEPPERMINT PARFAITS

6 (1-ounce) squares semisweet chocolate
2 eggs
2 egg yolks
¼ cup sugar
½ teaspoon peppermint extract
1 cup whipping cream
3 tablespoons Kahlúa
¾ cup whipping cream
¼ cup crushed peppermint candy
½ cup mint cream-filled chocolate sandwich cookie crumbs
Fresh mint leaves (optional)

Melt chocolate in top of a double boiler. Remove from heat; set aside.

Combine eggs, egg yolks, sugar, and peppermint extract in the container of an electric blender; process at medium-high speed 2 minutes. Add 1 cup whipping cream and Kahlúa, and process 30 seconds. Add chocolate, and process until smooth.

Beat ¾ cup whipping cream until soft peaks form; fold in candy.

Spoon about 2 teaspoons cookie crumbs into each of six 6-ounce parfait glasses; top with about 2½ tablespoons chocolate mousse and 2 tablespoons whipped cream mixture. Repeat layers, ending with whipped cream mixture. Chill 8 hours. Garnish with mint, if desired. Yield: 6 servings.
Dorothy Cordell
Gadsden, Alabama

MINTED MINIATURE ÉCLAIRS

¾ cup whipping cream
2 teaspoons powdered sugar
1 tablespoon green crème de
  menthe
12 ladyfingers, split
½ cup commercial fudge topping
Mint leaves (optional)

Beat whipping cream until foamy; gradually add sugar, beating until soft peaks form. Add crème de menthe; beat until stiff peaks form.

Spread cream filling over bottom halves of ladyfingers. Cover with top halves. Spread 2 teaspoons fudge topping over top of each éclair. Garnish with mint leaves, if desired. Yield: 6 servings. *Joyce Orr*
Montevallo, Alabama

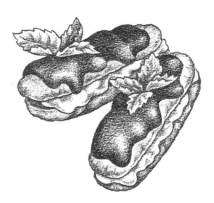

DINNER MINTS

½ cup butter
½ cup cocoa
½ cup sifted powdered sugar
1 egg, beaten
1 teaspoon vanilla extract
2 cups graham cracker crumbs
¼ cup plus 2 tablespoons butter,
  melted
⅓ cup crème de menthe
3 cups sifted powdered sugar
1½ cups semisweet chocolate
  morsels
¼ cup butter

Combine ½ cup butter and cocoa in top of a double boiler; bring water to a boil. Reduce heat to low; cook until butter melts. Remove from heat. Stir in ½ cup powdered sugar, egg, and vanilla; blend well. Stir in graham cracker crumbs. Press into bottom of ungreased 13- x 9- x 2-inch pan.

Combine ¼ cup plus 2 tablespoons butter and crème de menthe in a small bowl; beat at medium speed of an electric mixer. Gradually add 3 cups powdered sugar, and mix well. Spread over chocolate layer. Cover and chill 1 hour or until firm.

Combine last 2 ingredients in top of a double boiler; bring water to a boil. Reduce heat to low; cook until melted. Spread evenly over crème de menthe layer; chill 1 hour or until firm. Cut into 1-inch squares. Store in refrigerator. Yield: 8 dozen.
Mrs. William Fisher
Punta Gorda, Florida

MINT ICE-CREAM DESSERT

¾ cup vanilla wafer crumbs
2 (1-ounce) squares unsweetened
  chocolate
⅔ cup butter or margarine
2 cups sifted powdered sugar
2 eggs, separated
½ cup chopped pecans, toasted
1 teaspoon vanilla extract
½ gallon peppermint or
  mint-chocolate chip ice cream,
  softened
Chocolate syrup
Chopped pecans, toasted
  (optional)

Sprinkle vanilla wafer crumbs evenly in an ungreased 13- x 9- x 2-inch pan. Set aside.

Melt chocolate and butter in a heavy saucepan over low heat. Remove from heat; stir in powdered sugar, egg yolks, ½ cup pecans, and vanilla. Beat egg whites (at room temperature) at high speed of an electric mixer until soft peaks form; fold into chocolate mixture. Pour evenly over crumbs; cover and chill 1 hour or until firm.

Spread ice cream over chocolate layer; cover and freeze 8 hours or until ice cream is firm. Cut into squares; drizzle each piece with chocolate syrup, and sprinkle with toasted pecans, if desired. Yield: 15 to 18 servings. *Mike Singleton*
Scotts Hill, Tennessee

A Cheesecake With Distinction

Cheesecakes are popular desserts. Yet many menus are best complemented by a not-so-rich variety; that's why Daiquiri Chiffon Cheesecake is a delightful choice.

DAIQUIRI CHIFFON CHEESECAKE

1¼ cups graham cracker crumbs
½ cup sugar
¼ cup plus 2 tablespoons butter
  or margarine, melted
1 envelope unflavored gelatin
½ cup sugar
4 eggs, separated
½ cup rum
½ cup lime juice
2 teaspoons grated lime rind
1 teaspoon grated lemon rind
2 (8-ounce) packages cream
  cheese, softened
¼ cup sugar
1 cup whipping cream, whipped
Lime slices (optional)

Combine first 3 ingredients, mixing well. Reserve 2 tablespoons mixture; set aside. Press remaining crumb mixture into bottom and 1¾ inches up sides of a buttered 9-inch springform pan. Chill 45 minutes.

Combine gelatin and ½ cup sugar in a saucepan. Beat egg yolks; gradually stir yolks, rum, lime juice, lime rind, and lemon rind into gelatin mixture. Cook over medium heat, stirring constantly, until slightly thickened (8 to 10 minutes). Remove from heat. Cool about 30 minutes.

Beat cream cheese at medium speed of an electric mixer until smooth. Gradually add gelatin-lime mixture, beating until smooth.

Beat egg whites (at room temperature) at high speed of an electric mixer until foamy. Gradually add ¼ cup sugar, 1 tablespoon at a time, beating until stiff peaks form and sugar dissolves. Fold egg whites and whipped cream into gelatin mixture. Spoon into pan. Sprinkle reserved crumb mixture around edge of cheesecake. Cover and chill 8 hours.

To serve, carefully remove sides of springform pan. Garnish with lime slices, if desired. Yield: 10 to 12 servings.
Kathleen L. Hayes
Ballwin, Missouri

An Easy Menu For Eight

All of these recipes from Pat Sinick of Raleigh, North Carolina, appeal to the eye and the palate. They were natural choices for a simple menu.

Honey Chicken
Sesame Bites
Fried Rice
Peas and Snow Peas
Chocolate Silk Pie
Coffee

Plan: Make and freeze Sesame Bites; make Chocolate Silk Pie the night before. About 2 hours before guests arrive, start Honey Chicken, Fried Rice, and Peas and Snow Peas. Twenty minutes before serving, remove Sesame Bites from the freezer and bake; serve to guests as an appetizer.

HONEY CHICKEN

½ cup honey
½ cup prepared mustard
¼ cup butter or margarine, melted
1 teaspoon curry powder
2 (3-pound) broiler-fryers, cut up

Combine first 4 ingredients; set aside. Remove skin from chicken, if desired. Dip each piece of chicken in sauce, and place in a large greased roasting pan. Pour remaining sauce over chicken. Bake at 350° for 1 hour. Yield: 8 servings.

SESAME BITES

1 (16-ounce) loaf thinly sliced sandwich bread
1 (8-ounce) package cream cheese, softened
2 tablespoons chopped chives
¼ cup plus 2 tablespoons butter or margarine, melted
½ cup sesame seeds, toasted

Trim crust from bread; flatten each slice, using a rolling pin. Combine cream cheese and chives, mixing well. Spread mixture evenly on bread; roll up into a log. Brush log with butter, and roll in sesame seeds. Place seam side down on a baking sheet; cover and chill.

At serving time, slice each log into 3 pieces. Bake at 350° for 15 minutes. Yield: 5 dozen.

Note: Sesame Bites may be frozen before baking. To serve, place frozen on ungreased baking sheets; slice and bake at 350° for 20 minutes.

FRIED RICE

¼ cup plus 2 tablespoons butter or margarine
2 eggs, beaten
⅔ cup chopped green onions
⅔ cup chopped sweet red pepper
2⅔ cups cooked rice
⅔ cup water
¼ cup soy sauce

Melt butter in a skillet; add eggs, and cook over medium heat until almost set. Stir in next 3 ingredients; cook, stirring frequently, about 5 minutes or until lightly browned. Add water and soy sauce; cook 2 minutes. Yield: about 8 servings.

PEAS AND SNOW PEAS

2 (10-ounce) packages frozen tender tiny peas
2 tablespoons butter or margarine, melted
1 (6-ounce) package frozen snow pea pods
½ teaspoon dried whole dillweed
¼ teaspoon garlic powder

Sauté tiny peas in butter in a large skillet 5 minutes, stirring occasionally. Add snow pea pods, and cook over medium heat 5 minutes, stirring occasionally. Stir in dillweed and garlic powder, and cook mixture 2 minutes. Transfer to serving bowl. Yield: 8 servings.

CHOCOLATE SILK PIE

½ cup butter or margarine, softened
¾ cup sugar
1 (1-ounce) square unsweetened chocolate, melted
1 teaspoon vanilla extract
2 eggs, divided
Graham cracker crust (recipe follows)
Sweetened whipped cream

Cream butter; gradually add sugar, beating at medium speed of an electric mixer until well blended. Stir in chocolate and vanilla. Add 1 egg, and beat 4 minutes; add remaining egg, and beat 5 minutes. Spoon mixture into graham cracker crust. Chill at least 8 hours. Serve with whipped cream. Yield: one 9-inch pie.

Graham Cracker Crust

1½ cups graham cracker crumbs
3 tablespoons sugar
⅓ cup butter or margarine, melted

Combine all ingredients, mixing well. Press the mixture into a 9-inch pie-plate. Bake at 350° for 8 minutes. Cool. Yield: one 9-inch graham cracker crust.

Paella For The Entrée

When Mrs. Ben McKinley, Jr., of Dallas, Texas, wants a simple menu to serve, her Chicken-Seafood Paella is a natural choice. Saffron-flavored rice mixed with vegetables makes it a hearty dish.

CHICKEN-SEAFOOD PAELLA

¾ cup sliced mushrooms
½ cup finely chopped celery
3 tablespoons chopped onion
1 clove garlic, minced
2 tablespoons vegetable oil
1½ cups uncooked long-grain rice
2½ cups chicken broth
1 (6½-ounce) can minced clams, drained
½ teaspoon brown sugar
½ teaspoon salt
½ teaspoon pepper
⅛ teaspoon ground saffron
1 pound unpeeled medium-size fresh shrimp
1½ cups coarsely chopped cooked chicken
1 tablespoon grated Parmesan cheese
Celery leaves (optional)

Sauté mushrooms, celery, onion, and garlic in oil in a heavy ovenproof Dutch oven until tender. Add rice; cook until rice is straw colored. Add chicken broth and next 5 ingredients. Remove from heat; cover and bake at 350° for 30 minutes.

Peel and devein shrimp. Add shrimp, chicken, and Parmesan cheese to rice mixture, stirring well. Cover and bake an additional 30 minutes or until liquid is absorbed and rice is tender. Transfer to a large serving bowl, and garnish with celery leaves, if desired. Yield: 8 servings.

A Delicious Fruit Pie

Almonds in a creamy filling and mellow fruit nestled in a crunchy crust create a dynamic dessert. What makes this Crispy-Crust Fruit Pie special? The unusual crust is made with commercial phyllo pastry.

CRISPY-CRUST FRUIT PIE

6 sheets commercial frozen phyllo pastry, thawed
½ cup butter or margarine, melted
1 (8-ounce) package cream cheese, softened
3 tablespoons honey
1 teaspoon lemon juice
1 cup finely chopped almonds, toasted
1 cup strawberry halves
½ cup blueberries
¾ cup sliced peaches

Butter a 9-inch pieplate, and set aside. Place 1 sheet of phyllo on a damp towel (keep remaining phyllo covered). Lightly brush phyllo with melted butter; place phyllo, buttered side up, in pieplate, allowing ends to extend over sides. Repeat process with remaining phyllo, crisscrossing sheets alternately. Gently press phyllo so that layers conform to sides of pieplate.

Fold overhanging phyllo to inside of pieplate, forming a ridge on the rim of pastry. Bake at 350° for 10 minutes. Remove from oven. With back of a spoon, press bottom and sides of crust against pieplate. Bake an additional 15 minutes or until golden brown and crisp. Cool on a wire rack.

Combine cream cheese, honey, and lemon juice in a small bowl; beat at medium speed of an electric mixer until smooth. Stir in almonds; spread mixture evenly in crust. Serve immediately, or refrigerate up to 4 hours. Just before serving, arrange fruit on cream cheese mixture. Yield: one 9-inch pie.
Mrs. Steve Wortham
Hixson, Tennessee

Toppings Just For Fruit

With fresh fruit at its peak now, you want the right topping to enhance its flavor. These fruit toppings add just that touch.

TROPICAL FRUIT FLUFF

1 (8-ounce) carton commercial sour cream
¼ cup orange juice
¼ cup flaked coconut
¼ cup chopped walnuts
3 tablespoons peach, apricot, or pear preserves

Combine all ingredients; stir well. Chill 2 to 3 hours. Serve with assorted fresh fruit. Yield: 1¼ cups.
Gloria Patrick
Sweeny, Texas

NUTTY FRUIT DRESSING

1 (7-ounce) jar marshmallow cream
⅓ cup pineapple juice
1 teaspoon almond extract
2 teaspoons lemon juice
1 cup salted peanuts, coarsely chopped

Combine first 4 ingredients; mix well. Stir in peanuts. Chill well. Stir before serving. Serve over assorted fresh fruit. Yield: 1⅓ cups.
Leslie Ganszler
Roswell, Georgia

Right: *Stuffed Tenderloin (page 50) is garnished with watercress, mushrooms, and tomato roses.*

Page 72: *Bake a legendary dessert—General Robert E. Lee Orange-Lemon Cake (page 92).*

Above: *Enjoy the taste of grapefruit and crème de menthe in Minted Grapefruit (page 81), a simple yet elegant dish.*

Above right: *For breakfast or brunch, start your morning menu with Apricot-Citrus Slush (page 82).*

Left: *Take advantage of the season's fresh asparagus, and feature Eggs in Herb Sauce (page 80) at your next brunch.*

APRIL

One Basic Recipe Makes These Breads

Even if you've never baked bread before, now you can make homemade sandwich bread, French bread, dinner rolls, English muffins, or beautiful loaves of braided bread from one basic dough recipe. The various techniques for shaping, glazing, and baking the dough offer different results. First, familiarize yourself with the basics of making yeast dough; then follow the directions for shaping and baking the bread you want.

Making The Dough

This recipe follows the rapid-mix method—mixing the yeast with some of the dry ingredients before adding the liquid ingredients. This eliminates the need to dissolve the yeast first.

Invest in a good thermometer for measuring the temperature of the liquid, as temperatures are crucial when working with yeast. Liquids that are too hot will kill the yeast, and the dough won't rise at all; liquids that are too cool might not dissolve the yeast properly and might stunt the rising.

Kneading

Give your bread a fine, even texture by kneading the dough properly. Turn the dough out onto a lightly floured surface. With floured hands, lift the edge of the dough that is farthest from you, and fold it toward you. Using the heel of your hand, press the dough down and away from you. Give the dough a quarter-turn, and repeat the kneading process until the dough begins to feel smooth and elastic, adding extra flour as necessary to prevent sticking. The kneading process takes about 10 minutes.

The Dough-Rising Process

Bread needs a draft-free environment of about 85° to rise properly. A gas oven with a pilot light or an electric oven containing a large pan of hot water is a convenient choice. After kneading, shape the dough into a ball, and place it in a well-greased bowl, turning to grease all sides.

Cover the bowl with plastic wrap, and let dough rise about one hour or until doubled in bulk.

To test for proper rising, lightly press a finger ½ inch into the dough. If the indentation remains, the dough is ready for final preparation.

BASIC YEAST DOUGH

5 to 5½ cups all-purpose flour, divided
3 tablespoons sugar
2 teaspoons salt
1 package dry yeast
1½ cups milk
½ cup water
3 tablespoons butter or margarine

Combine 2 cups flour, sugar, salt, and yeast in a large mixing bowl; stir well. Combine milk, water, and butter in a saucepan; cook over low heat until butter melts, stirring occasionally. Cool to 120° to 130°.

Gradually add liquid mixture to flour mixture, beating well at high speed of an electric mixer. Beat an additional 2 minutes at high speed. Gradually add ¾ cup flour, beating well. Gradually stir in enough remaining flour to make a soft dough.

Turn dough out onto a floured surface, and knead until smooth and elastic (about 10 minutes). Shape into a ball, and place in a well-greased bowl, turning to grease top. Cover and let rise in a warm place (85°), free from drafts, 1 hour or until doubled in bulk.

Punch dough down; turn out onto a lightly floured surface, and knead lightly 4 or 5 times. Shape and bake dough as directed for the individual recipe you are making. Yield: enough dough for two 9-inch loaves or about 3½ dozen rolls.

■ **Shaped Loaf Bread:** To shape a perfect loaf of bread, first roll the dough into a large rectangle; then roll

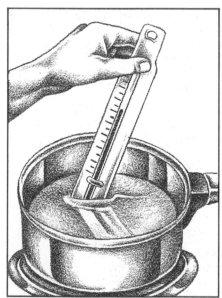

Measuring temperatures is critical for making yeast bread; liquid that is too hot will kill the yeast and keep the bread from rising.

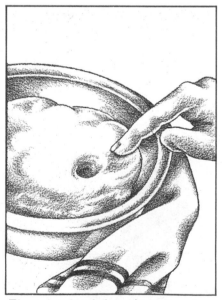

The yeast dough has risen enough when the indentation remains after lightly pressing a finger ½ inch into the dough.

it jellyroll fashion, and fit it into the loafpan. Let the dough rise in the pan, and bake as directed.

Remove the bread from the pan immediately after removal from the oven, and place it on a wire rack to cool. If bread cools in the pan too long, moisture will form, making the bread gummy.

OLD-FASHIONED LOAF BREAD

1 recipe Basic Yeast Dough
2 tablespoons butter or
   margarine, melted

Divide dough in half. Roll 1 portion of dough to a 14- x 7-inch rectangle on a lightly floured surface. Roll dough jellyroll fashion, starting at narrow edge, pressing firmly to eliminate all air pockets; pinch ends and seam to seal. Place dough, seam side down, in a well-greased 9- x 5- x 3-inch loafpan. Repeat procedure with remaining portion of dough.

Cover and let rise in a warm place (85°), free from drafts, 1 hour or until doubled in bulk. Bake at 375° for 35 to 45 minutes or until loaves sound hollow when tapped.

Remove bread from pans immediately; then brush top of loaves with melted butter. Cool on wire racks. Yield: 2 loaves.

■ **Glazed Bread:** Give a pretty shine and golden color to bread by brushing it with a mixture of beaten egg and milk after it rises and before it bakes.

Brush carefully to coat all surfaces for even browning, but do not drip egg mixture onto the baking sheet. (Egg mixture on the baking sheet usually burns onto the pan and the sides of the bread.) After brushing the egg mixture onto the dough, sprinkle lightly with poppy seeds or sesame seeds, if desired. In addition to glazing the bread, the egg mixture makes the seeds adhere.

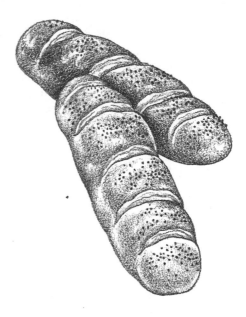

GLAZED FRENCH BREAD

1 recipe Basic Yeast Dough
1 egg, beaten
2 tablespoons milk
Poppy seeds or sesame seeds
   (optional)

Divide dough in half. Roll 1 portion of dough to a 13- x 8-inch rectangle on a lightly floured surface. Roll dough jellyroll fashion, starting at long edge, pressing firmly to eliminate all air pockets; pinch ends and seam to seal. Place loaf, seam side down, on a greased baking sheet. Repeat procedure with remaining dough.

Cover and let rise in a warm place (85°), free from drafts, about 45 minutes or until doubled in bulk. Carefully make diagonal slits about ¼ inch deep down the lengths of the loaves, using a sharp knife.

Combine egg and milk, beating with a fork until blended; gently brush over loaves. Sprinkle each loaf with poppy seeds, if desired. Bake at 400° for 20 to 25 minutes or until loaves sound hollow when tapped. Cool on wire racks. Yield: 2 loaves.

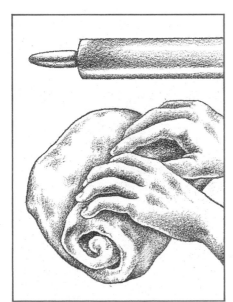

To shape loaf bread, first roll the dough into a large rectangle; next, roll it jellyroll fashion, and fit into a loafpan.

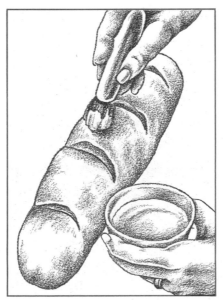

To glaze bread, brush with a mixture of beaten egg and milk, carefully coating all surfaces of the bread for even browning.

■ **Braided Bread:** Roll dough into thin ropes, and intertwine them. Vary the number of ropes you work with to change the look of the bread. For a simple twist, use just two ropes. Talented braiders use up to nine thin ropes to braid an intricate pattern. A small braid placed on top of a larger braid gives another interesting effect.

To seal the ropes as you begin and end the braid, pinch ropes together with just enough pressure to join them; then tuck the joint under.

After braiding, glaze the bread with an egg-and-milk mixture. You can also sprinkle the glaze on the braid with poppy seeds or sesame seeds, if desired.

BRAIDED BREAD

1 recipe Basic Yeast Dough
1 egg, beaten
2 tablespoons milk
Poppy seeds or sesame seeds
    (optional)

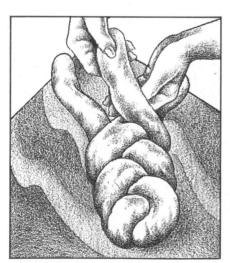

For Braided Bread, roll dough into thin ropes, and intertwine them.

Divide dough into thirds. Shape each third into a 20-inch rope. Place ropes on a greased baking sheet (do not stretch); pinch rope ends together at one end to seal. Braid ropes; pinch loose ends to seal. Cover and let rise in a warm place (85°), free from drafts, about 45 minutes or until doubled in bulk.

Combine egg and milk, beating with a fork until blended; gently brush over loaf. Sprinkle loaf with poppy seeds, if desired. Bake at 350° for 25 to 30 minutes or until loaf sounds hollow when tapped. Shield bread by loosely covering with a tent made of aluminum foil, if necessary, to keep loaf from overbrowning. Cool on a wire rack. Yield: 1 loaf.

■ **Shaped Pan Rolls:** Divide dough into small portions. Use kitchen shears to cut dough without stretching it; then roll dough into 1½-inch balls, and place in greased pans to rise. Keep in mind that because of their smaller size, rolls rise and bake quicker than bread loaves.

Once you master Pan Rolls, experiment with this same dough using different shapes, glazes, and sprinkles. Cloverleaf rolls, butterfans, and crescents are attractive shapes made in bakeries. Experiment with assorted herbs and Parmesan cheese to top dinner rolls.

PAN ROLLS

1 recipe Basic Yeast Dough
2 tablespoons butter or
    margarine, melted

Shape dough into 1½-inch balls, and place in 2 greased 9-inch square

pans. Cover and let rise in a warm place (85°), free from drafts, 35 minutes or until doubled in bulk.

Bake at 375° for 15 minutes or until rolls are golden brown. Brush rolls with butter. Yield: 3½ dozen.

■ **Fried Bread:** Give regular yeast bread a different look and texture by frying it into English Muffins in an electric skillet. Sprinkle the work surface with cornmeal to keep the dough from sticking and to help form the characteristically crunchy crust.

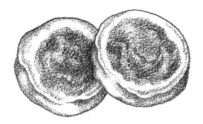

ENGLISH MUFFINS

1 recipe Basic Yeast Dough
Cornmeal

Divide dough in half. Turn 1 portion of dough out onto a smooth surface heavily sprinkled with cornmeal. Pat dough to a circle ½-inch thick, using palms of hands; cut dough into rounds, using a 2¾-inch cutter. (Cut carefully, as leftover dough should not be reused.) Repeat procedure with remaining dough.

Sprinkle 2 baking sheets with cornmeal. Transfer dough rounds to baking sheets, placing 2 inches apart with cornmeal side down (one side should remain free of cornmeal).

Cover and let rise in a warm place (85°), free from drafts, 30 minutes or until doubled in bulk. Using a wide spatula, transfer rounds to a preheated, lightly greased electric skillet (360°). Place rounds, cornmeal side down, in skillet; cook 5 to 6 minutes or until browned. Turn and cook 5 to 6 minutes. Cool on wire racks. Store muffins in an airtight container. To serve, split, and toast, if desired. Yield: 16 muffins.

BREAKFASTS & BRUNCHES

Top Of The Morning To You!

As the South shakes away the cold and welcomes warm weather, it's a time to plan brunches. Our Foods staff enthusiastically presents our 10th annual "Breakfasts & Brunches" special section.

In Decatur, Alabama, Jimmy and Jan Worthey have invited some friends over for a midmorning brunch and a few games of croquet. Jan spreads a table of appetizers and Bellinis, a champagne beverage of fresh peaches and apricot nectar.

Later, the guests gather in the Wortheys' sunroom for a buffet meal of Spinach-Ham Rolls, light, tempting Orange Rolls, Fruit Salad With Poppy Seed Dressing, and Crab-Stuffed Cherry Tomatoes.

Jan prepares her Orange Rolls ahead of time and adds the glaze just before serving. She makes Spinach-Ham Rolls ahead and refrigerates them, adding the cheese sauce right before baking. The fruit can be cut up the night before if it's dipped in lemon juice to prevent browning. And all appetizers and desserts are prepared beforehand with just a few last-minute touches.

Bellinis
Buttery Toasted Pecans
Cheese Straws
Cucumber Rounds
Spinach-Ham Rolls
Fruit Salad
With Poppy Seed Dressing
Crab-Stuffed Cherry Tomatoes
Orange Rolls
Fruited Mint Tea
Madeleines
Chocolate-Mint Brownies

BELLINIS

6 cups sliced fresh or frozen
   peaches
2 cups apricot nectar
6⅔ cups champagne

Combine half each of peaches and apricot nectar in container of an electric blender, and process until smooth. Repeat procedure with the remaining peaches and apricot nectar; freeze.

Remove peach-apricot mixture from freezer 30 minutes before serving. To serve, spoon about ⅔ cup mixture into each stemmed glass, and add ⅔ cup champagne. Yield: 10 servings (about 13 cups).

BUTTERY TOASTED PECANS

½ cup butter
4 cups pecan halves
½ teaspoon salt

Place butter in a 15- x 10- x 2-inch jellyroll pan. Heat at 325° for 5 minutes or until butter melts. Add pecans; stir until well coated. Sprinkle with salt; return to oven. Bake at 325° for 40 minutes or until toasted, stirring every 10 minutes. Drain on paper towels. Yield: 4 cups.

CHEESE STRAWS

4 cups (16 ounces) shredded
   sharp Cheddar cheese
½ cup butter or margarine,
   softened
2 cups all-purpose flour
½ teaspoon red pepper
¼ teaspoon salt
⅛ teaspoon dry mustard
   (optional)

Combine shredded Cheddar cheese and butter in a large mixing bowl; beat well at medium speed of an electric mixer. Set mixture aside.

Combine flour and remaining ingredients, stirring well. Gradually add flour mixture to cheese mixture; beat until dough is no longer crumbly. Press dough through a cookie press fitted with a star-tip disc; make long strips on ungreased baking sheets. Cut into 2-inch strips. Bake at 350° for 15 minutes or until strips are light brown. Remove strips from baking sheets, and let cool completely on wire racks. Store in an airtight container. Yield: 14 dozen.

CUCUMBER ROUNDS

1 large cucumber
1 (8-ounce) package cream
   cheese, softened
1½ teaspoons mayonnaise
⅛ teaspoon seasoned salt
1 loaf multi-grain bread
Parsley sprigs

Cut cucumber in half horizontally. Peel, seed, and shred half of cucumber. Measure ⅓ cup shredded cucumber. Slice remaining cucumber for garnish. Cut cucumber slices in half; set aside.

Combine cream cheese, mayonnaise, and seasoned salt, mixing until blended. Stir in shredded cucumber.

Cut two 2-inch rounds from each bread slice. Spread each round with 1 teaspoon cucumber spread. Garnish each sandwich with a thin half slice of cucumber and a sprig of parsley. Yield: 48 sandwiches.

SPINACH-HAM ROLLS

1 cup cottage cheese
¾ cup commercial sour cream
1 (10-ounce) package frozen
   chopped spinach, thawed and
   drained
1½ cups herb-seasoned stuffing
   mix
1 egg, beaten
¼ cup minced onion
½ teaspoon dry mustard
12 (⅛-inch-thick) slices ham
   (about 1½ pounds)
Cheese sauce (recipe follows)
Paprika
Green onion tops, sliced
Parsley sprigs

Combine cottage cheese and sour cream in container of an electric blender; process until smooth.

Combine sour cream mixture, spinach, and next 4 ingredients; mix well. Spoon ¼ cup of mixture on each slice of ham. Roll up, and place rolls, seam side down, in a lightly greased 13- x 9- x 2-inch baking dish. Top with cheese sauce; sprinkle with paprika. Bake at 350° for 20 to 25 minutes. Garnish with onion tops and parsley. Yield: 12 servings.

Cheese Sauce

1 tablespoon cornstarch
1 cup milk
2 tablespoons butter or margarine
¼ teaspoon salt
⅛ teaspoon pepper
1 cup (4 ounces) shredded
   Cheddar cheese

Combine cornstarch and milk, stirring until smooth. Cook over medium heat, stirring constantly, until mixture comes to a boil. Boil 1 minute. Add butter, salt, pepper, and cheese, stirring until smooth. Yield: 1¼ cups.

FRUIT SALAD WITH POPPY SEED DRESSING

2 cups blueberries
2 kiwifruit, sliced
2 red apples, sliced
2 green apples, sliced
1 bunch seedless green grapes
1 bunch seedless red grapes
1 cup strawberry halves
1 fresh pineapple, peeled, cored,
   and sliced or 1 (20-ounce) can
   sliced pineapple, drained and
   cut in half
Poppy Seed Dressing

Arrange fruit on a serving platter. Serve with Poppy Seed Dressing. Yield: 12 servings.

Poppy Seed Dressing

¾ cup sugar
⅓ cup vinegar
1½ tablespoons onion juice
1 teaspoon dry mustard
½ teaspoon salt
1 cup vegetable oil
1½ tablespoons poppy seeds

Combine first 5 ingredients in container of an electric blender; process on low speed 30 seconds. With blender on high, gradually add oil in a slow steady stream. Blend about 30 seconds or until thickened. Stir in poppy seeds. Yield: 1½ cups.

CRAB-STUFFED CHERRY TOMATOES

1 (6-ounce) can all-white
   crabmeat, drained
1 cup (6 ounces) chopped seafood
   blend (imitation crabmeat)
2 green onions, chopped
⅛ teaspoon red pepper
1 tablespoon lemon juice
¼ cup mayonnaise
30 large cherry tomatoes
Parsley sprigs

Position knife blade in food processor bowl; combine first 6 ingredients in processor bowl. Top with cover. Process 30 seconds or until smooth.

Cut an X on the bottom of each tomato, cutting to within ½ inch of stem end. Carefully spread out sections of each tomato to form a cup.

Spoon or pipe crab mixture into each tomato; top with parsley sprig. Yield: 2½ dozen.

Note: Instead of using food processor, you can dice crabmeat.

Tip: *When making coffee for a crowd, allow 1 pound of coffee and 2 gallons water for 40 servings.*

ORANGE ROLLS

2 packages dry yeast
¼ cup warm water (105° to 115°)
5 to 6 cups all-purpose flour, divided
1 cup sugar
1 teaspoon salt
2 eggs
½ cup butter or margarine, melted
⅔ cup warm water (105° to 115°)
1 (5-ounce) can evaporated milk
Melted butter or margarine
1 cup flaked coconut, toasted
¾ cup sugar
1½ tablespoons grated orange rind
Glaze (recipe follows)

Dissolve yeast in ¼ cup warm water in a large mixing bowl; let stand 5 minutes. Add 3 cups flour, 1 cup sugar, salt, eggs, ½ cup melted butter, ⅔ cup warm water, and evaporated milk; beat at low speed of an electric mixer until smooth. Gradually stir in enough remaining flour to make a soft dough.

Place dough in a well-greased bowl, turning to grease top. Cover and let rise in a warm place (85°), free from drafts, for 1 hour.

Punch dough down; turn out onto a lightly floured surface, and knead 4 or 5 times. Divide dough into 6 portions. Roll 1 portion to an 8-inch circle; brush with melted butter. Combine coconut, ¾ cup sugar, and orange rind; sprinkle one-sixth of mixture over dough. Cut circle into 8 wedges; roll each wedge tightly, beginning at wide end. Seal points, and place on a greased baking sheet, point side down, curving into a half-moon shape. Repeat with remaining dough and coconut mixture.

Cover and let rise in a warm place (85°), free from drafts, 1 hour or until doubled in bulk. Bake at 325° for 20 minutes or until lightly browned. Pour glaze over warm rolls. Yield: 4 dozen.

Glaze

¼ cup butter or margarine, melted
½ cup commercial sour cream
2 tablespoons orange juice
3 to 3½ cups sifted powdered sugar

Combine all ingredients, mixing well. Yield: 2 cups.

FRUITED MINT TEA

1 quart water
7 fresh mint sprigs
8 regular tea bags
2 cups sugar
1 (12-ounce) can frozen orange juice concentrate, thawed and undiluted
⅓ cup lemon juice
Additional mint leaves (optional)
Orange slices (optional)

Place water in a saucepan; bring to a boil. Add 7 mint sprigs; boil 2 minutes. Remove from heat; add tea bags. Cover and let stand 10 minutes. Remove mint and tea bags. Stir in sugar.

Combine tea mixture, orange juice concentrate, and lemon juice; add enough water to make 1 gallon. Serve over ice. If desired, garnish with mint leaves and orange slices. Yield: 1 gallon.

MADELEINES

1 (18.25-ounce) package yellow cake mix without pudding
½ teaspoon grated orange rind
¼ cup orange juice
¼ cup lemon juice
1 (1-pound) package powdered sugar, sifted
Powdered sugar

Prepare cake mix according to package directions. Spoon batter, 1 tablespoon at a time, into greased and floured madeleine molds. Bake at 400° for 8 to 10 minutes or until lightly browned. Cool in molds 3 minutes. Remove from molds, and cool on a wire rack, flat sides down.

Combine orange rind and next 3 ingredients in a medium bowl; beat at medium speed of an electric mixer until smooth. Spoon 1½ teaspoons glaze over each madeleine. Sprinkle with powdered sugar immediately before serving. Yield: 8 dozen.

CHOCOLATE-MINT BROWNIES

2 (1-ounce) squares unsweetened
  chocolate
½ cup butter or margarine
2 eggs
1 cup sugar
½ cup all-purpose flour
¼ teaspoon baking powder
¼ teaspoon salt
½ cup chopped pecans
1 teaspoon vanilla extract
Mint Frosting
1 (1-ounce) square unsweetened
  chocolate
1 tablespoon butter or margarine

Combine 2 squares chocolate and ½ cup butter in a small heavy saucepan; cook over low heat, stirring constantly, until melted. Let stand 10 minutes.

Beat eggs at medium speed of an electric mixer until blended; gradually add sugar, beating well. Combine flour, baking powder, and salt. Add chocolate mixture and flour mixture to creamed mixture. Stir in chopped pecans and vanilla.

Spoon mixture into a lightly greased and floured 13- x 9- x 2-inch pan. Bake at 350° for 15 minutes or until a wooden pick inserted in center comes out clean. Let brownies cool 10 minutes; spread Mint Frosting over top of brownies.

Combine 1 square chocolate and 1 tablespoon butter in a small heavy saucepan; cook over low heat, stirring constantly, until melted. Drizzle over frosting. Cut into 2- x 1-inch bars. Remove from pan, and chill at least 1 hour. Store brownies in an airtight container in refrigerator. Yield: 4½ dozen.

Mint Frosting

¼ cup butter or margarine,
  melted
2 tablespoons whipping cream
2 cups sifted powdered sugar
1½ teaspoons peppermint
  flavoring

Combine melted butter and whipping cream; stir in powdered sugar and peppermint flavoring, mixing until smooth. Yield: 1 cup.

Rise To These Egg Entrées

Whether it's breakfast for the family or a brunch for friends, these recipes offer entrées to suit the occasion. All feature eggs as the main dish.

Our recipe for Chile Eggs offers a solution for cooks who like to start preparations the night before. Put the casserole together, and refrigerate it unbaked for at least 8 hours. Bake it just before serving time.

EGGS IN HERB SAUCE
(pictured on page 70)

24 fresh asparagus spears
¼ cup mayonnaise
1 (8-ounce) carton commercial
  sour cream
Juice of 1 lemon
½ teaspoon salt
¼ teaspoon white pepper
¼ teaspoon sugar
2 teaspoons minced fresh parsley
1 teaspoon minced fresh dillweed
1 teaspoon minced fresh chives
8 hard-cooked eggs, divided
1 (12-ounce) package cooked
  6- x 4-inch ham slices
Fresh dillweed

Snap off tough ends of asparagus. Remove scales, if desired, with a knife or vegetable peeler. Cook asparagus, covered, in boiling water 6 to 8 minutes; drain. Cover and chill.

Combine mayonnaise, sour cream, lemon juice, salt, white pepper, sugar, parsley, minced dillweed, and chives; mix well. Mash 1 hard-cooked egg; add to mayonnaise mixture, and mix well. Cover and chill.

Place 4 asparagus spears on 2 ham slices. Roll ham around asparagus; secure with a wooden pick. Place ham-wrapped asparagus on a serving platter. Repeat procedure with remaining ham and asparagus. Slice 6 eggs; arrange slices over ham. Spoon about ¼ cup herb sauce over each serving. Sieve 1 remaining egg. Sprinkle over each serving. Garnish with fresh dillweed. Serve chilled. Yield: 6 servings.

Rosmarie Brautigam
Florence, South Carolina

CHILE EGGS

8 slices white bread
¼ cup butter or margarine,
  melted
1 cup (4 ounces) shredded sharp
  Cheddar cheese
1 (8-ounce) can chopped green
  chiles, drained
8 eggs, separated
½ teaspoon salt
⅛ teaspoon pepper
2 cups milk

Trim crust from bread; brush both sides of slices with butter, and arrange in a greased 13- x 9- x 2-inch baking dish. Sprinkle evenly with cheese and chiles.

Beat egg whites (at room temperature) until stiff. Beat egg yolks until lemon colored. Fold whites into yolks; add salt, pepper, and milk. Mix well. Pour evenly over casserole. Cover and refrigerate at least 8 hours. Bake at 300° for 50 to 60 minutes or until set. Serve immediately. Yield: 8 servings.

Sue Syers
Louisville, Kentucky

EASY EGGS RANCHEROS

1 (8-ounce) can tomato sauce
1 teaspoon chili powder
¼ teaspoon ground cumin
8 eggs
¼ teaspoon freshly ground pepper
¼ teaspoon paprika
1 cup (4 ounces) shredded
    Cheddar cheese
4 commercial tostada shells
Commercial sour cream
Jalapeño pepper slices (optional)

Combine tomato sauce, chili powder, and cumin in a lightly greased 9-inch quiche dish. Break eggs over sauce, arranging evenly in dish. Sprinkle with pepper and paprika. Cover and bake at 350° for 15 to 20 minutes. Sprinkle with cheese, and bake an additional 5 minutes or to desired degree of doneness. Spoon eggs onto tostada shells; top with a dollop of sour cream. Garnish with jalapeño pepper slices, if desired. Yield: 4 servings.   *Mrs. John R. Allen*
Dallas, Texas

Fruit-Filled Side Dishes

Bring on the fruit. Sauced, topped, and minted, our collection of fruit dishes will please even the pickiest eaters on your guest list.

MINTED GRAPEFRUIT
(pictured on page 71)

3 medium-size pink grapefruit
2 medium-size white grapefruit
2 to 3 tablespoons white crème
    de menthe
Fresh mint sprigs

Cut grapefruit in half; clip membranes, and carefully remove fruit sections (do not puncture bottom).

Combine grapefruit sections and crème de menthe, stirring well; chill at least 2 hours. Spoon fruit mixture into grapefruit shells to serve, if desired. Garnish with fresh mint. Yield: 4 to 6 servings.   *Debbie Slaton*
Cleveland, Georgia

FRUIT COMPOTE
WITH RASPBERRY PUREE

1 medium pineapple, peeled and
    cubed
1 papaya, peeled, seeded, and
    cubed
3 kiwifruit, peeled and cut into
    wedges
1 large banana, thickly sliced
¼ cup kirsch or other cherry-
    flavored brandy, divided
1 (10-ounce) package frozen
    raspberries in syrup, thawed

Combine first 4 ingredients in a large bowl. Add 2 tablespoons kirsch; gently toss to mix. Cover and chill.

Position knife blade in food processor bowl; add raspberries. Top with cover; process a few seconds until raspberries are smooth. Strain raspberries; discard seeds. Add remaining 2 tablespoons kirsch; mix well.

Spoon fruit into serving compotes, and top with raspberry puree. Yield: 8 servings.   *Mrs. C. D. Marshall*
Boston, Virginia

GREEN GRAPES SUPREME

¼ cup firmly packed light brown
    sugar
½ cup commercial sour cream
5 cups seedless green grapes,
    washed and stemmed
Mint sprigs (optional)

Combine brown sugar and sour cream in a large mixing bowl. Stir in grapes. Chill several hours. Spoon into individual serving dishes. Garnish with mint, if desired. Yield: 6 to 8 servings.   *Carol S. Noble*
Burgaw, North Carolina

Refreshing Beverages For Spring

Not too long ago the choices of breakfast beverages were limited to coffee or tea and orange or tomato juice. With the increasing popularity of weekend brunches, breakfast beverages have multiplied to include punches, slushes, coffees, and juices.

The bases for two of the slushes featured here can be made ahead and kept in the freezer. Immediately before serving, add the carbonated beverage and stir.

GRAPEFRUIT COOLER

2 cups grapefruit juice, chilled
1½ cups orange juice, chilled
1 (12-ounce) can apricot nectar,
    chilled
1 cup club soda, chilled
Crushed ice
Grapefruit slices (optional)

Combine first 3 ingredients. Add club soda just before serving. Pour over crushed ice; garnish with grapefruit slices, if desired. Yield: about 1½ quarts.   *Lorraine E. Zeigler*
Hollywood, Florida

PINEAPPLE SLUSH

1 (5¼-ounce) can pineapple
  tidbits, undrained
1 medium banana, chilled
¼ cup milk
2 cups pineapple sherbet

Combine all ingredients in container
of an electric blender; process until
mixture is smooth. Yield: 3 cups.
Kathe Waller
Birmingham, Alabama

MORNING PUNCH

1 (6-ounce) can frozen orange
  juice concentrate, thawed and
  undiluted
1 (6-ounce) can frozen grapefruit
  juice concentrate, thawed and
  undiluted
⅓ cup grenadine syrup
1 cup water
2 (33.8-ounce) bottles ginger ale,
  chilled
Fresh strawberries (optional)

Combine first 4 ingredients; mix
well, and chill. Add ginger ale just
before serving. Garnish each glass
with a strawberry, if desired. Yield:
2½ quarts. *Elizabeth M. Haney*
Dublin, Virginia

APRICOT-CITRUS SLUSH
(pictured on page 71)

1½ cups sugar
9 cups water
1 (12-ounce) can frozen lemonade
  concentrate, thawed and
  undiluted
1 (12-ounce) can frozen orange
  juice concentrate, thawed and
  undiluted
2 cups apricot or peach brandy
3⅓ cups lemon-lime carbonated
  beverage, chilled
Mint sprigs (optional)

Combine sugar and water in a large
Dutch oven. Bring to a boil, stirring
until sugar dissolves. Remove from
heat, and cool.

Add lemonade and orange juice
concentrates and brandy, stirring
until blended. Freeze 8 hours. Remove from freezer 20 minutes before
serving. Stir in carbonated beverage.
Garnish glasses with mint sprigs, if
desired. Yield: 13½ cups.
Kathleen Schoenfelder
Bradenton, Florida

ORANGE-MINT LEMONADE

1½ to 2 cups sugar
2½ cups water
Grated rind of 1 orange
⅔ cup orange juice
1⅓ cups lemon juice
¾ cup mint leaves
7 cups cold water
Orange slices (optional)
Mint sprigs (optional)

Combine sugar and water in a heavy
saucepan; bring to a boil. Cover, re-
duce heat, and simmer 5 minutes.
Add orange rind and next 3 ingre-
dients. Cover and let stand 1 hour.
Strain mixture. Stir in cold water.
Serve over ice. If desired, garnish
with orange slices and mint sprigs.
Yield: 3 quarts. *Mrs. Bob Maupin*
Fort Payne, Alabama

STREETCAR CHAMPAGNE
PUNCH

2 cups cranberry juice cocktail
2 cups orange juice
¼ cup lemon juice
½ cup sugar
1½ cups white wine, chilled
1 (25.4-ounce) bottle champagne,
  chilled
Orange slices (optional)

Combine fruit juices and sugar, stirring until sugar dissolves; chill. Pour
fruit mixture into a punch bowl. Add
wine and champagne; stir. Garnish
with orange slices, if desired. Yield:
2¼ quarts. *Vicki Sledge*
San Antonio, Texas

VODKA SLUSH

1 (6-ounce) can frozen orange
  juice concentrate, thawed and
  undiluted
1 (12-ounce) can frozen lemonade
  concentrate, thawed and
  undiluted
2 (6-ounce) cans frozen limeade
  concentrate, thawed and
  undiluted
½ cup sugar
3½ cups water
2 cups vodka
2 (32-ounce) bottles lemon-lime
  carbonated beverage, chilled

Combine all ingredients except
lemon-lime beverage; stir well.
Freeze 8 hours. Spoon ¾ cup frozen
mixture into a glass. Add ¾ cup
chilled lemon-lime beverage. Yield:
16 cups. *Carol Barclay*
Portland, Texas

TASTY TODDY

3 cups chicken broth
⅔ cup tomato puree
⅔ cup orange juice
¼ cup lemon juice
¾ teaspoon garlic powder
¾ teaspoon celery seeds
½ teaspoon ground cinnamon

Combine all ingredients in a 1½-quart
saucepan; mix well. Cook over medium heat until hot. Serve immediately. Yield: 4½ cups.
Mrs. Joel Allard
San Antonio, Texas

BRANDY MILK PUNCH

3 cups milk
¾ to 1 cup brandy
½ cup sugar
2 tablespoons vanilla extract
Orange Whipped Cream
Ground nutmeg

Combine first 4 ingredients; stir well. Pour into serving cups. Top each serving with a dollop of Orange Whipped Cream; sprinkle with nutmeg. Yield: 4 cups.

Orange Whipped Cream

1 cup whipping cream
1 teaspoon grated orange rind
2 tablespoons sugar

Beat whipping cream and grated orange rind until foamy; gradually add sugar, beating until soft peaks form. Yield: 2 cups. *Mrs. Michael Elliott*
River Ridge, Louisiana

COFFEE PUNCH

4 cups cold coffee
2 tablespoons rum
⅛ teaspoon salt
1 pint vanilla ice cream, softened
1 pint chocolate ice cream, softened
1 cup whipping cream
Ground nutmeg

Combine coffee, rum, and salt. Add ice creams and whipping cream; stir gently. Sprinkle with nutmeg. Yield: 9 cups. *Dorothy C. Taylor*
Palm City, Florida

CHOCOLATE SIPPER

4 eggs
1 pint chocolate ice cream
2 cups half-and-half
½ cup chocolate syrup
Whipped cream (optional)

Combine first 4 ingredients in container of an electric blender; process until smooth. Garnish with whipped cream, if desired. Serve immediately. Yield: 5 cups. *Heather Riggins*
Nashville, Tennessee

Biscuits: Hot From The Oven

What Southerner doesn't have a weakness for biscuits? Hot, steaming, right out of the oven, biscuits beg for a pat of butter and a hearty appetite.

WHOLE WHEAT BISCUITS

1 cup whole wheat flour
1 cup all-purpose flour
2 teaspoons baking powder
½ teaspoon salt
1 tablespoon sugar
⅓ cup shortening
1 egg, beaten
¾ cup milk

Combine first 5 ingredients; cut in shortening with a pastry blender until mixture resembles coarse meal.
Combine egg and milk. Add milk mixture to flour mixture, stirring until dry ingredients are moistened. Turn dough out onto a lightly floured surface, and knead 4 or 5 times.
Roll dough to ½-inch thickness; cut with a 2-inch biscuit cutter. Place on a lightly greased baking sheet. Bake at 450° for 12 minutes. Yield: 20 biscuits.
Mrs. Douglas Harper Jr.
Shreveport, Louisiana

BREAKFAST DROP SCONES

3 cups biscuit mix
2 tablespoons sugar
½ cup currants or chopped raisins
1 cup milk
Cinnamon Glaze

Combine biscuit mix, sugar, and currants; add milk, stirring until dry ingredients are moistened. Drop dough by heaping tablespoonfuls onto a lightly greased baking sheet. Bake at 425° for 10 minutes. Brush with Cinnamon Glaze, and bake 2 to 5 minutes or until browned. Yield: 2 dozen biscuits.

Cinnamon Glaze

3 tablespoons sugar
¼ teaspoon ground cinnamon
1 tablespoon butter or margarine, melted
1 tablespoon half-and-half

Combine all ingredients, mixing until blended. Yield: about ¼ cup.
Margie G. Phillips
Jonesboro, Louisiana

BLUE CHEESE BISCUITS

¼ cup butter or margarine
2 tablespoons crumbled blue cheese
1 teaspoon lemon juice
1 (10-ounce) package refrigerated biscuits

Combine butter and blue cheese in a small saucepan; cook over low heat, stirring constantly, until butter and cheese melt. Stir in lemon juice, and cook over medium heat 1 minute or until slightly thickened. Pour mixture into a 9-inch round cakepan.
Cut each biscuit into quarters, and place on top of mixture. Bake at 400° for 10 to 12 minutes or until browned. Yield: 10 servings.
Elinor T. Doyle
Wheeling, West Virginia

BREAKFASTS BRUNCHES

BACON-CHEESE BISCUITS

2 cups self-rising flour
1 tablespoon sugar
⅓ cup shortening
1 cup buttermilk
½ teaspoon baking soda
¾ pound sliced bacon, cooked and crumbled
1 cup (4 ounces) shredded Cheddar cheese

Combine flour and sugar in large bowl; cut in shortening with a pastry blender until mixture resembles coarse meal. Set aside.

Combine buttermilk and soda in a small bowl, stirring until soda dissolves. Add buttermilk mixture, crumbled bacon, and shredded cheese to flour mixture, stirring until dry ingredients are moistened. Turn dough out onto a lightly floured surface, and knead lightly 4 or 5 times.

Roll dough to ½-inch thickness; cut with a 2-inch biscuit cutter. Place on a lightly greased baking sheet. Bake at 425° for 10 to 12 minutes. Yield: about 1½ dozen.

Kathy Jean Brown
Tupelo, Mississippi

COOKING LIGHT®

A Light Menu For Brunch

A spring brunch is the perfect occasion to treat your guests to this elegant, light menu. From the Egg Roulade With Mushroom Filling to the Mixed Fruit Ice, this meal is as pretty as it is flavorful. Your guests will be surprised to know that this menu is less than 450 calories and provides a healthy balance of carbohydrate, protein, and fat. As with all "Cooking Light" menus, about 50% of calories come from carbohydrates, 20% from protein, and 30% from fat.

**Egg Roulade
With Mushroom Filling
Spiced Carrots Polynesian
Grapefruit Refresher
Mixed Fruit Ice
Orange Biscuits**

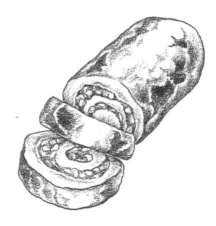

EGG ROULADE WITH MUSHROOM FILLING

Vegetable cooking spray
¼ cup reduced-calorie margarine
¼ cup all-purpose flour
¼ teaspoon salt
⅛ teaspoon ground nutmeg
⅛ teaspoon pepper
¾ cup skim milk
6 eggs, separated
¼ teaspoon cream of tartar
Mushroom Filling
3 tablespoons grated Parmesan cheese
½ cup (2 ounces) shredded low-fat Swiss cheese, divided
Parsley sprigs (optional)
Tomato rose (optional)

Coat bottom and sides of a 15- x 10- x 1-inch jellyroll pan with cooking spray; line with wax paper, and coat wax paper with cooking spray.

Melt margarine in a heavy saucepan over low heat; add flour, salt, nutmeg, and pepper, stirring until smooth. Cook 1 minute, stirring constantly. Gradually add skim milk; cook over medium heat, stirring constantly, until thickened and bubbly.

Beat egg yolks slightly in a large mixing bowl; gradually add white sauce. Set aside.

Beat egg whites (at room temperature) until foamy; add cream of tartar, beating until stiff but not dry. Stir a small amount of whites into sauce mixture; fold in remaining whites. Spread batter into prepared pan. Bake at 350° for 15 to 18 minutes or until puffy and firm in center.

Cover a baking sheet with aluminum foil; spray with cooking spray. Turn out roulade onto aluminum foil; carefully remove wax paper. Spread with Mushroom Filling; sprinkle with Parmesan cheese and ¼ cup Swiss cheese. Starting at short end, roll up roulade, ending with seam side down. Sprinkle remaining ¼ cup Swiss cheese over roulade. Broil about 4 inches from heat 1 to 2 minutes or until cheese melts. Cut roulade into 1-inch slices. If desired, garnish with parsley sprigs and tomato rose. Yield: 10 servings (127 calories per 1-inch slice).

☐ *7.6 grams protein, 7.8 grams fat, 6 grams carbohydrate, 166 milligrams cholesterol, 271 milligrams sodium, 112 milligrams calcium.*

Mushroom Filling

Vegetable cooking spray
¾ pound mushrooms, chopped
¼ cup sliced green onions
1 teaspoon all-purpose flour
⅛ teaspoon salt
¼ teaspoon dried whole tarragon
¼ cup skim milk

Coat a large skillet with cooking spray; place over medium heat until hot. Add mushrooms and green onions; sauté until vegetables are tender and liquid is absorbed.

Combine flour and remaining 3 ingredients in a small bowl; stir well. Add to mushroom mixture; cook 1 minute, stirring constantly. Remove from heat. Yield: 1¼ cups.

Libby Idom
Houston, Texas

SPICED CARROTS POLYNESIAN

2 tablespoons reduced-calorie margarine
½ cup unsweetened pineapple juice
1 tablespoon brown sugar
½ teaspoon ground nutmeg
⅛ teaspoon salt
⅛ teaspoon white pepper
1⅓ cups sliced onions, separated into rings
4 cups sliced carrots
2 tablespoons chopped parsley

Melt margarine in a Dutch oven over medium heat. Add remaining ingredients except parsley; cover, reduce heat, and simmer 10 to 12 minutes or until carrots are crisp-tender. Top with parsley. Yield: 8 servings (65 calories per ½-cup serving).

☐ *0.9 gram protein, 2.2 grams fat, 10.4 grams carbohydrate, 0 milligrams cholesterol, 75 milligrams sodium, and 25 milligrams calcium.*
Mrs. Henry A. Tucker
Stockton, Missouri

Tip: *Steaming fresh vegetables over boiling water preserves more vitamins than cooking in boiling water.*

GRAPEFRUIT REFRESHER

2 (6-ounce) cans unsweetened grapefruit juice concentrate, thawed and undiluted
¼ cup water
1 (33.8-ounce) bottle club soda, chilled

Combine first 2 ingredients in a pitcher; stir well. Slowly add club soda; stir gently. Serve immediately. Yield: 6 cups (62 calories per ¾-cup serving).

☐ *0.8 gram protein, 0.2 gram fat, 14.8 grams carbohydrate, 0 milligrams cholesterol, 26 milligrams sodium, and 17 milligrams calcium.*

MIXED FRUIT ICE

1 (16-ounce) can unsweetened apricots
1 (15¼-ounce) can unsweetened crushed pineapple
1 (16-ounce) package unsweetened frozen strawberries, thawed and sliced
3 cups diced banana
1 (6-ounce) can frozen orange juice, undiluted
2 tablespoons lemon juice

Drain liquid from apricots and pineapple, reserving ½ cup each. Chop apricots. Combine apricots, pineapple, reserved liquid, and remaining ingredients in a bowl; stir well.

Spoon into an 8-inch square dish; cover. Freeze until firm.

Remove from freezer about 20 minutes before serving. Break into small pieces. Scoop into serving compotes, and serve immediately. Yield: 14 servings (104 calories per ½-cup serving).

☐ *1.2 grams protein, 0.4 gram fat, 25.9 grams carbohydrate, 0 milligrams cholesterol, 2 milligrams sodium, and 21 milligrams calcium.*

ORANGE BISCUITS

1 cup plus 2 tablespoons all-purpose flour
2 tablespoons baking powder
¼ teaspoon baking soda
1 tablespoon sugar
3 tablespoons margarine
1 egg, slightly beaten
⅓ cup 2% low-fat cottage cheese
1 tablespoon grated orange rind
3 tablespoons reduced-calorie orange marmalade
Vegetable cooking spray

Combine first 4 ingredients in a medium bowl; cut in margarine with a pastry blender until mixture resembles coarse meal. Set aside.

Combine egg, cottage cheese, orange rind, and marmalade in a small bowl; stir well. Add egg mixture to flour mixture, stirring until dry ingredients are moistened.

Drop by tablespoonfuls onto a baking sheet that has been lightly coated with cooking spray. Bake at 400° for 15 minutes or until golden. Yield: 14 biscuits (72 calories per biscuit).

☐ *2.2 grams protein, 3.1 grams fat, 8.9 grams carbohydrate, 20 milligrams cholesterol, 200 milligrams sodium, and 95 milligrams calcium.*
Betty Manente
Lighthouse Point, Florida

Take A Fresh Look At Onions

Can you imagine cooking without onions? Whether in salads, relishes, side dishes, or entrees, versatile onions know no limits. With these tasty onion recipes, you're bound to agree. (For information on onions, see "From Our Kitchen to Yours" on page 87.)

ONION-CHEESE PIE

2⅓ cups chopped Spanish or
 Vidalia onion
1 tablespoon butter or margarine,
 melted
¾ cup (3 ounces) shredded sharp
 Cheddar cheese
Cheesy Crumb Crust
3 eggs, beaten
1 cup milk
½ teaspoon Italian seasoning
¼ teaspoon salt
⅛ teaspoon pepper
Onion rings (optional)
Parsley sprigs (optional)

Sauté chopped onion in 1 tablespoon butter until tender; remove from heat. Stir in cheese; spoon into prepared Cheesy Crumb Crust.

Combine eggs, milk, and seasonings; stir well. Pour over onion-cheese mixture; bake at 375° for 25 to 30 minutes or until set. Let stand 10 minutes before serving. If desired, garnish with onion rings and parsley. Yield: one 9-inch pie.

Cheesy Crumb Crust

1¾ cups cheese-flavored cracker
 crumbs
¼ cup plus 2 tablespoons butter
 or margarine, melted

Combine cracker crumbs and butter; mix well. Press into bottom and up sides of a 9-inch quiche dish or pieplate; bake at 350° for 5 minutes. Yield: one 9-inch pie shell.

Millicent D. Linn
Sarasota, Florida

BARBECUED ONIONS

1 cup catsup
¾ cup water
¼ cup cider vinegar
2 cloves garlic, minced
1 tablespoon Worcestershire
 sauce
1 tablespoon sugar
1 teaspoon salt
1 teaspoon celery seeds
¼ teaspoon hot sauce
3 cups sliced yellow onion

Combine all ingredients except onion in a large saucepan; bring to a boil, stirring occasionally. Cover, reduce heat, and simmer 4 to 5 minutes. Stir in onion; cover and simmer 3 minutes. Cover and chill. Serve with vegetables or barbecued meats. Yield: 4 cups.

Margaret L. Hunter
Princeton, Kentucky

VEGETABLE MEDLEY SALAD

4 green onions, cut into 1-inch
 slices
2 medium tomatoes, cubed
1 small cucumber, cut into
 ½-inch slices and quartered
1 (14-ounce) can artichoke
 hearts, drained and quartered
½ cup crumbled feta cheese
¼ cup chopped green pepper
¼ cup pitted ripe olives, halved
 (optional)
¼ cup plus 2 tablespoons olive
 oil
2 tablespoons lemon juice
1 teaspoon minced fresh parsley
1 teaspoon minced fresh
 coriander
¼ teaspoon freshly ground pepper
2 to 3 cups coarsely shredded
 iceberg lettuce

Combine first 6 ingredients and, if desired, ripe olives in a large bowl; set aside.

Combine oil, lemon juice, parsley, coriander, and pepper in a jar. Cover

tightly, and shake vigorously. Pour mixture over vegetables; toss gently. Chill at least 2 hours.

Add lettuce, and toss gently. Serve immediately. Yield: 6 to 8 servings.

Caro B. Ostlund
Potomac, Maryland

LEEKS IN ORANGE SAUCE

12 leeks
1 teaspoon salt
2 cups orange juice
1½ tablespoons cornstarch
¼ cup butter or margarine
¼ teaspoon white pepper
Orange slice (optional)
Leek strips (optional)

Remove roots, tough outer leaves, and tops from leeks. Split leeks in half lengthwise; wash well.

Combine leeks and salted water to cover in a large heavy skillet; bring to a boil. Cover, reduce heat, and simmer 12 to 14 minutes or until leeks are tender; drain. Plunge them into cold water, and drain.

Combine orange juice and cornstarch in a large skillet, stirring well. Add butter and pepper; bring to a boil, and cook 1 minute. Return leeks to skillet, and heat thoroughly. Arrange leeks in a serving dish. Spoon remaining sauce over leeks. If desired, garnish with an orange slice and leek strips. Serve immediately. Yield: 6 servings.

TENNESSEE-KILLED LETTUCE SALAD

7 cups torn leaf lettuce
1 bunch green onions, sliced
¼ cup butter or margarine
¼ cup vinegar
¼ teaspoon salt

Combine lettuce and green onions in a large bowl; set aside. Combine butter and remaining ingredients in a saucepan; bring to a boil. Pour over lettuce; toss gently. Serve immediately. Yield: 6 to 8 servings.

Joyce Dean Garrison
Charlotte, North Carolina

From Our Kitchen To Yours

Onions are virtually indispensable in food preparation. The skillful addition of members of the onion family to foods can produce a choice of flavors—pungent or subtle, strong or mild, sweet or tangy.

Identifying Onions

Onions are classified as dry or green. Dry onions, more fully developed than green onions, are easily identified by their brittle outer skins. All-purpose onions, called *Yellow Globe,* are usually 2 to 2½ inches in diameter. (The shape may vary, and the color can be white.) Their flavor is strong. Jumbo *Spanish* onions are round, yellow skinned, mild in flavor, and slightly sweet. *Granex* onions, better known as *Bermuda* onions, are medium to large, round or semiflat, white or yellow skinned, mild, and sweet. The long, slim yellow-skinned onions shaped like tops are the *Grano.*

Red or *purple onions,* the famous Southern *Vidalia* onions, *small white onions, shallots,* and *garlic* are also members of the dry onion group. Shallots are small, brown-skinned clustered bulbs that taste like a cross between onion and garlic; their flavor is delicate and subtle yet tangy. The most pungent member of this group is garlic, which is composed of small white-skinned cloves.

Members of the green onion group are *scallions, green onions, leeks,* and *chives.* Harvested before the bulbs are fully developed, scallions have tender green tops. Definite bulb formations usually identify green onions. Similar in appearance to scallions, leeks have straight, thick white shanks instead of bulbs, and flat solid-green leaves. Their flavor is sweeter, milder, and more delicate than that of other onions. Chives have pencil-thin green tops and a delicate flavor.

Selecting Onions

When purchasing dry onions, select hard, well-shaped bulbs. Keep in mind that moisture at the neck and soft or spongy bulbs with fresh sprouts are signs of decay.

Green onion bunches should be crisp and tender with delicate bulb formations. Be sure to look for white, bleached stems up to about 3 inches from the roots.

Small or medium leeks are the most tender; choose well-balanced bunches with white color extending 2 to 3 inches from the shank base.

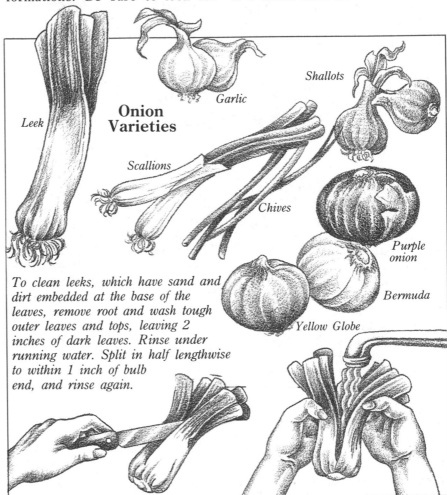

Onion Varieties

Leek

Garlic

Shallots

Scallions

Chives

Purple onion

Bermuda

Yellow Globe

To clean leeks, which have sand and dirt embedded at the base of the leaves, remove root and wash tough outer leaves and tops, leaving 2 inches of dark leaves. Rinse under running water. Split in half lengthwise to within 1 inch of bulb end, and rinse again.

Tips for Using Onions

■ To capture the full flavor of the onion, sauté chopped onion in a small amount of fat before adding to other ingredients.

■ Add chopped onion to an oil dressing one to two hours before mixing with other salad ingredients for increased flavor.

■ Cook garlic to mellow the sharp, potent herb and to lend a sweet, nutlike flavor to foods.

■ Use small white onions in pickles and stews, or in baked sauces that are cream based.

■ Use purple onions for salads and garnishes; they provide zest and color. If you cook them, they will disintegrate, lose their mild flavor, become watery, and bleed on other ingredients.

■ Use the green tops of leeks in soups and sauces, and use the white end plus 1 to 2 inches of the green in other dishes.

■ Extract onion juice by pressing the onion's raw surface against a fine grater; move back and forth, letting juice run into container.

New Appeal For An Old Favorite

If you think that all chicken salads taste alike, then you're in for a real treat with these recipes. To determine amount of chicken needed for a recipe, count on ½ cup of chopped cooked chicken per chicken breast half. A whole broiler-fryer yields 2½ to 3 cups of chopped chicken.

FRUITED CHICKEN SALAD
(pictured on page 105)

4 cups chopped cooked chicken
2 cups diced celery
2 cups halved seedless red or
   green grapes
1 (15¼-ounce) can pineapple
   tidbits, drained
1 (11-ounce) can mandarin
   oranges, drained
1 cup slivered almonds, toasted
½ cup mayonnaise
½ cup commercial sour cream
2 tablespoons lemon juice
¼ teaspoon salt
¼ teaspoon white pepper
Fresh escarole
Cheese Tart Shells

Combine first 6 ingredients, and toss well. Combine mayonnaise, sour cream, lemon juice, salt, and white pepper; add to chicken mixture, stirring well. Chill. To serve, arrange escarole around edges of Cheese Tart Shells; spoon chicken mixture on top. Yield: 8 servings.

Cheese Tart Shells

2 cups all-purpose flour
½ teaspoon salt
⅔ cup plus 2 tablespoons
   shortening
1 cup (4 ounces) shredded
   Cheddar cheese
4 to 5 tablespoons cold water

Combine flour and salt in a bowl; cut in shortening with pastry blender until mixture resembles coarse meal. Stir in cheese. Sprinkle cold water, 1 tablespoon at a time, evenly over surface; stir with a fork until dry ingredients are moistened. Shape into 8 balls; cover and chill.

Roll each ball of dough into a 6½-inch circle on a lightly floured surface. Line 8 (4½-inch) individual quiche dishes or tart pans with pastry; trim excess pastry with a knife. Bake at 450° for 8 to 10 minutes or until lightly browned. Yield: 8 tart shells.
Marie Bowers
Joaquin, Texas

ASPIC-TOPPED CHICKEN SALAD
(pictured on page 105)

1 envelope unflavored gelatin
½ cup cold water
3 cups tomato juice
3 cups finely chopped celery,
   divided
2 tablespoons chopped onion
1 tablespoon Worcestershire
   sauce
Dash of salt
¼ teaspoon white pepper
1 envelope unflavored gelatin
¼ cup cold water
1 cup mayonnaise
1 cup whipping cream, whipped
3 cups chopped cooked chicken
   (about 6 breast halves)
Lettuce leaves

Sprinkle 1 envelope gelatin over ½ cup cold water; let stand 1 minute. Combine tomato juice, 1 cup celery, and onion in a saucepan; bring to a boil, and cook 1 minute. Remove from heat; strain, discarding vegetables. Combine vegetable liquid and gelatin mixture, stirring until gelatin dissolves. Stir in Worcestershire sauce, salt, and pepper. Pour mixture into a lightly oiled 11-cup mold; chill until the consistency of unbeaten egg white.

Sprinkle 1 envelope gelatin over ¼ cup cold water in a small saucepan; let stand 1 minute. Cook over medium heat until gelatin dissolves. Remove from heat; cool. Fold mayonnaise and gelatin mixture into whipped cream. Fold in chicken and remaining 2 cups celery; gently spoon over aspic in mold. Chill until firm. Unmold onto a lettuce-lined serving dish. Yield: 8 servings.
Christine O. Roddy
Chattanooga, Tennessee

SOUTHWESTERN CHICKEN SALAD
(pictured on page 105)

4 chicken breast halves, skinned
1 teaspoon salt
¼ cup mayonnaise
¼ cup commercial sour cream
1 (4-ounce) can chopped green
   chiles, undrained
1 teaspoon ground cumin
¼ teaspoon salt
⅛ teaspoon pepper
¼ cup chopped onion
4 (8-inch) flour tortillas
1 cup (4 ounces) shredded
   Longhorn cheese
3 cups shredded lettuce
Commercial sour cream
1 small tomato, diced
Picante sauce

Place chicken in a Dutch oven; cover with water, and add 1 teaspoon salt. Bring to a boil. Cover, reduce heat, and simmer 30 minutes or until chicken is tender. Drain chicken, reserving broth for other uses. Bone chicken, and shred into small pieces. Set aside.

Combine mayonnaise and ¼ cup sour cream, stirring well. Add chiles and next 3 ingredients, stirring well.

Combine chicken and onion; add sour cream mixture, stirring to coat well. Cover and refrigerate 2 hours.

Place tortillas on a baking sheet; sprinkle cheese evenly over each tortilla. Bake at 300° for 10 minutes or until cheese melts; transfer to individual serving plates. Arrange lettuce over tortillas; top each with one-fourth of chicken mixture. Garnish with sour cream and tomato. Serve with picante sauce. Yield: 4 servings.
Bronwen M. Gibson
Birmingham, Alabama

COOKING LIGHT®

Pasta With A Light Twist

Pasta has been rediscovered as an elegant health food. New attitudes about the importance of complex carbohydrates in a healthy diet have helped increase pasta's popularity. Most nutrition experts agree that complex carbohydrates should be the backbone of a healthy diet because they are our bodies' most efficient source of energy. In addition, they contain good sources of B vitamins and dietary fiber, while being low in cholesterol, saturated fat, and sodium. Foods that are considered complex carbohydrates include pasta, potatoes, rice, breads, vegetables, and legumes.

The calories in pasta are not as much of a concern as the calories in the rich sauces that are usually eaten with it. Gram for gram, the calories from the carbohydrate in pasta are the same as calories in protein. (There are 4 calories in a gram of

each.) Fats, on the other hand, have 9 calories per gram, over twice as many calories as carbohydrates.

Pasta comes dried, fresh, or frozen, in over 600 different shapes, lengths, and sizes. The nutritional value of specialty pasta varies only slightly from conventional, with the exception of vitamin A in pasta with vegetables. Pasta prepared with egg or egg solids contains cholesterol.

Cooking pasta is as easy as boiling water. When the pasta is al dente (tender but firm), drain immediately. Keep in mind that it isn't necessary to rinse cooked pasta unless it is to be served cold.

CHICKEN PASTA SALAD

3 (4-ounce) boneless, skinless chicken breast halves
3½ cups cooked small macaroni shells (cooked without salt or fat)
3 cups fresh broccoli flowerets
1 cup sweet red pepper strips
6 ounces fresh snow pea pods, trimmed
¼ cup sliced green onions
¼ cup vegetable oil
¼ cup plus 1 tablespoon red wine vinegar
2 tablespoons honey
2 teaspoons sesame seeds, toasted
2 cloves garlic, minced
1 teaspoon hot sauce
½ teaspoon ground ginger
¼ teaspoon salt
6 lettuce leaves (optional)

Combine chicken and enough water to cover in a medium saucepan. Cook over medium heat 15 minutes or until tender; drain. Chop chicken into bite-size pieces.

Combine macaroni and chicken. Add broccoli, red pepper, snow peas, and green onions; toss gently.

Combine oil and next 7 ingredients in a jar. Cover tightly, and shake vigorously. Pour dressing over salad; toss gently. Cover and chill. Serve on lettuce-lined plates, if desired. Yield: 6 servings (330 calories per 1⅔-cup serving).

☐ *19.4 grams protein, 11.8 grams fat, 35.3 grams carbohydrate, 36 milligrams cholesterol, 152 milligrams sodium, 64 milligrams calcium.*
Joy L. Garcia
Bartlett, Tennessee

EASY CHICKEN WITH SPINACH FETTUCCINE

Vegetable cooking spray
4 (4-ounce) boneless, skinless chicken breast halves
¼ teaspoon freshly ground pepper
1 cup chopped onion
1 clove garlic, minced
1 (4-ounce) can mushroom stems and pieces, drained
1 (14½-ounce) can stewed tomatoes, undrained and chopped
1 bay leaf
¼ teaspoon salt
½ cup Chablis or other dry white wine
4 cups cooked spinach fettuccine (cooked without salt or fat)
1 tablespoon minced fresh parsley

Coat a large skillet with cooking spray; place over medium heat until hot. Cut chicken into bite-size pieces, and sprinkle with pepper; sauté chicken until lightly browned. Remove from skillet; set aside.

Sauté onion and garlic in skillet until browned. Add chicken, mushrooms, tomatoes, bay leaf, salt, and wine; stir well. Simmer, uncovered, 15 minutes.

Spoon fettuccine onto serving platter. Remove bay leaf. Arrange chicken and vegetables on fettuccine; sprinkle with parsley. Yield: 6 servings (271 calories per 1-cup serving).

☐ *23.6 grams protein, 4.3 grams fat, 33.5 grams carbohydrate, 48 milligrams cholesterol, 348 milligrams sodium, and 105 milligrams calcium.*
Bill Ripley
Bradenton, Florida

CHICKEN LASAGNA

Vegetable cooking spray
¼ cup chopped onion
2 cloves garlic, minced
2 (4-ounce) boneless, skinless
  chicken breast halves
½ teaspoon dried parsley flakes
½ teaspoon dried whole oregano
½ teaspoon dried whole basil
½ teaspoon salt
⅛ teaspoon pepper
1 (16-ounce) can no-salt-added
  tomatoes, undrained and
  chopped
6 cooked lasagna noodles (cooked
  without salt or fat)
1 (16-ounce) carton 1% low-fat
  cottage cheese
½ cup (2 ounces) shredded
  part-skim mozzarella cheese
⅓ cup grated Parmesan cheese
¼ cup (1 ounce) shredded
  40%-less-fat Cheddar cheese

Coat a large skillet with cooking spray; place over medium heat until hot. Add onion and garlic; sauté about 2 minutes. Cut chicken into bite-size pieces; add to skillet with parsley and next 5 ingredients. Stir well. Bring to a boil; reduce heat, and simmer, uncovered, 15 minutes. Remove from heat.

Coat a 10- x 6- x 2-inch baking dish with cooking spray; place 3 noodles in dish. Layer half each of cottage cheese, mozzarella cheese, chicken mixture, and Parmesan cheese. Repeat layers.

Cover and bake at 350° for 25 minutes. Remove cover, and sprinkle with Cheddar cheese. Bake an additional 5 minutes. Yield: 6 servings (232 calories per serving).

☐ *26 grams protein, 5.6 grams fat, 18.4 grams carbohydrate, 36 milligrams cholesterol, 735 milligrams sodium, and 244 milligrams calcium.*
Betty Fletcher
State Road, North Carolina

Tip: *When you use cheese as an ingredient in a recipe, do not overcook it as it will become stringy.*

PASTA PROVENÇALE

1 clove garlic, minced
¼ cup chopped onion
½ cup chopped green pepper
1 cup sliced mushrooms
3 cups sliced zucchini
1 tablespoon olive oil
¼ teaspoon salt
¼ teaspoon pepper
⅛ teaspoon dried whole oregano
¼ teaspoon dried whole basil
1 (14½-ounce) can stewed
  tomatoes, undrained and
  chopped
2 cups cooked rotini noodles
  (cooked without salt or fat)
¼ cup grated Parmesan cheese

Sauté first 5 ingredients in olive oil in a Dutch oven over medium heat 3 minutes. Add salt, pepper, oregano, basil, and tomatoes; stir well. Bring mixture to a boil; remove from heat. Add cooked noodles and Parmesan cheese; toss gently, and serve immediately. Yield: about 6 servings (139 calories per 1-cup serving).

☐ *5.5 grams protein, 3.8 grams fat, 21.5 grams carbohydrate, 3 milligrams cholesterol, 338 milligrams sodium, and 89 milligrams calcium.*
Beverly J. Donegon
Colorado Springs, Colorado

FETTUCCINE AND SPINACH

2 tablespoons olive oil
1 large clove garlic, crushed
1½ teaspoons minced fresh basil
¼ cup minced fresh parsley
1 (10-ounce) package frozen
  chopped spinach, thawed and
  drained
1 cup 1% low-fat cottage cheese
½ teaspoon salt
2 cups cooked thin fettuccine
  (cooked without salt or fat)
2 tablespoons grated Parmesan
  cheese

Heat oil in a large skillet over medium heat. Add garlic and next 5 ingredients, and stir well. Reduce heat, and cook about 3 minutes, stirring constantly.

Add fettuccine; toss gently. Sprinkle with Parmesan cheese; serve immediately. Yield: 6 servings (146 calories per ½-cup serving).

☐ *8.3 grams protein, 5.7 grams fat, 15.4 grams carbohydrate, 3 milligrams cholesterol, 397 milligrams sodium, and 83 milligrams calcium.*
Margaret Bauer
Jasper, Georgia

LINGUINE WITH CLAM SAUCE

2 (6½-ounce) cans chopped clams,
  undrained
2 teaspoons minced garlic
2 tablespoons olive oil
½ cup dry white wine
¼ teaspoon pepper
½ teaspoon crushed red pepper
  flakes
3 cups cooked linguine (cooked
  without salt or fat)
2 tablespoons minced fresh
  parsley
1 tablespoon plus 1 teaspoon
  grated Parmesan cheese

Drain clams, reserving liquid. Bring liquid to a boil in a medium saucepan; reduce heat, and simmer until reduced to about half. Add garlic and next 4 ingredients. Bring to a boil; reduce heat, and simmer about 4 minutes.

Combine linguine, clams, and clam sauce; toss well. Transfer to a serving platter, and sprinkle with parsley and Parmesan cheese. Serve immediately. Yield: 4 servings (296 calories per 1-cup serving).

☐ *17.3 grams protein, 9.6 grams fat, 34.2 grams carbohydrate, 46 milligrams cholesterol, 121 milligrams sodium, and 89 milligrams calcium.*
Mrs. William Alvine
Altamonte Springs, Florida

LINGUINE WITH GARLIC AND LEMON

1½ tablespoons reduced-calorie margarine
2 cloves garlic, crushed
2 tablespoons lemon juice
½ teaspoon pepper
¼ cup grated Parmesan cheese
2½ cups cooked linguine (cooked without salt or fat)

Melt margarine in a small saucepan; add garlic and next 3 ingredients. Add sauce to linguine, and toss gently. Serve immediately. Yield: 5 servings (143 calories per ½-cup serving).

□ 5 grams protein, 4 grams fat, 20.8 grams carbohydrate, 3 milligrams cholesterol, 97 milligrams sodium, and 66 milligrams calcium.

These Appetizers Start The Party

Whether you're serving appetizers for a party, a single snack for an informal gathering, or a more sophisticated prelude to a formal dinner, you'll find recipes here to suit the occasion.

Offer some unexpected choices for Chunky Pimiento Cheese. Use the dip to fill scooped-out cherry tomatoes and fresh snow peas, or to top tiny homemade biscuit halves. If you serve it as a spread, provide thin slices of apple instead of the standard party bread.

For a more formal occasion, try Drizzled Smoked Salmon. At an open house or buffet, serve the thin strips with sturdy crackers. Or for a seated dinner, arrange the salmon over lettuce on individual salad plates. When you purchase the salmon, you may find it labeled as lox. For this recipe, thin-sliced (sometimes called Nova-sliced) salmon works best.

CHUNKY PIMIENTO CHEESE

1 (3-ounce) package cream cheese, softened
1 (4-ounce) jar diced pimiento, drained
1 cup mayonnaise
1 tablespoon sugar (optional)
⅛ teaspoon pepper
4 cups (16 ounces) finely shredded sharp Cheddar cheese

Combine cream cheese and pimiento; stir well. Add mayonnaise and remaining ingredients; stir well. Cover and chill. Yield: 3½ cups.

Carolyn Webb
Jackson, Mississippi

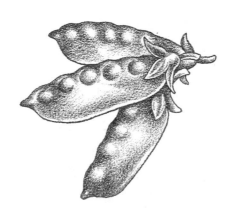

SUGAR SNAP DIP

¼ pound fresh Sugar Snap peas
1 (3-ounce) package cream cheese, softened
½ cup commercial clam dip
½ teaspoon Worcestershire sauce
⅛ teaspoon ground ginger
Additional fresh Sugar Snap peas

Trim ends from ¼ pound peas. Position knife blade in food processor bowl; add prepared peas. Process 5 to 10 seconds. Stop processor, and scrape down sides of bowl with a rubber spatula. Process an additional 10 seconds or until peas are finely chopped. Drain and set aside.

Beat cream cheese at high speed of an electric mixer until fluffy; stir in chopped peas, clam dip, Worcestershire sauce, and ginger. Serve with additional peas. Yield: 1 cup.

Mrs. Hugh F. Mosher
Huntsville, Alabama

DRIZZLED SMOKED SALMON

⅓ pound thinly sliced smoked salmon
2 tablespoons lemon juice
1 tablespoon vegetable oil
1 tablespoon capers
1 tablespoon chopped fresh parsley
½ teaspoon dried whole dillweed or 1½ teaspoons minced fresh dillweed
½ teaspoon pepper
Leaf lettuce

Cut salmon into 2- x 1-inch strips; place in a shallow 2-quart dish.

Combine lemon juice, vegetable oil, capers, parsley, dillweed, and pepper; drizzle over salmon. Cover and chill 2 hours.

To serve, arrange lettuce leaves on individual serving plates; top with salmon. Drizzle marinade over lettuce. Yield: 6 appetizer servings.

Charles R. Hosch
Marietta, Georgia

CHEESY HORS D'OEUVRE PIE

Pastry for a 9-inch pie
12 ounces cream cheese, softened
½ cup (2 ounces) crumbled blue cheese
½ cup mayonnaise
¼ teaspoon onion powder
4 ripe olives, sliced
15 small cherry tomatoes, halved
½ to ⅔ cup sliced mushrooms
1 tablespoon minced fresh parsley
2 hard-cooked eggs, chopped

Roll pastry to an 11-inch circle on a baking sheet. Prick well with a fork. Bake at 425° for 8 minutes or until lightly browned; cool. Place on a large serving tray.

Combine cheeses, mayonnaise, and onion powder; beat until smooth. Spread mixture evenly over pastry. Arrange olives and remaining ingredients over cream cheese mixture. Cut into wedges to serve. Yield: 10 to 12 appetizer servings.

Mrs. William Huffcut
Maxwell A.F.B., Alabama

Specialties Of The House

If you can't visit the Beaumont Inn in Kentucky or The Nutt House in Texas, you can still sample their old-time specialties in your own kitchen with these recipes.

■ Houseguests have savored these recipes at the **Beaumont Inn** in **Harrodsburg, Kentucky,** for over 70 years.

BEAUMONT FRIED CHICKEN

1 (3½- to 4-pound) broiler-fryer, cut up
¾ to 1 teaspoon salt
¼ to ½ teaspoon pepper
½ cup all-purpose flour
3 to 3½ cups shortening or lard
1 teaspoon water

Rinse chicken; pat dry. Sprinkle with salt and pepper. Place flour in a plastic bag; place 2 or 3 pieces of chicken at a time into bag. Close securely, and shake until pieces are evenly coated.

Heat shortening to 325° in a 10-inch iron skillet. Add chicken, and cook, uncovered, 25 to 30 minutes or until golden brown, turning once. Remove from heat; drain off fat. Return skillet to low heat; add water to chicken, cover, and allow chicken to steam 5 minutes. Yield: about 4 servings.

CORNMEAL MUFFINS

2 cups cornmeal
1 teaspoon baking soda
1 teaspoon salt
1 egg, beaten
1½ cups buttermilk

Combine first 3 ingredients in a medium bowl, mixing well. Combine egg and buttermilk, mixing well. Add to dry ingredients, stirring until batter is smooth.

Place a well-greased cast-iron muffin pan in a 500° oven for 2 minutes or until very hot. Remove pan from oven; spoon batter into pan, filling three-fourths full. Bake at 500° for 9 to 10 minutes or until lightly browned. Yield: 16 muffins.

GENERAL ROBERT E. LEE ORANGE-LEMON CAKE
(pictured on page 72)

2 cups sifted cake flour
1½ teaspoons baking powder
½ teaspoon cream of tartar
9 eggs, separated
2 cups sugar
½ cup vegetable oil
Grated rind and juice of 1 lemon
Pinch of salt
Orange-Lemon Frosting
Orange slices
Fresh mint leaves

Combine first 3 ingredients, and sift 6 times; set aside.

Combine egg yolks and sugar in a large mixing bowl; beat at high speed of an electric mixer until mixture is thick and lemon colored. Reduce speed to medium, and gradually add vegetable oil. Add flour mixture; mix until well blended. Stir in lemon rind and juice.

Beat egg whites (at room temperature) and salt until stiff peaks form. Fold whites into batter. Pour batter into 4 wax paper-lined and greased 8-inch round cakepans.

Bake at 325° for 20 to 25 minutes or until cake springs back when lightly touched. Cool in pans 10 minutes; loosen cake from sides of pan, using a small metal spatula. Remove cake from pan, and peel off wax paper. Cool layers completely on wire racks.

Spread Orange-Lemon Frosting between layers and on top and sides of cake. Store cake in refrigerator until serving time. Garnish cake with orange slices and fresh mint leaves. Yield: one 4-layer cake.

Orange-Lemon Frosting

½ cup butter, softened
3 egg yolks
2 (16-ounce) packages powdered sugar, sifted
Grated rind of 4 oranges
Grated rind of 2 lemons
2 tablespoons lemon juice
4 to 5 tablespoons orange juice

Cream butter; add egg yolks, and beat well. Add powdered sugar and grated rind alternately with juices, beating well. Yield: about 4 cups.

■ Country-style cooking brings folks from all over Texas to **The Nutt House** in **Granbury,** just for lunch.

BLACK-EYED PEA SALAD

3 (15.8-ounce) cans black-eyed peas, rinsed
1 (2-ounce) jar diced pimiento, drained
½ cup diced purple onion
¼ cup vinegar
¼ cup plus 2 tablespoons red wine vinegar
¼ cup plus 2 tablespoons sugar
¼ cup plus 2 tablespoons vegetable oil
¾ teaspoon ground red pepper
¼ teaspoon salt

Combine first 3 ingredients in a bowl; toss gently. Combine vinegar and remaining ingredients; stir well, and pour over pea mixture. Cover and chill at least 3 hours. Yield: 6 to 8 servings.

HOT WATER CORNBREAD

1 cup white cornmeal
1 cup yellow cornmeal
1 teaspoon salt
2 tablespoons shortening
2 cups water
½ teaspoon baking powder
2 tablespoons warm water

Combine first 3 ingredients in a bowl. Add shortening.

Bring 2 cups water to a rolling boil; add to cornmeal mixture, stirring well. Let cool 20 minutes. Combine baking powder and 2 tablespoons water. Add to cornmeal mixture; stir. Shape dough into 1-inch balls. Press each ball between two fingers to make a slight indention on two sides.

Carefully drop shaped dough into deep hot oil (375°); cook only a few at a time. Fry 1 to 2 minutes or until golden brown. Serve immediately. Yield: approximately 2½ dozen.

BUTTERMILK PIE

⅓ cup butter or margarine, softened
1½ cups sugar
3 eggs
3 tablespoons all-purpose flour
Dash of ground nutmeg
1 cup buttermilk
1 unbaked 9-inch pastry shell

Cream butter; gradually add sugar, beating at medium speed of an electric mixer. Add eggs, one at a time, beating well after each addition. Add flour and nutmeg, beating at low speed until blended. Add buttermilk, beating well. Pour into pastry shell; bake at 325° for 55 minutes or until pie is set. Cool on a wire rack. Yield: one 9-inch pie.

Rhubarb: A Spring Delicacy

Just once a year, tangy, tart rhubarb is at its flavor peak. The leggy stalks, resembling celery, are most often sweetened for use in pies and preserves. But our readers have found ways to enjoy rhubarb in salads, as a side dish, and even in a dessert mousse.

When you select rhubarb at the produce counter, be sure to look for stalks that are crisp and of medium thickness. If you puncture the stalk with your thumbnail and juice runs out, you know the rhubarb is fresh. Color, which varies from light pink to cherry red, does not indicate any difference in flavor.

Be sure to remove and discard any leaves that may be left on the stalks. The leaves can be toxic if consumed.

STRAWBERRY-RHUBARB COBBLER

2 cups cubed rhubarb (about 1 pound)
2 cups halved strawberries
1 cup sugar
1½ tablespoons quick-cooking tapioca
⅛ teaspoon salt
2 tablespoons butter or margarine
Pastry for one (8-inch) pie

Combine first 5 ingredients in a medium bowl; toss gently. Spoon into a lightly greased 8-inch square baking dish. Dot with butter.

Roll dough to ⅛-inch thickness on a lightly floured surface; cut into ½-inch-wide strips with a knife or pastry wheel. Arrange in a lattice design over rhubarb mixture.

Bake at 375° for 40 to 45 minutes or until pastry is golden brown. Yield: 6 servings.   *Betty Czebotar*
Baltimore, Maryland

RHUBARB MOUSSE

1 envelope unflavored gelatin
½ cup cold water, divided
3 cups chopped rhubarb (about 1½ pounds)
1 cup sugar
2 teaspoons lemon juice
Red food coloring (optional)
1 cup whipping cream
Additional whipped cream (optional)
Ground nutmeg (optional)

Sprinkle gelatin over ¼ cup cold water; let stand 5 minutes.

Combine rhubarb, sugar, and ¼ cup water in a medium saucepan; mix well, and bring to a boil. Reduce heat to low; simmer 10 minutes or until rhubarb is tender. Add gelatin mixture, stirring until gelatin dissolves. Stir in lemon juice. Stir in food coloring, if desired. Chill 45 minutes or until the consistency of unbeaten egg white, stirring occasionally.

Beat whipping cream until soft peaks form. Fold into gelatin mixture, and spoon into dishes; chill until firm. If desired, garnish with additional whipped cream and nutmeg. Yield: 8 servings.   *Maxine Hallars*
Vilas, North Carolina

RHUBARB AMBROSIA

5 cups chopped rhubarb (about 2½ pounds)
1⅓ cups sugar
2 tablespoons all-purpose flour
¼ teaspoon salt
1½ teaspoons grated orange rind, divided
1 orange, peeled, sectioned, and chopped
4 cups bread cubes, divided
¼ cup butter or margarine, melted and divided
½ cup flaked coconut

Combine first 4 ingredients; mix well. Add ¾ teaspoon orange rind, chopped orange, 2 cups bread cubes, and 2 tablespoons butter, mixing well. Spoon mixture into a lightly greased 8-inch square baking dish.

Combine remaining ¾ teaspoon orange rind, 2 cups bread cubes, 2 tablespoons butter, and coconut; sprinkle over rhubarb mixture. Bake at 375° for 40 minutes or until lightly browned. Serve warm. Yield: 6 servings.   *Mrs. John A. Shoemaker*
Louisville, Kentucky

CHILLED RHUBARB SAUCE

5 cups diced rhubarb (about 2 pounds)
¾ cup sugar
2 tablespoons water
1 tablespoon butter or margarine
2 tablespoons currant jelly

Combine first 4 ingredients in a saucepan; cover and cook over medium heat 10 minutes or until rhubarb is tender. Add jelly; stir until melted. Spoon mixture into container of an electric blender or food processor; process until smooth. Chill. Serve as a meat or dessert sauce. Yield: 3½ cups.

Chef Marcel Van Eeckhaut
Middleburg, Virginia

PINEAPPLE-RHUBARB SAUCE

5 cups diced rhubarb (about 2½ pounds)
4 cups sugar
1 (20-ounce) can unsweetened crushed pineapple, undrained
2 (3-ounce) packages strawberry-flavored gelatin

Combine rhubarb, sugar, and pineapple in a large, heavy saucepan; cook over medium heat, stirring often, 8 to 10 minutes or until rhubarb is tender. Remove from heat. Add gelatin, stirring until dissolved.

Quickly pour into hot sterilized jars, leaving ¼-inch headspace; cover at once with metal lids, and screw on bands. Process in boiling-water bath 10 minutes. Yield: 3½ pints.

Elizabeth M. Haney
Dublin, Virginia

Desserts With Fruit

No matter what the menu, fruit makes a tasty ending to a meal. Present one of these desserts to guests and you are sure to receive compliments.

CRÈME CELESTE

2 envelopes unflavored gelatin
¼ cup plus 2 tablespoons cold water
1 cup sugar
1 cup milk
1 teaspoon almond extract
1 (16-ounce) carton commercial sour cream
1 (8-ounce) carton frozen whipped topping, thawed
Fresh or canned fruit

Sprinkle gelatin over water; let stand 1 minute.

Combine sugar and milk in a saucepan; cook over medium heat, stirring constantly, until sugar dissolves. Remove from heat; stir in gelatin and almond extract. Fold in sour cream and whipped topping.

Pour into a lightly oiled 6½-cup ring mold; chill 8 hours. Unmold onto serving dish, and serve with fruit. Yield: 12 servings.

Sharry Swann
Tifton, Georgia

OLD-FASHIONED APPLE PIE

Double-crust pastry (recipe follows)
7 to 9 medium-size baking apples, peeled, cored, and sliced (about 8 cups)
1 cup sugar
2 tablespoons cornstarch
2 teaspoons vanilla extract
¼ teaspoon ground cinnamon
2 teaspoons butter or margarine
1 tablespoon milk
½ teaspoon sugar
¼ teaspoon ground cinnamon

Roll half of pastry to ⅛-inch thickness on a lightly floured surface. Fit into a 9-inch pieplate; set aside.

Combine apples, 1 cup sugar, cornstarch, vanilla, and ¼ teaspoon cinnamon, tossing to coat apples. Spoon mixture evenly into prepared pastry shell. Dot with butter.

Roll remaining pastry to ⅛-inch thickness, and place over filling. Trim edges; seal and flute. Cut several slits in top crust to allow steam to escape. Brush pastry with milk, and

sprinkle with ½ teaspoon sugar and ¼ teaspoon cinnamon. Bake at 425° for 15 minutes; reduce temperature to 350°, and bake 30 minutes. Yield: one 9-inch pie.

Double-Crust Pastry

2 cups all-purpose flour
½ teaspoon salt
½ cup shortening
½ cup cold water

Combine flour and salt; cut in shortening with pastry blender until mixture resembles coarse meal. Sprinkle cold water, 1 tablespoon at a time, evenly over surface; stir with a fork until dry ingredients are moistened. Shape into a ball; chill. Yield: pastry for one double-crust 9-inch pie.

Sandra Bird
Charleston, South Carolina

BLUEBERRY DREAM

2 cups graham cracker crumbs
⅔ cup butter or margarine, melted
2 (3-ounce) packages cream cheese
1 cup sifted powdered sugar
1 (2.8-ounce) package whipped topping mix
1 cup milk
1 teaspoon vanilla extract
1 (21-ounce) can blueberry pie filling

Combine cracker crumbs and butter; stir well. Set aside 2 tablespoons crumb mixture. Press remaining crumb mixture into an ungreased 12- x 8- x 2-inch baking dish. Bake at 350° for 8 minutes. Cool.

Place cream cheese in a large mixing bowl; beat at high speed of an electric mixer until fluffy. Add powdered sugar, and mix well. Set aside.

Combine whipped topping mix, milk, and vanilla in a large mixing bowl. Beat at high speed of electric mixer about 4 minutes or until topping is light and fluffy. Fold whipped topping into creamed mixture.

Spread half of whipped topping mixture over crust. Spoon pie filling over whipped topping mixture. Spread remaining whipped topping mixture over pie filling. Sprinkle reserved crumb mixture over top. Chill 8 hours. Yield: 12 servings.

Mrs. Doyle Register
Columbus, Georgia

STRAWBERRIES ROMANOFF

¼ cup sugar
¼ cup Grand Marnier or other
  orange-flavored liqueur
4 cups whole strawberries, hulled
1 cup whipping cream
2 tablespoons sugar
2 tablespoons Grand Marnier or
  other orange-flavored liqueur
⅛ teaspoon ground cinnamon
⅓ cup commercial sour cream
3 tablespoons chopped pistachios
  or toasted almonds

Combine ¼ cup sugar and ¼ cup Grand Marnier in a large bowl; stir until sugar dissolves. Add strawberries; toss gently, and set aside.

Beat whipping cream until foamy; gradually add 2 tablespoons sugar, 2 tablespoons Grand Marnier, and cinnamon, beating until soft peaks form. Fold in sour cream.

Spoon strawberries and syrup into serving dishes. Top each with a dollop of cream mixture; sprinkle with nuts. Yield: 8 servings. *Linda Keith*
Dallas, Texas

OLD-FASHIONED LEMON BREAD PUDDING

6 slices bread, cut into ½-inch
  cubes
1 tablespoon grated lemon rind
½ teaspoon salt
2 cups milk
1 cup sugar
3 tablespoons butter or margarine
4 eggs, separated
⅓ cup lemon juice
¼ cup sifted powdered sugar

Combine bread cubes, lemon rind, and salt in a large bowl; set aside.

Combine milk, 1 cup sugar, and butter in a saucepan; place over medium heat until butter melts, stirring occasionally. Pour mixture over bread cubes; let cool.

Beat egg yolks and lemon juice; add to bread mixture, stirring gently. Beat egg whites (at room temperature) until stiff peaks form; fold into bread mixture. Spoon into a lightly greased 2-quart casserole; dust with powdered sugar. Bake at 325° for 40 to 45 minutes or until set. Yield: 8 servings. *Mrs. J. A. Satterfield*
Fort Worth, Texas

Help Yourself To Antipasto

Serve antipasto when you want appetizers with an Italian flair. Antipasto refers to a variety of foods grouped together as an appetizer. Harriet O. St. Amant of Vienna, Virginia, sent us five recipes for a tray to serve 10 to 12 people.

STUFFED CHERRY TOMATOES

1 pint cherry tomatoes
1 (8-ounce) package cream
  cheese, softened
3 to 4 tablespoons whipping
  cream
2 tablespoons chopped chives
¼ teaspoon salt
¼ teaspoon white pepper

Wash tomatoes. Cut a thin slice from top of each tomato; carefully scoop out pulp, reserving pulp for other uses. Invert shells on paper towels to drain.

Combine cream cheese and remaining ingredients in a medium bowl; beat at low speed of an electric mixer until smooth. Spoon or pipe cream cheese mixture into tomato shells. Yield: about 2 dozen.

ALMOND-STUFFED OLIVES

1 (4-ounce) jar large pitted green
  olives
About 2 dozen whole blanched
  almonds

Drain olives, reserving liquid. Carefully stuff an almond into each olive; pour liquid over olives. Cover and chill 8 hours. Drain before serving. Yield: about 2 dozen.

MARINATED ARTICHOKE HEARTS

¼ cup olive oil
¼ cup white wine vinegar
⅛ teaspoon salt
⅛ teaspoon pepper
⅛ teaspoon dried parsley flakes
⅛ teaspoon dried whole oregano
⅛ teaspoon dried whole basil
⅛ teaspoon dried whole marjoram
1 (14-ounce) can artichoke
  hearts, drained and quartered

Combine first 8 ingredients in a jar. Cover tightly, and shake vigorously. Place artichokes in a single layer in a shallow dish; drizzle marinade over artichokes. Cover and chill at least 8 hours. Drain before serving. Yield: 12 appetizer servings.

STUFFED EGGS

12 hard-cooked eggs
3 tablespoons mayonnaise
1 tablespoon sugar
1 tablespoon Dijon mustard
1 tablespoon vinegar
1 teaspoon hot sauce
1 teaspoon Worcestershire sauce
⅛ teaspoon salt
Paprika
Fresh parsley sprigs

Slice eggs in half lengthwise, and carefully remove yolks. Mash yolks; add mayonnaise and next 6 ingredients. Stir well. Stuff egg whites with yolk mixture. Sprinkle with paprika, and garnish with fresh parsley. Yield: 2 dozen.

SALAMI-CHEESE SNACKS

2 (3-ounce) packages cream
  cheese, softened
1 (6-ounce) package 3-inch round
  hard salami

Spread 1 package of cream cheese
evenly on 5 slices of salami; stack
and top with another slice of salami.
Cover and chill 4 hours. Cut into 8
wedges.

For log-shaped snacks, spread remaining cream cheese evenly on each
remaining slice of salami. Roll each
slice jellyroll fashion; secure with
wooden picks. Cover and chill. Yield:
about 1½ dozen.

MICROWAVE COOKERY

A Menu Tailored
For Spring

If fresh produce whets your appetite,
you'll want to take advantage of this
easy menu. It's built around three
simple recipes, all cooked in the microwave. Commercial lemon sherbet
for dessert completes the meal.

Fruit Salad With Mint Sauce
Asparagus-and-Ham
   Melt Sandwiches
Spring Pea Soup
Commercial lemon sherbet

Plan: Microwave Mint Sauce, and
refrigerate. Cook asparagus, and prepare fruit salad. Make soup, and assemble sandwiches. During the
standing time for soup, microwave
the sandwiches.

FRUIT SALAD
WITH MINT SAUCE

4 oranges
1 grapefruit, peeled and sectioned
1 (15¼-ounce) can pineapple
  chunks, drained
Bibb lettuce leaves
Mint Sauce

Cut a thin slice from stem end of
each orange to level the base. Score
rind with a sharp knife to make a
shell with 4 petals; cut just through
the rind along scoring, ending 1 inch
from base.

Carefully pull each petal from fruit,
using a knife to separate pulp from
rind. Remove pulp intact, using
thumb to dislodge pulp; set shell
aside. With serrated knife, remove
white membrane from pulp. Section
orange. Combine orange sections,
grapefruit sections, and pineapple.
Line orange shell with lettuce; spoon
fruit into shell. Drizzle with Mint
Sauce. Yield: 4 servings.

Mint Sauce

½ cup chopped fresh mint leaves
½ cup light corn syrup
1 teaspoon lemon juice
1 tablespoon cornstarch
½ cup water

Combine mint leaves, corn syrup,
and lemon juice in a 1-quart glass
measure. Combine cornstarch and
water, stirring until blended; add to
mint mixture.

Microwave at HIGH 4 to 6 minutes or until mixture thickens and
bubbles, stirring once. Strain sauce,
if desired. Chill. Yield: about ¾ cup.

ASPARAGUS-AND-HAM
MELT SANDWICHES

1 pound fresh asparagus
2 tablespoons water
⅓ cup commercial sour cream
2 tablespoons Dijon mustard
½ teaspoon prepared horseradish
4 steak buns
4 (¼-inch-thick) slices cooked
  ham
4 (1-ounce) slices provolone
  cheese

Snap off tough ends of asparagus,
and remove scales, if desired. Combine asparagus and water in a shallow
2-quart casserole. Cover and microwave at HIGH 7 to 9 minutes, giving
dish a half-turn and stirring after 4
minutes. Drain and set aside.

Combine sour cream, mustard, and
horseradish in a small bowl; stir well.
Spread mixture on both sides of
steak buns.

Place 1 ham slice, 3 to 4 asparagus
spears, and 1 cheese slice on bottom
of each bun; cover with top bun.
Wrap each sandwich loosely in paper
towels. Microwave at HIGH 5 minutes or until cheese melts. Serve immediately. Yield: 4 servings.

SPRING PEA SOUP

1 small onion, sliced
3 tablespoons butter or margarine
¼ teaspoon garlic powder
1½ cups fresh English peas or 1
  (10-ounce) package frozen peas
1 (10¾-ounce) can chicken broth,
  undiluted
⅓ cup water
½ cup half-and-half
¼ teaspoon white pepper
Grated carrot (optional)

Combine onion, butter, and garlic
powder in a 2-quart casserole. Microwave at HIGH 1 minute or until
butter melts. Stir in peas, chicken
broth, and water; cover and microwave at HIGH 9 to 10 minutes or
until peas are tender, giving dish a
half-turn after 5 minutes.

Pour half of soup mixture into container of an electric blender, and process until mixture is smooth. Repeat
blending procedure with remaining
soup mixture.

Combine soup mixture, half-and-
half, and pepper in a 2-quart casserole. Microwave at MEDIUM HIGH
(70% power) 5 to 8 minutes or until
mixture is thoroughly heated, stirring
once. Cover and let stand 5 minutes.
Garnish with grated carrot, if desired. Yield: 3 cups.

Peas Fresh From The Pod

English peas are in season, and with them comes an array of new salad and side-dish recipes. If you buy green peas, look for large, bright-green pods. The pods should be filled and have a velvety texture. A pound of peas in the shell yields about 1 cup shelled. To store, refrigerate peas unshelled; they should keep three to five days.

SPECIAL PEAS

2 pounds fresh English peas
   (2 cups shelled)
2 tablespoons butter or margarine
2 cups shredded iceberg lettuce
¼ cup chopped onion
½ teaspoon salt
¼ teaspoon pepper
1 teaspoon minced fresh basil
Fresh basil (optional)

Shell and wash peas; cover with water in a saucepan. Bring to a boil; cover, reduce heat, and simmer 8 to 12 minutes or until tender. Drain and set aside.

Melt butter in a Dutch oven; add peas, lettuce, and next 4 ingredients. Toss lightly; cover and cook 3 minutes. Garnish with fresh basil, if desired. Serve immediately. Yield: 4 to 6 servings.
Jane Maloy
Wilmington, North Carolina

PEAS AND RICE

1 pound fresh English peas
   (1 cup shelled)
½ cup sliced mushrooms
1 tablespoon lemon juice
1 cup cooked rice
2 tablespoons diced onion
1 tablespoon diced pimiento
¼ cup mayonnaise
½ teaspoon salt
¼ teaspoon curry powder
⅛ teaspoon red pepper

Shell and wash peas; cover with water in a small saucepan. Bring to a boil over medium heat; cover and cook 10 minutes or until peas are tender. Drain and set aside.

Combine mushrooms and lemon juice in a medium bowl; toss gently, and let stand 5 minutes. Add peas, rice, and remaining ingredients to mushroom mixture; toss gently.

Spoon into a lightly greased 1-quart baking dish. Cover and bake at 350° for 20 minutes or until thoroughly heated. Yield: 4 servings.
Mrs. C. D. Marshall
Boston, Virginia

GREEN PEAS IN ORANGE SAUCE

2 pounds fresh English peas
   (2 cups shelled)
1 tablespoon butter or margarine
1 (12¼-ounce) jar white boiled
   onions, drained
1 tablespoon cornstarch
1 tablespoon sugar
½ teaspoon salt
½ teaspoon grated orange rind
½ cup orange juice
2 tablespoons minced fresh
   parsley

Shell and wash peas; cover with water in a medium saucepan. Bring to a boil over medium heat; cover and cook 12 minutes or until peas are tender. Drain well. Return peas to saucepan; stir in butter and onions.

Combine cornstarch and next 4 ingredients in a small bowl; stir well. Add to peas; cook over medium heat, stirring constantly, until mixture begins to boil; cook 1 minute, stirring constantly. Spoon into serving dish; sprinkle with parsley. Yield: 6 servings.
Iris Brenner
Fort McCoy, Florida

Spinach And Cheese For Brunch

Two kinds of cheeses, sour cream, and spinach make this layered dish a perfect brunch accompaniment. Joy M. Hall of Lucedale, Mississippi, spoons a mixture of ricotta cheese, eggs, and Cheddar cheese into a homemade cracker crust. After it bakes, she tops it with sour cream.

SPINACH-RICOTTA BAKE

⅓ cup chopped green onions
½ teaspoon dried whole basil,
   crushed
2 tablespoons butter or
   margarine, melted
1 (10-ounce) package frozen
   chopped spinach, thawed
1 (16-ounce) carton ricotta cheese
4 eggs, slightly beaten
½ cup (2 ounces) shredded sharp
   Cheddar cheese
¼ teaspoon salt
⅛ teaspoon ground nutmeg
Cracker Crust
1 cup commercial sour cream
2 teaspoons lemon juice
½ cup chopped parsley (optional)
¼ cup chopped green onions
   (optional)

Sauté ⅓ cup green onions and basil in butter. Drain spinach well; add to green onion mixture. Set aside.

Combine ricotta cheese and next 4 ingredients, mixing well. Add spinach mixture. Spoon into baked Cracker Crust. Bake, uncovered, at 375° for 30 minutes.

Combine sour cream and lemon juice, mixing well. Spread on top of spinach mixture. Bake at 375° for 10 minutes. Let stand 10 minutes before serving. If desired, combine parsley and ¼ cup green onions for garnish. Yield: 8 to 10 servings.

Cracker Crust

½ cup butter or margarine
3 cups saltine cracker crumbs
1 egg, slightly beaten
2 tablespoons cold water

Cut butter into cracker crumbs with a pastry blender; set aside. Combine egg and water, mixing well; add to crumb mixture, mixing well. Firmly press crumb mixture evenly over the bottom and up sides of a 12- x 8- x 2-inch baking dish. Bake at 375° for 10 minutes. Yield: one cracker crust.

Cook Pork With Confidence

Once described as the fattiest type of meat on the market, pork is leaner than ever today. Producers now breed pork to be lower in fat, keeping it a popular choice for the health-conscious consumer.

When selecting fresh pork, look for a bright-pink color; the meat takes on a gray color as it ages. Choose pork that has a high proportion of meat to fat or bone, and trim excess fat before cooking, if desired.

PORK-AND-NOODLE BAKE

6 ounces medium-size egg
   noodles
¾ cup cottage cheese
½ cup commercial sour cream
¼ cup chopped green onions
½ teaspoon Worcestershire sauce
¼ teaspoon garlic salt
1 pound ground pork
1 cup chopped fresh mushrooms
¼ cup chopped green onions
¼ cup chopped green pepper
2 tablespoons all-purpose flour
½ teaspoon salt
½ teaspoon Worcestershire sauce
⅛ teaspoon garlic salt
⅛ teaspoon ground nutmeg
1 teaspoon chicken-flavored
   bouillon granules
½ cup commercial sour cream
¼ cup water
½ cup (2 ounces) shredded
   Cheddar cheese

Cook noodles according to package directions, omitting salt. Drain. Combine noodles, cottage cheese, and next 4 ingredients in a large bowl; mix well. Spoon into a greased 9-inch pieplate. Using the back of a spoon, shape noodle mixture into a crust. Set aside.

Cook pork in a skillet over medium heat until browned, stirring to crumble. Drain pork, reserving 1 tablespoon drippings in skillet. Set pork aside. Add mushrooms, ¼ cup green onions, and green pepper to skillet; sauté until tender. Add flour, salt, Worcestershire sauce, ⅛ teaspoon garlic salt, nutmeg, and bouillon granules; blend well. Cook over medium heat, stirring constantly, until thickened. Remove from heat; stir in ½ cup sour cream, water, and pork. Spoon into noodle crust. Bake at 350° for 5 minutes. Remove from oven. Sprinkle with Cheddar cheese, and bake an additional 5 minutes. Let stand 5 minutes. Yield: 6 servings.
Grace Bravos
Timonium, Maryland

GLAZED SPARERIBS

½ cup catsup
¼ cup vinegar
2 tablespoons brown sugar
2 tablespoons Worcestershire
   sauce
1 teaspoon celery seeds
½ teaspoon chili powder
Dash of pepper
2 or 3 drops of hot sauce
2 pounds spareribs
Lemon slices (optional)
Fresh parsley sprigs

Combine first 8 ingredients in a saucepan; bring to a boil. Remove from heat, and set aside.

Cut ribs into serving-size pieces; place ribs, meaty side down, in a large shallow pan. Bake, uncovered, at 350° for 1 hour. Baste ribs with sauce; turn over, and bake 15 minutes. Baste with sauce; turn again, and bake 15 minutes. (Arrange lemon slices over ribs for last 30 minutes of baking, if desired.) Garnish with parsley. Yield: 3 to 4 servings.
Patricia Andrews
McAlester, Oklahoma

PORK CHOPS AND SAUERKRAUT

4 (½-inch-thick) pork chops
1 tablespoon vegetable oil
1 (14-ounce) can sauerkraut with
   caraway seeds
1 large tomato, peeled and cubed
½ teaspoon paprika

Brown chops on both sides in hot oil in a heavy skillet. Top with sauerkraut and tomato, and sprinkle with paprika. Cover and simmer 40 minutes or until chops are tender. Yield: 4 servings.
Hazel S. Stephenson
Denison, Texas

GRILLED PORK TENDERLOIN

2 tablespoons soy sauce
2 tablespoons hoisin sauce
2 tablespoons dry sherry
1 tablespoon light brown sugar
1 tablespoon peanut oil
1½ teaspoons honey
½ teaspoon garlic salt
½ teaspoon ground cinnamon
1 (1-pound) pork tenderloin
Commercial sweet-and-sour sauce

Combine first 8 ingredients in a large shallow container; stir well. Add tenderloin, turning to coat. Cover and chill 8 hours.

Remove tenderloin from marinade. Grill 6 inches from hot coals for 35 minutes or until done, turning often. To serve, slice thinly, and arrange on platter. Serve with sweet-and-sour sauce. Yield: 3 to 4 servings.
Mrs. E. W. Hanley
Palm Harbor, Florida

Make These Pies Anytime

Pies will always reign as a favorite dessert in the South. Even though some are made for special occasions, these recipes fit right into menus for family supper or company.

When the recipe calls for prebaking the pastry, prick it well with a fork to help the pastry keep its shape during baking. Metal pie weights or even uncooked dried beans placed in the pastry shell will prevent it from puffing during baking. Remove weights after pastry is set, and then bake just enough to brown.

To prevent sogginess, brush the pastry with beaten egg white before baking the pie. To absorb any additional liquid, you can also sprinkle cookie crumbs or breadcrumbs in the bottom of a fruit pie before adding the filling.

CHILLED CHOCOLATE PIE

1 (7-ounce) package
  marshmallows
2 ounces sweet baking chocolate,
  chopped
¾ cup milk
½ teaspoon vanilla extract
⅛ teaspoon salt
1 cup whipping cream, whipped
1 baked 9-inch pastry shell
Sweetened whipped cream
  (optional)
Chocolate shavings (optional)

Combine marshmallows and chocolate in top of a double boiler; bring water to a boil. Reduce heat to low; cook until melted, stirring occasionally. Add milk; stir well with a wire whisk. Remove from heat; let cool. Stir in vanilla and salt. Fold in whipped cream; spoon into pastry shell. Cover and chill 8 hours or until set. If desired, garnish with sweetened whipped cream and chocolate shavings. Yield: one 9-inch pie.

Freida Merrell
Magnolia, Arkansas

CHOCOLATE BOURBON PIE

3 eggs, beaten
½ cup light corn syrup
½ cup sugar
¼ cup firmly packed brown sugar
¼ cup butter or margarine,
  melted
2 tablespoons all-purpose flour
3 to 4 tablespoons bourbon
1 teaspoon vanilla extract
1 cup chopped walnuts
1 cup semisweet chocolate
  morsels
1 unbaked 9-inch pastry shell
Ice cream (optional)

Combine first 6 ingredients in a medium bowl; beat with an electric mixer just until blended. Add bourbon and vanilla, mixing well. Stir in walnuts and chocolate morsels. Spoon into pastry shell. Bake at 375° for 40 minutes or until set. Serve with ice cream, if desired. Yield: one 9-inch pie.

Mrs. Don Heun
Louisville, Kentucky

BUTTERMILK-LEMON CREAM PIE

¾ cup sugar
3 tablespoons cornstarch
1½ cups buttermilk
2 tablespoons butter or margarine
3 eggs, separated
1 tablespoon grated lemon rind
3 tablespoons lemon juice
1 baked 9-inch pastry shell
¼ teaspoon cream of tartar
⅓ cup sugar

Combine ¾ cup sugar and cornstarch in a heavy saucepan; mix well. Add buttermilk; cook over medium heat, stirring constantly, until mixture comes to a boil. Remove from heat; stir in butter. Beat egg yolks. Gradually stir about one-fourth of hot mixture into yolks; add to remaining hot mixture, stirring constantly. Boil 1 minute, stirring constantly. Remove from heat; stir in lemon rind and juice. Pour mixture immediately into pastry shell.

Beat egg whites (at room temperature) and cream of tartar at high speed of an electric mixer 1 minute. Gradually add ⅓ cup sugar, 1 tablespoon at a time, beating 2 to 4 minutes or until stiff peaks form and sugar dissolves.

Spread meringue over warm filling, sealing to edge of pastry. Bake at 375° for 10 minutes or until lightly browned. Cool before serving. Yield: one 9-inch pie.

Dora H. Brake
Asheville, North Carolina

APRICOT SURPRISE PIE

1 (6-ounce) package dried apricots
½ cup water
2 tablespoons sugar
1 baked 9-inch pastry shell
⅔ cup sugar
¼ cup cornstarch
3 eggs, separated
2 cups milk
1 teaspoon vanilla extract
2 tablespoons lemon juice
¼ teaspoon cream of tartar
2 tablespoons sugar

Combine dried apricots and water in a small saucepan; bring to a boil. Cover, reduce heat, and simmer 10 minutes, stirring occasionally. Drain, reserving 2 tablespoons liquid. Add 2 tablespoons sugar and reserved apricot liquid to apricots; stir until sugar dissolves. Spoon into pastry shell.

Combine ⅔ cup sugar and cornstarch in a heavy saucepan; stir well. Beat egg yolks; add yolks and milk to cornstarch mixture, stirring with a wire whisk until blended. Cook over medium heat, stirring constantly with a wooden spoon, until mixture thickens and comes to a boil. Add vanilla and lemon juice; boil 1 minute, stirring constantly. Pour immediately over apricot mixture in pastry shell. Cover with wax paper.

Beat egg whites (at room temperature) and cream of tartar at high speed of an electric mixer 1 minute. Gradually add 2 tablespoons sugar, beating 2 to 4 minutes until stiff peaks form and sugar dissolves. Remove wax paper from pie; spread meringue over hot filling, sealing to edge of pastry. Bake at 375° for 10 minutes or until lightly browned. Let cool. Yield: one 9-inch pie.

Roseanna Stevens
Jacksonville, Florida

Salads Perk Up Your Menu

Salads, whether served as a main dish or side dish, add variety to your menu. The ones we offer here combine meat, eggs, cheese, fruit, vegetables, and even rice for some refreshing ideas.

LAYERED SHRIMP SALAD

3 cups water
1 pound unpeeled fresh small shrimp
2 cups uncooked corkscrew macaroni
¼ cup chopped fresh parsley
3 cups coarsely shredded iceberg lettuce
2 cups unpeeled, chopped cucumber
1½ cups sliced celery
3 cups chopped tomatoes
1 (8-ounce) bottle bacon-and-tomato salad dressing
½ cup commercial sour cream

Bring water to a boil; add shrimp, and cook 3 to 5 minutes. Drain well; rinse with cold water. Chill. Peel and devein shrimp; set aside.

Cook macaroni according to package directions; drain. Rinse with cold water, and drain well. Add parsley; toss gently.

Layer lettuce, cucumber, macaroni mixture, celery, tomatoes, and shrimp in a large salad bowl.

Combine salad dressing and sour cream; stir well. Spread over top of salad, sealing to edge of bowl. Cover and chill. Toss salad before serving. Yield: 6 servings. *Cathy Darling*
Grafton, West Virginia

SPRINGTIME WILD RICE SALAD

1 (6-ounce) package long-grain and wild rice mix
2⅓ cups water
½ pound fresh asparagus, cut into 1-inch pieces
1 small sweet red or green pepper, cut into ½-inch pieces
¼ cup vegetable oil
2 tablespoons white wine vinegar
Lettuce leaves
1 small purple onion, sliced into rings

Combine rice mix and water in a heavy saucepan. Bring to a boil; cover, reduce heat, and simmer 20 minutes. Add asparagus, and cook an additional 5 minutes or until rice is tender and water is absorbed. Cover and chill. Stir in red pepper.

Combine oil and vinegar; stir into rice mixture. Cover and chill. Spoon onto a lettuce-lined dish, and garnish with onion rings. Yield: 6 servings.
Cathy Williams
Vale, North Carolina

CHUTNEYED RICE SALAD

1 cup uncooked long-grain rice
1 medium apple, chopped
½ cup chopped celery
¼ cup raisins
2 tablespoons chopped green onions
2 tablespoons chopped pecans, toasted
¼ cup vegetable oil
1 tablespoon lemon juice
¼ cup plus 2 tablespoons chutney
¼ teaspoon ground ginger
⅛ teaspoon white pepper

Cook rice according to package directions; cool.

Combine rice and next 5 ingredients in a large bowl; mix well. Combine oil, lemon juice, chutney, ginger, and pepper in a small bowl; pour over rice mixture, tossing gently to coat. Cover and chill at least 2 hours. Yield: 8 servings.
Sara A. McCullough
Broaddus, Texas

CRUNCHY-CREAMY SALAD

¾ cup crumbled blue cheese
¼ cup plus 2 tablespoons milk
3 tablespoons lemon juice
⅛ teaspoon Worcestershire sauce
4 cups torn lettuce
½ cup chopped celery
2 green onions, sliced
2 slices boiled ham, cut into strips
2 tomatoes, quartered
2 hard-cooked eggs, quartered
¼ teaspoon celery seeds (optional)
Crumbled blue cheese (optional)

Combine ¾ cup blue cheese, milk, lemon juice, and Worcestershire sauce in a small mixing bowl; stir well. Cover and chill.

Combine lettuce, celery, and green onions; toss gently. Arrange lettuce mixture on individual salad plates; place ham strips, tomatoes, and eggs on lettuce mixture. Spoon dressing over salad. If desired, sprinkle celery seeds and additional blue cheese over dressing. Yield: 4 servings.
Eleanor K. Brandt
Arlington, Texas

JIFFY WALDORF SALAD

½ (8-ounce) package cream cheese, softened
¼ cup milk
1 tablespoon lemon juice
2 teaspoons lemon juice
2 medium apples, cored and cut into wedges
1 cup seedless green grapes
½ cup pitted dates, halved
Lettuce leaves
½ cup chopped walnuts

Combine cream cheese, milk, and 1 tablespoon lemon juice; beat until smooth. Sprinkle 2 teaspoons lemon juice over apples.

Arrange apples, grapes, and dates on a lettuce-lined tray. Drizzle with cream cheese mixture, and sprinkle with walnuts. Yield: 4 servings.
Mrs. Don Walker
Delray Beach, Florida

Mexican Dip In Minutes

If you like chile con queso, a dip made with green chiles and cheese, you're sure to relish this version of the traditional Tex-Mex appetizer. Yvonne Greer of Greenville, South Carolina, uses jalapeño-flavored process cheese and spinach to make Easy Spinach con Queso.

EASY SPINACH CON QUESO

1 (10-ounce) package frozen chopped spinach, thawed
1 pound process cheese with mild jalapeño peppers, cut into cubes
½ cup milk
1 small onion, diced
1 (2-ounce) jar diced pimiento, drained
1 medium tomato, diced

Place spinach between paper towels, and squeeze until barely moist. Set spinach aside.

Combine cheese, milk, onion, and pimiento in top of a double boiler; bring water to a boil. Reduce heat to low; cook until cheese melts.

Add spinach and tomato, stirring well. Serve warm with tortilla chips. Yield: 2 cups.

Flavor Vegetables With Herbs

From black-eyed peas and broccoli to artichokes and leeks, these recipes showcase the seasoning power of herbs. Because you don't often find fresh herbs at this time of the year, these recipes call for dried. You can substitute fresh herbs when they're available by using three times the amount specified for dried.

ARTICHOKES VINAIGRETTE

2 (9-ounce) packages frozen artichoke hearts
1 (4-ounce) jar pimiento, drained and chopped
½ cup vegetable oil
½ cup white wine vinegar
2 tablespoons chopped sweet pickle
1 tablespoon dried whole oregano
½ teaspoon dried basil leaves

Cook artichokes according to package directions; drain. Place in a glass bowl. Add pimiento, and toss gently.

Combine oil and remaining ingredients in a jar; cover tightly, and shake vigorously. Pour over artichokes; toss gently. Chill until ready to serve. Serve with a slotted spoon. Yield: 6 to 8 servings.   *Bee Harper*
Naples, Florida

MARINATED BLACK-EYED PEAS

1 (16-ounce) package dried black-eyed peas
1 teaspoon salt
⅔ cup vegetable oil
¼ cup plus 1 tablespoon red wine vinegar
1 cup chopped onion
1 cup chopped fresh parsley
2 cloves garlic, crushed
2 teaspoons dried basil leaves
1 teaspoon dried whole oregano
½ teaspoon dry mustard
½ teaspoon pepper
Dash of crushed red pepper
Green pepper rings (optional)

Sort and wash peas; place in a Dutch oven. Cover with water 2 inches above peas, and soak 8 hours. Drain. Add salt to peas; cover with water. Cover and cook over low heat 45 minutes or until tender. Drain.

Combine oil and next 9 ingredients, stirring well; pour over peas, and toss gently. Cover and chill, stirring occasionally. Serve with a slotted spoon. Garnish with green pepper rings, if desired. Yield: 8 to 10 servings.   *Mrs. C. Gibson*
Brooksville, Florida

HERBED BROCCOLI

1½ pounds fresh broccoli
2 chicken-flavored bouillon cubes
1 cup water
¼ cup chopped onion
1 teaspoon dried marjoram leaves
1 teaspoon dried basil leaves
3 tablespoons butter or margarine, melted

Trim off large leaves of broccoli. Remove tough ends of lower stalks, and wash broccoli thoroughly. Cut into spears. Set aside.

Combine bouillon cubes and water in a large skillet; cook over medium heat until bouillon dissolves. Stir in onion, marjoram, and basil. Add broccoli; cover, reduce heat, and simmer 10 minutes or until tender. Drain and arrange broccoli on a serving platter; drizzle with melted butter. Yield: 6 servings.
Mrs. Joseph Laux
Toney, Alabama

DILLED GREEN BEANS

1 pound fresh green beans
1 teaspoon salt
⅓ cup sliced green onions
2 tablespoons vegetable oil
1 tablespoon red wine vinegar
2 teaspoons dried whole dillweed
½ teaspoon dry mustard
⅛ teaspoon freshly ground pepper

Wash beans; trim ends, and remove strings. Cut beans into 1½-inch pieces. Add water to a depth of 1 inch in a large saucepan; bring water to a boil over high heat. Add salt and beans. Cover, reduce heat, and simmer 10 to 12 minutes or until beans are crisp-tender.

Drain beans, and return to pan. Add green onions; keep beans and onions warm.

Combine oil, vinegar, dillweed, mustard, and pepper; stir vigorously, using a wire whisk. Pour dressing mixture over bean mixture, and toss gently. Yield: 4 servings.

Janet M. Filer
Arlington, Virginia

CARROT-AND-LEEK MEDLEY

1¼ cups water
¼ cup vegetable oil
Juice of 1 lemon
1 large clove garlic
1 small bay leaf
½ teaspoon salt
½ teaspoon dried whole thyme
½ teaspoon dried whole
   rosemary, crushed
¼ teaspoon white pepper
1 pound carrots, scraped and
   sliced
1 pound leeks, split lengthwise
   (about 4 medium)
Lemon slices
Sprig of fresh parsley

Combine first 9 ingredients in a large skillet; bring to a boil. Add carrots and leeks; cover, reduce heat, and simmer 5 minutes or until vegetables are crisp-tender. Remove garlic clove and bay leaf. Arrange vegetables on a serving platter. Spoon cooking liquid over vegetables, if desired. Garnish with lemon and parsley. Yield: 6 servings. *Mrs. C. D. Marshall*
Boston, Virginia

Everyday Entrées

Whether you're cooking for the family or friends, you'll enjoy preparing recipes that are substantial enough to be a meal in themselves. For any of these entrées, all you'll need to add is salad and bread.

CHILI BEAN ROAST

1 (3- to 3½-pound) beef round tip
   roast
1½ teaspoons spicy brown
   mustard
2 tablespoons brown sugar
1½ teaspoons chili powder
½ teaspoon salt
¼ teaspoon pepper
1 (15½-ounce) can Mexican-style
   chili beans, undrained
1 cup chopped onion

Trim excess fat from roast. Spread mustard on all sides of roast. Combine sugar, chili powder, salt, and pepper; rub on all sides of roast. Place roast in a Dutch oven; top with beans and onion. Cover and bake at 350° for 2½ hours or until done. Yield: about 8 servings.
Dorothy Nieman
Dunnellon, Florida

ROYAL MEATBALLS

2 pounds ground beef
1 cup finely chopped onion
1½ teaspoons ground ginger
1½ teaspoons ground coriander
1 teaspoon chili powder
1 teaspoon paprika
1 teaspoon lemon-pepper
   seasoning
1 teaspoon salt
1 teaspoon chopped fresh parsley
1 (32-ounce) jar spaghetti sauce
2 cups finely chopped onion
2 cloves garlic, minced
1 tablespoon plus 1 teaspoon
   paprika
2 teaspoons chili powder
2 teaspoons grated fresh
   gingerroot
1½ teaspoons ground coriander
Hot cooked spaghetti

Combine first 9 ingredients; mix well. Shape mixture into 1½-inch balls; place meatballs on broiler pan, and bake at 300° for 20 minutes, turning after 10 minutes. Remove from oven, and drain meatballs on paper towels; set aside.
Combine spaghetti sauce and next 6 ingredients in a large Dutch oven. Cover and cook over medium heat 10 minutes. Add meatballs, and cook an additional 5 minutes. Serve over cooked spaghetti. Yield: 8 servings.
Sambhu N. Banik
Bethesda, Maryland

CAJUN CHICKEN OVER RICE

1½ pounds boneless chicken
   breast halves, cut into 1-inch
   pieces
⅛ teaspoon garlic powder
5 large tomatoes, peeled and
   chopped
2 large onions, chopped
1 large green pepper, chopped
¼ cup Worcestershire sauce
¼ cup soy sauce
1 to 2 teaspoons pepper
1 teaspoon dried whole basil
1 teaspoon dried whole marjoram
1 teaspoon dried whole oregano
Hot cooked rice

Sprinkle chicken with garlic powder; set aside.
Combine tomatoes and remaining ingredients except rice in a large Dutch oven. Bring to a boil; reduce heat, and simmer 15 minutes. Add chicken; return to a boil. Cover, reduce heat, and simmer 30 minutes or until tender. Serve over rice. Yield: 6 servings. *K. Michelle Cobb*
Roxboro, North Carolina

THICK 'N' CRUSTY
CHICKEN POT PIE

1 (2½- to 3-pound) broiler-fryer
1 onion, quartered
1 stalk celery, cut into large
   pieces
1 teaspoon dried whole basil
1 teaspoon dried whole thyme
1 teaspoon dried whole rosemary
   leaves, crushed
1 teaspoon salt
1 bay leaf
1 cup finely chopped celery
1 cup finely chopped onion
1 cup finely chopped carrot
1 cup finely chopped potato
⅓ cup butter or margarine,
   melted
½ cup all-purpose flour
1½ cups half-and-half
½ teaspoon salt
¼ teaspoon pepper
Pastry (recipe follows)
1 egg
1 tablespoon milk

Combine first 8 ingredients in a Dutch oven. Cover with water, and bring to a boil; cover, reduce heat, and simmer 1 hour or until tender. Remove chicken from broth; strain broth, reserving 1½ cups. Cool chicken. Remove chicken from bone; chop meat.

Sauté 1 cup each of celery, onion, carrot, and potato in butter until crisp-tender. Add flour, stirring until smooth. Cook 1 minute, stirring constantly. Gradually add reserved broth and half-and-half; cook over medium heat, stirring constantly, until thickened and bubbly. Stir in ½ teaspoon salt, pepper, and chopped chicken.

Roll half of pastry to ⅛-inch thickness on a lightly floured surface. Fit into a 9½-inch deep-dish pieplate. Spoon chicken mixture into pastry.

Roll remaining pastry to ⅛-inch thickness, and place over chicken filling. Trim, seal, and flute edges. Roll out dough scraps, and cut into a chicken or desired shape. Dampen with water, and arrange over pastry, if desired. Cut slits in top of pastry to allow steam to escape.

Combine egg and milk; blend well. Brush over pastry. Bake at 400° for 30 minutes or until golden brown. Yield: 6 servings.

Pastry

3 cups all-purpose flour
1 teaspoon salt
1 cup shortening
1 egg, beaten
¼ cup plus 1 tablespoon ice
    water
1 tablespoon vinegar

Combine flour and salt; cut in shortening with pastry blender until mixture resembles coarse meal.

Combine egg, ice water, and vinegar; sprinkle evenly over surface, and stir with a fork until dry ingredients are moistened. Shape into a ball. Yield: enough for one double-crust 9-inch pie.   *Sally Murphy*
                    Allen, Texas

Tip: *Revive the flavor of long-dried herbs by soaking them for 10 minutes in lemon juice.*

SWEET-AND-SOUR SHRIMP AND CHICKEN

¼ cup firmly packed brown sugar
2 tablespoons cornstarch
¾ teaspoon ground ginger
¼ teaspoon garlic powder
¼ teaspoon curry powder
1 tablespoon Worcestershire
    sauce
1½ cups pineapple juice
⅓ cup wine vinegar
¼ cup soy sauce
¼ cup catsup
1½ pounds unpeeled medium-size
    fresh shrimp
1 tablespoon butter or margarine,
    melted
1 tablespoon olive oil
2 cups cubed cooked chicken
    (about 3 breast halves)
1 cup unsalted cashew nuts
Hot cooked rice

Combine first 10 ingredients in a saucepan. Cook over medium heat 5 minutes or until clear and thickened, stirring frequently. Set aside.

Peel and devein shrimp. Sauté in butter and oil in a skillet 3 minutes. Add chicken and nuts; sauté 2 minutes. Add sauce; cook until heated; stir occasionally. Serve over rice. Yield: 6 servings.   *Beth R. McClain*
                Grand Prairie, Texas

SPICY CHICKEN DISH

2½ pounds chicken breast halves
2 cups chopped onion
1 large green pepper, chopped
4 cloves garlic, minced
1 tablespoon olive oil
2 tablespoons all-purpose flour
2 (16-ounce) cans whole
    tomatoes, undrained and
    chopped
1 (6-ounce) can tomato paste
1½ tablespoons Worcestershire
    sauce
1¼ teaspoons salt
¾ teaspoon pepper
½ teaspoon chili powder
¼ teaspoon dried whole basil
1 bay leaf
4 cups hot cooked rice
⅓ cup chopped fresh parsley
Gumbo filé

Cook chicken in boiling salted water to cover 30 minutes. Drain chicken, reserving 3 cups broth; let chicken cool. Skin, bone, and chop chicken; set aside.

Sauté onion, green pepper, and garlic in hot oil in a large Dutch oven until tender. Stir in flour; cook 1 minute, stirring constantly. Gradually add reserved broth. Add tomatoes and next 7 ingredients; stir well. Bring to a boil, stirring constantly. Reduce heat, and simmer, uncovered, 1 hour. Add chicken; cook until heated. Remove bay leaf.

Combine rice and parsley; stir well. Serve chicken mixture over rice; sprinkle with filé powder. Yield: 6 to 8 servings.   *Mrs. Phillip Rose*
                Harrisonburg, Virginia

Zesty Watercress

Watercress is somewhat of a mystery to most of us. It's a vegetable we've heard of and seen in the grocery store, but few of us eat it regularly. Before dismissing it as just another salad green or garnish, take a closer look.

Keep in mind that the dark green color of watercress is evidence of its richness in vitamins and minerals. Sold in bunches, it is usually available year-round.

WATERCRESS SPREAD

2 (3-ounce) packages cream
    cheese
2 tablespoons milk
½ cup minced watercress
¼ teaspoon onion powder
¼ teaspoon dry mustard
¼ teaspoon white pepper

Combine all ingredients in a small bowl; stir well. Spread on party bread. Yield: 1¾ cups.

WATERCRESS MOUSSE

1 envelope unflavored gelatin
¼ cup cold water
1 cup chicken broth
½ teaspoon salt
½ teaspoon white pepper
¼ teaspoon dried whole
  rosemary, crushed
3 egg yolks, beaten
3 cups finely chopped cooked
  chicken
1½ cups watercress, trimmed and
  torn
3 tablespoons lemon juice
1 cup whipping cream
Additional watercress (optional)

Sprinkle unflavored gelatin over cold water; let stand 5 minutes.

Heat chicken broth in top of a double boiler; add salt, pepper, and rosemary. Add gelatin mixture; cook over low heat until gelatin dissolves. Gradually stir one-fourth of hot mixture into egg yolks; add to remaining hot mixture, stirring constantly. Cook, stirring constantly, until mixture thickens and coats a metal spoon; cool. Chill until consistency of unbeaten egg white. Stir in chicken, 1½ cups torn watercress, and lemon juice. Beat whipping cream until stiff peaks form; fold into mixture.

Pour into a lightly oiled 5-cup mold; chill until mixture is firm. Unmold onto a serving plate. Garnish mousse with additional watercress, if desired. Yield: 6 servings.

WATERCRESS SOUP

¼ cup butter or margarine
¼ cup all-purpose flour
1½ cups milk
1 chicken-flavored bouillon cube
1 cup water
1 cup watercress leaves
¼ cup thinly sliced green onions
2 tablespoons minced celery
Additional watercress (optional)
Commercial sour cream (optional)

Melt butter in a medium saucepan over low heat; add flour, stirring until smooth. Cook 1 minute, stirring constantly. Gradually add milk; cook

over medium heat, stirring constantly, until slightly thickened. Add bouillon cube and next 4 ingredients; cook 5 minutes. Spoon mixture into container of an electric blender; process until smooth. If desired, garnish with watercress and sour cream. Serve immediately. Yield: 3 cups.

WATERCRESS-AND-MUSHROOM SALAD

9 cups watercress, trimmed and
  torn (about ½ pound)
½ pound fresh mushrooms, sliced
½ cup vegetable oil
¼ cup white wine vinegar
1 clove garlic, crushed
½ teaspoon dry mustard
½ teaspoon salt
½ teaspoon sugar
¼ teaspoon pepper

Combine watercress and mushrooms in a bowl; cover and chill.

Combine oil and remaining ingredients in a jar. Cover tightly, and shake vigorously. Just before serving, shake dressing, and pour over salad; toss gently. Yield: 6 to 8 servings.
Anna Robinson
Oak Ridge, Tennessee

Sausage To Suit Your Taste

Many people pick a favorite brand of bulk sausage and look for it each time they shop. But Louise Denmon of Silsbee, Texas, likes the kind she makes at home best of all. She serves Basic Sausage for breakfast and skillfully adds herbs and spices for different flavors.

Sausage made at home using lean ground pork often contains less fat than many commercial brands. The amount of fat can be reduced even more by buying a lean cut of pork and asking the butcher to trim all visible fat before grinding the meat.

BASIC SAUSAGE

1 pound ground pork
2 teaspoons rubbed sage
1 teaspoon salt
½ teaspoon pepper

Combine all ingredients, mixing well. Shape into 6 patties about ½-inch thick. Cook patties in a large skillet over medium heat 5 to 7 minutes on each side. Drain. Yield: 6 servings.

Garlic Sausage: Add 1 clove garlic, minced, to Basic Sausage mixture; mix well.

Italian Sausage: Add 2 teaspoons paprika and ½ teaspoon fennel seeds to Basic Sausage mixture; mix well.

Country Sausage: Add ½ teaspoon ground marjoram and ¼ teaspoon ground thyme to Basic Sausage mixture; mix well.

Spiced Country Sausage: Add ¼ teaspoon ground cloves and ¼ teaspoon ground mace to Basic Sausage mixture; mix well.

Right: *At your next luncheon, serve (clockwise from front) Southwestern Chicken Salad, Fruited Chicken Salad, or Aspic-Topped Chicken Salad. (Recipes, page 88.)*

Pages 106 and 107: *A Southern fish fry includes (left to right) French-Fried Onion Rings, Crisp-Fried Catfish, Fried Okra, and Peppery Hush Puppies. Fried Frog Legs (inset) are a delicacy. (Recipes begin on page 110.)*

Page 108: *Peppers are the main ingredient in Southwestern fare. For identification, see page 115.*

MAY

Take Pride In Southern Fried

Whether it's a fish fry, a barbecue, a Sunday dinner, or a backyard gathering of friends, our Southern heritage dictates that some of our favorite foods be crisp-fried and golden brown. For years, we've proudly fried foods, using one of two methods—deep-frying or pan-frying. Deep-frying involves immersing the entire piece of food in hot oil; less oil is used to pan-fry.

See "From Our Kitchen to Yours," on page 112 for more information about both methods of frying.

CRISP-FRIED CATFISH
(pictured on pages 106 and 107)

1 quart water
¼ cup vinegar
3 tablespoons salt
6 (10- to 12-ounce) catfish, cleaned and dressed
1½ cups cornmeal
½ cup all-purpose flour
½ teaspoon salt
½ teaspoon onion powder
1 teaspoon seasoned salt
Vegetable oil
1 medium onion, sliced (optional)
Parsley sprigs (optional)
Lemon slices (optional)

Combine first 3 ingredients in a large bowl. Soak catfish in vinegar mixture 4 to 5 hours in the refrigerator.

Combine cornmeal, flour, ½ teaspoon salt, onion powder, and seasoned salt in a plastic bag, shaking to mix. Add catfish, one at a time, and shake until completely coated. Pour oil to depth of 2 to 3 inches into a Dutch oven; heat to 375°. Fry catfish 4 minutes on each side or until golden brown. Drain well.

If desired, dredge onion slices in cornmeal mixture; fry onion slices in hot oil until golden brown. Drain well. Serve immediately. If desired, garnish fish with parsley sprigs and lemon slices. Yield: 6 servings.
*E. G. Dosier
Sparta, North Carolina*

FRIED FROG LEGS
(pictured on page 107)

2 pounds frog legs
2 eggs, beaten
2 tablespoons mayonnaise
1 tablespoon cornstarch
1 tablespoon lemon juice
½ teaspoon baking powder
¼ teaspoon salt
⅛ teaspoon pepper
⅔ cup all-purpose flour
⅓ cup seasoned dry breadcrumbs
Vegetable oil

Arrange frog legs in a shallow container. Combine eggs, mayonnaise, cornstarch, lemon juice, baking powder, salt, and pepper; stir until smooth. Pour over frog legs; cover and chill for at least 30 minutes.

Combine flour and breadcrumbs in a plastic bag. Remove legs from marinade, shaking off excess; place 2 or 3 legs at a time in flour mixture. Close bag securely; shake until legs are well coated. Pour oil to depth of 2 to 3 inches into a Dutch oven; heat to 375°. Fry legs 1 to 2 minutes or until dark golden brown; drain on paper towels. Yield: 6 servings.

Note: Two pounds orange roughy fillets, cut into fingers, or two pounds peeled shrimp may be substituted for frog legs. Yield: 6 servings.
*Susie Pharr
New Iberia, Louisiana*

SUNDAY DINNER FRIED CHICKEN

1 cup all-purpose flour
¼ cup cornmeal
1 teaspoon salt
½ teaspoon pepper
1 (2½- to 3-pound) broiler-fryer, cut up
½ cup vegetable oil
2 tablespoons butter or margarine
2 tablespoons all-purpose flour
1¼ cups milk
¼ teaspoon salt
⅛ teaspoon pepper

Combine flour, cornmeal, 1 teaspoon salt, and ½ teaspoon pepper in a plastic bag; shake to mix. Place 2 or 3 chicken pieces in bag; shake well. Repeat with remaining chicken pieces.

Heat oil and butter in a large skillet. Add chicken, and brown on both sides over high heat (375°). Cover, reduce heat to medium, and cook 20 minutes. Uncover chicken, and cook an additional 10 minutes or until golden brown. Drain chicken on paper towels, reserving 2 tablespoons drippings in skillet.

Add 2 tablespoons flour to drippings, stirring until smooth. Cook 1 minute, stirring constantly. Gradually add milk; cook over medium heat, stirring constantly, until mixture is thickened and bubbly. Stir in ¼ teaspoon salt and ⅛ teaspoon pepper. Serve gravy with chicken. Yield: 4 servings.
*Catherine Bearden
Bostwick, Georgia*

CHICKEN-FRIED STEAKS

1 egg, slightly beaten
½ cup buttermilk
½ cup water
1 teaspoon Worcestershire sauce
⅔ cup dry breadcrumbs
1⅓ cups all-purpose flour
½ teaspoon salt
½ teaspoon pepper
6 (4-ounce) cubed steaks
Vegetable oil
¼ cup all-purpose flour
2 cups milk
½ teaspoon salt
½ teaspoon pepper

Combine first 4 ingredients, mixing well. Set aside.

Combine breadcrumbs, 1⅓ cups flour, ½ teaspoon salt, and ½ teaspoon pepper, mixing well. Dip steaks in buttermilk mixture; dredge in flour mixture. Let stand 10 minutes on paper towels. Pour vegetable oil to depth of ¼ inch into heavy skillet. Fry steaks in hot oil (375°) over medium-high heat until browned, adding oil as necessary. Remove and drain on paper towels; set aside. Pour off pan drippings, reserving 3 tablespoons in skillet.

Add ¼ cup flour to drippings; stir over medium heat until bubbly. Boil 1 minute, stirring constantly. Add 2 cups milk; cook until thickened, stirring constantly. Stir in remaining salt and pepper. Add steaks; cover and simmer 5 minutes. Yield: 6 servings.
Norma Cowden
Shawnee, Oklahoma

SOUTHERN FRIED OYSTERS

1 cup self-rising cornmeal
1 cup self-rising flour
¼ teaspoon red pepper (optional)
2 eggs
2 tablespoons milk
2 (12-ounce) containers fresh
   Select oysters, drained
Vegetable oil

Combine cornmeal, flour, and, if desired, pepper, stirring well. Combine eggs and milk, beating well with a fork. Dip oysters in egg mixture, and dredge in flour mixture. Pour oil to depth of 2 to 3 inches into Dutch oven. Heat to 375°. Fry oysters in oil until golden, turning once. Drain on paper towels. Yield: 6 servings.
Betty Howlett
Homewood, Alabama

FRIED OKRA
(pictured on pages 106 and 107)

1 pound fresh okra
2 eggs, beaten
¼ cup buttermilk
1 cup self-rising flour
1 cup self-rising cornmeal
Vegetable oil

Wash and slice okra; pat dry with paper towels. Combine eggs and buttermilk; add okra, and let stand for 10 minutes.

Combine flour and cornmeal. Drain okra, small portions at a time, using a slotted spoon. Dredge okra, small portions at a time, in flour mixture. Pour oil to depth of 2 to 3 inches into a Dutch oven or heavy saucepan. Heat to 375°. Fry okra until golden brown. Drain on paper towels, and serve immediately. Yield: 4 servings.
Peggy Hardy
Huntsville, Alabama

FRENCH-FRIED ONION RINGS
(pictured on pages 106 and 107)

2 large Spanish onions
2¼ cups all-purpose flour, divided
1¼ teaspoons baking powder
1¼ teaspoons salt
¼ teaspoon white pepper
2 cups buttermilk
1½ tablespoons vegetable oil
2 eggs, separated
Vegetable oil

Peel onions; cut into ½-inch slices, and separate into rings. Place in a plastic or paper bag; add 1 cup flour. Shake until rings are coated.

Combine remaining 1¼ cups flour, baking powder, and next 4 ingredients; stir in egg yolks, mixing well. Beat egg whites (at room temperature) until stiff peaks form; fold into batter. Dip onion rings in batter. Pour oil to depth of 2 to 3 inches into a Dutch oven; heat to 375°. Fry, turning once, until golden brown. Drain on paper towels, and serve immediately. Yield: 4 servings.
Mrs. Theron Trimble
Warrington, Florida

FRIED EGGPLANT

2 eggs
1 cup milk
1 large eggplant, peeled and cut
   into ½-inch slices
2 cups seasoned dry breadcrumbs
Vegetable oil

Combine eggs and milk; beat well. Dip eggplant slices in egg mixture; dredge in breadcrumbs.

Pour oil to depth of ½ inch into a heavy skillet. Heat to 350°. Fry eggplant, about 8 slices at a time, over medium heat 2 minutes on each side or until golden. Repeat with remaining eggplant, adding oil as needed. Drain on paper towels. Yield: 6 to 8 servings.
Pam Hidalgo
Iberville, Louisiana

PEPPERY HUSH PUPPIES
(pictured on pages 106 and 107)

2 cups cornmeal
½ cup pancake mix
1 teaspoon baking powder
2½ teaspoons sugar
1 teaspoon salt
½ cup diced onion
½ cup diced green pepper
2 jalapeño peppers, seeded and
   diced
1 egg
1 cup buttermilk
2 tablespoons vegetable oil
⅛ teaspoon hot sauce
Vegetable oil

Combine first 8 ingredients; stir well. Add egg, buttermilk, 2 tablespoons oil, and hot sauce, stirring well.

Pour oil to depth of 2 to 3 inches into a Dutch oven or heavy saucepan. Heat to 375°. Carefully drop batter by rounded tablespoonfuls into oil; cook only a few at a time, turning once. Fry 1 to 2 minutes on each side or until golden brown. Drain on paper towels, and serve immediately. Yield: about 4 dozen. *Pam Clayton*
Ferriday, Louisiana

Tip: *Use tongs to turn frying foods. Food can easily slip off a fork and splatter the grease.*

GREEN ONION HOECAKES

1 egg, slightly beaten
1½ cups self-rising cornmeal
1¼ cups buttermilk
1 tablespoon vegetable oil
¼ cup chopped green onions
¼ cup vegetable oil

Combine first 5 ingredients; mix.

Heat ¼ cup oil to 375° in a large skillet over high heat. For each hoecake, pour ¼ cup batter into skillet. Fry 3 minutes on each side or until browned, adding extra oil as needed. Yield: 8 servings.   *Jan Hayes*
Rural Hall, North Carolina

PINEAPPLE FRITTERS

1¼ cups all-purpose flour
1½ teaspoons baking powder
¼ teaspoon salt
2 teaspoons sugar
1 egg, slightly beaten
¼ cup plus 2 tablespoons milk
1 tablespoon vegetable oil
1 (8-ounce) can crushed
  pineapple, drained
Vegetable oil
Glaze (recipe follows)

Combine flour, baking powder, salt, and sugar in a large bowl; stir well. Set mixture aside.

Combine egg and next 3 ingredients in a small bowl; mix well. Add to dry ingredients; stir mixture just until moistened.

Pour oil to depth of 2 to 3 inches into a Dutch oven or heavy saucepan; heat to 375°. Carefully drop batter by rounded tablespoonfuls into oil; cook only a few at a time, turning once. Fry 2 to 3 minutes or until fritters are golden brown. Drain well on paper towels. Pour glaze over fritters. Drain on a wire rack. Yield: 1½ dozen fritters.

Glaze

1 cup sifted powdered sugar
2 tablespoons milk

Combine ingredients, mixing well. Yield: about ¼ cup.
Connie L. Simpson
Lebanon, Missouri

SOPAIPILLAS

1 package dry yeast
2 tablespoons warm water (105°
  to 115°)
3 cups all-purpose flour
½ teaspoon salt
1 tablespoon shortening
1¼ to 1½ cups buttermilk
Vegetable oil

Dissolve yeast in warm water; let stand 5 minutes.

Combine flour and salt; cut in shortening. Make a well in center of mixture. Add yeast mixture and enough buttermilk to make a soft dough. Turn dough out onto a floured surface, and knead 5 or 6 times. Place in a well-greased bowl, turning to grease top. Cover and let rise in a warm place (85°), free from drafts, 1 hour or until doubled in bulk.

Punch dough down; cover and let rise in a warm place, free from drafts, 30 to 45 minutes or until doubled in bulk.

Punch dough down. Turn out onto a lightly floured surface. Roll dough to ⅛-inch thickness; cut with a 2½-inch cutter.

Pour oil to depth of 2 to 3 inches into Dutch oven or heavy saucepan; heat to 375°. Fry a few at a time in oil until puffed and browned, turning once. Drain on paper towels. Serve with honey. Yield: about 3 dozen.
Sonya J. Grob
Norman, Oklahoma

FRIED APPLE PIES

1 (8-ounce) package dried apples
1 cup water
⅓ cup sugar
1 tablespoon butter or margarine
1 (10-ounce) can flaky biscuits
Vegetable oil

Combine apples and water in a saucepan; bring to a boil. Cover, reduce heat, and simmer 30 minutes or until tender. Cool. Mash slightly, if necessary. Stir in sugar and butter; set mixture aside.

Roll each biscuit into a 5-inch circle on a lightly floured surface. Place about 2 tablespoons apple mixture on half of each biscuit circle. To seal pies, dip fingers in water and moisten edges of circle; fold in half, making sure edges are even. Using a fork dipped in flour, press edges firmly together.

Pour oil to depth of ½ inch into a heavy skillet. Fry pies in hot oil (375°) over medium-high heat on both sides until golden, turning once. Drain well on paper towels. Yield: 10 turnovers.

Note: Three cooking apples may be substituted for dried apples. Peel and chop apples; combine apple and ½ cup water in a saucepan. Cook 10 minutes or until soft; drain. Stir in ⅓ cup sugar and 1 tablespoon butter; set aside. Follow remaining instructions.
Clairiece Gilbert Humphrey
Charlottesville, Virginia

From Our Kitchen To Yours

A whiff of sizzling fried food floats through the air, whetting the appetite with images of golden brown delicacies. Southerners have long craved these mouth-watering morsels (see "Take Pride in Southern Fried" beginning on page 110). The sought-after crispness and nongreasy texture of these foods are obtained by using the correct cooking fat, frying technique, and temperature.

Food can be deep-fried or pan-fried. Deep-frying involves immersing food in hot oil, which rapidly browns the exterior while leaving the food moist on the inside. Pan-frying is a fast method of cooking thin strips of tender food. A thin layer of oil prevents sticking and adds flavor. Some foods pan-fry at a high initial temperature to brown and continue to cook at a reduced temperature.

Frying Techniques

If the oil is hot enough, a brittle shell forms around the food—preventing oil absorption, sealing in natural juices, and yielding food that is neither greasy nor soggy. This technique can be tricky. A temperature that is too high browns the surface before the inside is done; too low a temperature takes longer for the food to cook, resulting in fat absorption and an overcooked exterior. The ideal temperature for frying ranges from 325° to 400°. To keep an accurate oil temperature, use a thermometer and avoid fluctuations by adding small amounts of food at a time. All pieces should float freely.

Which Cooking Fat?

Fat used for frying should be odorless, bland tasting, and capable of reaching high temperatures. When overheated or smoking, fat begins to decompose and could burst into flame. Keep in mind that butter cannot be heated above 250°; vegetable shortening is limited to 370°. Vegetable oil is a good all-purpose cooking oil; peanut oil and corn oil may also be used for frying.

When properly cared for, oil can be reused at least once. Cool the hot oil, and pour through a sieve or several thicknesses of cheesecloth into clean, dry glass or heavy plastic containers. Cover and refrigerate oil. Discard when the color darkens or if foaming occurs when adding food.

Proper Equipment

A well-balanced container with proper depth, such as an electric deep-fryer or a 4- to 5-quart Dutch oven, is mandatory for deep-frying. For pan-frying, a deep, heavy skillet can be used.

Another important piece of equipment, a deep-fry thermometer takes the guesswork out of frying by registering the exact oil temperature. (The oil amount used in pan-frying is often too shallow for a thermometer.) In our test kitchens, we use a thermometer with an adjustable metal clip that attaches to the side of the Dutch oven or skillet, preventing the tip from touching the pan bottom.

Snappy Entrées

When time is short and everyone's hungry, a quick, nourishing entrée is in order. These entrée recipes offer heartiness and fast preparation.

GRILLED PORK CHOPS

4 (¾- to 1-inch-thick) pork chops
¼ teaspoon salt
¾ teaspoon lemon-pepper seasoning
½ teaspoon dried whole oregano

Sprinkle pork chops with salt, lemon-pepper, and oregano.

Place chops, 4 to 5 inches from coals. Grill over low to medium-hot coals 25 minutes or until the chops are no longer pink, turning once. Yield: 4 servings. *Lillian Mackay Lexington, South Carolina*

PEPPER STEAK

1½ pounds boneless sirloin steak
2 tablespoons vegetable oil
1 (10¾-ounce) can beef broth, undiluted
1 medium onion, sliced
2 medium-size green peppers, cut into ¼-inch strips
½ teaspoon garlic salt
½ teaspoon ground ginger
1 tablespoon plus 1 teaspoon cornstarch
2 teaspoons sugar
2 tablespoons soy sauce
2 medium tomatoes, peeled and cut into wedges
Hot cooked rice

Partially freeze steak; slice across grain into 2- x ¼-inch strips.

Brown steak in oil in a skillet over medium-high heat 4 to 6 minutes. Add beef broth and next 4 ingredients. Reduce heat, and simmer 5 minutes or until crisp-tender.

Combine cornstarch, sugar, and soy sauce, stirring well; add to beef

mixture. Bring to a boil; boil 1 minute, stirring constantly. Remove from heat. Add tomato wedges; toss gently. Serve over rice. Yield: 6 servings. *M. DeMello Hollywood, Florida*

VEAL PAPRIKA

1 pound veal cutlets
¼ cup all-purpose flour
Dash of salt
⅛ teaspoon pepper
1 to 2 tablespoons butter or margarine
1 to 2 tablespoons olive oil
1 small onion, sliced and separated into rings
1 tablespoon butter or margarine
1 teaspoon paprika
⅔ cup chicken broth
2 teaspoons lemon juice
Dash of salt
¼ teaspoon white pepper
⅓ cup commercial sour cream
2 teaspoons chopped fresh parsley
Hot cooked rice

Cut veal into 3- x ½-inch strips.

Combine flour, dash of salt, and ⅛ teaspoon pepper in a plastic bag; add veal, and shake until well coated.

Heat 1 tablespoon butter and 1 tablespoon olive oil in a large skillet. Add half of veal; brown on all sides. Remove from pan, and repeat procedure with remaining veal, adding more butter and olive oil if needed. Remove veal from pan.

Sauté onion in 1 tablespoon butter in skillet. Return veal to skillet; add paprika and next 4 ingredients. Bring to a boil; cover, reduce heat, and simmer 5 minutes. Stir in sour cream and parsley; cook just until thoroughly heated (do not boil). Serve over rice. Yield: 4 servings.

Sally Murphy Allen, Texas

EASY MEXICAN OMELET

3 eggs
½ teaspoon salt
¼ teaspoon pepper
1 tablespoon water
1 tablespoon butter or margarine
¾ cup (3 ounces) shredded
  Monterey Jack cheese
2 tablespoons sliced jalapeño
  peppers
2 tablespoons salsa

Combine first 4 ingredients; stir with a wire whisk just until blended.

Heat a heavy 8-inch skillet over medium heat until hot enough to sizzle a drop of water. Add butter, and rotate skillet to coat bottom. Pour egg mixture into skillet; sprinkle with cheese and jalapeño peppers. As mixture starts to cook, gently lift edges of omelet with a spatula, and tilt pan so that uncooked portion flows underneath. Fold omelet in half, and transfer to plate. Top with salsa. Yield: 1 or 2 servings.

Carole A. Brock
Mount Holly, Virginia

Fired Up About Peppers

Peppers, chiles, or chile peppers? Almost every pepper can claim several names depending on the stage of development or even the geographic region in which it was grown. Experts haven't agreed on official names for the specific types of peppers or even when to use the terms "chiles" or "peppers" or "chile peppers." Although there are some strong preferences for various definitions, "pepper" often refers to a sweet variety, and "chile" is a popular reference to any hot variety.

Generally, some type of chile seasons at least one dish in every Tex-Mex menu. The most commonly used are serranos, jalapeños (both about the size of your little finger), and long green chiles, often called Californias or Anaheims.

Poblanos (resembling darker, misshapen sweet bell peppers), anchos (leatherlike dried poblanos), and mulatos (resembling poblanos, but with blackish green skin) are the ones most used in Mexican recipes.

Knowing What's Hot

There's a rule of thumb to identify mild chiles—usually, the lighter green the skin and the blunter the tip, the milder the chile. Small dark-green chiles with pointed tips are often very hot.

Chile heat is determined by a substance called capsaicin, found mainly in the veins. The stem end of the chile is the hottest portion. Unfortunately, there's no way to determine the heat of an individual chile. A mild one and a blistering hot one can grow on the same plant.

Although heat may vary, common hot peppers are serranos, jalapeños, yellow wax peppers, and sometimes long green or red chiles. Poblanos, anchos, and mulatos have mild to medium pungency.

Removing the seeds and veins of the chile will make the flavor milder, but plastic gloves are recommended when handling hot peppers.

Cooking With Peppers

One of the most popular uses for peppers is in salsas (the Spanish word meaning sauces). In Texas, salsa usually means a chunky sauce consisting of a combination of pepper, onion, and tomato used to season foods. It can be spooned over tacos, scrambled eggs, refried beans, or served as a dip with crisp, home-fried tostados.

Chiles Rellenos is one of the most traditional pepper recipes you'll find. Chiles are stuffed with cheese or a spicy beef mixture, dipped in batter, and pan-fried or deep-fried. Deep-frying retains a prettier chile shape.

Making Chiles Rellenos is time-consuming, but a few pointers might make it easier. First, the chiles should be parched and peeled. Then, seeds and veins may be removed, but this is difficult to do without tearing the peppers. If the chiles do tear, the torn pieces should be overlapped and held carefully while battering. During frying, the batter will crust over the tear.

Fresh Chile Substitutes

If you can't find fresh peppers in your area, processed versions, sold in jars or cans, make good substitutes.

Canned green chiles, sold whole or chopped, can be interchanged with Anaheim green chiles or other varieties of **long green chiles.** They can be substituted for fresh in almost any recipe; however, Chiles Rellenos is one recipe that works best with fresh chiles.

If you've never peeled your own fresh chiles, you may be surprised to know that the result is identical to the chiles you'll find in the cans. One advantage of using the canned chiles is that they are already peeled, seeded, and destemmed.

You may find slight heat differences when substituting canned chiles. Canned ones are a little hotter.

Pickled jalapeños, sold in jars, make a good substitute for fresh **jalapeños** or even **serranos.** Even though the chiles are labeled "pickled," there is no pickle flavor. They have the same heat intensity as fresh. Although jalapeños are milder than yellow hot peppers, the jalapeños in jars can substitute for fresh **yellow hot peppers** also.

For **poblano chiles,** sweet green bell peppers make the best substitute, even though the bell peppers have no heat at all. Ground chili powder can be substituted for **ancho chiles,** the dried red version of poblanos. Use ½ teaspoon chili powder for each ancho chile.

Common peppers used in Southern recipes: **1.** *Anaheim green* **2.** *yellow wax* **3.** *jalapeño* **4.** *poblano/ancho* **5.** *serrano* **6.** *sweet green bell* **7.** *yellow bell* **8.** *red bell.* *(See page 108 for color photograph of these eight peppers.)*

Parching Chiles

Poblanos and long green chiles traditionally used for chiles rellenos generally need to be parched and peeled before using in cooked recipes. This is done to remove the tough transparent skin on the chiles. In some Southwestern or Mexican recipes the procedure is called roasting or blistering. Follow these instructions for parching:

—With a knife, pierce each chile near the stem to prevent bursting during roasting.

—Place the chiles on a baking sheet, and broil 4 to 5 inches from the heat source in a gas oven or 6 inches from heat in an electric oven. (The chiles may be parched on a gas grill 5 inches from heat.)

—Broil, turning chiles with tongs. Be sure the chiles blister rather than burn. Plunge parched chiles in ice water, or place them in a plastic bag, and seal to steam. Leave the chiles in the bag 10 to 15 minutes to loosen skins. For crisper chiles, place them in a sink or bowl, and cover with cracked ice.

Once chiles have been cooled or steamed, peel them, beginning at the stem ends, and pull the skin off. Then they are ready to use.

If the chiles specified in the following recipes are not available in your area, you can grow your own or use a chile similar in size and heat. For example, serranos and jalapeños can be used interchangeably. Sweet green peppers have no heat value, but they can replace poblanos if the recipe calls for fresh, chopped poblanos in a salad or sauce.

MEXICAN-STYLE CEVICHE

⅔ pound red snapper fillets, skinned and cut into ½-inch cubes
½ cup lime juice
1½ cups chopped onion
2 medium tomatoes, peeled and chopped
½ cup chopped fresh cilantro
1 (5-ounce) jar pimiento-stuffed olives
3 jalapeño peppers, seeded and chopped
3 tablespoons olive oil
3 tablespoons vinegar
1 teaspoon pepper
1 teaspoon ground oregano
1 teaspoon ground cumin
Lime slices
Additional fresh cilantro

Combine fish and lime juice in a shallow glass (not metal) dish, stirring to coat. Cover and chill 6 hours. Drain.

Layer onion, tomatoes, ½ cup cilantro, olives, and jalapeños over fish. Combine oil, vinegar, pepper, oregano, and cumin; stir well. Pour over layered ingredients (do not stir). Cover and chill 2 hours. Stir gently about 1 hour before serving time. Garnish with lime slices and cilantro. Yield: 8 appetizer servings.
Carol Barclay
Portland, Texas

SHRIMP-STUFFED JALAPEÑOS

1 cup water
⅓ pound unpeeled fresh medium shrimp
1 (3-ounce) package cream cheese, softened
1 tablespoon grated onion
1 teaspoon Worcestershire sauce
⅛ teaspoon garlic powder
Dash of salt
Dash of pepper
¼ pound jalapeño peppers
Additional red and green jalapeño pepper slices

Bring water to a boil in a 1-quart saucepan; add shrimp, and cook 3 to 5 minutes. Drain well; rinse with cold water. Peel and devein shrimp; chop.

Beat cream cheese until fluffy; stir in shrimp, grated onion, and next 4 ingredients. Chill.

Rinse peppers; remove stem ends. Cut ¼ pound peppers in half lengthwise; remove seeds. (Wear rubber gloves when working with peppers.) Stuff pepper halves with cream cheese mixture, and garnish with additional pepper slices. Yield: 14 appetizer servings.
Ruth Wilson
Normangee, Texas

HOT CHILE SALSA WITH HOMEMADE TOSTADOS

3 to 4 fresh yellow hot peppers
1 (14.5-ounce) can whole tomatoes, drained and chopped
1 small clove garlic, minced
½ teaspoon salt
12 corn tortillas
Vegetable oil

Remove stems from peppers; finely chop peppers. Combine chopped peppers and next 3 ingredients. Chill.

Cut each tortilla into four wedges. Fry pieces, a few at a time, in ¼ inch hot oil (375°) for 20 seconds on each side or until golden brown. Drain on paper towels. Serve with salsa. Yield: 48 appetizer servings.
Willette Rawlins
Dallas, Texas

PUERCO EN ADOBO

4 pounds country-style pork ribs
5 dried ancho chiles
6 serrano chiles, stems removed
1 (4-ounce) can chopped green
  chiles, drained
1 clove garlic
¾ cup vinegar
1 teaspoon salt
¼ teaspoon ground cumin
¼ teaspoon ground oregano
1 avocado, chopped (optional)
Radish slices (optional)

Place ribs in a large Dutch oven, and cover with water. Bring to a boil; cover, reduce heat, and simmer 1 hour. Drain.

Remove stems from ancho chiles; remove seeds. Tear each chile into several pieces; place in a saucepan, and cover with water. Bring to a boil; cover, reduce heat, and simmer 5 minutes. Drain. Combine ancho and serrano chiles in container of an electric blender; process until finely chopped. Add green chiles and next 5 ingredients; process until smooth.

Place ribs on a broiler rack; broil 6 inches from heat 10 to 15 minutes, turning once and brushing with sauce. If desired, garnish with chopped avocado and radish slices. Yield: 4 to 6 servings.

Edna Chadsey
Corpus Christi, Texas

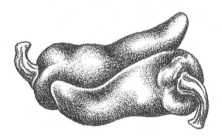

CHILES RELLENOS

12 fresh Anaheim green chiles
8 ounces Monterey Jack cheese
3 eggs, separated
¼ cup all-purpose flour
Vegetable oil
Tomato sauce (recipe follows)

Place chiles on a baking sheet; broil 5 to 6 inches from heat, turning often

with tongs, until chiles are blistered on all sides. Immediately place in a plastic storage bag; fasten securely, and let steam 10 to 15 minutes. Remove peel of each chile (chiles will be limp). If desired, carefully remove seeds, leaving sides of chiles and stem ends intact.

Cut cheese into ¼-inch-thick strips; place inside chiles, trimming strips to fit chiles, if necessary. (If chiles are torn, overlap torn sides; eggs and flour will hold them.)

Beat egg whites (at room temperature) until stiff peaks form; beat yolks until thick and lemon colored. Fold yolks into whites.

Dredge filled chiles in flour, coating well; dip in eggs. Fry chiles on both sides in 2 inches hot oil (375°) for 3 to 5 minutes or until browned. Drain. Serve warm with tomato sauce. Yield: 6 servings.

Tomato Sauce

1 small onion, sliced and
  separated into rings
2 tablespoons butter or
  margarine, melted
2 cups commercial tomato puree
1 teaspoon sugar
1 teaspoon dried parsley flakes
⅛ teaspoon ground cloves

Sauté onion in butter until tender. Stir in remaining ingredients; cook until thoroughly heated. Yield: about 2¼ cups.
Mrs. J. M. Paul
Amarillo, Texas

Stir Up
An Icy Refresher

The reputation of sorbets and granitas is as glittery as the ice crystals that make up these frozen concoctions. Hailing from Europe, they are spectacular presentations in the finest restaurants. And they're easy to make at home, too.

First cousins to ice cream and sherbet, these frozen treats don't contain milk and eggs (except for an occasional egg white added to sorbets to smooth the texture). The Italian version of an ice, **granitas** are coarser in texture than sorbets. They're stirred several times during freezing to help develop their granular appearance.

Smoother in texture and almost like sherbet, **sorbets** are the French ice. They're often mixed in a food processor after freezing to smooth out the ice crystals.

Traditionally, sorbets and granitas were served between courses to cleanse the palate. Sweeter versions, however, often double as dessert. You'll find that versions not so sweet work well as an appetizer.

But no matter when you serve them, most granitas and sorbets are considered prime choices by those who choose light cuisine. They're often made from fresh ingredients, they usually have no cholesterol, and most have little or no added sugar per individual serving.

PEAR-LEMON SORBET

1 (16-ounce) can sliced pears in
  light syrup, undrained
½ teaspoon grated lemon rind
3 tablespoons lemon juice
Thin slices of canned or fresh
  pear (optional)

Position knife blade in food processor bowl. Combine first three ingredients in processor bowl, and process until smooth. Chill thoroughly.

Pour pear mixture into freezer tray or an 8-inch square pan, and freeze until almost firm. Break mixture into large pieces, and place in processor bowl; process several seconds or until fluffy but not thawed. Return to freezer tray, and freeze until firm. Use an ice-cream scoop to serve. Garnish each serving with a pear slice, if desired. Yield: 2¼ cups.

BANANA-ORANGE SORBET

⅔ cup sugar
½ cup water
2 large bananas
½ teaspoon grated orange rind
1 cup orange juice
3 tablespoons dark rum

Combine sugar and water in a saucepan; bring to a boil, and boil until sugar dissolves, stirring occasionally. Remove from heat, and let cool to room temperature.

Position knife blade in food processor bowl. Peel bananas, and cut into chunks; place chunks in processor bowl, and add orange rind and juice. Top bowl with cover, and process 1 minute or until mixture is smooth. Combine syrup, banana mixture, and rum; chill thoroughly.

Pour banana mixture into freezer tray or an 8-inch square pan, and freeze until almost firm. Break mixture into large pieces, and place in processor bowl; process several seconds or until fluffy but not thawed. Return to freezer tray, and freeze until firm. Use an ice-cream scoop to serve. Yield: 3 cups.

STRAWBERRY SORBET

½ cup sugar
⅔ cup water
2½ pints fresh strawberries
2 tablespoons lemon juice
Fresh strawberry halves (optional)

Combine sugar and water in a saucepan; bring to a boil, and boil until sugar dissolves, stirring occasionally. Remove from heat, and let cool to room temperature.

Position knife blade in food processor bowl. Place 2½ pints strawberries, small portions at a time, into food processor bowl; top with cover, and process 1 minute or until strawberries are pureed. Press pureed strawberries through a sieve or several layers of cheesecloth to extract juice; discard pulp. Combine syrup, strawberry juice, and lemon juice; chill thoroughly.

Pour strawberry mixture into freezer tray or an 8-inch square pan, and freeze until almost firm. Break mixture into large pieces, and place in processor bowl; process several seconds or until fluffy but not thawed. Return to freezer tray, and freeze until firm. Use an ice-cream scoop to serve. Garnish each serving with strawberry halves, if desired. Yield: 3 cups.

AVOCADO SORBET

¾ cup sugar
⅔ cup water
2 large avocados
3 tablespoons lime juice
⅛ teaspoon salt
⅛ teaspoon hot sauce
Thin slices avocado (optional)

Combine sugar and water in a saucepan; bring to a boil, and boil until sugar dissolves, stirring occasionally. Remove from heat, and let cool to room temperature.

Position knife blade in food processor bowl. Peel and coarsely chop avocados, and place in processor bowl; add lime juice, salt, and hot sauce. Process 1 minute or until mixture is smooth. Combine syrup and avocado mixture; chill thoroughly.

Spoon avocado mixture into freezer tray or an 8-inch square pan, and freeze until almost firm. Break mixture into large pieces, and return to processor bowl; process several seconds or until fluffy but not thawed. Return to freezer tray, and freeze until firm. Use an ice-cream scoop to serve. Garnish each serving with an avocado slice, if desired. Yield: 3 cups.

MINT TEA GRANITA

2 quarts boiling water
4 family-size tea bags
1½ cups sugar
12 mint sprigs
¼ cup lemon juice

Pour boiling water over tea bags; cover and let steep 5 minutes. Remove tea bags, squeezing gently. Stir in sugar, mint sprigs, and lemon juice; cover and steep 25 minutes. Strain and let cool to room temperature. Chill thoroughly.

Pour tea mixture into three freezer trays or two 9-inch square pans, and freeze until almost firm, stirring several times during freezing process.

Remove mixture from freezer 10 minutes before serving. Scrape with a fork to loosen ice crystals; spoon into serving containers. Serve immediately. Yield: 11 cups.

RASPBERRY LIQUEUR GRANITA

3 (10-ounce) packages frozen raspberries, thawed
⅓ cup sugar
1½ cups water
⅔ cup raspberry liqueur

Press raspberries through a sieve or food mill to extract juice; discard seeds and pulp. Set juice aside.

Combine sugar and water in a saucepan; bring mixture to a boil, and boil until sugar dissolves, stirring occasionally. Remove from heat, and let cool to room temperature.

Combine syrup, raspberry juice, and raspberry liqueur; chill thoroughly. Pour raspberry mixture into two freezer trays or a 12- x 8- x 2-inch pan, and freeze until almost firm, stirring several times during freezing process.

Remove mixture from freezer 10 minutes before serving. Scrape with a fork to loosen ice crystals; spoon into serving containers. Serve immediately. Yield: 5 cups.

COFFEE-KAHLÚA GRANITA

½ cup sugar
1 cup water
1 (3-inch) stick cinnamon
2½ cups brewed coffee
½ cup Kahlúa

Combine first 3 ingredients in a saucepan; bring to a boil, and boil until sugar dissolves, stirring occasionally. Remove from heat; let cool to room temperature. Remove cinnamon stick. Combine syrup, coffee, and Kahlúa; chill thoroughly.

Pour coffee mixture into two freezer trays or a 9-inch square pan, and freeze until almost firm, stirring several times during freezing process. Remove from freezer about 10 minutes before serving. Scrape with a fork to loosen ice crystals, and spoon into serving containers. Serve immediately. Yield: 4 cups.

Making Sorbets And Granitas

To make sorbets or granitas, keep the following in mind:

■ To help develop the desired icy consistency of these sweets, always chill the ingredients before freezing.

■ Cover sorbets and granitas while they freeze; otherwise, they may pick up flavors from other foods or moisture that can make them sticky.

■ To obtain the granular texture of granitas, stir several times during the freezing process.

■ For the smooth but icy consistency of sorbets, process mixture in the food processor just until fluffy after the mixture is almost frozen. Return it to freezer, and freeze until it's firm again.

■ Sorbets left in the freezer more than a few days can become too crystalline. If this happens, partially thaw sorbet and process it again in food processor. Refreeze and use it within 24 hours.

GRAPE GRANITA

1 (12-ounce) can frozen grape juice concentrate, thawed and undiluted
4 cups water
3 tablespoons lemon juice

Combine all ingredients, stirring well; chill thoroughly. Pour grape mixture into two freezer trays or a 12- x 8- x 2-inch pan, and freeze until almost firm, stirring several times during freezing process.

Remove mixture from freezer about 10 minutes before serving. Scrape mixture with a fork to loosen ice crystals, and spoon into serving containers. Serve immediately. Yield: 5½ cups.

ORANGE GRANITA

½ cup sugar
1 cup water
3 oranges
¼ cup frozen orange juice concentrate, thawed and undiluted
2 tablespoons lemon juice
Mint leaves

Combine sugar and water in a saucepan; bring to a boil, and boil until sugar dissolves, stirring occasionally. Remove from heat, and let cool to room temperature.

Slice oranges in half crosswise; cut a zigzag design on edges, if desired. Carefully juice oranges, keeping rinds intact to make a decorative shell. Scrape out pulp; place shells in plastic bags, and chill. Set aside ¾ cup orange juice; reserve remaining juice for other uses.

Combine syrup, orange juice concentrate, ¾ cup orange juice, and lemon juice; chill thoroughly. Pour orange mixture into freezer tray or an 8-inch square pan, and freeze until almost firm, stirring several times during freezing process.

Remove mixture from freezer 10 minutes before serving. Scrape mixture with a fork to loosen ice crystals, and spoon into reserved orange shells. Garnish with mint leaves. Serve immediately. Yield: 2¼ cups.

Tangy Lemon Adds Flavor

What's low in calories, high in vitamin C, and a good replacement for salt? Lemon, of course. Besides having these nutritious qualities, lemon also enhances the natural flavor of most foods.

LEMONY PORK CHOPS

4 (¾-inch-thick) pork chops
¼ teaspoon salt
⅛ teaspoon pepper
4 lemon slices
¼ cup firmly packed brown sugar
⅓ cup catsup
⅓ cup water

Sprinkle chops with salt and pepper; arrange in a 9-inch square baking pan. Place a lemon slice on center of each chop. Top each lemon slice with 1 tablespoon brown sugar.

Combine catsup and water, mixing well. Pour sauce around chops.

Bake, uncovered, at 350° for 1 hour or until tender. Yield: 4 servings.   *Trudie Young*
Johns Island, South Carolina

LEMON CHICKEN AND VEGETABLES

3 tablespoons vegetable oil, divided
4 chicken breast halves, skinned, boned, and cut into ½-inch strips
1 lemon, sliced
½ cup sliced celery
½ medium onion, sliced
1 cup sliced yellow squash or zucchini
½ cup sliced mushrooms
½ cup red pepper strips
½ cup frozen English peas, thawed
½ cup fresh snow pea pods
1 teaspoon pepper
1 tablespoon lemon juice

Heat 1½ tablespoons oil to medium-high heat in a large skillet. Add chicken and lemon slices, and stir-fry 2 minutes or until lightly browned. Remove from skillet. Set aside.

Heat remaining oil to medium high in skillet. Add celery, onion, squash, mushrooms, and pepper strips; stir-fry 2 minutes or until crisp-tender.

Add chicken, peas, and remaining ingredients to skillet. Stir-fry on medium high until thoroughly heated. Serve immediately. Yield: 4 servings.
Mildred Sherrer
Bay City, Texas

LEMON BROCCOLI

1 (1½-pound) bunch fresh broccoli
½ cup butter or margarine
2 tablespoons lemon juice
½ teaspoon dried whole oregano
¼ teaspoon freshly ground pepper
¼ teaspoon garlic powder

Trim off large leaves of broccoli. Remove tough ends of lower stalks, and wash broccoli thoroughly. Separate into spears. Arrange broccoli in steaming rack with stalks to center of rack. Place over boiling water; cover and steam 8 to 10 minutes. Set aside.

Combine butter and remaining ingredients in a saucepan; bring to a boil. Pour over broccoli. Yield: 6 servings.
Marianne Eastland
Doddsville, Mississippi

LEMON MUFFINS

1¾ cups all-purpose flour
1 teaspoon baking powder
¾ teaspoon baking soda
¼ teaspoon salt
¾ cup sugar
1 tablespoon grated lemon rind
1 egg, beaten
1 (8-ounce) carton lemon yogurt
¼ cup plus 2 tablespoons butter or margarine, melted
1 tablespoon lemon juice
Glaze (recipe follows)

Combine first 6 ingredients in a large bowl; make a well in center of mixture, and set aside.

Combine egg, yogurt, butter, and lemon juice; stir well. Add to dry

ingredients; stir just until moistened. Spoon batter into greased muffin pans, filling three-fourths full. Bake at 400° for 20 minutes or until lightly browned. Cool in pans 5 minutes. Remove from pans, and place on wire rack. While muffins are warm, prick with a wooden pick; pour glaze over muffins. Yield: 16 muffins.

Glaze

¼ cup sugar
2 teaspoons grated lemon rind
⅓ cup lemon juice

Combine all ingredients in a small saucepan. Cook over medium heat, stirring constantly, until sugar dissolves. Yield: ⅓ cup.
Linda Magers
Clemmons, North Carolina

Pretty, Little Tea Cookies

In the South, the traditional tea is one of the finest occasions for expressing hospitality and joy. An assortment of dainty delights abounds with tea cookies as the highlight.

ORANGE-PECAN COOKIES

½ cup butter or margarine, softened
⅓ cup sugar
1½ teaspoons grated orange rind
1 cup all-purpose flour
1 cup minced pecans
Orange Frosting

Cream butter; gradually add sugar, beating at medium speed of an electric mixer until mixture is light and fluffy. Add grated orange rind, flour, and minced pecans; mix well. Cover mixture, and chill 1 hour.

Roll dough to ⅛- to ¼-inch thickness on a lightly floured surface. Cut with a 2-inch cutter, and place on ungreased cookie sheets. Bake at 350° for 8 minutes or until lightly

browned. Cool on wire racks. Decorate cookies with Orange Frosting. Yield: 4 dozen.

Orange Frosting

¼ cup butter or margarine, melted
¼ cup Triple Sec or other orange-flavored liqueur
2 to 2½ cups sifted powdered sugar
Food coloring (optional)

Combine first 3 ingredients in a small bowl; beat at medium speed of an electric mixer until smooth. Add food coloring, if desired. Yield: 1 cup.
Helen J. Seine
Austin, Texas

SURPRISE BONBON COOKIES

2 cups all-purpose flour
½ teaspoon salt
¾ cup butter or margarine, softened
½ cup sugar
2 egg yolks
1 (3.5-ounce) package almond paste or ⅓ cup almond paste
1 teaspoon vanilla extract
48 semisweet chocolate- or vanilla-flavored baking pieces or 6 (1-ounce) squares semisweet chocolate or vanilla, each cut into 8 pieces
8 ounces chocolate-flavored candy coating, melted

Combine flour and salt in a small bowl; set mixture aside.

Cream butter; add sugar, beating at medium speed of an electric mixer until light and fluffy. Add egg yolks, almond paste, and vanilla; beat well. Add flour mixture, mixing well.

Shape 1 rounded teaspoon dough around each chocolate piece, forming a 1-inch ball. Place on lightly greased cookie sheets. Bake at 350° for 12 to 14 minutes or until lightly browned. Cool. Drizzle candy coating over cookies, or pipe in desired design, using metal tip No. 2. Yield: 4 dozen.
Henri Sue Kennard
Starkville, Mississippi

FLORENTINE LACE COOKIES

¼ cup butter or margarine
¼ cup shortening
⅔ cup firmly packed light brown
  sugar
½ cup light corn syrup
1 cup all-purpose flour
1 cup finely chopped pecans
3 cups whipping cream
¾ cup sifted powdered sugar

Combine first 4 ingredients in a heavy saucepan; bring to a boil, stirring constantly. Remove from heat; stir in flour and pecans. Cool.

Shape dough into ¾-inch balls; place 2 inches apart on greased cookie sheets; bake at 350° for 8 minutes. Cool 30 seconds. Quickly roll each cookie around the handle of a wooden spoon or other cylindrical object. Cool on wire racks.

Beat whipping cream until foamy; gradually add powdered sugar, beating until soft peaks form.

Just before serving, place a finger over one end of a cookie; fill cookie by piping with whipped cream. Repeat with remaining cookies. Serve immediately. Yield: about 5 dozen.

Note: If too firm to roll, reheat for 30 seconds.
Gwen Louer
Roswell, Georgia

ALMOND-FILLED WAFERS

1 cup butter or margarine,
  softened
2¼ cups all-purpose flour
⅓ cup whipping cream
½ cup sugar
¼ cup butter or margarine,
  softened
¾ cup sifted powdered sugar
½ teaspoon almond extract
1 or 2 drops of food coloring
  (optional)

Cream 1 cup butter at medium speed of an electric mixer until light and fluffy. Gradually add flour alternately with whipping cream, beginning and ending with flour. Shape dough into a ball; cover and chill 2 hours.

Divide dough in half; store 1 portion in refrigerator. Roll dough to ⅛-inch thickness on a lightly floured surface. Cut with a 1½-inch round cutter. Use a ¼- to ⅜-inch cutter to cut out heart or other decorative design in center of half of cookies. Sprinkle both sides of cookies with sugar, and place on ungreased cookie sheets. Repeat procedure with remaining dough. Bake at 375° for 7 to 9 minutes or until very lightly browned. Cool on wire racks.

Combine ¼ cup butter, powdered sugar, and almond extract, mixing well. Add food coloring, if desired. Spread each solid cookie with a thin layer of filling. Top with decorative cookie. (Cookies are very delicate and must be handled carefully.) Yield: about 4½ dozen.
Betty Tucker
Birmingham, Alabama

COOKING LIGHT®

Light And Shapely Congealed Salads

Congealed salads can add variety and flavor to meals as appetizers, side dishes, or desserts. Unflavored gelatin is used in these recipes to keep calories, fat, and cholesterol low.

Gelatin is an incomplete protein. If it is eaten alone, your body cannot take full advantage of it as a protein source. However, if it is combined with other protein-containing foods, a complete protein will be formed and your body can use it.

Unlike flavored gelatins that contain about 85% sugar and 10% gelatin, unflavored gelatin contains no sugar and only about 28 calories per envelope. It absorbs 5 to 10 times its weight in water and can be used as a stabilizer, thickener, or texturizer.

THREE-LAYER ASPIC

1 envelope unflavored gelatin
¼ cup water
1 tablespoon lemon juice
1 (8-ounce) carton plain low-fat
  yogurt
Vegetable cooking spray
1 envelope unflavored gelatin
1 cup water
1 tablespoon lemon juice
1 teaspoon reduced-sodium
  Worcestershire sauce
1 cup diced green pepper
1 (14½-ounce) can stewed
  tomatoes, undrained
1 (12-ounce) can vegetable
  cocktail juice
1 tablespoon sugar
1 teaspoon celery salt
1 teaspoon reduced-sodium
  Worcestershire sauce
¼ teaspoon hot sauce
2 tablespoons lemon juice
1 bay leaf
2 envelopes unflavored gelatin
1 cup thinly sliced celery
Lettuce leaves
Lemon slices (optional)

Sprinkle 1 envelope gelatin over ¼ cup water in a small saucepan; let stand 1 minute. Cook over medium heat, stirring constantly, until gelatin dissolves; remove from heat. Stir in 1 tablespoon lemon juice and yogurt. Pour into a 6-cup mold that has been coated with cooking spray; cover and chill until firm.

Sprinkle 1 envelope gelatin over 1 cup water in a small saucepan; let stand 1 minute. Cook over medium heat, stirring constantly, until gelatin dissolves; remove from heat. Stir in 1 tablespoon lemon juice and 1 teaspoon Worcestershire sauce; chill until the consistency of unbeaten egg white. Stir in green pepper. Spoon mixture over yogurt layer. Cover and chill until firm.

Drain tomatoes, reserving liquid; chop tomatoes. Combine liquid, tomatoes, vegetable juice, and next 6 ingredients in a saucepan. Cook over low heat 30 minutes; remove from heat. Remove bay leaf. Sprinkle 2 envelopes gelatin over hot mixture; stir until gelatin dissolves.

Chill until the consistency of unbeaten egg white. Stir in celery; spoon mixture over green pepper layer. Cover and chill until firm. Unmold onto lettuce leaves. Garnish with lemon slices, if desired. Yield: 12 servings (48 calories per ½-cup serving).

□ 3.8 grams protein, 0.5 gram fat, 7.8 grams carbohydrate, 1 milligram cholesterol, 392 milligrams sodium, and 58 milligrams calcium.

ASPARAGUS SALAD

1 (10½-ounce) can asparagus
1 envelope unflavored gelatin
1 cup water
¼ cup lemon juice
½ cup reduced-calorie
    mayonnaise
½ (8-ounce) package low-fat
    cream cheese
1 tablespoon diced onion
⅓ cup chopped pecans

Drain asparagus, reserving ¼ cup liquid. Chop asparagus; set aside.
Sprinkle gelatin over water in a small saucepan; let stand 1 minute. Cook over medium heat, stirring constantly, until gelatin dissolves; remove from heat, and pour into container of an electric blender. Add ¼ cup reserved asparagus liquid, lemon juice, mayonnaise, cream cheese, and onion; blend until smooth. Stir in pecans and asparagus. Spoon into an 8-inch square dish. Cover and chill until firm. Yield: 9 servings (100 calories per serving).

□ 3.1 grams protein, 8.6 grams fat, 4 grams carbohydrate, 4 milligrams cholesterol, 247 milligrams sodium, and 27 milligrams calcium.
Mary Ruth Cayson
Tupelo, Mississippi

SPICY CHILE-TOMATO SALAD

2 envelopes unflavored gelatin
1 (24-ounce) can vegetable
    cocktail juice, divided
1 tablespoon lemon juice
½ teaspoon hot sauce
¼ cup diced celery
2 tablespoons canned diced green
    chiles
Vegetable cooking spray
Lettuce leaves

Sprinkle gelatin over 1 cup vegetable cocktail juice in a small saucepan; let stand 1 minute. Cook over medium heat, stirring constantly, until gelatin dissolves; remove from heat. Stir in remaining cocktail juice, lemon juice, and hot sauce. Chill until the consistency of unbeaten egg white. Fold in celery and chiles. Spoon into a 4-cup mold that has been coated with cooking spray. Cover and chill until firm. Unmold onto a lettuce-lined plate. Yield: 6 servings (35 calories per ½-cup serving).

□ 3 grams protein, 0.2 gram fat, 6.2 grams carbohydrate, 0 milligrams cholesterol, 431 milligrams sodium, and 18 milligrams calcium.
Virginia Porterfield
Bermuda Run, North Carolina

CUCUMBER MOUSSE

2 envelopes unflavored gelatin
1½ cups chicken broth, divided
1 tablespoon lemon juice
1 teaspoon prepared horseradish
¾ cup shredded, unpeeled
    cucumber
½ cup reduced-calorie
    mayonnaise
¼ cup sliced green onions
1 (12-ounce) container 1% low-fat
    cottage cheese
Vegetable cooking spray

Sprinkle gelatin over ½ cup chicken broth in a small saucepan; let stand 1 minute. Cook over medium heat, stirring constantly, until gelatin dissolves; remove from heat. Add remaining 1 cup chicken broth, lemon

juice, and horseradish. Chill until the consistency of unbeaten egg white. Stir in cucumber and next 3 ingredients; spoon into a 4-cup mold coated with cooking spray. Cover and chill. Yield: 8 servings (87 calories per ½-cup serving).

□ 7.8 grams protein, 4.7 grams fat, 3 grams carbohydrate, 7 milligrams cholesterol, 405 milligrams sodium, and 32 milligrams calcium.

APPLE-APRICOT SALAD

1 envelope unflavored gelatin
2 cups unsweetened apple juice,
    divided
2 teaspoons lemon juice
1½ cups chopped apple
8 canned apricot halves in
    extra-light syrup, drained and
    chopped
Vegetable cooking spray
Lettuce leaves
Apple wedges (optional)

Sprinkle gelatin over 1 cup apple juice in a small saucepan; let stand 1 minute. Cook over medium heat, stirring constantly, until gelatin dissolves; remove from heat. Add remaining 1 cup apple juice and lemon juice. Chill until the consistency of unbeaten egg white. Fold in chopped apple and apricots; spoon into seven ½-cup molds that have been coated with cooking spray. Cover and chill until firm.
Unmold onto lettuce-lined plates. Garnish with apple wedges, if desired. Yield: 7 servings (67 calories per ½-cup serving).

□ 1.3 grams protein, 0.3 gram fat, 15.5 grams carbohydrate, 0 milligrams cholesterol, 5 milligrams sodium, and 13 milligrams calcium.
Louise L. Holmes
Winchester, Tennessee

Tip: *Use leftover liquid from canned or cooked fruit and vegetables in frozen desserts, gelatin molds, soups, stews, sauces, or casseroles.*

TRIPLE APPLE SALAD

1 envelope unflavored gelatin
1 tablespoon sugar
1 cup unsweetened apple juice
¼ teaspoon almond extract
1 cup unsweetened applesauce
1 cup diced apple
Vegetable cooking spray
Apple wedges (optional)
Fresh mint sprigs (optional)

Sprinkle gelatin and sugar over apple juice in a small saucepan; let stand 1 minute. Cook over medium heat, stirring constantly, until gelatin dissolves; remove from heat. Stir in almond extract and applesauce. Chill until the consistency of unbeaten egg white. Stir in diced apple. Spoon into a 3-cup mold coated with cooking spray. Cover and chill until firm.

Unmold onto serving plate. If desired, garnish with apple wedges and mint sprigs. Yield: 7 servings (51 calories per ⅓-cup serving).

□ 1 gram protein, 0.2 gram fat, 11.9 grams carbohydrate, 0 milligrams cholesterol, 3 milligrams sodium, and 5 milligrams calcium.　Jan Hughes
Batesville, Arkansas

GRAPEFRUIT SALAD

1 (16-ounce) can unsweetened grapefruit sections
1 envelope unflavored gelatin
2 tablespoons sugar
2 tablespoons lemon juice
¼ cup diced celery
¼ cup diced apple
1 teaspoon diced crystallized ginger
Vegetable cooking spray
Lettuce leaves

Drain grapefruit, reserving liquid; add water to liquid to measure 1¼ cups. Sprinkle gelatin and sugar over liquid mixture in a small saucepan; let stand 1 minute. Cook over medium heat, stirring constantly, until gelatin dissolves; remove from heat. Stir in lemon juice. Chill until the consistency of unbeaten egg white. Fold in grapefruit, celery, apple, and ginger.

Spoon mixture into a 3-cup mold that has been coated with cooking spray. Cover and chill until firm. Unmold salad onto a lettuce-lined plate. Yield: 5 servings (69 calories per ½-cup serving).

□ 2 grams protein, 0.3 gram fat, 16 grams carbohydrate, 0 milligrams cholesterol, 11 milligrams sodium, and 23 milligrams calcium.
Mrs. M. L. Shannon
Fairfield, Alabama

Vegetable Dishes To Savor

If you want to turn an ordinary meal into a memorable one, offer any of these vegetable side dishes. In Corn-and-Cheese Soufflé, the delicate soufflé texture is combined with corn to give the dish extra body. Remember that as soufflés cool, they tend to deflate or fall, but the flavor will be the same.

GARDEN CASSEROLE

1 large onion, sliced
1 medium-size sweet red pepper, cut into strips
2 cloves garlic, minced
3 tablespoons butter or margarine, melted
¼ cup all-purpose flour
6 small baking potatoes, unpeeled and sliced
1 (10-ounce) package frozen cut green beans, thawed
2 cups (8 ounces) shredded Swiss cheese
1 cup half-and-half
½ teaspoon dried whole rosemary
½ teaspoon salt
¼ teaspoon pepper
16 strips sweet red pepper

Sauté first 3 ingredients in butter until crisp-tender. Add flour; cook 1 minute, stirring constantly. Spoon

half of onion mixture into a lightly greased 13- x 9- x 2-inch baking dish. Layer half each of potato slices, green beans, and cheese over onion mixture. Repeat layers of onion mixture, potatoes, and green beans. Combine half-and-half, rosemary, salt, and pepper; pour over vegetables. Cover and bake at 375° for 1 hour or until potatoes are tender; sprinkle with remaining cheese, and garnish with 16 red pepper strips. Bake an additional 5 minutes. Yield: 8 to 10 servings.　Edith Askins
Greenville, Texas

CORN-AND-CHEESE SOUFFLÉ

¼ cup plus 2 tablespoons butter or margarine
¼ cup all-purpose flour
⅓ cup milk
1 (17-ounce) can cream-style corn
1½ cups (6 ounces) shredded sharp Cheddar cheese
½ cup (2 ounces) shredded provolone cheese
⅛ teaspoon garlic powder
⅛ teaspoon red pepper
5 eggs, separated
¼ teaspoon cream of tartar

Cut a piece of aluminum foil long enough to fit around a 1½-quart soufflé dish, with a 1-inch overlap; fold foil lengthwise into thirds. Oil one side of foil and bottom of dish. Wrap oiled side of foil around outside of dish, allowing it to extend 3 inches above rim; secure with string.

Melt butter in a heavy saucepan over low heat. Add flour; stir until smooth. Cook 1 minute, stirring constantly. Gradually add milk; cook over medium heat, stirring until thickened. Stir in corn, cheeses, and seasonings.

Beat egg yolks until thick and lemon colored; add to mixture, and stir. Beat egg whites (at room temperature) and cream of tartar until stiff peaks form; fold into mixture. Spoon into prepared soufflé dish. Bake at 350° for 55 to 60 minutes. Remove collar, and serve. Yield: 6 to 8 servings.　Sharon McClatchey
Muskogee, Oklahoma

VEGGIES CASSEROLE

2 (15-ounce) cans asparagus
   spears, drained and divided
2 (17-ounce) cans small English
   peas, drained
1 (8-ounce) can sliced water
   chestnuts, drained
1 (4-ounce) can sliced
   mushrooms, drained
1 (10¾-ounce) can cream of
   chicken soup, undiluted
¾ cup (3 ounces) shredded
   Cheddar cheese
2 tablespoons minced onion
1 cup soft breadcrumbs
2 tablespoons butter or
   margarine, melted

Arrange half of asparagus spears in a
lightly greased 12- x 8- x 2-inch baking dish. Combine peas and next 5
ingredients, stirring gently. Spoon
half of mixture over asparagus. Repeat layers.
   Combine breadcrumbs and butter;
sprinkle over pea mixture. Bake, uncovered, at 350° for 20 minutes or
until thoroughly heated. Yield: 8 to
10 servings.
             Larry Miller
        Ashland, Kentucky

GREEN BEAN-AND-CORN CASSEROLE

1 (12-ounce) can Mexican-style
   corn, drained
1 (16-ounce) can French-cut green
   beans, drained
½ cup diced celery
½ cup diced onion
½ cup (2 ounces) shredded sharp
   Cheddar cheese
½ cup commercial sour cream
1 (10¾-ounce) can cream of
   celery soup, undiluted
¼ teaspoon white pepper
¼ cup butter or margarine,
   melted
½ cup slivered almonds
1 cup herb-seasoned stuffing mix

Combine first 8 ingredients in a medium bowl; stir well. Spoon mixture
into a lightly greased 8-inch square
baking dish.

Combine butter, almonds, and
stuffing mix in a bowl; toss gently.
Sprinkle over casserole. Bake, uncovered, at 350° for 45 minutes.
Yield: 6 servings.   *Millie Givens*
        Savannah, Georgia

Entrées Just For Two

What's the biggest problem when
cooking for two? Probably leftovers.
To avoid leftovers with every meal,
it takes some planning, and these
main dishes are designed accordingly.
They're also easy to prepare.

ORANGE BARBECUED CHICKEN

2 chicken breast halves, skinned
¼ teaspoon salt
¼ teaspoon pepper
1 tablespoon vegetable oil
1 tablespoon all-purpose flour
¼ cup commercial barbecue sauce
1 tablespoon brown sugar
1½ teaspoons minced crystallized
   ginger
⅛ teaspoon hot sauce
½ cup orange juice
Hot cooked rice
Parsley sprigs (optional)
2 orange slices (optional)

Sprinkle both sides of chicken with
salt and pepper. Cook chicken in hot
oil in a small skillet over medium
heat until browned, turning once.
   Combine flour and barbecue sauce;
stir until smooth. Stir in brown
sugar, ginger, hot sauce, and orange
juice; pour over chicken. Cover, reduce heat, and simmer 30 minutes or
until done, basting occasionally.
   Spoon rice onto serving plate; arrange chicken over rice. Spoon sauce
over chicken. If desired, garnish with
parsley sprigs and orange slices.
Yield: 2 servings.   *Kathryn Knight*
        Sarasota, Florida

STEAK AND SHRIMP

6 unpeeled fresh jumbo shrimp
1 clove garlic, sliced
1 tablespoon butter or margarine,
   melted
3 tablespoons Chablis or other
   dry white wine
2 (1-inch-thick) beef tenderloin
   steaks
Parsley sprigs

Peel shrimp, leaving tails intact; devein shrimp. Set aside.
   Sauté garlic in butter in a small
skillet over medium heat 1 minute.
Add shrimp; cook just until shrimp
are pink, stirring constantly. Remove
shrimp from skillet. Add wine to skillet; stir well. Remove from heat.
Return shrimp to skillet, and cover
to keep warm.
   Place steaks on broiler rack; broil
6 inches from heat about 4 to 5 minutes on each side or to desired degree of doneness.
   Place steaks on individual serving
plates. Arrange shrimp on steaks;
spoon wine mixture over shrimp.
Garnish with parsley. Yield: 2
servings.   *Marguerite Schaeffer*
        Long Beach, Mississippi

TURKEY-APPLE SALAD

1 cup cooked turkey strips
1 apple, unpeeled and diced
3 tablespoons vegetable oil
2 tablespoons white wine vinegar
1 small clove garlic, minced
¼ teaspoon dry mustard
⅛ teaspoon ground ginger
Dash of pepper
2 cups torn lettuce leaves
2 tablespoons slivered almonds,
   toasted

Combine turkey and apple in a bowl.
Combine oil and next 5 ingredients in
a jar; cover tightly, and shake vigorously. Pour over turkey and
apples, tossing to coat well. Cover
and refrigerate.
   Just before serving, toss mixture
with lettuce, and sprinkle with almonds. Yield: 2 servings.
       Margaret Defournette
    Thurmond, North Carolina

Brioche Boasts A Filling

Many Southern cooks bake brioche because they relish the rich flavor of the extra butter and eggs added to dough. But Dorothy Akers of Vinton, Virginia, bakes brioche to take advantage of the unique shape of the bread. She twists off the characteristic top knot, carves out the center a little, and then spoons in a tasty curried chicken filling. She replaces the top knot, and serves the little concoctions as appetizers.

Although brioche is usually baked in pans with fluted sides, straight-sided pans work just as well. Brioche typically has a top knot and is round in shape. It can range in size from a single large round loaf, to the traditional dinner-roll size, to the miniature ones that work so well for appetizers.

If you've never made brioche, don't be intimidated. It looks more complicated than it is.

Step 1: *After the dough is made and chilled, punch it down, and knead until smooth and elastic. Divide dough as directed.*

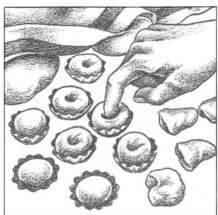

Step 2: *Place dough in greased brioche pans; make an indentation in each ball of dough, using a floured finger.*

Step 3: *Brush with egg yolk mixture; gently press 1 ball of dough into each indentation. Brush again with yolk mixture; let rise, and bake.*

Step 4: *Twist off top knots of brioche; spoon out bread to leave a ½-inch-thick shell. Spoon in chicken filling, and replace knots.*

BRIOCHE CHICKEN CURRY

1 package dry yeast
¼ cup warm water (105° to 115°)
½ cup butter or margarine,
 softened
¼ cup sugar
¼ teaspoon salt
5 eggs
3½ cups all-purpose flour, divided
1 egg yolk
1 tablespoon water
Curried Chicken Filling
Curly endive

Dissolve yeast in warm water; let stand 5 minutes.

Combine butter, sugar, and salt in a large mixing bowl; mix well. Add yeast mixture, eggs, and 1 cup flour. Beat at medium speed of an electric mixer 3 minutes or until smooth, scraping sides of bowl occasionally. Gradually stir in remaining flour. (Dough will be sticky.) Cover and refrigerate 8 hours.

Punch dough down. Turn dough out onto a well-floured surface, and knead until smooth and elastic (about 5 minutes). Divide dough into 4 equal portions; set 1 portion aside. Divide each of 3 portions into 16 pieces; shape each piece into a ball.

Place in well-greased 1¾-inch brioche or muffin pans. Make a deep indentation in center of each, using a floured finger. Combine egg yolk and 1 tablespoon water, beating well; gently brush over dough in pans.

Divide reserved portion of dough into 48 pieces, and shape into balls.

Gently press 1 ball in each indentation. Brush with additional yolk mixture. Cover and let rise in a warm place (85°), free from drafts, 30 to 50 minutes or until dough is doubled in bulk. Bake at 375° for 12 minutes or until golden brown. Remove brioche from pans immediately, and let cool on wire racks.

Twist off top knots, and scoop out enough bread to leave a ½-inch-thick shell. Fill shells with Curried Chicken Filling. Replace tops. Garnish with endive. Yield: 4 dozen.

Curried Chicken Filling

2 (3-ounce) packages cream
  cheese, softened
⅔ cup plain yogurt
1 tablespoon plus 1 teaspoon
  curry powder
1 tablespoon plus 1 teaspoon
  lemon juice
¼ teaspoon salt
⅛ teaspoon pepper
2 cups finely chopped cooked
  chicken
¾ cup raisins
⅔ cup finely chopped almonds,
  toasted
½ cup flaked coconut

Beat cream cheese until smooth in a large bowl at medium speed of an electric mixer. Add yogurt (at room temperature), curry powder, lemon juice, salt, and pepper; mix well. Stir in chicken and remaining ingredients; cover and chill. Yield: 2¾ cups.

Note: For 2 dozen larger brioche, divide each of the 3 portions of dough into 8 pieces. Place into 2½-inch brioche or muffin pans. Divide reserved portion of dough into 24 pieces. Assemble and bake like smaller brioche.

Tip: *When a recipe calls for a "greased pan," be sure to grease the pan with solid shortening or an oil unless specified.*

MICROWAVE COOKERY

Quick Ideas For Supper

These microwave recipes will get you out of the kitchen in a hurry. They combine meat and vegetables to serve as the entrée and need only bread or one other side dish to complete a light meal.

SESAME CHICKEN WITH NOODLES

4 chicken breast halves, skinned
  and boned
¼ cup firmly packed light brown
  sugar
⅓ cup soy sauce
¼ cup dry sherry
2 tablespoons white wine vinegar
2 tablespoons sesame oil
1 teaspoon minced fresh ginger
1 clove garlic, minced
¼ teaspoon pepper
¼ teaspoon ground red pepper
2 teaspoons cornstarch
1 sweet red pepper, cut into
  strips
¼ cup sliced scallions or green
  onions
1 cup shredded red cabbage
½ cup coarsely chopped walnuts
2 tablespoons sesame seeds
2 tablespoons minced fresh
  parsley
8 ounces cooked spinach noodles
  or egg noodles

Cut chicken into 3- x ½-inch strips; set aside.

Combine brown sugar and next 8 ingredients in a 2-quart shallow casserole. Add chicken; toss gently to coat. Cover and chill 30 minutes. Drain chicken, reserving ¼ cup marinade; return chicken to casserole. Combine reserved marinade and cornstarch; pour over chicken, and toss. Cover with heavy-duty plastic wrap, turning back one corner to vent; microwave at HIGH 5 minutes.

Stir in sweet red pepper and scallions. Cover with plastic wrap, venting corner; microwave at HIGH 2 to 3 minutes or until chicken is done. Stir in cabbage and remaining ingredients except noodles. Cover and let stand 1 minute. Serve over noodles. Yield: 4 servings.

Betty Beske
Arlington, Virginia

CHICKEN DIVAN QUICHE

½ cup uncooked long-grain rice
1¼ cups water
¼ teaspoon salt
2 eggs, slightly beaten
1½ cups (6 ounces) shredded
  Cheddar cheese, divided
1 (10-ounce) package frozen
  chopped broccoli
3 tablespoons chopped sweet red
  pepper
3 tablespoons chopped onion
1 tablespoon all-purpose flour
1 (6¾-ounce) can chunk chicken,
  drained
4 eggs, slightly beaten
1 cup half-and-half
1 tablespoon Worcestershire
  sauce
½ teaspoon salt
¼ teaspoon ground red pepper

Combine rice, water, and ¼ teaspoon salt in a 1½-quart casserole. Cover with heavy-duty plastic wrap, and microwave at HIGH 5 minutes. Cook, covered, at MEDIUM HIGH (70% power) 12 minutes or until rice is tender. Cool.

Combine rice, 2 eggs, and ½ cup cheese; stir well. Spread on bottom and sides of a 9-inch quiche dish.

Microwave broccoli according to package directions; drain well. Combine broccoli, sweet red pepper, onion, and flour; stir well, and spoon into quiche dish. Top with chicken and ½ cup cheese. Combine 4 eggs and next 4 ingredients; mix well. Pour mixture over chicken, and microwave at MEDIUM HIGH 8 minutes. Give dish a half-turn; microwave at MEDIUM HIGH 9 to 10 minutes or until set. Sprinkle with remaining ½ cup cheese; let stand 10 minutes. Yield: 6 servings.

MANDARIN PORK-AND-SPINACH SALAD

1 (1½-pound) pork tenderloin
½ cup teriyaki sauce
2 tablespoons brown sugar
2 tablespoons bourbon
1 pound fresh spinach, torn
1 (11-ounce) can mandarin
    oranges, drained
1 red apple, cored and cubed
½ cup thinly sliced green onions
Dressing (recipe follows)
Apple wedges (optional)

Partially freeze tenderloin. Trim excess fat from tenderloin; cut crosswise into ¼-inch slices, and cut each slice in half. Place pork in a 12- x 8- x 2-inch baking dish. Combine teriyaki sauce, sugar, and bourbon; pour over pork. Cover and refrigerate 2 to 4 hours.

Drain pork; discard marinade. Cover dish with wax paper, and microwave at MEDIUM (50% power) 12 to 14 minutes or until done, stirring every 4 minutes. Drain.

Combine spinach, oranges, cubed apple, and green onions in a large bowl. Top with pork. Pour hot dressing over salad. Toss and serve immediately. Garnish with apple wedges, if desired. Yield: 6 servings.

Dressing

¼ cup vegetable oil
2 tablespoons red wine vinegar
1½ tablespoons sugar
1 tablespoon sesame seeds
¼ teaspoon salt
¼ teaspoon dry mustard
¼ teaspoon paprika
⅛ teaspoon hot sauce

Combine all ingredients in a 2-cup glass measure; stir well. Microwave at HIGH 1 to 2 minutes; stir well. Yield: ½ cup.

Tip: *Don't be tempted to increase the amount of seasonings called for in a microwave recipe. You can easily overdo it because there's usually less liquid to reduce their flavor; you can add more seasoning after tasting.*

Give Grits A Topping

You'll have to stay south of the Mason-Dixon line to enjoy these dishes. Our readers have paired two saucy entrées with grits, and the results are delicious!

GRILLADES AND GRITS

1 (4-pound) veal or beef boneless
    rump roast
½ cup bacon drippings, divided
½ cup all-purpose flour
1 cup chopped onion
2 cups chopped green onions
¾ cup chopped celery
1½ cups chopped green pepper
2 cloves garlic, minced
2 cups peeled and chopped
    tomatoes
½ teaspoon tarragon leaves
1 teaspoon dried whole thyme
1 cup water
1 cup Burgundy or other dry red
    wine
1 teaspoon salt
½ teaspoon pepper
2 bay leaves
½ teaspoon hot sauce
2 tablespoons Worcestershire
    sauce
3 tablespoons fresh chopped
    parsley
Garlic-Cheese Grits

Remove fat from meat; cut into ½-inch slices. Sauté meat in ¼ cup bacon drippings in a heavy Dutch oven 2 to 3 minutes on each side or until browned. Remove to a serving platter, and repeat until all meat is browned. Set aside.

Add remaining ¼ cup bacon drippings to Dutch oven. Add flour; cook over medium heat, stirring constantly, until roux is the color of caramel. Add onion, green onions, celery, green pepper, and garlic to roux; cook until tender. Add tomatoes, tarragon, and thyme. Cook 3 minutes, stirring constantly. Add water and next 6 ingredients, stirring until blended.

Return meat to Dutch oven, stirring well. Bring to a boil; cover, reduce heat, and simmer 1 hour, stirring occasionally. Uncover and simmer 30 minutes. Remove bay leaves; stir in parsley. Serve chopped mixture over Garlic-Cheese Grits. Yield: 12 servings.

Garlic-Cheese Grits

8 cups boiling water
1 teaspoon salt
2 cups uncooked quick-cooking
    grits
2 (6-ounce) rolls process cheese
    food with garlic

Bring water and salt to a boil in a Dutch oven; stir in grits. Return to a boil; reduce heat, and cook 4 minutes, stirring occasionally. Add cheese, stirring until melted. Yield: 12 servings. *Mary Hamblen*
New Orleans, Louisiana

SHRIMP STEW OVER GRITS

2 (10¾-ounce) cans cream of
    celery soup, undiluted
1 medium-size green pepper,
    diced
1 medium onion, chopped
1 tablespoon Worcestershire
    sauce
1 tablespoon hot sauce
1 bay leaf
⅛ teaspoon pepper
1 (16-ounce) package peeled
    frozen small shrimp
Cooked buttered grits

Combine first 7 ingredients in a Dutch oven; stir well. Bring to a boil over medium heat; reduce heat, and simmer, uncovered, 20 minutes. Add shrimp, and cook 5 to 7 minutes, stirring occasionally. Remove bay leaf. Serve over buttered grits. Yield: 8 servings. *Harry M. Bayne*
Oxford, Mississippi

Chilled Desserts To Tempt You

Dessert is a breeze when you prepare it the day before, especially if your schedule is a hectic one. Here's a selection of chilled make-ahead desserts, including flavors from chocolate to a refreshing fruit combination.

ICE CREAM PIE WITH MERINGUE-PECAN CRUST

1 egg white
¼ cup sugar
1½ cups chopped pecans
1 quart vanilla ice cream, softened
Pecan halves (optional)
Caramel-Raisin Sauce

Beat egg white (at room temperature) at high speed of an electric mixer; gradually add sugar, 1 tablespoon at a time, beating until stiff peaks form and sugar dissolves. Fold in chopped pecans. Spread mixture on bottom and sides of a buttered 9-inch pieplate. Bake at 400° for 12 minutes or until lightly browned. Cool completely.

Spread ice cream evenly over crust; cover and freeze until ice cream is firm. Garnish with pecan halves, if desired. To serve, spoon Caramel-Raisin Sauce over each serving. Yield: one 9-inch pie.

Caramel-Raisin Sauce

3 tablespoons butter or margarine
1 cup firmly packed light brown sugar
½ cup whipping cream
½ cup golden raisins
1 teaspoon vanilla extract

Melt butter in a small saucepan. Add sugar and cream; stir over low heat until sugar dissolves. Add raisins and vanilla; stir well. Yield: 1½ cups.

Diane King
Egypt, Mississippi

QUICK CRÈME DE MENTHE PIE

1 (3½-ounce) package vanilla instant pudding mix
¾ cup milk
¼ cup green crème de menthe
½ cup milk
½ teaspoon vanilla extract
1 (1.4-ounce) package whipped topping mix
1 (9-inch) graham cracker crust
Additional whipped topping (optional)
Fresh mint leaves (optional)

Combine first three ingredients; beat 1 minute at medium speed of an electric mixer. Set aside.

Combine ½ cup milk, vanilla, and whipped topping mix; beat at high speed of an electric mixer 4 minutes or until light and fluffy.

Fold whipped topping into pudding mixture; pour into graham cracker crust. Cover and chill 8 hours or until firm. If desired, serve with additional whipped topping and fresh mint leaves. Yield: one 9-inch pie.

Mrs. William R. Roberts II
Jacksonville, Florida

LEMON-STRAWBERRY PIE

1 cup sugar
2 tablespoons plus 2 teaspoons cornstarch
1 cup water
2 egg yolks, beaten
¼ cup butter or margarine
¼ cup plus 2 tablespoons lemon juice
1 baked 9-inch pastry shell
2 cups sliced fresh strawberries
2 (3-ounce) packages cream cheese, softened
¼ cup sifted powdered sugar
⅓ cup flaked coconut
¾ cup whipping cream, whipped
¼ cup flaked coconut, toasted

Combine 1 cup sugar and cornstarch in a heavy saucepan; gradually stir in water, egg yolks, and butter. Cook over medium heat until mixture comes to a boil; cook 1 minute, stirring constantly. Remove from heat, and stir in lemon juice. Pour into cooled pastry shell; cool. Arrange strawberries on top of filling.

Combine cream cheese and powdered sugar, beating at medium speed of an electric mixer until smooth. Fold ⅓ cup coconut and whipped cream into cream cheese mixture. Carefully spread over strawberries, and sprinkle with ¼ cup toasted coconut. Cover and chill. Yield: one 9-inch pie.

Jill Rorex Curtis
Monroeville, Pennsylvania

FROZEN OZARK PUDDING

1 egg
¾ cup sugar
3 tablespoons all-purpose flour
1½ teaspoons baking powder
½ cup chopped pecans
½ cup chopped, peeled apple
½ gallon coffee ice cream, divided
1 cup whipping cream, whipped
Chopped pecans

Beat egg at high speed of an electric mixer; gradually add sugar, and continue beating until mixture is thick and lemon colored.

Combine flour and baking powder; fold into egg mixture. Fold in pecans and apple. Spoon into a buttered 9-inch pieplate. Bake at 325° for 35 minutes; cool. Crumble mixture into small pieces.

Spread 1 quart of ice cream in an 8-inch square pan. Sprinkle crumbled mixture evenly over ice cream. Top with remaining ice cream. Cover and freeze until firm. Cut into squares. Garnish with whipped cream and chopped pecans. Yield: 9 servings.

Louise McGehee
Montevallo, Alabama

PUMPKIN CHIFFON DESSERT

1¾ cups gingersnap crumbs
¼ cup butter or margarine, melted
1 (8-ounce) package cream cheese, softened
2 eggs
½ cup sugar
2 (3½-ounce) packages vanilla instant pudding mix
¾ cup milk
1 (16-ounce) can pumpkin or 2 cups mashed cooked pumpkin
1 teaspoon ground cinnamon
¼ teaspoon ground cloves
½ teaspoon ground nutmeg
1 (8-ounce) carton frozen whipped topping, thawed and divided
½ teaspoon ground cinnamon
¼ cup chopped pecans, toasted

Combine gingersnap crumbs and butter; stir well. Press into a 13- x 9- x 2-inch baking pan.

Combine cream cheese, eggs, and sugar; beat at medium speed of an electric mixer until smooth. Spread over crumb mixture; bake at 350° for 18 to 20 minutes or until set. Cool.

Combine pudding mixes and milk; beat 1½ minutes at medium speed of an electric mixer (mixture will be very thick). Add pumpkin, 1 teaspoon cinnamon, cloves, and nutmeg; beat until smooth. Fold in 1 cup whipped topping; chill at least 1 hour. Fold ½ teaspoon cinnamon into remaining whipped topping; spread over pumpkin layer. Sprinkle with pecans. Cover and chill until serving time. Yield: 15 servings.

Polly Hughes
Tarpon Springs, Florida

CHOCOLATE ANGEL CAKE

1 (14.5-ounce) package angel food cake mix
1 (12-ounce) package semisweet chocolate morsels
2 tablespoons milk
3 eggs, separated
3 tablespoons powdered sugar
1½ cups whipping cream, whipped
½ cup chopped walnuts

Prepare and bake cake mix according to package directions, using a 10-inch tube pan. Invert pan on funnel or bottle about 2 hours or until cake is completely cooled.

Loosen cake from sides of tube pan, using a small metal spatula. Remove from pan; split cake horizontally into 3 layers. Set aside.

Combine chocolate and milk in top of a double boiler; bring water to a boil. Reduce heat to low; cook until chocolate melts, stirring occasionally.

Combine egg yolks and powdered sugar; beat well at medium speed of an electric mixer. Gradually add chocolate, beating well after each addition. Beat egg whites (at room temperature) until stiff; fold into chocolate mixture. Fold in whipped cream; chill at least 1 hour.

Spread whipped cream filling between layers and on top and sides of cake. Sprinkle layers and top with walnuts. Chill at least 4 hours. Yield: one 10-inch cake.

Ann Fearns
Crystal River, Florida

HEAVENLY CHOCOLATE CREAM

2 (4-ounce) packages sweet baking chocolate
2 tablespoons hot coffee
4 eggs, separated
2 tablespoons powdered sugar
1 teaspoon vanilla extract
2 (3-ounce) packages ladyfingers
2 cups whipping cream
2 teaspoons powdered sugar
Shaved chocolate (optional)

Place chocolate and coffee in top of a double boiler; bring water to a boil. Reduce heat to low; cook until chocolate melts, stirring occasionally.

Beat egg yolks slightly; gradually add powdered sugar, beating at high speed of an electric mixer until thick and lemon colored. Gradually stir about one-fourth of chocolate mixture into yolks; add to remaining chocolate mixture, stirring constantly. Stir in vanilla.

Beat egg whites (at room temperature) at high speed of an electric mixer until stiff peaks form; fold into chocolate mixture.

Line bottom and sides of a 9- x 5- x 3-inch loafpan with aluminum foil. Split ladyfingers, and set 7 aside. Place remaining ladyfingers on bottom and sides of prepared pan. Spoon chocolate mixture into pan. Top chocolate mixture with reserved ladyfingers. Cover and chill until firm.

Remove dessert from pan; place on serving tray. Beat whipping cream at medium speed of an electric mixer until foamy. Gradually add 2 teaspoons sugar, beating until soft peaks form. Frost sides and top of dessert with whipped cream. Garnish with shaved chocolate, if desired. Yield: 8 servings.

Alice McNamara
Eucha, Oklahoma

Self-Rising Flour: A Southern Tradition

The South is famous for biscuits, muffins, and hush puppies. And it's the love of these quick-to-make breads that keeps self-rising flour in demand in our region.

In recipes for biscuits, cakes, or quick breads, you can use self-rising flour interchangeably with all-purpose flour. Remember that each cup of self-rising flour contains 1½ teaspoons of baking powder and 1 teaspoon of salt; adjust the baking powder and salt amounts accordingly. If the original recipe uses leavening other than baking powder, you may need to make additional adjustments.

SPICY FRIED CHICKEN

2 cups water
2 tablespoons hot sauce
6 chicken breast halves, skinned and boned
1 cup self-rising flour
1 teaspoon garlic salt
½ teaspoon pepper
1 teaspoon paprika
1 teaspoon red pepper
Vegetable oil

Combine water and hot sauce; pour over chicken breasts, and marinate 1 hour in refrigerator turning once.

Combine flour and next 4 ingredients. Remove chicken from marinade, and dredge each piece in flour mixture, coating well.

Heat 1 inch of oil in a skillet to 350°; add chicken, and fry 5 to 6 minutes on each side or until golden brown. Yield: 6 servings.

Cindy Rooks
Columbus, Georgia

BLUEBERRY MUFFINS WITH STREUSEL TOPPING

2 cups self-rising flour
⅓ cup sugar
1 egg, beaten
¾ cup milk
¼ cup vegetable oil
1 cup fresh or frozen blueberries
¼ cup firmly packed brown sugar
2 tablespoons self-rising flour
1 tablespoon butter or margarine, softened

Combine 2 cups flour and ⅓ cup sugar in a large bowl, mixing well. Reserve 2 tablespoons mixture, and set aside. Make a well in center of remaining flour mixture.

Combine egg, milk, and oil; stir well. Add to dry ingredients, stirring just until moistened.

Combine blueberries and reserved 2 tablespoons flour mixture, tossing gently to coat. Stir blueberries into batter just until blended. Spoon batter into greased muffin pans, filling three-fourths full.

Combine brown sugar, 2 tablespoons flour, and butter; mix until crumbly. Sprinkle over batter. Bake at 400° for 15 to 18 minutes or until browned. Yield: 1 dozen.

Note: If frozen blueberries are used, rinse and drain thawed berries; pat berries dry.

Beth Evins
Atlanta, Georgia

HEARTY CORNMEAL PANCAKES

2 cups self-rising flour
½ cup regular cornmeal
2 teaspoons baking soda
2 eggs, beaten
3 cups buttermilk
¼ cup vegetable oil

Combine flour, cornmeal, and soda in a large bowl; make a well in center of mixture. Combine eggs, buttermilk, and oil; add to dry ingredients, stirring until smooth.

For each pancake, pour ¼ cup batter onto a hot, lightly greased griddle. Turn pancakes when tops are covered with bubbles and edges look cooked. Yield: 24 (4-inch) pancakes.

Janice A. Hampton
Marietta, Georgia

Enjoy A Menu Hot From The Grill

Because Mary Hoppe of Kitty Hawk, North Carolina, cooks out frequently in the warm months, she's perfected a menu that feeds six. Everything but the dessert can be placed on one large grill.

Remember that grilling requires smart food handling. During preparation, be sure to use a separate cutting board and knife for vegetables and meats. When you're finished grilling, place the meat and vegetables on clean plates.

Bourbon Barbecue
Charcoal Potatoes
Vegetables à la Grill
Frozen Lemon Soufflé
With Raspberry-Amaretto Sauce

BOURBON BARBECUE

1 (2½-pound) sirloin roast
1 (5-ounce) bottle soy sauce
¼ cup firmly packed brown sugar
¼ cup bourbon
1 tablespoon lemon juice
1 teaspoon Worcestershire sauce
½ cup water

Place roast in a large shallow dish. Combine remaining ingredients, stirring well. Pour marinade over meat; cover and marinate for 8 hours in refrigerator.

Drain meat, reserving marinade. Place on grill about 5 inches from medium-hot coals. Cook meat 20 minutes on each side or to desired degree of doneness, brushing often with marinade. Yield: 6 servings.

CHARCOAL POTATOES

6 medium potatoes
½ cup plus 2 tablespoons butter or margarine, softened
3 (.25-ounce) envelopes instant onion soup mix

Scrub potatoes; do not peel. Slice lengthwise into ½-inch slices. Arrange slices of each potato on a square of heavy-duty aluminum foil to make individual bundles.

Combine butter and soup mix, mixing well. Divide mixture evenly, and spread on each potato. Fold foil edges over, and wrap securely. Grill over medium-hot coals 50 to 60 minutes, turning once. Yield: 6 servings.

VEGETABLES À LA GRILL

2 tomatoes, cut into wedges
1 zucchini, cut into ¼-inch slices
1 yellow squash, cut into ¼-inch
    slices
6 broccoli flowerets
6 cauliflower flowerets
1 onion, thinly sliced
1 teaspoon beef-flavored bouillon
    granules
3 tablespoons butter, cut into
    pieces
1 tablespoon brown sugar
¼ teaspoon salt
¼ teaspoon fennel seeds, crushed
⅛ teaspoon pepper

Combine all ingredients in a large bowl; toss gently.

Place vegetables on large piece of heavy-duty aluminum foil. Fold edges over, and wrap securely.

Place on grill about 5 inches from medium-hot coals. Cook 12 to 15 minutes or until vegetables are tender. Yield: 6 servings.

FROZEN LEMON SOUFFLÉ WITH RASPBERRY-AMARETTO SAUCE

1 envelope unflavored gelatin
½ cup lemon juice
3 eggs, separated
¾ cup sugar, divided
2 teaspoons grated lemon rind
⅛ teaspoon salt
1 cup whipping cream, whipped
3 coconut macaroon cookies,
    crumbled
Raspberry-Amaretto Sauce

Sprinkle gelatin over lemon juice in a small saucepan; let stand 1 minute. Cook over low heat, stirring until gelatin dissolves; set aside.

Beat egg yolks and ¼ cup sugar in a large bowl at medium speed of an electric mixer until thick and lemon colored. Add gelatin mixture, remaining ½ cup sugar, and grated lemon rind, stirring well.

Beat egg whites (at room temperature) and salt until stiff peaks form.

Gently fold egg whites and whipped cream into lemon mixture.

Spoon three-fourths of mixture into a 1-quart soufflé dish. Sprinkle with macaroon crumbs, and spoon remaining lemon mixture over crumbs. Cover and freeze.

To serve, spoon into individual dishes; top with Raspberry-Amaretto Sauce. Yield: 6 servings.

Raspberry-Amaretto Sauce

1 pint fresh raspberries
¼ cup water
1 tablespoon lemon juice
½ cup sugar
2 tablespoons amaretto

Combine raspberries, water, and lemon juice in food processor or electric blender. Process until pureed. Strain. Discard seeds.

Pour raspberry puree into a saucepan; add sugar. Bring to a boil over medium heat; reduce heat, and simmer 10 minutes. Stir in amaretto. Refrigerate until ready to serve. Yield: 1 cup.

Note: 1 (10-ounce) package frozen raspberries can be substituted for the fresh berries. Thaw raspberries, and reserve ¼ cup juice for use in place of ¼ cup water.

Asparagus Is Something Special

May is a good time for asparagus, so put away the canned and frozen to enjoy the fresh while it's available. Fresh asparagus can be cooked by steaming, boiling, or microwaving.

In addition to having a delicate flavor, asparagus is low in calories and a good source of vitamins A and C, niacin, and potassium. To preserve these nutrients, use asparagus as soon after purchasing as possible.

MARINATED ASPARAGUS SPEARS

2 pounds fresh asparagus
½ cup sugar
½ cup cider vinegar
1½ tablespoons lemon juice
1 teaspoon salt
⅛ teaspoon seasoned pepper

Snap off tough ends of asparagus. Remove scales with a vegetable peeler or knife, if desired. Cook asparagus, covered, in boiling water 6 to 8 minutes or until crisp-tender; drain, reserving ½ cup liquid. Place asparagus in a large shallow container; set aside.

Combine reserved ½ cup asparagus liquid and remaining ingredients in a small saucepan; stir well. Bring to a boil, stirring constantly; pour over asparagus. Cover; chill 8 hours. Yield: 8 servings.

Mrs. John B. Wright
Greenville, South Carolina

CHILLED ASPARAGUS IN MUSTARD SAUCE

1 pound fresh asparagus
½ cup plain yogurt
2½ tablespoons Dijon mustard
2 tablespoons mayonnaise
1 tablespoon minced fresh
    dillweed
1 tablespoon minced fresh chives
⅛ teaspoon freshly ground pepper
Lettuce leaves
Cherry tomatoes (optional)

Snap off tough ends of asparagus. Remove scales with a vegetable peeler or knife, if desired. Cook asparagus, covered, in a small amount of boiling water 5 minutes or until crisp-tender; drain. Rinse with cold water; drain. Place asparagus in refrigerator to chill.

Combine yogurt and next 5 ingredients; chill.

Place asparagus on a lettuce-lined plate, and top with yogurt mixture. Garnish with cherry tomatoes, if desired. Yield: 4 servings.

Jackie Garrison
Lauderhill, Florida

ASPARAGUS MERINGUE

2 pounds fresh asparagus
¾ cup mayonnaise
¼ cup commercial sour cream
1½ teaspoons Dijon mustard
1 teaspoon lemon juice
1½ tablespoons minced chives
4 egg whites
½ teaspoon salt
¼ teaspoon pepper

Snap off tough ends of asparagus. Remove scales with a vegetable peeler or knife, if desired. Cook asparagus, covered, in boiling water 6 to 8 minutes or until crisp-tender. Drain. Arrange asparagus on an ovenproof platter, alternating tips.

Combine mayonnaise and next 4 ingredients in a large bowl. Beat egg whites (at room temperature) until foamy; add salt and pepper, and continue beating until soft peaks form. Fold egg whites into mayonnaise mixture. Spoon mixture over asparagus, leaving tips exposed. Bake at 375° for 10 minutes, and serve. Yield: 6 servings.

Mrs. Randall L. Wilson
Louisville, Kentucky

EASY ASPARAGUS SALAD

1 pound fresh asparagus
Lettuce leaves
2 small tomatoes, sliced
2 hard-cooked eggs, sliced
1 small purple onion, sliced and separated into rings
Commercial ranch-style salad dressing

Snap off tough ends of asparagus. Remove scales with a vegetable peeler or knife, if desired. Cook asparagus, covered, in a small amount of boiling water 6 to 8 minutes or until crisp-tender; drain. Chill asparagus 1 to 2 hours.

Line individual salad plates with lettuce leaves; arrange asparagus, tomato slices, egg slices, and onion rings on top. Serve with dressing. Yield: 4 servings.
Betty Wall
Austin, Texas

Spinach Appetizers Make Sense

It's no surprise that many cooks turn to spinach when preparing appetizers these days. You'll find dips, spreads, and a host of other nibbles that cast the familiar green color served often and with good reason.

While some appetizers offer only "empty calories," adding spinach boosts the nutrient count a great deal. The vegetable is loaded with vitamins A and C.

And thanks to the frozen food industry, it's easy to cook with spinach. The vegetable is available frozen in chopped and leaf forms, as well as blended into tasty, ready-to-bake soufflés.

Just remember to read your recipe and select your spinach carefully. Most appetizer recipes that use spinach call for it in the chopped form. Cooks who mistakenly use the leaf form end up with unspreadable spreads and undippable dips.

SPINACH SQUARES

2 (10-ounce) packages frozen chopped spinach, thawed
3 eggs, beaten
¼ cup butter or margarine, melted
1 cup all-purpose flour
1 teaspoon baking powder
½ teaspoon seasoned salt
¼ teaspoon pepper
1 cup milk
4 cups (16 ounces) shredded mozzarella cheese
2 tablespoons chopped onion

Drain spinach well, and press between paper towels until barely moist; set aside.

Combine eggs and butter. Add flour, baking powder, salt, and pepper, stirring well. Gradually add milk, stirring until smooth. Stir in spinach, cheese, and onion. Spoon mixture

into a lightly greased 13- x 9- x 2-inch baking dish. Bake at 350° for 35 minutes or until lightly browned. Cut into 1-inch squares. Yield: 9¾ dozen.

Note: To freeze, bake spinach squares as directed; let cool. Wrap in aluminum foil, and freeze. To serve, let thaw; bake in foil at 325° for 10 minutes or until heated.
Pauline S. Morgan
St. Albans, West Virginia

SPINACH-STUFFED MUSHROOMS

1 (12-ounce) package frozen spinach soufflé
1 cup soft breadcrumbs, lightly toasted
1 teaspoon dried minced onion
¼ teaspoon salt
2 teaspoons lemon juice
24 large fresh mushrooms
1 tablespoon butter or margarine, melted
1½ tablespoons grated Parmesan cheese
Leaf spinach
Fresh parsley sprigs
Pimiento rose

Bake soufflé, uncovered, at 350° for 15 to 18 minutes or until slightly warmed. Combine spinach, breadcrumbs, onion, salt, and lemon juice; stir well.

Clean mushrooms with damp paper towels. Remove mushroom stems, and reserve for other uses. Place mushroom caps, bottom side up, in a shallow pan; brush mushrooms with melted butter.

Spoon spinach mixture evenly into mushroom caps; sprinkle with Parmesan cheese. Bake, uncovered, at 350° for 15 minutes. Arrange mushrooms on spinach leaves; garnish with parsley and pimiento rose. Yield: 2 dozen.
Jackie Pippin
Louisville, Kentucky

SPINACH SPREAD

1 (10-ounce) package frozen
   chopped spinach, thawed
3 green onions, chopped
½ cup mayonnaise
1 teaspoon Worcestershire sauce
½ teaspoon salt
¼ teaspoon hot sauce

Drain spinach well, and press between paper towels until barely moist. Combine spinach and remaining ingredients; stir well. Chill at least 2 hours. Serve with assorted crackers. Yield: about 1 cup.

Mary-Hannah Taft
Greenville, North Carolina

CREAMY SPINACH DIP

1 (10-ounce) package frozen
   chopped spinach, thawed
1 (8-ounce) package cream
   cheese, softened
1 (8-ounce) carton commercial
   sour cream
2 tablespoons milk
1 (6¾-ounce) can chunk ham,
   drained
1½ teaspoons minced onion
½ teaspoon garlic salt
½ teaspoon pepper

Drain spinach well, and press between paper towels until barely moist; set aside.

Combine cream cheese, sour cream, and milk in a mixing bowl; beat at medium speed of an electric mixer until smooth. Stir in spinach, ham, and remaining ingredients. Cover and chill. Serve with chips or cut vegetables. Yield: 4 cups.

Ginny Munsterman
Garland, Texas

This Cook Loves The Dramatic

Phillip Myers-Reid has a flair for the unusual. Once a full-time actor and now the managing director of the 2,300-seat Aycock Auditorium on the campus of the University of North Carolina at Greensboro, Phillip also has a reputation for being a whiz in the kitchen. He confesses, "I'm always tempted to try something a little bit different."

CHICKEN LIVER PÂTÉ

1 pound chicken livers
1 cup water
1 teaspoon beef-flavored bouillon
   granules
6 slices bacon
½ cup pecan pieces
2 hard-cooked eggs
½ small onion
¼ cup dry sherry
½ cup mayonnaise
¼ teaspoon salt
¼ teaspoon pepper

Combine livers, water, and bouillon granules in a 4-cup glass measure. Cover with heavy-duty plastic wrap, and microwave at HIGH 6 to 8 minutes. Let stand 5 minutes; drain.

Place bacon on a rack in a 12- x 8- x 2-inch baking dish; cover with paper towels. Microwave at HIGH 5 to 7 minutes or until bacon is crisp. Drain bacon; crumble and set aside.

Position knife blade in food processor bowl; add pecan pieces. Top with cover, and pulse 2 or 3 times until pecans are chopped. Remove from bowl; set aside. Place hard-cooked eggs in processor bowl; pulse 2 or 3 times until eggs are chopped. Remove eggs from bowl, and set aside.

Place chicken livers, onion, and sherry in processor bowl; process 1 minute or until pureed. Combine chicken liver mixture, bacon, pecans, eggs, and remaining ingredients. Spoon into a lightly oiled 3-cup mold. Chill at least 3 hours. Unmold and serve with crackers. Yield: 3 cups.

OVEN-BARBECUED PORK RIBS

Vegetable cooking spray
4 pounds country-style pork ribs
½ cup dry sherry
½ cup water
1 teaspoon salt
1 teaspoon celery seeds
1 teaspoon chili powder
⅛ teaspoon pepper
½ cup firmly packed brown sugar
1 (12-ounce) bottle chili sauce
¼ cup vinegar
¼ cup Worcestershire sauce
2 cups water
1 medium onion, chopped
1 lemon, thinly sliced (optional)
Parsley sprigs (optional)

Coat a large nonstick skillet with cooking spray; place over medium-high heat until hot. Brown ribs on both sides. Add sherry and ½ cup water. Cover, reduce heat, and simmer 1½ hours.

Combine salt, celery seeds, and next 8 ingredients in a 2-quart saucepan. Simmer, uncovered, over medium heat 1 hour.

Transfer ribs to a 13- x 9- x 2-inch baking dish; pour sauce over ribs. Bake, uncovered, at 300° for 1 hour. If desired, garnish with lemon slices and parsley. Yield: 6 servings.

WINDSOR MUSHROOM BAKE

1 cup chopped celery
1 cup chopped onion
3 tablespoons butter, melted
½ pound fresh mushrooms, sliced
9 slices bread, cubed and toasted
1 cup (4 ounces) shredded Colby
   cheese
1 cup (4 ounces) shredded
   Monterey Jack cheese
2 eggs, beaten
2 cups milk
¼ teaspoon salt
¼ teaspoon pepper
⅛ teaspoon Italian seasoning

Sauté celery and onion in butter 5 minutes. Add sliced mushrooms; sauté 5 minutes.

Layer half each of bread cubes, cheeses, and sautéed vegetables in a buttered 2½-quart casserole. Repeat layers; set aside.

Combine eggs, milk, and seasonings; stir well. Pour over sautéed vegetables; bake at 350° for 55 to 60 minutes. Remove from oven, and let stand 5 minutes before serving. Yield: 8 servings.

Bread Made With Beer

Mrs. E. W. Hanley of Palm Harbor, Florida, eliminates time-consuming mixing and measuring with her Hearty Beer Bread recipe. She begins with a hot roll mix.

HEARTY BEER BREAD

1¼ cups beer
¼ cup butter or margarine
1 (16-ounce) package hot roll mix
½ cup nutlike cereal nuggets
2 tablespoons sugar
½ teaspoon salt
1 to 2 teaspoons milk

Combine beer and butter in a saucepan; cook over medium heat, stirring constantly, until butter melts. Cool to 105° to 115°. Add yeast packet from roll mix; stir until dissolved. Add roll mix, cereal nuggets, sugar, and salt; stir well.

Turn dough out onto a floured surface, and knead until smooth and elastic (about 5 minutes). Place in a well-greased bowl, turning to grease top. Cover and let rise in a warm place (85°), free from drafts, 1½ hours or until doubled in bulk.

Punch dough down; invert onto a floured surface. Cover and let stand 15 minutes. Shape into a 6-inch ball, and place on a lightly greased baking sheet. Cover and let rise in a warm place, free from drafts, one hour and 15 minutes or until doubled in bulk.

Gently brush dough with milk; bake at 375° for 25 to 30 minutes or until loaf sounds hollow when tapped. Yield: one 10-inch round loaf.

Southern Sunday Dinner

Sunday dinner is a special time when family and friends gather to visit and enjoy favorite recipes.

The menu we have put together includes Marinated Baked Ham; the orange juice-and-ginger ale marinade seems to take out some of the salt and leaves the ham tender and juicy.

MARINATED BAKED HAM

1 (8-pound) smoked fully cooked ham half
2 cups orange juice
2 cups ginger ale
⅓ cup firmly packed brown sugar
¼ cup orange marmalade
1 teaspoon dry mustard

Place ham in a large roasting bag; pour orange juice and ginger ale over ham. Tie bag tightly. Place ham in a large bowl, and refrigerate 8 hours, turning occasionally.

Remove ham from marinade, reserving marinade. Place ham on a rack in a shallow roasting pan; insert meat thermometer, making sure it does not touch fat or bone. Bake at 325° for 2½ hours; baste occasionally with marinade.

Remove ham from oven; remove skin. Score fat on ham in a diamond design, if desired. Combine brown sugar, marmalade, and mustard; mix well. Coat exposed portion of ham with sugar mixture. Bake, uncovered, an additional 30 minutes or until meat thermometer registers 140°. Place ham on platter. Yield: 16 servings.
Faye Hicks
Charleston, West Virginia

SPINACH SALAD WITH CITRUS DRESSING

Juice of 1 grapefruit (⅔ cup)
1½ teaspoons sugar
½ teaspoon salt
½ teaspoon pepper
½ teaspoon dry mustard
½ teaspoon dried whole dillweed
½ teaspoon parsley flakes
½ teaspoon onion powder
½ teaspoon dried whole basil
¾ cup vegetable oil
½ cup cider vinegar
2 pounds fresh spinach, torn
2 carrots, grated
4 slices bacon, cooked and crumbled
½ cup (2 ounces) shredded Cheddar cheese

Combine first 11 ingredients in a jar. Cover and shake vigorously. Chill.

Combine spinach and carrots in a salad bowl; sprinkle with bacon and cheese. Serve with dressing. Yield: 12 servings.
Beryle Wyatt
Columbia, Missouri

ASPARAGUS CAESAR

3 pounds fresh asparagus spears
¼ cup plus 2 tablespoons butter or margarine, melted
¼ cup plus 2 tablespoons lemon juice
¼ cup plus 2 tablespoons grated Parmesan cheese
Paprika
Lemon slices (optional)

Snap off tough ends of asparagus; remove scales with a knife or vegetable peeler, if desired. Cook asparagus, covered, in a small amount of boiling water 6 to 8 minutes or until crisp-tender. Drain.

Place asparagus in a 12- x 8- x 2-inch baking dish. Combine butter and lemon juice; pour over asparagus. Sprinkle cheese and paprika over asparagus. Place under broiler until browned. Garnish asparagus with lemon slices, if desired. Yield: 12 servings.
Eleanor Brandt
Arlington, Texas

HERB POTATOES

½ cup butter or margarine,
   melted
2 tablespoons chopped fresh
   chives
2 tablespoons chopped fresh
   parsley
¼ teaspoon paprika
1 teaspoon salt
¼ teaspoon pepper
½ teaspoon fines herbes
4½ pounds potatoes, unpeeled
   and cut into ¼-inch slices
Grated Parmesan cheese
   (optional)

Combine first 7 ingredients in a large bowl; add potatoes, tossing to coat.

Cover and bake at 425° for 1 hour, stirring at 15-minute intervals. Top with Parmesan cheese, if desired. Yield: 12 servings.   *Grace Bravos*
Timonium, Maryland

LAYERED LEMON DESSERT

½ cup butter or margarine
1 cup all-purpose flour
½ cup chopped pecans
1 (8-ounce) package cream
   cheese, softened
1½ cups sifted powdered sugar
1 (8-ounce) container frozen
   whipped topping, thawed and
   divided
2 cups sugar
¼ cup plus 2 tablespoons
   cornstarch
¼ teaspoon salt
2 cups water, divided
3 eggs, beaten
¼ cup vinegar
¼ cup lemon juice
1 tablespoon butter or margarine
1 teaspoon lemon extract
Additional chopped pecans
   (optional)

Cut butter into flour with a pastry blender until mixture resembles coarse meal; stir ½ cup pecans into flour mixture. Press pecan mixture in bottom of a 13- x 9- x 2-inch pan. Bake at 350° for 15 minutes or until golden brown.

Combine cream cheese and powdered sugar; beat at medium speed of an electric mixer until fluffy. Fold 1½ cups whipped topping into cheese mixture. Spread over crust; chill.

Combine sugar, cornstarch, and salt in a heavy saucepan; add ¼ cup water, stirring to make a smooth paste. Add eggs, vinegar, lemon juice, and remaining 1¾ cups water, stirring well. Cook over medium heat, stirring constantly, until mixture boils. Boil 1 minute. Remove from heat; add butter and lemon extract. Cool.

Spread lemon filling over cream cheese layer. Top each serving with remaining whipped topping. Sprinkle with pecans, if desired. Yield: 15 servings.   *Wilmoth Cunningham*
Lexington, Kentucky

Processor Crêpes And Fillings

By using the food processor and planning ahead, you can make elegant crêpes for your next brunch. Traditional crêpe batter—a mixture of eggs, flour, milk, and butter or oil—can be whirled for a few seconds in the processor or blender for a smooth creamy mixture. If lumps occur when the batter is hand mixed, the batter must be sieved. This problem isn't likely to occur using the food processor.

Once the batter is mixed, it needs to sit 1 to 2 hours before cooking to allow the flour particles to expand and the air bubbles to collapse. It's easy to overprocess the batter; remember that 4 to 6 seconds should be sufficient.

The crêpe recipes we've included here are basic, but you can add your own touches. For example, you might add savory herbs to batter for crêpes that will wrap around meat or vegetables. Liqueurs and extracts give a flavor lift to dessert crêpes.

Use moderate heat to cook crêpes. The pan is hot enough when a few drops of water bounce and sizzle in the pan. Don't worry if you don't have a traditional crêpe pan—any low-sided pan with a 6- to 8-inch diameter cooking surface will do.

To save time when you entertain, make the crêpes ahead. They'll keep in the refrigerator up to 3 days and in the freezer for 4 months. To freeze, place wax paper between each crêpe, and wrap in aluminum foil. Then sandwich the stack between two paper plates, and wrap in foil. This will keep the edges of the crêpes from breaking off.

DESSERT CRÊPES

1½ cups all-purpose flour
1 tablespoon sugar
¼ teaspoon salt
½ teaspoon ground cinnamon
   (optional)
2 tablespoons butter or
   margarine, chilled
3 eggs
2 cups milk
1 teaspoon vanilla extract
Vegetable oil

Position knife blade in food processor bowl. Place flour, sugar, salt, and, if desired, cinnamon in bowl. Top with cover, and pulse 2 or 3 times to blend. Add butter; process until mixture resembles coarse meal.

Add eggs through food chute, one at a time, and process just until blended. Combine milk and vanilla. With processor running, pour milk mixture through food chute, and process until smooth. Refrigerate 1 to 2 hours. (This allows flour particles to swell and soften so that the crêpes are light in texture.)

Brush bottom of 6-inch crêpe pan or heavy skillet with oil; place over medium heat just until skillet is hot. Pour 2 tablespoons batter into pan; quickly tilt pan in all directions so that batter covers pan in a thin film. Cook 1 minute or until lightly browned. Lift edge of crêpe to test for doneness.

Crêpe is ready for flipping when it can be shaken loose from pan. Flip crêpe, and cook about 30 seconds on other side. (This side is usually spotty brown and is the side on which the filling is placed.) Repeat until all batter is used.

Place crêpes on a towel to cool. Stack between layers of wax paper to prevent sticking. Yield: approximately 2 dozen crêpes.

STRAWBERRY ICE CREAM CRÊPES

¼ cup sugar
Rind of ½ lemon
1 (10-ounce) package frozen
    strawberries, partially thawed
¼ teaspoon vanilla extract
¾ cup whipping cream, chilled
6 (6-inch) Dessert Crêpes
Berry Sauce
Fresh strawberries (optional)

Position knife blade in food processor bowl. Add sugar and lemon rind; process until rind is finely chopped. Add partially thawed strawberries and vanilla; process 10 to 15 seconds or until strawberries are cut into small chunks. With machine running, pour whipping cream through food chute, and process 10 seconds or until mixture reaches a smooth, creamy consistency (some strawberry chunks may remain, if desired).

Immediately spoon about ⅓ cup ice cream in center of each crêpe; roll up, and place seam side down on individual serving plates. Top with Berry Sauce, and, if desired, garnish with fresh strawberries. Serve immediately. Yield: 6 servings.

Berry Sauce

1 (10-ounce) package frozen
    strawberries, thawed
1 tablespoon kirsch or other
    cherry-flavored liqueur

Position knife blade in food processor bowl. Add strawberries and kirsch to processor. Top with cover, and process until strawberries are pureed. Chill. Yield: about 1 cup.

BASIC PROCESSOR CRÊPES

1½ cups all-purpose flour
¼ teaspoon salt
2 tablespoons butter or
    margarine, chilled
3 eggs
2 cups milk
Vegetable oil

Position knife blade in food processor bowl. Place flour, salt, and butter in processor bowl. Top with cover, and process until mixture resembles coarse meal. Add eggs through food chute, one at a time, processing just until blended. With processor running, pour milk through food chute, and process until smooth. Refrigerate batter 1 to 2 hours. (This allows flour particles to swell and soften so the crêpes will be light in texture.)

Brush bottom of a 6- or 8-inch crêpe pan or heavy skillet with oil; place the pan over medium heat just until hot, not smoking.

Pour 2 to 3 tablespoons batter into pan; quickly tilt pan in all directions so batter covers pan in a thin film. Cook about 1 minute or until lightly browned. Lift edge of crêpe to test for doneness. Crêpe is ready for flipping when it can be shaken loose from pan. Flip crêpe, and cook about 30 seconds on other side. (This side is usually spotty brown and is the side on which the filling is placed.) Repeat until all batter is used.

Place crêpes on a towel to cool. Stack between layers of wax paper to prevent sticking. Yield: 24 (6-inch) crêpes or 18 (8-inch) crêpes.

MUSHROOM-CHEESE CRÊPES

2 small shallots, cut in half
½ pound fresh mushrooms
3 tablespoons butter or
    margarine, melted
1 (8-ounce) package cream
    cheese, softened
1 egg, beaten
Swiss Cheese Sauce
14 (6-inch) Basic Processor
    Crêpes
¼ cup (1 ounce) shredded Swiss
    cheese

Position knife blade in food processor bowl, and top with cover. With processor running, drop shallots through food chute, and process until minced. Remove knife blade, and leave shallots in processor bowl.

Position slicing disc in processor, and top with cover. Slice off one side of two mushroom caps. Arrange these mushrooms in food chute, cut side down. Stack remaining mushrooms sideways in chute, alternating stems and caps. Slice, using firm pressure.

Sauté shallots and mushrooms in butter in a heavy skillet about 3 minutes or until vegetables are tender. Drain and set aside.

Position knife blade in processor bowl. Cut cream cheese into 1-inch pieces, and add to processor. Add egg to processor; top with cover, and process about 10 seconds or until smooth. Combine cream cheese mixture, vegetables, and 1¾ cups Swiss Cheese Sauce.

Spread ¼ cup mushroom filling in center of each crêpe; roll up, and place seam side down in a greased 13- x 9- x 2-inch baking dish. Spread remaining Swiss Cheese Sauce over crêpes, and sprinkle with cheese. Bake at 375° for 15 minutes. Yield: 7 servings.

Swiss Cheese Sauce

¼ cup butter or margarine
¼ cup plus 1 tablespoon
    all-purpose flour
2¾ cups milk
¼ cup whipping cream
¾ cup (3 ounces) shredded Swiss
    cheese
⅛ teaspoon ground nutmeg
⅛ teaspoon pepper
Pinch of salt

Melt butter in a heavy saucepan over low heat; add flour, stirring with a wire whisk until smooth. Cook 1 minute, stirring constantly. Gradually add milk; cook over medium heat, stirring constantly, until thickened and bubbly. Stir in whipping cream, Swiss cheese, nutmeg, pepper, and salt; cook over low heat, stirring constantly, until cheese melts. Yield: about 3½ cups.

Wonderful Strawberry Desserts

If you're looking for colorful, fancy, desserts, search no more. These desserts feature luscious strawberries, the favorite berries of people all over the South.

For a quick ending to a meal, you can prepare English Toffee Dessert in 15 minutes. It captures the flavor of strawberries and combines it with sour cream and toffee.

STRAWBERRY MERINGUE TORTE

¼ cup butter or margarine, softened
½ cup sugar
2 eggs, separated
1¾ cups sifted cake flour
2 teaspoons baking powder
Dash of salt
½ cup milk
¼ teaspoon vanilla extract
¼ teaspoon almond extract
½ cup sugar
1 quart strawberries, sliced
¼ to ½ cup sugar

Cream softened butter; gradually add ½ cup sugar, beating well at medium speed of an electric mixer. Add egg yolks, one at a time, beating after each addition.

Combine flour, baking powder, and salt; add to creamed mixture alternately with milk, beginning and ending with flour mixture. Mix after each addition. Stir in vanilla and almond flavorings. Spoon batter into two greased and wax paper-lined 8-inch cakepans. Set aside.

Beat egg whites (at room temperature) at high speed of an electric mixer 1 minute. Gradually add ½ cup sugar, 1 tablespoon at a time, beating until stiff peaks form and sugar dissolves. Spread half of meringue over cake batter in each pan. Bake at 350° for 25 minutes. Cool in pans 10 minutes; remove cake layers from pans. Remove wax paper, and cool cake layers, meringue side up, on wire racks.

Combine strawberries and ¼ to ½ cup sugar in a bowl. Place one cake layer, meringue side up, on a serving plate; spoon half of strawberries over cake layer. Top with second cake layer, meringue side up; spoon remaining strawberries over cake layer. Chill. Yield: one 8-inch cake.
Mrs. M. L. Shannon
Fairfield, Alabama

ENGLISH TOFFEE DESSERT

¾ cup sugar
½ cup whipping cream
¼ cup light corn syrup
2 tablespoons butter or margarine
2 (1⅛-ounce) English toffee-flavored candy bars, crushed
4 cups fresh strawberries, halved
1 cup commercial sour cream

Combine first 4 ingredients in a small saucepan; cook over medium heat until mixture comes to a boil. Boil 1 minute, stirring constantly. Remove from heat; add candy. Stir well; cool. (Sauce thickens as it cools.)

Place strawberries in serving dishes; dollop each serving with 2 tablespoons sour cream. Top with 2 to 3 tablespoons toffee sauce. Yield: 8 servings.
Eleanor K. Brandt
Arlington, Texas

A FAVORITE STRAWBERRY SHORTCAKE

4 cups strawberries, sliced
¼ to ⅓ cup sugar
2 tablespoons shortening
½ cup sugar
1 egg
1½ cups self-rising flour
½ cup milk
1 teaspoon vanilla extract
1 cup whipping cream, whipped

Combine strawberries and ¼ to ⅓ cup sugar; chill.

Cream shortening; gradually add ½ cup sugar, beating well at medium speed of an electric mixer. Add egg, beating well. Add flour to creamed mixture alternately with milk, beginning and ending with flour. Mix after each addition. Stir in vanilla. Spoon batter into a greased and floured 9-inch cakepan. Bake at 350° for 25 minutes or until golden brown. Remove from pan. Cool on wire rack.

Slice shortcake crosswise into 2 equal parts. Place bottom half of shortcake, cut side up, on a serving plate; spoon half of strawberries onto bottom layer. Top with second layer of shortcake, cut side down; spoon on remaining strawberries. Top with whipped cream. Yield: 6 to 8 servings.
Thelma Brooks
Winter Haven, Florida

STRAWBERRY ANGEL PIE

1 (3-ounce) package wild strawberry-flavored gelatin
1 cup boiling water
½ cup cold water
1 (8-ounce) container frozen whipped topping, thawed
1 cup fresh sliced strawberries
1 (9-inch) graham cracker crust
Additional sliced strawberries

Dissolve gelatin in boiling water; add cold water, stirring well. Chill until the consistency of unbeaten egg white. Fold in whipped topping and 1 cup strawberries. Spoon into graham cracker crust. Chill at least 4 hours. Arrange additional strawberry slices on top of pie. Yield: one 9-inch pie.
Sherri Rape
Lancaster, South Carolina

STRAWBERRY COCONUT NESTS

1½ cups sliced fresh strawberries
1 tablespoon sugar
1 (8-ounce) package cream cheese, softened
½ cup sugar
2 teaspoons milk
1 teaspoon vanilla extract
6 (3-inch) commercial shortcake cups
½ cup flaked coconut, toasted

Combine strawberries and 1 tablespoon sugar; stir gently. Set aside.

Combine cream cheese, ½ cup sugar, milk, and vanilla; beat at medium speed of an electric mixer until smooth. Spread over top and sides of shortcake cups; sprinkle with coconut. Place on individual serving dishes; spoon ¼ cup strawberries into each. Serve immediately. Yield: 6 servings.
Kay Hall
Mineral Wells, Texas

Cool Desserts Ready When You Are

On hot summer days, you don't want to heat up the kitchen any more than is absolutely necessary. With one of these desserts in the refrigerator or freezer, you'll have a ready-to-serve cool refreshment to end the meal.

PEACHES 'N' CREAM CHEESECAKE

¾ cup all-purpose flour
1 teaspoon baking powder
1 (3⅛-ounce) package vanilla pudding mix
3 tablespoons butter or margarine, softened
1 egg
½ cup milk
1 (16-ounce) can sliced peaches, undrained
1 (8-ounce) package cream cheese, softened
½ cup sugar
1½ teaspoons sugar
¼ teaspoon ground cinnamon

Combine first 6 ingredients in a mixing bowl; beat at medium speed of an electric mixer until batter is smooth. Pour mixture into a greased 8-inch round cakepan. Drain peaches, reserving 3 tablespoons peach liquid.

Set peach liquid aside. Arrange peach slices over batter.

Combine cream cheese, ½ cup sugar, and reserved peach liquid. Beat 2 minutes at medium speed of an electric mixer. Spoon mixture over peaches in center of cake, leaving a 1-inch border around edge of cakepan.

Combine 1½ teaspoons sugar and cinnamon; sprinkle over cream cheese filling. Bake at 350° for 35 minutes; remove from oven, and cool to room temperature on a wire rack. Chill. Yield: one 8-inch cheesecake.
Merle Dunson
Greenville, South Carolina

FROZEN PEANUT BUTTER DELIGHT

½ cup peanut butter
¼ cup butter or margarine, softened
½ cup firmly packed brown sugar
1 cup all-purpose flour
1 (8-ounce) package cream cheese, softened
½ cup sugar
¼ cup peanut butter
1 teaspoon vanilla extract
2 eggs
1 cup whipping cream, whipped
1 (6-ounce) package semisweet chocolate morsels

Cream ½ cup peanut butter and butter; add ½ cup brown sugar, beating at medium speed of an electric mixer until mixture is light and fluffy. Add flour; mix well. (Mixture will be crumbly.) Reserve 1 cup of mixture for topping. Lightly press remaining crumbs in an ungreased 13- x 9- x

2-inch baking pan. Bake at 350° for 8 to 10 minutes or until golden brown; cool. Set aside.

Combine cream cheese, ½ cup sugar, ¼ cup peanut butter, and vanilla. Beat at medium speed of an electric mixer until mixture is light and fluffy. Add eggs, one at a time, beating well after each addition. Fold whipped cream into cheese mixture. Spoon over crust.

Place chocolate morsels in top of a double boiler; bring water to a boil. Reduce heat to low, and cook until chocolate melts. Drizzle melted chocolate over filling; cut through with a knife to marble. Sprinkle with the reserved crumbs.

Cover and freeze 8 hours or until firm. Cut into squares to serve. Yield: 12 to 15 servings.
Barbara L. Boyle
Germantown, Maryland

BAVARIAN CREAM WITH FRESH FRUIT

1 envelope unflavored gelatin
½ cup sugar, divided
⅛ teaspoon salt
2 eggs, separated
1¼ cups milk
½ teaspoon vanilla extract
1 cup whipping cream, whipped
Strawberry slices
Kiwifruit slices
Blueberries

Combine gelatin, ¼ cup sugar, and salt in top of a double boiler. Combine egg yolks and milk, mixing well; add to gelatin mixture. Cook over boiling water, stirring constantly, until gelatin dissolves. Remove mixture from heat, and stir in vanilla. Chill until the consistency of unbeaten egg white.

Beat egg whites (at room temperature) until foamy. Gradually add remaining ¼ cup sugar, 1 tablespoon at a time, beating until stiff peaks form. Fold egg whites and whipped cream into gelatin mixture. Pour into a lightly greased 4-cup mold; chill until firm. Unmold and garnish with fruit. Yield: 6 servings.
Teresa Sands
Irmo, South Carolina

Mangoes And Papayas Are Tropical Treats

Mangoes and papayas are no longer rare tropical fruits that are seen only in the Caribbean or Hawaii. Although these fruits are stocked regularly in supermarkets, many people still haven't tasted them. Both have exotic and distinctive flavors that are reminiscent of more familiar fruits.

Nutritionally, they are good sources of vitamins A and C. Low in sodium, they add potassium and fiber to the diet. One cup of papaya contains only 55 calories, and mango is about 110 calories per cup.

MANGO-BEEF AND RICE

1 pound top sirloin steak
1 medium-size green pepper, cut into strips
1 medium onion, chopped
2 tablespoons vegetable oil
2 cups water
¼ cup soy sauce
1 cup uncooked rice
1 medium-size ripe mango, peeled and sliced
½ cup sliced almonds, toasted

Partially freeze steak; slice diagonally across grain into ¼-inch strips.

Sauté meat, green pepper, and onion in oil in a large skillet over medium-high heat until meat is browned, stirring often. Add water, soy sauce, and rice. Bring to a boil, and stir well.

Arrange mango slices over top of rice mixture; cover, reduce heat, and simmer 20 minutes or until rice is tender. Sprinkle almonds over mangoes, and serve. Yield: 4 servings.

Nita Grochowski
Bokeelia, Florida

PAPAYA BREAD

1 cup shredded firm papaya
½ cup butter or margarine, softened
1 cup sugar
2 eggs
1½ cups all-purpose flour
1 teaspoon baking powder
¼ teaspoon baking soda
½ teaspoon salt
½ teaspoon ground cinnamon
½ teaspoon ground allspice
½ teaspoon ground ginger
½ cup raisins
¼ cup chopped walnuts

Drain papaya well on paper towels.

Cream butter at medium speed of an electric mixer; gradually add sugar, beating well. Add eggs, one at a time.

Combine flour and next 6 ingredients; add to creamed mixture, stirring well. Stir in papaya, raisins, and chopped walnuts.

Spoon batter into a greased and floured 8½- x 4½- x 3-inch loafpan. Bake at 350° for 1 hour and 10 minutes or until done. Let cool in pan 10 minutes; remove bread from pan, and let cool completely on a wire rack. Yield: 1 loaf.

Lily Shapiro
Weslaco, Texas

MANGO-GINGER PIE

2 medium-size ripe mangoes, peeled and sliced
1 (14-ounce) can sweetened condensed milk
⅓ cup lime juice
2 egg yolks, beaten
Ginger Snap Crust
1 tablespoon ginger snap crumbs
Mango slices (optional)
Lime slice (optional)

Place mangoes in container of a food processor or electric blender; process until smooth. Combine 1 to 1½ cups of mango puree and next 3 ingredients; stir well. Pour into Ginger Snap Crust; cover and chill at least 6 hours. Sprinkle with 1 tablespoon crumbs. If desired, garnish with mango slices and lime slice. Yield: one 9-inch pie.

Ginger Snap Crust

1½ cups ginger snap crumbs
¼ cup sugar
¼ cup plus 1 tablespoon butter or margarine, melted

Combine all ingredients; mix well. Press into a 9-inch pieplate. Chill crust. Yield: one 9-inch crumb crust.

Meat Makes A Salad A Meal

Prepare any of these salads, and supper will be ready when you are. Each recipe offers "cover and chill" convenience as well as enough meat and fruit or vegetables to make the salad a meal in itself.

HAM-AND-CHEESE SALAD

8 ounces uncooked corkscrew macaroni
½ pound cooked ham, cut into 2-inch julienne strips
1 cup broccoli flowerets
1 cup frozen English peas, thawed
1 small yellow squash, thinly sliced
1 small sweet red pepper, cut into thin strips
4 ounces Swiss cheese, cubed
½ cup mayonnaise or salad dressing
¼ cup Dijon mustard
¼ cup milk
¼ cup grated Parmesan cheese

Cook macaroni according to package directions; drain. Rinse with cold water; drain.

Combine macaroni and next 6 ingredients in a large bowl.

Combine mayonnaise, mustard, and milk; stir well. Add to vegetable mixture, tossing gently. Sprinkle with Parmesan cheese. Cover and chill at least 2 hours. Yield: 6 servings.

Mrs. Harland J. Stone
Ocala, Florida

HAM-AND-APPLE SALAD

2 cups diced cooked ham
1 large red apple, unpeeled,
  cored, and diced
1 stalk celery, sliced
1 green onion, minced
¾ cup raisins
¼ cup mayonnaise
½ teaspoon poppy seeds
⅛ teaspoon curry powder
Dash of white pepper
1 tablespoon lemon juice
Lettuce leaves
Apple slices (optional)
Parsley sprigs (optional)

Combine first 5 ingredients, tossing
well. Combine mayonnaise, poppy
seeds, curry powder, pepper, and
lemon juice, stirring well; add to ham
mixture, and toss well. Cover and
chill. Serve on lettuce leaves. If desired, garnish with apple slices and
parsley. Yield: 4 servings.

Barbara S. Davis
Erwin, Tennessee

SHRIMP VERMICELLI SALAD

5 cups water
1½ pounds unpeeled medium-size
  fresh shrimp
1 (12-ounce) package vermicelli
3 hard-cooked eggs, chopped
1½ cups chopped green onions
1 cup chopped dill pickle
¼ cup minced fresh parsley
1 small green pepper, chopped
1 (2-ounce) jar diced pimiento,
  drained
1 (10-ounce) package tiny English
  peas, thawed and drained
1 cup mayonnaise
1 (8-ounce) carton commercial
  sour cream
¼ cup lemon juice
2 tablespoons prepared mustard
1 teaspoon celery seeds
1 teaspoon salt
¼ teaspoon pepper
Leaf lettuce
¼ to ½ teaspoon paprika

Bring water to a boil; add shrimp,
and cook 3 to 5 minutes. Drain well;
rinse with cold water. Chill. Peel and
devein shrimp.

Break vermicelli into 3-inch pieces.
Cook according to package directions; drain. Add shrimp, eggs,
onions, pickle, parsley, green pepper, pimiento, and peas; set aside.

Combine mayonnaise and next 6
ingredients; stir well. Pour over
shrimp mixture; toss gently. Cover
and chill 2 hours. Serve on a lettuce-
lined platter; sprinkle with paprika.
Yield: 8 servings. *Susan W. Pajcic*
Jacksonville, Florida

Pick A Sandwich That's Good For You

You'll find sandwiches a popular
menu item during the summer because they're quick to make and easy
to eat. One drawback for the health-
conscious cook, however, is that
many versions are full of saturated
fat, cholesterol, and calories. Not so
with these.

CHICKEN SALAD IN A POCKET

4 chicken breast halves, skinned
4 cups water
1 bay leaf
½ teaspoon dried minced onion
Dash of garlic powder
4 medium-size sweet pickles,
  chopped
2 celery hearts, chopped
1 large carrot, grated
1 medium onion, chopped
1 medium apple, chopped
½ cup raisins
1 cup mayonnaise
1 tablespoon curry powder
½ teaspoon salt
¼ teaspoon white pepper
6 (6-inch) pita bread rounds, cut
  in half
2 cups alfalfa sprouts

Combine first 5 ingredients in a large
saucepan. Bring to a boil; cover, reduce heat, and simmer 30 minutes or
until tender. Drain chicken, and let
cool. Bone chicken, and cut into ½-
inch pieces. Combine chicken, pickles, celery hearts, carrot, onion,
apple, and raisins.

Combine mayonnaise, curry powder, salt, and pepper, stirring well;
add to chicken mixture, and toss
gently. Cover and chill.

To serve, fill each pita bread half
with equal portions of chicken salad
and alfalfa sprouts. Yield: 6
servings. *Maria Evans Lilly*
Charleston, West Virginia

TUNA POCKETS

⅔ cup cottage cheese
⅔ cup plain yogurt
¼ cup chopped fresh parsley
1 tablespoon lemon juice
1 teaspoon garlic powder
1 teaspoon prepared mustard
1 (6½-ounce) can tuna, drained
  and flaked
6 (1-ounce) slices Swiss cheese
3 (6-inch) pita bread rounds, cut
  in half
1½ cups alfalfa sprouts

Process cottage cheese in food processor or electric blender until
smooth. Combine cottage cheese,
yogurt, and next 5 ingredients.

Place a slice of Swiss cheese in
each pita bread half; spoon ¼ cup
tuna mixture into each. Wrap sandwiches individually in aluminum foil,
and place on a baking sheet. Bake at
300° for 15 minutes or until cheese
melts. Place alfalfa sprouts in each
sandwich. Serve immediately. Yield:
3 servings. *B. M. Meyer*
Fort Worth, Texas

PEANUT-CHEESE-RAISIN SANDWICHES

10 slices cinnamon-raisin bread
1 tablespoon butter or margarine, softened
½ cup chunky peanut butter
¾ cup (3 ounces) shredded Cheddar cheese
¼ cup milk
½ cup raisins

Spread one side of bread slices with butter; broil 6 inches from heat until lightly browned. Set aside.

Combine peanut butter and remaining ingredients, stirring well. Spread mixture on untoasted side of 5 bread slices; top each with another slice, toasted side up. Yield: 5 servings.
*Audrey Bledsoe
Smyrna, Georgia*

Summertime Turkey Entrées

For easy turkey entrées, use pre-packaged fillets, or purchase a turkey breast and have the butcher slice it. Try deli-cut turkey for a quick Curried Turkey Salad.

CHILLED TURKEY-AND-PEPPER STIR-FRY SALAD

4 (2-ounce) slices uncooked fresh turkey breast (about ¼-inch thick)
½ cup commercial Italian salad dressing, divided
1 small red pepper, cut into ¼-inch strips
1 small green pepper, cut into ¼-inch strips
2 cups torn lettuce leaves

Cut turkey slices lengthwise into ½-inch-wide strips; set aside.

Heat ¼ cup dressing in a skillet. Add turkey and pepper strips; stir-fry 3 to 4 minutes or until done.

Remove from heat, and add remaining ¼ cup dressing, stirring well. Cover and chill at least 3 hours.

Drain mixture, reserving marinade. Spoon mixture onto lettuce-lined plates; drizzle with marinade. Yield: 2 servings.
*Sara A. McCullough
Broaddus, Texas*

TURKEY-AND-FRUIT KABOBS

8 (2-ounce) slices uncooked fresh turkey breast
¼ cup vegetable oil
2 tablespoons lemon juice
½ teaspoon salt
⅛ teaspoon white pepper
1 large green pepper, cut into 16 pieces
1 (8-ounce) can pineapple chunks, drained
1 (11-ounce) can mandarin oranges, drained
½ cup pineapple preserves
2 tablespoons barbecue sauce
Hot cooked rice

Cut each turkey slice in half lengthwise, and arrange in a shallow dish. Combine oil and next 3 ingredients; stir well, and drizzle over turkey. Cover and chill 1 to 2 hours.

Soak 12 (12-inch) wooden skewers in water at least 30 minutes.

Remove turkey strips, reserving marinade. Arrange strips on 8 skewers alternately with green pepper and pineapple chunks. Arrange mandarin oranges on 4 skewers, and set aside.

Combine reserved marinade, pineapple preserves, and barbecue sauce; stir well. Place turkey kabobs on a lightly greased rack in a shallow roasting pan. Brush with preserve mixture. Broil 5 inches from heat for 5 minutes. Turn kabobs; add orange kabobs, and brush with preserve mixture. Broil an additional 5 minutes

or until turkey is tender. Serve over rice. Yield: 4 servings.

Note: Turkey kabobs may be grilled over medium coals 5 minutes on each side and orange kabobs just until thoroughly heated. Chicken may be substituted for turkey. *Cheryl Zack
Lawrenceville, Georgia*

CURRIED TURKEY SALAD

2 cups unpeeled, diced red apples
2 tablespoons lemon juice
2 cups cubed cooked turkey
1 cup thinly sliced celery
1 cup chopped pecans
½ cup raisins
2 tablespoons minced onion
½ to 1 teaspoon salt
¼ teaspoon pepper
⅓ cup whipping cream
2 teaspoons curry powder
½ cup salad dressing or mayonnaise
Lettuce leaves
2 medium avocados, peeled and sliced
Lemon juice
¼ cup flaked coconut, toasted

Combine apples and lemon juice; toss gently. Add turkey and next 6 ingredients; toss gently, and set aside.

Combine cream and curry powder; beat at medium speed of an electric mixer until soft peaks form. Fold in salad dressing. Fold dressing mixture into turkey mixture. Chill.

Spoon turkey mixture onto lettuce-lined plates. Brush avocado with lemon juice, and arrange on each plate; sprinkle with coconut. Yield: 6 servings.
*Mrs. Harland J. Stone
Ocala, Florida*

Tip: *Save lemon and orange rinds. Store in the freezer, and grate as needed for pies, cakes, breads, and cookies. Or the rinds can be candied for holiday uses.*

JUNE

A Bounty Of Summer Squash

Summer squash—yellow, zucchini, and pattypan—offer vivid additions to all kinds of menus. The delicate flavors of squash go well with a variety of herbs, seasonings, and other vegetables. There's another bonus, too—the attractive shapes of squash make pretty, edible containers.

Large squash are best for stuffing, but for other uses choose small sizes that are crisp and unblemished. Yellow squash and zucchini offer the best flavor and texture if they are harvested before they get to be 7 inches long, and the smaller the better. Pattypan should be firm and less than 4 inches wide. All varieties should be handled with care because the tender skins bruise easily.

Don't confuse summer and winter varieties. Summer squash, with their tender, edible skins, will stay fresh for only a few days when properly wrapped and refrigerated. Winter squash, on the other hand, have thick skins and will keep from the time they're harvested in summer and fall through the winter months.

CAJUN SQUASH

1 medium onion, sliced
1 clove garlic, minced
1 tablespoon olive oil
1 medium zucchini, sliced
2 medium-size yellow squash, sliced
2 tomatoes, peeled and quartered
¼ teaspoon salt
⅛ teaspoon pepper
⅛ teaspoon dried whole oregano
⅛ teaspoon dried whole thyme
¼ teaspoon hot sauce

Sauté onion and garlic in olive oil in a skillet until crisp-tender. Add zucchini and yellow squash; cook vegetable mixture over medium-high heat, stirring constantly, 5 minutes. Add tomatoes and remaining ingredients; cook, stirring constantly, 2 minutes. Serve immediately. Yield: 6 servings. *Mrs. Randall L. Wilson*
Louisville, Kentucky

Tip: *Remember that overcooking destroys nutrients in vegetables. Warm leftovers carefully in a double boiler or a microwave. Even better, just mix them cold in a salad.*

TANGY MARINATED VEGETABLE KABOBS

1 large zucchini
2 medium-size yellow squash
1 sweet red pepper, cut into 12 (1-inch) pieces
1 (14-ounce) can artichoke hearts, drained and halved
½ cup olive oil
¼ cup lemon juice
1 large clove garlic, crushed
¼ teaspoon salt
¼ teaspoon freshly ground pepper

Cut zucchini and yellow squash into 2-inch slices. Cut each slice into 4 wedges. Combine wedges with sweet red pepper and artichoke hearts in a shallow dish.

Combine oil and remaining ingredients in a small bowl; stir well. Pour over vegetables; cover and chill 3 hours, occasionally tossing gently.

Soak 12 (6-inch) wooden skewers in water 30 minutes.

Drain vegetables, reserving marinade. Place vegetables on skewers. Grill kabobs over medium-hot coals 8 to 10 minutes turning frequently; baste with marinade. Yield: 6 servings. *Shirley M. Draper*
Winter Park, Florida

STUFFED PATTYPAN SQUASH

1 cup grated zucchini
1 cup grated yellow squash
⅛ teaspoon salt
6 small pattypan squash
1 tablespoon butter or margarine
½ teaspoon dried whole basil
⅛ teaspoon pepper
1 tablespoon grated Parmesan cheese

Combine zucchini, yellow squash, and salt; stir gently. Let stand 30 minutes. Drain well, and press between layers of paper towels. Set aside.

Cook pattypan squash in boiling salted water to cover 8 to 10 minutes or until tender but firm. Drain and let cool to touch. Cut a ½-inch slice from stem end of each squash. Scoop out seeds, leaving shells intact. Place shells in a 13- x 9- x 2-inch pan.

Melt butter in a skillet. Add zucchini, yellow squash, basil, and pepper; sauté 2 minutes. Remove from heat; spoon evenly into shells. Sprinkle with Parmesan cheese; bake at 400° for 15 minutes or until thoroughly heated. Yield: 6 servings. *Mrs. C. D. Marshall*
Boston, Virginia

SQUASH CROQUETTES

2 pounds yellow squash, sliced
2 to 2½ cups fine, dry breadcrumbs, divided
½ cup minced green onions
2 eggs
2 tablespoons grated Parmesan cheese
1 teaspoon salt
½ teaspoon pepper
1 cup cornmeal
Vegetable oil

Cook squash in a small amount of water until tender; drain and mash. Add 2 cups breadcrumbs and next 5 ingredients. Add more breadcrumbs if mixture is too soft. Shape mixture into 18 logs; roll in cornmeal. Deep-fry in hot oil (375°) until golden. Yield: 8 servings. *Bunnie George*
Birmingham, Alabama

ITALIAN VEGETABLE MEDLEY

¼ cup chopped onion
2 tablespoons butter or
   margarine, melted
4 medium zucchini, thinly sliced
4 medium ears corn, cut from cob
1 teaspoon salt
¾ teaspoon dried whole oregano,
   crushed
½ teaspoon sugar
¼ teaspoon pepper
Dash of garlic powder
3 medium tomatoes, peeled and
   chopped
½ cup seasoned croutons
   (optional)
½ cup (2 ounces) shredded
   mozzarella cheese

Sauté onion in butter in a large skillet until tender. Add zucchini, corn, and seasonings; cook over medium heat 8 minutes, stirring often. Add tomatoes; cook 4 minutes, stirring often. Spoon into serving dish; sprinkle with croutons, if desired, and cheese. Let stand until cheese melts. Yield: 8 to 10 servings.
Beth Canaday
Suffolk, Virginia

SQUASH-AND-GREEN CHILE QUICHE

1 unbaked 9-inch deep-dish pastry
   shell
¼ teaspoon salt
3 cups grated yellow squash
   (about ¾ pound)
¾ cup sliced green onions
1½ tablespoons butter or
   margarine, melted
1 tablespoon all-purpose flour
1 (4-ounce) can chopped green
   chiles, drained
1½ cups (6 ounces) shredded
   Cheddar cheese, divided
3 eggs, slightly beaten
1 cup whipping cream
¼ teaspoon salt
⅛ teaspoon freshly ground pepper

Prick bottom and sides of pastry with a fork. Bake at 400° for 3 minutes; remove pastry from oven, and gently prick with a fork. Bake an additional 5 minutes.

Sprinkle ¼ teaspoon salt on squash. Let stand 30 minutes. Drain well; pat dry.

Sauté onions in butter in a skillet until tender. Add squash; heat just until squash is glazed with butter. Add flour, and cook 1 minute over medium-high heat, stirring constantly. Spoon into pastry shell. Sprinkle with chiles and 1 cup cheese.

Combine eggs and next 3 ingredients, stirring well. Pour over cheese. Bake at 400° for 15 minutes. Reduce heat to 350°, and bake 20 minutes. Remove from oven. Sprinkle remaining ½ cup cheese on quiche; bake an additional 5 minutes. Let cool 15 minutes. Yield: one 9-inch quiche.
Sheree S. Garvin
Wilkesboro, North Carolina

SUMMER SQUASH WITH ROSEMARY

1 tablespoon olive oil
1 medium onion, thinly sliced and
   separated into rings
1 clove garlic, minced
4 medium zucchini, thinly sliced
½ teaspoon dried whole
   rosemary, crushed
1 medium tomato, peeled and
   chopped
⅓ cup chicken broth
⅛ teaspoon salt
¼ teaspoon pepper
1 tablespoon grated Parmesan
   cheese (optional)

Heat olive oil in a skillet; add onion and garlic, and stir-fry 2 minutes. Add zucchini and rosemary; stir-fry 8 minutes or until zucchini is crisp-tender. Add tomato, broth, salt, and

pepper; gently stir-fry just until thoroughly heated. Spoon into serving dish. Sprinkle with Parmesan cheese, if desired. Serve immediately. Yield: 6 servings.
Joy L. Garcia
Bartlett, Tennessee

Tomatoes, As You Like Them

Oh, the joy of summer that fresh tomatoes bring. Sliced in a sandwich, added to a salad, or cooked in a casserole, tomatoes offer a pleasing combination of flavor and nutrition.

HERBED TOMATO-CHEESE BREAD

2 cups biscuit mix
⅔ cup milk
3 medium tomatoes, peeled and
   sliced
1 medium onion, chopped
2 tablespoons butter or
   margarine, melted
¾ cup commercial sour cream
⅓ cup mayonnaise
½ teaspoon salt
¼ teaspoon pepper
¼ teaspoon dried whole oregano
Pinch of ground sage
1 cup (4 ounces) shredded
   Cheddar cheese
Paprika

Combine biscuit mix and milk, stirring until dry ingredients are moistened. Turn out onto a floured surface; knead 3 or 4 times. Press into bottom and up sides of a lightly greased 13- x 9- x 2-inch baking dish. Top with tomato slices.

Sauté onion in butter until tender; stir in remaining ingredients except paprika. Spoon mixture over tomatoes, and sprinkle with paprika. Bake at 400° for 20 to 25 minutes. Let stand 10 minutes. Yield: about 12 servings.
Grace Bravos
Timonium, Maryland

TOMATO DUMPLINGS

1 cup all-purpose flour
2 teaspoons baking powder
1 teaspoon salt
1 tablespoon shortening
½ cup milk
5 cups peeled, chopped tomatoes
1 medium onion, finely chopped
1 tablespoon butter or margarine
2 teaspoons sugar
½ teaspoon dried whole basil,
  crushed
1 teaspoon salt
½ teaspoon pepper
½ teaspoon garlic powder

Combine first 3 ingredients; mix well. Cut in shortening with a pastry blender until mixture resembles coarse meal. Add milk, stirring until dry ingredients are moistened.

Combine tomatoes and remaining ingredients in a Dutch oven; bring to a boil, stirring occasionally. Drop dough by tablespoonfuls into boiling mixture. Cover, reduce heat, and simmer 12 minutes without stirring. Yield: about 6 servings.

Doris J. Phillips
Springdale, Arkansas

SCALLOPED TOMATO CASSEROLE

3½ cups peeled, chopped
  tomatoes
1 cup chopped onion
½ cup cheese-flavored cracker
  crumbs
1½ teaspoons sugar
½ teaspoon salt
1 (8-ounce) carton commercial
  sour cream
1½ cups seasoned croutons
1 tablespoon butter, melted

Layer half each of tomatoes, onion, cracker crumbs, sugar, and salt in a greased 1½-quart casserole. Repeat layers. Bake at 325° for 20 minutes. Spread sour cream on top; sprinkle croutons over sour cream. Drizzle melted butter over croutons. Bake an additional 10 minutes. Yield: 6 servings.

Sally Murphy
Allen, Texas

FRIED HERB TOMATOES

1 large ripe tomato, cut into
  ¼-inch slices
1½ cups crushed herb-seasoned
  stuffing mix
1 egg, beaten
2 tablespoons vegetable oil
2 tablespoons (½ ounce) shredded
  Cheddar cheese

Coat tomato slices with stuffing mix; dip in egg; coat again with mix.

Heat oil in a heavy skillet. Add tomato slices; cook until brown, turning once. Immediately transfer to serving dish, and sprinkle with cheese. Yield: 2 servings.

Dolly G. Northcott
Fairfield, Alabama

Pork Barbecue, North Carolina Style

What does it take to make a really good barbecue? In North Carolina, it depends on whether you're from the eastern or western part of the state. Passions run deep over just how pork should be prepared, what cut of meat to use, and whether the pork should be chunked, sliced, or chopped. The biggest bone of contention, however, is usually over the barbecue sauce, with easterners favoring a clear, vinegar-based sauce, while those from the west prefer the sweet-and-sour taste that catsup and sugar add.

Barbecue Tips

Whatever the preferences for sauce, barbecue enthusiasts don't have to be grilling experts to enjoy the tangy taste of barbecue—Carolina style. In our test kitchens, we scaled down the prizewinning recipes of Roger and David Lambert of Franklinville, North Carolina, and Willis Peaden and Jim Elder of Havelock, North Carolina, to make them suitable for backyard cooking. Although none of these champions of the North Carolina Pork Cookoff would give us their secret recipe (some family members don't even know the exact proportions), they promise these versions are close.

Use hickory or charcoal to achieve the flavor most characteristic of North Carolina barbecue. Gas can be used. Whatever fuel you use, insert a meat thermometer in the pork to check the internal temperature before removing it from the grill.

Flare-ups occur when the meat is first placed on the grill. To avoid this, place the meat about 4 to 5 inches from coals (more if possible). Then shut the lid tightly on the grill. Keep air vents at the base open to keep the fire burning, but close vents at the top. Air flow into the grill feeds the flare-up, and the meat's outer crust will char. Remove this crust before chopping or slicing the meat and adding sauce.

The meat cooks best when the grill temperature stays between 225° and 300°. Some grill temperatures may even reach 400° or above. To check the temperature of the grill, place an oven thermometer alongside the meat, and close the lid. Check the temperature in about 5 minutes, and remove the thermometer from the grill. Thermometers left in the grill for the entire cooking time become smoky and unreadable. If you are cooking with hickory, you may find the temperature in the grill will drop about halfway through the cooking time. If this happens, simply remove the meat rack from the grill and add hickory coals started outside the cooker. Replace the meat, close the grill, and continue cooking.

Although the suggested internal temperature for pork is 160°, the shoulders may be cooked to an internal temperature of 185°. This higher temperature allows fat to cook out of the meat, making a leaner barbecue.

When you take the meat off the grill, allow it to cool for 1 hour. Then remove the charred outer covering and chop, shred, or slice the meat. Add the sauce of your choice, and enjoy that Carolina barbecue.

HOME-STYLE BARBECUE

8 to 12 (1-foot) pieces of hickory
   wood (about 4 inches in
   diameter) or 10 pounds
   charcoal
1 (12- to 13-pound) pork shoulder

Prepare fire in grill; let burn until coals are white. Place pork shoulder on grill, fat side down. Cover with lid; cook 4 to 5 hours or until internal meat thermometer registers 160°, turning every hour.

Let meat cool; slice, chop, or shred. Serve with barbecue sauce. Yield: 8 to 10 servings.

Note: Hot coals may be added halfway through cooking time to keep the temperature in the grill between 250° and 300°.

EASTERN-STYLE BARBECUE SAUCE

7¼ cups vinegar
¾ cup ginger ale
3 tablespoons plus 1 teaspoon
   crushed red pepper
2 tablespoons ground red pepper

Combine all ingredients. Stir well, and serve over pork barbecue. Yield: 2 quarts.

WESTERN-STYLE BARBECUE SAUCE

2 quarts vinegar
2 cups sugar
1 cup catsup
¼ cup Worcestershire sauce
2 tablespoons hot sauce
¼ cup plus 1 tablespoon salt
¼ cup plus 1 tablespoon pepper

Combine all ingredients. Stir well, and serve over pork barbecue. Yield: 3 quarts.

From Our Kitchen To Yours

Summer with its longer days and warmer weather lures Southerners to their grills. To help you become a master backyard chef, here are the answers to some common questions.

■ **What factors affect grilling temperature and cooking time?** In our recipes, cooking temperature and time are guidelines. There are many variables—wind velocity, outside temperature, doneness preference, thickness of the meat, open or closed cover, distance between the heat source and the food, and food's temperature when placed on the grill. Extra charcoal briquets, a cover, and a longer cooking time are often required on cold or windy days. Cooking two or more items at the same time can also lengthen time.

■ **How do you gauge cooking temperature?** Allow approximately 30 minutes for briquets to become hot and almost completely covered with ash. To measure accurate temperature, place an oven thermometer on the grid and close cover for five minutes. You can also hold your hand, palm side down, at cooking height over the coals. If you can keep your hand in place for only two seconds, the coals are hot; three seconds, medium hot; four seconds, medium; five seconds, low.

■ **How can cooking temperature be controlled?** To lower temperature, raise the grid, spread charcoal briquets farther apart, or close vents halfway. To increase heat, lower the grid, open vents, tap ash from briquets, or push briquets closer together. Adding new briquets, a few at a time, keeps the fire hot for several hours; place these along the outer edges of the hot briquets. Do not add more starter fluid; the new briquets will ignite as long as the edges are touching. Gas grills are preheated 10 minutes at high or medium setting; the gas control knobs are then easily adjusted to the proper temperature.

■ **What is the difference between direct and indirect cooking methods?** Cooking food directly above the heat source (direct method) is possible on any kind of grill. Like broiling, this method sears food; it is used for foods that cook in 30 minutes or less, such as steaks, chops, burgers, and some vegetables. These foods will have the charcoal flavor that comes from smoking caused by juices and fat dripping onto the hot charcoal or gas briquets.

Similar to baking or oven roasting, the indirect method cooks food by circulating hot air. For dual-burner gas grills and large, covered charcoal grills, simply light one side; place food on the opposite cooking grid, and close the cover. On single-burner grills and small charcoal grills, line half the cooking grid with a double thickness of heavy-duty aluminum foil; place a rack on the foil, add food, and close the cover. Use indirect cooking for larger cuts of meat. Juices and fat do not drip onto the hot briquets; therefore, smoking that creates the charcoal flavor does not occur.

■ **How can more flavor be added when using the indirect cooking method?** Wood chips or chunks and fresh or dried herbs add subtle flavor. Soak a handful of chips (hickory, oak, or mesquite) or herbs (fennel, tarragon, bay leaves, basil, or rosemary) in water at least 15 minutes. Sprinkle drained chips or herbs over hot charcoal briquets. For a gas grill, wrap chips or herbs lengthwise in a piece of aluminum foil, leaving ends open, and place on hot lava rocks.

■ **How can flare-up be minimized?** Some flare-up is desirable because it adds to the charcoal flavor, but excessive flaring chars food. High fat content, some marinades and sauces, and grease or food buildup on grids cause flaring. To reduce flare-up, trim excess fat, raise the grid, cover the grill, close vents, and clean grids after each use. It is also helpful to use the indirect cooking method, reposition food away from flare-ups, or place a foil drip pan directly under food to catch drippings. Using a gas grill, you can also turn off the burner or lower the setting until flaming subsides. As a last resort, remove food from the grid, and mist flames with water.

■ **When should basting sauce be brushed on food?** To prevent excess browning and burning, apply sweet or tomato-based sauces during the final 10 to 30 minutes of cooking.

■ **What are tips for cooking kabobs?** Leave ¼ inch between each piece of food to allow even cooking and thorough basting. Placing flavorful vegetables next to meat increases flavor. Larger vegetables, such as onions or peppers, need to be parboiled before skewering. Cherry tomatoes should be added to the end of skewers during last few minutes. To prevent wooden skewers from scorching, soak them in water for 30 minutes before grilling.

■ **How often do lava rocks in gas grills need replacing?** Some lava rocks or ceramic briquets are used for the lifetime of the grill, while others are replaced after several years. How often the grill is used and cleaned are determining factors. Lava rocks and ceramic briquets should be turned occasionally to allow even heating.

■ **How difficult is grilling with wood?** Cooking with wood is trickier than using charcoal. Lighting the fire requires skill and time. Start the fire base using dry paper and small twigs. Once you have a hot base, keep adding larger pieces of wood. Building a fire and letting it burn to a hot bed of coals can take about two hours and much wood. Building a wood fire in a small grill is not recommended.

MICROWAVE COOKERY

It's Easy To Cook Cheese

Microwave cooking techniques take the guesswork out of cooking with cheese, yielding tasty sauces and side dishes. When cooking cheese conventionally, cooks usually handle it with care, using low temperatures and short cooking times. With a microwave, those rules still hold true to a certain extent; however, microwave techniques are easier, and these recipes are foolproof.

For Macaroni and Cheese, a basic cheese sauce is made by stirring shredded cheese into a microwaved white sauce. The heat in the sauce melts the cheese, yielding a creamy, smooth sauce. (The same proportions and cooking instructions will also make a cheese sauce for vegetables.) The sauce is then poured over macaroni and heated at MEDIUM HIGH (70% power).

The sauce for Creamy Cheese Potatoes is somewhat different. Shredded Cheddar and American cheeses are added to the white sauce before microwaving because of the large quantity of cheese in the recipe.

If cheese is stirred into a casserole, the contents of the recipe determine the power setting. For example, Broccoli Casserole can be microwaved at HIGH because the food is dense and no delicate sauces are included.

Adding a cheese topping is especially simple. After removing a casserole from the oven, place cheese slices on top, and cover the dish with aluminum foil. The cheese slices will melt during standing time.

BROCCOLI CASSEROLE

6 cups coarsely chopped fresh
  broccoli
¼ cup water
1 (10¾-ounce) can cream of
  mushroom soup, undiluted
¼ cup (1 ounce) shredded sharp
  Cheddar cheese
¼ cup mayonnaise
1½ teaspoons lemon juice
⅓ cup round buttery cracker
  crumbs

Combine broccoli and water in a 2-quart casserole; cover and microwave at HIGH 4 minutes. Drain.

Place broccoli in a lightly greased 2-quart casserole. Combine soup and next 3 ingredients in a medium bowl; stir well. Spoon mixture over broccoli. Cover with heavy-duty plastic wrap, and microwave at HIGH 4 to 5 minutes. Sprinkle cracker crumbs over top. Rotate dish, and microwave at HIGH 4 to 5 minutes. Yield: 6 servings.
    Margaret Ajac
    Raleigh, North Carolina

CREAMY CHEESE POTATOES

6 slices bacon
6 baking potatoes, peeled and
  cubed (about 4 pounds)
¼ cup water
½ teaspoon salt
½ teaspoon seasoned salt
⅓ cup chopped onion
2 cups (8 ounces) shredded
  Cheddar cheese
2 cups (8 ounces) diced process
  American cheese
2 teaspoons all-purpose flour
1 (8-ounce) carton commercial
  sour cream
½ cup milk
1 teaspoon Worcestershire sauce

Place bacon on a rack in a 12- x 8- x 2-inch baking dish; cover with paper towels. Microwave at HIGH 5 to 7 minutes or until bacon is crisp. Drain bacon, reserving 1 tablespoon drippings; set bacon aside.

Combine potatoes, water, and salt in a large microwave-safe mixing bowl. Cover with heavy-duty plastic wrap; microwave at HIGH 16 to 18 minutes or until tender, stirring every 4 minutes. Remove from microwave, and drain. Sprinkle with seasoned salt; keep warm.

Place reserved bacon drippings in a 1-quart glass measuring cup; microwave at HIGH 1 minute or until hot. Stir in onion; microwave at HIGH 1 to 1½ minutes or until onion is transparent. Stir in cheeses and flour; cover with heavy-duty plastic wrap, and microwave at HIGH 3½ to 4 minutes or until cheeses melt, stirring after 2 minutes. Add sour cream, milk, and Worcestershire sauce; stir with a whisk until smooth. Pour over potatoes, tossing gently to coat; cover and microwave at HIGH 1 minute or until thoroughly heated. Transfer to a serving dish, if desired; crumble bacon, and sprinkle over top. Yield: 8 to 10 servings.

Gayle Wager
Baton Rouge, Louisiana

MACARONI AND CHEESE

1 (8-ounce) package uncooked
   elbow macaroni
3 cups water
1 teaspoon salt
¼ cup butter or margarine
¼ cup plus 2 tablespoons
   all-purpose flour
1 teaspoon salt
2 cups milk
2 cups (8 ounces) shredded
   Cheddar cheese
Paprika

Combine macaroni, water, and 1 teaspoon salt in a 2-quart baking dish; cover with heavy-duty plastic wrap. Microwave at HIGH 10 to 12 minutes or until macaroni is done, stirring after 5 minutes. Drain macaroni, and return to baking dish. Set aside.

Place butter in a 1-quart glass measure; microwave at HIGH 55 seconds or until melted. Blend in flour and 1 teaspoon salt; stir until smooth. Gradually stir in milk; microwave at HIGH 5½ to 7 minutes or until mixture is thickened, stirring at 1-minute intervals. Add cheese; stir until melted.

Stir cheese sauce into macaroni, mixing well. Cover and microwave at MEDIUM HIGH (70% power) 7 to 8 minutes, stirring after 4 minutes. Sprinkle with paprika. Let stand 2 minutes. Yield: 6 servings.

COOKING LIGHT®

The Taste Of Mexico Goes Light

Bursting with color and flavor, Mexican food has become a favorite ethnic food of Southerners. It's often avoided, however, because of its high fat content. We've chosen some recipes that preserve unique Mexican flavors while keeping calories, fat, and cholesterol to a minimum.

The staples of Mexican cooking—beans, rice, and corn—provide both fiber and complex carbohydrates (starches). Contrary to widespread belief, carbohydrates are not "the bad guys" when it comes to calories. The fiber in complex carbohydrates aids in digestion.

BAKED CHILE CHICKEN WITH SALSA

1 medium onion, chopped
1 medium carrot, coarsely
   chopped
1 stalk celery, coarsely chopped
1 bay leaf
¼ teaspoon salt
¼ teaspoon freshly ground pepper
5 cups water
8 (4-ounce) boneless and skinless
   chicken breast halves
2 (4-ounce) cans green chiles,
   undrained
12 fresh tomatillas, cored and
   halved
½ cup chopped onion
2 cloves garlic
¼ cup firmly packed fresh
   cilantro
Vegetable cooking spray
10 (6-inch) corn tortillas
2 cups (8 ounces) shredded
   part-skim mozzarella cheese
2 cups (8 ounces) shredded 40%
   less-fat Cheddar cheese
Salsa (recipe follows)

Combine first 7 ingredients in a large Dutch oven; bring to a boil over high heat. Add chicken; cover, reduce heat, and simmer 5 minutes or until tender. Remove from heat. Remove chicken, and chop into bite-size pieces; set aside. Strain broth mixture, reserving 1 cup; set aside.

Position knife blade in food processor bowl; add green chiles and next 4 ingredients. Top with cover; process about 1 minute or until chile mixture is smooth.

Coat a skillet with cooking spray; place over medium heat until hot. Add chile mixture, and cook, stirring constantly, about 5 minutes; gradually add reserved broth; stir well.

Cut tortillas into ½-inch strips; place in a single layer on a baking sheet. Bake at 350° for 15 minutes or until strips are crisp. Remove from oven; cool.

Coat a 13- x 9- x 2-inch baking dish with cooking spray. Layer half each of tortilla strips, chicken, and sauce mixture, and all of mozzarella cheese; repeat layers of tortilla strips, chicken, and sauce mixture. Cover and chill 8 hours.

Bake at 350°, uncovered, for 40 minutes. Add Cheddar cheese, and bake an additional 5 minutes. Serve with salsa. Yield: 12 servings (242 calories per serving).

☐ *27.4 grams protein, 7.7 grams fat, 14.8 grams carbohydrate, 55 milligrams cholesterol, 515 milligrams sodium, and 306 milligrams calcium.*

Salsa

2½ cups chopped tomatoes
2 (4-ounce) cans chopped green
   chiles, undrained
¼ cup diced onion
2 tablespoons minced cilantro
¼ teaspoon salt
¼ teaspoon sugar

Combine all ingredients in a medium bowl; stir well. Cover and chill 2 hours before serving. Yield: 3 cups (3 calories per tablespoon).

☐ *0.1 gram protein, 0 grams fat, 0.7 gram carbohydrate, 0 milligrams cholesterol, 18 milligrams sodium, and 1 milligram calcium.* Susan D. Spain
Charleston, West Virginia

LIGHT CHILE VERDE

1 (5-pound) boneless center-cut
  pork roast
Vegetable cooking spray
1 (14½-ounce) can stewed
  tomatoes, undrained
1 (28-ounce) can crushed
  tomatoes, undrained
1 (22-ounce) container tomato
  sauce
2 cups chopped onion
1 tablespoon garlic powder
4 cups hot water
5 (4-ounce) cans diced green
  chiles, undrained
1½ tablespoons seeded, diced
  jalapeño peppers
1 tablespoon sugar
¼ teaspoon ground cloves
2 teaspoons ground cumin
¼ teaspoon salt
¼ cup lemon juice
½ cup dried parsley flakes

Trim excess fat from roast; place on
a rack in a shallow roasting pan
coated with cooking spray. Bake at
325° for 2 hours or until meat thermometer registers 160°. Remove
from pan; let cool.

Combine stewed tomatoes and
next 5 ingredients in a Dutch oven.
Bring to a boil over medium heat;
simmer, uncovered, 20 minutes.

Chop pork roast; add meat to tomato mixture. Stir in green chiles
and remaining ingredients; cover and
simmer 45 minutes. Yield: 5 quarts
(186 calories per ¾-cup serving).

Note: If desired, chile may be frozen
in airtight container for 3 months.

☐ *18.4 grams protein, 8.9 grams fat,
7.5 grams carbohydrate, 48 milligrams cholesterol, 318 milligrams sodium, and 29 milligrams calcium.*
                    Sheral Cade
                    Dallas, Texas

FRIJOLES RANCHEROS

1½ cups dried pinto beans
6 cups water
½ cup chopped cooked lean ham
⅔ cup chopped onion
½ teaspoon pepper
½ teaspoon crushed red pepper
1 tablespoon minced garlic
2 bay leaves
Rancheros Sauce

Sort and wash beans; place in a
Dutch oven. Add water, and bring to
a boil; boil 2 minutes. Remove from
heat; cover and let stand 1 hour.

Add ham and next 5 ingredients to
Dutch oven; bring to a boil. Reduce
heat, and simmer, uncovered, 1 to
1½ hours, stirring occasionally. Remove bay leaves; serve with Rancheros Sauce. Yield: 7 servings (169
calories per ½-cup serving).

☐ *11.7 grams protein, 1.3 grams fat,
28.5 grams carbohydrate, 9 milligrams cholesterol, 13 milligrams sodium, and 62 milligrams calcium.*

Rancheros Sauce

Vegetable cooking spray
½ cup chopped onion
1½ cups chopped tomato
1 teaspoon dried whole oregano
1 tablespoon reduced-sodium
  Worcestershire sauce

Coat a skillet with cooking spray;
place over medium heat until hot.
Add onion, and sauté. Stir in tomato
and oregano; cook 3 minutes. Stir in
Worcestershire sauce, and remove
from heat. Yield: ¾ cup (8 calories
per tablespoon).

☐ *0.3 gram protein, 0.1 gram fat,
1.8 grams carbohydrate, 0 milligrams
cholesterol, 2 milligrams sodium, and
6 milligrams calcium.*

                    Julia A. Boggs
                Buckhannon, West Virginia

MEXICAN MARINATED STEAK

1 (2½-pound) boneless lean top
  sirloin steak, 2 inches thick
¼ cup vegetable oil
1 large clove garlic, halved
½ teaspoon dried whole basil
½ teaspoon chili powder
½ teaspoon pepper
Vegetable cooking spray
Fresh cilantro (optional)
Lime (optional)
Salsa Cruda

Trim excess fat from steak; pierce
meat every ½ inch with a fork. Place
meat in a 13- x 9- x 2-inch baking
dish; set aside.

Heat oil in a small skillet over medium heat. Add garlic, basil, chili
powder, and pepper, and stir well.
Pour hot mixture over meat in baking
dish. Cover and let stand at room
temperature 1 hour.

Remove meat from marinade;
place on a rack in a shallow roasting
pan coated with cooking spray. Discard marinade.

Broil steak 5 inches from heat 10
minutes on each side or to desired
degree of doneness. Remove steak
from oven; let stand 10 minutes before slicing. Place on a serving platter; if desired, garnish with fresh
cilantro and lime. Serve steak with
Salsa Cruda. Yield: 8 servings (183
calories per 3-ounce serving).

☐ *24.8 grams protein, 8.6 grams fat,
1.1 grams carbohydrate, 66 milligrams cholesterol, 59 milligrams sodium, and 8 milligrams calcium.*

Salsa Cruda

2 (14½-ounce) cans whole
  tomatoes, drained and diced
¼ cup thinly sliced green
  onions
1 teaspoon diced pickled
  jalapeño peppers
1½ teaspoons lime juice
1 teaspoon olive oil
¼ teaspoon salt

Combine all ingredients in a small
bowl, and stir well. Cover and let
stand 20 to 30 minutes before serving. Yield: 1½ cups (6 calories per
tablespoon).

□ *0.2 gram protein, 0.2 gram fat, 1 gram carbohydrate, 0 milligrams cholesterol, 59 milligrams sodium, and 6 milligrams calcium.*

Koenia Pereira
Newark, Texas

RED SNAPPER VERACRUZ

6 (4-ounce) skinless red snapper fillets
½ cup lime juice
½ teaspoon salt
1 cup sliced onion
1 teaspoon vegetable oil
1 (4-ounce) jar diced pimiento, drained
2 cups chopped tomatoes
1 teaspoon canned chopped green chiles
½ teaspoon capers
1 parsley sprig
Lime slices (optional)
6 parsley sprigs (optional)

Arrange fillets in a shallow dish; drizzle lime juice and sprinkle salt over fillets. Cover and chill 2 hours.

Sauté onion in oil in a skillet over medium heat. Add pimiento, tomatoes, chiles, capers, and 1 parsley sprig. Cover and cook 7 minutes. Remove fillets from marinade; discard marinade. Arrange fillets on tomato mixture. Cover and cook 6 minutes on each side or until fish flakes easily when tested with a fork.

Remove snapper fillets to a serving plate; keep fillets warm. Continue cooking tomato mixture, uncovered, until liquid has been absorbed (about 10 minutes). Remove parsley sprig. Spoon ¼ cup tomato mixture over each fillet. If desired, garnish snapper with lime slices and 6 parsley sprigs. Yield: 6 servings (139 calories per serving).

□ *23.4 grams protein, 1.9 grams fat, 6.6 grams carbohydrate, 62 milligrams cholesterol, 299 milligrams sodium, and 31 milligrams calcium.*

Patra Collins Sullivan
Columbia, South Carolina

SPICY MEXICAN RICE

Vegetable cooking spray
1 teaspoon vegetable oil
½ cup uncooked long-grain rice
½ cup chopped onion
1 cup chopped tomato
⅓ cup chopped green pepper
¼ teaspoon garlic powder
¼ teaspoon ground red pepper
½ teaspoon chili powder
1 teaspoon beef-flavored bouillon granules
1 to 1¼ cups water

Coat a large skillet with cooking spray; add oil, and place over medium heat. Add rice and onion; sauté about 3 minutes. Add tomato and remaining ingredients to rice mixture; bring to a boil. Cover, reduce heat, and simmer 25 minutes or until tender. Yield: 5 servings (95 calories per ½-cup serving).

□ *1.9 grams protein, 1.4 grams fat, 18.5 grams carbohydrate, 0 milligrams cholesterol, 190 milligrams sodium, and 13 milligrams calcium.*

Susie M. E. Dent
Saltillo, Mississippi

MEXICAN TORTA

¼ teaspoon salt
4 cups sliced zucchini
Vegetable cooking spray
⅔ cup diced onion
1 cup peeled, seeded, and chopped tomato
1 clove garlic, minced
½ teaspoon dried whole oregano
1 (4-ounce) can green chiles, drained
3 eggs, separated
1 cup (4 ounces) shredded part-skim mozzarella cheese, divided

Sprinkle salt over sliced zucchini; toss gently, and let stand 10 minutes. Drain zucchini between layers of paper towels.

Coat a large skillet with cooking spray; place over medium heat until hot. Sauté zucchini, onion, tomato, and garlic until vegetables are crisp-tender; add oregano and green chiles. Set aside.

Beat egg whites (at room temperature) until stiff peaks form. Add egg yolks slowly, beating well.

Spoon half of vegetable mixture into a shallow 2-quart baking dish that has been coated with cooking spray. Spoon half of egg mixture over vegetables, and top with ½ cup cheese. Repeat vegetable and egg layers. Bake at 350°, uncovered, for 20 minutes; top with remaining cheese, and bake an additional 5 minutes. Yield: 10 servings (71 calories per ½-cup serving).

□ *5.5 grams protein, 3.7 grams fat, 4.2 grams carbohydrate, 89 milligrams cholesterol, 147 milligrams sodium, and 96 milligrams calcium.*

Traci Myers
Boca Raton, Florida

LIGHT MEXICAN CUSTARD

2 eggs
⅛ teaspoon salt
2½ tablespoons sugar
1 tablespoon all-purpose flour
1 teaspoon vanilla extract
½ teaspoon maple extract
1 cup 1% low-fat milk
1 cup evaporated skim milk
Ground cinnamon

Combine all ingredients except cinnamon in container of an electric blender; process at high speed 5 seconds. Pour mixture into six 6-ounce custard cups; sprinkle with cinnamon. Place custard cups in a 13- x 9- x 2-inch pan; pour hot water to depth of 1 inch into pan. Cover with aluminum foil. Bake at 325° for 1 hour or until a knife inserted in center comes out clean. Remove cups from water. Serve warm or cold. Yield: 6 servings (105 calories per serving).

□ *6.7 grams protein, 2.4 grams fat, 13.6 grams carbohydrate, 95 milligrams cholesterol, 141 milligrams sodium, and 187 milligrams calcium.*

Seafood Starts The Party

If you're planning a party, why not tempt your guests with a mouth-watering seafood appetizer? These recipes offer a choice of shrimp or crabmeat served in a variety of interesting ways.

DILLED SHRIMP

1¾ pounds unpeeled large fresh shrimp
1 tablespoon minced garlic
2 tablespoons minced shallots
2 tablespoons butter or margarine, melted
1 tablespoon olive oil
2 tablespoons lemon juice
1 tablespoon plus 1 teaspoon finely chopped fresh dillweed
⅛ teaspoon salt
⅛ teaspoon pepper
Fresh dillweed (optional)
Lemon slices (optional)

Peel and devein shrimp. Set aside. Sauté garlic and shallots in butter and olive oil in a large skillet until tender. Stir in shrimp; cook over medium heat, stirring occasionally, 3 minutes or until cooked. Add lemon juice and next 3 ingredients, stirring well. Serve warm or cold. If desired, garnish with dillweed and lemon. Yield: 8 to 10 appetizer servings.

Mrs. Stephen Donald Johnson
St. Petersburg, Florida

LUSCIOUS LEMON SHRIMP

20 unpeeled large fresh shrimp
¼ cup butter or margarine
¾ cup fresh crabmeat, drained and flaked
¼ cup vermouth
2 tablespoons minced fresh parsley
2 cloves garlic, minced
1½ tablespoons lemon juice
Parsley sprigs (optional)
Lemon wedges (optional)

Peel shrimp, leaving tails intact; devein and set aside.

Melt butter in a large skillet; add shrimp, crabmeat, and next 4 ingredients. Bring to a boil; reduce heat, and simmer 4 to 5 minutes. Spoon mixture into 4 individual serving dishes; arrange shrimp around crabmeat. If desired, garnish with parsley sprigs and lemon wedges. Yield: 4 servings.

Mrs. Joan Collins
Cross Lanes, West Virginia

CRABMEAT CANAPÉS

2 (20-count) packages small party rolls
1 (6-ounce) can white crabmeat, drained
1½ cups (6 ounces) shredded Cheddar cheese
¼ cup chopped ripe olives
¼ cup mayonnaise
2 green onions, chopped
1 teaspoon lemon juice
⅛ teaspoon pepper
Sliced ripe olives, cut in half (optional)
Parsley sprigs (optional)

Scoop out the center of each roll with a melon baller, and reserve for other uses. Set rolls aside.

Combine crabmeat and next 6 ingredients, stirring well. Spoon about 2 teaspoons crabmeat mixture into each roll. Bake at 325° for 10 minutes or until cheese melts. If desired, garnish with ripe olives and parsley sprigs. Yield: 40 appetizers.

Note: Canapés can be made a day ahead, covered with foil, and refrigerated. To serve, remove foil, and bake at 325° for 10 minutes or until cheese melts.

Sharon McClatchey
Muskogee, Oklahoma

CRABMEAT BALLS

¼ cup butter or margarine, melted
1 teaspoon dry mustard
½ teaspoon salt
⅛ teaspoon ground mace
⅛ teaspoon ground nutmeg
½ teaspoon Old Bay seasoning
2 tablespoons chopped fresh parsley
½ cup soft breadcrumbs
1 pound fresh crabmeat, drained and flaked
2 egg yolks, beaten
¼ cup all-purpose flour
Vegetable oil

Combine first 8 ingredients; stir well. Stir in crabmeat and egg yolks; cover and chill 1 to 2 hours.

Shape into 1-inch balls; dredge balls in flour. Pour oil to depth of 2 to 3 inches in Dutch oven or heavy saucepan. Heat to 375°. Fry balls in oil until golden. Drain on paper towels. Serve immediately. Yield: 28 appetizer servings.

Mary G. Knighton
Catonsville, Maryland

Chicken Is So Versatile

Chicken is hard to beat. There seems to be no end to the many ways it can be served. Whether you're planning a cookout or an elegant dinner, you can depend on it.

SPICY ALMOND CHICKEN

3 tablespoons butter or margarine
1 (3- to 3½-pound) broiler-fryer, cut up and skinned
1 (14-ounce) jar red currant jelly
½ cup prepared mustard
½ cup slivered almonds
3 tablespoons brown sugar
2 tablespoons lemon juice
½ teaspoon ground cinnamon

Melt butter in a large skillet over medium heat. Add chicken, and cook about 10 minutes or until lightly browned on all sides. Place chicken in a lightly greased 13- x 9- x 2-inch baking dish. Add jelly and remaining ingredients to skillet; cook over medium heat until jelly dissolves, stirring occasionally. Pour over chicken; cover and bake at 350° for 30 minutes. Uncover and bake an additional 10 minutes or until done. Yield: 4 servings.

Winifred Martin
Norfolk, Virginia

TIPSY CHICKEN AND DRESSING

1 (8-ounce) package cornbread stuffing mix
2 eggs
3 slices bread, crumbled
1 (14½-ounce) can chicken broth, undiluted
1 small onion, finely chopped
1 stalk celery, finely chopped
1 (14-ounce) can artichoke hearts, drained and quartered
8 chicken breast halves, boned and skinned
8 (1-ounce) slices Swiss cheese
1 (10¾-ounce) can cream of celery soup, undiluted
1 cup white wine
½ teaspoon dried whole basil
4 mushrooms, sliced
¼ cup grated Parmesan cheese
2 tablespoons minced parsley
Parsley sprigs

Combine first 6 ingredients; mix well. Divide mixture among 8 lightly greased individual 2-cup casserole dishes. Place 3 artichoke quarters in the middle of dressing mixture; place chicken over artichokes. Top with Swiss cheese. Combine soup, wine, and basil; pour over chicken. Top with mushrooms, Parmesan cheese, and minced parsley.

Cover and bake at 350° for 40 minutes. Uncover and bake an additional 10 minutes. Garnish with parsley sprigs. Yield: 8 servings.

Irene R. Smith
Covington, Georgia

BREAST-OF-CHICKEN FIESTA

1 cup Cheddar cheese cracker crumbs
2 tablespoons taco seasoning mix
8 chicken breast halves, skinned and boned
4 green onions, chopped
2 tablespoons butter or margarine, melted
2 cups whipping cream
1 cup (4 ounces) shredded Monterey Jack cheese
1 cup (4 ounces) shredded Cheddar cheese
1 (4-ounce) can chopped green chiles, drained
½ teaspoon chicken-flavored bouillon granules

Combine cracker crumbs and seasoning mix in a small bowl, stirring well. Dredge chicken in crumb mixture; place in a greased 13- x 9- x 2-inch baking dish.

Sauté green onions in butter in a skillet until tender. Stir in whipping cream and remaining ingredients; pour over chicken. Bake, uncovered, at 350° for 45 minutes. Yield: 8 servings.

Sharron Kay Johnston
Fort Worth, Texas

CHICKEN TAMALES

2 dozen dried cornhusks
2 (2½- to 3-pound) broiler-fryers, cut up
1 medium onion, chopped
1 tablespoon vegetable oil
1 (4-ounce) can taco sauce
1 teaspoon salt
1 teaspoon ground cumin
1 cup shortening
2 teaspoons chili powder
½ teaspoon salt
2½ cups instant corn masa
Commercial salsa

Cover dried cornhusks with hot water; let stand 1 hour or until softened. Drain well, and pat with paper towels to remove excess water.

Cook chicken in boiling water to cover 45 minutes or until tender; drain, reserving 1 cup broth. Bone chicken, and finely chop to make 4 cups. Set chopped chicken aside.

Sauté onion in hot oil in a large skillet until tender. Stir in chicken, taco sauce, 1 teaspoon salt, and cumin. Set aside.

Cream shortening; add reserved 1 cup broth, chili powder, and salt, mixing well. Gradually add corn masa, mixing well; beat 10 minutes at medium speed of a heavy-duty electric mixer until light and fluffy.

Cut each cornhusk to make a 4-inch square. Place about 2 tablespoons masa dough in center of each husk, spreading to within ½ inch of edges. Place about 2 tablespoons chicken mixture on dough, spreading evenly. Fold in one edge; roll up tamales, starting with an adjoining side, leaving opposite end open. Tie with string or narrow strip of softened cornhusk.

Place a cup in center of a steaming rack or metal colander in a large pot. Add just enough water to fill pot below rack level to keep tamales above water. Stand tamales on folded ends around the cup. Bring water to a boil. Cover and steam 1 hour or until tamale dough pulls away from husks; add more water as necessary. Serve with salsa. Yield: 2 dozen.

Lynda Gottschalk
Winters, Texas

Tip: *Fresh meat, poultry, and fish should be loosely wrapped and refrigerated; use in a few days. Loosely wrap fresh ground meat, liver, and kidneys; use in one or two days. Frankfurters, bacon, and sliced sandwich meats can be stored in original wrappings in the refrigerator. Store all meat in the coldest part of the refrigerator.*

BIRD'S-NEST CHICKEN

8 nested-style angel hair pasta
  bundles
8 chicken breast halves, skinned
  and boned
1 teaspoon salt
½ teaspoon pepper
1 (6-ounce) can sliced
  mushrooms, drained
1 (10-ounce) package frozen
  chopped spinach, thawed and
  well drained
1 (10¾-ounce) can cream of
  chicken soup, undiluted
⅔ cup water
3 ounces Monterey Jack cheese,
  diced
3 ounces Cheddar cheese, diced

Cook angel hair pasta nests according to package directions; drain well, keeping nests intact.

Sprinkle chicken with salt and pepper; arrange in a lightly greased 13-x 9- x 2-inch baking dish. Spoon mushrooms and chopped spinach over chicken. Arrange cooked pasta nests over spinach.

Combine soup and water in a small saucepan; bring to a boil, stirring constantly. Pour sauce evenly over pasta nests. Bake at 375° for 1 hour.

Combine Monterey Jack and Cheddar cheeses; sprinkle over pasta. Bake an additional 5 minutes. Yield: 8 servings.
  Jo Ann Bridges
  Birmingham, Alabama

Herbed Cheese For A Party

Heather Riggins of Nashville, Tennessee, makes a flavorful cheese filling for appetizers. She prefers piping the mixture into fresh snow pea pods, but the cheese flavor is versatile enough to use with any fresh vegetable. It's even tasty served as a spread with party bread slices or crackers.

HERBED CHEESE

2 (8-ounce) packages cream
  cheese, softened
1 large clove garlic, minced
2 teaspoons minced fresh chives
2 teaspoons dried whole basil
  leaves
1 teaspoon dried whole dillweed
1 teaspoon lemon-pepper
  seasoning

Combine all ingredients; stir well. Use the cheese as a filling for snow peas, cherry tomato shells, celery sticks, or cucumber slices, or use it as a spread for party-size bread. Yield: about 2 cups.

Plum Delicious Recipes

Plums are ripe, juicy, and full of flavor this time of year. You'll find them in the produce section of the supermarket or at the farmers' market. Better yet, pick them fresh from the tree. Then try these recipes.

PLUM BUTTER

12 to 14 pounds ripe plums
3 cups sugar

Remove pits from plums (do not peel), and place in a large kettle; cover. Bring to a boil over medium heat, and simmer 15 minutes or until plums are tender, stirring occasionally. Drain. Press plums through a sieve or food mill; measure 6 cups of puree. Combine puree and sugar in a Dutch oven. Cook, uncovered, over medium heat 1 hour or until mixture thickens, stirring frequently.

Remove from heat, and skim off foam. Pour hot plum mixture into hot sterilized jars, leaving ¼-inch headspace. Cover at once with metal lids, and screw on bands. Process mixture in boiling-water bath for 10 minutes. Yield: 6 pints.
  Gladys Stout
  Elizabethton, Tennessee

PLUM SAUCE

1½ pounds fresh plums, pitted
  and quartered
2 tablespoons water
¾ cup applesauce
½ cup apricot preserves
½ cup crushed pineapple
2 tablespoons sugar
1 tablespoon vinegar
½ teaspoon grated fresh
  gingerroot
¼ teaspoon crushed garlic
¼ to ½ teaspoon crushed red
  pepper

Combine plums and water in a saucepan. Cover and cook over medium-low heat 10 minutes or until soft, stirring occasionally. Press plums through a sieve or food mill. Combine puree, applesauce, and remaining ingredients, mixing well; chill at least 2 hours. Yield: about 3⅔ cups.

Note: Ground ginger (¼ teaspoon) may be substituted for ½ teaspoon grated fresh gingerroot.
  Linda E. Whitt
  Missouri City, Texas

CRUNCHY PLUM COBBLER

2 pounds fresh plums, pitted and
  quartered
¾ cup firmly packed brown sugar
1 cup all-purpose flour
¼ cup sugar
½ teaspoon ground cinnamon
1 egg, beaten
¼ cup butter or margarine,
  melted
Ice cream or sweetened whipped
  cream (optional)

Arrange plums in a lightly greased 10- x 6- x 2-inch baking dish; sprinkle with brown sugar.

Combine flour, sugar, and cinnamon; add egg, stirring with a fork until crumbly. Sprinkle flour mixture evenly over brown sugar; drizzle with butter. Bake at 375° for 45 minutes. Serve with ice cream or sweetened whipped cream, if desired. Yield: 6 servings.
  Betty R. Butts
  Kensington, Maryland

STREUSEL-TOPPED PLUM PIE

1½ pounds fresh plums, pitted
   and quartered
⅓ cup water
¾ cup sugar
3 tablespoons cornstarch
¼ teaspoon salt
1 unbaked 9-inch pastry shell
⅓ cup all-purpose flour
⅓ cup sugar
½ teaspoon ground cinnamon
¼ teaspoon ground nutmeg
2 tablespoons butter or margarine
Whipped cream (optional)

Combine plums and water in a saucepan; bring to a boil, and cook 4 minutes. Combine ¾ cup sugar, cornstarch, and salt; stir into plum mixture. Cook over low heat until mixture thickens and comes to a boil. Boil 1 minute, stirring constantly. Remove from heat; cool. Spoon mixture into pastry shell.

Combine flour, ⅓ cup sugar, cinnamon, and nutmeg; cut in butter with a pastry blender until mixture resembles coarse meal. Sprinkle over plum mixture; bake at 375° for 25 to 30 minutes or until golden brown. Cool before serving. Serve with whipped cream, if desired. Yield: one 9-inch pie.
Lona B. Shealy
Leesville, South Carolina

Pancakes And Waffles Take To Dessert

The next time you crave pancakes or waffles, hold the syrup and sausage in favor of a new line of accompaniments. Toppings—such as fruit and nut sauces and flavored whipped cream—transform these common breakfast foods into festive desserts.

For best results, cook the batter within one hour after mixing. If you're preparing them for a large group, it's often difficult to keep the first batches from cooling and softening while you complete the cooking. Keep freshly cooked pancakes and waffles warm and firm by placing them on an ovenproof platter in a 200° oven as you cook the rest. If you need to prepare them in advance, let cool completely, seal them in a plastic bag, and store at room temperature up to two days. Reheat on a wire rack at 350° just before serving. Pancakes and waffles are good candidates for freezing, as well.

Most pancakes have a natural indicator to let you know when they're ready to turn. When the top surface is covered with bubbles and the edges begin to look cooked, they're ready to turn. Thicker batters won't follow the bubble test; in that case, check the edges for doneness. Usually the second side will take only a minute or two to cook. Most waffle irons have a signal light to tell you when they're done.

DESSERT GINGER PANCAKES

1 cup all-purpose flour
1 teaspoon baking powder
¼ teaspoon baking soda
½ teaspoon ground ginger
½ teaspoon ground cinnamon
¼ teaspoon ground nutmeg
1 egg
1 cup buttermilk
⅓ cup molasses
2 tablespoons butter or
   margarine, melted
¼ cup firmly packed brown sugar
Apricot-Walnut Hard Sauce

Combine flour, baking powder, soda, and spices in a large mixing bowl.

Beat egg; add buttermilk, molasses, butter, and brown sugar, stirring until blended. Add to flour mixture, stirring just until dry ingredients are moistened (mixture will be lumpy).

For each pancake, pour about 2 tablespoons batter onto a hot, lightly greased griddle. Turn pancakes when edges look cooked. Serve 3 pancakes per serving with Apricot-Walnut Hard Sauce. Yield: 6 servings.

Apricot-Walnut Hard Sauce

⅓ cup butter or margarine,
   softened
½ cup sifted powdered sugar
½ cup diced fresh or canned
   apricots
¼ cup chopped walnuts
1 teaspoon lemon juice

Cream butter in a small bowl at medium speed of an electric mixer; add sugar, and beat until light and fluffy. Fold in remaining ingredients. Serve at room temperature. Yield: 1 cup.

CHOCOLATE WAFFLES WITH STRAWBERRY CREAM

¾ cup plus 2 tablespoons
   all-purpose flour
½ teaspoon baking soda
⅛ teaspoon salt
¼ cup plus 2 tablespoons sugar
3 tablespoons cocoa
1 egg, separated
1 cup buttermilk
2 tablespoons butter or
   margarine, melted
Strawberry Cream
8 strawberry fans

Combine flour, soda, salt, sugar, and cocoa in a large bowl. Combine egg yolk, buttermilk, and butter; add to flour mixture, stirring until dry ingredients are moistened.

Beat egg white (at room temperature) until stiff peaks form; carefully fold into batter. Bake in preheated, oiled waffle iron.

Cut waffles to make eight 4-inch squares. Serve waffle squares with Strawberry Cream. Garnish each serving with a strawberry fan. Yield: 8 servings.

Strawberry Cream

¾ cup whipping cream
⅓ cup sifted powdered sugar
2 cups sliced strawberries

Beat whipping cream until foamy; gradually add powdered sugar, beating until soft peaks form. Fold sliced strawberries into whipped cream. Yield: 2 cups.

LUAU DESSERT PANCAKES

1 cup all-purpose flour
1 teaspoon baking powder
½ teaspoon baking soda
¼ teaspoon salt
2 tablespoons sugar
1 (8-ounce) can crushed
  pineapple, undrained
1 egg
½ cup buttermilk
2 tablespoons vegetable oil
⅓ cup flaked coconut
Rum Cream
1 (8-ounce) can pineapple
  rings, drained and halved
⅓ cup flaked coconut,
  toasted

Combine flour, baking powder, soda, salt, and sugar in a large bowl.

Drain crushed pineapple, reserving juice; add enough water to juice to make ½ cup liquid.

Beat egg; add ½ cup pineapple liquid, buttermilk, and oil, stirring well. Add to flour mixture, stirring until dry ingredients are moistened (batter will be lumpy).

Combine crushed pineapple and ⅓ cup flaked coconut; set aside.

For each pancake, pour ⅓ cup batter onto a hot, lightly greased griddle. Sprinkle each pancake with 1 tablespoon pineapple mixture. Turn pancakes when tops are covered with bubbles and edges look cooked. To serve, dollop Rum Cream over each pancake, and top with halved pineapple rings and toasted coconut. Yield: 6 servings.

Rum Cream

1 cup whipping cream
2 tablespoons powdered sugar
2 tablespoons light rum
1 teaspoon vanilla extract

Combine all ingredients; beat until firm peaks form. Yield: 2 cups.

Tip: *If only drained fruit is called for in a recipe, use quarters and halves rather than the more costly whole fruit.*

Wild About Blueberries

The abundance of plump, juicy blueberries inspires some distinctive treats. When purchasing blueberries, select firm, plump, purplish-blue ones free of moisture. They maintain their quality for several days if refrigerated. Rinse just before using.

BLUEBERRY BREAD PUDDING

2 tablespoons butter or margarine
4 eggs, beaten
2½ cups milk
¾ cup sugar
2 tablespoons lemon juice
8 cups (½-inch) French bread
  cubes
2 cups fresh blueberries
1 teaspoon grated lemon rind
Custard Sauce

Melt butter in a 13- x 9- x 2-inch baking dish; set aside.

Combine eggs and next 3 ingredients; beat well. Add bread cubes, and let stand 5 minutes. Fold in blueberries and lemon rind; spoon into prepared dish. Bake at 350° for 35 minutes or until lightly browned and puffed. Serve warm with Custard Sauce. Yield: 10 servings.

Custard Sauce

2 eggs
2 tablespoons sugar
Dash of salt
1 cup milk, scalded
½ teaspoon vanilla extract
½ teaspoon grated lemon rind

Combine eggs, sugar, and salt in top of a double boiler, beating well. Gradually stir about ½ cup milk into egg mixture; add remaining milk, stirring constantly.

Bring water in bottom of double boiler to a boil. Reduce heat to low; cook custard over hot water, stirring occasionally, about 15 minutes or until mixture thickens. Cool slightly. Add vanilla and grated lemon rind. Yield: 1⅓ cups.   *Elton Darby*
Tunica, Mississippi

BLUEBERRY STREUSEL COFFEE CAKE

1 cup fresh blueberries
2 tablespoons all-purpose flour
½ cup butter or margarine,
  softened
2 cups all-purpose flour
2 teaspoons baking powder
¼ teaspoon salt
1 cup sugar
¾ cup milk
1 egg
Streusel Topping

Combine blueberries and 2 tablespoons flour; toss gently. Set aside.

Combine butter and next 5 ingredients in a large bowl; beat at medium speed of an electric mixer 2 minutes. Add egg; beat 1 minute. Fold in blueberries. Spread batter evenly in a greased and floured 9-inch square pan. Sprinkle with topping. Bake at 350° for 50 minutes. Yield: 9 servings.

Streusel Topping

½ cup sugar
⅓ cup all-purpose flour
½ teaspoon ground cinnamon
¼ cup butter or margarine,
  softened

Mix first 3 ingredients; cut in butter until mixture resembles coarse meal. Yield: 1 cup.   *Ernestine Elder*
Gainesville, Texas

BLUEBERRY-CREAM CHEESE PIE

1 (8-ounce) package cream
  cheese, softened
¼ cup sugar
¼ cup commercial sour cream
½ teaspoon vanilla extract
1 baked 9-inch pastry shell
1 cup fresh blueberries
½ cup water
½ cup sugar
2 tablespoons cornstarch
1 tablespoon lemon juice
1½ cups fresh blueberries
Commercial sour cream
2 tablespoons powdered sugar
Dash of ground cinnamon
Blueberries
Grated nutmeg

Combine first 4 ingredients; beat at medium speed of an electric mixer 1 minute or until smooth. Spread mixture in baked pastry shell; cover and chill for 1 hour.

Place 1 cup blueberries in a small saucepan; mash with a potato masher. Add water; bring to a boil. Reduce heat, and simmer 3 minutes. Remove from heat. Strain berry mixture. If necessary, add water to juice to make 1 cup; return to saucepan.

Combine ½ cup sugar and cornstarch; stir into berry liquid. Bring to a boil, and boil 1 minute, stirring constantly. Stir in lemon juice; cool.

Place 1½ cups blueberries over cream cheese mixture; pour glaze over top. Chill 2 to 3 hours.

To serve, dollop each slice with sour cream. Combine powdered sugar and cinnamon; sprinkle mixture over sour cream. Garnish with blueberries and grated nutmeg. Yield: one 9-inch pie.
Lois Hansen
Niceville, Florida

BLINTZ SOUFFLÉ

1 (8-ounce) package cream
   cheese, softened
2 cups small-curd cottage cheese
2 egg yolks
1 tablespoon sugar
1 teaspoon vanilla extract
6 eggs
1½ cups commercial sour cream
½ cup orange juice
½ cup butter or margarine,
   softened
1 cup all-purpose flour
⅓ cup sugar
2 teaspoons baking powder
1 teaspoon grated orange rind
Blueberry Sauce

Combine first 5 ingredients in a small bowl; beat at medium speed of an electric mixer until smooth. Set mixture aside.

Combine 6 eggs, sour cream, orange juice, and butter in container of an electric blender; blend until smooth. Add flour, ⅓ cup sugar, baking powder, and orange rind; blend until smooth. Pour half of batter into a greased 13- x 9- x 2-inch

baking dish. Spoon cream cheese mixture evenly over batter, and spread carefully with knife. Pour remaining batter over cream cheese mixture. Bake at 350° for 50 to 60 minutes or until puffy and golden. Serve immediately with Blueberry Sauce. Yield: 8 to 10 servings.

Blueberry Sauce

⅔ cup sugar
2 tablespoons cornstarch
Dash of ground cinnamon
Dash of ground nutmeg
1 cup water
2 cups fresh blueberries
2 tablespoons lemon juice

Combine first 4 ingredients in a heavy saucepan. Gradually stir in water. Cook over medium heat, stirring constantly, until mixture comes to a boil. Boil 1 minute; stir in blueberries and lemon juice. Serve warm. Yield: 2¼ cups.
Janet S. Wilkins
Baton Rouge, Louisiana

New Ideas
For Fresh Beets

When you plan meals, be sure to include beets, one of the sweetest vegetables, especially when they are young and tender. And they're available year-round, with the best selection during summer months.

The skin easily slips off cooked beets. To remove beet stains, rub hands and nonporous surfaces with table salt.

BEETS AND APPLES

1½ pounds fresh beets, peeled
   and grated
1 large apple, peeled, cored, and
   grated
1 tablespoon water
1 teaspoon lemon juice
½ teaspoon sugar
Pinch of salt
1 tablespoon commercial sour
   cream
⅛ teaspoon freshly ground pepper

Combine first 6 ingredients in a saucepan. Cover and cook over low heat 30 minutes or until beets are tender, stirring occasionally. Stir in sour cream and pepper, and cook until thoroughly heated. Yield: 4 servings.
Gwen Louer
Roswell, Georgia

STUFFED BEETS

6 medium-size fresh beets
1 cup English peas, cooked and
   drained
2 stalks celery, chopped
1 green onion, chopped
¼ teaspoon salt
¼ teaspoon pepper
2 tablespoons mayonnaise
Beet leaves (optional)
Celery leaves (optional)

Leave root and 1 inch of stem on beets; scrub with a brush. Arrange beets in a steamer basket or colander in a Dutch oven with 1 inch of water. Bring to a boil; cover, reduce heat, and simmer 35 to 40 minutes or until tender. Drain. Pour cold water over beets, and drain. Cool. Trim off beet stems and roots, and rub off skins. Cut a slice from top of each beet. Gently scoop out pulp, leaving ½-inch shells; reserve pulp for other uses. Chill beets.

Combine peas and next 5 ingredients; coat well. Chill. Just before serving, fill beet cavities with pea mixture. If desired, serve on beet leaves and garnish with celery leaves. Yield: 6 servings.
Charlotte Pierce
Greensburg, Kentucky

POTATO-BEET SOUP

1½ pounds fresh beets
4 large leeks, quartered and diced
3 tablespoons butter or margarine, melted
3 large potatoes, peeled and diced
6 cups chicken broth
¾ cup half-and-half
¾ cup milk
¼ teaspoon salt
¼ teaspoon white pepper

Leave root and 1 inch of stem on beets; scrub with a brush. Place beets in a saucepan; add water to cover. Bring to a boil; cover, reduce heat, and simmer 35 to 40 minutes or until beets are tender. Drain. Pour cold water over beets, and drain. Cool. Trim off beet stems and roots, and rub off skins. Dice beets. Measure 2 cups; reserve remainder for another use. Set aside.

Sauté leeks in butter in a large Dutch oven 3 minutes or until wilted. Add potatoes and chicken broth; cover and cook 20 minutes or until potatoes are tender. Spoon half of mixture into container of an electric blender; process until smooth. Repeat with remaining potato mixture.

Return potato mixture to Dutch oven; stir in half-and-half, milk, salt, and pepper. Cook over low heat, stirring constantly, until mixture is thoroughly heated.

Place 2 cups beets in container of electric blender; process until beets are smooth. Drizzle beets into potato soup, and swirl gently with a knife. Yield: 8 cups.

Note: One (16-ounce) can of beets, drained, may be substituted for fresh beets.   *Mrs. Harland J. Stone*
Ocala, Florida

Tip: *Use a stiff vegetable brush to scrub vegetables rather than peel them. Peeling is not necessary for many vegetables, and it causes a loss of vitamins found in and just under the vegetable skin.*

Stir-Fry Vegetables In Minutes

Stir-frying fits today's lifestyle; it's nutritious and quick. The key is cooking at a high temperature for a short period of time, stirring continuously to ensure even cooking. Some vegetables, though, may require a few minutes of steaming after the initial stir-frying.

SKILLET-FRIED VEGETABLES

2 tablespoons vegetable oil
2 large green peppers, cut into strips
1 large onion, cut into strips
1 (8-ounce) package fresh mushrooms, sliced
½ teaspoon seasoned salt
¾ cup (3 ounces) shredded mozzarella cheese

Heat electric wok or skillet at 325° for 2 to 3 minutes; add oil, and heat 1 minute. Add green peppers and onion; stir-fry 2 minutes. Add mushrooms, and stir-fry 2 to 4 minutes or until vegetables are crisp-tender. Sprinkle with seasoned salt and cheese. Serve immediately. Yield: 6 servings.   *Dolly Prince*
Front Royal, Virginia

STIR-FRY MEDLEY

2 tablespoons vegetable oil
½ stalk celery, sliced
1 medium onion, chopped
1 stalk broccoli, cut into flowerets
2 cups coarsely chopped green cabbage
2 cups coarsely chopped red cabbage
¼ teaspoon salt
⅛ teaspoon white pepper
2 teaspoons Worcestershire sauce

Heat electric wok or skillet at 325° for 2 to 3 minutes; add oil, and heat 1 minute. Add celery, onion, and broccoli; stir-fry 2 minutes. Add cabbages, and stir-fry 3 minutes. Cover

and cook vegetables over low heat 3 minutes. Stir in salt, pepper, and Worcestershire sauce. Serve immediately. Yield: 6 servings.
Rubie Mae Walker
Lynchburg, Virginia

STIR-FRY ZUCCHINI TOSS

2 tablespoons vegetable oil
4 stalks celery, cut into ½-inch pieces
1 large green pepper, cut into strips
1 medium onion, cut into strips
3 medium zucchini, cut into ¼-inch slices
2 tablespoons chopped fresh parsley
1 teaspoon seasoned salt
1 teaspoon paprika

Heat electric wok or skillet at 325° for 2 to 3 minutes; add oil, and heat 2 minutes. Add celery, green pepper, and onion; stir-fry 2 minutes. Add zucchini, and stir-fry 5 minutes or until crisp-tender. Stir in parsley and seasonings. Serve immediately. Yield: 6 to 8 servings.   *Anita Cox*
Fort Worth, Texas

LEMON-BUTTER CABBAGE

1½ tablespoons butter or margarine
1½ tablespoons vegetable oil
1 teaspoon caraway seeds
1 medium head cabbage (about 1½ pounds), coarsely chopped
1 teaspoon grated lemon rind
2 tablespoons lemon juice
¼ teaspoon salt
⅛ teaspoon pepper

Heat electric wok or skillet at 325° for 2 to 3 minutes; add first 3 ingredients, and heat 1 minute. Add cabbage; stir-fry 3 to 4 minutes. Cover, reduce heat, and steam 2 to 3 minutes or until tender. Add lemon rind and remaining ingredients, tossing gently. Serve immediately. Yield: 6 servings.   *Madeline Gibbons*
Little Rock, Arkansas

JULY

Sandwiches For The Summer Season

These open-faced sandwiches come together easily. Try them for a quick brunch, a casual supper, or a filling snack. To serve meaty sandwiches, consider the convenience and attractive appearance of sliced deli meats. Thin layers of ham can easily be substituted for one thicker slice of meat.

SEAFOOD HOT BROWN

½ pound unpeeled medium-size fresh shrimp
2 tablespoons butter or margarine
3 tablespoons butter or margarine
3 tablespoons all-purpose flour
1½ cups milk
1 packet instant broth and seasoning
1 teaspoon Old Bay seasoning
4 slices sandwich bread, toasted
½ cup (2 ounces) shredded Cheddar cheese
4 slices tomato
4 slices bacon, cooked and crumbled

Peel and devein shrimp. Melt 2 tablespoons butter in a heavy saucepan; add shrimp, and cook over medium heat about 5 minutes, stirring occasionally. Remove shrimp, and set aside.

Add 3 tablespoons butter to saucepan. Melt butter over low heat; add flour, stirring until smooth. Cook 1 minute, stirring constantly. Gradually add milk; cook over medium heat, stirring constantly, until thickened and bubbly. Stir in instant broth and Old Bay seasoning. Place toast in a shallow baking dish; place 3 shrimp on each piece of toast. Spoon sauce over shrimp. Top with cheese and tomato. Bake at 450° for 12 to 15 minutes or until bubbly. Top with bacon, and serve. Yield: 4 servings.
W. W. Davis
Lexington, Kentucky

TEMPTING TUNA MELTS

1 (6½-ounce) can tuna, drained and flaked
3 hard-cooked eggs, chopped
⅓ cup sweet pickle relish
¼ cup chopped onion
2 tablespoons commercial mustard/mayonnaise sauce
3 tablespoons mayonnaise
3 hamburger buns, split and toasted
1 cup (4 ounces) shredded Monterey Jack cheese

Combine first 5 ingredients, stirring well. Spread mayonnaise evenly on cut sides of hamburger buns; top each half with tuna mixture, and sprinkle with cheese. Broil sandwiches 6 inches from heat until cheese melts. Yield: 6 servings.
Lynn Walker Wright
Ocoee, Florida

GUMBO JOES

1 pound lean ground beef
1 (10¾-ounce) can chicken gumbo soup, undiluted
2 tablespoons prepared mustard
2 tablespoons catsup
4 hamburger buns, split and toasted
¼ cup sliced green onions

Cook ground beef in a large skillet over medium heat until meat is browned, stirring to crumble. Drain well. Add soup, mustard, and catsup; stir. Cook, uncovered, over medium heat 5 to 10 minutes, stirring often. Serve mixture over hamburger buns; sprinkle with green onions. Yield: 4 servings.
Mrs. Ralph Hatfield
Kansas City, Missouri

ORANGE BLOSSOM SPECIAL

2 tablespoons commercial mustard/mayonnaise sauce
4 slices whole wheat bread, toasted
1 (2½-ounce) jar sliced dried beef
2 oranges, peeled and cut into 8 slices
1 cup (4 ounces) shredded Monterey Jack cheese
4 fresh strawberries (optional)

Spread mustard/mayonnaise sauce on bread; top each with 5 slices of beef and 2 orange slices. Sprinkle cheese on sandwiches; broil 6 inches from heat until cheese melts. Garnish with strawberries, if desired. Yield: 4 servings.
Mrs. Wesley Hull
Dallas, Texas

HAM AND EGGS À LA SWISS

4 English muffins
3 tablespoons butter or margarine, softened
½ pound thinly sliced deli ham
4 hard-cooked eggs, sliced
½ cup commercial sour cream
½ cup mayonnaise
1 cup (4 ounces) shredded Swiss cheese
Paprika (optional)
16 jalapeño pepper slices
Sweet red pepper strips (optional)
Squash cups (optional)
Lettuce (optional)

Split English muffins; spread with butter. Toast muffins until lightly browned. Place ham on English muffin halves. Arrange 2 egg slices on each sandwich. Set aside.

Combine sour cream and mayonnaise, mixing well. Spoon 2 tablespoons of mixture over each sandwich; sprinkle sandwiches with shredded cheese. Sprinkle sandwiches with paprika, if desired, and garnish with two jalapeño slices. Broil sandwiches about 6 inches from heat until cheese melts and sandwiches are heated. If desired, garnish with sweet red pepper strips, squash cups, and lettuce. Yield: 4 servings.

Peggy Sisson
Wimberley, Texas

MEAL-IN-ONE BAGELS

¼ cup spicy mustard
2 tablespoons honey
4 bagels, split lengthwise
16 slices Canadian bacon
1 (3-ounce) package cream
  cheese, softened
2 teaspoons minced fresh chives

Combine mustard and honey in a small bowl; spread on each bagel half. Top each with 2 slices of Canadian bacon. Place on an ungreased baking sheet; cover with aluminum foil. Bake at 400° for 10 minutes. Remove from oven, and spread with cream cheese. Sprinkle each with ¼ teaspoon chives. Yield: 4 servings.

Diana Krizan
Sugar Land, Texas

OPEN-FACED ZUCCHINI SANDWICHES

1 medium zucchini, diagonally
  sliced
1 small onion, sliced and
  separated into rings
2 individual French bread loaves,
  split lengthwise
1 (6-ounce) package provolone
  cheese, shredded
6 slices bacon, cooked and
  crumbled
¼ teaspoon dried whole oregano
Lettuce (optional)

Combine zucchini and onion in steaming rack. Place rack over boiling water; cover and steam 3 minutes or until vegetables are crisp-tender. Drain well on paper towels.

Place bread, cut side up, on an ungreased baking sheet; sprinkle with provolone cheese. Arrange zucchini and onion in rows alternately with crumbled bacon on top of cheese. Sprinkle with oregano. Bake at 350° for 5 minutes or until cheese melts. Serve on lettuce-lined plate, if desired. Yield: 4 servings.

Mary Kay Menees
White Pine, Tennessee

TOMATOES WITH CHEESE SAUCE OVER TOAST

½ cup all-purpose flour
¼ teaspoon salt
¼ teaspoon pepper
4 firm tomatoes
2 tablespoons vegetable oil
¼ cup butter or margarine
¼ cup all-purpose flour
½ teaspoon prepared mustard
2 cups milk
1 cup (4 ounces) shredded
  American cheese
¼ teaspoon salt
¼ teaspoon pepper
12 (¾-inch) slices French bread,
  toasted
Paprika (optional)
Parsley (optional)

Combine ½ cup flour, ¼ teaspoon salt, and ¼ teaspoon pepper. Cut each tomato into 3 thick slices; dredge tomatoes in flour mixture. Heat oil in a heavy skillet; add tomatoes, and fry slowly until browned, turning once. Remove tomatoes from skillet, and keep warm.

Melt butter in a heavy saucepan over low heat; add ¼ cup flour and mustard, stirring until smooth. Cook 1 minute, stirring constantly. Gradually add milk; cook over medium heat, stirring constantly, until mixture is thickened and bubbly. Stir in cheese, ¼ teaspoon salt, and ¼ teaspoon pepper.

Arrange 2 slices of bread on each serving plate. Top bread with 2 tablespoons cheese sauce and 2 slices fried tomato. Spoon remaining cheese sauce over sandwiches. If desired, garnish with paprika and parsley. Serve immediately. Yield: 6 servings.

Helen Wampler
Knoxville, Tennessee

TANGY WELSH RAREBIT

¾ cup milk
1½ cups (6 ounces) shredded
  mild Cheddar cheese
¾ teaspoon dry mustard
⅛ teaspoon red pepper
½ teaspoon prepared horseradish
1 egg, well beaten
4 (1-inch-thick) slices French
  bread, toasted
4 slices bacon, cooked and
  crumbled

Combine first 5 ingredients in top of a double boiler; bring water to a boil. Reduce heat to low; cook, stirring constantly, until cheese melts. Slowly stir about one-fourth of hot cheese mixture into beaten egg; add to remaining hot mixture, stirring constantly. Cook over low heat, stirring constantly, until mixture thickens and just begins to simmer. Spoon over toast; sprinkle with crumbled bacon. Serve immediately. Yield: 4 servings.

CUCUMBER SANDWICHES

1 (8-ounce) package cream
  cheese, softened
1 tablespoon Italian salad
  dressing mix
2 tablespoons milk
6 slices rye bread
1 large cucumber, sliced

Combine first 3 ingredients, mixing well. Spread mixture on rye bread, and top with cucumber slices. Yield: 6 servings.

Pam Wondolowski
Corpus Christi, Texas

Put The Chill On Summer Soups

It's just habit to ice down the watermelon or to serve the tea or lemonade frosty cold. But you can now add soup—fruit or vegetable—to your list of favorite chilled summer treats.

Cold soups are an excellent choice for sack lunches or picnics. Just store in a thermos to keep them cold.

COLD TOMATO SOUP

5 to 7 large tomatoes, peeled and seeded
2 cups chicken broth
1 to 2 tablespoons red wine vinegar
1 tablespoon olive oil
1 clove garlic, crushed
⅛ teaspoon salt
¼ teaspoon pepper
⅛ teaspoon ground cumin
1 medium cucumber, unpeeled
¼ cup thinly sliced leeks

Quarter tomatoes, and place in container of a food processor or electric blender; process until smooth. Combine 4 cups tomato puree, broth, and next 6 ingredients, and stir well. Quarter cucumber lengthwise, and slice thinly. Stir cucumber and leek slices into tomato mixture. Cover and chill for at least 2 hours. Yield: 7½ cups.
Carolyn Hill
Alpine, Alabama

COLD POTATO-CUCUMBER SOUP

3 medium potatoes, peeled and thinly sliced
1 quart water
6 medium cucumbers, peeled, seeded, and thinly sliced
1 small onion, chopped
3 tablespoons butter or margarine, melted
4 chicken-flavored bouillon cubes
2 cups milk
Chopped fresh chives (optional)

Combine potatoes and water in a large saucepan; cover and cook over medium heat 20 minutes or until tender. Set aside. Do not drain.

Sauté cucumbers and onion in butter in a large skillet until tender; add to potatoes. Stir in bouillon cubes and milk. Cook over medium heat 10 minutes, stirring occasionally. Cool.

Spoon one-third of mixture into container of a food processor or electric blender; process until smooth. Repeat procedure twice with remaining mixture. Cover and chill thoroughly. Ladle into soup bowls; garnish with chopped chives, if desired. Yield: 10 cups.
David Darst
Tallahassee, Florida

AVOCADO SOUP

1 cup chopped onion
¾ cup chopped celery
1 (5-ounce) can chicken, drained
2 cups chicken broth
1½ cups half-and-half
¾ cup commercial sour cream
3 medium avocados, peeled and mashed
½ teaspoon hot sauce
¼ teaspoon salt
¼ teaspoon pepper
½ cup dry white wine
¼ cup chopped fresh parsley

Combine first 4 ingredients in a saucepan. Bring to a boil; cover, reduce heat, and simmer 20 minutes.

Pour half of broth mixture into container of an electric blender; process until smooth. Add half each of half-and-half and sour cream. Process until blended. Set aside. Repeat procedure with remaining broth mixture, half-and-half, and sour cream. Combine mixtures; cover and chill. Stir in avocados, hot sauce, salt, pepper, and wine. Chill at least 1 hour. Garnish each serving with parsley. Yield: 7 cups.
Mrs. J. A. Allard
San Antonio, Texas

CANTALOUPE SOUP

8 cups cubed cantaloupe, chilled (about 2 medium)
¾ cup sweet white wine, chilled
¼ cup whipping cream
Fresh mint sprigs

Place half of cantaloupe in container of an electric blender; process until smooth. With blender running, add half each of wine and whipping cream; process until smooth. Repeat procedure with remaining cantaloupe, wine, and whipping cream. Ladle into soup bowls; garnish with mint. Yield: 6½ cups.
Clare Hall Smith
Bethesda, Maryland

CHILLED FRESH FRUIT SOUP

2 tablespoons cornstarch
1 cup cold water, divided
¾ cup maple-flavored syrup
¾ cup white wine
1 teaspoon lemon juice
2 cups sliced fresh peaches, cut into bite-size pieces
1 cup sliced strawberries
1 cup fresh blueberries

Combine cornstarch and ¼ cup water in a saucepan. Add remaining ¾ cup water, syrup, wine, and lemon juice, mixing well. Cook over medium heat, stirring constantly, until mixture comes to a boil. Boil 1 minute. Remove from heat; cool completely.

Stir in fruit; cover and chill. Yield: 5 cups.
Cathy Darling
Grafton, West Virginia

STRAWBERRY SOUP

2 cups strawberries, sliced
1 cup commercial sour cream
1 cup half-and-half
¼ cup sugar
2 tablespoons brandy
½ teaspoon vanilla extract
Strawberry fans or slices

Combine first 6 ingredients in container of an electric blender; process until smooth. Pour into chilled soup bowls; garnish each serving with a strawberry fan or strawberry slices. Yield: 3½ cups. *Eleanor K. Brandt*
Arlington, Texas

summer Suppers

Celebratin' Summer

We're eager to share our 12th "Summer Suppers" special section. As always, it's filled with delicious recipes from our readers; their endless supply of food ideas is proof that there's no better place to experience summer than in the South. For recipes to make ahead, there are ice cream cakes and pies or fruit and cheese appetizers; each of these recipes will make entertaining easier. For those who have never smoked meat, we offer information on trying this process at home. We include a delectable "Cooking Light" menu, as well as side dishes to accompany a barbecue or cookout.

Join us in taking advantage of these opportunities to do what Southerners do best and love most—entertaining. There's no better place to do it than outdoors, so let's head to the backyard of Mag and Jim Stein in Nashville, Tennessee.

Peach Smash
Mushroom Tarts
Grilled Chicken With Dill Sauce
Special Scalloped Potatoes
Marinated Beets, Green Beans,
and Carrots
Baked Stuffed Tomatoes
Sally Lunn
Fresh Berries
With Raspberry Custard Sauce
Mocha Meringue Pie
Minted Tea

MUSHROOM TARTS

1 pound fresh mushrooms,
  chopped
1 cup chopped onion
3 tablespoons butter or
  margarine, melted
¼ teaspoon dried whole thyme
½ teaspoon salt
⅛ teaspoon pepper
2 tablespoons all-purpose flour
¼ cup commercial sour cream
1 tablespoon sherry
1 (10-ounce) package frozen patty
  shells, thawed

Sauté mushrooms and onion in butter 3 minutes or until tender. Add thyme, salt, pepper, and flour, mixing well. Stir in sour cream; cook over low heat until mixture thickens. Stir in sherry, and set mixture aside.

Roll out each pastry shell to form a 5-inch circle. Cut each circle in half. Fit each half into a regular-size muffin pan.

Fill with mushroom filling. Bake at 400° for 15 to 18 minutes or until done. Remove from pan. Cool 15 minutes. Yield: 12 tarts.

Tip: *Read labels to learn the weight, quality, and size of food products. Don't be afraid to experiment with new brands. Store brands can be equally good in quality and nutritional value, yet lower in price than well-known brands. Lower grades of canned fruit and vegetables are as nutritious as higher grades. Whenever possible, buy most foods by weight or cost per serving rather than by volume or package size.*

PEACH SMASH

2 cups unpeeled, sliced peaches
  (2 or 3 peaches)
½ cup light rum or tequila
¼ cup frozen pineapple juice
  concentrate, thawed
4 maraschino cherries
1 tablespoon maraschino cherry
  juice
Ice cubes

Combine peaches, rum, pineapple juice concentrate, cherries, and cherry juice in container of an electric blender; process until mixture is smooth.

Gradually add enough ice cubes to make mixture measure 5 cups in blender; process until peach mixture is smooth and thickened. Serve immediately. Yield: 5 cups.

GRILLED CHICKEN WITH DILL SAUCE

8 boneless chicken breast halves
¼ cup plus 2 tablespoons butter
   or margarine, melted
½ teaspoon pepper
Grape clusters
Small yellow squash
Orange slices
Parsley sprigs
Dill Sauce

Brush chicken with butter; sprinkle with pepper. Place chicken on grill over medium coals. Cover and grill 5 to 8 minutes on each side, basting frequently with butter. Garnish with grapes, squash, orange slices, and parsley sprigs. Serve with Dill Sauce. Yield: 8 servings.

Dill Sauce

2 cups commercial sour cream
2 tablespoons dried whole
   dillweed
2 tablespoons lemon juice
¼ teaspoon salt
½ teaspoon pepper

Combine all ingredients, stirring well. Yield: 2 cups.

SPECIAL SCALLOPED POTATOES

1 large clove garlic, minced
1 shallot, chopped
½ teaspoon crushed red pepper
3 tablespoons butter or
   margarine, melted
1¼ cups milk
1½ cups whipping cream
½ teaspoon salt
¼ teaspoon freshly ground pepper
2½ pounds red potatoes, unpeeled
   and cut into ⅛-inch slices
1 cup (4 ounces) shredded
   Gruyère cheese or Swiss
   cheese
¼ cup grated Parmesan cheese

Sauté garlic, shallot, and crushed red pepper in butter in a Dutch oven 2 minutes. Add milk and next 3 ingredients, stirring well. Add potatoes; bring to a boil over medium heat, stirring occasionally. Spoon into a lightly greased 12- x 8- x 2-inch baking dish. Sprinkle with Gruyère and Parmesan cheeses. Bake at 350° for 45 minutes or until bubbly and golden brown. Let stand 30 minutes before serving. Yield: 8 servings.

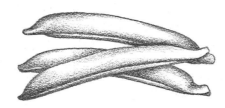

MARINATED BEETS, GREEN BEANS, AND CARROTS

2 pounds fresh small green beans
2 (16-ounce) cans small whole
   beets, drained
2 (16-ounce) cans small whole
   carrots, drained
1 (10¾-ounce) can tomato soup,
   undiluted
1 clove garlic, minced
¾ cup vegetable oil
¾ cup vinegar
⅓ cup sugar
1 tablespoon Worcestershire
   sauce
1 teaspoon grated onion
½ teaspoon paprika
½ teaspoon pepper
⅛ teaspoon salt
Canned apple rings
Lettuce

Arrange green beans in a steaming rack. Place rack over boiling water in a Dutch oven; cover and steam 8 to 10 minutes or until crisp-tender. Cool. Place beans, beets, and carrots in separate shallow dishes.

Combine tomato soup and next 9 ingredients in a jar. Cover tightly, and shake vigorously. Pour equal amounts over vegetables; toss. Cover and chill at least 8 hours, stirring once.

Drain vegetables, and place on a serving platter. Garnish with apple rings and lettuce. Yield: 8 servings.

BAKED STUFFED TOMATOES

8 medium-size tomatoes
1¼ teaspoons salt, divided
2 cups finely chopped zucchini
2 small onions, chopped
¼ cup finely chopped green
   pepper
2 cloves garlic, minced
½ teaspoon sugar
3 tablespoons olive oil, divided
½ cup soft breadcrumbs
¼ cup chopped fresh parsley,
   divided
¼ cup chopped fresh basil
2 teaspoons red wine vinegar
¾ teaspoon freshly ground pepper
Collard green leaves
Endive

Cut top quarter off each tomato. Chop top quarter, and set aside. Scoop out pulp, reserving pulp for other uses. Sprinkle inside of each tomato with ⅛ teaspoon salt, and invert on paper towels to drain.

Combine zucchini, onions, green pepper, garlic, sugar, reserved chopped tomato, and 2 tablespoons olive oil in a large skillet. Cook over medium heat until vegetables are tender (about 5 minutes).

Remove from skillet with a slotted spoon. Add remaining 1 tablespoon olive oil to skillet; add breadcrumbs, and cook until crumbs are golden. Add crumbs to vegetable mixture. Stir in 2 tablespoons parsley, basil, vinegar, pepper, and remaining ¼ teaspoon salt.

Spoon mixture into tomato shells, and place in a lightly greased 13- x 9- x 2-inch baking dish. Sprinkle stuffed tomatoes with remaining 2 tablespoons parsley, and bake at 350° for about 10 minutes. Remove stuffed tomatoes to a serving platter, and garnish with collard leaves and endive. Yield: 8 servings.

SALLY LUNN

1 package dry yeast
½ cup warm water (105° to 115°)
2 eggs, beaten
1 cup warm milk (105° to 115°)
½ cup butter or margarine, melted
4 cups all-purpose flour
3 tablespoons sugar
1 teaspoon salt

Dissolve yeast in warm water in a large mixing bowl; let stand 5 minutes. Add eggs, milk, and melted butter, beating well at medium speed of an electric mixer.

Combine flour, sugar, and salt; gradually add to yeast mixture, mixing until smooth.

Cover batter, and let rise in a warm place (85°), free from drafts, 45 minutes or until batter is doubled in bulk.

Spoon batter into a well-greased and floured 10-inch Bundt pan. Cover and let rise in a warm place, free from drafts, 30 minutes or until batter is doubled in bulk. Bake at 350° for 45 to 50 minutes. Remove bread from pan, and let cool on a wire rack. Serve with butter. Yield: one 10-inch ring.

Note: To freeze, bake bread as directed; let cool. Wrap in aluminum foil, and freeze. To serve, let bread thaw; reheat in foil at 250° for 10 to 15 minutes.

FRESH BERRIES WITH RASPBERRY CUSTARD SAUCE

4 egg yolks
⅓ cup sugar
1¾ cups half-and-half
2 to 3 tablespoons black raspberry liqueur
¼ teaspoon vanilla extract
4 pints fresh raspberries, strawberries, or blueberries

Beat egg yolks in a heavy saucepan until thick and lemon colored; gradually add sugar, beating well. Stir in half-and-half. Cook over low heat, stirring constantly, until mixture thickens and coats a metal spoon (about 10 minutes). Stir in liqueur and vanilla; cool. Cover and chill 8 hours. Serve with berries. Yield: 8 servings.

MOCHA MERINGUE PIE

3 egg whites
½ teaspoon baking powder
¾ cup sugar
Pinch of salt
1 cup chocolate wafer crumbs
½ cup chopped pecans
1 teaspoon vanilla extract
1 quart coffee ice cream, softened
1 cup whipping cream
¼ cup powdered sugar
Sweet chocolate shavings
½ cup Kahlúa

Beat egg whites (at room temperature) in a large mixing bowl until frothy; add baking powder, beating slightly. Gradually add ¾ cup sugar and salt; continue beating until stiff peaks form. Fold in chocolate wafer crumbs, pecans, and vanilla.

Spoon meringue into a buttered 9-inch pieplate, forming a shell; swirl sides high. Bake at 350° for 30 minutes; cool.

Spread ice cream evenly over meringue crust; cover and freeze at least 8 hours.

Beat whipping cream in a medium mixing bowl until foamy; gradually add powdered sugar, beating until soft peaks form. Spread sweetened whipped cream over ice cream. Garnish with chocolate shavings; cover and freeze until pie is firm.

Let pie stand at room temperature 10 minutes before slicing. Pour 1 tablespoon Kahlúa over each serving. Yield: one 9-inch pie.

MINTED TEA

1¾ cups sugar
2 cups water
8 regular-size tea bags
8 sprigs fresh mint
1 quart boiling water
2 quarts cold water
2 cups orange juice
¾ cup lemon juice
Fresh mint sprigs (optional)

Combine sugar and 2 cups water in a saucepan; stir well. Bring to a boil; boil 5 minutes. Remove from heat.

Add tea bags and 8 sprigs fresh mint to 1 quart boiling water; cover and let stand 10 minutes. Remove tea bags and mint.

Combine sugar water, tea mixture, 2 quarts cold water, orange juice, and lemon juice; stir well. Serve over ice. Garnish with mint sprigs, if desired. Yield: about 1 gallon.

Entrées In 30 Minutes

When it's warm outside, you don't want to spend hours in the kitchen. You need recipes that will minimize your time cooking over a hot stove. These selections from our readers will help you prepare entrées in 30 minutes or less, from start to finish.

Fish is always a good choice for a quick entrée because it can cook in as few as 10 minutes; the recipe for Macadamia Mahi Mahi is an example. If you can't find mahi mahi (a type of dolphin, but not the type you see in sea animal shows), you can substitute firm-fleshed fish, such as amberjack, flounder, or halibut.

While it helps to use particularly quick-cooking recipes, you can trim preparation time for meals by planning ahead. Keep ground beef frozen in the correct amounts for use in some of your favorite recipes. If you want to freeze chicken breasts, first skin, bone, and pound to flatten; then wrap as individual pieces. Freezer paper or wax paper between the chicken pieces makes them easy to separate.

MACADAMIA MAHI MAHI

2 pounds mahi mahi fillets
½ teaspoon salt
⅛ teaspoon pepper
2 tablespoons butter or margarine, melted
2 tablespoons lemon juice
¼ cup butter or margarine
1 cup macadamia nuts, chopped
1 tablespoon chopped fresh parsley

Cut fish into serving-size portions. Sprinkle both sides of fish with salt and pepper; place fillets on rack of a well-greased broiler pan. Combine 2 tablespoons butter and lemon juice, and brush over fish; reserve remaining mixture for basting.

Broil 5 to 6 inches from heat for 5 minutes. Turn fish; baste with butter mixture. Broil an additional 4 to 5 minutes or until fish flakes easily when tested with a fork. Transfer to a serving platter.

Melt ¼ cup butter in a skillet; add nuts, and cook, stirring constantly, until nuts are lightly browned. Remove from heat; add parsley. Pour over fish. Serve immediately. Yield: 6 servings.
Heather Riggins
Nashville, Tennessee

SALMON PATTIES WITH SAUCE

1 (15½-ounce) can salmon, undrained
⅓ cup finely chopped onion
1 egg
½ cup all-purpose flour
1½ teaspoons baking powder
1½ cups vegetable oil
3 tablespoons butter or margarine
¼ cup all-purpose flour
1½ cups milk
¼ teaspoon salt
⅛ teaspoon pepper
1 (8-ounce) can English peas, drained

Drain salmon, reserving 2 tablespoons liquid. Set reserved salmon liquid aside.

Flake salmon; add onion and egg. Stir in ½ cup flour. Add baking powder to reserved salmon liquid, stirring well. Add to salmon mixture, mixing well. Shape salmon mixture into 4 patties, and fry in hot oil (375°) in a skillet until golden brown (about 5 minutes). Drain.

Melt butter in a heavy saucepan over low heat; add ¼ cup flour, stirring constantly. Gradually add milk; cook over medium heat, stirring constantly, until mixture is thickened and bubbly. Stir in salt, pepper, and peas. Serve over patties. Yield: 4 servings.
Edith Askins
Greenville, Texas

CURRIED BEEF AND RICE

1 pound ground beef
¾ cup chopped onion
½ cup uncooked long-grain rice
2 cups beef broth
1 (4-ounce) can mushrooms, drained
1 teaspoon curry powder
1 teaspoon Worcestershire sauce
1 (16-ounce) can French-style or whole green beans, drained

Cook ground beef in a large skillet over medium-high heat until meat is browned, stirring to crumble. Drain off pan drippings. Stir in onion and next 5 ingredients; bring to a boil. Cover, reduce heat, and simmer 20 minutes or until rice is done. Add green beans; toss gently, and cook just until beans are thoroughly heated. Serve immediately. Yield: 4 servings.
Nancy Wallace
Pasadena, Texas

ITALIAN SAUSAGE SUPPER

1 cup uncooked shell macaroni
3 cups boiling water
1 pound hot Italian sausage
1 cup chopped onion
1 clove garlic, crushed
2 tablespoons all-purpose flour
¾ cup evaporated milk
¼ cup water
1 cup frozen English peas
1 cup chopped, peeled tomato
2 tablespoons grated Parmesan cheese

Cook macaroni in boiling water 8 to 10 minutes or until tender; drain and set aside.

Remove casings from sausage. Cook sausage, onion, and garlic in a large skillet over medium-high heat until sausage is browned, stirring to crumble. Drain. Stir in flour. Gradually add milk and water; add peas. Reduce heat to medium, and cook, stirring constantly, about 5 minutes or until mixture is thickened and bubbly. Add macaroni and tomato; cook just until thoroughly heated.

Spoon into serving dish; sprinkle with cheese. Yield: 4 servings.

Mrs. Earl L. Faulkenberry
Lancaster, South Carolina

CHICKEN AND VEGETABLES

1 to 2 tablespoons vegetable oil
2 carrots, scraped and sliced
¼ cup chopped onion
2 boneless chicken breast halves, cut into ¼-inch strips
¼ teaspoon dried whole basil
¼ teaspoon garlic powder
⅛ teaspoon salt
⅛ teaspoon pepper
¼ cup chicken broth
2 tablespoons white wine
1 (6-ounce) package frozen snow pea pods, thawed and drained
1 medium tomato, cut into 8 pieces
⅓ cup minced fresh parsley

Heat 1 tablespoon oil in a large skillet over medium heat. Add carrots and onion; sauté vegetables 8 minutes. Remove from skillet, reserving pan drippings. Set vegetables aside.

Add chicken to skillet; sprinkle with basil, garlic powder, salt, and pepper. Sauté chicken 3 to 4 minutes on each side or until browned, adding 1 tablespoon oil if needed. Add reserved vegetables, chicken broth,

and wine. Cover, reduce heat, and simmer 10 minutes. Stir in snow peas, tomato, and parsley, and cook until thoroughly heated. Yield: 2 servings.

Carolyn Look
El Paso, Texas

From Our Kitchen To Yours

Summertime meal preparation need not be hectic. A nutritious meal can be ready in as little as 30 minutes. As our home economists tested recipes in "Entrées in 30 Minutes," on page 164, they streamlined cooking techniques and reduced the amount of cooking equipment.

You can use these recipes to plan weekly menus, keeping in mind that time is the important factor. Vegetables and fruits can balance the meal and brighten plates in simple ways. To decrease time spent in the kitchen, choose recipes with few ingredients, quick preparation, easy-to-follow directions, and swift cleanup. One-dish meals, such as Curried Beef and Rice (page 164), are ideal. Recipes using chicken or seafood are speedy as well as delectable.

With advance planning and preparation you can come home to a dinner that's just about ready. Prepare the recipe the night before, and refrigerate until time to cook or reheat. Or try preparing part of the recipe ahead, such as the sauce in Salmon Patties With Sauce (page 164). Marinating food overnight adds flavor and requires little effort. On weekends or when you have extra time, cook double batches, freezing the extras; just one time to market and one cleanup saves time. All you have to do is

defrost foods such as meat sauces, breads, waffles, cookies, cakes, soups, and meat loaf in the microwave oven or overnight in the refrigerator; then heat. You can also use your microwave oven for side dishes or reheating. Stir-fry meals, such as Chicken and Vegetables (this page), are convenient when time is short. On frenzied days, use leftovers, filling in with convenience products or deli foods.

After planning weekly menus, make your tentative shopping list. Try to use supplies in your pantry or freezer while quality and nutritive value are at their best. On your list group similar items together—baking items, produce, meats, cleaning supplies, dairy products, canned vegetables and soups, canned fruits, frozen foods, and specialty items. Organize the list so that it corresponds to the store's layout. For example, if the frozen food section is last, list frozen food items last.

Tips for Quick Meals

■ Keep ingredients on hand for one simple meal.

■ Freeze chopped fresh herbs, chopped green pepper, chopped onion, breadcrumbs, and shredded cheese in plastic bags or freezer containers to add to quick meals.

■ Keep a small notebook with a list of ingredients of favorite easy recipes for a quick shopping trip.

■ Slice meats and vegetables into serving-size portions.

■ Make salads ahead of time; refrigerate the dressing and other ingredients separately.

■ Sandwiches, soups, or main-dish salads make quick use of leftover salad ingredients along with commercial breads.

■ Gather all necessary ingredients and utensils for the recipe you are preparing.

Make A Meal Of Vegetables

When you return home from a long day of working or playing in the summer sun, you're sure to enjoy the lightness and freshness that these vegetable recipes offer. The vegetables and bread are unmistakably Southern.

COLORFUL COLESLAW

1 small cabbage, shredded
1 small onion, chopped
1 carrot, shredded
½ cup chopped green pepper
½ cup chopped red pepper
3 tablespoons minced fresh
  parsley
½ cup cider vinegar
½ cup vegetable oil
3 tablespoons sugar
½ teaspoon salt
¼ teaspoon white pepper
1 large cabbage (optional)

Combine first 6 ingredients in a bowl; set aside.

Combine vinegar, oil, sugar, salt, and pepper in a small bowl; stir well. Add to cabbage mixture; toss gently. Cover and chill.

Serve coleslaw in a decorative cabbage shell, if desired. To make shell, trim core end of cabbage to form a flat base. Fold back several outer leaves of cabbage, if desired. Cut a crosswise slice from the top, making it wide enough to remove about one-fourth of the head; then lift out enough inner leaves from the cabbage to form a shell about 1-inch thick. (Reserve slice and inner leaves of cabbage for other uses.) Yield: 6 to 8 servings.   *Lona B. Shealy*
Leesville, South Carolina

YELLOW SQUASH CASSEROLE

2 pounds yellow squash, sliced
1 cup water
2 small onions, minced
2 tablespoons butter or
  margarine, melted
1 cup round buttery cracker
  crumbs, divided
1½ cups (6 ounces) shredded
  Cheddar cheese
2 eggs, beaten
¼ cup bacon bits
1 (2-ounce) jar diced pimiento,
  drained
¼ teaspoon salt
¼ teaspoon pepper

Combine squash and water in a medium saucepan; bring to a boil. Cover, reduce heat, and simmer 10 minutes or until squash is tender. Drain well, and mash; set aside.

Sauté onions in butter until tender. Combine onions, squash, ¾ cup cracker crumbs, cheese, and remaining ingredients. Spoon into a lightly greased 2-quart casserole. Sprinkle with remaining ¼ cup cracker crumbs. Bake at 350° for 45 minutes. Yield: about 6 servings.
Laurie McIntyre
Lake Jackson, Texas

JALAPEÑO BLACK-EYED PEAS

9 slices bacon, cut into ½-inch
  pieces
1 small onion, chopped
4 cloves garlic, minced
4 cups water
2 pounds fresh black-eyed peas,
  shelled (about 6 cups)
1 small jalapeño pepper, chopped
½ teaspoon pepper
1 cup minced cooked ham
¼ cup chopped green onions

Cook bacon in a Dutch oven until crisp; remove bacon with a slotted spoon, reserving 2 tablespoons drippings in Dutch oven. Drain bacon, and set aside.

Sauté onion and garlic in reserved drippings until tender. Add water, peas, jalapeño, and pepper. Bring to a boil. Cover, reduce heat, and simmer 1 hour. Add bacon, ham, and green onions, and cook an additional 15 minutes. Yield: 6 to 8 servings.
Keith deVille
Dallas, Texas

SOUTHERN CORNCAKES

1½ cups self-rising cornmeal
1 tablespoon sugar
1 cup buttermilk
1 egg, slightly beaten
1 tablespoon vegetable oil
3 to 4 tablespoons vegetable oil

Combine cornmeal and sugar. Add buttermilk, egg, and 1 tablespoon oil; mix well.

Heat 3 tablespoons oil in a large, heavy skillet over high heat. For each corncake, pour about ¼ cup batter into hot oil. Fry about 3 minutes on each side or until browned. Add additional oil to skillet, if necessary. Yield: 8 corncakes.
Gladys Stout
Elizabethton, Tennessee

Summer Calls For Ice Cream Desserts

If you want to prepare a dessert in advance but you fear that someone around your house will get the munchies before company comes, try a sneaky approach. Make one of these ice cream concoctions when your family is away, and hide it in the freezer until it's needed.

summer Suppers

FROZEN PUMPKIN DESSERT

1½ cups graham cracker crumbs
½ cup sugar
½ cup butter or margarine, melted
1¼ cups canned mashed pumpkin
¼ cup firmly packed brown sugar
1 teaspoon ground cinnamon
½ teaspoon ground ginger
⅛ teaspoon ground cloves
¼ teaspoon salt
1 quart vanilla ice cream, softened
Sweetened whipped cream (optional)
Chopped pecans (optional)

Combine first 3 ingredients, stirring well. Press mixture into bottom of a 9-inch square pan. Bake at 350° for 10 minutes; let cool.

Combine pumpkin, brown sugar, cinnamon, ginger, cloves, and salt, stirring until blended; fold in ice cream. Pour mixture into prepared pan. Cover and freeze 8 hours. If desired, serve with sweetened whipped cream, and sprinkle with pecans. Yield: 9 servings.
Pearle E. Evans
Myrtle Beach, South Carolina

HOT FUDGE SUNDAE CAKE PUDDING

1 cup all-purpose flour
2 teaspoons baking powder
¼ teaspoon salt
¾ cup sugar
2½ tablespoons cocoa
½ cup milk
2 tablespoons shortening, melted
1 teaspoon vanilla extract
1 cup chopped pecans or walnuts
¾ cup firmly packed brown sugar
¼ cup cocoa
1¾ cups hot water
1 quart vanilla ice cream

Combine first 8 ingredients, stirring until blended. Stir in pecans. Spread mixture into a lightly greased 9-inch square pan.

Sprinkle mixture with brown sugar and ¼ cup cocoa; pour water over mixture. (Do not stir.) Bake at 350° for 40 to 45 minutes.

To serve, cut into squares, and invert each square onto an individual dessert dish. Top with a scoop of vanilla ice cream, and spoon sauce remaining in the pan over top. Yield: 9 servings. *Mrs. Farmer L. Burns*
New Orleans, Louisiana

CHOCOLATE MINT FREEZE

1¼ cups vanilla wafer crumbs
¼ cup butter or margarine, melted
1 quart peppermint ice cream, softened
2 (1-ounce) squares unsweetened chocolate
½ cup butter or margarine
1½ cups sifted powdered sugar
1 teaspoon vanilla extract
½ cup chopped pecans
3 eggs, separated

Combine vanilla wafer crumbs and melted butter; stir well. Set aside ¼ cup crumb mixture. Press remaining crumb mixture into bottom of an ungreased 9-inch square pan. Bake at 350° for 8 minutes; let cool.

Spread ice cream over crust; cover and freeze until firm.

Combine chocolate and ½ cup butter in a saucepan; cook over low heat until melted. Remove from heat. Add powdered sugar, vanilla, and pecans; beat at medium speed of an electric mixer until smooth. Add egg yolks; beat mixture until smooth.

Beat egg whites (at room temperature) until stiff peaks form; fold into chocolate mixture. Spread chocolate mixture over ice cream; sprinkle with reserved crumb mixture. Cover and freeze at least 8 hours. Yield: 9 servings. *Mary Andrew*
Winston-Salem, North Carolina

FUDGE-PEANUT ICE CREAM DESSERT

1 (12-ounce) can evaporated milk
3 cups sifted powdered sugar
½ cup cocoa
½ cup butter or margarine
1¼ teaspoons vanilla extract
2 cups cream-filled chocolate sandwich cookie crumbs (about 24 cookies)
½ cup butter or margarine, melted
½ gallon vanilla ice cream (rectangular carton)
¾ cup coarsely chopped dry-roasted peanuts

Combine evaporated milk, powdered sugar, cocoa, and ½ cup butter in a heavy saucepan; cook over medium heat until mixture boils. Reduce heat, and simmer until mixture thickens. Remove from heat; stir in vanilla. Set aside to cool.

Combine chocolate cookie crumbs and melted butter, stirring well. Press crumb mixture into a 13- x 9- x 2-inch pan.

Cut ice cream crosswise into ½-inch-thick slices. Arrange over crust. Spoon fudge sauce over ice cream; sprinkle with chopped peanuts. Cover and freeze until firm.

Let dessert stand at room temperature 5 minutes before serving. Yield: 15 servings.
Polly Ann Hughes
Tarpon Springs, Florida

CHOCOLATE DATE-NUT DELIGHT

1 cup all-purpose flour
½ cup firmly packed brown sugar
½ cup butter or margarine, softened
1 cup firmly packed brown sugar
2 tablespoons all-purpose flour
½ teaspoon baking powder
¼ teaspoon salt
2 eggs, beaten
1 teaspoon vanilla extract
¾ cup chopped pitted dates
¾ cup chopped pecans
1 (6-ounce) package semisweet chocolate morsels
1 quart coffee or praline ice cream

Combine 1 cup flour and ½ cup brown sugar, stirring well. Cut butter into flour mixture with pastry blender until mixture resembles coarse meal. Press mixture into bottom of a 9-inch square pan. Bake at 350° for 10 minutes.

Combine 1 cup brown sugar, 2 tablespoons flour, baking powder, and salt; add eggs and vanilla, stirring until blended. Stir in dates, pecans, and chocolate morsels. Pour mixture into prepared pan. Bake at 350° for 20 minutes. Cool. Cut into squares, and serve with a scoop of ice cream. Yield: 12 servings.

Margaret S. Dallas
Martinsville, Virginia

NEAPOLITAN CAKE

1 (14.5-ounce) package angel food cake mix
½ gallon Neapolitan ice cream, softened
1 (2.8-ounce) package whipped topping mix
Fresh strawberries

Prepare cake mix according to package directions. Immediately invert cake; let stand 1 hour or until completely cooled. Remove cake from pan. Slice cake horizontally into 4 layers. Place the bottom layer on a serving plate.

Slice ice cream into 3 layers according to flavors. Spread chocolate ice cream over first cake layer. Top with second cake layer; spread vanilla ice cream over cake. Top with third cake layer; spread strawberry ice cream over cake. Place remaining cake layer, cut side down, on top of cake. Cover and freeze 1 hour.

Prepare whipped topping mix according to package directions. Remove cake from freezer, and spread whipped topping on sides and top of cake. Cover dessert loosely, and freeze until firm.

Let dessert stand at room temperature 10 minutes before serving. Garnish with strawberries. Yield: one 10-inch cake. *Mrs. P. J. Davis*
Drexel, North Carolina

Smoke Flavors The Meat

Smoldering aromatic wood imparts a succulent flavor to foods, particularly meats. While special meat smokers are available just for smoke-cooked taste, you can use charcoal or gas grills for the same result.

Smoked Cornish Hens and Smoked Turkey Breast are cooked in a smoker. As with most smoked poultry, the meat has a pinkish color, but this is typical of smoked meats. It's best to use a meat thermometer to test for doneness.

Mesquite chips in a charcoal grill add the rich smoked taste to Smoked Ribs. Pile the coals on one end of the grill and place the meat on the opposite end. Soaked wood chips should be placed directly on the coals. Because a covered grill has a smaller space to heat than a larger smoker, the meat will cook faster.

Gas grills can also be used for smoking; the type with two burners works best. Heat one side of the grill, and arrange soaked wood chips directly on the hot lava rocks or on a rack below the cooking rack. Place the meat on the cool side of the grill. Meat cooks slightly faster on a gas grill than on a charcoal grill because the heat is more consistent throughout the cooking time.

SMOKED CORNISH HENS

4 (1¼- to 1½-pound) Cornish hens
½ cup butter or margarine
4 small onions
Hickory chips
2 to 3 cups white wine
Water

Remove giblets from hens; reserve giblets for other uses. Rinse hens with cold water, and pat dry. Place 2 tablespoons butter and 1 onion in cavity of each hen.

Prepare charcoal fire in meat smoker; let fire burn 15 to 20 minutes. Soak hickory chips in water 15 minutes; place soaked hickory on coals. Place water pan in smoker; add wine to pan. Add water to wine until liquid reaches fill line.

Place hens, breast side down, on rack. Cover with smoker lid; cook 3 to 4 hours or until juices run clear and drumsticks are easy to move. Refill water pan with wine and water, and add more charcoal as needed during cooking. Yield: 4 servings.

Stan Sands
Irmo, South Carolina

SMOKED TURKEY BREAST

1 (5- to 6-pound) turkey breast
2 teaspoons seasoned salt
Hickory chips
½ cup zesty Italian salad
  dressing
Hot water

Debone turkey breast. (Most butchers will do this for you.) Rinse turkey with cold water; pat dry. Sprinkle turkey with seasoned salt.
  Prepare charcoal fire in meat smoker; let burn 15 to 20 minutes.
  Soak hickory chips in water at least 15 minutes; place soaked hickory chips on coals. Place water pan in smoker; add salad dressing to pan. Add hot water to dressing until liquid reaches fill line on pan.
  Place turkey on rack. Cover with smoker lid; cook 4 to 5 hours or until meat thermometer reaches 170° when inserted in thickest part of breast. Refill water pan, and add more charcoal as needed during cooking time. Yield: 12 to 16 servings.
Jim Hayward
Birmingham, Alabama

SMOKED RIBS

Mesquite chips
1 teaspoon Creole seasoning
½ teaspoon pepper
3½ pounds pork ribs

Soak mesquite chips in water for 1 to 24 hours.
  Prepare charcoal fire by piling charcoal in one end of grill; let burn 15 to 20 minutes or until flames disappear and coals are white. Add 6 to 8 pieces of soaked mesquite to coals.
  Sprinkle Creole seasoning and pepper on ribs. Arrange ribs away from coals on opposite end of the grill; cover with grill hood. Open the air vents halfway.

Cook 2½ hours or until tender, turning ribs every 30 minutes. Place additional wood chips on the coals, if necessary. Yield: 4 servings.
Donald Sutton
Gadsden, Alabama

Pour A Cool Beverage

Whether you're looking for an afternoon thirst quencher or a before-dinner cocktail, you'll find just the right recipe here. Fruit juices, tea, and champagne are just a few of the delectable ingredients our readers used to create these beverages.

MINTED APPLE COOLER

¼ cup plus 2 tablespoons
  chopped fresh mint
1 cup sugar
1½ cups water
1 cup orange juice
½ cup lemon juice
4 cups apple juice
Fresh mint sprigs (optional)

Combine chopped fresh mint, sugar, and water in a small saucepan; bring to a boil. Reduce heat, and simmer 5 minutes; cool. Strain syrup mixture into a large pitcher; discard mint. Add remaining juices, and stir well. Serve over ice. Garnish with mint sprigs, if desired. Yield: 7¼ cups.
Carrie Bartlett
Gallatin, Tennessee

CRANBERRY-APPLE TEA

1 cup boiling water
3 regular-size tea bags
1 (32-ounce) bottle cranberry
  juice cocktail, chilled
2 cups apple juice, chilled
1 tablespoon lemon juice
1½ tablespoons light corn syrup
1 lemon, sliced

Pour boiling water over tea bags; cover. Let stand 5 minutes. Discard tea bags; cool tea.
  Combine tea and next 4 ingredients in a large pitcher; stir well. Add lemon slices, and serve over ice. Yield: 1¾ quarts.
Carolyn Norman
Old Hickory, Tennessee

SPARKLING STRAWBERRY MIMOSA

2½ cups orange juice, chilled
1 (10-ounce) package frozen
  strawberries, partially thawed
1 (26.4-ounce) bottle dry
  champagne, chilled
Whole strawberries (optional)

Combine orange juice and partially thawed strawberries in container of an electric blender. Process until pureed. Pour into a pitcher. Add champagne; stir gently. Garnish each serving with a whole strawberry, if desired. Serve immediately. Yield: about 8 cups.
R. Patricia Saylor
Crofton, Maryland

SOUTHERN SANGRÍA

⅓ cup sugar
⅓ cup lemon juice
⅓ cup orange juice
1 (25.4-ounce) bottle sparkling red grape juice, chilled

Combine first 3 ingredients in a large pitcher, stirring until sugar dissolves. Add grape juice, and gently stir to mix well. Serve over crushed ice. Yield: 5 cups.   *Marion Hall*
Knoxville, Tennessee

COOKING LIGHT ®

Welcome Guests To A Light Menu

Come summertime, light, healthy meals are a refreshing respite from the heat. We've put together a menu that is ideal for serving guests on the terrace and yet portable enough to take on a picnic.

Tomato Soup Plus
Lemon-Frosted Chicken
Marinated Vegetables
Honey Bran Muffins
Strawberries Marsala

TOMATO SOUP PLUS

7¾ cups no-salt-added vegetable juice
¼ cup lemon juice
½ teaspoon salt
½ teaspoon white pepper
¼ to ½ teaspoon hot sauce
Shredded carrot (optional)

Combine first 5 ingredients in a large bowl; stir well. Cover and chill. Garnish with shredded carrot, if desired. Yield: 8 cups (46 calories per 1-cup serving).

☐ *2.2 grams protein, 0.2 gram fat, 9.5 grams carbohydrate, 0 milligrams cholesterol, 192 milligrams sodium, and 33 milligrams calcium.*
Wilmina R. Smith
St. Petersburg, Florida

LEMON-FROSTED CHICKEN

8 (4-ounce) boneless and skinless chicken breast halves
2 stalks celery, quartered
1 medium onion, quartered
1 clove garlic
1 bay leaf
⅔ cup light processed cream cheese product, softened
3 tablespoons reduced-calorie mayonnaise
2 teaspoons lemon juice
¾ teaspoon grated lemon rind
2¼ teaspoons fresh or ¾ teaspoon dried whole dillweed
Lettuce leaves
24 almond slices, lightly toasted
Lemon curls (optional)
Fresh dillweed (optional)

Combine first 5 ingredients in a large Dutch oven; add water to cover. Bring to a boil; cover, reduce heat, and simmer 15 minutes or until chicken is tender. Refrigerate chicken in broth.

Combine cream cheese and next 4 ingredients; stir well. Remove chicken from broth, and pat dry; discard broth. Spread mixture over top and sides of chicken.

Cover and chill up to 2 hours. When ready to serve, place each chicken breast on lettuce leaves; arrange 3 almond slices on each breast. If desired, garnish with lemon curls and fresh dillweed. Yield: 8 servings (215 calories per frosted chicken breast half).

☐ *28.7 grams protein, 9.5 grams fat, 2.6 grams carbohydrate, 74 milligrams cholesterol, 218 milligrams sodium, and 51 milligrams calcium.*

MARINATED VEGETABLES

1½ cups broccoli flowerets
⅔ cup reduced-calorie Italian salad dressing
1½ cups cauliflower flowerets
2 cups small cherry tomatoes
1 cup sliced yellow squash
1 cup sliced unpeeled cucumber
¾ cup sliced carrot
1 (14-ounce) can artichoke hearts, drained and quartered
2 cups cooked small shell macaroni (cooked without salt or fat)
Lettuce leaves (optional)

Place broccoli in a large bowl; drizzle dressing over broccoli, and toss gently. Add cauliflower and remaining ingredients except lettuce leaves; toss gently. Cover and chill 8 hours; toss. Serve on lettuce leaves, if desired. Yield: 8 servings (78 calories per 1½-cup serving).

☐ *3.5 grams protein, 0.4 gram fat, 16.7 grams carbohydrate, 0 milligrams cholesterol, 248 milligrams sodium, and 34 milligrams calcium.*

HONEY BRAN MUFFINS

½ cup shreds of wheat bran
   cereal
¼ cup morsels of bran cereal
¼ cup boiling water
½ cup low-fat cultured buttermilk
¼ cup honey
¼ cup egg substitute
2 tablespoons vegetable oil
½ teaspoon baking soda
½ cup all-purpose flour
½ cup unprocessed wheat bran
½ teaspoon baking powder
⅛ teaspoon salt

Combine first 3 ingredients; let stand about 3 minutes. Stir in buttermilk, honey, egg substitute, oil, and soda.

Combine flour and remaining ingredients in a large bowl; make a well in center of mixture. Add cereal mixture to dry ingredients, stirring just until moistened. Spoon into paper-lined muffin cups, filling three-fourths full. Bake at 350° for 20 to 25 minutes or until a wooden pick inserted in center comes out clean. Yield: 8 muffins (127 calories per muffin).

☐ *3.6 grams protein, 3.8 grams fat, 22.2 grams carbohydrate, 1 milligram cholesterol, 213 milligrams sodium, and 47 milligrams calcium.*

STRAWBERRIES MARSALA

2 tablespoons plus 2 teaspoons
   Marsala wine
1 tablespoon plus 1 teaspoon
   sugar
½ teaspoon lemon juice
8 cups fresh strawberries, capped

Combine first 3 ingredients in a large bowl; add strawberries, and toss gently. Cover and chill 8 hours. Toss before serving. Yield: 8 servings (58 calories per 1-cup serving).

☐ *0.9 gram protein, 0.6 gram fat, 12.6 grams carbohydrate, 0 milligrams cholesterol, 2 milligrams sodium, and 21 milligrams calcium.*
Sandra Hensley
San Antonio, Texas

Slaw Or Potato Salad Completes The Menu

Potato salad and coleslaw are favorites you'll find at almost every summer gathering. Whether they're made to accompany a cookout or a covered-dish dinner, these side dishes are appealing.

CREAMY POTATO SALAD

8 medium-size red potatoes,
   unpeeled
½ cup commercial Italian salad
   dressing
½ cup sliced celery
⅓ cup sliced green onions
½ cup commercial sour cream
½ cup mayonnaise
½ cup commercial cucumber
   salad dressing
Chopped green onion tops
   (optional)

Wash potatoes, and cut into ¼-inch slices. Cook in boiling water to cover 15 minutes or until tender. Drain.

Combine potatoes and Italian salad dressing; chill. Carefully stir celery and green onions into potato mixture. Combine sour cream, mayonnaise, and cucumber salad dressing; stir well. Pour mixture over potatoes; toss gently. Garnish with green onion tops, if desired. Yield: 8 to 10 servings.
Mrs. Lewis Self
Sylvania, Georgia

FRENCH-STYLE POTATO SALAD

12 to 14 small new potatoes,
   unpeeled (about 1½ pounds)
3 tablespoons Chablis or other
   dry white wine
¼ cup olive oil
2 tablespoons wine vinegar
1 to 2 tablespoons Dijon mustard
¼ teaspoon salt
¼ teaspoon dried whole tarragon
¼ teaspoon white pepper
¼ cup thinly sliced green onions
¼ cup minced fresh parsley
Lettuce leaves

Wash potatoes, and cook in boiling water to cover 12 to 15 minutes or until tender; drain and cool slightly. Cut potatoes into ¼-inch slices. Add wine; toss gently, and let stand 10 minutes.

Combine olive oil and next 5 ingredients; stir well. Pour over potato mixture. Add onions and parsley; toss gently. Chill, if desired. Serve on a lettuce-lined platter. Yield: about 6 servings.
Mrs. Earl Maurer
Christmas, Florida

Tip: *Add garlic flavor to salads by rubbing halved garlic cloves around the insides of the salad bowls.*

TEXAS MUSTARD SLAW

1 large cabbage
1 cup chopped dill pickle
¾ cup chopped onion
1 cup mayonnaise
2 tablespoons prepared mustard
2 teaspoons sugar
1 teaspoon celery seeds
2 teaspoons vinegar
⅛ teaspoon pepper

Shred enough cabbage to make 12 cups. Combine cabbage, dill pickle, and onion in a large bowl; set aside.

Combine mayonnaise and remaining ingredients in a bowl; stir well. Pour over cabbage mixture; toss. Cover and chill. Yield: 14 to 16 servings.
Laurie McIntyre
Lake Jackson, Texas

CURRIED PINEAPPLE COLESLAW

2 cups grated cabbage
1 cup grated carrot
1 (8-ounce) can crushed pineapple, drained
½ cup mayonnaise or salad dressing
1 teaspoon curry powder
1 teaspoon celery seeds

Combine cabbage, carrot, and pineapple; set aside.

Combine mayonnaise and remaining ingredients; stir well. Pour over cabbage mixture; toss well. Cover and chill. Yield: 4 servings.
Mrs. George Lance
Madison, Tennessee

Dress Ups For French Bread

Wouldn't you like to serve bread that looks and tastes special without spending a lot of time preparing it? Then try one of these tempting recipes for dressed French bread.

CHEESY FRENCH BREAD

½ cup mayonnaise
¼ cup grated Parmesan cheese
1 clove garlic, minced
¼ cup (1 ounce) shredded Cheddar cheese
1½ teaspoons milk
¼ teaspoon paprika
1 (16-ounce) loaf French bread

Combine mayonnaise, Parmesan cheese, and garlic in a small bowl; stir well. Set aside.

Combine Cheddar cheese, milk, and paprika in a small saucepan over low heat; stir constantly until cheese melts. Remove from heat, and stir in mayonnaise mixture.

Slice bread in half lengthwise, and toast cut sides. Spread cheese mixture on toasted side of bread halves. Broil 6 inches from heat 2 minutes or until cheese is bubbly. Yield: about 8 to 10 servings.
Alma Ray
Tulsa, Oklahoma

SNACKWICHES

1 (3-ounce) package cream cheese, softened
2 tablespoons butter or margarine, softened
1 egg yolk
1 teaspoon grated onion
¼ teaspoon rubbed sage
8 (¾-inch) slices French bread

Combine first 5 ingredients, mixing until well blended. Spread 1 tablespoon mixture on each bread slice, and place on a baking sheet. Broil 6 inches from heat 2 to 3 minutes or until hot and bubbly. Yield: 8 servings.
Mae McClaugherty
Marble Falls, Texas

HERB-VEGETABLE-CHEESE BREAD

1 cup (4 ounces) shredded mozzarella cheese
½ cup grated carrot
2 green onions, sliced
½ teaspoon dried Italian seasoning
¼ cup mayonnaise
8 (¾-inch) slices French bread

Combine first 5 ingredients in a medium bowl; stir well, and set aside.

Place bread on an ungreased baking sheet; broil 2 to 3 minutes or until lightly browned. Turn and spread mixture on untoasted side. Bake at 350° for 15 minutes or until cheese melts. Serve immediately. Yield: 8 servings.
Judi Grigoraci
Charleston, West Virginia

Fruit Complements The Cheese

Creative cooks enhance cream cheese with a variety of spices and fruits, as well as Cheddar and blue cheeses, for some unusual and tasty combinations. These cream cheese recipes are best served with crisp

summer Suppers

pear or apple slices, strawberries, and lightly sweetened whole grain crackers or gingersnaps.

You may want to check the gourmet section of your grocery store or a wine and cheese shop for the best selection of crackers and cookies to serve with these recipes. Saltine and herb-seasoned crackers will overpower their delicate flavors.

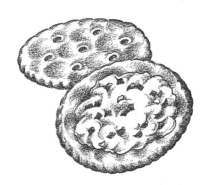

EAST INDIAN CHEESE LOGS

2 (8-ounce) packages cream
  cheese, softened
1 cup cottage cheese
1 teaspoon curry powder
1 cup finely chopped green onions
1 cup unsalted dry-roasted
  peanuts, coarsely chopped
1 cup golden raisins
½ cup flaked coconut
¾ cup mango chutney
¼ cup flaked coconut, toasted
  (optional)
Mango slices (optional)

Combine first 3 ingredients in a large mixing bowl; beat at medium speed of an electric mixer until smooth. Add green onions, peanuts, raisins, and ½ cup coconut; beat at low speed until mixed well. Stir in mango chutney. Cover and chill slightly. Divide cheese mixture in half; shape each portion into a 12-inch log. Wrap in wax paper, and chill 6 hours or until cheese logs are firm.

Place cheese logs on a serving tray; if desired, garnish with toasted coconut and mango slices. Serve with toasted pita bread triangles, crackers, or apple slices. *Thelma Peedin*
Newport News, Virginia

WALDORF CHEESE SPREAD

1 (8-ounce) package cream
  cheese, softened
½ cup mayonnaise
1 tablespoon sugar
1 cup (4 ounces) shredded sharp
  Cheddar cheese
1 large apple, unpeeled and diced
½ cup diced celery
¼ cup diced walnuts

Combine first 3 ingredients, and beat at medium speed of an electric mixer until smooth. Stir in Cheddar cheese and remaining ingredients. Cover and chill at least 1 hour. Serve with apple wedges or crackers. Yield: 1¾ cups.

Note: Mixture may be chilled up to 24 hours. *Mary H. Windell*
Fort Mill, South Carolina

ALMOND CHEESE

1 (8-ounce) package cream
  cheese, softened
1 (3-ounce) package cream
  cheese, softened
½ cup butter or margarine,
  softened
½ cup commercial sour cream
2 tablespoons sugar
1 envelope unflavored gelatin
¼ cup water
1 cup slivered almonds, toasted
  and coarsely chopped
½ cup golden raisins
1 teaspoon grated lemon rind
½ teaspoon almond extract
Strawberry halves

Combine cream cheese and butter, and beat at medium speed of an electric mixer until smooth. Add sour cream and sugar, mixing well.

Combine gelatin and water in a small saucepan; let stand 1 minute. Cook and stir over low heat until gelatin dissolves, about 1 minute. Add to cream cheese mixture, stirring well. Stir in almonds, raisins, lemon rind, and almond extract. Spoon mixture into a lightly greased 1-quart mold, and chill until firm. Unmold onto serving platter, and garnish with strawberries. Serve with gingersnaps or lightly sweetened crackers. Yield: 4 cups. *Carol Barclay*
Portland, Texas

CREAMY BLUE CHEESE

1 (3-ounce) package cream
  cheese, softened
1 (3-ounce) package blue cheese,
  softened
¼ cup butter or margarine,
  softened
1 tablespoon brandy

Combine cream cheese, blue cheese, and butter; beat at medium speed of an electric mixer until smooth. Add brandy, mixing well. Serve with crackers or sliced apples or pears. Yield: 1 cup. *Ashley Adams*
Birmingham, Alabama

Tip: *Most cheeses should be wrapped in moisture-proof airtight wrappers. (One exception is "moldy" cheeses, such as blue cheese, which need to breathe and should be kept in covered containers with the tops loosened a bit.) Remember, too, that all cheeses keep best on the bottom shelf of the refrigerator.*

COOKING LIGHT®

Puddings And Custards Add Calcium

Smooth, creamy puddings and custards—always chock-full of dairy products—offer an appealing way to add calcium to the diet.

Calcium is a vital mineral needed throughout life. Along with phosphorus, vitamins, and protein, it gives strength and hardness to bones and helps the heart beat, muscles contract, and blood clot.

Bones act like a calcium bank for the body. They regularly absorb calcium from the diet to rebuild and strengthen themselves and release it whenever the body needs it. This banking system won't work properly if there's not enough calcium in the diet. When the body withdraws more calcium than it deposits, bones can become weak and brittle.

Milk and dairy products are the best food sources of calcium. Low-fat and skim milk products used in "Cooking Light" recipes contain as much calcium as their higher fat counterparts. In fact, in many cases, skim milk products contain slightly more calcium because nonfat milk solids are added to fortify and improve appearance.

ALMOST BANANA PUDDING

⅓ cup sugar
2 tablespoons cornstarch
3 tablespoons water
2 egg yolks, slightly beaten
1½ cups evaporated skim milk
1 teaspoon vanilla extract
2 medium bananas, sliced
3 egg whites
¼ teaspoon cream of tartar
1 tablespoon sugar

Combine ⅓ cup sugar and cornstarch in a heavy saucepan; add water, and stir well. Add egg yolks and milk.

Cook over medium heat, stirring constantly, until mixture begins to bubble. Boil 1 minute, stirring constantly. Remove from heat; stir in vanilla. Let cool slightly. Fold in banana slices; spoon mixture into six 6-ounce custard cups. Set aside.

Combine egg whites (at room temperature) and cream of tartar in a small mixing bowl. Beat at high speed of an electric mixer until soft peaks form. Gradually add 1 tablespoon sugar, beating until stiff peaks form. Spread meringue over individual puddings, sealing to edge of cups. Bake at 400° for 8 to 10 minutes or until golden brown. Serve warm or at room temperature. Yield: 6 servings (178 calories per serving).

☐ *7.8 grams protein, 2.2 grams fat, 32.4 grams carbohydrate, 93 milligrams cholesterol, 110 milligrams sodium, and 198 milligrams calcium.*

ORANGE CUSTARD PUDDING

¼ cup sugar
¼ cup cornstarch
⅛ teaspoon salt
¼ cup plus 2 tablespoons egg substitute
2 teaspoons grated orange rind
2 cups orange juice
1 (8-ounce) carton plain low-fat yogurt
2 cups orange sections
Fresh mint sprigs (optional)
Orange rind curls (optional)

Combine first 3 ingredients in a heavy saucepan; stir in egg substitute, grated orange rind, and orange juice. Cook over medium heat, stirring constantly, until mixture begins to boil; boil 1 minute, stirring constantly. Remove from heat, and let

cool slightly. Stir a small amount of custard into yogurt; gently fold yogurt mixture into custard. Cover and chill thoroughly.

Place orange sections in serving dishes; spoon custard over oranges. If desired, garnish with mint and orange rind curls. Yield: 8 servings (114 calories per ⅓ cup custard pudding with ¼ cup orange sections).

☐ *3.4 grams protein, 0.6 gram fat, 24.6 grams carbohydrate, 2 milligrams cholesterol, 74 milligrams sodium, and 82 milligrams calcium.*

Frank H. Fogg
Tulsa, Oklahoma

ALMOND CREME CUSTARD WITH RASPBERRIES

3 tablespoons brown sugar
2 cups evaporated skim milk
2 eggs, slightly beaten
1 teaspoon almond extract
4 cups fresh raspberries

Combine brown sugar and milk in a heavy saucepan; cook over medium heat until mixture is hot. Gradually stir about one-fourth of hot mixture into eggs; add to remaining hot mixture, stirring constantly. Cook, stirring constantly, about 3 minutes or until mixture thickens. Remove from heat; stir in almond extract. Cover and chill.

Spoon raspberries into serving dishes; stir custard with a wire whisk, and spoon over raspberries. Yield: 8 servings (114 calories per ⅓ cup custard with ½ cup raspberries).

☐ *6.9 grams protein, 1.9 grams fat, 17.8 grams carbohydrate, 71 milligrams cholesterol, 92 milligrams sodium, and 209 milligrams calcium.*

Tip: *To conserve energy, use pans with flat bottoms to absorb heat, and use covers that fit tightly. Food will continue to cook 3 to 5 minutes after you turn off the electrical unit.*

PEACHY BREAD PUDDING

4 eggs, slightly beaten
2 cups skim milk
2½ tablespoons sugar
¼ teaspoon ground cinnamon
¼ teaspoon ground nutmeg
2 teaspoons vanilla extract
1 (16-ounce) can sliced peaches,
   in extra-light syrup
4 slices bread, cubed
Vegetable cooking spray

Combine first 6 ingredients; stir well. Drain peaches; coarsely chop, and add to milk mixture. Add bread, and stir. Spoon into five 10-ounce custard cups coated with cooking spray. Bake at 350° for 45 to 50 minutes or until a knife inserted in center comes out clean. Serve warm. Yield: 5 servings (217 calories per serving).

☐ 10.5 grams protein, 5.5 grams fat, 30.5 grams carbohydrate, 222 milligrams cholesterol, 211 milligrams sodium, and 166 milligrams calcium.
            H. J. Cox
            Hope, Arkansas

OLD-FASHIONED BREAD PUDDING

2 eggs, slightly beaten
⅓ cup firmly packed brown sugar
2 cups skim milk
1 teaspoon vanilla extract
¼ teaspoon ground cinnamon
4 slices raisin bread, cubed
Vegetable cooking spray

Combine first 5 ingredients; add bread, and stir well. Spoon mixture into an 8-inch square baking dish that has been coated with cooking spray. Place dish in a larger shallow pan; add water to a depth of 1 inch. Bake at 350° for 35 to 40 minutes or until a knife inserted in center comes out clean. Yield: 5 servings (179 calories per ½-cup serving).

☐ 7.3 grams protein, 3.1 grams fat, 30.4 grams carbohydrate, 112 milligrams cholesterol, 157 milligrams sodium, and 166 milligrams calcium.
            V. Butcher
            Stuart, Florida

APPLE-RAISIN BREAD PUDDING

8 slices raisin bread, cut in half
2 eggs, slightly beaten
⅓ cup chunky applesauce
2 tablespoons brown sugar
1 tablespoon reduced-calorie
   margarine, melted
¼ teaspoon vanilla extract
Dash of ground cinnamon
⅛ teaspoon ground nutmeg
¾ cup skim milk
1 (8-ounce) carton vanilla low-fat
   yogurt
Vegetable cooking spray

Position knife blade in food processor bowl; top with cover. Drop bread through food chute with processor running; process 5 to 10 seconds or until bread is crumbled. Set aside. Combine eggs and next 7 ingredients; stir well. Fold in yogurt and breadcrumbs. Spoon mixture into a 1-quart casserole that has been coated with cooking spray. Bake, uncovered, at 350° for 25 minutes; stir and bake an additional 20 minutes or until a knife inserted in center comes out clean. Serve warm or at room temperature. Yield: 7 servings (164 calories per ½-cup serving).

☐ 6.2 grams protein, 4 grams fat, 26.4 grams carbohydrate, 81 milligrams cholesterol, 176 milligrams sodium, and 122 milligrams calcium.

CHOCOLATE CUSTARD CAKE

2 tablespoons cocoa
1 tablespoon vegetable oil
⅓ cup sugar
3 tablespoons all-purpose flour
2 egg yolks
2 cups evaporated skim milk
1 teaspoon vanilla extract
4 egg whites
Vegetable cooking spray

Combine cocoa and oil in a small bowl; stir well, and set aside. Combine sugar and next 4 ingredients in container of an electric blender; process at medium speed until smooth. With blender running, pour cocoa mixture into blender; process until smooth. Pour into a large bowl.
    Beat egg whites (at room temperature) until stiff peaks form. Stir a small amount of whites into chocolate mixture; fold in remaining whites.
    Spoon mixture into a 2-quart baking dish coated with cooking spray. Place dish in a larger shallow pan; add water to a depth of 1 inch. Bake at 325° for 40 to 45 minutes or until a knife inserted in center comes out clean. Cover and chill. Spoon into individual compotes. Yield: 9 servings (123 calories per ⅔-cup serving).

☐ 6.8 grams protein, 3.1 grams fat, 16.7 grams carbohydrate, 63 milligrams cholesterol, 89 milligrams sodium, and 177 milligrams calcium.

Crisp, Tangy Marinated Vegetables

Marinated vegetables can be a good friend during warm-weather months. Once they're combined, they can be tucked away in the refrigerator, ready to add a refreshing touch to any plate.

HERBED MUSHROOMS

1 (4-ounce) jar diced pimiento, drained
½ teaspoon dried whole oregano
½ teaspoon dried whole marjoram
½ teaspoon dried parsley flakes
¼ teaspoon coarsely ground pepper
¼ cup olive oil
2 tablespoons garlic-flavored red wine vinegar
½ pound fresh large mushrooms, sliced

Combine first 7 ingredients; mix well. Pour over sliced mushrooms, and toss gently to coat. Cover and refrigerate 1 to 2 hours, stirring occasionally. Yield: 4 to 6 servings.

Lorraine F. Boyer
Little Switzerland, North Carolina

CUCUMBER-AND-PEPPER COMBO

3 medium cucumbers, peeled and sliced
1 onion, sliced and separated into rings
1 sweet red pepper, sliced into strips
½ cup vinegar
¼ cup sugar
2 tablespoons lemon juice
1 teaspoon celery seeds
1 teaspoon salt
⅛ teaspoon pepper

Toss cucumbers, onion, and red pepper in a bowl.
Combine vinegar, sugar, lemon juice, celery seeds, salt, and pepper in a jar. Cover tightly, and shake vigorously. Pour marinade over vegetables. Cover and refrigerate 8 hours, stirring occasionally. Yield: 6 to 8 servings.

Katherine Saltz
Pisgah Forest, North Carolina

BRIGHT TOMATO MARINADE

½ cup vegetable oil
¼ cup plus 2 tablespoons vinegar
1 tablespoon sugar
1 tablespoon Worcestershire sauce
1 tablespoon minced fresh basil or 1 teaspoon dried whole basil
½ teaspoon salt
¼ teaspoon coarsely ground pepper
¾ teaspoon minced fresh thyme or ¼ teaspoon dried whole thyme
5 medium tomatoes, cut into wedges
1 medium onion, diced

Combine first 8 ingredients in a jar. Cover tightly, and shake vigorously. Combine tomatoes and onion in a shallow container; pour marinade over vegetables. Cover and refrigerate 2 hours. To serve, use a slotted spoon. Yield: 8 to 10 servings.

Mary Jane Yost
Huntsville, Alabama

MARINATED CARROT STRIPS

4 cups (1 pound) carrots, scraped and cut into 1-inch julienne strips
½ cup olive oil
2 tablespoons white wine vinegar
1 teaspoon dried whole basil
¼ teaspoon finely chopped garlic
½ teaspoon salt
Dash of freshly ground pepper

Heat 1 inch water to boiling. Add carrots; return to boil. Cover; simmer 7 minutes. Drain. Combine with oil and remaining ingredients. Cover; refrigerate 8 hours, tossing occasionally. Yield: 6 servings.

Mrs. Peter Rosato III
Memphis, Tennessee

TANGY CORN SALAD

1 (16-ounce) package frozen shoepeg corn, cooked and drained
⅔ cup chopped green pepper
⅓ cup finely chopped celery
⅓ cup white wine vinegar
⅓ cup vegetable oil
¼ cup sugar
2 green onions, chopped
2 tablespoons chopped fresh parsley
¾ teaspoon seasoned salt
¼ teaspoon garlic powder

Combine all ingredients; mix well. Cover and refrigerate 8 hours, tossing occasionally. Yield: 6 to 8 servings.

Mrs. Bill Anthony
Poteau, Oklahoma

Tip: *Onions offer outstanding nutritive value. They are a good source of calcium and vitamins A and C. They contain iron, riboflavin, thiamine, and niacin; have a high percentage of water; and supply essential bulk. They are low in calories and have only a trace of fat.*

Simplify Your Sauce Making

If you've never made sauces in your microwave oven, give the technique a try. You'll appreciate the speed and convenience the microwave adds to these recipes for popular meat, vegetable, and dessert sauces.

When made in the microwave, sauces usually don't fall prey to some of the common problems—sticking, scorching, and lumping—of conventionally cooked sauces. Microwave sauces don't need constant attention, but they do need occasional stirring to mix the cooked outer part with the less cooked center portion; stirring keeps them from lumping.

Remember that it's easy to overcook sauces in the microwave, especially those that contain eggs and dairy products. Most of our microwave recipes suggest a time range; always check for doneness at the lower end of the range to prevent overcooking. Sauces that are overcooked tend to break down.

Glass measuring cups or casseroles work well for cooking sauces in the microwave. Just be sure that the container is deep enough to prevent the sauce from boiling over. A large glass measuring cup is ideal to use because the ingredients can be measured, mixed, cooked, and poured, using the same container.

HOLLANDAISE SAUCE

⅓ cup butter or margarine
1½ tablespoons lemon juice
2 egg yolks, slightly beaten
⅛ teaspoon salt
Dash of red pepper

Place butter in a 1-quart glass bowl; microwave at HIGH 1 minute or until melted. Add lemon juice; stir well.
Combine egg yolks, salt, and red pepper; gradually add to butter mixture, stirring constantly with a wire

whisk. Microwave at MEDIUM LOW (30% power) 1 to 1½ minutes, stirring with a wire whisk at 30-second intervals. Serve over cooked meat or vegetables. Yield: ½ cup.

Note: For béarnaise sauce, add 1 tablespoon white wine vinegar, ½ teaspoon dried whole tarragon, and ⅛ teaspoon pepper to prepared Hollandaise Sauce; stir mixture with a wire whisk.

CREAMY HORSERADISH-MUSTARD SAUCE

1 tablespoon butter or margarine
1 tablespoon all-purpose flour
½ cup milk
3 tablespoons Dijon mustard
½ to ¾ teaspoon prepared horseradish

Place butter in a 2-cup glass measure. Microwave at HIGH 35 seconds or until melted. Add flour, stirring until smooth. Gradually add milk, stirring well. Microwave at HIGH 1½ minutes or until thickened and bubbly. Stir in mustard and horseradish; microwave at HIGH 30 seconds. Serve over vegetables. Yield: ⅔ cup.

LEMONY BARBECUE SAUCE

2 tablespoons butter or margarine
½ cup chopped onion
1 clove garlic, minced
½ cup catsup
¼ cup lemon juice
2 tablespoons molasses
1 tablespoon Worcestershire sauce
½ teaspoon dry mustard
½ teaspoon salt
¼ teaspoon pepper
¼ teaspoon ground cumin
5 thin slices lemon, seeded and quartered

Place butter in a 1½-quart casserole. Microwave at HIGH 45 seconds or

until melted. Add onion and garlic; cover with lid, and microwave at HIGH 2 minutes. Add catsup and remaining ingredients; cover and microwave at HIGH 3 to 4 minutes or until mixture is thoroughly heated, stirring once. Use as a basting sauce when grilling beef, pork, or chicken. Yield: about 1 cup.

ALMOND-VANILLA CUSTARD SAUCE

1 egg, beaten
¾ cup half-and-half
2 tablespoons sugar
½ teaspoon vanilla extract
¼ teaspoon almond extract

Combine all ingredients in a 2-cup glass measure, mixing well. Microwave at MEDIUM (50% power) 4 to 7 minutes or until thickened, stirring with a wire whisk after 2 minutes and every minute thereafter. Stir well; cover and chill. Serve over pound cake or fruit. Yield: 1 cup.

CREAMY CHOCOLATE SAUCE

1 (6-ounce) package semisweet chocolate morsels
½ cup half-and-half
1 cup marshmallow cream
½ teaspoon vanilla extract

Combine chocolate morsels and half-and-half in a 1-quart glass measure; microwave at HIGH 2 minutes or until chocolate is almost melted, stirring after 1 minute. Stir until smooth. Spoon marshmallow cream into chocolate mixture; microwave at HIGH 45 seconds to 1 minute or until marshmallow cream softens. Add vanilla; stir with a wire whisk until smooth. Serve warm over ice cream or pound cake. Yield: 2 cups.

Cherries—Ripe For These Recipes

Shiny, ruby-red cherries are ripe for the picking now that midsummer is here. Enjoy the flavor of fresh, sweet varieties in desserts and salads, or bake tart ones into a luscious pie.

Sweet dark cherries are the type most available in the markets. You'll know them by their plump size and garnet-red color.

Tart, bright-red cherries are especially good to use in pies. Use them also for sauces or other cooked recipes when you want great flavor.

For these recipes, a pound of unpitted cherries equals about 2 cups of pitted cherries. You'll find them at their best right after picking, but they may be stored unwashed in a plastic bag in the refrigerator for a few days.

BLACK FOREST CHERRY TORTE

½ cup butter or margarine, softened
2 cups sifted powdered sugar
1 egg yolk
1 (8-ounce) loaf commercial angel food cake
Cherry filling (recipe follows)
1 (1-ounce) square semisweet chocolate, grated

Cream butter; gradually add powdered sugar, beating at medium speed of an electric mixer. Add egg yolk, beating until light and fluffy; set frosting aside.

Slice cake horizontally into two layers. Place one cake layer on serving platter; spread top and sides with frosting. Top evenly with cherry filling. Place second cake layer over cherries; spread top and sides with frosting.

Pipe or spoon dollops of frosting around top edge and base of torte. Sprinkle top of torte with grated chocolate. Refrigerate until ready to serve. Yield: 6 to 8 servings.

Cherry Filling

½ cup sifted powdered sugar
¼ cup kirsch or other cherry-flavored brandy
2 cups pitted fresh sweet cherries (about 1 pound)
1½ tablespoons cornstarch

Combine powdered sugar and kirsch; stir well. Pour over cherries; toss gently, and let stand 2 hours. Drain cherry liquid into a medium saucepan; add cornstarch, and stir well. Add cherries; place over medium heat, and cook, stirring constantly, until mixture begins to thicken. Boil 1 minute. Remove from heat; set aside to cool. Yield: 2 cups.

Louise Walker
Lexington, Tennessee

CHERRIES SABAYON

2 cups pitted fresh sweet cherries (about 1 pound)
2 egg yolks
⅓ cup dry white wine
¼ cup sugar
¾ teaspoon grated orange rind

Place ½ cup cherries in each of 4 individual serving dishes; set aside.

Combine egg yolks, wine, sugar, and orange rind in top of a double boiler; stir well. Place over boiling water; cook 8 to 10 minutes or until thickened, beating constantly with a wire whisk. Spoon one-fourth of warm mixture over each serving of cherries. Serve immediately. Yield: 4 servings.

Mrs. Bruce Fowler
Woodruff, South Carolina

FRESH CHERRY PIE

1¼ cups sugar
2 tablespoons tapioca
⅛ teaspoon salt
4 cups pitted fresh red tart cherries (about 2 pounds)
Double-crust pastry (recipe follows)

Combine first 3 ingredients in a large bowl; add cherries, stirring until cherries are well coated.

Roll half of pastry to ⅛-inch thickness on a lightly floured surface. Place in a 9-inch pieplate. Spoon cherry mixture into pastry shell.

Roll remaining pastry to ⅛-inch thickness; transfer to top of pie. Trim off excess pastry. Fold edges under, and flute. Cut slits in top crust. Bake at 375° for 55 to 60 minutes. Cool before serving. Yield: one 9-inch pie.

Double-Crust Pastry

2¼ cups all-purpose flour
1 teaspoon salt
¾ cup shortening
5 to 5½ tablespoons milk

Combine flour and salt; cut in shortening with a pastry blender until mixture resembles coarse meal. Sprinkle milk (1 tablespoon at a time) evenly over surface; stir with a fork until dry ingredients are moistened. Shape dough into a ball. Yield: pastry for one double-crust pie.

Wilma Ernsberger
Lynchburg, Virginia

Creamy Blackberry Pie

If your supply of blackberries is a little shy of what's needed to make a traditional double-crusted blackberry pie, you'll appreciate Creamy Blackberry Pie. In this easy-to-make recipe, a sour cream mixture helps fill the pastry shell. Browned streusel topping crowns the pie and adds a crunchy texture.

CREAMY BLACKBERRY PIE

3 cups fresh blackberries
1 unbaked 9-inch deep-dish pastry
    shell
1 cup sugar
⅓ cup all-purpose flour
⅛ teaspoon salt
2 eggs, beaten
½ cup commercial sour cream
½ cup sugar
½ cup all-purpose flour
¼ cup butter or margarine
Additional blackberries (optional)
Fresh mint leaves (optional)

Place 3 cups blackberries in pastry shell. Set aside.

Combine 1 cup sugar, ⅓ cup flour, and salt. Add eggs and sour cream, stirring until blended. Spoon over blackberries.

Combine ½ cup sugar and ½ cup flour; cut in butter with pastry blender until mixture resembles coarse meal. Sprinkle evenly over sour cream mixture. Bake at 350° for 50 to 55 minutes or until lightly browned. If desired, garnish with blackberries and mint leaves. Yield: one 9-inch pie.

Light-As-Air Orange Cake

When the weather is warm, Tassie Bradley of Sparta, Tennessee, pulls out her recipe for Fresh Orange Chiffon Cake. Cake flour and beaten egg whites make the cake delightfully tender. As with any chiffon cake, it's important to beat the egg whites until stiff peaks form—this is the secret to the fluffy texture and rising of the cake.

Fresh orange juice and rind add a tangy citrus flavor to the cake. Tassie suggests substituting lemon rind and lemon juice, if a different taste is desired. "And it's really good with a scoop of sherbet the same flavor as the cake," she adds.

FRESH ORANGE CHIFFON CAKE

2½ cups sifted cake flour
1 tablespoon baking powder
1 teaspoon salt
1⅓ cups sugar, divided
½ cup vegetable oil
3 egg yolks, beaten
3 tablespoons grated orange rind
¾ cup orange juice
5 egg whites
½ teaspoon cream of tartar
Fresh Orange Glaze

Combine flour, baking powder, salt, and ⅔ cup sugar. Make a well in center; add oil, egg yolks, orange rind, and orange juice. Beat at high speed of an electric mixer about 5 minutes or until satiny smooth.

Beat egg whites (at room temperature) and cream of tartar in a large mixing bowl until soft peaks form. Add remaining ⅔ cup sugar, 2 tablespoons at a time, beating until stiff peaks form.

Pour egg yolk mixture in a thin, steady stream over entire surface of egg whites, and gently fold whites into yolk mixture.

Pour batter into an ungreased 10-inch tube pan, spreading evenly with a spatula. Bake at 325° for 1 hour or until cake springs back when lightly touched. Invert pan; cool 40 minutes. Loosen cake from sides of pan, using a narrow metal spatula; remove from pan. Place cake on a cake plate; drizzle top with Fresh Orange Glaze. Yield: one 10-inch cake.

Fresh Orange Glaze

3 cups sifted powdered sugar
⅛ teaspoon salt
2¼ teaspoons grated orange rind
¼ teaspoon orange extract
3½ to 4 tablespoons orange juice

Combine all ingredients; stir until smooth. Yield: about 1¼ cups.

Dill Spruces Up Vegetables

There was a time when folks thought only of pickles when dill was mentioned, but this aromatic herb carries broader fame these days. It commonly flavors sauces, fish and seafood, and egg dishes, and it's especially well known for seasoning vegetables this time of year.

If you don't grow dill in your own garden, you can often find it sold in bunches at grocery stores or farmers markets. In its dried form, what's referred to as dillweed comes from the leaves of the plant; dillseed comes from the dried fruit. When substituting dried dillweed for fresh, remember that 1 teaspoon of the dried herb equals 1 tablespoon of the chopped fresh.

DILLED VEGETABLE STICKS

2 cups water
¾ cup vinegar
½ cup sugar
1 teaspoon salt
1½ tablespoons chopped fresh
    dillweed or 1½ teaspoons dried
    whole dillweed
1 teaspoon onion powder
¼ teaspoon garlic powder
½ pound fresh whole green beans
3 large carrots, cut into julienne
    strips
3 stalks celery, cut into julienne
    strips

Combine first 7 ingredients in a large saucepan. Bring to a boil; cover, reduce heat, and simmer 15 minutes. Add beans, carrots, and celery. Return mixture to a boil; cover, reduce heat, and simmer 5 minutes. Place vegetables in a shallow container; pour vinegar mixture over vegetables. Cover and chill at least 8 hours. Yield: 4 to 6 servings.

Peggy Fowler Revels
Woodruff, South Carolina

DILLED BRUSSELS SPROUTS

2 (10-ounce) packages frozen
   brussels sprouts
1 cup zesty Italian dressing
2 tablespoons sliced green
   onions
1 tablespoon chopped fresh
   dillweed or 1 teaspoon
   dried whole dillweed

Cook brussels sprouts according to
package directions, omitting salt;
drain well.

Combine brussels sprouts, Italian
dressing, sliced green onions, and
dillweed in a medium mixing bowl,
tossing gently. Cover and refrigerate
for at least 8 hours.

Serve brussels sprouts, using a
slotted spoon. Yield: about 8
servings.

Evelyn Snellings
Richmond, Virginia

DILLY ASPARAGUS

1 (10-ounce) package frozen
   asparagus spears
¼ cup vinegar
¼ cup olive oil
1 tablespoon sugar
½ teaspoon salt
¼ teaspoon coarsely ground
   pepper
1 tablespoon chopped fresh
   parsley
2 teaspoons chopped fresh
   dillweed or ¾ teaspoon dried
   whole dillweed
2 teaspoons dried minced onion
1 (2-ounce) jar diced pimiento,
   drained

Cook asparagus according to package
directions, omitting salt; drain.

Combine vinegar and remaining ingredients in a jar; cover tightly, and
shake vigorously.

Place asparagus in a shallow container; pour marinade over asparagus. Cover and chill 8 hours. To
serve, drain asparagus, and arrange
on serving platter. Drain pimiento
mixture, using a slotted spoon, and
spoon over asparagus. Yield: 3 to 4
servings.

Margot Foster
Hubbard, Texas

Looks Like Spaghetti, Tastes Like Squash

Many people are now looking for
spaghetti squash when they shop.
They've heard about this unusual
vegetable that tastes like squash but
separates into thin strands when the
cooked pulp is scraped with a fork.

SPAGHETTI SQUASH WITH MEAT SAUCE

½ pound ground turkey
½ pound ground pork
1 medium onion, chopped
1 clove garlic, minced
1½ teaspoons mixed pickling
   spices
1 (8-ounce) can tomato sauce
⅓ cup Burgundy or other dry
   red wine
¼ cup water
1 (2-inch) stick cinnamon
¼ teaspoon salt
½ teaspoon pepper
1 (3-pound) spaghetti squash
¼ cup water
2 tablespoons butter or
   margarine, melted
⅛ teaspoon salt
⅛ teaspoon pepper
1 avocado, peeled, seeded, and
   sliced (optional)
1 tomato, cut into wedges
   (optional)
2 tablespoons grated Parmesan
   cheese
2 tablespoons chopped fresh
   parsley

Combine turkey, pork, onion, and
garlic in a Dutch oven. Cook until
meat is browned, stirring to crumble
meat; drain.

Place pickling spices in a tea ball
or tie securely in a cheesecloth bag.
Add pickling spices, tomato sauce,
wine, ¼ cup water, cinnamon stick,
¼ teaspoon salt, and ½ teaspoon
pepper to meat mixture in skillet.
Bring mixture to a boil; cover, reduce heat, and simmer about 1 hour,
stirring occasionally. Remove and
discard pickling spices and cinnamon
stick. Keep meat sauce warm.

Cut spaghetti squash in half lengthwise, and remove seeds. Place
squash halves, cut side down, in a
large baking dish; add ¼ cup water
to dish. Cover dish with plastic wrap,
and microwave at HIGH 8 to 10 minutes or until tender. Drain squash.
Using a fork, remove spaghetti-like
strands of squash. Drizzle squash
with melted butter, and sprinkle with
⅛ teaspoon salt and ⅛ teaspoon
pepper; toss until squash is well
coated.

Spoon squash onto a serving platter; spoon warm meat sauce over
squash. If desired, garnish with avocado slices and tomato wedges.
Sprinkle Parmesan cheese and
chopped parsley evenly over squash.
Yield: 4 servings.

Note: To bake squash in a conventional oven, cut squash in half, and
seed as directed above. Place squash
halves, cut side down, in a shallow
baking pan. Add water to a depth of
1½ inches in pan. Bake squash at
350° for 45 minutes.

Rose Durham
Holliday, Texas

Tip: *Use your microwave to make a
quick and easy job of drying herbs.
To dry fresh herbs in the microwave
oven, first remove stems from parsley, chives, basil, sage, and other
herbs; rinse and pat dry. Then
spread ½ to 1 cup of the rinsed
herbs between two sheets of paper
towel, and microwave at HIGH for
2 to 2½ minutes. Store dried herbs
in airtight containers.*

AUGUST

Cool Melons At Their Peak

One of the best things about summer is that it brings plenty of sweet melons to the South. Containing 90% water, melons are some of the juiciest treats of summer. A bonus is that they are low in calories yet surprisingly nutritious.

You may want to read "From Our Kitchen to Yours" on the facing page for clues to selecting melons.

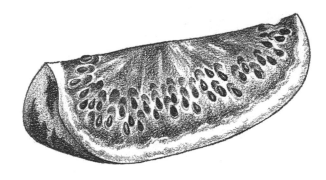

MELON SALAD WITH DILL DRESSING

1 (4-ounce) package sliced
   prosciutto or ham
¼ pound thinly sliced brick or
   Muenster cheese
2 medium honeydew melons or
   cantaloupes
1 small cucumber, unpeeled
1 cup fresh pineapple chunks
Lettuce leaves
Dill Dressing

Place one slice prosciutto on each slice of cheese; roll tightly, jellyroll fashion. Chill 1 hour. Cut into ½-inch slices, using a sharp knife.

Cut honeydew melons in half, and remove seeds. Carefully scoop out melon balls, leaving a 1-inch-thick shell. Scallop edges of melon shells, if desired. Set melon balls aside.

Cut cucumber in half lengthwise. Scoop out seeds with spoon. Cut into ¼-inch slices. Set aside.

Combine cheese pinwheels, melon balls, cucumber, and pineapple in a large bowl. Line melon shells with lettuce leaves. Spoon salad over lettuce. Serve salad with Dill Dressing. Yield: 4 servings.

Dill Dressing

½ cup mayonnaise
½ cup plain yogurt
⅛ teaspoon dillweed
⅛ teaspoon white pepper
¼ teaspoon hot sauce

Combine all ingredients, stirring well. Chill. Yield: 1 cup.

MIDSUMMER FRUIT MEDLEY

¾ cup sugar
½ cup water
1 tablespoon grated lemon rind
1 tablespoon grated orange rind
¼ cup lemon juice
3 tablespoons lime juice
1 large cantaloupe
1 large honeydew melon
½ large watermelon
1 cup seedless green grapes
2 cups strawberries, halved
Fresh mint sprigs (optional)

Combine first 6 ingredients in a small saucepan. Cook, stirring constantly, until sugar dissolves; boil 5 minutes. Let cool and refrigerate.

Cut cantaloupe and honeydew melon in half, and remove seeds. Carefully scoop out cantaloupe, melon, and watermelon balls. Combine with grapes and strawberries in a large bowl. Serve chilled citrus dressing over fruit. Garnish with mint sprigs, if desired. To serve, use a slotted spoon. Yield: 12 servings.

Sara F. Stuart
Donalsonville, Georgia

MELLOWED-OUT MELON BALLS

1½ cups cantaloupe balls
1½ cups honeydew melon balls
¼ cup amaretto
½ cup slivered almonds, toasted

Combine first 3 ingredients; toss gently to coat. Chill 1 hour. Spoon into individual compotes; sprinkle with almonds, and serve immediately. Yield: 4 servings.

Sonya H. Davis
Huntington, West Virginia

CANTALOUPE MERINGUE PIE

1 unbaked 9-inch pastry shell
1 egg white, beaten
4 eggs, separated
½ teaspoon cream of tartar
½ cup sugar
2 cups pureed cantaloupe
1 cup sugar
¼ cup cornstarch
½ cup milk
¾ cup evaporated milk
¼ cup butter or margarine
⅛ teaspoon salt
2 teaspoons vanilla extract

Prick pastry shell; bake at 450° for 9 to 11 minutes. Remove from oven; brush immediately with beaten egg white to seal pricks. Let cool.

Beat 4 egg whites (at room temperature) and cream of tartar at high speed of an electric mixer 1 minute. Gradually add ½ cup sugar, 1 tablespoon at a time, beating until stiff peaks form and sugar dissolves (2 to 4 minutes); set aside.

Combine egg yolks, cantaloupe, and next 6 ingredients in a heavy saucepan; stir well. Cook over medium heat, stirring constantly, until thickened and bubbly. Remove from heat; stir in vanilla. Pour mixture into prepared pastry shell. Spread meringue over hot filling, sealing to edge of pastry. Bake at 400° for 8 to 10 minutes or until golden brown. Let cool. Yield: one 9-inch pie.

Toni R. Riley
Waco, Texas

CANTALOUPE SHERBET

4 cups cantaloupe chunks (1 small cantaloupe)
4 cups milk, divided
2 envelopes unflavored gelatin
¾ cup light corn syrup
½ cup sugar
¼ teaspoon salt
Cantaloupe slices (optional)
Mint sprigs (optional)

Combine cantaloupe chunks and 1 cup milk in container of an electric blender; top with cover, and process until smooth.

Combine 1 cup milk and gelatin in a saucepan; cook over low heat, stirring constantly, until gelatin dissolves. Combine gelatin mixture, cantaloupe puree, remaining 2 cups milk, syrup, sugar, and salt, stirring well. Pour into a 13- x 9- x 2-inch pan. Cover and freeze 3 hours. Spoon sherbet into a large mixing bowl; beat at low speed of an electric mixer until smooth. (Do not overbeat or mixture will melt.) Pour back into pan; cover and freeze until firm. If desired, serve with cantaloupe slices, and garnish with mint sprigs. Yield: 2 quarts. *Julie Earhart*
St. Louis, Missouri

From Our Kitchen To Yours

Magnificent melons bursting with naturally sweet flavor and the heady perfumes of summer offer simple refreshment for hot, sunny days. Here are suggestions for selecting the sweetest, juiciest melon.

Selecting Melons

Avoid melons with soft, discolored spots, cuts, or punctures. Check for mold growth, particularly on the stem end; dark water-soaked spots indicate decay, which spreads quickly inside melons.

A melon picked before it fully matures does not ripen properly; it is also not as flavorful because the sugar content hasn't completely developed. A mature melon has a smooth, shallow basin at the stem end. If part of the stem remains or the stem scar is jagged or torn, the melon is probably not mature.

If you plan to use the melon within a day or two, select a fully ripe one. Buy a slightly underripe melon if you're not going to use it for a few days. The best guidelines are smell and touch. Ripe cantaloupe and honeydew melons have faint, fragrant aromas, and the blossom ends are slightly soft.

Watermelon and honeydew have smooth, velvety surfaces that are slightly dull. When buying cut pieces, be sure they are from a ripe melon, because the melon will not ripen once it's cut.

Cantaloupe, generally available year-round, is sweetest and most fragrant during June, July, and August. As you pick through the cantaloupe display, look for a melon with an oval-shaped, gray-brown or taupe rind with lighter taupe netting.

The netting (the veinlike network of lines running randomly across the rind) should be thick, coarse, and well raised. The smooth, rounded depression, or stem scar, has a light-yellow tint. When it is cut, the flesh, or meat, of the cantaloupe is salmon colored.

Named for its refreshing taste and color, the **honeydew** is abundant June through October. This large, bluntly oval-shaped melon is generally smooth with occasional traces of surface netting. Select a honeydew that has a firm rind ranging in color from creamy white to creamy yellow. A stark-white rind tinged with green indicates an unripe honeydew.

Watermelon is available May through September with peak supplies in June, July, and August. It is difficult to select a ripe whole watermelon. Round or oblong, a whole watermelon should be firm and symmetrically shaped; depending on the variety, the rind colors may vary from dark green to pale green, or they may be dark- or light-green striped.

A yellowish underside where the melon touched the ground is a good sign of ripeness, although it may not always be totally reliable. If you are uncertain that the watermelon you have selected is ripe, ask the produce manager to cut it in half so that you can see the inside. A ripe, cut watermelon has firm, juicy, bright-red flesh, free from white streaks. Pale-colored flesh, white streaks, and whitish seeds are signs of immaturity; dry, mealy flesh or watery, stringy flesh indicates that the melon is overripe.

Storing Melons

Fresh melons can be damaged by improper handling and storage, especially improper refrigeration. For your family to enjoy maximum flavor, serve melons within a few days after ripening. If the melons are firm when purchased, give your kitchen an attractive, homey feeling by storing them at room temperature in bowls or baskets on the table or counter.

After one or two days, the blossom ends will yield to gentle thumb pressure, and the ripe melons should be placed in the refrigerator. Ripe cantaloupe and honeydew will keep two to three days in the refrigerator; uncut watermelon keeps about one week, while cut watermelon keeps up to two days.

The Best Of Summer In A Salad

With the scorching heat of summer comes a tempting crop of tender, juicy fruit. Filled with flavor, fruit salads make the soaring temperatures far more bearable.

FRESH FRUIT AMBROSIA

4 oranges
2 unpeeled apples, cubed
2 cups fresh pineapple chunks
1 cup seedless green grapes, halved
1 cup orange juice
⅓ cup sugar
2 tablespoons Grand Marnier or cream sherry
¼ teaspoon vanilla extract
¼ teaspoon almond extract
2 cups sliced strawberries
Flaked coconut

Peel oranges, and slice crosswise; cut each slice into quarters.

Combine oranges, apples, pineapple, and grapes in a bowl. Combine orange juice and sugar, stirring until sugar dissolves. Add Grand Marnier and flavorings; pour over fruit. Cover and chill 2 to 3 hours.

To serve, stir in strawberries, and spoon into individual serving dishes. Top ambrosia with coconut. Yield: 8 servings.   *Janet S. Wilkins*
Baton Rouge, Louisiana

GINGERED FRUIT COMPOTE

1 tablespoon cornstarch
1 tablespoon sugar
⅛ teaspoon ground ginger
1 cup pineapple juice or orange juice
1 cup fresh blueberries
1½ cups fresh strawberries
1½ cups fresh pineapple chunks
1 cup sliced peaches

Combine first 3 ingredients in a small saucepan; gradually add pineapple juice, stirring until smooth. Bring mixture to a boil over medium heat; boil 1 minute, stirring constantly. Remove from heat, and cool.

Combine fruit in a large bowl. Pour sauce over fruit; toss gently. Chill. Yield: 8 servings.   *Brenda Rohe*
Charlotte, North Carolina

CANTALOUPE-CHEESE SALAD

2 cups cantaloupe balls
1½ cups cubed, unpeeled apple
½ cup chopped celery
¼ cup seedless green grapes
¼ cup commercial sour cream
3 tablespoons mayonnaise
¼ cup crumbled blue cheese
Leaf lettuce
Additional crumbled blue cheese (optional)

Combine first 4 ingredients. Combine sour cream, mayonnaise, and ¼ cup blue cheese; stir well. Pour over cantaloupe mixture; toss gently.

Arrange lettuce leaves on individual salad plates; spoon cantaloupe mixture on top. Garnish with additional blue cheese, if desired. Yield: 4 to 6 servings.

Mrs. R. V. McBrayer
Chattanooga, Tennessee

EASY PATIO FRUIT SALAD

1 large unpeeled apple, cubed
1 tablespoon lemon juice
1 cup fresh pineapple chunks
1 large orange, peeled, seeded, and sectioned
5 apricots, peeled, seeded, and sliced
½ cup chopped celery
¼ cup slivered almonds, toasted
½ cup commercial sour cream
2 tablespoons apricot brandy
1 cup torn iceberg lettuce

Combine apple and lemon juice in a large bowl; toss gently to coat well. Add pineapple and next 4 ingredients; cover and refrigerate fruit mixture 1 to 2 hours.

Combine sour cream and apricot brandy; stir well. Cover and chill at least 1 hour.

Add lettuce to fruit mixture; toss. Spoon sauce on top; toss gently to coat well. Serve immediately. Yield: 6 servings.   *Mrs. R. L. McKeithan*
Hamlet, North Carolina

Tip: *When buying fresh citrus, look for fruit with smooth, blemish-free skins. Indications of high juice content are that fruit feel firm and are heavy for their size.*

MICROWAVE COOKERY

Vegetables Great For The Microwave

If you think saving time is the greatest advantage to microwave cooking, you may change your mind when you sample these vegetable recipes. With conventional cooking methods, vegetable flavor can be lost as the cooking liquid evaporates, taking valuable nutrients and freshness with it. But when cooked in the microwave, vegetables retain more nutrients, more flavor, and a brighter color because the rapid cooking promotes minimal loss of cooking liquid.

You also save vegetable nutrients and flavor by using just a few tablespoons of water, if any, for cooking during microwaving. This way, the flavor and nutrients stay in the vegetables instead of being released into the cooking liquid.

You'll find that vegetables with uniform shapes and sizes, such as corn kernels, will cook more evenly. To cook vegetables of uneven lengths, such as green beans, cut them into similar lengths as in the recipe for Nutty Green Beans. For unevenly shaped vegetables, such as carrots, cut slices of equal thickness or chop into uniform-size pieces.

Covering vegetables as they cook prevents oven splatters and excessive liquid loss. If the vegetables are very watery naturally, such as tomatoes, you may want to cover loosely with wax paper to allow some liquid to escape during cooking. Covering tightly with heavy-duty plastic wrap is helpful for vegetables that have low moisture content, such as beans. Just remember to always fold back an edge of the plastic wrap to serve as a steam vent. Lima beans and black-eyed peas are lower in moisture than most vegetables and require more water and a surprisingly long cooking time, even in the microwave.

For basic microwave cooking times and instructions for your favorite vegetables, see the microwave chart on page 186. You may want to keep the chart near your microwave oven for handy reference. Just remember that cooking times will vary with the amount of vegetables cooked at one time and with the wattage of your microwave.

OKRA MEDLEY

5 slices bacon, cut into ½-inch pieces
2 cups sliced fresh okra (about ½ pound)
2 medium tomatoes, chopped
1 cup fresh corn, cut from cob
½ cup chopped onion
¼ cup chopped celery
¼ teaspoon salt
5 drops hot sauce

Place bacon pieces in a 2-quart casserole. Cover with wax paper; microwave at HIGH 5 minutes or until crisp. Remove bacon, and discard drippings. Crumble bacon, and return to casserole.

Stir in okra and remaining ingredients. Cover and microwave at HIGH 10 minutes, stirring after 5 minutes. Yield: 6 to 8 servings.

BASIL SNOW PEAS AND TOMATOES

1 pound fresh snow pea pods
2 tablespoons butter or margarine
¼ cup chopped onion
1 tablespoon soy sauce
1½ tablespoons minced fresh basil or 1½ teaspoons dried whole basil
½ teaspoon salt
2 medium tomatoes, coarsely chopped

Wash snow pea pods; trim ends, and remove any tough strings. Set aside.

Place butter in a shallow 2½-quart casserole; microwave at HIGH 45 seconds or until melted. Add snow peas, chopped onion, soy sauce, basil, and salt; toss gently.

Cover and microwave at HIGH 3 minutes. Add chopped tomatoes, stirring gently. Cover and microwave at HIGH 4 to 5 minutes. Yield: about 8 servings.

The recipes in the "Microwave Cookery" special section and in the monthly "Microwave Cookery" column are tested in *Southern Living* test kitchens in microwave ovens with wattages of 650 and 700. Cooking times for these recipes may need to be increased if prepared in lower wattage ovens.

MICROWAVING TIMES FOR VEGETABLES

Vegetable	Amount	Procedure
BEANS Green/Wax	1 pound	Wash beans; trim ends, and remove strings. Cut into 1-inch pieces. Combine beans and ½ cup water in a 1½-quart casserole. Cover and microwave at HIGH 14 to 15 minutes or until tender. Drain.
Lima beans (shelled)	1 pound	Combine beans and 1 cup water in a 1½-quart casserole. Cover and microwave at HIGH 5 minutes. Reduce to MEDIUM HIGH (70% power), and microwave 25 to 30 minutes or until tender. Drain.
BROCCOLI	1 pound	Remove tough ends, and divide into spears. Combine spears (stem ends toward the outside) and ½ cup water in a 12- x 8- x 2-inch baking dish. Cover and microwave at HIGH 7 to 8 minutes or until broccoli is tender. Drain.
CARROTS	1 pound	Slice carrots. Combine carrots and ¼ cup water in a 1-quart casserole. Cover and microwave at HIGH 9 to 10 minutes or until tender. Let stand 2 minutes. Drain.
CAULIFLOWER	1 medium or 2 pounds	Separate into flowerets. Combine flowerets and ½ cup water in a 1½-quart casserole. Cover and microwave at HIGH 10 to 11 minutes or until tender. Let stand 2 minutes. Drain.
CORN Kernels	2 cups or 4 ears	Combine kernels and ¼ cup water. Cover and microwave at HIGH 9 to 10 minutes or until tender. Drain.
On cob (in husks)	1 ear (3 to 5 minutes) 2 ears (6 to 9 minutes) 3 ears (9 to 12 minutes) 4 ears (12 to 16 minutes)	Peel back husks, leaving them attached. Remove silks, if desired; re-arrange attached husks over corn ears. Arrange corn spoke-fashion on paper towels. Microwave at HIGH for time indicated. Remove husks.
On cob (without husks)	1 ear (2 to 4 minutes) 2 ears (5 to 9 minutes) 3 ears (7 to 12 minutes) 4 ears (8 to 15 minutes)	Remove husks and silks. Wrap each ear in heavy-duty plastic wrap (or place in a tightly covered baking dish with ¼ cup water). Microwave at HIGH for time indicated. Drain, if necessary.
EGGPLANT	1 pound or 1 medium	Peel eggplant, and cut into cubes. Place cubes in a 12- x 8- x 2-inch baking dish. Cover and microwave at HIGH 6 to 8 minutes or until tender. Drain.
OKRA	1 pound	Cut okra into thin slices. Combine okra and ¼ cup water in a 1-quart casserole. Cover and microwave at HIGH 8 to 10 minutes or until okra is tender.
ONIONS	1 pound	Peel onions; cut into quarters. Place in a 1-quart baking dish. Cover and microwave at HIGH 6 to 8 minutes or until crisp-tender. Drain.
PEAS Black-eyed (shelled)	2 pounds or 4 cups	Combine peas and 1¼ cups water in a 2-quart casserole. Cover and microwave at HIGH 4 minutes. Reduce to MEDIUM (50% power), and microwave 35 to 40 minutes.
English (shelled)	1 pound or 1½ cups	Combine peas and 2 tablespoons water in a 1-quart casserole. Cover and microwave at HIGH 6 to 7 minutes. Drain.
Snow peas	1 pound	Trim ends, and remove strings. Place peas and 2 tablespoons water in a 1½-quart casserole. Cover and microwave at HIGH 3 to 4 minutes or until crisp-tender. Drain.
PEPPERS	2 medium	Cut peppers into thin strips. Place in a 1-quart casserole. Cover and microwave at HIGH 4 to 5 minutes or until crisp-tender. Drain.

MICROWAVE COOKERY

MICROWAVING TIMES FOR VEGETABLES

Vegetable	Amount	Procedure
POTATOES Baking or sweet potatoes	1 potato (4 to 6 minutes) 2 potatoes (7 to 8 minutes) 3 potatoes (9 to 11 minutes) 4 potatoes (12 to 14 minutes)	Prick scrubbed potatoes with a fork. Arrange spoke-fashion on paper towels. Microwave at HIGH for time indicated. Let stand 5 minutes.
New potatoes	1 pound	Scrub and peel, if desired. Combine potatoes and ¼ cup water in a 1½-quart casserole. Cover and microwave at HIGH 8 to 10 minutes or until tender. Drain.
SUMMER SQUASH Pattypan	1 pound	Cut off tops, and remove seeds. Combine squash and 2 tablespoons water in an 8-inch baking dish. Cover and microwave at HIGH 8 to 10 minutes or until tender. Drain.
Yellow or zucchini	1 pound	Cut squash into thin slices. Combine squash and ¼ cup water in a 1½-quart casserole. Cover and microwave at HIGH 7 to 8 minutes or until tender. Drain.

VEGETABLE PLATTER

1 pound fresh broccoli, cut into
    ½-inch pieces
½ head cauliflower, cut into
    flowerets
1 medium zucchini, cut into
    ¼-inch slices
2 tablespoons water
¼ cup butter or margarine
½ teaspoon garlic salt
2 medium tomatoes, cut into
    wedges
½ cup freshly grated Parmesan
    cheese

Arrange broccoli and cauliflower around outer edge of a 12-inch round pizza plate; place zucchini in center of plate, and sprinkle with water. Cover tightly with heavy-duty plastic wrap; fold back a small edge of wrap to allow steam to escape. Microwave at HIGH 5 to 7 minutes or until crisp-tender, rotating plate once. Let stand, covered, 2 minutes.

Combine butter and garlic salt in a 1-cup glass measure. Microwave at HIGH 55 seconds; mix well.

Lift plastic wrap from one side of plate, and drain. Remove plastic wrap. Arrange tomato wedges around edge of plate; drizzle butter mixture over vegetables. Sprinkle with cheese, and microwave at HIGH 1 to 2 minutes. Yield: 8 servings.

Kay Swanner
Montgomery, Alabama

NUTTY GREEN BEANS

1 pound fresh green beans
½ cup water
3 tablespoons butter or margarine
⅓ cup coarsely chopped pecans
2 tablespoons chopped onion
1 clove garlic, crushed
¼ teaspoon salt

Wash beans, and remove strings. Cut beans into 1-inch pieces. Place in a 1½-quart casserole; add water. Cover and microwave at HIGH 16 to 17 minutes or until crisp-tender. Drain and keep warm.

Place butter in a pieplate. Microwave at HIGH 50 seconds or until melted. Add pecans and remaining ingredients; microwave at HIGH 2 to 3 minutes or until onion is tender, stirring after each minute.

Pour butter mixture over beans, tossing to coat. Yield: 4 servings.

PARMESAN CORN ON THE COB

4 ears fresh corn
¼ cup butter or margarine,
    softened
¼ cup grated Parmesan cheese
1½ teaspoons chopped fresh
    parsley
¼ teaspoon dried whole salad
    herbs

Remove husks and silks from corn just before cooking. Combine butter and remaining ingredients, stirring well. Spread mixture on corn, and place each ear on a piece of heavy-duty plastic wrap. Roll wrap lengthwise around each ear, and twist wrap at each end. Arrange ears of corn, spoke-fashion, on a microwave-safe glass plate. Microwave corn at HIGH 10 to 13 minutes, rearranging ears occasionally.

Note: Cooking time will vary depending on size of ears.

Tip: *Add salt to taste after cooking to prevent dark spots from forming on microwaved vegetables.*

HOT VEGETABLE PEPPER CUPS

4 medium-size sweet red peppers
4 slices bacon
1½ cups sliced okra
1½ cups fresh corn, cut from cob
1 jalapeño pepper, chopped
3 tablespoons water
¼ teaspoon salt
⅛ teaspoon pepper

Cut off tops of peppers, and remove seeds. Wash peppers, and place cut side down in an 8-inch square baking dish. Cover and microwave at HIGH 4 to 5 minutes or until peppers are crisp-tender, giving dish a half-turn at 2-minute intervals.

Place bacon on a rack in a 12- x 8- x 2-inch baking dish. Cover with wax paper; microwave at HIGH 4 minutes or until crisp. Remove bacon, reserving 1 tablespoon drippings. Crumble bacon, and set aside.

Add okra, corn, jalapeño, and water to bacon drippings. Cover and microwave at HIGH 8 to 9 minutes or until tender. Stir in salt, pepper, and half of crumbled bacon.

Fill pepper cups with corn mixture; set filled peppers on a microwave-safe serving platter. Cover and microwave at HIGH 1 minute or until peppers are thoroughly heated. Sprinkle cups with remaining crumbled bacon. Yield: 4 servings.

Speed Up Yeast Bread

Many sources say bread isn't a good candidate for baking in a microwave. It doesn't brown or develop a crust like conventionally baked bread. But some breads developed especially for microwaving receive raves when baked this way.

Even though bread doesn't brown in a microwave, adding a naturally colored ingredient such as the chocolate in Chocolate Loaf Bread makes the loaf look more appetizing. Using dark flour, such as whole wheat or rye, will also color the dough.

Sprinkling cornmeal, poppy seeds, or sesame seeds on top or adding a brown sugar topping makes a crunchier crust. Adding a powdered sugar glaze as in Chocolate Loaf Bread also helps compensate for the lack of a crisp crust.

One of the biggest bonuses of teaming yeast bread and your microwave is that you can cut the bread's rising time in half.

Place the dough in a well-greased bowl, turning to grease top. Set the bowl in a larger, shallow dish; pour hot water to a depth of 1 inch in the bottom dish. Cover the dough loosely with wax paper. Microwave at MEDIUM LOW (30% power) 2 minutes; let it stand in microwave 5 minutes. Repeat microwaving and standing 3 times or until dough is doubled in bulk, giving the dish a quarter-turn after each microwaving period. Carefully turn the dough over in the bowl if the dough's surface appears to be drying out. When rising is complete, punch the dough down and proceed as directed in the recipe.

CHOCOLATE LOAF BREAD

½ cup milk
¼ cup butter or margarine
¼ cup sugar
¾ teaspoon salt
1½ (1-ounce) squares unsweetened chocolate
1 package dry yeast
¼ cup warm water (105° to 115°)
2 eggs, beaten
3 to 3¼ cups all-purpose flour, divided
Vegetable cooking spray
Glaze (recipe follows)

Combine milk, butter, sugar, and salt in a small glass bowl; microwave at HIGH 1½ to 2 minutes or until butter melts. Cool to 105° to 115°.

Place chocolate in a custard cup. Microwave at MEDIUM (50% power) 2 to 2½ minutes or until softened; stir well. Let cool.

Dissolve yeast in warm water in a large mixing bowl. Stir in milk mixture, chocolate, eggs, and 2 cups flour; beat at medium speed of an electric mixer until smooth. Stir in enough remaining flour to make a soft dough.

Turn dough out onto a lightly floured surface, and knead until smooth and elastic. Place in a well-greased bowl, turning to grease top. Set bowl in a larger, shallow dish; pour hot water to depth of 1 inch in bottom dish. Cover dough loosely with wax paper. Microwave at MEDIUM LOW (30% power) 2 minutes; let stand in microwave 5 minutes. Repeat microwaving and standing 3 times or until dough is doubled in bulk, giving dish a quarter-turn after each microwaving period. Carefully turn dough over in bowl if surface appears to be drying out during microwaving period. Remove from oven, and punch dough down.

Turn dough out onto a floured surface, and roll to an 18- x 9-inch rectangle. Roll up dough, jellyroll fashion, starting at short end. Place roll, seam side down, in a greased 9- x 5- x 3-inch loaf dish. Return loaf to dish with hot water; cover dough loosely with wax paper sprayed with vegetable cooking spray. Microwave at MEDIUM LOW 2 minutes; let stand 5 minutes. Repeat microwaving and standing 2 or 3 times or until doubled in bulk, giving dish a quarter-turn each time you microwave.

Place dish on an inverted saucer in microwave oven. Microwave at MEDIUM (50% power) 7 to 8 minutes or until top springs back when lightly touched with finger, giving dish a quarter-turn after every 3 minutes. Invert bread onto a serving platter, and let stand 10 minutes before serving. Drizzle glaze over warm loaf. Yield: one loaf.

Glaze

1 cup sifted powdered sugar
1½ tablespoons milk
½ teaspoon vanilla extract

Combine all ingredients, stirring well. Yield: about ⅓ cup.

Note: Bread may be baked in a conventional oven if a crisper crust is desired. After dough rises in dish, bake at 350° for 30 minutes or until loaf sounds hollow when tapped.

Classic Recipes For The Microwave

One of the most exciting things to come along in recent years is the discovery of microwave cooking. We now know that it can do more than melt butter and heat water. It has become a major cooking tool, allowing us to produce flaky fish, crisp-tender vegetables, moist chicken, and wonderful candies.

Southern Living has been sharing microwave recipes with our readers since 1979. From the very beginning, we aimed to provide clear, concise recipes along with useful hints to help you get the best possible results from your microwave oven. We believe that you will find this same high quality in *The Southern Living Microwave Cookbook*.

This complete guide to cooking in the microwave oven is packed with hints and tempting recipes, which range from those that are just right for beginning microwave users to those that are more challenging.

We've also converted some favorite traditional recipes from conventional to microwave procedures.

Recipes reprinted from *The Southern Living Microwave Cookbook*, copyright 1988, Oxmoor House, Inc. Reproduced with permission.

GROUPER WITH CONFETTI VEGETABLES

1 (1-pound) grouper fillet
¼ cup lemon juice
1 small onion, chopped
1 small green pepper, chopped
1½ tablespoons butter or margarine
1 small tomato, seeded and chopped
¼ teaspoon salt
⅛ teaspoon pepper
¼ cup sliced ripe olives
1 cup (4 ounces) shredded mozzarella cheese

Cut fillet into four equal portions. Place fish in a shallow container, and add lemon juice. Cover and refrigerate 2 hours.

Place onion, green pepper, and butter in a 9-inch pieplate. Microwave, uncovered, at HIGH 2 to 3 minutes or until vegetables are crisp-tender. Add tomato; microwave, uncovered, at HIGH 1 minute. Drain and set aside.

Remove fish from lemon juice, and arrange in a 9-inch baking dish with thickest portions toward outside of dish. Sprinkle with salt and pepper. Cover with wax paper, and microwave at HIGH 6 to 7 minutes or until fish flakes easily when tested with a fork. Drain off any excess liquid. Spoon vegetable mixture over fish; sprinkle with sliced olives and cheese. Cover and microwave at MEDIUM HIGH (70% power) 2 minutes or just until cheese melts. Serve immediately. Yield: 4 servings.

PARTY PAELLA

2 (10¾-ounce) cans chicken broth, undiluted
1 bunch green onions, chopped
1 medium-size green pepper, chopped
½ cup sliced ripe olives
¼ cup finely chopped fresh parsley
¼ teaspoon ground saffron
2 cloves garlic, minced
2½ cups uncooked instant rice
2 medium tomatoes, peeled and chopped
4 (8-ounce) chicken breast halves, skinned, boned, and cut into 8 pieces
1 tablespoon dried whole oregano
2 teaspoons ground cumin
1 teaspoon chili powder
1 dozen unpeeled jumbo fresh shrimp, peeled and deveined
14 to 16 fresh littleneck clams
Fresh parsley sprigs (optional)

Combine first 7 ingredients in a large bowl. Microwave, uncovered, at HIGH 10 to 12 minutes or until mixture is boiling. Stir in instant rice; let stand 5 minutes. Stir in chopped tomatoes; set aside.

Arrange chicken in a 3½-quart shallow baking dish with thickest portions toward outside of dish. Combine oregano, cumin, and chili powder, mixing well. Sprinkle over chicken. Cover dish tightly with heavy-duty plastic wrap; fold back a small edge of wrap to allow steam to escape, and microwave at HIGH 12 to 15 minutes or until tender, rotating dish a half-turn every 5 minutes.

Spoon rice mixture over chicken. Arrange shrimp on top of rice; arrange clams around outer edges of dish with hinge ends in rice. Cover and microwave at HIGH 5 to 7 minutes or until clam shells begin to open. Let stand, covered, 5 minutes. Garnish with parsley sprigs, if desired. Serve immediately. Yield: 8 servings.

HERBED GREEN BEANS

½ pound fresh green beans
½ cup water
⅓ cup chopped green pepper
¼ cup sliced green onions
1 tablespoon vegetable oil
1 medium tomato, peeled and
   diced
¾ teaspoon minced fresh basil or
   ¼ teaspoon dried whole basil
½ teaspoon salt
¼ teaspoon sugar
¼ teaspoon minced fresh
   rosemary or ⅛ teaspoon dried
   whole rosemary

Wash beans; trim ends, and remove strings. Cut beans into 1½-inch pieces. Combine beans and water in a 1½-quart casserole. Cover tightly with heavy-duty plastic wrap; fold back a small edge of wrap to allow steam to escape. Microwave at HIGH 9 to 10 minutes or until crisp-tender, stirring after 3 minutes. Let stand, covered, 2 minutes; drain.

Place green pepper, onions, and oil in a small bowl. Cover with heavy-duty plastic wrap, and microwave at HIGH 3 to 4 minutes or until tender.

Add green pepper mixture, tomato, and remaining ingredients to beans; mix well. Cover and microwave at HIGH 2 to 3 minutes or until thoroughly heated. Yield: 4 servings.

PARMESAN-POTATO FANS

⅓ cup grated Parmesan cheese
1½ teaspoons dried parsley flakes
¼ teaspoon garlic powder
¼ teaspoon onion salt
¼ teaspoon paprika
6 medium baking potatoes
¼ cup plus 2 tablespoons butter
   or margarine
Lemon slices (optional)
Fresh parsley sprigs (optional)

Combine first 5 ingredients in a small bowl; set aside. Wash potatoes, and pat dry. Cut each potato crosswise into ¼-inch-thick slices, cutting to, but not through, bottom of potato. Allow potatoes to stand in ice water for 10 minutes.

Place butter in a 1-cup glass measure; microwave, uncovered, at HIGH 1 minute or until melted. Drain potatoes, and pat dry. Arrange potatoes, cut side up, in a 13- x 9- x 2-inch baking dish. Brush top and sides of potatoes with butter. Cover tightly with heavy-duty plastic wrap; fold back a small edge of wrap to allow steam to escape. Microwave at HIGH 20 to 24 minutes or until tender, rearranging potatoes every 5 minutes and brushing with remaining butter. Sprinkle potatoes with cheese mixture. Let stand, covered, 5 minutes. If desired, garnish with lemon slices and parsley. Serve immediately. Yield: 6 servings.

MACARONI AND CHEESE

1 (8-ounce) package elbow
   macaroni
3 cups water
¼ teaspoon salt
¼ cup butter or margarine
¼ cup plus 2 tablespoons
   all-purpose flour
¼ teaspoon salt
2 cups milk
2 cups (8 ounces) shredded
   Cheddar cheese
1 (2-ounce) jar diced pimiento,
   drained
1 tablespoon butter or margarine
⅓ cup fine, dry breadcrumbs
½ teaspoon dried parsley flakes

Combine macaroni, water, and ¼ teaspoon salt in a deep 2-quart casserole. Cover tightly with heavy-duty plastic wrap; fold back a small edge of wrap to allow steam to escape. Microwave at HIGH 10 to 12 minutes or until macaroni is tender, stirring after 5 minutes. Drain well, and set aside.

Place ¼ cup butter in a 4-cup glass measure; microwave, uncovered, at HIGH 55 seconds or until melted. Blend in flour and ¼ teaspoon salt, stirring until smooth. Gradually stir in milk; microwave, uncovered, at HIGH 5 to 6 minutes or until thickened, stirring after every minute. Add cheese, stirring until melted; stir in pimiento.

Add cheese sauce to macaroni, stirring well. Place macaroni mixture in a 1½-quart casserole; cover tightly with heavy-duty plastic wrap. Fold back a small edge of wrap to allow steam to escape. Microwave at MEDIUM HIGH (70% power) 7 to 8 minutes or until thoroughly heated, stirring after 4 minutes.

Place 1 tablespoon butter in a 1-cup glass measure; microwave, uncovered, at HIGH 35 seconds or until melted. Stir in breadcrumbs and parsley flakes; sprinkle over macaroni mixture. Let stand, uncovered, 1 minute. Serve immediately. Yield: 6 servings.

QUICK-AND-EASY FUDGE

1 (16-ounce) package powdered
   sugar, sifted
½ cup cocoa
¼ cup milk
1 tablespoon vanilla extract
¼ teaspoon salt
¼ teaspoon ground cinnamon
½ cup butter or margarine
1 cup chopped pecans

Line bottom of an 8-inch square baking dish with wax paper; set aside. Combine first 6 ingredients in a 2-quart casserole, stirring gently. Add butter; microwave, uncovered, at HIGH 2 to 3 minutes or until thoroughly heated. Stir until smooth. Stir in pecans. Pour mixture into prepared dish. Refrigerate until firm; cut into squares. Yield: 16 squares.

COOKING LIGHT®

Healthy Fish Dishes In Minutes

Naturally low in calories, sodium, fat, and cholesterol, fish offers many tasty options on a healthy diet. The omega-3 fatty acids found in fish have recently received attention because of their link in the prevention of heart disease. To get your fair share of omega-3 fatty acids, simply put fish on your menu two or more times a week.

Because it has no connective tissue like beef, pork, or poultry, fish cooks quickly in the microwave. The combination of quick cooking and steam, created by covering, helps fish retain its delicate texture and moistness.

Arrange halibut steaks for Halibut Steaks Italiano with the thickest portion to the outside of the dish to prevent thinner areas from overcooking. When the steaks turn opaque, they are done. The center may be slightly translucent, but it will finish cooking after the fish is taken out of the oven.

HALIBUT STEAKS ITALIANO

¾ cup chopped tomato
1½ cups sliced fresh mushrooms
¼ cup chopped onion
¼ cup chopped green pepper
2 tablespoons minced fresh parsley
1 clove garlic, minced
½ teaspoon dried whole oregano
1 tablespoon lemon juice
4 (4-ounce) halibut steaks, with skin
¼ teaspoon pepper
Fresh parsley sprigs (optional)
Lemon slices, halved (optional)

Combine tomato, mushrooms, onion, green pepper, minced parsley, garlic, oregano, and lemon juice in a 12- x 8- x 2-inch baking dish; stir well, and distribute vegetables evenly in dish. Cover with heavy-duty plastic wrap; fold back a small edge of wrap to allow steam to escape, and microwave at HIGH 4 minutes, giving dish a half-turn after 2 minutes. Spoon vegetables to one side of dish. Arrange fish with thickest portion to outside of dish. Sprinkle with pepper, and spoon vegetable mixture evenly over fish.

Cover with heavy-duty plastic wrap, and microwave at HIGH 4 minutes, giving dish a half-turn after 2 minutes. Cook until fish turns opaque. Let stand, covered, 3 to 5 minutes. Fish is done if it flakes easily when tested with a fork. If desired, garnish with parsley sprigs and lemon slices. Yield: 4 servings (133 calories per serving).

☐ 23.5 grams protein, 1.7 grams fat, 4.9 grams carbohydrate, 57 milligrams cholesterol, 66 milligrams sodium, and 29 milligrams calcium.

HADDOCK FILLETS WITH ZUCCHINI STUFFING

1 cup soft breadcrumbs
½ cup unpeeled shredded zucchini
½ cup diced onion
¼ cup diced celery
1 tablespoon minced fresh parsley
¼ teaspoon dried whole tarragon
¼ teaspoon pepper
⅛ teaspoon dried whole rosemary
1 teaspoon vegetable oil
4 (4-ounce) skinned haddock fillets
4 (¼-inch) tomato slices
Fresh parsley sprigs (optional)

Combine first 9 ingredients in bowl; toss gently. Cover with wax paper, and microwave at HIGH 4 minutes.

Pull up short ends of each fish fillet, forming a cylinder, and secure with wooden picks. Arrange fish with open area upward in an 8-inch square dish. Fill center of cylinder with stuffing mixture. Cover with wax paper; microwave at HIGH 4 minutes, giving dish a half-turn after 2 minutes. Cook until fish turns opaque. Let stand, covered, 3 to 5 minutes. Fish is done if it flakes easily when tested with a fork.

Place tomato slices on a serving platter; microwave at HIGH 1 to 2 minutes or until heated. Place fish rolls on top of tomato slices; garnish with parsley sprigs, if desired, and serve. Yield: 4 servings (172 calories per serving).

☐ 23.2 grams protein, 2.7 grams fat, 14.2 grams carbohydrate, 69 milligrams cholesterol, 184 milligrams sodium, and 60 milligrams calcium.

MICROWAVE COOKERY

ORANGE ROUGHY WITH SPINACH PESTO

1 (10-ounce) package frozen chopped spinach
1 cup (4 ounces) shredded part-skim mozzarella cheese, divided
¼ cup grated Parmesan cheese
1 small clove garlic, minced
2 tablespoons chopped onion
1 tablespoon pine nuts
2 teaspoons dried whole basil leaves
¼ teaspoon dried whole marjoram leaves
⅛ teaspoon white pepper
3 tablespoons Chablis or other dry white wine
⅓ cup plain low-fat yogurt
6 (4-ounce) skinned orange roughy fillets or other lean white fish

Remove wrapper from spinach package; place package in a flat baking dish, and pierce with a fork. Microwave at HIGH 4 minutes or until thawed. Drain spinach; press between layers of paper towels.

Combine spinach, ½ cup mozzarella cheese, and next 9 ingredients in container of an electric blender. Process at medium speed until mixture is smooth.

Arrange fish in a single layer in a 12- x 8- x 2-inch baking dish; spread spinach mixture evenly over fish. Cover with wax paper, and microwave at HIGH 3 minutes. Give dish a half-turn, and sprinkle fish with remaining ½ cup mozzarella cheese. Microwave at HIGH 3 to 4 minutes or until fish turns opaque; let stand, covered, 3 to 5 minutes. Fish is done if it flakes easily when tested with a fork. Yield: 6 servings (278 calories per serving).

☐ *29.7 grams protein, 15.1 grams fat, 5.1 grams carbohydrate, 78 milligrams cholesterol, 260 milligrams sodium, and 275 milligrams calcium.*

APPLE-CARROT STUFFED FILLETS

½ cup peeled, shredded apple
½ cup shredded carrot
¼ cup diced onion
2 tablespoons minced parsley
1 tablespoon lemon juice
1 teaspoon vegetable oil
¼ teaspoon dried whole thyme
⅛ teaspoon ground ginger
⅛ teaspoon salt
⅛ teaspoon white pepper
4 (4-ounce) skinned grouper fillets or other lean white fish
¼ cup Chablis or other dry white wine
Carrot curls (optional)
Fresh parsley sprigs (optional)

Combine apple, carrot, onion, minced parsley, lemon juice, oil, thyme, ginger, salt, and pepper in a 12- x 8- x 2-inch baking dish. Cover with wax paper, and microwave at HIGH 5 to 6 minutes or until vegetables are crisp-tender.

Tuck fillet ends under to make a thicker portion of fish. On top side, make a diagonal slit from lower left to upper right, cutting almost through fillet. Stuff each fillet with ¼ cup vegetable mixture.

Arrange fillets, filling side up, in an 8-inch square baking dish; add wine, and cover with wax paper. Microwave at HIGH 6 minutes, giving dish a half-turn after 3 minutes. Cook until fish fillets turn opaque; let stand, covered, 3 to 5 minutes. Fish is done if it flakes easily when tested with a fork.

Transfer fish to a serving dish. If desired, garnish with carrot curls and fresh parsley sprigs. Yield: 4 servings (140 calories per serving).

☐ *17.6 grams protein, 1.8 grams fat, 13.2 grams carbohydrate, 49 milligrams cholesterol, 141 milligrams sodium, and 41 milligrams calcium.*
Sara A. McCullough
Broaddus, Texas

Big Show, Little Trouble

Friends will jockey for position when you serve this easy cake. Whipped cream flavored with Kahlúa coats layers of microwaved chocolate cake and coffee ice cream. The cake is quick to assemble, and you can keep the necessary ingredients on hand to use whenever you need them.

ICE CREAM CAKE FOR GROWN-UPS

1 (8.6-ounce) package microwave chocolate cake mix with pan
1 pint coffee ice cream
1 cup whipping cream
2 tablespoons Kahlúa or other coffee-flavored liqueur
¼ cup chopped pecans
½ cup commercial chocolate sauce (optional)

Prepare cake according to package directions. Cool completely. Split the cake horizontally, making 2 layers; set aside.

Soften ice cream by microwaving at MEDIUM LOW (30% power) 30 to 45 seconds.

Place one layer of cake on cake plate, and spread with softened ice cream; freeze. Top with second cake layer. Cover and freeze 8 hours.

Beat whipping cream until foamy; gradually add 2 tablespoons Kahlúa, beating until stiff peaks form. Frost sides and top of cake with 1 cup whipped cream. Pipe remaining whipped cream decoratively around top and base of cake.

Place pecans in a pieplate; microwave at HIGH 3 minutes, stirring once. Cool. Sprinkle pecans on top of cake. Serve immediately with chocolate sauce, if desired, or freeze, thawing 15 minutes before serving. Yield: one 8-inch cake.

Quick! Make A Salad

If the thought of stewing chicken for a salad causes you to rethink your menu plan, take heart. Our recipe for Special Chicken Salad offers a quick method of microwaving the meat that takes only 10 minutes.

The same ease and good nutrition are found in our other microwave salad recipes.

SPECIAL CHICKEN SALAD

4 chicken breast halves, skinned
2 tablespoons chopped onion
¼ cup water
1 lemon
¾ cup mayonnaise
1 teaspoon dry mustard
½ teaspoon curry powder
1 (2-ounce) package slivered almonds
1 (11-ounce) can mandarin oranges, drained
1 cup seedless grapes, halved
Bibb lettuce leaves

Arrange chicken in a 2-quart shallow casserole, placing thickest portions to outside of dish; sprinkle with onion. Add water; cover with heavy-duty plastic wrap. Microwave at HIGH 5 minutes. Give dish a half-turn, and microwave at HIGH 4 to 5 minutes or until chicken is done; drain. Let cool. Remove chicken from bone, and chop.

Microwave lemon at HIGH 30 seconds. Cut lemon in half, and juice; discard seeds. Combine lemon juice, mayonnaise, mustard, and curry powder; stir well.

Spread almonds in a glass pieplate. Microwave at HIGH 3 minutes, stirring once. Set aside 2 tablespoons almonds. Combine chicken, oranges, grapes, and remaining almonds. Add mayonnaise mixture; toss. Arrange on lettuce leaves; sprinkle with reserved 2 tablespoons almonds. Yield: 4 to 6 servings.

ARTICHOKES WITH ORZO SALAD

1 quart water
¼ teaspoon salt
½ cup orzo, uncooked
1 carrot, diced
2 green onions, sliced
8 pitted ripe olives
1 tablespoon chopped fresh basil
⅛ teaspoon salt
⅛ teaspoon pepper
2 tablespoons Creamy Lemon Dressing
4 artichokes
Lemon wedge
½ cup water
2 teaspoons lemon juice
2 teaspoons vegetable oil
Ripe olive slices (optional)
Chopped fresh parsley

Combine 1 quart water and ¼ teaspoon salt in a 2½-quart casserole. Cover with heavy-duty plastic wrap; fold back a small edge of wrap to allow steam to escape. Microwave at HIGH 6 minutes or until water boils. Add orzo; cover and microwave at HIGH 6 minutes. Stir well. Cover and microwave at HIGH 1 to 2 minutes or until orzo is tender; drain. Rinse with cold water; drain.

Combine orzo and next 7 ingredients, mixing well. Cover and chill.

Wash artichokes by plunging them up and down in cold water. Cut off stem ends, and trim about ½ inch from top of each artichoke. Remove any loose bottom leaves. With scissors, trim away about one-fourth of each outer leaf. Rub top and edge of leaves with a lemon wedge to prevent discoloration.

Place artichokes upside down in a 2½-quart casserole. Add ½ cup water, lemon juice, and oil. Cover and microwave at HIGH 14 minutes, giving dish a quarter-turn halfway through cooking time. Let stand, covered, 5 minutes. Plunge into cold water. Drain. Spread leaves apart; scrape out fuzzy thistle center (choke) with a spoon. Spoon mixture into cavities. Garnish with olive slices, if desired. Serve with remaining Creamy Lemon Dressing. Sprinkle with parsley. Yield: 4 servings.

Creamy Lemon Dressing

2 tablespoons lemon juice
2 tablespoons red wine vinegar
1 tablespoon brown mustard
¼ teaspoon garlic powder
1 egg yolk
½ cup vegetable oil

Combine first 4 ingredients in bowl of a food processor fitted with a steel blade. Process 15 seconds; add egg yolk, and process 15 seconds. With processor running, gradually add oil in a slow, steady stream, mixing just until well blended. Yield: ⅔ cup.

Tip: *Heavy-duty plastic wrap holds in steam and heat and is recommended for microwaving vegetables and fish. It is also useful for bowls that have no covers. Place the plastic wrap loosely over the dish, and fold back one corner to prevent excessive steam buildup.*

GERMAN-STYLE
POTATO SALAD

5 new potatoes (about 1½
  pounds), unpeeled and sliced
¼ cup water
6 slices bacon
½ cup chopped onion
2 tablespoons all-purpose flour
1 tablespoon plus 1 teaspoon
  sugar
¾ teaspoon salt
½ teaspoon celery seeds
½ teaspoon pepper
¾ cup water
¼ cup vinegar

Place potatoes in a 2-quart casserole, and add ¼ cup water. Cover with heavy-duty plastic wrap, and microwave at HIGH 7 to 8 minutes, stirring once. Let stand, covered, 5 minutes. Drain, and set aside.

Place bacon on a rack in a 12- x 8- x 2-inch baking dish. Cover with paper towels. Microwave at HIGH 5 to 7 minutes or until bacon is crisp. Drain bacon, reserving drippings in dish; crumble bacon, and set aside.

Add onion to bacon drippings; microwave at HIGH 1 to 2 minutes or until onion is transparent. Stir in flour and next 4 ingredients. Microwave at HIGH 1½ minutes, and stir until smooth. Add ¾ cup water and vinegar to onion mixture, mixing well. Microwave at HIGH 3 to 4 minutes, stirring after 2 minutes. Add potatoes and half of crumbled bacon, mixing well. Garnish with remaining bacon. Serve warm. Yield: 6 servings.   *Anne McCrory*
             Birmingham, Alabama

Tip: *Reheat single servings in a microwave or toaster oven; these use less energy than a standard range.*

Microwave
Cookware Basics

If you've just bought a microwave oven, you'll be happy to know that you won't have to restock your kitchen with cookware. Probably much of what you already have is ideal for using in the microwave. Paper towels, plastic foam plates, straw plates or baskets (for warming), wooden cutting boards, most stoneware, and heat-resistant glass casseroles and bowls are safe.

When choosing microwave cookware, remember that round dishes provide more even microwave cooking. And glass cookware uses two methods of cooking; once the microwaves heat the food in the dish, the glass becomes hot and the heat retained in the container provides additional cooking. The hard plastic-type microwave cookware will not hold as much heat as glass.

Many manufacturers are producing cookware made of a variety of materials that is safe for both conventional and microwave cooking. To be certain, check the labels for any cooking recommendations.

Basic Cookware

If you plan to use your microwave for more than just reheating and defrosting, there are a few pieces of cookware that most microwave cooks find invaluable. These are the ones our home economists consider basic.
- 1-, 2-, and 4-quart casseroles with covers
- 2- and 4-cup glass measures
- 8-inch round glass cake dish or 9-inch round glass pieplate
- Six 4-ounce custard cups
- Four to six 10-ounce custard cups
- Bacon or roasting rack
- 2-quart mixing bowl with handle
- 12-inch round glass plate
- 1½- or 2-cup microwave-safe storage containers
- 12- x 8-inch oval or rectangular baking dish

Experienced microwave cooks also enjoy the following microwave equipment: temperature probe, browning tray, microwave cakepans, turntable, popcorn popper, steamer, muffin pan, 2-quart saucepan with lid, teapot, Bundt cake pan, divided plate with cover, and wooden whisk. (A wooden whisk saves time when microwaving sauces; you can leave the whisk in the sauce while it cooks.)

Items with more than one use are particularly economical and helpful with storage space. For example, in addition to baking muffins in a muffin pan, you can use it as a container for microwaving apples or potatoes. A bacon rack can be used to cook chicken pieces, fish, or corn on the cob, as well as bacon.

How To Tell If It's
Microwave Safe

Today most cookware and dinnerware is marked if it's suitable for the microwave. If you have some older unmarked cookware, you can try this simple test to determine if you can use it for microwave cooking.

Fill a microwave-safe glass measure or bowl with ½ cup water. Place the dish to be tested in the microwave oven, and place the container of water in the dish or beside it. Microwave at HIGH for 1 minute. If the water is hot and the dish is cool, the dish is microwave safe. If the dish is warm, it's best not to use it for microwaving.

You may find that some plastic containers that are not marked as microwave safe seem to be fine for reheating foods. Be careful about using these, however; food with a high fat or sugar content may cause them to melt during microwaving.

Desserts Shaped Like Shells

When you present these shell-shaped desserts, your guests will recognize some of the flavors, such as strawberry shortcake and lemon pie, but the looks will surprise them.

Each of these recipes is baked or molded in fluted, 4- to 5-inch baking shells typically used for seafood dishes. If you don't own a set of these, you can find them in most large department stores, kitchen specialty shops, or mail-order catalogs that specialize in kitchenware. They're sturdy, ovenproof, and so versatile you'll use them often.

Grease the baking shells as directed in the recipe before pouring in cakelike batters. Don't grease the shells when shaping pastry dough around them because this dough contains a larger proportion of fat.

LEMON TART SHELLS

1½ cups all-purpose flour
2 tablespoons sugar
½ cup butter or margarine
1 egg, beaten
1 tablespoon water
2 cups sugar
1½ teaspoons grated lemon rind
½ cup lemon juice
1 cup butter or margarine
4 eggs, beaten
Lemon slices (optional)
Sweetened whipped cream

Combine flour and 2 tablespoons sugar; cut in ½ cup butter with a pastry blender until mixture resembles coarse meal. Stir 1 beaten egg into mixture. Sprinkle water evenly over surface; stir with a fork until dry ingredients are moistened. Shape dough into a ball; cover and chill.

Divide dough into 8 equal portions. Roll each portion of dough to ⅛-inch thickness on a lightly floured surface. Press each portion of dough firmly onto back of an ungreased 4- to 5-inch baking shell. Trim dough ⅛ inch smaller than shells on all sides.

Arrange shells on baking sheets, dough side up. Prick pastry generously with a fork. Bake at 400° for 14 minutes or until lightly browned. Immediately remove pastry from shells, and let cool on wire racks.

Combine 2 cups sugar and next 3 ingredients in a heavy saucepan. Cook over low heat, stirring constantly, until butter melts.

Gradually stir about one-fourth of hot mixture into 4 beaten eggs; add to remaining hot mixture, stirring constantly. Cook over low heat, stirring constantly, 5 minutes or until thickened. Cover and chill mixture at least 2 hours.

To serve, spoon lemon mixture into pastry shells; garnish with lemon slices, if desired, and top with a dollop of sweetened whipped cream. Yield: 8 servings.

BROWNIE ICE CREAM SANDWICH SHELLS

½ cup water
¼ cup butter or margarine
¼ cup cocoa
¼ cup vegetable oil
1 cup all-purpose flour
1 cup sugar
⅛ teaspoon salt
¼ cup buttermilk
1 egg, beaten
½ teaspoon baking soda
½ teaspoon vanilla extract
Mint or vanilla ice cream
Powdered sugar
Mint sprigs (optional)

Combine water, butter, and cocoa in a small saucepan; cook over medium heat, stirring frequently, until mixture comes to a boil. Remove from heat. Stir in vegetable oil.

Combine flour, 1 cup sugar, and salt in a large bowl; add cocoa mixture, stirring well. Stir in buttermilk, egg, soda, and vanilla.

Grease eight 4- to 5-inch baking shells. Set baking shells on top of muffin pans, arranging shells so that they sit level. Spoon batter evenly into prepared shells to within ¼ inch of edges. Bake at 350° for 15 to 20 minutes or until a wooden pick inserted in center comes out clean. Immediately invert cakes onto a wire rack, and let cool.

To prepare sandwiches, slice shells in half horizontally. Spoon ice cream onto cut surface of smooth-sided shells; top with ridged shells. Sprinkle lightly with powdered sugar. Garnish with mint sprigs, if desired. Serve sandwiches immediately. Yield: 8 servings.

CHOCOLATE SHELLS WITH KAHLÚA CREAM

1 (12-ounce) package semisweet chocolate morsels
2 teaspoons shortening
2 cups whipping cream
¼ to ⅓ cup sifted powdered sugar
2 tablespoons cocoa
2 tablespoons Kahlúa
1 teaspoon vanilla extract
Chocolate curls (optional)

Combine chocolate morsels and shortening in top of a double boiler; bring water to a boil. Stir until chocolate melts and mixture is smooth. Let cool until mixture begins to thicken.

Tear off eight (8-inch) sheets of plastic wrap. Stretch a sheet of plastic wrap over back of each 4- to 5-inch baking shell, twisting ends of wrap together and taping to bowl side of shell.

Using a narrow spatula, spread slightly thickened chocolate over back of each shell, leaving a ¼-inch margin. Place shells on a baking sheet, chocolate side up, and chill until chocolate is firm. Carefully untape plastic wrap, and peel plastic wrap from chocolate. (Keep shells refrigerated until ready to serve.)

Combine whipping cream and next 4 ingredients in a large mixing bowl; beat at medium speed of an electric mixer until soft peaks form.

To serve, pipe or spoon cream mixture into chocolate shells, and garnish each with chocolate curls, if desired. Yield: 8 servings.

STRAWBERRY SHORTCAKE SHELLS

5 egg whites
1½ teaspoons cream of tartar
¼ teaspoon salt
½ cup sugar
½ cup sifted cake flour
¾ teaspoon vanilla extract
Vegetable cooking spray
Brandied Strawberry Sauce
Sweetened whipped cream
8 strawberry fans

Beat egg whites (at room temperature) until foamy. Add cream of tartar and salt; beat until soft peaks form. Add sugar, 2 tablespoons at a time, beating until stiff peaks form. Sprinkle half of flour at a time over egg white mixture, and fold in carefully. Fold in vanilla.

Coat eight 4- to 5-inch baking shells with cooking spray. Set baking shells on top of muffin pans, arranging the shells so that they sit level. Spoon batter evenly into prepared shells to within ¼ inch of edges. Bake at 375° for 9 to 12 minutes or until cake springs back when lightly touched. Immediately invert cakes onto a baking sheet. If desired, broil 4 inches from heat 30 seconds or until cakes are lightly browned.

To serve, spoon about 3 tablespoons Brandied Strawberry Sauce onto each of 8 dessert plates, and spread thinly with the back of a spoon. Place cake shells, smooth side down, on sauce on dessert plates, and top shells with whipped cream and strawberry fans. Yield: 8 servings.

Brandied Strawberry Sauce

2 (10-ounce) packages frozen
   sliced strawberries, thawed
2 teaspoons cornstarch
⅓ cup red currant jelly
2 tablespoons brandy

Drain strawberries, reserving ½ cup juice; reserve remaining juice for other uses. Press strawberries through a sieve; discard pulp, and set sieved strawberries aside.

Combine cornstarch and ½ cup reserved strawberry juice, stirring until smooth. Set aside.

Melt jelly over low heat in a heavy saucepan; add cornstarch mixture. Cook over medium heat, stirring constantly, until mixture comes to a boil. Boil 1 minute. Stir in sieved strawberries and brandy. Yield: 1⅓ cups.

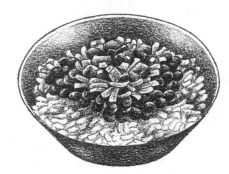

Main Dishes, Minus The Meat

Eating meatless entrées doesn't necessarily mean settling for less. Each of these recipes offers complete proteins necessary for the building of healthy muscles and tissues. Complete proteins are found in animal products, such as eggs, milk, and cheese, and all kinds of meat. Incomplete proteins from plant sources—such as beans, lentils, rice, and other grains—are made complete when they're combined.

CUBAN BLACK BEANS

1 pound dried black beans
1 large onion, chopped
1 green pepper, chopped
6 cloves garlic, minced
1 (4-ounce) jar diced pimiento,
   drained
¼ cup olive oil
5 cups water
1 (6-ounce) can tomato paste
1 tablespoon vinegar
2 teaspoons salt
1 teaspoon sugar
1 teaspoon pepper
Hot cooked rice
Shredded Cheddar cheese
Chopped tomatoes
Chopped green onions

Sort and wash beans; place in a large Dutch oven. Cover with water 2 inches above beans; let soak 8 hours. Drain well.

Sauté onion, green pepper, garlic, and pimiento in olive oil until tender.

Combine beans, sautéed vegetables, 5 cups water, and next 5 ingredients; bring to a boil. Cover, reduce heat, and simmer 1½ hours or until beans are tender, stirring occasionally. Serve over rice. Garnish with cheese, tomatoes, and green onions. Yield: about 8 servings.

Susan Simonson
Greenville, South Carolina

LASAGNA FLORENTINE

2 chicken-flavored bouillon cubes
¼ cup water
½ cup butter or margarine
⅓ cup all-purpose flour
⅛ teaspoon salt
⅛ teaspoon dried Italian
   seasoning
Dash of garlic powder
Dash of ground nutmeg
¼ teaspoon white pepper
¼ teaspoon lemon-pepper
   seasoning
1 cup whipping cream
1 cup half-and-half
¾ cup chopped onion
1 tablespoon butter or margarine,
   melted
2 (10-ounce) packages frozen
   chopped spinach, thawed
1 egg, slightly beaten
1½ cups (6 ounces) shredded
   mozzarella cheese
1 (8-ounce) carton commercial
   sour cream
9 lasagna noodles
½ teaspoon salt
½ cup grated Parmesan cheese

Dissolve bouillon cubes in water; set aside. Melt ½ cup butter in a heavy saucepan over low heat. Add flour and next 6 ingredients, stirring until smooth. Cook 1 minute, stirring constantly. Gradually add bouillon mixture, cream, and half-and-half; cook over medium heat, stirring until thickened and bubbly. Remove from heat; set aside.

Sauté onion in 1 tablespoon butter until tender. Drain spinach well by pressing between layers of paper towels. Combine spinach, sautéed onion, egg, mozzarella cheese, and sour cream; stir well, and set mixture aside.

Cook lasagna noodles according to package directions, adding ½ teaspoon salt; drain.

Layer 3 noodles in a lightly greased 12- x 8- x 2-inch baking dish. Spread with spinach mixture; repeat with 3 noodles. Spread with half of cream sauce; repeat with remaining noodles. Spread with remaining cream sauce; sprinkle with Parmesan cheese. Bake, uncovered, at 350° for 30 minutes. Yield: 6 servings.   *Ann Hall Harden*
Pleasant Garden, North Carolina

PASTA STUFFED WITH FIVE CHEESES

8 ounces jumbo pasta shells (about 32 shells)
1 (8-ounce) package cream cheese, softened
1 cup low-fat cottage cheese
1 cup (4 ounces) shredded mozzarella cheese
1 egg, slightly beaten
¼ cup grated Parmesan and Romano cheese topping
2 tablespoons chopped fresh parsley
2 teaspoons dried whole basil
½ teaspoon dried whole oregano
½ teaspoon dried whole thyme
⅛ teaspoon lemon rind
Pinch of ground nutmeg
1 (14½-ounce) can stewed tomatoes, undrained
1 (8-ounce) can tomato sauce
1 cup white wine
1 (8-ounce) can mushroom stems and pieces, drained
1 teaspoon dried whole oregano
1 teaspoon dried whole thyme
1 clove garlic, minced
Parsley sprigs (optional)

Cook pasta shells according to package directions; drain and set aside.

Combine cream cheese and next 10 ingredients, mixing well. Stuff cheese mixture into shells.

Arrange stuffed shells in a lightly greased 12- x 8- x 2-inch baking dish. Cover and bake at 350° for 25 minutes or until thoroughly heated.

Puree stewed tomatoes; combine tomatoes, tomato sauce, wine, mushrooms, 1 teaspoon oregano, 1 teaspoon thyme, and garlic in a saucepan. Simmer 25 minutes or until sauce is thickened. Spoon sauce onto plates; arrange pasta shells on sauce. Garnish with parsley sprigs, if desired. Yield: 6 servings.
Margaret Cotton
Franklin, Virginia

LENTIL TACOS

1½ cups dried lentils
3½ to 5 cups water
1 bay leaf
1 stalk celery
1 clove garlic, crushed
½ teaspoon salt
⅛ teaspoon dried whole thyme
1½ cups tomato sauce
1 tablespoon taco seasoning mix
8 commercial taco shells
1½ cups shredded lettuce
1 medium onion, diced
1 cup (4 ounces) shredded Cheddar cheese
1 large tomato, chopped

Sort and wash lentils. Combine lentils, 3½ cups water, and next 5 ingredients in a Dutch oven. Bring to a boil; cover, reduce heat, and simmer 1½ hours, stirring occasionally. Add additional water, if necessary. Remove and discard bay leaf and celery.

Combine tomato sauce and taco seasoning in a small bowl; stir well.

Heat taco shells according to package directions. Spoon lentils into each shell; top with lettuce, onion, cheese, tomato, and sauce. Yield: 4 servings.   *Erma Jackson*
Huntsville, Alabama

MUSHROOMS AND EGGS IN PATTY SHELLS

1 (10-ounce) package frozen patty shells
½ pound fresh mushrooms, sliced
2 tablespoons chopped onion
2 tablespoons butter or margarine, melted
¼ cup butter or margarine
3 tablespoons all-purpose flour
1½ cups milk
¾ teaspoon salt
⅛ teaspoon red pepper
3 tablespoons dry white wine
5 hard-cooked eggs, chopped
1 hard-cooked egg, cut into 6 wedges (optional)

Bake patty shells according to package directions; set aside.

Sauté mushrooms and onion in 2 tablespoons butter 4 to 5 minutes; remove from skillet. Set aside.

Melt ¼ cup butter in skillet over low heat; add flour, and stir until smooth. Cook 1 minute, stirring constantly. Gradually add milk; cook over medium heat, stirring constantly, until thickened and bubbly. Stir in salt, pepper, and wine. Add vegetables and chopped eggs; stir. Spoon into patty shells; garnish with hard-cooked egg wedges, if desired. Yield: 6 servings.
Susan Kamer Shinaberry
Charleston, West Virginia

Tip: *After purchasing fresh mushrooms, refrigerate immediately in their original container. If mushrooms are in a plastic bag, make a few holes in the bag for ventilation.*

CHEDDAR-LEEK QUICHE

Pastry for a 10-inch pie
4 leeks
2 tablespoons butter or
  margarine, melted
4 cups (16 ounces) shredded
  Cheddar cheese
4 eggs, well beaten
2 cups half-and-half
½ teaspoon salt
⅛ teaspoon pepper
1¼ teaspoons Worcestershire
  sauce
Leek strips (optional)
Tomato rose (optional)

Line a 10-inch pieplate with pastry; trim edges.

Trim leeks to 3 inches in length, reserving remainder for other uses. Wash leeks, and cut in half; thinly slice. Sauté leeks in butter until crisp-tender; drain. Spoon leeks into pastry shell; sprinkle cheese over leeks. Combine eggs and next 4 ingredients, mixing well; pour into pastry shell. Bake at 375° for 50 minutes or until set. Let stand 15 minutes. If desired, garnish with leek strips and a tomato rose. Yield: one 10-inch quiche.
Harriet St. Amant
Vienna, Virginia

These Pies Feature Vegetables

To make the most of summer's bounty of fresh vegetables, try these pies and quiches. They offer delicious ways to serve asparagus, tomatoes, peppers, zucchini, and eggplant.

To save time, substitute a commercial pie shell for homemade pastry. If using a frozen pie shell, be sure to select one labeled "deep-dish" because a regular 9-inch frozen pie shell is more shallow than homemade pastry baked in a standard pieplate. A ready-made, folded piecrust from the dairy case can be used for Asparagus-Tomato Quiche, baked in a 10-inch quiche dish.

RATATOUILLE PIE

Pastry for 9-inch deep-dish pie
½ pound mild Italian link
  sausage
2 cups peeled, diced eggplant
1 cup sliced zucchini
1 cup peeled, diced tomato
½ cup green pepper strips
¼ cup diced onion
1 cup (4 ounces) shredded
  mozzarella cheese
½ teaspoon dried whole oregano
½ teaspoon dried whole basil
½ teaspoon dried Italian
  seasoning
½ teaspoon dried parsley flakes
3 eggs, beaten
⅓ cup milk
Tomato rose (optional)
Parsley (optional)

Line a 9-inch quiche dish with pastry. Trim excess pastry around edges. Prick bottom and sides of pastry with a fork. Bake at 400° for 3 minutes; remove from oven, and gently prick with a fork. Bake 5 minutes.

Remove casing from sausage; cook sausage until browned, stirring to crumble. Drain well. Combine sausage and next 10 ingredients; spoon into prepared pastry.

Combine eggs and milk, stirring well. Pour into pastry shell. Bake at 325° for 50 minutes or until set. Let stand 10 minutes before serving. If desired, garnish with tomato rose and parsley. Yield: one 9-inch pie.
Mrs. James A. Tuthill
Virginia Beach, Virginia

TOMATO PIE

3 medium tomatoes, peeled and
  sliced
Pastry (recipe follows)
¾ cup mayonnaise
1 cup (4 ounces) shredded
  Cheddar cheese
1 (4-ounce) can sliced
  mushrooms, drained
1 tablespoon chopped onion
1 tablespoon chopped green
  pepper

Arrange half of tomato slices in pastry shell.

Combine mayonnaise, cheese, mushrooms, onion, and green pepper, stirring well. Spread half of mixture over tomato slices. Repeat layers with remaining tomatoes and mayonnaise mixture. Bake at 350° for 30 to 35 minutes. Yield: one 9-inch pie.

Pastry

1¼ cups all-purpose flour
2 teaspoons baking powder
½ teaspoon salt
½ teaspoon dried whole basil
½ cup shortening
½ cup commercial sour cream

Combine first 4 ingredients; cut in shortening with pastry blender until mixture resembles coarse meal. Add sour cream; stir with a fork. Shape into a ball. Chill.

Roll pastry to ⅛-inch thickness on a lightly floured surface. Place in a 9-inch pieplate; trim off excess pastry along edges. Fold edges under, and flute. Yield: one 9-inch pastry shell.
Elinor Zollinger
Louisville, Kentucky

ASPARAGUS-TOMATO QUICHE

Pastry for 10-inch pie
1 pound fresh asparagus spears,
  divided
2 cups (8 ounces) shredded Swiss
  cheese
4 eggs, beaten
1½ cups half-and-half
3 tablespoons all-purpose flour
1 teaspoon paprika
1 teaspoon salt
½ teaspoon dry mustard
1 medium tomato
1 tablespoon butter or margarine,
  melted

Line a 10-inch quiche dish with pastry. Trim excess pastry around edges. Prick bottom and sides of pastry with a fork. Bake at 400° for 3 minutes; remove from oven, and gently prick with a fork. Bake an additional 5 minutes.

Snap off tough ends of asparagus. Remove scales from stalks with a knife or vegetable peeler. Set aside 6 spears. Cut remaining asparagus into 1-inch pieces; place in pastry shell. Sprinkle cheese over asparagus.

Combine eggs and next 5 ingredients in a bowl, stirring well; pour over cheese in pastry shell. Bake at 375° for 25 minutes. Remove from oven. Cut tomato into 3 slices, and cut slices in half. Arrange reserved asparagus and tomato in a wagon-wheel pattern on quiche. Brush tomato and asparagus with butter. Bake quiche an additional 30 minutes or until set. Let stand 10 minutes before serving. Yield: one 10-inch quiche. *Clare Hall Smith* *Bethesda, Maryland*

COOKING LIGHT®

Light Meals In A Skillet

Skillet meals are known for being quick to make, but often they're laden with cholesterol, fat, and calories. They don't have to be.

The ingredients determine the cholesterol, fat, and calorie content. If lean meat, poultry, or fish is used, with complex carbohydrates such as rice, pasta, and corn added, the result will be a one-dish meal that's healthy, quick to prepare, and filling.

The nutritional value of these meals can be increased further by cooking them in a cast-iron skillet. Iron from the skillet combines with the food as it cooks and is absorbed by the body.

MEXICAN BEEF-AND-RICE DINNER

1 pound ground chuck
1 (14½-ounce) can Mexican-style tomatoes
1 (6-ounce) can tomato juice
1 cup water
½ teaspoon chili powder
¼ teaspoon salt
¼ teaspoon dried whole oregano
¼ teaspoon freshly ground pepper
1 small clove garlic, minced
1 (10-ounce) package frozen whole kernel corn
1¾ cups uncooked instant rice

Cook ground chuck in a large non-stick skillet over medium heat until browned, stirring to crumble. Drain meat in a colander, and pat dry with paper towels. Wipe pan drippings from skillet with a paper towel.

Combine tomatoes and next 8 ingredients in skillet; bring to a boil, and cook 2 minutes. Stir in meat and rice. Cover and remove from heat; let stand 5 minutes. Fluff with a fork before serving. Yield: 4 servings (451 calories per ½-cup serving).

□ *34.7 grams protein, 9.3 grams fat, 58 grams carbohydrate, 86 milligrams cholesterol, 623 milligrams sodium, and 54 milligrams calcium.*

PORK-AND-NOODLES SKILLET DINNER

Vegetable cooking spray
1½ pounds boneless lean pork, cut into bite-size pieces
1 cup sliced carrot
1 cup (½-inch) celery slices
½ cup chopped onion
2 (8-ounce) cans no-salt-added tomato sauce
2 cups water
⅓ cup catsup
½ cup sliced fresh mushrooms
½ teaspoon salt
¼ teaspoon garlic powder
¼ teaspoon dried whole basil
¼ teaspoon pepper
4 ounces uncooked noodles

Coat a large skillet with cooking spray; place over medium-high heat

until hot. Add pork, and cook until browned. Drain pork in a colander, and pat dry with paper towels. Wipe pan drippings from skillet with a paper towel.

Coat skillet with cooking spray; place over medium-high heat until hot. Add carrot, celery, and onion; sauté until tender. Stir in tomato sauce and remaining ingredients.

Bring to a boil; cover, reduce heat, and simmer 30 minutes, stirring occasionally. Yield: 4 servings (400 calories per 1½-cup serving).

□ *30.6 grams protein, 13 grams fat, 40.3 grams carbohydrate, 104 milligrams cholesterol, 662 milligrams sodium, and 64 milligrams calcium.*

SKILLET FISH DINNER

2 teaspoons vegetable oil
¾ cup onion slices
1 large clove garlic, crushed
2⅔ cups peeled tomato wedges
1 (16-ounce) package frozen fish fillets, thawed
3 medium ears corn
12 Greek olives
1 teaspoon dried whole dillweed
¼ teaspoon pepper

Heat oil in a large skillet over medium heat. Add onion and garlic; sauté until onion is crisp-tender. Add tomatoes; cover, reduce heat, and simmer about 3 minutes. Cut fish into 4 equal portions; place on vegetables. Cut each ear of corn into 4 pieces; add to vegetables. Add olives, dillweed, and pepper; cover and simmer 10 to 15 minutes or until fish turns opaque. Fish is done when it flakes easily when tested with a fork. Yield: 4 servings (237 calories per 1 piece fish, 3 olives, 3 pieces corn, and ¼ cup vegetable mixture).

□ *22.3 grams protein, 7.9 grams fat, 22 grams carbohydrate, 0 milligrams cholesterol, 451 milligrams sodium, and 43 milligrams calcium.*

Ruby Kirkes *Tuskahoma, Oklahoma*

TURKEY-ASPARAGUS PILAF

2 cups water
2 tablespoons reduced-calorie
  margarine
1 (6¾-ounce) package instant
  long-grain and wild rice
1 (10-ounce) package frozen
  asparagus
3 cups chopped cooked turkey
⅓ cup no-salt-added chicken
  broth
2 tablespoons dry sherry
2 tablespoons white wine vinegar
3 tablespoons sliced almonds,
  toasted

Combine water, margarine, and rice seasoning packet in a skillet. Bring to a boil; stir in rice. Cover; remove from heat. Let stand 7 minutes. Cook asparagus according to package directions (omitting fat and salt); drain. Cut spears into thirds. Add asparagus, turkey, and next 3 ingredients to rice; toss. Sprinkle with almonds. Yield: 4 servings (442 calories per 1¾-cup serving).

☐ *40.6 grams protein, 12 grams fat, 41.5 grams carbohydrate, 86 milligrams cholesterol, 932 milligrams sodium, and 76 milligrams calcium.*
Margaret Stallings
Ardmore, Oklahoma

CHICKEN-AND-SAUSAGE JAMBALAYA

1 pound boned, skinned chicken
  breasts
¼ teaspoon pepper
¼ teaspoon red pepper
3 tablespoons oil-free Italian
  dressing
12 ounces turkey sausage
Vegetable cooking spray
2¼ cups chopped celery
2½ cups chopped onion
1¾ cups sliced green onions
1 cup chopped green pepper
2 cloves garlic, minced
2 chicken-flavored bouillon cubes
3 cups water
½ teaspoon browning-and-
  seasoning sauce
1½ cups uncooked long-grain rice

Cut chicken into bite-size pieces; season with pepper and red pepper. Add dressing to an electric skillet; heat to medium high (325°) 1 minute. Add chicken, and cook 3 minutes, stirring often. Remove chicken.

Cook sausage in skillet over medium heat until browned, stirring to crumble meat. Drain in a colander, and pat dry with paper towels.

Coat a large nonstick skillet with cooking spray; place over medium-high heat. Add celery and next 4 ingredients; sauté until vegetables are crisp-tender. Add chicken; cover, reduce heat, and simmer 15 minutes.

Dissolve bouillon cubes in water; add browning-and-seasoning sauce. Pour into skillet, and bring to a boil. Stir in rice and sausage; cover, reduce heat, and simmer 20 minutes or until rice is tender. Yield: 6 servings (400 calories per 1⅔-cup serving).

☐ *23.8 grams protein, 12.1 grams fat, 48.6 grams carbohydrate, 57 milligrams cholesterol, 778 milligrams sodium, and 120 milligrams calcium.*
Celia Pope
Baton Rouge, Louisiana

SPICY CHICKEN AND RICE

3½ cups water
2 teaspoons chicken-flavored
  bouillon granules
1½ cups uncooked brown rice
6 (4-ounce) boned, skinned
  chicken breast halves
1 (28-ounce) can whole tomatoes,
  undrained and chopped
1 cup sliced green pepper
1 cup chopped onion
2 cloves garlic, minced
2 tablespoons chopped fresh
  green chile pepper
1 teaspoon chili powder
¼ teaspoon salt
½ teaspoon pepper
¼ teaspoon ground saffron
1 bay leaf
1 cup frozen English peas,
  thawed

Combine water and bouillon granules in an electric skillet; bring to a boil over high heat. Add rice, and return to a boil. Cover, reduce heat, and simmer 30 minutes.

Cut chicken into bite-size pieces, and add to skillet. Add tomatoes and next 9 ingredients. Stir well, and cook 20 minutes or until rice is tender. Remove bay leaf. Add peas; toss gently. Yield: 6 servings (360 calories per 1⅓-cup serving).

☐ *33.1 grams protein, 3.1 grams fat, 48.9 grams carbohydrate, 66 milligrams cholesterol, 745 milligrams sodium, and 81 milligrams calcium.*
Mrs. John W. Wood
Norman, Oklahoma

Hot Dog Recipes You'll Use Year-Round

Franks, frankfurters, and wieners all describe one thing—hot dogs. Children especially enjoy them, no matter how they are prepared.

HOT DOGGIE CASSEROLE

4 medium potatoes
¼ cup plus 2 tablespoons butter
  or margarine
½ cup chopped onion
¼ cup all-purpose flour
1½ cups milk
2 cups (8 ounces) shredded
  Cheddar cheese, divided
1 (10-ounce) package frozen
  chopped spinach
1 pound frankfurters
Parsley

Cook potatoes in boiling salted water to cover for 30 minutes or until tender. Drain and cool slightly. Peel and cut potatoes into ¼-inch slices. Set aside.

Melt butter in a heavy saucepan over low heat; add onion, and cook until tender. Add flour, stirring well. Cook 1 minute, stirring constantly. Gradually add milk; cook over medium heat, stirring constantly, until mixture is thickened and bubbly. Remove from heat; add 1½ cups cheese. Stir until smooth.

Cook spinach according to package directions; drain well, and add to cheese sauce, stirring well.

Reserve 4 frankfurters; cut remaining frankfurters into ½-inch pieces.

Place half of potatoes in a lightly greased 12- x 8- x 2-inch baking dish; top with frankfurter pieces and half of spinach mixture. Top with remaining potatoes and spinach mixture. Cut remaining 4 frankfurters lengthwise into four thin pieces, leaving one end intact. Fan frankfurters on top of casserole; cover and bake at 350° for 40 minutes. Sprinkle with remaining ½ cup cheese, and bake an additional 5 minutes. Garnish with parsley. Yield: 6 to 8 servings.
Frances Kuykendall
Columbia, Mississippi

SAUCY FRANKS

5 slices bacon, cut into small
  pieces
¼ cup diced green onions
¼ cup chopped green pepper
1 (16-ounce) package jumbo
  frankfurters, cut diagonally
  into 1-inch pieces
1 cup pineapple juice
¾ cup catsup
¼ cup water
⅛ teaspoon chili powder
Hot cooked rice (optional)

Combine bacon, green onions, and green pepper in a large skillet; cook over medium-high heat until bacon is crisp and vegetables are tender. Drain. Add frankfurters, juice, catsup, water, and chili powder. Bring

mixture to a boil; reduce heat, and simmer 15 minutes. Serve franks over rice, if desired. Yield: 4 to 6 servings.
Shelby Niven Crump
Memphis, Tennessee

FRANKARONI POTLUCK DISH

1 (8-ounce) package elbow
  macaroni
½ cup butter or margarine
1 cup chopped onion
1 cup thinly sliced celery
2 tablespoons all-purpose flour
2½ cups milk
1 pound turkey frankfurters, cut
  diagonally into 1-inch pieces
2 cups (8 ounces) shredded
  Cheddar cheese, divided
1 tablespoon prepared mustard
½ teaspoon salt
Dash of pepper

Cook macaroni according to package directions. Drain well, and set aside.

Melt butter in a heavy saucepan over low heat. Add onion and celery; cook until tender, stirring occasionally. Add flour, stirring well. Cook 1 minute, stirring constantly. Gradually add milk; cook over medium heat, stirring constantly, until thickened and bubbly. Add frankfurters, 1⅓ cups cheese, mustard, salt, and pepper; stir until cheese melts. Spoon mixture into a lightly greased 2½-quart casserole. Bake at 350° for 30 minutes; add remaining cheese, and bake an additional 5 minutes. Yield: 6 servings.
Bessie McMillan
Sparta, North Carolina

STOVE-TOP
FRANKS 'N' BEANS

1 pound jumbo frankfurters, cut
  into thirds
½ cup chopped onion
2 tablespoons butter or
  margarine, melted
2 (16-ounce) cans pork and beans
¼ cup catsup
2 tablespoons brown sugar
2 tablespoons prepared mustard
1 tablespoon Worcestershire
  sauce

Sauté frankfurters and onion in butter in a large skillet until frankfurters are lightly browned. Add pork and beans and remaining ingredients to skillet; stir gently. Cook over medium heat 10 minutes or until thoroughly heated, stirring often. Yield: 6 servings.
Myrtle Hudson
Ennis, North Carolina

Shortcut Desserts

These desserts will satisfy the most insistent sweet tooth as well as your busy schedule. They are as tempting as they are quick and easy.

EASY STRAWBERRY TRIFLE

1 (7-ounce) package jellyrolls
1 (3½-ounce) package vanilla
  instant pudding mix
1½ cups milk
3 cups frozen whipped topping,
  thawed and divided
2 cups sliced fresh strawberries
Additional strawberries (optional)

Cut each jellyroll into 3 slices; arrange cut sides of slices around sides and bottom of a 2½-quart soufflé or trifle dish. Fill in with remaining jellyroll slices.

Prepare pudding mix according to package directions, using 1½ cups milk; let stand 5 minutes. Fold in 1 cup whipped topping.

Arrange half of sliced strawberries over jellyroll slices; top with pudding mixture. Arrange remaining sliced strawberries over pudding mixture; dollop or pipe remaining whipped topping on top. Garnish with additional strawberries, if desired. Yield: about 8 servings.
Carol W. Hybart
Hybart, Alabama

CHERRIES À LA MODE

1 (21-ounce) can cherry pie filling
3 tablespoons lemon juice
2 tablespoons brown sugar
⅛ teaspoon salt
Vanilla ice cream
Commercial pound cake slices

Combine first 4 ingredients in a small saucepan; cook over medium heat 3 minutes or until mixture is thoroughly heated.

To serve, scoop ice cream onto cake slices; top with sauce. Yield: 8 to 10 servings.
Gwen Louer
Roswell, Georgia

PINEAPPLE 'N' CREAM

1 medium-size fresh pineapple
1 (8-ounce) carton commercial
   sour cream
2 tablespoons apricot preserves
¼ cup flaked coconut, toasted
2 tablespoons chopped pecans,
   toasted

Peel and core pineapple; cut pulp into bite-size pieces. Spoon into individual compotes.

Combine sour cream and preserves; stir well. Spoon over pineapple. Sprinkle with coconut and pecans. Yield: 6 servings.
Mrs. R. D. Walker
Garland, Texas

PINK LEMONADE
ICE CREAM LOAF

1 (8-ounce) loaf angel food cake
1 quart vanilla ice cream,
   softened
1 (6-ounce) can frozen pink
   lemonade concentrate,
   unthawed
1 cup whipping cream
3 tablespoons powdered sugar
1 pint fresh strawberries, sliced
Additional fresh strawberries
   (optional)
Fresh mint (optional)

Slice cake horizontally into 3 layers; set aside. Combine ice cream and frozen lemonade concentrate; swirl gently. Spread half of ice cream mixture on bottom layer of cake. Top with second cake layer, and spread with remaining ice cream mixture. Place the third layer over ice cream, and freeze loaf 30 minutes.

Beat whipping cream until foamy; gradually add powdered sugar, beating until soft peaks form.

Frost top and sides of cake with whipped cream. Freeze until firm. Slice cake, and serve with sliced strawberries; if desired, garnish with additional strawberries and mint. Yield: 10 servings.

Note: Two cups frozen whipped topping, thawed, may be substituted for whipped cream.
Mrs. Robert L. Scofield
Clarksville, Tennessee

CARAMEL SURPRISE

1 quart vanilla ice cream
4 (1⅛-ounce) English
   toffee-flavored candy bars,
   frozen and crushed
¼ cup plus 2 tablespoons Kahlúa
   or other coffee-flavored liqueur

Spoon alternate layers of ice cream and crushed candy into 6 parfait glasses. Top each with 1 tablespoon Kahlúa. Yield: 6 servings.
Curt Treloar
Largo, Florida

Churn Out
The Ice Cream

Maxine Pinson of Savannah, Georgia, sent us her favorite recipe for ice cream, and it was, indeed, one of the most unusual we've ever received.

Maxine's recipe included directions for making not just one flavor, but an additional 20 variations of ice cream, 15 of which are presented here.

BASIC VANILLA ICE CREAM

2 (14-ounce) cans sweetened
   condensed milk
1 quart half-and-half
1 tablespoon plus 1 teaspoon
   vanilla extract

Combine all ingredients, mixing well. Pour ice cream mixture into freezer can of a 1-gallon hand-turned or electric freezer. Freeze according to manufacturer's instructions. Ripen ice cream 1 hour, if desired. Yield: 2½ quarts.

Rainbow Candy Ice Cream: Stir 1½ cups candy-coated milk chocolate pieces into ice cream mixture just before freezing.

Coffee Ice Cream: Combine ⅔ cup hot water and 1 tablespoon instant coffee granules, stirring until granules dissolve. Let cool slightly. Stir coffee mixture into ice cream mixture just before freezing.

Mocha Ice Cream: Combine 1 cup hot water and 1 tablespoon instant coffee granules, stirring until granules dissolve. Let mixture cool slightly. Stir coffee mixture and 1 (5.5-ounce) can chocolate syrup (½ cup) into ice cream mixture just before freezing.

Toffee Ice Cream: Stir 1 (6-ounce) package toffee-flavored candy pieces into ice cream mixture just before freezing.

Mint-Chocolate Chip Ice Cream: Stir ½ cup green crème de menthe and 1 (6-ounce) package semisweet chocolate mini-morsels (1 cup) into ice cream mixture before freezing.

Butter Pecan Ice Cream: Add 1 tablespoon butter flavoring and 2 cups coarsely chopped toasted pecans to ice cream mixture just before freezing.

Lemonade Ice Cream: Add 1 (6-ounce) can frozen lemonade concentrate, thawed and undiluted, to ice cream mixture before freezing.

Cherry-Pecan Ice Cream: Substitute 1 teaspoon almond extract for vanilla, and add ⅓ cup maraschino cherry juice to ice cream mixture; freeze ice cream as directed. Stir ¾ cup quartered maraschino cherries and ¾ cup chopped pecans into ice cream after freezing.

Strawberry-Banana-Nut Ice Cream: Stir 3 bananas, mashed; 1 pint strawberries, coarsely chopped; and ¾ cup chopped pecans into ice cream mixture just before freezing.

Peanut Butter Ice Cream: Stir ¾ cup chunky peanut butter into ice cream mixture just before freezing. Serve ice cream with chocolate syrup, if desired.

Blueberry Ice Cream: Stir 2 cups fresh or frozen blueberries into ice cream mixture just before freezing.

Double-Chocolate Ice Cream: Stir 1 (5.5-ounce) can chocolate syrup (½ cup) and 1 (6-ounce) package semisweet chocolate mini-morsels (1 cup) into ice cream mixture just before freezing.

Black Forest Ice Cream: Stir 1 (5.5-ounce) can chocolate syrup (½ cup) and 1 (16½-ounce) can pitted Bing cherries, drained and halved, into ice cream mixture just before freezing.

Chocolate-Covered Peanut Ice Cream: Stir 1 (5.5-ounce) can chocolate syrup (½ cup) and 2 (7-ounce) packages chocolate-covered peanuts (2 cups) into ice cream mixture just before freezing.

Cookies and Cream Ice Cream: Break 15 cream-filled chocolate sandwich cookies into small pieces; stir into ice cream mixture just before freezing.

Tip: *At least once a year, vacuum the coils of your freezer and refrigerator. A buildup of dust can interfere with efficient cooling.*

Oats Add Whole Grain Goodness

Crunchy goodness, nutty flavor, nutrient richness, and high fiber content have long made oats a breakfast favorite. But this natural whole grain is versatile and economical for other cooking purposes.

Regular and quick-cooking oats are essentially interchangeable, but regular oats add chewy texture and are ideal for granola, cookies, desserts, and pie crust. Quick-cooking oats, cut into smaller flakes during processing, are less noticeable. For a nuttier flavor, use toasted oats for recipes. To toast, spread oats on a baking sheet; bake at 350° for 10 minutes.

CRISPY OAT COOKIES

1 cup butter or margarine, softened
1 cup sugar
1 cup firmly packed brown sugar
1 egg
1 cup vegetable oil
1 teaspoon vanilla extract
3½ cups all-purpose flour
1 teaspoon baking soda
½ teaspoon salt
1 cup regular oats, uncooked
1 cup crushed corn flakes
½ cup flaked coconut
½ cup chopped pecans or walnuts

Cream butter; gradually add sugars, beating well at medium speed of an electric mixer. Add egg, and beat well; add oil and vanilla, mixing well.

Combine flour, soda, and salt; add to creamed mixture, mixing well. Stir in oats and remaining ingredients.

Shape dough into 1-inch balls. Place on ungreased cookie sheets, and flatten each ball with tines of a fork. Bake at 325° for 15 minutes. Cool slightly; remove from cookie sheets, and cool completely on wire racks. Yield: 10 dozen.
Dorothy C. Taylor
Palm City, Florida

MOLASSES GINGERBREAD

⅔ cup molasses
½ cup butter or margarine
1 cup all-purpose flour
½ teaspoon baking soda
⅔ cup regular oats, uncooked
1 tablespoon sugar
1 teaspoon grated lemon rind
½ teaspoon ground ginger
¼ teaspoon ground cloves
⅔ cup milk
Sweetened whipped cream

Combine molasses and butter in a saucepan; heat until butter melts. Pour into a large bowl. Combine flour and next 6 ingredients; add to molasses mixture alternately with milk, beginning and ending with flour mixture. Mix after each addition.

Pour batter into a lightly greased and floured 8-inch square pan. Bake at 350° for 35 minutes or until a wooden pick inserted in center comes out clean. Serve with a dollop of sweetened whipped cream. Yield: 9 servings.
Mrs. Paul Raper
Burgaw, North Carolina

OATMEAL-BROWN SUGAR PANCAKES

1 egg
1 cup milk
2 tablespoons vegetable oil
1 cup all-purpose flour
1 teaspoon baking powder
½ teaspoon baking soda
½ teaspoon salt
¼ cup firmly packed brown sugar
½ cup quick-cooking oats, uncooked

Beat egg; add milk and oil, mixing well. Combine flour and next 4 ingredients; add to egg mixture, mixing until blended. Stir oats into batter.

For each pancake, pour about ¼ cup batter onto a hot, lightly greased griddle. Turn pancakes when tops are covered with bubbles and edges look cooked. Yield: 10 (4½-inch) pancakes.
Alex Lowery
Baker, Florida

Make These Pies Year-Round

Pie is a favorite dessert in the South, and Southern cooks think nothing of whipping one up. Most of the ingredients for these recipes are probably already in your pantry.

Orange Chess Pie boasts a new flavor for an old favorite. As the pie bakes, the filling puffs, but it falls while it cools.

A crunchy macaroon-like mixture rises to the top of Coconut Macaroon Pie, leaving a delicate custard on the bottom.

BANANA PIE WITH HOT BUTTERED RUM SAUCE

Pastry for double-crust 9-inch pie
7 to 8 bananas, cut into ⅛-inch
  slices
2 tablespoons lemon juice
½ cup sugar
2 tablespoons all-purpose flour
½ teaspoon ground cinnamon
2 tablespoons butter or margarine
Dash of ground nutmeg
Vanilla ice cream
Hot Buttered Rum Sauce

Roll half of pastry to ⅛-inch thickness on a lightly floured surface. Place in a 9-inch pieplate; trim off excess pastry along edges.

Combine bananas and lemon juice, tossing gently to coat bananas. Combine sugar, flour, and cinnamon, mixing well; add to bananas, stirring gently. Spoon bananas into pastry shell. Dot with butter, and sprinkle with nutmeg.

Roll remaining pastry to ⅛-inch thickness; transfer to top of pie. Trim off excess pastry along edges. Fold edges under, and flute. Cut slits in top of crust for steam to escape.

Bake at 450° for 30 minutes or until pie is golden brown. Serve with a scoop of vanilla ice cream and Hot Buttered Rum Sauce. Yield: one 9-inch pie.

Hot Buttered Rum Sauce

1 cup sugar
2 tablespoons all-purpose flour
1 cup water
¼ cup butter or margarine
2 oranges, unpeeled and sliced
2 teaspoons rum extract

Combine sugar and flour in a saucepan; add water and butter. Bring to a boil over medium heat. Reduce heat; add orange slices, and simmer 10 minutes, stirring occasionally. Remove orange slices; add rum extract, stirring well. Yield: 1⅔ cups.

Stephanie J. Foskey
Washington, North Carolina

NO-CRUST APPLE PIE

6 cooking apples, peeled, cored,
  and cut into eighths
½ cup sugar
½ cup water
1 teaspoon ground cinnamon
½ teaspoon ground allspice
½ cup all-purpose flour
¼ cup firmly packed brown sugar
½ teaspoon baking powder
¼ teaspoon salt
3 tablespoons butter or margarine
Vanilla ice cream (optional)

Combine first 5 ingredients in a large saucepan; bring to a boil. Cover, reduce heat, and simmer 8 to 10 minutes or until apples are almost tender. Spoon mixture into a deep-dish 9-inch pieplate.

Combine flour, brown sugar, baking powder, and salt; cut in butter with a pastry blender until mixture resembles coarse meal.

Crumble brown sugar mixture over apples. Bake at 350° for 30 minutes or until top is browned. Serve with ice cream, if desired. Yield: one 9-inch pie.

Patricia Hill
Roan Mountain, Tennessee

COCONUT MACAROON PIE

3 eggs, separated
1 cup sugar
¼ cup milk
2 tablespoons butter or
  margarine, melted
¼ teaspoon salt
1 teaspoon lemon juice
1 teaspoon vanilla extract
¼ teaspoon almond extract
1½ cups flaked coconut
1 unbaked 9-inch pastry shell

Beat egg yolks in a large mixing bowl until thick and lemon colored; gradually add sugar, beating well. Stir in milk and next 5 ingredients.

Beat egg whites (at room temperature) until soft peaks form. Fold egg whites and coconut into yolk mixture; pour into pastry shell. Bake at 375° for 35 minutes or until a knife inserted in center comes out clean. Cool on a wire rack. Yield: one 9-inch pie.

Ida T. Ramsey
Viola, Tennessee

ORANGE CHESS PIE

½ cup butter or margarine,
  softened
1 cup sugar
3 eggs, beaten
3 tablespoons cornmeal
1 tablespoon plus 1 teaspoon
  grated orange rind
½ cup orange juice
1 tablespoon lemon juice
1 unbaked 9-inch pastry shell
Orange slice (optional)
Mint sprig (optional)

Cream butter; gradually add sugar, beating well at medium speed of an electric mixer. Add eggs, and beat until blended. Add cornmeal, orange rind, and juices; beat well.

Pour into pastry shell. Bake at 350° for 45 minutes or until a knife inserted in center of pie comes out clean. If desired, garnish with orange slice and mint. Yield: one 9-inch pie.

Mrs. Paul Raper
Burgaw, North Carolina

SEPTEMBER

Be Inventive With Fried Chicken

Everyone appreciates the crispness and flavor of fried chicken. There's no way to improve upon this Southern classic, but there are several ways to add a new twist. The color and crust produced by these recipes are familiar, but the fillings, sauces, and serving options will make you want to put fried chicken on the menu more often.

FRIED CHEESE-STUFFED CHICKEN THIGHS

8 chicken thighs, skinned and boned
½ (8-ounce) package Swiss cheese
8 slices bacon, partially cooked
2 egg whites, slightly beaten
1½ tablespoons lemon juice
¾ cup all-purpose flour
1½ teaspoons lemon-pepper seasoning
Vegetable oil

Place each chicken thigh between 2 sheets of heavy-duty plastic wrap, and flatten to ¼-inch thickness, using a meat mallet or a rolling pin.

Slice cheese lengthwise to make 8 even strips. Place 1 strip of cheese in center of each chicken thigh. Fold long sides of chicken over cheese; fold ends of chicken over, and wrap each with a strip of bacon. Secure with wooden picks.

Combine beaten egg whites and lemon juice; combine flour and lemon-pepper seasoning. Dip each chicken thigh in egg mixture; dredge in flour mixture.

Pour oil to depth of 1 inch into a heavy skillet. Fry stuffed chicken thighs in hot oil 15 minutes or until golden, turning once. Drain on paper towels. Yield: 8 servings.

CRISPY CHICKEN CROQUETTES

2 tablespoons chopped onion
1 tablespoon butter or margarine, melted
1 tablespoon all-purpose flour
¾ cup water
1¼ teaspoons chicken-flavored bouillon granules
½ teaspoon dry mustard
½ teaspoon pepper
4 cups finely chopped cooked chicken
1 egg, beaten
3 tablespoons dry white wine
1 cup round buttery cracker crumbs
Vegetable oil
Peppery Cream Sauce

Sauté onion in butter in a large saucepan until tender. Add flour, stirring until smooth. Cook 1 minute, stirring constantly. Gradually add water; cook over medium heat, stirring constantly, until sauce is thickened and bubbly. Stir in bouillon granules and next 5 ingredients. Cook over medium heat 3 to 5 minutes, stirring constantly. Remove from heat; cover and chill.

Shape mixture into croquettes, and roll in cracker crumbs. Pour oil to depth of 3 to 4 inches into a Dutch oven; heat to 350°. Fry chicken until golden brown. Drain on paper towels. Serve with Peppery Cream Sauce. Yield: 10 croquettes.

Peppery Cream Sauce

3 tablespoons butter or margarine
3 tablespoons all-purpose flour
1½ cups milk
½ teaspoon salt
½ teaspoon pepper

Melt butter in a heavy saucepan over low heat; add flour, stirring until smooth. Cook 1 minute, stirring constantly. Gradually add milk; cook over medium heat, stirring constantly, until sauce is thickened and bubbly. Stir in salt and pepper. Yield: 1½ cups.

FRIED SPINACH-STUFFED CHICKEN BREASTS

1 (10-ounce) package frozen chopped spinach, thawed and well drained
¼ cup commercial sour cream
½ teaspoon salt
¼ teaspoon ground nutmeg
⅛ teaspoon red pepper
1 cup all-purpose flour
2 teaspoons pepper
1 teaspoon salt
1 teaspoon paprika
½ teaspoon poultry seasoning
¼ teaspoon garlic powder
6 chicken breast halves, skinned and boned
1 egg, beaten
½ cup milk
Vegetable oil

Combine spinach, sour cream, ½ teaspoon salt, nutmeg, and red pepper, stirring well; set aside.

Combine flour and next 5 ingredients, stirring well; set aside.

Place each chicken breast half between 2 sheets of heavy-duty plastic wrap; flatten to ¼-inch thickness, using a meat mallet or rolling pin. Place about 1½ tablespoons spinach mixture in center of each chicken breast. Fold long sides of chicken over spinach mixture; fold ends over, and secure with a wooden pick.

Combine egg and milk; mix well. Dredge chicken in flour mixture, and dip in egg mixture; dredge again in flour mixture.

Pour oil to depth of 1 inch into a large heavy skillet. Fry chicken in hot oil 15 minutes or until golden brown, turning once. Drain on paper towels. Yield: 6 servings.

FRIED CHICKEN DRUMMETTES WITH HORSERADISH SAUCE

2½ pounds chicken wings
¾ cup buttermilk
½ teaspoon salt
¼ teaspoon pepper
1 cup self-rising flour
Vegetable oil
Horseradish Sauce

Cut chicken wings at joints; discard tips. Place chicken in a shallow dish.

Combine buttermilk, salt, and pepper; stir well, and pour over chicken. Cover and let stand 20 minutes; turn once. Drain. Dredge chicken in flour.

Pour oil to depth of 2 inches into a Dutch oven; heat to 325°. Fry chicken 15 minutes or until golden; turn once. Drain on paper towels. Serve with Horseradish Sauce. Yield: 3 dozen.

Horseradish Sauce

1 (8-ounce) carton commercial
  sour cream
2 tablespoons milk
1½ tablespoons prepared
  horseradish

Combine all ingredients; stir well. Yield: 1 cup.

Tip: *New cast-iron cookware should always be seasoned before using. Rub the interior of the utensil with oil or shortening, and place in a 250° or 300° oven for several hours. Wipe off oily film, and store. If scouring is necessary after using the utensil, reseason the surface immediately to prevent rusting.*

Sweet Potatoes: A Southern Fancy

Known as Indian potatoes or Tuckahocs, sweet potatoes have earned the endearing name of "yams." Discover how our readers use these gems in a variety of breads, desserts, and side dishes.

It's no coincidence that one of them comes from Opelousas, Louisiana, the original yam capital and home of the Yambilee, an annual October festival held since 1945 to celebrate the Louisiana yam harvest.

To learn more about cooking sweet potatoes, see "From Our Kitchen to Yours" on page 208.

CANDIED SWEET POTATOES

6 medium-size sweet potatoes
  (about 4½ pounds)
⅓ cup firmly packed brown
  sugar
½ cup sugar
2 tablespoons all-purpose flour
1 teaspoon ground cinnamon
¼ teaspoon ground nutmeg
¼ teaspoon ground allspice
¾ cup pineapple juice
⅓ cup light corn syrup
2 tablespoons orange juice
¼ cup butter or margarine
½ cup chopped pecans

Cook sweet potatoes in boiling water 20 to 25 minutes or until fork-tender. Let cool to touch; peel and cut potatoes lengthwise into ¼-inch slices. Set aside.

Combine brown sugar and next 5 ingredients in a saucepan; stir in pineapple juice, syrup, orange juice, and butter. Cook over medium heat about 10 minutes, stirring occasionally. Place half of sweet potatoes in a lightly greased 13- x 9- x 2-inch baking dish. Pour half of sugar mixture over sweet potatoes; repeat layers. Sprinkle with pecans. Bake at 350° for 30 minutes or until bubbly. Yield: 8 to 10 servings. *Claire Hollier*
Opelousas, Louisiana

APPLE-STUFFED SWEET POTATOES

6 medium-size sweet potatoes
  (about 4½ pounds)
2 tablespoons butter or
  margarine
1 teaspoon grated orange rind
2 tablespoons brown sugar
¼ teaspoon salt
¼ teaspoon ground cinnamon
2 tablespoons orange juice
1 cup peeled, finely chopped
  apple

Wash sweet potatoes; bake at 375° for 1 hour or until done. Allow potatoes to cool to touch.

Cut a 1-inch lengthwise strip from top of each sweet potato; carefully scoop out pulp, leaving shells intact.

Mash sweet potato pulp; combine with butter, orange rind, brown sugar, salt, cinnamon, orange juice, and chopped apple, mixing well. Stuff shells with sweet potato mixture. Bake at 350° for 25 minutes. Yield: about 6 servings.

Mrs. Lee Stringfield
Cottageville, South Carolina

SWEET POTATO-ORANGE PIE

2 cups cooked, mashed sweet
  potatoes (about 2 large sweet
  potatoes)
1 cup finely chopped pitted dates
3 eggs, slightly beaten
¾ cup firmly packed brown sugar
¾ cup orange juice
3 tablespoons butter or
  margarine, melted
½ teaspoon salt
½ teaspoon ground nutmeg
1 unbaked 9-inch pastry shell
Orange slices (optional)
Orange rind (optional)

Combine sweet potatoes, dates, eggs, sugar, orange juice, butter, salt, and nutmeg, mixing well. Spoon mixture into pastry shell. Bake at 350° for 45 minutes or until set. Cool. If desired, garnish with orange slices and orange rind. Yield: one 9-inch pie. *Clairiece Gilbert Humphrey*
Charlottesville, Virginia

SWEET POTATO WAFFLES

2 cups all-purpose flour
1 tablespoon baking powder
1 teaspoon salt
¼ teaspoon ground cinnamon
3 eggs, separated
1½ cups milk
¼ cup vegetable oil
¾ cup cooked, mashed sweet
  potato (about 1 medium sweet
  potato)
¼ cup chopped walnuts

Combine first 4 ingredients; set aside. Beat egg yolks in a medium bowl; add milk and oil, mixing well. Stir in sweet potato. Add to flour mixture, stirring briskly until blended.

Beat egg whites (at room temperature) at high speed of an electric mixer until stiff peaks form; fold into batter. Pour about one-fourth of batter into a preheated, lightly oiled waffle iron. Sprinkle 1 tablespoon walnuts evenly over batter. Cook about 5 minutes or until done. Repeat procedure with remaining batter and walnuts. Yield: 4 (8-inch) waffles.
Mrs. J. Michael Cheek
Leesburg, Florida

From Our Kitchen To Yours

Appreciation for Southern fare usually begins with our earliest childhood memories of the good food shared around the family table. The coppery-skinned sweet potato is an ingredient in many remembered classic recipes. This fall vegetable is a storehouse of essential nutrients and a natural companion to apples, pork, and turkey.

Many varieties of sweet potatoes thrive in our climate. The two basic types most familiar to us are the dry, somewhat mealy sweet potato with pale-orange flesh and the soft, moist sweet potato with deep-orange flesh. The moist sweet potato, sometimes referred to as a yam, is high in natural sugar. You can use the various types of sweet potatoes interchangeably in recipes.

Select thick, plump, medium-size sweet potatoes that taper toward the ends; they should be bright, clean, and blemish free. Generally, the darker the skin, the sweeter and moister the flesh. Avoid those with shriveled, discolored ends or other signs of decay.

As a general rule, this vegetable doesn't keep well uncooked. It decays more rapidly than the white potato and can be stored for only a day or two. Store in a cool, dry, well-ventilated spot. Do not place in the refrigerator; temperatures below 55° cause the core to harden and an undesirable taste to develop.

The skin is delicate and needs careful handling. To clean sweet potatoes, scrub with a soft brush under cold running water. Any bruised or woody portions need trimming. If the vegetables are damaged in spots, it is best for you to peel the whole potato before cooking in water.

When recipes call for cooked slices or mashed sweet potato, cook the potatoes in the jacket to save nutrients and to allow the natural sugars just under the skin to caramelize for a delicious flavor. When this protective peel is removed before cooking, some of the nutrients and sweetness dissolve in the cooking water. However, if you must peel before cooking, remember that sweet potatoes may darken unless they are cooked immediately or soaked in lightly salted water.

Canned sweet potatoes may be substituted for fresh. Three medium-size sweet potatoes (about 2¼ pounds) are equivalent to 1 (16-ounce) can sweet potatoes or 2 cups cooked and mashed.

Baking And Boiling Sweet Potatoes

	Baking Time at 375° (in minutes)	Boiling Time (in minutes)
Small sweet potatoes (about ½-pound each)	45	15 to 20
Medium-size sweet potatoes (about ¾-pound each)	60	25 to 30
Large sweet potatoes (about 1-pound each)	75 to 85	45 to 50

Beverages To Boost Team Spirit

After a long afternoon of cheering, quench your thirst with one of these beverages. During the first of the season while the weather is still warm, try refreshing frozen Mock Margaritas. Keep the base in the freezer, and simply mix it with club soda before serving. As the weather cools, drink Hot Buttered Lemonade to keep you warm all over.

HOT BUTTERED LEMONADE

½ cup sugar
¼ teaspoon grated lemon rind
½ cup lemon juice
¼ cup light rum or bourbon
3 cups water
1 tablespoon butter or margarine
Cinnamon sticks (optional)

Combine all ingredients except cinnamon sticks in a large saucepan. Cook over medium heat until butter melts and mixture is hot. Serve with cinnamon stick stirrers, if desired. Yield: 3¾ cups.
Madeline Gibbons
Little Rock, Arkansas

MOCK MARGARITAS

1 (12-ounce) can frozen lemonade
  concentrate, thawed and
  undiluted
1 (12-ounce) can frozen limeade
  concentrate, thawed and
  undiluted
1 cup powdered sugar
4 egg whites
6 cups crushed ice
Lime wedges
Coarse salt
3 cups club soda

Combine first 5 ingredients in a 4-quart plastic container, mixing well. Freeze mixture, stirring occasionally. Remove container from freezer 30 minutes before serving.

Rub rims of stemmed glasses with wedge of lime. Place salt in saucer; spin rim of each glass in salt. Set prepared glasses aside.

Spoon 2 cups slush mixture into container of an electric blender; add 1 cup club soda. Blend to desired consistency. Repeat procedure twice.

Pour beverage into prepared glasses; garnish each glass with a wedge of lime. Yield: 9 cups.

Marion Pool
Groom, Texas

AUTUMN PUNCH

1½ cups honey
¾ cup lemon juice
6 whole cardamom seeds
3 (3-inch) sticks cinnamon
1 teaspoon whole allspice
2 teaspoons whole cloves
1½ quarts cranberry juice
5 cups apple juice
5 cups apricot nectar
3 quarts ginger ale
Crushed ice

Combine first 6 ingredients in a saucepan; bring to a boil, reduce heat, and simmer 10 minutes. Strain and discard spices. Chill. Combine chilled mixture with remaining juices and ginger ale. Serve over crushed ice. Yield: 7½ quarts.

Mrs. Carl Smith
Melbourne, Florida

PINEAPPLE-MINT PUNCH

2 cups boiling water
4 regular-size tea bags
1 cup sugar
2 cups orange juice
¾ cup lemon juice
2 tablespoons lime juice
2 cups mint leaves
2 (33.8-ounce) bottles sparkling
  water, chilled
1 (67.6-ounce) bottle ginger ale,
  chilled
1 (15¼-ounce) can chunk
  pineapple, undrained
Mint sprigs (optional)

Pour boiling water over tea bags; cover. Let stand 10 minutes; discard bags. Add sugar and next 4 ingredients, stirring until sugar dissolves. Chill. Strain mint from tea mixture; discard mint. To serve, combine tea mixture, sparkling water, ginger ale, and pineapple, stirring well. Garnish with mint sprigs, if desired. Yield: 1½ gallons.

Mrs. R. S. Trent
Waverly, Missouri

No-Fuss Desserts

Our readers have found a myriad of ways to make luscious desserts and spend only a small amount of time in the kitchen. If you keep such products as whipped topping, cake mix, and pie filling on hand, you'll never be caught without something quick—and elegant—to serve.

BLACK FOREST TORTE

1 (18¼-ounce) package devil's
  food cake mix with pudding
1 (8-ounce) container frozen
  whipped topping, thawed
1 (21-ounce) can cherry pie filling

Prepare cake mix according to package directions. Spoon batter into a greased and floured 10-inch tube pan;

bake according to package directions. Cool in pan 10 minutes; remove from pan, and let cool completely on a wire rack.

Slice cake horizontally to make 3 layers. Place bottom layer on cake platter; spread with about 1 cup whipped topping, and top with one-third of cherry pie filling. Repeat process with second and third layers. Chill well. Yield: one 10-inch cake.

Libby Winstead
Nashville, Tennessee

STRAWBERRY SHORTCAKE JUBILEE

2 cups fresh strawberries, hulled
  and sliced
⅓ cup sugar
1 cup biscuit mix
1 tablespoon sugar
¼ cup milk
1 tablespoon butter or margarine,
  melted
¼ cup frozen whipped topping,
  thawed

Combine strawberries and ⅓ cup sugar; stir gently. Cover and chill at least 45 minutes.

Combine biscuit mix and next 3 ingredients in a small bowl; stir to make a soft dough. Turn out onto a lightly floured surface; knead about 5 times. Roll out to ½-inch thickness; cut into two 3-inch circles. Place circles on an ungreased baking sheet; bake at 425° for 10 to 12 minutes or until golden.

Split warm shortcakes horizontally; place each on an individual dessert plate. Spoon sweetened strawberries between layers and on top. Dollop with whipped topping. Yield: 2 servings.

Alice McNamara
Eucha, Oklahoma

APPLE PIE WITH HOT CINNAMON SAUCE

1 (26-ounce) frozen double-crust
  apple pie
¼ cup sugar
2 tablespoons all-purpose flour
1 cup water
3 tablespoons lemon juice
1 tablespoon butter or margarine
1 teaspoon ground cinnamon
½ teaspoon ground nutmeg
¼ teaspoon ground allspice

Bake pie according to directions on package.

Combine sugar and flour in a small saucepan; add water and lemon juice, mixing well. Cook over medium heat, stirring constantly, until mixture thickens. Add butter, cinnamon, nutmeg, and allspice. Serve sauce warm over pie. Yield: one 9-inch pie.

Jane Ryan
Birmingham, Alabama

LEMON-BLUEBERRY TRIFLE

1 (10¾-ounce) frozen pound cake,
  thawed
1 (3½-ounce) package lemon
  instant pudding mix
1 (21-ounce) can blueberry pie
  filling
1 (8-ounce) container frozen
  whipped topping, thawed
2 tablespoons sliced almonds,
  toasted

Cut pound cake into ½-inch cubes; arrange in a 2-quart dessert bowl. Prepare pudding mix according to package directions; pour over pound cake. Spoon pie filling over pudding, and spread whipped topping over pie filling. Chill. Sprinkle with toasted almonds. Yield: 10 servings.

Note: A 4-ounce package chocolate instant pudding mix and cherry pie filling can be substituted for lemon pudding mix and blueberry pie filling to make a Chocolate-Cherry Trifle.

Faye Williams
Pineville, Louisiana

COOKING LIGHT®
Light Party Fare

Food is often the icebreaker at parties, and what better way to get conversation flowing than with outstanding, light appetizers.

CHICKEN-MUSHROOM APPETIZERS

1 (5-ounce) can chunk chicken,
  drained and chopped
1 (2.5-ounce) jar sliced
  mushrooms, drained and
  chopped
1 tablespoon minced fresh parsley
2 tablespoons minced onion
2 teaspoons reduced-sodium
  Worcestershire sauce
2 tablespoons reduced-calorie
  mayonnaise
16 melba toast rounds

Combine first 6 ingredients in a small bowl; stir well. Cover and chill. Spread 1 tablespoon chicken mixture on each melba toast round. Yield: 16 appetizers (33 calories each).

☐ *2.5 grams protein, 1.5 grams fat, 2.4 grams carbohydrate, 1 milligram cholesterol, 99 milligrams sodium, and 2 milligrams calcium.*

Joyce-Anne Pottorff
Pine Bluff, Arkansas

STUFFED MUSHROOM APPETIZERS

30 medium mushrooms (1½
  pounds)
Vegetable cooking spray
½ pound turkey sausage
¼ cup chopped green onions
1 clove garlic, minced
¼ cup soft breadcrumbs
1 egg, beaten
2 tablespoons grated Parmesan
  cheese
½ teaspoon dried Italian
  seasoning

Clean mushrooms with damp paper towels. Remove stems, and chop finely; set mushroom caps aside.

Coat a large nonstick skillet with cooking spray; place over medium-high heat until hot. Add sausage, onions, garlic, and mushroom stems; cook until sausage is browned, stirring to crumble. Drain, if necessary. Stir in breadcrumbs, egg, cheese, and Italian seasoning. Spoon 1 teaspoon sausage mixture into each mushroom cap. Place stuffed mushrooms in a 15- x 10- x 1-inch jellyroll pan; bake at 350° for 10 minutes. Serve immediately. Yield: 2½ dozen (32 calories each).

☐ *1.8 grams protein, 2.2 grams fat, 1.5 grams carbohydrate, 14 milligrams cholesterol, 71 milligrams sodium, and 17 milligrams calcium.*

MUSHROOM-ALMOND PASTRY CUPS

3 sheets commercial frozen phyllo
  pastry, thawed
Butter-flavored vegetable cooking
  spray
¼ cup slivered almonds, toasted
2½ cups chopped fresh
  mushrooms
1 clove garlic, crushed
1 teaspoon dry sherry
¼ teaspoon dried whole thyme
Dash of white pepper
2 tablespoons reduced-calorie
  mayonnaise
1 tablespoon minced green onions

Place 1 sheet of phyllo on a damp towel (keep remaining phyllo covered). Coat phyllo with cooking spray. Layer 2 more sheets phyllo on first sheet, spraying each with cooking spray. Cut stack of phyllo into 3-inch squares, using kitchen shears.

Coat miniature muffin pans with cooking spray. Place 1 square of layered phyllo into each muffin cup, pressing gently in center to form a pastry shell. Bake at 350° for 8 minutes or until golden. Remove shells from pan; let cool on a wire rack.

Place almonds in blender or food processor; process until ground, and set aside.

Sauté mushrooms and garlic in a nonstick skillet that has been coated with cooking spray; sauté until liquid evaporates. Add sherry, thyme, and pepper; simmer until mushrooms are dry. Add reserved ground almonds and mayonnaise, mixing well. Spoon about ½ tablespoon mushroom filling into each pastry shell. Garnish with minced green onions. Yield: 20 appetizers (28 calories each).

☐ 0.9 gram protein, 1.6 grams fat, 2.9 grams carbohydrate, 0 milligrams cholesterol, 22 milligrams sodium, and 6 milligrams calcium.

CHEESE TARTLETS

8 slices light wheat sandwich
   bread
¾ cup (3 ounces) shredded
   low-fat Swiss cheese
¼ cup grated Parmesan cheese
1 tablespoon minced fresh parsley
1 teaspoon Dijon mustard
⅛ teaspoon garlic powder
Dash of hot sauce
3 egg whites
2 tablespoons diced pimiento,
   drained

Remove crust from bread; cut each slice into 4 squares. Gently press each bread square into a miniature muffin pan; bake at 400° for 3 to 4 minutes. Set aside.

Combine Swiss cheese and next 5 ingredients in a small bowl; set aside. Beat egg whites (at room temperature) in a large mixing bowl until stiff; fold in cheese mixture. Spoon 1 teaspoon mixture into each tart shell; bake at 400° for 6 to 8 minutes or until filling is slightly puffed.

Remove from pans. Garnish each tartlet with diced pimiento; serve immediately. Yield: 32 appetizers (17 calories each).

☐ 1.6 grams protein, 0.6 gram fat, 1.5 grams carbohydrate, 1 milligram cholesterol, 70 milligrams sodium, and 31 milligrams calcium.

HAM-STUFFED NEW POTATOES

15 (1⅛ pounds) small unpeeled
   new potatoes
1 cup diced cooked lean ham
⅓ cup part-skim ricotta cheese
⅓ cup light process cream
   cheese product
1 tablespoon minced onion
1 tablespoon Dijon mustard
Paprika
Fresh parsley sprigs

Arrange potatoes in a vegetable steamer over boiling water. Cover and steam 15 to 20 minutes or until tender. Remove from steamer; let cool. Scoop out center of potatoes with a melon-ball scoop. Reserve potato pulp for other uses.

Combine ham and next 4 ingredients; stir well. Fill center of each potato with ham mixture. Sprinkle each with paprika; garnish with a parsley sprig. Yield: 15 appetizers (67 calories each).

☐ 5.1 grams protein, 2.2 grams fat, 6.7 grams carbohydrate, 10 milligrams cholesterol, 249 milligrams sodium, and 28 milligrams calcium.

TABBOULEH

¾ cup cracked wheat
3 cups diced tomato
1½ cups minced fresh parsley
1 cup sliced green onions
2 tablespoons firmly packed
   minced fresh mint
2 tablespoons minced green
   pepper
2 tablespoons minced celery
2 tablespoons minced ripe olives
2 tablespoons olive oil
¼ cup lemon juice
1 teaspoon salt
¼ teaspoon pepper
Pita bread triangles (recipe
   follows)

Place cracked wheat in a large bowl; cover with hot water 2 inches above wheat. Let soak 1 hour. Drain thoroughly. Add diced tomato and next

10 ingredients; stir well. Cover and chill at least 2 hours, stirring occasionally. Serve with pita bread triangles. Yield: 5 cups (12 calories per tablespoon).

☐ 0.3 gram protein, 0.4 gram fat, 1.8 grams carbohydrate, 0 milligrams cholesterol, 32 milligrams sodium, and 4 milligrams calcium.

Pita Bread Triangles

3 (6-inch) whole wheat pita bread
   rounds

Separate each pita bread into 2 rounds; cut each into 8 wedges to make 48 triangles. Place on an ungreased baking sheet; bake at 350° for 20 minutes or until lightly browned. Let cool. Yield: 48 triangles (4 calories each).

☐ 0.1 gram protein, 0 grams fat, 0.8 gram carbohydrate, 0 milligrams cholesterol, 15 milligrams sodium, and 1 milligram calcium.

BLUE CHEESE-STUFFED BEETS

2½ tablespoons blue cheese
¼ cup plus 1½ tablespoons light
   process cream cheese product
2 (16-ounce) cans whole,
   medium-size beets, drained
Fresh parsley sprigs

Combine cheeses in a small bowl; stir well, and let stand 1 to 2 hours.

Scoop out center of each beet, using a melon-ball scoop; reserve beet pulp for other uses. Fill center of each beet with 1 teaspoon cheese filling. Garnish with parsley sprigs. Serve immediately. Yield: 2 dozen (12 calories each).

☐ 0.6 gram protein, 0.8 gram fat, 0.8 gram carbohydrate, 1 milligram cholesterol, 44 milligrams sodium, and 11 milligrams calcium.

Mrs. John C. Hamel
Lake Worth, Florida

STUFFED CHERRY TOMATOES

36 small cherry tomatoes
¼ cup grated cucumber
1 (8-ounce) package
    reduced-calorie cream cheese,
    softened
1 tablespoon lemon juice
1 tablespoon reduced-calorie
    mayonnaise
¼ teaspoon onion powder
¼ teaspoon salt
2 tablespoons minced fresh
    parsley

Cut top off each tomato; scoop out pulp, reserving pulp for other uses. Invert tomato shells on paper towels to drain.

Place cucumber between 2 paper towels, and pat dry.

Combine softened cream cheese and next 4 ingredients, mixing well. Stir in grated cucumber.

Spoon 1½ teaspoons cucumber mixture into each tomato shell. Sprinkle each tomato with parsley. Yield: 3 dozen (16 calories each).

☐ 0.7 gram protein, 1.2 grams fat, 0.8 gram carbohydrate, 0 milligrams cholesterol, 54 milligrams sodium, and 10 milligrams calcium.

Zoe Newton
Fort Smith, Arkansas

SPINACH-RICOTTA PHYLLO TRIANGLES

Butter-flavored vegetable cooking
    spray
½ cup minced onion
1 (10-ounce) package frozen
    chopped spinach, thawed and
    drained well
¼ teaspoon garlic powder
¼ teaspoon salt
¼ teaspoon freshly ground pepper
½ teaspoon dried whole oregano
1 tablespoon dry sherry
¼ cup (1¾ ounces) crumbled feta
    cheese
⅓ cup part-skim ricotta cheese
21 sheets commercial frozen
    phyllo pastry, thawed

Coat a nonstick skillet with cooking spray; place over medium-high heat

until hot. Add onion, and sauté until tender. Add spinach and next 7 ingredients; stir well.

Coat a flat surface with cooking spray; place 1 sheet of phyllo on surface (keep remaining phyllo covered). Coat phyllo with cooking spray. Layer 2 more sheets phyllo on first sheet, spraying each with cooking spray. Cut into 7 strips (about 2⅓ inches wide). Place 1 teaspoon spinach mixture at base of each strip; fold right bottom corner of each strip over to form a triangle. Continue folding back and forth into a triangle, gently pressing corners together to end of strip. Repeat with remaining phyllo and filling.

Place triangles, seam side down, on a baking sheet coated with cooking spray. Lightly spray tops of triangles with cooking spray. Bake at 350° for 30 to 40 minutes or until golden. Serve hot. Yield: 49 appetizers (39 calories each).

Note: Phyllo triangles may be frozen before baking. Place unbaked triangles on baking sheets in freezer until frozen. Store in airtight container in freezer. Bake as directed above.

☐ 1.4 grams protein, 0.9 gram fat, 6.3 grams carbohydrate, 1 milligram cholesterol, 66 milligrams sodium, and 19 milligrams calcium.

ZUCCHINI PIZZAS

¾ cup commercial spaghetti
    sauce
½ cup (2 ounces) shredded
    part-skim mozzarella cheese
2 tablespoons grated Parmesan
    cheese
2 tablespoons minced green
    onions
¼ teaspoon freshly ground pepper
¼ teaspoon dried whole oregano
24 (½-inch) slices fresh zucchini
24 slices fresh mushrooms
24 slices ripe olives

Combine first 6 ingredients; stir well. Spoon 1½ teaspoons cheese mixture

on each zucchini slice. Top each with a slice of mushroom and a slice of olive. Broil 6 inches from heat 3 to 5 minutes or until thoroughly heated. Serve immediately. Yield: 2 dozen appetizers (19 calories each).

☐ 1.1 grams protein, 1.1 grams fat, 1.5 grams carbohydrate, 2 milligrams cholesterol, 29 milligrams sodium, and 26 milligrams calcium.

ZUCCHINI CAVIAR

2 tablespoons olive oil
2 cups shredded, unpeeled
    zucchini
½ cup diced sweet red pepper
¼ cup diced onion
1 clove garlic, minced
1 teaspoon celery seeds
½ teaspon dried whole basil
½ teaspoon dried whole oregano
2 tablespoons minced fresh
    parsley
2 cups diced tomato
1 teaspoon grated lemon rind
1½ teaspoons reduced-sodium
    Worcestershire sauce
¼ teaspoon salt
¼ teaspoon freshly ground pepper
2 tablespoons lemon juice
Pita bread triangles (recipe on
    page 211)

Heat oil in a large nonstick skillet over medium heat until hot. Add next 8 ingredients; sauté until vegetables are crisp-tender. Remove from heat; stir in diced tomato and next 4 ingredients. Chill several hours. Add lemon juice; toss gently, and chill thoroughly. Serve with pita bread triangles. Yield: 4 cups (6 calories per tablespoon).

☐ 0.1 gram protein, 0.5 gram fat, 0.6 gram carbohydrate, 0 milligrams cholesterol, 10 milligrams sodium, and 3 milligrams calcium.

APPLE-PHYLLO ROLLS

Butter-flavored vegetable cooking spray
2 cups diced apple
½ teaspoon ground cinnamon
¼ teaspoon ground nutmeg
1 tablespoon plus 1½ teaspoons brown sugar
9 sheets commercial frozen phyllo pastry, thawed
3 tablespoons sifted powdered sugar
1 teaspoon vanilla extract
½ teaspoon water

Coat a nonstick skillet with butter-flavored vegetable cooking spray; place over medium heat until skillet is hot. Add diced apple; sauté 8 to 10 minutes, stirring often.

Add cinnamon, nutmeg, and brown sugar to sautéed apple; stir well, and cook apple mixture an additional 3 minutes. Remove from heat, and let apple mixture cool.

Coat a flat surface with vegetable cooking spray; place 1 sheet of phyllo pastry on surface (keep remaining phyllo pastry covered). Coat phyllo with cooking spray. Layer 2 more sheets phyllo pastry on first sheet, coating each with cooking spray. Cut stacked phyllo pastry vertically into 5 equal strips; cut strips in half to make 10 pieces. Repeat layering and cutting procedure with remaining phyllo sheets, spraying each sheet with cooking spray.

Spoon 1½ teaspoons apple mixture onto phyllo dough at base of each strip, and roll up jellyroll fashion. Place phyllo rolls, seam side down, on a baking sheet coated with butter-flavored cooking spray. Bake at 375° for 30 to 35 minutes or until rolls are golden. Cool slightly on wire rack.

Combine powdered sugar and remaining ingredients in a small mixing bowl, and stir well. Drizzle 1½ teaspoons glaze over each roll. Serve rolls warm. Yield: 30 appetizers (30 calories each).

□ *0.6 gram protein, 0.3 gram fat, 6.4 grams carbohydrate, 0 milligrams cholesterol, 26 milligrams sodium, and 2 milligrams calcium.*

MICROWAVE COOKERY

Build Quick Menus Around Ground Meat

You've probably defrosted ground beef in your microwave oven, but have you tried ground turkey or bulk pork sausage? Both are also easy to defrost—and make good additions to a variety of recipes.

Turkey-Bean Chili has the same fresh aroma and spicy-hot flavor of a chili that's been simmering for several hours, but it's ready in about 30 minutes. Hearty Stuffed Peppers takes a little longer to prepare, but convenient ingredients, such as tomato soup, sour cream, and commercial stuffing mix, make this recipe easy to assemble. Bulk pork sausage adds a different flavor.

TURKEY-BEAN CHILI

1 pound ground turkey
1 cup chopped onion
1 clove garlic, crushed
1 (15-ounce) can tomato sauce
1 (15½-ounce) can Mexican-style chili beans, undrained
¼ teaspoon salt
⅛ teaspoon pepper
2 tablespoons chili powder
1 tablespoon ground cumin
Commercial sour cream (optional)
Chopped green onions (optional)

Combine first 3 ingredients in a 3-quart casserole. Cover and microwave at HIGH 5 to 6 minutes or until meat is no longer pink, stirring once; drain well.

Add tomato sauce, beans, salt, pepper, chili powder, and cumin. Cover and microwave at HIGH 10 to 12 minutes, stirring after 6 minutes. If desired, garnish with sour cream and green onions. Yield: 5 cups.

MICROWAVE TACOS

1 pound ground beef
½ cup chopped onion
½ cup chopped green pepper
1 clove garlic, minced
1 (8-ounce) can tomato sauce
1 teaspoon Worcestershire sauce
1 teaspoon chili powder
¼ teaspoon ground red pepper
½ teaspoon salt
1 dozen commercial taco shells
3 cups shredded lettuce
2 medium tomatoes, chopped
1½ cups (6 ounces) shredded Cheddar cheese
Commercial taco sauce

Crumble beef into a 1½-quart casserole; add chopped onion, chopped green pepper, and minced garlic. Cover tightly with heavy-duty plastic wrap; fold back a small edge of wrap to allow steam to escape.

Microwave at HIGH 6 to 7 minutes or until beef is browned, stirring every 2 minutes. Drain. Stir in tomato sauce and next 4 ingredients; cover and microwave at HIGH 3 minutes or until thoroughly heated.

Spoon about 2 tablespoons meat mixture into each taco shell; top meat with lettuce, chopped tomato, cheese, and taco sauce. Serve immediately. Yield: 12 servings.

Mrs. Earl L. Faulkenberry
Lancaster, South Carolina

Defrosting Ground Meat

*Ground Meat (1 pound)	Time
Ground chuck	10 to 12 minutes
Ground turkey	8 to 10 minutes
Bulk pork sausage	5 to 7 minutes

*Microwave at defrost (30% power).

Stir meat to crumble at 3-minute intervals. Remove defrosted portions to speed defrosting and to avoid cooking.

EASY MEAT LOAF

1½ pounds lean ground beef
1 cup quick-cooking oats,
    uncooked
2 eggs, beaten
1 small onion, chopped
1 (1.4-ounce) envelope vegetable
    soup mix
3 (1-ounce) slices Swiss cheese

Combine first 5 ingredients, mixing well. Shape meat mixture into 6 loaves. Place on a rack in a 12- x 8- x 2-inch baking dish. Cover with wax paper. Microwave at HIGH 10 minutes, rearranging loaves after 5 minutes. Microwave at HIGH an additional 2 minutes or until done.

Slice cheese in half diagonally. Place a cheese triangle on each loaf. Cover loosely with foil; let stand 5 minutes. Yield: 6 servings.

HEARTY STUFFED PEPPERS

8 medium-size green peppers
    (about 4 pounds)
1 pound bulk pork sausage
1½ cups chopped onion
½ pound fresh mushrooms,
    chopped
1 (6-ounce) package
    herb-seasoned stuffing mix
1 (8-ounce) carton commercial
    sour cream
2 cups chopped fresh tomato
1 (10¾-ounce) can tomato soup
¾ cup water
2 teaspoons salt-free
    herb-and-spice blend

Cut off tops of green peppers, and remove seeds. Wash peppers, and set aside.

Crumble sausage into a 2½-quart casserole. Add chopped onion and mushrooms; stir well. Cover tightly with heavy-duty plastic wrap; fold back a small edge of wrap to allow steam to escape.

Microwave at HIGH 7 to 8 minutes or until sausage is browned, stirring once. Drain well; set aside. Add stuffing mix, including seasoning packet, and sour cream; stir well. Add chopped tomato, and stir gently.

Stuff peppers with sausage mixture, and place in a lightly greased 12- x 8- x 2-inch baking dish. Combine soup and remaining ingredients. Stir well; pour over peppers. Cover tightly with heavy-duty plastic wrap; fold back a small edge to allow steam to escape. Microwave at HIGH 20 to 22 minutes, giving dish a half-turn after 10 minutes. Yield: 8 servings.
Wini Orr
Greenville, South Carolina

A Tender Approach To Round Steak

For an ideal way to stretch your food budget, give round steak a try. Three cuts come from a full round steak; each varies in price and tenderness, so it pays to be familiar with them all. Top round, the most expensive, is the most tender and suitable for broiling or pan-frying.

The bottom round (referred to simply as round steak) and eye of round are less-tender cuts. But proper cooking techniques can turn these cuts into entrées suitable for family meals or guests.

RED PEPPER ROUND STEAK

1 (1-pound) round steak
½ teaspoon salt
⅛ teaspoon pepper
2 tablespoons chopped onion
2 tablespoons vegetable oil
1 large sweet red pepper,
    chopped
1 beef-flavored bouillon cube
1 cup hot water
1 (14½-ounce) can tomato
    wedges, drained
1 tablespoon cornstarch
¼ cup water
2 teaspoons soy sauce
Hot cooked noodles or rice

Partially freeze steak; slice diagonally across grain into ¼-inch-wide strips. Cut strips into 2-inch pieces. Sprinkle steak with salt and pepper.

Sauté steak and onion in oil in a skillet until steak is browned. Add chopped red pepper.

Dissolve bouillon cube in 1 cup hot water; add to steak, and bring to a boil. Cover, reduce heat, and simmer 40 minutes. Add tomatoes.

Combine cornstarch, ¼ cup water, and soy sauce, stirring well; stir into steak mixture. Bring to a boil, and cook 1 minute, stirring constantly. Serve over noodles or rice. Yield: 4 servings.
Billie Taylor
Fort Union, Virginia

BEEF AND BROCCOLI WITH CHIVE GRAVY

1 (1-pound) top round steak
1½ pounds fresh broccoli
3 tablespoons water
1 tablespoon vegetable oil
½ pound fresh mushrooms, sliced
1 tablespoon vegetable oil
1 (8-ounce) carton commercial
    sour cream
1 tablespoon minced chives
½ teaspoon salt
⅛ teaspoon pepper

Partially freeze steak; slice diagonally across grain into ⅛- to ¼-inch strips; set aside.

Wash and trim broccoli, and cut into 2- x 1-inch pieces; set aside. Bring water to a boil in a large skillet. Add broccoli; cover and cook 8 to 10 minutes or until broccoli is crisp-tender. Drain.

Heat 1 tablespoon oil in skillet over medium heat until hot. Add mushrooms, and sauté until tender; remove from skillet.

Heat 1 tablespoon oil in skillet over medium heat until hot. Add steak; sauté 2 to 3 minutes. Add broccoli and mushrooms; stir well. Reduce heat, and stir in sour cream and remaining ingredients. Cook until thoroughly heated. Yield: 4 servings. *Monnie Sandra Richmond*
St. Marys, West Virginia

ROQUEFORT BEEF ROULADES

1 (3-ounce) can sliced
  mushrooms, undrained
2 (1-pound) round steaks
¼ teaspoon pepper
½ cup chopped onion, divided
1 (4-ounce) package Roquefort
  cheese, divided
2 tablespoons all-purpose flour
2 tablespoons vegetable oil
1 (12-ounce) can vegetable juice
2 tablespoons Worcestershire
  sauce
Hot cooked noodles or rice

Drain mushrooms, reserving liquid. Set aside.

Trim excess fat from steak. Cut each steak into 3 pieces, and pound to ¼-inch thickness, using a smooth-surfaced meat mallet. Sprinkle steaks with pepper. Sprinkle mushrooms, half of onion, and half of cheese on steaks; roll up, and secure with wooden picks. Dredge steaks in flour, coating evenly. Brown steaks in hot oil in a large skillet; drain.

Return steaks to skillet, and add vegetable juice, reserved mushroom liquid, Worcestershire sauce, and remaining onion. Bring to a boil; cover, reduce heat, and simmer 45 minutes. Arrange steaks on a platter over hot cooked noodles. Add remaining cheese to sauce, stirring until blended. Spoon cheese sauce over steaks. Yield: 6 servings.

Margot Foster
Hubbard, Texas

Snacks
For Children

Sometimes it's hard to find snack recipes that please both parents and children. These recipes are a snap to prepare and they combine flavors no one can resist.

Applesauce Snack Cakes is a tasty make-ahead recipe. The batter can be stored in the refrigerator for up to two weeks and baked as needed.

No-Recipe Snacks

- Spread peanut butter on slices of apple, pear, or banana.
- Freeze juice in Popsicle molds.
- Toast English muffin halves, and melt cheese on top.
- Spread cream cheese or shredded cheese on a flour or corn tortilla, and heat. Roll up like a jellyroll.
- Combine cereal, nuts, and raisins, and store mixture in zip-top plastic bags.
- Spread applesauce over graham crackers.

BANANA-BERRY FLIP

1 cup strawberry-flavored
  carbonated beverage
1 cup vanilla ice cream
1 medium-size ripe banana,
  quartered
1 teaspoon vanilla extract

Combine all ingredients in container of an electric blender; process mixture until smooth. Serve immediately. Yield: about 3½ cups.

Cathy Williams
Vale, North Carolina

APPLESAUCE SNACK CAKES

1 cup butter or margarine,
  softened
2 cups sugar
2 eggs
2 teaspoons baking soda
1 teaspoon vanilla extract
1 (16-ounce) can applesauce
4 cups all-purpose flour
1½ teaspoons ground cinnamon
1 teaspoon ground allspice
½ teaspoon ground cloves

Cream butter; gradually add sugar, beating well at medium speed of an electric mixer. Add eggs, one at a time, beating well after each addition.

Stir soda and vanilla into applesauce. Combine flour and spices; add to creamed mixture alternately with applesauce mixture, mixing after each addition. Cover batter, and store in refrigerator up to 2 weeks.

When ready to bake, spoon batter into paper-lined muffin pans, filling two-thirds full. Bake at 400° for 17 to 19 minutes or until a wooden pick inserted in center comes out clean. Remove from pans, and let cool on wire racks. Yield: 2½ dozen.

Evelyn Howell
Orange, Texas

Fresh Salads
For Fall

When summer's harvest starts dwindling, don't think your opportunities to make fresh fruit and vegetable salads diminish, too. Fall and winter are peak seasons for a variety of produce that's perfect for tossing into salads.

MARINATED MUSHROOM
SALAD

1 pound fresh mushrooms
¾ cup sliced green onions
½ cup vegetable oil
¼ cup white wine vinegar
¼ cup (1 ounce) shredded Swiss
  cheese
1 tablespoon Greek seasoning

Clean mushrooms with damp paper towels. Remove mushroom stems, and reserve for other uses. Slice mushrooms; combine mushrooms and sliced green onions.

Combine oil and remaining ingredients, stirring well; pour over mushroom mixture, tossing gently. Cover and chill. Serve, using a slotted spoon. Yield: 8 to 10 servings.

Mrs. Alton R. Lower
Birmingham, Alabama

NUTTY APPLE SLAW

2 large green apples, unpeeled
  and chopped
1½ teaspoons lemon juice
2 cups coarsely shredded red
  cabbage
¼ cup chopped walnuts
1 stalk celery, thinly sliced
6 large radishes, thinly sliced
3 tablespoons raisins
¼ cup commercial sour cream
¼ cup chopped walnuts

Toss chopped apple with lemon juice
in a large bowl. Stir in cabbage and
next 4 ingredients; add sour cream,
stirring until blended. Sprinkle with
¼ cup chopped walnuts. Cover and
chill 2 hours. Yield: 6 to 8
servings.   *Mary Pappas*
                    Richmond, Virginia

CAULIFLOWER-BROCCOLI CRUNCH

1 head cauliflower, broken into
  flowerets
1 pound broccoli, broken into
  flowerets
½ cup chopped onion
¾ cup mayonnaise
1 tablespoon sugar
3 tablespoons evaporated milk
1 teaspoon vinegar
½ teaspoon salt
¼ teaspoon pepper

Combine cauliflower, broccoli, and
onion; toss well. Combine mayonnaise and remaining ingredients, mixing well; pour over vegetables. Toss
gently; cover and chill 4 hours. Yield:
10 servings.   *Freda Cantrell*
                    Fairland, Oklahoma

It's Time For Muscadines

Grapes are grown in various areas
across the U.S., but one species—
the muscadine—is unique to the
Southeast. Thick vines that can reach
the tops of tall trees bear purplish-
black, reddish-black, or bronze
(sometimes known as white) fruit.

The scuppernong, which is bronze,
is the best known and most widely
grown selection. And the sweet nectar of muscadines is prized for its
distinctive flavor in wine, jelly, pie,
and juice. Southerners are undoubt-
edly the experts when it comes to
using muscadines, and these recipes
show the fruit's versatility.

PEARS IN MUSCADINE SAUCE

2 to 3 cups muscadines
3 cups water
4 medium-size firm, ripe pears
¾ cup sugar
1 tablespoon plus 1 teaspoon
  cornstarch

Rinse muscadines; combine muscadines and water in a medium saucepan. Bring to a boil; cover, reduce
heat, and simmer 45 minutes. Remove from heat; mash muscadines
with a potato masher. Strain through
a jelly bag, reserving 1¼ cups juice;
set aside.

Peel pears, leaving stems intact.
Cut a thin slice from bottoms, so that
pears stand upright. Place pears in a
steamer in an upright position; cover
and simmer 15 to 20 minutes or until
pears are tender.

Combine sugar and cornstarch in a
small saucepan; gradually add reserved muscadine juice, stirring well.
Bring mixture to a boil, and cook 1
minute, stirring constantly. Remove
from heat.

Place pears in individual compotes;
pour sauce over pears. Yield: 4
servings.   *Hattie Culbreth*
                Rutherfordton, North Carolina

SCUPPERNONG ICE CREAM

6 cups scuppernongs (about 3
  pounds)
2 (14-ounce) cans sweetened
  condensed milk
1 quart half-and-half

Rinse and crush scuppernongs; place
in a medium saucepan. Bring to a
boil; cover, reduce heat, and simmer
10 minutes. Remove from heat;
mash scuppernongs with a potato
masher, and strain through a jelly
bag. Set aside 2 cups juice, and let
cool completely. Reserve any remaining juice for other uses.

Combine reserved 2 cups juice and
remaining ingredients in a large bowl;
stir well.

Pour mixture into freezer can of a
1-gallon hand-turned or electric
freezer. Freeze ice cream according
to manufacturer's instructions. Let
ripen about 2 hours before serving.
Yield: ½ gallon.   *Tina Brooks*
                    Damascus, Georgia

SCUPPERNONG PIE

4 cups scuppernongs (about 2
  pounds)
1 cup sugar
¼ cup all-purpose flour
⅛ teaspoon salt
1 tablespoon lemon juice
1½ tablespoons butter or
  margarine, melted
1 unbaked 9-inch pastry shell
Crumb Topping

Rinse scuppernongs; drain well.

Remove skins from scuppernongs;
separate and set both aside. Place
pulp in a heavy saucepan, and bring
to a boil. Reduce heat, and simmer,
uncovered, 5 minutes. Press pulp
through a sieve to remove seeds.
Combine pulp, skins, sugar, and next
4 ingredients; stir well. Pour into
pastry shell. Sprinkle Crumb Topping
over pie. Bake at 400° for 40 minutes. Yield: one 9-inch pie.

Crumb Topping

½ cup all-purpose flour
¼ cup sugar
⅓ cup butter or margarine

Combine flour and sugar; stir well. Cut in butter with pastry blender until mixture resembles coarse meal. Yield: about 1 cup.

Helen J. Wright
Leesville, South Carolina

Chocolate Cookies Are The Best

Nothing satisfies a sweet tooth like a plateful of chocolate cookies and a tall glass of milk. The recipes here offer a variety of flavor combinations for any occasion.

DATE-AND-ALMOND BROWNIES

2 (1-ounce) squares unsweetened baking chocolate
⅓ cup butter or margarine
2 eggs, beaten
1 cup sugar
¾ cup all-purpose flour
½ teaspoon baking powder
¼ teaspoon salt
½ cup chopped almonds, toasted
½ cup chopped dates
1 teaspoon vanilla extract

Combine chocolate and butter in top of a double boiler; bring water to a boil. Reduce heat to low; cook until chocolate melts. Remove from heat, and cool.

Combine eggs and sugar; beat well at medium speed of an electric mixer. Add chocolate mixture; beat until blended. Combine flour, baking powder, and salt; stir into batter.

Set aside 2 tablespoons almonds. Stir remaining almonds, dates, and vanilla into batter.

Spoon batter into a greased and floured 8-inch square pan; sprinkle with reserved almonds. Bake at 350° for 20 to 25 minutes or until a wooden pick inserted in center comes out clean. Cool on a wire rack; cut into squares. Yield: 16 brownies. *Mrs. L. W. Mayer*
Richmond, Virginia

CHOCOLATE-NUT FREEZER COOKIES

⅓ cup butter or margarine, softened
⅓ cup shortening
½ cup sugar
½ cup firmly packed brown sugar
1 egg
2 (1-ounce) squares semisweet chocolate, melted
1 tablespoon milk
1 teaspoon vanilla extract
2 cups all-purpose flour
1 teaspoon baking powder
½ teaspoon salt
1 cup chopped pecans

Cream butter and shortening; gradually add sugars, beating well at medium speed of an electric mixer. Add egg, melted chocolate, milk, and vanilla, beating well.

Combine flour, baking powder, and salt; add to creamed mixture, mixing well. Stir in pecans. Shape dough into two 9-inch logs.

Cut dough into ¼-inch-thick slices, and place on ungreased cookie sheets. Bake at 350° for 8 to 10 minutes. Transfer cookies to wire racks to cool completely.

Note: To freeze before baking, wrap logs in heavy-duty plastic wrap, and freeze. To serve, thaw dough, slice, and bake cookies as directed. Yield: 5 dozen. *Jean Pashby*
Memphis, Tennessee

CHOCOLATE MACAROON COOKIES

1 (4-ounce) package sweet baking chocolate
2 egg whites
½ cup sugar
¼ teaspoon vanilla extract
1 (7-ounce) can flaked coconut

Place chocolate in top of a double boiler; bring water to a boil. Reduce heat to low; cook until chocolate melts, stirring occasionally. Remove from heat, and cool.

Beat egg whites (at room temperature) at high speed of an electric mixer 1 minute. Gradually add sugar, 1 tablespoon at a time, beating until stiff peaks form and sugar dissolves (about 2 to 4 minutes). Add melted chocolate and vanilla; beat well. Stir in coconut.

Drop by teaspoonfuls onto cookie sheets lined with brown paper. Bake at 350° for 12 to 15 minutes. Transfer cookies, leaving them on brown paper, to wire rack to cool. Carefully remove cookies from brown paper. Yield: 4½ dozen. *Susan W. Pajcic*
Jacksonville, Florida

SUPER CHOCOLATE CHUNK COOKIES

1 cup butter or margarine, softened
1 cup sugar
½ cup firmly packed brown sugar
2 eggs
2 teaspoons vanilla extract
2 cups all-purpose flour
1 teaspoon baking powder
½ teaspoon salt
1 (12-ounce) package semisweet chocolate chunks
1 cup chopped walnuts

Cream butter; gradually add sugars, beating well at medium speed of an electric mixer. Add eggs and vanilla, beating well.

Combine flour, baking powder, and salt; add to creamed mixture, mixing well. Stir in semisweet chocolate chunks and walnuts. Refrigerate dough at least 1 hour.

Drop dough by tablespoonfuls onto ungreased cookie sheets. Bake at 350° for 12 to 15 minutes or until lightly browned. Cool slightly on cookie sheets; transfer to wire racks to cool completely. Yield: 4 dozen.

Yvonne M. Greer
Greenville, South Carolina

A Winning World Series Party

It's almost time for the World Series, so plan now to invite some guests for a party. With this menu, which serves six, food preparation is easy.

The Day Before: Make Onion-Cheese Buns, and store in an airtight container. Marinate, cook, then refrigerate the Barbecued Brisket. (It slices easier when cold.) Mix up the barbecue sauce.

Game Day Strategy: While Scalloped Corn bakes, make Nutty Cabbage Slaw. Fix Chili Dip right before your guests arrive.

Chili Dip
Barbecued Brisket
Onion-Cheese Buns
Scalloped Corn
Nutty Cabbage Slaw

CHILI DIP

1 (15-ounce) can chili without
  beans
1 (8-ounce) package cream
  cheese, softened
½ cup green chile sauce or
  jalapeño salsa
1 (2¼-ounce) can sliced black
  olives, drained

Combine chili and cream cheese in a medium saucepan. Cook over low heat until cheese melts, stirring occasionally. Stir in sauce and olives. Serve dip warm with assorted chips. Yield: 3 cups.
Rose Durham
Holliday, Texas

BARBECUED BRISKET

1 (3½- to 4-pound) beef brisket
¼ cup plus 2 tablespoons liquid
  smoke
1 teaspoon salt
1 tablespoon onion powder
1 tablespoon garlic powder
Barbecue Sauce

Line a 13- x 9- x 2-inch baking pan with a 36-inch piece of heavy-duty aluminum foil, leaving a 9-inch overhang at short ends.

Trim excess fat from brisket. Place in prepared pan; sprinkle with liquid smoke and salt. Bring long sides of foil together, and fold down. Fold up short ends; crimp to seal. Chill 8 hours.

Unwrap brisket, and sprinkle with onion powder and garlic powder. Rewrap brisket, and bake at 300° for 4 hours. Remove from pan, discarding juices; thinly slice brisket, and serve with Barbecue Sauce. Yield: 6 to 8 servings.

Barbecue Sauce

1 cup catsup
½ cup water
2 tablespoons butter or margarine
2½ tablespoons brown sugar
2½ teaspoons dry mustard
¾ teaspoon celery salt
3 tablespoons Worcestershire
  sauce

Combine all ingredients in a saucepan. Bring mixture to a boil; reduce heat, and simmer 15 minutes. Yield: 1½ cups.
Lois Hansen
Niceville, Florida

ONION-CHEESE BUNS

½ cup finely chopped onion
1 tablespoon butter, melted
1 (16-ounce) package hot roll mix
1 cup hot water (120° to 130°)
1 egg
½ cup grated Parmesan cheese
1 teaspoon dried parsley flakes
¼ teaspoon garlic powder

Sauté onion in butter; cool. Combine roll mix, water, and egg; mix well. Stir in cheese, parsley flakes, garlic powder, and sautéed onion.

Turn dough out onto a well-floured surface; knead 5 minutes or until smooth and elastic. Shape into a ball. Place dough in a well-greased bowl, turning to grease top. Cover and let rise in a warm place (85°), free from drafts, 30 to 40 minutes or until doubled in bulk.

Punch dough down. Shape dough into 12 smooth balls. Place on a greased baking sheet. Flatten each ball to form a bun. Cover and let rise in a warm place (85°), free from drafts, 20 minutes or until doubled in bulk. Bake at 375° for 15 to 20 minutes or until golden. Yield: 12 buns.

SCALLOPED CORN

½ cup chopped green onions
2 tablespoons butter or
  margarine, melted
1 (17-ounce) can cream-style corn
1 (7-ounce) can whole kernel
  corn, drained
1 cup cracker crumbs
1 cup milk
2 eggs, slighty beaten
½ teaspoon salt

Sauté green onions in butter until tender. Stir in corn and remaining ingredients. Spoon mixture into a lightly greased 1½-quart casserole. Bake, uncovered, at 350° for 1 hour and 10 minutes. Yield: 6 servings.
Joyce B. Andrews
Washington, Virginia

NUTTY CABBAGE SLAW

½ cup mayonnaise
2 tablespoons sugar
2 tablespoons vinegar
4 cups coarsely shredded cabbage
1 cup salted Spanish peanuts,
  chopped
Cabbage leaves (optional)

Combine mayonnaise, sugar, and vinegar; mix well. Chill 2 hours.

Combine cabbage and peanuts; add dressing mixture, and toss gently. Serve on cabbage leaves, if desired. Yield: 6 servings.
Janie Wallace
Seguin, Texas

OCTOBER

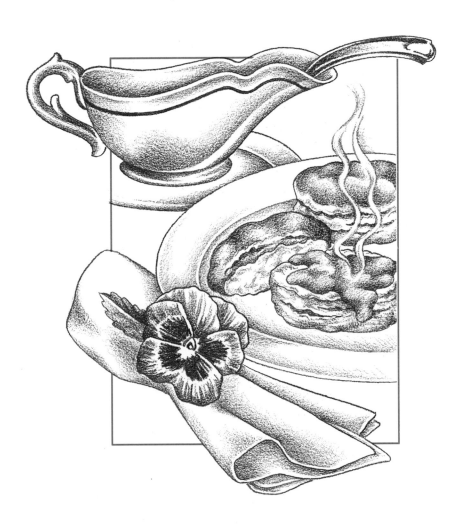

Country Breakfast Fare

Breakfast in the South has traditionally been taken seriously. You've no doubt been awakened by the aroma of frying bacon or maybe the appetizing smell of chicken, steak, pork chops, or fish drifting from the kitchen. Sausage-and-biscuit or fruit-and-cereal breakfasts seem meager in comparison. Until recent times, the traditional "country" menu was similar in many Southern homes, regardless of their proximity to the city. While health concerns and career demands have changed this daily custom, many Southerners savor this ample fare on weekends, holidays, and special occasions. And for some, a traditional, hearty breakfast menu remains a daily ritual, or it is served as a favorite quick supper.

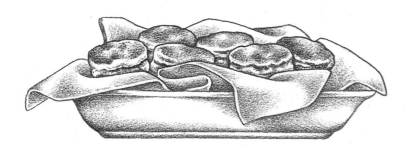

SEASONED FRIED QUAIL
(pictured on page v)

8 quail, cleaned
1 cup buttermilk
1 tablespoon hot sauce
2 tablespoons Worcestershire
 sauce
1 teaspoon dried whole thyme
1 teaspoon pepper
½ teaspoon salt
1 cup all-purpose flour
1 teaspoon salt
½ teaspoon pepper
¼ teaspoon red pepper
1 teaspoon paprika
Vegetable oil
½ cup chicken broth
¼ cup all-purpose flour
2 cups milk
1 tablespoon Worcestershire
 sauce
¼ teaspoon salt
½ teaspoon pepper
Tomato slices (optional)
Parsley sprigs (optional)

Split quail to, but not through, the breast bone. Combine buttermilk and next 5 ingredients in a large shallow dish, mixing well. Add quail; cover and marinate 8 hours in refrigerator. Remove quail from marinade, reserving marinade.

Combine 1 cup flour and next 4 ingredients; dredge quail in flour mixture, dip in reserved marinade, and dredge again in flour mixture.

Heat ¼ inch of oil in a skillet; add quail, and cook over medium heat 10 minutes or until golden, turning occasionally. Drain on paper towels.

Pour off all but ¼ cup oil from skillet. Add broth and quail; cover and cook over medium heat 15 minutes. Transfer quail to a serving platter. Drain off drippings, reserving ¼ cup in skillet.

Add ¼ cup flour to drippings in skillet; cook over low heat, stirring until smooth. Cook 1 minute, stirring constantly. Gradually add 2 cups milk, and cook over medium heat, stirring constantly, until thickened and bubbly. Stir in Worcestershire sauce, ¼ teaspoon salt, and ½ teaspoon pepper. Serve quail with gravy. If desired, garnish quail with tomato slices and parsley. Yield: 4 servings.

Cheryl Midgley
Gadsden, Alabama

GRILLED BREAKFAST QUAIL

½ cup butter or margarine,
 melted
⅛ teaspoon garlic powder
⅛ teaspoon salt
8 quail, cleaned
8 slices bacon

Combine butter, garlic powder, and salt; brush on all sides of quail. Wrap 1 slice bacon around each quail; secure with wooden picks.

Grill quail over hot coals 45 to 50 minutes or until done, turning once. Remove wooden picks, and serve immediately. Yield: 4 servings.

John-Michael Van Dyke
Hilton Head Island, South Carolina

SPECIAL FRIED CHICKEN

6 (6-ounce) chicken breast halves,
 skinned
1 (8-ounce) bottle commercial
 Italian salad dressing
2 eggs
¼ cup water
1½ cups all-purpose flour
1½ tablespoons paprika
1½ teaspoons curry powder
¾ teaspoon salt
¾ teaspoon pepper
Vegetable oil

Place chicken in a large shallow container; pour salad dressing over chicken. Cover and marinate in refrigerator 8 hours.

Combine eggs and water; mix well. Combine flour, paprika, curry powder, salt, and pepper in a plastic bag; shake to mix.

Drain chicken, and discard marinade. Place 2 or 3 pieces of chicken in flour mixture; shake well. Dip in egg mixture; return to flour mixture, and shake again. Repeat with remaining chicken breasts.

Heat ½ inch oil in a large skillet to 350°; add chicken, and fry 20 to 25 minutes or until golden brown, turning to brown both sides. Drain on paper towels. Yield: 6 servings.

Mrs. George B. Lance
Madison, Tennessee

HAM AND RED-EYE GRAVY

2 (½-inch-thick) ham steaks
  (about 1 pound each)
1½ cups milk
2 tablespoons vegetable oil,
  divided
1 cup strong black coffee
¼ teaspoon pepper
Hot biscuits

Place ham in a large shallow container; pour milk over ham. Cover and refrigerate 8 hours. Remove ham from milk. Cut slashes in fat to keep ham from curling.

Cook 1 slice of ham in 1 tablespoon oil in a heavy skillet over low heat until light brown, turning once. Remove from skillet, and keep warm. Drain off pan drippings, reserving for gravy. Repeat procedure with remaining oil and ham.

Add pan drippings, coffee, and pepper to skillet; bring to a boil, stirring constantly. Reduce heat, and simmer 3 minutes. Serve gravy with ham and hot biscuits. Yield: 4 servings.
Shelby Green
Princeton, West Virginia

New Look, New Taste For Old Favorites

To Southerners, menus at upscale restaurants all over the South have added a sophisticated flair to regional staples. Country ham, shrimp, grits, crowder peas, corn pudding, venison, quail, cornbread, and even crawfish touch heartstrings of the local folks. It's the combinations—such as pork tenderloins with grits timbales, fresh quail stuffed with cornbread and pecans, grits with country ham, leeks, and shrimp, blue crab tart, soft-shell crawfish served on eggplant, or Virginia ham mousse—that may cause a raised eyebrow. The recipes here are good examples of how Southern specialties are being presented in new ways.

■ Owner and chef Frank Stitt of **Highlands: A Bar & Grill** in Birmingham, Alabama, has received national acclaim for his outstanding work as a regional chef. He says, "The trend is now to find the old recipes and traditions of your own area and update them." Try a sampling of his creative recipes.

ROAST PORK LOIN

1 (4- to 5-pound) pork loin roast
3 cloves garlic, crushed
3 tablespoons olive oil
2 teaspoons chopped fresh thyme
2 teaspoons chopped fresh
  rosemary
½ teaspoon salt
¼ teaspoon pepper
Aioli

Trim excess fat from roast; place roast on a rack in a roasting pan. Rub garlic over roast; brush with olive oil, and sprinkle with herbs. Cover roast, and refrigerate for at least 2 hours.

Sprinkle roast with salt and pepper. Bake at 500° for 15 minutes. Insert meat thermometer so that it does not touch fat or bone. Reduce heat to 325°; bake 1 hour and 20 minutes or until meat thermometer registers 160°. Allow roast to rest 15 minutes before carving. Serve with Aioli. Yield: 8 servings.

Aioli (garlic mayonnaise)

2 egg yolks
4 large cloves garlic, crushed
¼ teaspoon salt
1½ cups extra-virgin olive oil
¼ cup lemon juice
¼ teaspoon red pepper

Combine first 3 ingredients in a deep narrow bowl, and beat at high speed of an electric mixer until thick and lemon colored. Add oil, 1 tablespoon at a time, beating until mixture begins to thicken. Gradually add lemon juice, beating until thickened. Add pepper, stirring well. Store in a nonmetal container in the refrigerator. Yield: 1¾ cups.

BLACK-EYED PEA SALAD

2 sweet red peppers
2 yellow peppers
2 (16-ounce) packages frozen
  black-eyed peas or 2 pounds
  fresh black-eyed peas
2 cups water
1 ham shank
1 onion, halved
2 dried hot peppers
2 bay leaves
4 sprigs fresh thyme
2 tablespoons olive oil
½ teaspoon salt
¼ teaspoon freshly ground pepper
8 ounces fresh mozzarella cheese
  or goat cheese, cut into
  wedges
¼ pound slab bacon or
  thick-sliced bacon, cut into
  ⅛-inch cubes, cooked and
  drained
Fresh sorrel
8 hard-cooked quail eggs, halved

Place red and yellow peppers on a baking sheet. Broil 3 to 4 inches from heat, turning often with tongs, until blistered on all sides. Immediately place peppers in a plastic bag; seal and let stand 10 minutes to loosen skins.

Peel peppers; remove core and seeds. Cut into 2-inch-wide strips. Combine black-eyed peas and next 6 ingredients in a Dutch oven. Bring to a boil; cover, reduce heat, and simmer 45 minutes or until tender. Drain and cool; remove ham shank, onion, hot peppers, bay leaves, and thyme sprigs.

Combine peas, olive oil, salt, and pepper. Arrange peas in center of plate; place pepper strips diagonally across peas. Arrange cheese wedges on peppers; sprinkle peas with bacon. Garnish with sorrel and hard-cooked quail eggs. Yield: 8 servings.

Tip: *Plan your menus for the week, but stay flexible enough to substitute good buys when you spot them. By planning ahead, you can use leftovers in another day's meal.*

■ Chef John Wagner says he highlights local seafood on his menu at **Flamingo Café** in Destin, Florida. Veering from the traditional deep-fried seafood fare, John says he adds a Louisiana flair to the recipes.

SOFT-SHELL CRAWFISH ON EGGPLANT

20 whole soft-shell crawfish
   (about ¾ pound)
1 cup all-purpose flour
2 tablespoons Old Bay Seasoning
2 tablespoons paprika
1 tablespoon black pepper
1 tablespoon white pepper
1½ teaspoons red pepper
1½ teaspoons garlic powder
1 egg, slightly beaten
½ cup milk
4 (¾-inch-thick) slices eggplant
Vegetable oil
½ cup Hollandaise Sauce
½ cup Lemon Meunière Sauce
½ cup Garlic Beurre Blanc Sauce
¾ cup Glazed Nuts
Carrot flowers (optional)
Lemon wedges (optional)
Onion fans (optional)

Remove crawfish heads, including small ball. Leave shell and tails intact, and set aside.

Combine flour and next 6 ingredients; set aside. Combine egg and milk; stir well. Dip eggplant into egg mixture; dredge in flour mixture. Pour oil to depth of 1 inch in a heavy saucepan; heat oil to 350°. Fry eggplant 2 to 3 minutes or until golden brown. Drain.

Dip crawfish in egg mixture; dredge in flour mixture. Pour oil to depth of 1 inch in a heavy saucepan; heat to 350°. Fry crawfish about 2 minutes or until shells are bright in color and batter is golden brown. Drain on paper towels.

Spoon 2 tablespoons of each sauce onto each serving plate. Place a slice of eggplant in center of plate; top with 5 crawfish. Sprinkle 3 tablespoons Glazed Nuts over crawfish. If desired, garnish each plate with carrot, lemon, and onion. Yield: 4 appetizer servings.

Hollandaise Sauce

6 egg yolks
1 tablespoon dry white wine
2 tablespoons lemon juice
1½ cups butter, melted

Combine egg yolks, wine, and lemon juice in top of a double boiler. Place over boiling water, and cook, beating at medium speed of an electric mixer, 3 minutes or until thickened.

Remove from heat. Add butter, 1 tablespoon at a time, beating at medium speed of an electric mixer until thickened. Yield: 2 cups.

Lemon Meunière Sauce

3 tablespoons lemon juice
2 tablespoons white wine
1 tablespoon white vinegar
1 shallot, chopped
¼ cup plus 2 tablespoons
   whipping cream
2 cups butter, softened
¼ teaspoon browning-and-
   seasoning sauce

Combine first 4 ingredients in a saucepan; bring to a boil. Boil 2 minutes or until 95% of liquid evaporates. Add cream, and bring to a boil; boil 1 minute. Remove from heat; cool 2 minutes. Return to low heat. Add butter, 2 tablespoons at a time, stirring with a wire whisk until butter is incorporated. Keep temperature at 160°. Stir in browning-and-seasoning sauce. Sauce will separate if reheated. Yield: 2 cups.

Garlic Beurre Blanc Sauce

2 tablespoons white wine
1 tablespoon white vinegar
6 cloves garlic, chopped
1 shallot, chopped
½ cup whipping cream
2 cups butter, softened

Combine first 4 ingredients in a saucepan; bring to a boil. Boil 2 minutes or until 95% of liquid evaporates. Add whipping cream, and bring to a boil; boil 1 minute. Remove from heat. Cool 2 minutes. Return to low heat. Add butter, 2 tablespoons at a time, stirring with a wire whisk until butter is incorporated. Keep sauce temperature at 160°. Sauce will separate if reheated. Yield: 2 cups.

Glazed Nuts

3¾ cups pecan pieces
3 cups slivered almonds
½ cup sugar
⅛ teaspoon seasoned salt
¼ cup vegetable oil

Combine all ingredients in a large heavy skillet; cook over medium heat about 5 minutes or until golden brown, stirring constantly. Immediately spread nuts in a thin layer on a jellyroll pan; cool. Stir occasionally to separate nuts. Yield: 6¾ cups.

SNAPPER DESTIN

1 cup all-purpose flour
2 tablespoons Old Bay Seasoning
2 tablespoons paprika
1 tablespoon black pepper
1 tablespoon white pepper
1½ teaspoons red pepper
1½ teaspoons garlic powder
2 pounds red snapper fillets (cut
   into 4 to 6 pieces)
¼ cup butter or margarine,
   melted
Vegetable cooking spray
8 to 12 unpeeled jumbo fresh
   shrimp
1 pound fresh lump crabmeat,
   drained and flaked
2 to 3 tablespoons butter or
   margarine
½ to ¾ cup Hollandaise Sauce
   (recipe above)
½ to ¾ cup Lemon Meunière
   Sauce (recipe above)
½ to ¾ cup Garlic Beurre Blanc
   Sauce (recipe above)
Carrot flowers (optional)
Lemon wedges (optional)
Onion fans (optional)

Combine first 7 ingredients, mixing well. Dredge fillets in flour mixture; dip fillets in ¼ cup melted butter.

Spray a fish basket with cooking spray; place fish in basket. Grill over medium-hot coals 10 minutes on each side or until fish flakes easily when tested with a fork.

Peel and devein shrimp, leaving tails intact. Sauté shrimp and crabmeat in 2 to 3 tablespoons butter.

Spoon 2 tablespoons of each sauce onto each plate; place fillet on sauces. Top each with ¼ cup crabmeat and 2 shrimp. If desired, garnish with carrot flowers, lemon wedges, and onion fans. Yield: 4 to 6 servings.

■ "It's Southern food," says Jenny Fitch about the recipes served at **Fearrington House,** just south of Chapel Hill, North Carolina. But she and chef Cory Mattson give the old-time favorites a classical touch.

MEDAILLIONS OF PORK WITH VEGETABLES

3 cups chicken broth
2 cups Chablis or other dry white wine
¼ cup plus 2 tablespoons butter
2 tablespoons tomato paste
3 (1-pound) pork tenderloins
1 tablespoon corn oil
40 fresh or frozen asparagus spears (about 1¼ pounds)
2 medium-size yellow squash
2 medium carrots
Grits Timbales

Simmer chicken broth in a saucepan over medium heat until reduced to about ½ cup; set aside. Simmer wine in a saucepan over medium heat until reduced to ½ cup; set aside.

Melt butter over low heat in a small saucepan; skim off white froth from top. Strain off clear butter into a skillet (discard milky sediment).

Add tomato paste to butter; cook over medium heat until smooth and dark, stirring frequently. Add reduced ½ cup broth and ½ cup wine; stir well.

Cut pork tenderloins into 24 (2-ounce) medaillions. Heat oil in a large ovenproof skillet until very hot; add pork medaillions, and sauté 1 to 2 minutes. Turn medaillions over; place skillet in oven, and bake at 425° for 10 to 12 minutes. Keep pork warm.

Snap off tough ends of asparagus. Remove scales from stalks with a knife or vegetable peeler, if desired.

Cut squash in half lengthwise; scoop out seeds. Cut squash into ¼-inch slices.

Cut carrots in half; cut each half into julienne strips. Place vegetables in steaming rack over boiling water. Cover and steam 6 to 8 minutes.

Place a Grits Timbale in center of each plate; arrange 3 pork medaillions around timbale. Divide vegetables evenly, and arrange on each plate. Spoon sauce over meat and vegetables. Yield: 8 servings.

Grits Timbales

6 cups water
1½ cups uncooked regular grits
2 teaspoons salt
2 cloves garlic, minced
1½ cups (6 ounces) shredded sharp Cheddar cheese
2 tablespoons grated Parmesan cheese
½ teaspoon salt
½ teaspoon freshly ground pepper
3 egg yolks, slightly beaten
½ cup whipping cream
2 tablespoons grated Parmesan cheese

Bring water to a boil in a Dutch oven; add grits and 2 teaspoons salt. Cook according to package directions. Remove from heat. Stir in garlic, Cheddar cheese, 2 tablespoons Parmesan cheese, ½ teaspoon salt, and pepper. Combine yolks and cream; stir into grits.

Spoon mixture into 12 (4-ounce) buttered ramekins. Place ramekins in a large pan; pour hot water to a depth of 1 inch in pan. Cover with aluminum foil, and bake at 350° for

30 minutes. Remove from oven, and let cool. Remove timbales from ramekins; place upside down on a greased baking sheet. Sprinkle with 2 tablespoons Parmesan cheese; broil about 3 minutes or until browned. Yield: 12 servings.

POACHED PEARS WITH RASPBERRY SAUCE

6 medium-size firm, ripe pears
1 (25.4-ounce) bottle red wine
2 cups water
½ cup sugar
1 teaspoon whole cloves
½ teaspoon vanilla extract
1 (10-ounce) package frozen raspberries, thawed
¼ to ½ cup sugar
1 tablespoon Grand Marnier
Chocolate curls
Fresh raspberries (optional)

On each of 6 pears, cut a downward slash on either side of stem about 1½ inches from top, forming a V. Remove tops, and set aside. Peel bottom portion of pears, and cut a thin slice from bottoms so that pears stand upright.

Combine wine, water, ½ cup sugar, cloves, and vanilla in a Dutch oven; bring to a boil. Add pears; cover, reduce heat, and simmer 20 minutes. Remove pears; set aside.

Put thawed raspberries through a sieve, and strain. Discard seeds. Combine raspberry puree, ¼ cup sugar, and Grand Marnier.

Divide Raspberry Sauce among 6 dessert plates, and set pears in center of sauce. Replace uncooked pear tops. Garnish with chocolate curls and, if desired, raspberries. Yield: 6 servings.

RUM-ORANGE COCONUT CAKE

2 cups water
½ cup sugar
¼ cup grated orange rind
¾ cup butter or margarine, softened
2 cups sugar
3 egg yolks
2 cups all-purpose flour
2 teaspoons baking powder
¼ teaspoon salt
¾ cup milk
2 egg whites
Orange Filling
Rum Cream
1 small fresh coconut, grated, or ½ cup flaked coconut

Combine water and ½ cup sugar in a small saucepan; bring mixture to a boil. Add orange rind, and cook 3 minutes. Drain well. Set orange rind aside for batter and filling.

Cream butter; gradually add 2 cups sugar, beating well at medium speed of an electric mixer. Add egg yolks, one at a time; beat well after each addition.

Combine flour, baking powder, and salt. Add flour mixture to creamed mixture alternately with milk, beginning and ending with flour mixture.

Beat egg whites (at room temperature) until stiff peaks form; fold egg whites and 2 tablespoons orange rind into batter.

Grease two 9-inch round cakepans, and line with wax paper; grease and flour wax paper. Pour batter into prepared pans; bake at 350° for 25 to 30 minutes. Cool 10 minutes; remove from pans, and cool completely on wire racks.

Split cake layers in half horizontally to make 4 layers. Spread Orange Filling between layers; spread Rum Cream on top and sides of cake, and sprinkle with coconut. Chill. Yield: one 4-layer cake.

Orange Filling

1 cup sugar
¼ cup cornstarch
¼ teaspoon salt
1 cup orange juice
2 tablespoons butter or margarine
2 tablespoons lemon juice

Combine sugar, cornstarch, and salt in a heavy saucepan; gradually stir in orange juice. Bring to a boil; cook over medium heat, stirring constantly, until thickened. Remove from heat; stir in butter, lemon juice, and 2 tablespoons reserved orange rind. Cool. Yield: 1½ cups.

Rum Cream

1 cup whipping cream
⅓ cup sugar
2 teaspoons rum

Beat whipping cream until soft peaks form. Add sugar and rum; beat until stiff peaks form. Yield: 2½ cups.

Apples & Pears Better With A Crust

When autumn brings crisp air and colorful trees to the South, it signals that apples and pears are ready for picking. The flavors and textures of both are just as varied as the colors, making these two fall specialties popular with almost everyone.

When you're choosing apples and pears from the market or your backyard tree, you'll find that some are better than others for cooking. The best cooking or all-purpose apples are Golden Delicious, Winesap, Rome Beauty, York Imperial, and Stayman. These hold their shapes and retain their flavors during cooking. Apples can be stored in the vegetable crisper or plastic bag on the refrigerator shelf. They will ripen faster if left at room temperature.

Pears are classified into two groups—dessert or cooking. Dessert pears have a wonderfully sweet flavor and are excellent served fresh. Cooking pears, such as Anjou and Bosc, hold their shapes well during baking and cooking.

Unlike apples, pears are best picked from the tree just before they ripen. The tree-ripened pears develop a coarser texture than those allowed to ripen at room temperature after picking. In fact, pears to be used in baked or cooked desserts are best when firm.

APPLE DUMPLINGS WITH ORANGE HARD SAUCE
(pictured on page 237)

2 cups all-purpose flour
2 teaspoons sugar
Pinch of salt
¾ cup shortening
1 egg, beaten
½ cup ice water
6 medium-size Granny Smith or cooking apples
½ cup sugar
1 teaspoon ground cinnamon
3 tablespoons butter or margarine, divided
2 tablespoons sugar
1½ cups water
½ cup sugar
1 teaspoon grated lemon rind
1 tablespoon lemon juice
¼ teaspoon ground cinnamon
Orange Hard Sauce

Combine first 3 ingredients; cut in shortening with a pastry blender until mixture resembles coarse meal. Combine egg and ice water; gradually add to flour mixture, stirring to make a soft dough. Cover and chill. Roll pastry to a 21- x 14-inch rectangle on a floured surface; cut into six 7-inch squares. Peel and core apples; reserve apple peel. Place one apple on each pastry square.

Combine ½ cup sugar and 1 teaspoon cinnamon; fill core of each apple with sugar-cinnamon mixture. Dot each apple with 1 teaspoon butter. Moisten edges of each dumpling with water; bring corners to center, pinching edges to seal. Use extra pastry to shape apple stems and leaves, if desired. Place dumplings in a 12- x 8- x 2-inch baking dish. Cover and chill 1 hour. Sprinkle 2 tablespoons sugar over dumplings.

Combine reserved apple peel and 1½ cups water in a saucepan; bring to a boil. Cover, reduce heat, and simmer 30 minutes. Drain, reserving liquid, and press apple skins through a sieve or food mill. Combine reserved liquid, apple puree, ½ cup sugar, remaining 1 tablespoon butter, lemon rind, lemon juice, and ¼ teaspoon cinnamon; pour over apples. Bake, uncovered, at 400° for 10 minutes. Reduce heat to 350°; bake 30 minutes. Serve hot with Orange Hard Sauce. Yield: 6 servings.

Orange Hard Sauce

½ cup butter, softened
2 cups sifted powdered sugar
1 teaspoon grated orange rind
2 teaspoons orange juice
½ teaspoon orange extract

Combine softened butter and powdered sugar; add remaining ingredients, stirring until smooth. Yield: about 1 cup. *Mrs. Joe H. Emersen*
Winnfield, Louisiana

LUSCIOUS APPLE ROLLS
(pictured on page 237)

2 cups sugar
2 cups water
¼ teaspoon ground cinnamon
¼ teaspoon ground nutmeg
2 tablespoons butter or margarine
2 cups all-purpose flour
2 teaspoons baking powder
1 teaspoon salt
⅔ cup shortening
½ cup milk
2½ cups shredded cooking apples
Vanilla ice cream (optional)

Combine first 4 ingredients in a saucepan. Cook over medium heat, stirring constantly, until sugar dissolves; stir in butter. Set aside.

Combine flour, baking powder, and salt; cut shortening into flour mixture with a pastry blender until mixture resembles coarse meal. Add milk, stirring just until dry ingredients are moistened. Turn dough out onto a lightly floured surface, and knead lightly 4 or 5 times.

Roll dough to a 12- x 9-inch rectangle. Spread apples evenly over dough; roll up jellyroll fashion, beginning with long side. Cut into 12 (1-inch) slices; place slices, cut side down, in a well-greased 13- x 9- x 2-inch pan. Pour sugar syrup around slices; bake at 375° for 40 minutes or until golden brown. If desired, serve warm with vanilla ice cream. Yield: 12 servings. *Nancy Bettis-Worsham*
Grapevine, Texas

FRIED APPLE PIES

4 medium-size cooking apples, peeled and sliced
½ cup sugar
¼ teaspoon ground allspice
Pastry (recipe follows)
Vegetable oil

Place apples in a saucepan with a small amount of water. Cook over medium heat, stirring occasionally, about 20 minutes or until tender. Drain well. Mash slightly, and measure 2⅓ cups apples, reserving remaining apples for other uses. Combine apples, sugar, and allspice, stirring well. Set aside.

Divide pastry into 7 portions; roll each portion to a 7-inch circle. Spoon ⅓ cup apple mixture onto half of each circle. Fold circles in half; press edges together with a fork dipped in flour to seal. (Fry pies immediately after filling.)

Heat ½ inch oil in a large skillet over medium-high heat. Cook pies, two at a time, until golden, turning once; drain on paper towels. Yield: 7 (7-inch) pies.

Pastry

⅓ cup shortening
2 cups self-rising flour
⅔ cup cold water

Cut shortening into flour until mixture resembles coarse meal. Sprinkle water (1 tablespoon at a time) evenly over surface; stir with a fork until all ingredients are moistened. Shape into a ball. Yield: enough pastry for 7 (7-inch) pies. *Gladys Stout*
Elizabethton, Tennessee

APPLE TART
WITH CHEESE PASTRY
(pictured on page 237)

1½ cups all-purpose flour
½ teaspoon salt
½ cup shortening
1 cup (4 ounces) shredded Cheddar cheese
4 to 5 tablespoons ice water
½ cup powdered non-dairy coffee creamer
½ cup firmly packed brown sugar
½ cup sugar
⅓ cup all-purpose flour
¼ teaspoon salt
1 teaspoon ground cinnamon
½ teaspoon ground nutmeg
¼ cup butter or margarine
About 6 cups (½-inch-thick) apple slices
2 tablespoons lemon juice

Combine 1½ cups flour and ½ teaspoon salt; cut in shortening with a pastry blender until mixture resembles coarse meal. Stir in cheese. Sprinkle water over flour mixture, and stir with a fork until dry ingredients are moistened. Shape into a ball. Roll dough to ⅛-inch thickness on a floured surface. Place in a 12-inch tart pan or pizza pan. Set aside.

Combine coffee creamer and next 6 ingredients; sprinkle half of mixture evenly over pastry. Cut butter into remaining mixture; set aside.

Arrange apple slices in a circle in pastry shell, overlapping slices. Sprinkle with lemon juice and remaining sugar mixture. Bake at 450° for 30 minutes or until apples are tender. Remove from tart pan to serve. Yield: one 12-inch tart.
Erma Jackson
Huntsville, Alabama

UPSIDE-DOWN SOUTHERN APPLE PIE

¼ cup butter or margarine, softened
⅔ cup pecan halves
⅔ cup firmly packed brown sugar
Pastry for double-crust 9-inch pie
6 cups peeled and sliced cooking apples (about 1¾ pounds)
Juice of 1 lemon
⅓ cup firmly packed brown sugar
1 tablespoon all-purpose flour
¼ teaspoon salt
½ teaspoon ground cinnamon
½ teaspoon ground nutmeg

Spread butter in bottom of a 9-inch, deep-dish pieplate. Arrange pecan halves, rounded sides down, on bottom of pieplate; gently press into butter. Sprinkle ⅔ cup brown sugar over pecans, and press gently.

Roll half of pastry to ⅛-inch thickness on a lightly floured surface; transfer to pieplate, and press firmly onto bottom and sides of pieplate. Trim off excess pastry along edges; set aside.

Combine apples and lemon juice in a bowl. Combine ⅓ cup brown sugar and remaining ingredients. Sprinkle over apple mixture; toss gently. Spoon filling into pastry shell.

Roll remaining pastry to ⅛-inch thickness; transfer to top of pie. Trim off excess pastry along edges. Fold edges under, and flute. Prick top of crust with a fork for steam to escape. Bake at 450° for 10 minutes. Reduce temperature to 350°, and bake 30 to 40 minutes. Cool 5 minutes. Place plate on top of pie, and invert. Yield: one 9-inch pie.

Pat Boschen
Ashland, Virginia

PEAR MINCEMEAT PIE

Pastry for double-crust 9-inch pie
2 cups pear mincemeat (recipe follows)

Roll half of pastry to ⅛-inch thickness on a lightly floured surface. Place in a 9-inch pieplate. Spoon prepared mincemeat evenly into prepared shell.

Roll remaining pastry to ⅛-inch thickness; transfer to top of pie. Trim off excess pastry along edges; fold edges under, and flute. Cut slits in top crust for steam to escape.

Bake at 350° for 45 minutes. If necessary, cover edges of pastry with strips of aluminum foil to prevent excessive browning. Yield: one 9-inch pie.

Pear Mincemeat

7½ pounds pears, peeled, cored, and cut into eighths
1 lemon, unpeeled and cut into eighths
2 (15-ounce) packages raisins
4½ cups sugar
1½ teaspoons ground cloves
1½ teaspoons ground cinnamon
1½ teaspoons ground allspice

Position knife blade in food processor bowl. Add about 1 cup pears; process until finely chopped. Repeat with remaining pears and lemon.

Combine chopped fruit and remaining ingredients in a Dutch oven. Bring to a boil; reduce heat, and simmer, uncovered, 30 minutes.

Pour hot mixture into hot sterilized jars, leaving ¼-inch headspace. Wipe jar rims. Cover at once with metal lids, and screw on bands. Process in boiling-water bath for 20 minutes. Serve as a relish, or use to make Pear Mincemeat Pie. Yield: 8 pints.

Velma Bryant
Johnson City, Tennessee

DELICIOUS PEAR PIE

Pastry for double-crust 9-inch pie
¼ cup sugar
1 tablespoon all-purpose flour
¾ teaspoon ground cinnamon
½ teaspoon ground nutmeg
6 medium baking pears, peeled and thinly sliced
½ cup sugar
3 tablespoons all-purpose flour
3 tablespoons butter or margarine

Roll half of pastry to ⅛-inch thickness on a lightly floured surface. Place in a 9-inch pieplate; set aside.

Combine ¼ cup sugar, 1 tablespoon flour, cinnamon, and nutmeg in a bowl; stir well. Add pears; stir well. Spoon into pastry shell.

Combine ½ cup sugar and 3 tablespoons flour; cut in butter until mixture resembles coarse meal. Sprinkle over top of pears.

Roll remaining pastry to ⅛-inch thickness; transfer to top of pie. Trim off excess pastry along edges. Fold edges under, and flute. Cut slits in top crust for steam to escape.

Bake at 425° for 45 to 50 minutes. Cover edges of pastry with strips of aluminum foil to prevent excessive browning, if necessary. Serve warm or cool. Yield: one 9-inch pie.

Jodie McCoy
Tulsa, Oklahoma

NATURAL PEAR-APPLE PIE
(pictured on page 237)

3 large cooking apples, peeled and sliced
¾ cup dark or golden raisins
¼ cup plus 2 tablespoons sugar
1 tablespoon whole wheat flour
¼ teaspoon ground cinnamon
¼ teaspoon ground nutmeg
2 medium pears, peeled and sliced
Pastry for double-crust 9-inch pie
1 tablespoon dark rum or cognac
1½ tablespoons butter or margarine, melted
2 tablespoons finely chopped black walnuts

Combine first 6 ingredients in a bowl; toss. Cover and chill 20 minutes.

Cook pears in a small amount of water in a saucepan 5 minutes or until tender. Drain and mash; set pears aside.

Roll half of pastry to ⅛-inch thickness on a lightly floured surface. Place in a 9-inch deep-dish pieplate. Spoon half of apple mixture into pastry shell. Spread half of pears over apple mixture. Repeat procedure with remaining apple mixture and pears. Sprinkle with rum, butter, and black walnuts.

Roll remaining pastry to ⅛-inch thickness; transfer to top of pie.

Trim off excess pastry. Fold edges under, and flute. Cut slits in top crust for steam to escape. Bake at 425° for 45 minutes. Cover edges of pastry with aluminum foil to prevent excessive browning, if necessary. Yield: one 9-inch pie.

Mrs. Ronald D. Smith
Houston, Texas

Invite Spooky Friends To This Party

If little ghosts and goblins reside in your home, why not plan a party just for them prior to trick-or-treating this year? The recipes on our menu are simple to prepare and open up great opportunities for carrying out the theme in decorations.

QUICK LITTLE PIZZAS

1 pound ground beef
½ cup chili sauce
½ teaspoon dried Italian seasoning
5 English muffins, split and toasted
1 medium onion, thinly sliced (optional)
10 (1-ounce) slices sharp process cheese

Cook ground beef in a large skillet until meat is browned, stirring to crumble meat; drain well. Stir in chili sauce and Italian seasoning. Spoon ¼ cup beef mixture onto each English muffin half. Arrange onion slices over beef, if desired. Cut each cheese slice into 4 strips; arrange lattice-fashion over onion slices. Bake at 400° for 8 to 10 minutes or until cheese melts. Yield: 10 servings.

Dawn Lolley
Double Springs, Alabama

NUTTY POPCORN BALLS

1 (15-ounce) jar cane syrup
3 tablespoons butter or margarine
⅛ teaspoon cream of tartar
1 cup chopped pecans
4 quarts popped corn

Combine first 4 ingredients in a saucepan; cook over low heat, stirring gently, until butter melts. Cook over medium heat, without stirring, to soft crack stage (290°). Remove from heat.

Place popped corn in a large pan. Carefully pour hot syrup mixture over top, stirring well with a wooden spoon. Grease hands with butter, and shape mixture into 3½-inch balls. Place on wax paper to dry. Wrap in plastic wrap, and store in a cool, dry place. Yield: about 15 balls.

Note: One (5-ounce) bag seasoned popped corn may be substituted for plain home-popped corn, if desired.

Theresa Johnson Blount
Baton Rouge, Louisiana

GINGERBREAD MAN COOKIES

½ cup shortening
½ cup firmly packed brown sugar
½ cup molasses
½ teaspoon vinegar
½ cup buttermilk
3½ cups all-purpose flour
1 teaspoon baking soda
½ teaspoon salt
2 teaspoons ground ginger
2 teaspoons ground cinnamon
Orange candy-coated chocolate pieces or candy corn

Cream shortening; gradually add sugar, beating at medium speed of an electric mixer until light and fluffy. Add molasses, beating well.

Combine vinegar and buttermilk.

Combine flour, soda, salt, and spices. Add 1 cup flour mixture to creamed mixture; beat well. Add remaining flour mixture alternately with buttermilk mixture, beginning and ending with dry ingredients. Cover and chill dough at least 1 hour.

Roll dough to ¼-inch thickness on a lightly floured surface. Cut with a

5-inch gingerbread man cutter. Place on ungreased cookie sheets; bake at 375° for 10 minutes. Remove from oven, and quickly press candies into dough as desired. Return to oven 1 minute. Cool on wire racks. Store in an airtight container. Yield: 20 cookies.

Sandra Russell
Gainesville, Florida

Halloween Party Tips

For a Halloween party that is fun for the children and sets the mood for ghosts and goblins, follow some of these suggestions. Most items can be found at a novelty or department store.

■ Purchase a witch's hat as the centerpiece of your table. Black and orange paper plates and cups are fun to decorate with magic markers.

■ A pumpkin cookie jar filled with candy corn will hold Gingerbread Man Cookies upright.

■ An inexpensive glass bucket makes a clever punch bowl, and jelly jars act as glasses.

■ Black vinyl is a perfect table covering because it creates a mood and is waterproof.

■ Ceramic ghosts and pumpkins placed randomly over the tabletop create a whimsical mood.

■ Don't forget that a chandelier or hanging light fixture is the perfect prop for suspending popcorn ghosts with black thread.

■ Complete your Halloween table setting with handmade place cards cut out of construction paper and personalized with names, using a black fine-point marker.

GOBLIN PUNCH

2 cups water
½ cup sugar
2½ cups orange juice
1 cup pineapple juice
1½ teaspoons grated lemon rind
6 cups apple cider, chilled

Combine water and sugar in a saucepan; cook over medium heat until sugar dissolves. Cool. Add orange juice, pineapple juice, and lemon rind. Cover and chill. Add cider just before serving. Yield: 11½ cups.

Marcia Jeffries
Oklahoma City, Oklahoma

Bring In The Flavor Of Autumn

After the glaring heat of summer comes the cool crispness of fall. Under the soil, a cache of sleepy vegetables wakens to the call of the season: long, slender parsnips; fat, round turnips; and hard, purple rutabagas. Aboveground, squash appear in all shapes and sizes, some vibrant with color and others somewhat paler—but all are good to eat.

Parsnips look like carrots except they're white and taste sweeter. A starchy vegetable, parsnips are often substituted for potatoes. If they grow too large, the texture becomes woody.

Rutabagas and turnips are members of the cabbage family. Round, and heavy for their size, these vegetables are actually roots. Select those that are firm and free of decay. The waxy coating on rutabagas can be removed with the peeling.

The season's offering of squash includes turban, butternut, and acorn. These squash are sweeter vegetables and lend themselves not only to side dishes but to entrées and soups as well. Turn to "From Our Kitchen to Yours" on page 229 for tips on how to identify and cut them.

CREAMED BUTTERNUT-AND-APPLE SOUP

1 (2½-pound) butternut squash, peeled and diced
¾ pound cooking apples, peeled, cored, and quartered
4 cups chicken broth
1 (1½-inch) stick cinnamon
1 cup half-and-half
¼ cup unsalted butter or margarine, melted
2 tablespoons maple syrup
¼ teaspoon salt
¼ teaspoon ground nutmeg
¼ teaspoon ground ginger
Apple slices (optional)
Ground nutmeg (optional)

Combine squash, apples, broth, and cinnamon stick in a Dutch oven. Bring to a boil; cover, reduce heat, and simmer 20 to 30 minutes or until squash is tender. Remove cinnamon stick. Spoon mixture into container of an electric blender, and process until smooth.

Return squash mixture to Dutch oven; stir in half-and-half and next 5 ingredients. Cook over low heat, stirring constantly, until well heated. Serve hot. If desired, garnish with apple slices and ground nutmeg. Yield: 8 cups.

La Juan Coward
Jasper, Texas

APPLE-AND-PECAN-FILLED SQUASH

2 medium acorn squash (about 1¼ pounds each)
¼ cup firmly packed brown sugar
¼ cup butter or margarine, melted
1 cup chopped, unpeeled apple
¼ cup chopped pecans, toasted

Cut acorn squash in half, and remove seeds. Place squash, cut side up, in a shallow baking dish. Add boiling water to a depth of ½ inch to pan.

Combine brown sugar, butter, and chopped apple; spoon into squash shells. Cover and bake at 350° for 1 hour or until squash is tender. Sprinkle with pecans. Yield: 4 servings.

Iris Brenner
Fort McCoy, Florida

STUFFED TURKS TURBAN SQUASH

1 turban squash (3½ to 4 pounds)
4 cups water
1 pound hot bulk pork sausage
1 large onion, chopped
2 large cloves garlic, minced
⅓ cup minced parsley
1 egg, slightly beaten
½ teaspoon salt
¼ teaspoon pepper
⅛ teaspoon red pepper
½ to ¾ cup dry breadcrumbs
Vegetable oil

Cut vertically with a sharp knife around crown of squash. Remove crown; discard fiber and seeds. Place base and crown in a large kettle, cut sides up. Add water; cover and bring to a boil. Reduce heat, and simmer about 30 minutes. Remove crown, and continue to cook larger squash portion 15 minutes or until tender. Remove from water; drain squash, cut side down, on paper towels. Let cool to touch.

Brown sausage in a skillet, stirring to crumble; remove from skillet, and drain well, reserving drippings. Sauté onion, garlic, and parsley in reserved drippings until onion is tender. Combine sausage, sautéed vegetables, egg, salt, pepper, and red pepper; stir well.

Scoop out squash pulp, leaving 1¼-inch shell; add to sausage mixture, and stir well. Sprinkle inside of crown portion with about 2 tablespoons breadcrumbs. Add remaining breadcrumbs to sausage mixture, and stir well. Spoon sausage mixture into squash shell. Turn filled crown portion upside down on top of base. Place in a 13- x 9- x 2-inch baking pan. Bake at 350° for 45 minutes. Let stand about 10 minutes; rub with oil, remove crown shell, and serve. Yield: 8 to 10 servings.

Sara Cairns
Montevallo, Alabama

Tip: *Store spices in a cool place and away from any direct source of heat, as the heat will destroy their flavor. Red spices will maintain flavor and retain color longer if refrigerated.*

WILTED CABBAGE

4 slices bacon
½ cup chopped onion
2 tablespoons sugar
¼ cup vinegar
½ teaspoon salt
⅛ teaspoon pepper
4 cups shredded cabbage

Cook bacon in a large skillet until crisp; remove bacon, reserving drippings in skillet. Crumble bacon, and set aside. Add onion and next 4 ingredients to drippings in skillet, stirring until blended. Stir in cabbage. Cook over medium heat, uncovered, 15 minutes, stirring occasionally. Sprinkle with reserved bacon. Yield: 4 to 6 servings.   *Linda Davidson*
Midland, Texas

TURNIPS AU GRATIN

1 pound medium turnips, cut
   into ¼-inch slices
2 medium onions, cut into
   ¼-inch slices
¼ teaspoon sugar
1 tablespoon butter or
   margarine
1 tablespoon all-purpose flour
1 cup milk
⅛ teaspoon red pepper
⅛ teaspoon white pepper
¼ teaspoon salt
½ cup (2 ounces) shredded
   American cheese
1 tablespoon butter or margarine,
   melted
¼ teaspoon paprika
⅔ cup soft breadcrumbs

Combine turnips, onion, and sugar in a Dutch oven; cover with water, and bring to a boil. Cover, reduce heat, and simmer 8 minutes or until vegetables are crisp-tender. Drain well, and set aside.

Melt 1 tablespoon butter in a heavy saucepan over low heat; add flour, stirring constantly. Gradually add milk; cook over medium heat, stirring constantly, until thickened and bubbly. Add red pepper and next

3 ingredients; stir until cheese melts. Remove from heat.

Layer half of onion-turnip mixture and cheese sauce in a greased 1-quart casserole; repeat layers.

Combine 1 tablespoon butter, paprika, and breadcrumbs; sprinkle over casserole. Bake at 350° for 25 minutes or until hot and bubbly. Yield: 4 to 6 servings.

GLAZED RUTABAGA

3 cups peeled, cubed rutabaga
2 cups water
2 tablespoons butter or margarine
1 tablespoon brown sugar
2 tablespoons soy sauce
1 tablespoon lemon juice
1 teaspoon Worcestershire sauce

Combine rutabaga and water in a large skillet. Bring to a boil; reduce heat, and simmer 15 minutes or until tender. Remove rutabaga, and drain.

Combine butter and remaining ingredients in skillet. Return rutabaga to skillet. Cook over medium heat, stirring constantly, until rutabaga is glazed. Yield: 4 servings.

Dorothy Nieman
Dunnellon, Florida

SUGAR-CRUSTED PARSNIPS

1 pound parsnips
2 tablespoons butter or margarine
1 tablespoon brown sugar
Dash of grated nutmeg
¼ teaspoon salt
⅛ teaspoon pepper

Wash and scrape parsnips; cut into julienne strips. Cover and cook in a small amount of boiling water 5 minutes or until tender; drain well.

Melt butter in a large skillet; add brown sugar, and stir until blended. Add parsnips; cook over medium heat about 2 minutes, stirring constantly, until parsnips are glazed. Add nutmeg, salt, and pepper. Yield: 4 to 6 servings.   *Edith Askins*
Greenville, Texas

From Our Kitchen To Yours

Stacks of winter squash bring autumn's exuberant, colorful blaze to Southern markets. Inside these warm-colored and uniquely shaped vegetables you'll discover delicious flavor. And the unexpected sweet pulp of hard-rind squash offers variety for any meal.

For the smoothest texture and sweetest flavor, choose butternut or hubbard. If you want a lighter gold color and a mellower flavor, consider acorn, banana, or turban squash. The tan, bottle-shaped **butternut** averages 2 to 4 pounds and makes delectable pies. Dark green or blue gray describes the bumpy skin of the massive **hubbard;** this squash is 12 to 16 inches long and has a well-rounded shape with tapered ends. Shaped like its name, the **acorn** has a deep-ridged, dark-green rind tinged with orange; suitable for baking and stuffing, one squash usually serves two. The long cylindrical **banana** squash has a small seed cavity; during storage, its pale olive-gray color transforms to a creamy pink. Orange with green variegations, the regal **turban** appears to have a crown or looks like a turban-topped bowl.

Although winter squash is available all year, it is abundant October through February. You can select a ripe squash by the color and toughness of the rind. Check for characteristic color; avoid an acorn squash that is more than half orange and a butternut squash with green-tinted skin. If your thumbnail cannot penetrate the hard, thick rind, the squash is mature. As you pick up the squash, it should feel heavy in relation to its size. The tough outer covering should be without cuts, punctures, or sunken spots.

The number of servings needed determines how much to buy. An average 2- to 3-pound squash serves 4.

The thick rind of winter squash enables it to be stored for several weeks in a cool, dry, well-ventilated place. Use squash within one week if it is kept at room temperature. Wrap cut pieces in heavy-duty plastic wrap, and store in the refrigerator for one to two days.

All winter squash can be baked or boiled. Cutting through the rind is often difficult; using a mallet and a sharp knife makes the task easier. To prepare winter squash for cooking, cut in half, and remove the seeds with a large metal spoon; scrape the pulp to remove any clinging fibers.

To bake, place cut side down in a shallow baking dish, and add ½ inch water. Bake, uncovered, at 400° for 30 minutes. Turn and season or fill; bake an additional 20 to 30 minutes or until tender. To boil, cook, covered, in boiling water 20 to 25 minutes or until tender. Loss of nutrients and flavor will result from overcooking.

MICROWAVE COOKERY

Quick Magic With Pumpkins

Pumpkins are not just for carving and decorating. Cooked pumpkin is used in making breads, pies, and other baked goodies. To make these treats quick and easy to prepare, we give instructions on using the microwave to cook both the raw pumpkin and the recipes. Save the pumpkin seeds and toast them in the microwave for a snack that's ready in minutes.

TOASTED PUMPKIN SEEDS

1 cup pumpkin seeds
1 tablespoon butter or margarine
¼ teaspoon seasoned salt

Remove any fiber clinging to pumpkin seeds; wash and drain well. Spread seeds in a single layer to dry, stirring occasionally.

Line a 9-inch pieplate with two layers of paper towels; sprinkle seeds on towels in a single layer. Microwave at HIGH 13 to 14 minutes or until seeds are dry but still white, stirring every 5 minutes. Let stand 5 minutes.

Place butter in a 2-cup glass measure; microwave at HIGH 35 seconds or until melted. Add seeds and salt; stir to coat. Serve toasted seeds as a snack. Yield: 1 cup.

COOKED FRESH PUMPKIN

1 (5- to 6-pound) pumpkin

Cut pumpkin in half crosswise; remove seeds, and set aside. Peel and cut pumpkin into 1-inch cubes; place in a shallow 2-quart dish. Cover tightly with heavy-duty plastic wrap; fold back a small edge of wrap to allow steam to escape. Microwave at HIGH 20 to 25 minutes or until tender, giving dish a quarter-turn every 5 minutes. Mash pumpkin, if desired. Yield: about 3 to 4½ cups mashed pulp or 5 to 6 cups cubes.

QUICK PUMPKIN PIE

¼ cup plus 2 tablespoons butter or margarine
¾ cup chopped walnuts
¾ cup quick-cooking oats, uncooked
¾ cup graham cracker crumbs
¼ cup sugar
2 cups cooked mashed pumpkin
¾ cup firmly packed brown sugar
1 cup half-and-half
3 eggs, slightly beaten
2 tablespoons brandy
1 teaspoon ground cinnamon
½ teaspoon ground ginger
¼ teaspoon salt
Sweetened whipped cream (optional)

Place butter in a 9-inch pieplate; microwave at HIGH 1 to 1½ minutes or until butter melts. Stir in walnuts, oats, cracker crumbs, and ¼ cup sugar, mixing well. Press mixture evenly into bottom and up sides of pieplate; microwave at HIGH 1 to 2 minutes.

Combine pumpkin and next 7 ingredients in a 4-quart bowl, mixing well. Microwave at HIGH 6 to 8 minutes or until mixture begins to thicken, stirring every 2 minutes. Pour mixture into crust; microwave at MEDIUM (50% power) 10 to 15 minutes or until set, giving pieplate a quarter-turn every 5 minutes. Serve with sweetened whipped cream, if desired. Yield: one 9-inch pie.

AUTUMN FRUIT CHUTNEY

½ cup orange juice
½ cup firmly packed dark brown sugar
1 tablespoon lemon juice
¼ teaspoon ground ginger
1 (3-inch) stick cinnamon
1 cup cubed apple
1 cup cooked pumpkin cubes (about ½-inch pieces)
½ cup golden raisins

Combine first 5 ingredients in a 2-quart casserole. Stir in cubed apple. Cover tightly with heavy-duty plastic wrap; fold back a small edge of wrap to allow steam to escape. Microwave at HIGH 2 minutes or until apple is crisp-tender. Add pumpkin and raisins; cover and microwave at HIGH 2 minutes or until thoroughly heated, stirring after 1 minute. Remove cinnamon stick. Serve chutney with roasted pork, poultry, or ham. Yield: 2½ cups.

Breakfast On The Run

If your schedule requires a quick breakfast, these recipes offer practical, home-baked alternatives to restaurant fast foods. Many of these items can be started the night before or mixed up quickly in the morning. For instance, roll up Sausage-Cheese Turnovers the night before, using commercial biscuits. Bake them in the morning and you've got a quick breakfast.

SAUSAGE-CHEESE TURNOVERS

10 (1-ounce) link sausages
2 ounces sharp Cheddar cheese
1 (11-ounce) can refrigerated
   biscuits
2 tablespoons cornmeal

Cook sausage in a skillet until browned; drain well. Set aside.

Cut cheese to 2- x ½- x ¼-inch strips; set aside.

Roll each biscuit to a 4-inch circle on wax paper sprinkled with cornmeal. Place a cheese strip and a sausage in center of each biscuit. Fold over, and pinch edges to seal. Press edges together with a fork dipped in flour. Place on a lightly greased baking sheet; bake at 400° for 10 minutes. Yield: 10 servings.

Nita Brown
Oklahoma City, Oklahoma

BREAKFAST SCONES

⅓ cup currants
¾ cup buttermilk
2 cups all-purpose flour
2 teaspoons baking powder
¼ teaspoon baking soda
2 tablespoons sugar
1 tablespoon grated orange rind
Pinch of salt
¼ cup plus 1 tablespoon butter
   or margarine
Milk
Sugar

Soak currants in buttermilk in a small mixing bowl. Set aside.

Combine flour and next 5 ingredients, mixing well. Cut in butter with a pastry blender until mixture resembles coarse meal. Gradually add currants and buttermilk, stirring just until dry ingredients are moistened. Turn dough out onto a lightly floured surface, and knead lightly 4 or 5 times.

Roll dough to ½-inch thickness; cut with a 3-inch biscuit cutter. Place on a lightly greased baking sheet. Brush scones with milk, and sprinkle with sugar. Bake at 400° for 16 minutes or until lightly browned. Yield: 10 scones.

Ella C. Stivers
Houston, Texas

FRUITED HONEY-YOGURT SMOOTHIE

1 (8-ounce) carton plain or
   flavored yogurt
1 (6-ounce) can frozen orange
   juice concentrate, thawed and
   undiluted
1 cup water
⅓ cup honey
1½ teaspoons vanilla extract
Ice cubes

Combine first 5 ingredients in container of an electric blender; add enough ice cubes to bring mixture to 5-cup level. Process until frothy. Yield: 5 cups.

Frieda Harris
Leesville, Louisiana

MINCEMEAT-SPICE BARS

1 cup shortening
½ cup firmly packed brown sugar
½ cup sugar
2 eggs
2¼ cups all-purpose flour
1 teaspoon baking soda
1 teaspoon salt
¼ teaspoon ground cinnamon
¼ teaspoon ground nutmeg
⅛ teaspoon ground mace
2 cups commercial mincemeat
   with rum and brandy
1 cup chopped pecans
1 cup quick-cooking oats,
   uncooked
1 teaspoon vanilla extract

Cream shortening; gradually add sugars, beating well at medium speed of an electric mixer. Add eggs, one at a time, beating after each addition. Combine flour, soda, salt, and spices;

gradually add to creamed mixture. Stir in mincemeat and remaining ingredients. Spoon batter into a greased and floured 15- x 10- x 1-inch jellyroll pan. Bake at 350° for 25 to 30 minutes or until lightly browned. Cool; cut into bars. Yield: 4 dozen.

Mary Ellen Springer
Springfield, Virginia

No-Fuss Fajitas

When Jan Ramsey of Quitaque, Texas, wants to fix something quick and easy, she makes Chicken Fajitas. "I put the chicken in to marinate before I go to work, then it's ready to cook when I get home," she says.

CHICKEN FAJITAS

2 tablespoons lemon juice
½ teaspoon salt
¼ teaspoon coarsely ground
   pepper
¼ teaspoon garlic powder
½ teaspoon liquid smoke
3 chicken breast halves, skinned,
   boned, and cut into strips
6 (6-inch) flour tortillas
2 tablespoons vegetable oil
1 green or sweet red pepper, cut
   into strips
1 medium onion, sliced and
   separated into rings

Combine first 5 ingredients in a small bowl. Add chicken; stir to coat. Cover and chill at least 30 minutes. Drain chicken, reserving marinade.

Wrap tortillas in aluminum foil; bake at 350° for 15 minutes.

Heat oil in a heavy skillet. Add chicken; cook 2 to 3 minutes, stirring constantly. Add marinade, pepper, and onion; sauté until vegetables are crisp-tender. Remove from heat. Divide mixture evenly, and spoon a portion onto each tortilla. If desired, top with any of the following: chopped tomato, green onions, lettuce, guacamole, sour cream, shredded cheese, and picante sauce; then wrap. Yield: 3 servings.

Light And Lean Beef

For more than a decade, nutritionists have urged limiting the amount of red meat eaten because of its high fat and cholesterol content. But today's leaner breeding of cattle and closer trimming of fat by supermarkets make beef a good choice for healthy eating.

Lean beef is considered nutrient dense; that is, it has a relatively high level of specific nutrients for the number of calories it contains. Lean beef adds a substantial amount of protein and iron to the diet and is also a good source of zinc and vitamins B12, niacin, and riboflavin.

More than 40% of the iron in beef is heme iron—the type used most readily by the body. Moreover, the presence of heme iron in a meal increases the absorption of nonheme iron found in milk, eggs, cheese, and vegetables. Eating a food that contains vitamin C at the same meal enhances iron absorption.

There are more than 50 cuts and 3 grades of beef available at the meat counter. The three USDA grades are a good gauge of marbling: Prime grade (usually found only in restaurants) has the most marbling, Select grade the least, and Choice grade (the grade most often seen in the supermarket) falls in between.

The cut of meat actually has more to do with the fat content of beef than the grade. For example, even the leanest prime rib tends to be fatty, and the fattiest top sirloin tends to be lean. The lean cuts described on page 234 generally have little marbling and seam fat. Even though the cut may be lean, it's important to trim fat before cooking.

To keep beef lean and tender, use low-fat cooking techniques, such as braising, roasting, broiling, baking, grilling, or stir-frying. Lean meats cook faster than fattier meats, so cook them for a shorter time.

ITALIAN-STUFFED STEAK

2 (¾-pound) lean boneless top round steaks
1½ cups water
¾ cup uncooked risotto
½ teaspoon ground turmeric
Vegetable cooking spray
½ cup diced onion
½ cup diced green pepper
½ cup diced sweet red pepper
1 clove garlic, minced
1 tablespoon minced fresh parsley
½ teaspoon dried Italian seasoning
¼ teaspoon salt
¼ teaspoon pepper
2 (8-ounce) cans no-salt-added tomato sauce
¼ teaspoon salt
1 teaspoon dried Italian seasoning
¼ teaspoon dried whole fennel seeds
⅛ teaspoon garlic powder
1 tablespoon Parmesan cheese
Fresh parsley sprigs (optional)
Sweet red pepper strips (optional)

Trim fat from steaks; place each piece of meat between two sheets of heavy-duty plastic wrap, and pound to ¼-inch thickness, using a meat mallet. Overlap edges of meat to make one large piece.

Combine water, risotto, and turmeric in a medium saucepan. Bring to a boil; cover, reduce heat, and simmer 25 to 30 minutes or until tender; set aside.

Coat a skillet with cooking spray; place over medium heat until hot. Add onion, diced green and red pepper, and minced garlic; sauté until tender. Remove from heat. Add risotto, minced parsley, and next 3 ingredients; stir well.

Spread stuffing mixture in center of meat within 1 inch of sides. Roll up jellyroll fashion, starting with long side. Secure at 2-inch intervals with string. Place seam side down in a shallow roasting pan.

Combine tomato sauce and next 4 ingredients in a small bowl; stir well. Pour over steak roll. Cover and bake at 350° for 1 hour, basting occasionally. Uncover and bake an additional 30 minutes, basting occasionally.

Transfer steak to a serving platter. Let stand 15 minutes; remove strings, and slice steak roll. Spoon remaining sauce over meat, and sprinkle with Parmesan cheese. If desired, garnish with parsley sprigs and red pepper strips. Yield: 6 servings (303 calories per 3-ounce serving meat plus stuffing and sauce).

☐ *31 grams protein, 6 grams fat, 29.4 grams carbohydrate, 74 milligrams cholesterol, 284 milligrams sodium, and 43 milligrams calcium.*

STEAK AU POIVRE

6 (4-ounce) beef tenderloin steaks
1 clove garlic, crushed
1 teaspoon crushed black peppercorns
Vegetable cooking spray
⅓ cup chopped onion
1 cup green pepper strips
1 cup sweet red pepper strips
1 cup yellow pepper strips
1 clove garlic, minced
½ teaspoon beef-flavored bouillon granules
½ teaspoon paprika
½ teaspoon crushed black peppercorns
½ cup water
½ cup evaporated skim milk
3 tablespoons brandy

Trim fat from steaks. Combine crushed garlic and 1 teaspoon crushed peppercorns; press a small amount of mixture into each side of steaks. Coat a large nonstick skillet with cooking spray; place over medium heat until hot. Arrange steaks in skillet, and cook to desired degree of doneness, turning once. Remove steaks to a serving platter, and keep steaks warm.

Wipe skillet with paper towels; coat with cooking spray, and place over medium heat until hot. Add onion and next 4 ingredients; sauté until vegetables are crisp-tender. Spoon pepper mixture over steaks, and keep warm.

Combine bouillon granules, paprika, ½ teaspoon crushed peppercorns, water, and milk in a small bowl; stir well. Pour into skillet, and cook over medium heat, stirring often, until mixture is reduced to ⅔ cup. Place brandy in a small, long-handled saucepan; heat until warm (do not boil). Remove from heat. Ignite with a long match; pour into sauce mixture, and stir until flames die down. Spoon sauce over each steak, and serve. Yield: 6 servings (214 calories per 3-ounce serving, ⅓ cup vegetables, and 1½ tablespoons sauce).

☐ *26.5 grams protein, 8.3 grams fat, 7.1 grams carbohydrate, 71 milligrams cholesterol, 143 milligrams sodium, and 16 milligrams calcium.*

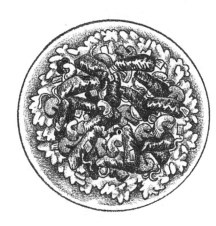

FLANK STEAK SUKIYAKI

1 (1-pound) flank steak
1 tablespoon sugar
1 teaspoon chopped fresh ginger
½ teaspoon beef-flavored bouillon granules
¼ teaspoon crushed red pepper
2 tablespoons dry sherry
¼ cup reduced-sodium soy sauce
½ cup water
2 teaspoons vegetable oil
¾ cup thinly sliced onion
½ cup diagonally sliced celery
⅓ cup bamboo shoots
⅓ cup sliced water chestnuts
⅓ cup diagonally sliced green onions
⅓ cup sliced fresh mushrooms
2 cups torn fresh spinach
1 cup fresh bean sprouts
2½ cups hot cooked rice (cooked without fat or salt)

Trim fat from steak, and partially freeze. Slice diagonally across grain into thin strips; set aside.

Combine sugar and next 6 ingredients in a saucepan. Cook over medium heat until sugar dissolves, stirring often; remove from heat.

Add oil to a preheated wok; heat oil to about 325°. Add meat, and cook just until meat browns. Remove from wok.

Add onion, celery, and half of sauce mixture to wok; cook 3 minutes, stirring constantly. Add bamboo shoots and water chestnuts; cook 3 minutes, stirring constantly. Add green onions, mushrooms, spinach, and bean sprouts; cook 1 to 2 minutes, stirring constantly. Add meat and remaining sauce; cook until thoroughly heated. Serve immediately over hot cooked rice. Yield: 5 servings (321 calories per 1-cup serving with ½ cup rice).

☐ *22.5 grams protein, 10.8 grams fat, 33 grams carbohydrate, 45 milligrams cholesterol, 590 milligrams sodium, and 52 milligrams calcium.*

BEEF FAJITAS

1 (1-pound) flank steak
¼ cup chopped fresh cilantro
⅛ teaspoon pepper
⅛ teaspoon red pepper
1 large clove garlic, minced
⅓ cup lime juice
2 (6-ounce) cans no-salt-added cocktail vegetable juice
Vegetable cooking spray
1 cup sweet red pepper strips
1 cup green pepper strips
¾ cup sliced red onion
8 (6-inch) flour tortillas
¾ cup diced tomato
¾ cup commercial salsa

Trim fat from steak; slice diagonally across grain into thin strips. Place in a shallow dish. Combine cilantro and next 5 ingredients; stir well, and pour over meat. Toss gently; cover and marinate in refrigerator 4 hours.

Remove meat from marinade. Place meat on rack coated with cooking spray; place rack in a broiler pan.

Broil 2 inches from heat 3 minutes; turn meat, and broil 1 additional minute. Remove from oven, and keep meat warm.

Coat a nonstick skillet with cooking spray; place over medium heat until hot. Add red and green pepper strips and onion; sauté until crisp-tender. Combine vegetables and meat strips, and keep warm.

Seal tortillas in aluminum foil, and bake at 325° for 15 minutes. Place ¼ cup meat mixture and 1 tablespoon tomato on each tortilla, and wrap. Serve with salsa. Yield: 8 servings (250 calories per fajita with 1½ tablespoons salsa).

☐ *14.8 grams protein, 9.1 grams fat, 29.5 grams carbohydrate, 31 milligrams cholesterol, 49 milligrams sodium, and 49 milligrams calcium.*

MARINATED STEAK

1 (1½-pound) flank steak
⅔ cup Burgundy or other dry red wine
1 tablespoon reduced-sodium soy sauce
⅛ teaspoon pepper
⅛ teaspoon dried whole oregano
⅛ teaspoon dried whole marjoram
Vegetable cooking spray

Trim fat from flank steak; place in a large shallow dish. Combine wine and next 4 ingredients; pour over steak. Cover and marinate in refrigerator 8 hours, turning steak occasionally.

Remove steak from marinade; pat each side dry with paper towels. Place steak on a rack coated with cooking spray; place rack in a broiler pan. Broil 4 inches from heat 5 to 6 minutes on each side or to desired degree of doneness.

To serve, thinly slice steak diagonally across grain. Yield: 6 servings (216 calories per 3-ounce serving).

☐ *22.2 grams protein, 13.1 grams fat, 0.1 gram carbohydrate, 61 milligrams cholesterol, 87 milligrams sodium, and 5.7 milligrams calcium.*
Phyllis Dupont
Concord, Virginia

BURGUNDY BEEF STEW

2 pounds top boneless round
   steak
¼ teaspoon pepper
¼ teaspoon garlic powder
Vegetable cooking spray
½ cup chopped onion
2½ cups sliced fresh mushrooms
3 cups water
1 teaspoon beef-flavored bouillon
   granules
1 bay leaf
1 tablespoon minced fresh parsley
⅛ teaspoon ground cumin
½ cup Burgundy or other dry red
   wine
2 cups cubed potato
1⅔ cups sliced carrot (½-inch
   pieces)
4 small onions, halved (about ⅓
   pound)
1½ cups sliced celery (1-inch
   pieces)
¼ cup all-purpose flour
½ cup water
Minced fresh parsley (optional)

Trim fat from steak; cut into 1-inch cubes. Combine pepper and garlic powder; sprinkle over meat.

Coat a Dutch oven with cooking spray; place over medium-high heat until hot. Add meat and chopped onion; sauté until meat is browned. Add sliced mushrooms, and sauté 3 to 4 minutes.

Add 3 cups water and next 5 ingredients; stir well. Cover, reduce heat, and simmer 35 minutes. Add potato, carrot, onion halves, and celery; stir well. Cover and simmer 20 minutes or until vegetables are tender.

Combine flour and ½ cup water, stirring until smooth. Add to hot vegetable mixture, and stir well. Cook 10 minutes or until mixture is thickened, stirring often. Remove and discard bay leaf.

Spoon beef stew into serving bowls; sprinkle with minced fresh parsley, if desired. Yield: 9 cups (206 calories per 1-cup serving).

☐ *25.3 grams protein, 4.5 grams fat, 15.3 grams carbohydrate, 57 milligrams cholesterol, 197 milligrams sodium, and 30 milligrams calcium.*

COMPANY BEEF AND VEGETABLES

½ teaspoon dried parsley
   flakes
½ teaspoon garlic powder
½ teaspoon dried whole basil
½ teaspoon dried whole
   oregano
¼ teaspoon pepper
1 (4½-pound) eye-of-round beef
   roast
Vegetable cooking spray
2 cups water
12 new potatoes (about 2¼
   pounds)
12 boiling onions (about 1¼
   pounds)
2 cups julienne-cut carrots

Combine first 5 ingredients in a small bowl; mix well. Divide herb mixture in half, and set aside.

Trim fat from roast; place roast on a rack coated with cooking spray; place rack in broiler pan. Sprinkle half of herb mixture over roast, and bake at 325° for 50 minutes.

Pour water into broiler pan. Arrange potatoes and onions around roast in a single layer; cover with aluminum foil. Bake at 325° for 25 minutes. Remove foil; add carrots. Sprinkle remaining herb mixture over vegetables; cover and bake an additional 45 minutes or until vegetables are tender and meat thermometer registers 150° for medium-rare, 160° for medium, or 170° for well done.

Transfer roast to a serving platter; let stand 10 minutes before cutting into thin slices. Arrange baked vegetables around roast. Yield: 12 servings (343 calories per 3-ounce serving of beef roast with 1 potato, 1 onion, and ⅓ cup carrots).

☐ *43.1 grams protein, 9.3 grams fat, 19.6 grams carbohydrate, 96 milligrams cholesterol, 100 milligrams sodium, and 37 milligrams calcium.*

Guide to Lean Cuts of Beef

(Nutrition analysis based on a 3-ounce cooked serving)

Eye of Round

156 calories
5.5 grams total fat
2.1 grams saturated fat
59 milligrams cholesterol

Round Tip Roast

162 calories
6.4 grams total fat
2.3 grams saturated fat
69 milligrams cholesterol

Top Loin (Strip Steak)

173 calories
7.6 grams total fat
3 grams saturated fat
65 milligrams cholesterol

Top Round

162 calories
5.3 grams total fat
1.8 grams saturated fat
71 milligrams cholesterol

Top Sirloin Steak

177 calories
7.4 grams total fat
3 grams saturated fat
76 milligrams cholesterol

Tenderloin Steak

173 calories
7.9 grams total fat
3.1 grams saturated fat
71 milligrams cholesterol

Flank Steak

207 calories
12.7 grams total fat
5.9 grams saturated fat
60 milligrams cholesterol

Loaves For Sandwich Lovers

For a recipe that's suitable for breakfast, lunch, or outings such as picnics and football games, try Sausage-Cheese Loaves, from Wanda Jones of Bon Aqua, Tennessee.

SAUSAGE-CHEESE LOAVES

½ pound bulk pork sausage
2 cups self-rising flour
¼ cup shortening
¾ cup buttermilk
½ (11-ounce) package summer sausage, sliced and cut into quarters
1 cup (4 ounces) shredded mozzarella cheese
Melted butter or margarine

Cook pork sausage in a skillet until browned, stirring to crumble meat. Drain and set aside.

Place flour in a large mixing bowl; cut in shortening with a pastry blender until mixture resembles coarse meal. Add buttermilk, stirring to form a dough. Turn dough out onto a lightly floured surface, and knead lightly 4 or 5 times.

Divide dough into fourths; roll each portion to an 8- x 6-inch rectangle. Layer one-fourth each of cooked sausage, summer sausage, and cheese onto each rectangle. Fold long sides to center, sealing edges; fold ends 1 inch toward center. Place loaves on a greased baking sheet, seam side down. Brush tops with butter. Bake at 350° for 30 minutes or until lightly browned. Yield: 4 servings.

Tip: *Refrigerate cheese in its original wrap until opened. After opening, rewrap the cheese tightly in plastic wrap, plastic bags, or aluminum foil, or place in airtight containers and refrigerate.*

Hearty Soups For The Season

When the days start to shorten and the nights start to chill, thoughts turn to hearty soups that warm you up. Nothing does the job better than hot Chicken-and-Rice Soup like Grandma used to make; it's simple but satisfying for a cool evening.

For another offering that's unique to our region, try Kentucky Burgoo. It's made from a variety of meats and vegetables that makes the soup a meal in itself. Serve cornbread on the side for a Southern feast.

KENTUCKY BURGOO

1 (3- to 3½-pound) broiler-fryer
1 pound boneless beef, cut into 1-inch cubes
1 pound boneless veal, cut into 1-inch cubes
1 pound boneless pork, cut into 1-inch cubes
1 gallon water
3 medium potatoes, peeled and cubed
3 medium carrots, scraped and sliced
1 large onion, chopped
1 large green pepper, chopped
1 cup frozen cut okra
1 cup shredded cabbage
1 cup frozen whole kernel corn
1 cup frozen lima beans
1 cup chopped fresh parsley
½ cup finely chopped celery
1 hot red pepper
2 cups tomato puree
2 tablespoons salt
1 teaspoon red pepper
1 to 1½ teaspoons hot sauce

Combine first 5 ingredients in a large Dutch oven; bring to a boil. Cover, reduce heat, and simmer 2 hours or until meat is tender.

Remove meat from broth, reserving broth; cool meat completely. Skin, bone, and chop chicken. Coarsely chop meat; set aside.

Skim off and discard fat from surface of broth. Measure broth, and return 3 quarts to Dutch oven. Add chopped meats, potato, and remaining ingredients. Bring mixture to a boil. Reduce heat, and simmer, uncovered, 4 hours, stirring often. Add additional reserved broth and water, if necessary, to make desired consistency. Discard red pepper pod. Yield: 5 quarts.

SPLIT PEA SOUP

1 cup dried split peas
3 cups water
1 meaty ham hock
4 cups water
½ cup chopped celery
¼ cup chopped onion
¼ cup chopped carrot
¼ teaspoon pepper
Dash of paprika
2 tablespoons all-purpose flour
1½ cups diluted canned beef broth, divided

Sort and wash peas; place in a Dutch oven. Add 3 cups water; cover and let soak 8 hours. Drain peas, and return to Dutch oven.

Add ham hock and 4 cups water to peas; bring to a boil. Cover, reduce heat, and simmer 1 hour, stirring occasionally. Add celery and next 4 ingredients; cover and simmer 1 hour. Remove ham hock. Remove meat from bone; chop meat, and set aside.

Pour half of soup mixture into container of an electric blender, and process until smooth. Repeat procedure with remaining half of soup mixture. Return soup to Dutch oven.

Combine flour and ½ cup beef broth, stirring until smooth; stir in remaining beef broth. Gradually add broth mixture to soup, stirring well. Add chopped ham. Cook over medium heat until slightly thickened. Yield: 7 cups.
Bonnie Ovimette
Tallahassee, Florida

CHICKEN-AND-RICE SOUP

1 (3½- to 4-pound) broiler-fryer,
   cut up and skinned
2 quarts water
1 medium onion, chopped
2 stalks celery, thinly sliced
1½ teaspoons salt
1 to 1½ teaspoons pepper
1 bay leaf
¾ cup uncooked long-grain rice
1 carrot, diced

Combine first 7 ingredients in a Dutch oven. Bring to a boil; cover, reduce heat, and simmer 45 minutes. Remove chicken from Dutch oven, reserving broth. Discard bay leaf. Set chicken aside.

Add rice and carrot to broth; bring to a boil. Cover, reduce heat, and simmer 20 minutes or until rice is tender.

Bone chicken, and cut into bite-size pieces. Add chicken to broth; heat thoroughly. Yield: 9 cups.

Flavor The Recipe With Applesauce

If you have a jar of applesauce on the pantry shelf, then you're probably ready to make the recipes here.

You'll find Applesauce Spice Muffins moist and flavorful. The batter makes seven dozen miniature muffins, which is convenient if you're serving a large breakfast or luncheon crowd. For everyday use, you can store the batter in the refrigerator for up to two weeks and bake just the amount that you want.

APPLE CUSTARD PIE

3 eggs, beaten
½ cup sugar
½ teaspoon salt
½ cup milk
2 cups applesauce
1 teaspoon vanilla extract
1 unbaked 9-inch pastry shell
¼ teaspoon ground nutmeg

Combine first 6 ingredients; stir well. Pour into pastry shell; sprinkle with nutmeg. Bake at 450° for 15 minutes. Reduce heat to 350°, and bake 45 minutes or until set. Cool on a wire rack. Yield: one 9-inch pie.

Janet G. Comegys
Doraville, Georgia

APPLESAUCE CAKE WITH BOURBON FROSTING

1 cup butter or margarine,
   softened
1 cup sugar
2 eggs
2 cups golden raisins
1 cup chopped walnuts
3¼ cups all-purpose flour, divided
1 teaspoon baking soda
Pinch of salt
2 teaspoons ground cloves
2 teaspoons ground nutmeg
1 teaspoon ground cinnamon
2 cups applesauce
Bourbon Frosting
Walnut halves

Cream butter; gradually add sugar, beating at medium speed of an electric mixer until light and fluffy. Add eggs, one at a time, beating well after each addition.

Dredge raisins and chopped walnuts in ½ cup flour; set aside.

Combine remaining flour and next 5 ingredients; add to creamed mixture alternately with applesauce, beginning and ending with flour mixture. Mix well after each addition. Stir in raisins and chopped walnuts.

Pour batter into a greased and floured 10-inch tube pan. Bake at 350° for 1 hour and 5 minutes or until a wooden pick inserted in center comes out clean. Cool cake in pan 10 minutes; remove from pan, and let cool completely on a wire rack.

Spread Bourbon Frosting on top and sides of cake; garnish with walnut halves. Yield: one 10-inch cake.

Bourbon Frosting

¼ cup plus 2 tablespoons butter
   or margarine, softened
3 cups sifted powdered sugar
2 tablespoons bourbon
2½ tablespoons milk

Cream butter at medium speed of an electric mixer; gradually add sugar, bourbon, and milk, beating until mixture reaches spreading consistency. Yield: frosting for a 10-inch cake.

Peggy Wilson Witherow
Pelham, Alabama

APPLESAUCE SPICE MUFFINS

1 cup butter or margarine,
   softened
2 cups sugar
2 eggs
2 cups applesauce
4 cups all-purpose flour
2 teaspoons baking soda
1 teaspoon salt
1 tablespoon ground cinnamon
2 teaspoons ground allspice
½ teaspoon ground cloves
1 cup chopped pecans
Powdered sugar

Cream butter; gradually add 2 cups sugar, beating well at medium speed of an electric mixer. Add eggs, one at a time, beating after each addition. Add applesauce, mixing well.

Combine flour and next 5 ingredients; add to creamed mixture, mixing well. Stir in pecans. Fill greased miniature (1¾-inch) muffin pans about three-fourths full. Bake at 350° for 14 minutes or until done. Transfer from pans to wire racks; sprinkle with powdered sugar. Yield: 7 dozen.

Note: Batter will keep in refrigerator for two weeks. *Carolyn G. Brown*
Montgomery, Alabama

Right: *(Clockwise from bottom left) Luscious Apple Rolls, Natural Pear-Apple Pie, Apple Dumplings With Orange Hard Sauce, and Apple Tart With Cheese Pastry are ripe with just-picked fall flavor. (Recipes begin on page 224.)*

Above: *You'll find rich-tasting Mocha-Chocolate Cheesecake (page 258), which contains sour cream, coffee, Kahlúa, and chocolate, a fitting dessert for the holidays.*

Inset: *Shrimp Dip (page 261), sweet red and green peppers, endive, and breadsticks add holiday color to the tray.*

Left: *Any meal can be special with Venison Kabobs (page 249). Serve the meat and vegetables atop a bed of nutty-tasting wild rice.*

Above: *Plain shortbread boasts some new looks (clockwise from front left): Orange Shortbread Madeleines, Spiced Shortbread Cookies, Cocoa Shortbread Wafers, Praline Shortbread Cookies, and Old-Fashioned Shortbread Cookie. (Recipes begin on page 242; see identification sketch page 242.)*

NOVEMBER

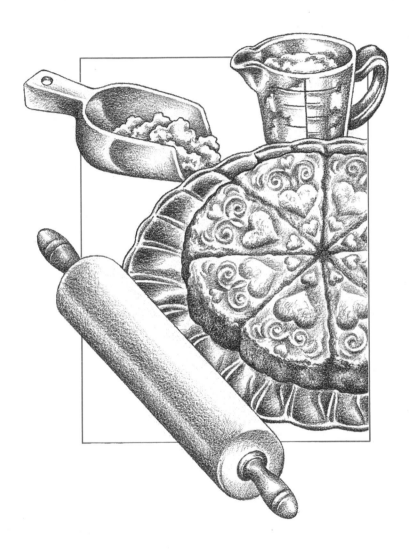

Shortbread Takes On Shape And Flavor

It's hard to imagine something so rich and tasty being made from such a few basic ingredients, but that's the story of shortbread. Original recipes simply called for butter, sugar, and enough flour to make the dough a good consistency. And while we don't claim to make a better shortbread with these recipes, we do add a lot of interest.

Stir either a little cocoa, orange rind, ground pecans, or spices into the dough and you'll be delighted with the new creations. Then turn the dough into cookie or madeleine molds, press it with indented cookie stamps, or cut it into shapes with a fluted pastry wheel.

You can vary the dough with other spices and flavorings as desired. Just keep the original amounts of dry ingredients just about the same.

The shaping techniques that accompany each recipe are interchangeable, too. Consider making several flavors of shortbread to pack into gift boxes for hostess or holiday gifts in the weeks ahead.

ORANGE SHORTBREAD MADELEINES
(pictured on page 240)

1 cup butter, softened
¾ cup sifted powdered sugar
1 teaspoon grated orange rind
1 teaspoon orange extract
1¾ cups all-purpose flour
Vegetable cooking spray

Cream butter; gradually add sugar, beating at medium speed of an electric mixer until light and fluffy. Add orange rind and extract. Stir in flour. (Dough will be stiff.)

Press about 1½ tablespoons dough into madeleine molds lightly sprayed with cooking spray. Bake at 325° for 20 minutes or until done. Invert onto wire racks to cool. Yield: 2½ dozen.

OLD-FASHIONED SHORTBREAD COOKIE
(pictured on page 240)

1 cup butter, softened
¾ cup sifted powdered sugar
¼ cup cornstarch
1¾ cups all-purpose flour

Cream butter; gradually add powdered sugar and cornstarch, beating at medium speed of an electric mixer until light and fluffy. Stir in flour. (Dough will be stiff.)

PRALINE SHORTBREAD COOKIES
(pictured on page 240)

1 cup butter, softened
¾ cup firmly packed dark brown sugar
1½ cups all-purpose flour
½ cup ground pecans

Cream butter; gradually add brown sugar, beating at medium speed of an electric mixer until light and fluffy. Stir in flour and ground pecans. (Dough will be stiff.)

Divide dough into 6 equal portions; pat each portion to a 6-inch circle on lightly greased cookie sheets. Score dough into 8 wedges, using a fluted pastry wheel. Press outside edges of dough with tines of a fork. Bake at 325° for 20 minutes or until cookies are lightly browned. Let cool on cookie sheets; break into wedges. Yield: 4 dozen.

SPICED SHORTBREAD COOKIES
(pictured on page 240)

1 cup butter or margarine, softened
⅔ cup sifted powdered sugar
½ teaspoon ground nutmeg
½ teaspoon ground cinnamon
½ teaspoon ground ginger
2 cups all-purpose flour

Cream butter; gradually add sugar, beating at medium speed of an electric mixer until light and fluffy. Add spices, and beat well. Stir in flour. (Dough will be stiff.)

Shape dough into 1¼-inch balls, and place 2 inches apart on lightly greased cookie sheets. Lightly press cookies with a floured cookie stamp or fork to flatten to ¼-inch thickness. Bake at 325° for 15 to 18 minutes or until done. Let cool on wire racks. Yield: 2½ dozen.

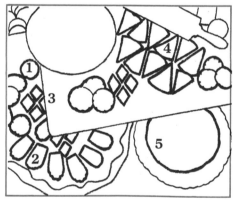

Plain shortbread boasts some new looks. (See color photo, page 240.) 1. *Spiced Shortbread Cookies* 2. *Orange Shortbread Madeleines* 3. *Cocoa Shortbread Wafers* 4. *Praline Shortbread Cookies and* 5. *Old-Fashioned Shortbread Cookie.*

Firmly press dough into a lightly greased and floured 9-inch cookie mold or cakepan. Bake at 325° for 30 to 35 minutes or until done. Invert cookie from pan, and let cool on wire rack. Yield: 1 (9-inch) cookie.

Note: May be baked in 5-inch cookie molds. Firmly press about ¼ cup dough into lightly greased and floured molds, and invert onto lightly greased cookie sheets. Bake at 325° for 15 to 20 minutes or until done. Yield: about 10 cookies.

COCOA SHORTBREAD WAFERS
(pictured on page 240)

1 cup butter, softened
¾ cup sifted powdered sugar
¼ cup cocoa
1½ cups all-purpose flour
Sugar

Cream butter; gradually add powdered sugar, beating at medium speed of an electric mixer until light and fluffy. Add cocoa, and beat mixture well. Stir in flour. (Dough will be stiff.)

Press dough into a lightly greased 15- x 10- x 1-inch jellyroll pan; prick all over with a fork. Bake at 300° for 30 minutes or until done. While warm, cut into 1½-inch diamonds, using a fluted pastry wheel, and sprinkle with sugar. Let cool in pan. Yield: about 7½ dozen.

Holiday Entrées On A Grand Scale

Golden brown and basted with home-made scuppernong jelly, the Roast Duckling With Scuppernong Jelly is Elaine Harvell's secret to entertaining. "When I entertain, I like for everyone to enjoy the meal—even the cook," Elaine says. "Duck can be easier to fix than many other entrées, and it doesn't require a large number of ingredients to enhance the flavor of the meat." The extra Wine Jelly can also be used for gifts throughout the holiday season.

Elegant Beef Tenderloin is a favorite recipe of Marian Brown, who says, "I serve it with a large antipasto using artichoke hearts, asparagus, hearts of palm, mushrooms, raw vegetables, and ripe olives—all marinated in Italian dressing."

ROAST DUCKLING WITH WINE JELLY
(pictured on page 307)

1 (3½- to 5-pound) dressed domestic duckling
Salt and pepper
2 large apples, cored and quartered
1 cup Wine Jelly
Grapes (optional)
Apple slices (optional)

Remove giblets and neck from duckling; reserve for other uses. Sprinkle cavity and body with salt and pepper. Stuff with quartered apple. Close cavity of duckling with skewers; truss. Prick skin with a fork at 2-inch intervals. Place duckling, breast side up, on a rack in a shallow roasting pan. Melt jelly in a small saucepan over low heat. Brush duckling generously with jelly.

Bake, uncovered, at 350° for 2½ to 3 hours or until a meat thermometer registers 185°, basting occasionally. After 1½ hours, cover duck loosely with aluminum foil to prevent overbrowning. If desired, garnish with grapes and apple slices before serving. Yield: 2 servings.

Wine Jelly

3 cups sugar
2 cups scuppernong wine
1 (3-ounce) package liquid pectin

Combine sugar and wine in a large Dutch oven; bring to a boil, stirring constantly. Stir in pectin; boil 1 minute, stirring constantly. Remove from heat, and skim off foam with a metal spoon.

Quickly pour jelly into hot sterilized jars, leaving ¼ inch headspace; wipe jar rims. Cover at once with metal lids, and screw on bands. Process in boiling-water bath 5 minutes. Yield: about 3½ cups.

Elaine Harvell
Fort Mill, South Carolina

GRILLED CORNISH HENS

2 Cornish hens
2 shallots
1 teaspoon Greek seasoning
1 teaspoon dried bouquet garni or dried whole rosemary, crushed
½ cup butter or margarine, melted
¼ teaspoon hot sauce
¼ teaspoon Worcestershire sauce

Remove giblets from hens; reserve for other uses. Rinse hens with cold water, and pat dry. Place a shallot in cavity of each hen; sprinkle hen with Greek seasoning and bouquet garni.

Combine butter and remaining ingredients; brush Cornish hens with butter mixture.

Prepare fire in grill; let burn until coals are white. Rake coals to one end of grill. Place hens at opposite end; cover with lid, and cook 1 hour and 15 minutes or until meat thermometer registers 185°, basting occasionally with butter mixture. Yield: 2 servings.

Eugenia W. Bell
Louisville, Kentucky

ROASTED LAMB ROSEMARY

1 (6- to 7-pound) leg of lamb,
  boned
5 cloves garlic, minced
1 tablespoon fresh rosemary
  leaves, crushed
1 teaspoon salt, divided
½ teaspoon pepper, divided
½ cup water
2 tablespoons plus 1½ teaspoons
  cornstarch
2 tablespoons water

Sprinkle cut side of lamb with garlic, rosemary, ½ teaspoon salt, and ¼ teaspoon pepper. Fold sides of lamb together; tie securely with heavy string at 2- to 3-inch intervals. Sprinkle outside with remaining ½ teaspoon salt and ¼ teaspoon pepper.

Place lamb in a lightly greased, shallow roasting pan. Pour ½ cup water into pan; cover with aluminum foil. Punch a hole in foil; insert meat thermometer into thickest part of roast, making sure thermometer does not touch foil. Bake at 325° for 2½ to 3¾ hours or until meat thermometer registers 140° (rare) or 160° (medium). Remove lamb to a serving platter, reserving pan drippings in roasting pan.

Pour pan drippings into measuring cup; add water to make 2 cups. Combine cornstarch and 2 tablespoons water in a saucepan; add pan drippings. Cook over medium heat, stirring constantly, until mixture thickens. Boil 1 minute, stirring constantly. Serve with lamb. Yield: 6 to 8 servings.   *Emily Danho*
Birmingham, Alabama

BAKED HAM WITH CRANBERRY-RAISIN SAUCE

1 (5-pound) smoked fully cooked
  ham half
About 20 whole cloves
1 (14-ounce) jar cranberry-orange
  sauce
½ cup raisins
1 teaspoon lemon juice
¼ teaspoon ground cinnamon

Slice skin from ham; place ham, fat side up, on rack in a shallow roasting pan. Score fat in a diamond design, and stud with cloves. Insert meat thermometer, making sure it does not touch fat or bone. Bake ham at 325° for 1 hour and 50 minutes. Remove ham from oven.

Combine cranberry-orange sauce and remaining ingredients; spread half of cranberry mixture over ham. Bake ham an additional 20 minutes or until meat thermometer registers 140°. Serve remaining sauce with ham. Yield: 8 to 10 servings.
Mrs. Kenneth B. Waldron
Mountain Rest, South Carolina

LEG OF PORK WITH CRANBERRY GLAZE

1 (5- to 6-pound) half pork leg
  (fresh ham)
1 large clove garlic, crushed
1 teaspoon dried whole rosemary,
  crushed
¼ teaspoon pepper
1 carrot, sliced
2 stalks celery, sliced
1 large onion, chopped
Vegetable cooking spray
Cranberry Glaze
2 (16-ounce) cans peach halves,
  drained
Fresh parsley (optional)

Rub meat with garlic. Combine rosemary and pepper; sprinkle over meat. Arrange carrot, celery, and onion in center of a roasting pan coated with cooking spray. Place meat on top of vegetables. Insert meat thermometer, making sure it does not touch fat or bone. Bake, uncovered, at 325° for 2½ to 3 hours or until meat thermometer registers 160°. Remove meat thermometer.

Brush about ½ cup Cranberry Glaze over meat; bake an additional 15 minutes. Place meat on serving platter; discard vegetables. Arrange peach halves around meat; spoon remaining Cranberry Glaze into peaches. Garnish with parsley, if desired. Yield: 8 to 10 servings.

Cranberry Glaze

1 (16-ounce) can whole-berry
  cranberry sauce
2 tablespoons grated orange rind
¼ cup orange juice
2 teaspoons diced crystallized
  ginger
1 orange, sectioned and chopped

Combine all ingredients in a small saucepan; stir well. Simmer over medium heat 25 minutes, stirring occasionally. Yield: about 2 cups.
Mildred Sherrer
Bay City, Texas

ELEGANT BEEF TENDERLOIN

1 (5-pound) beef tenderloin,
  trimmed
1¼ teaspoons garlic salt
1 cup Burgundy wine
¼ cup soy sauce
¾ cup butter
1 teaspoon lemon-pepper
  seasoning
Grapes (optional)
Celery leaves (optional)
Lemon zest (optional)

Place meat on a lightly greased, shallow roasting pan; sprinkle with garlic salt. Bake at 425° for 10 minutes.

Combine wine, soy sauce, butter, and lemon-pepper seasoning in a small saucepan; cook until mixture is thoroughly heated. Pour over tenderloin; bake an additional 30 to 40 minutes or until a thermometer registers 140° (rare), basting occasionally with pan drippings. (Bake until thermometer registers 150° for medium rare or 160° for medium.) If desired, garnish beef with grapes, celery leaves, and lemon zest. Yield: 10 servings.
Marian C. Brown
Simpsonville, South Carolina

Celebrate The Holidays In Style

Think back to your most memorable holidays. Perhaps it was with family and close friends gathered around a table filled with turkey and all the trimmings, or maybe it was an evening of caroling, hot chocolate, and cookies. Your family's pride might have swelled when the entrée was the result of a successful hunt, or perhaps romantic thoughts still linger at the memory of a cozy holiday meal shared by just two of you.

If any of these scenarios are part of your celebration of the season, then you'll want to scan the pages of this section for some delicious recipe ideas. If you're traveling to the home of friends or family, take along a jar of tea mix or one of the other hostess gift recipes featured. The take-along gifts also make a nice "something extra" to give to neighbors.

When folks are coming to your house, you'll be prepared with recipes for make-ahead salads and turkey with all the trimmings. Even if the menu is just for two of you this year, there are some recipes provided for your convenience.

If a big party during the season is traditional, then our open-house buffet menu may be ideal. Or entertain as David and Nancy Wilson of Austin, Texas, do: They make it an annual tradition to invite their friends and family to partake of a unique Southwestern-style menu.

Entertaining year-round is a favorite pastime of Nancy's. "I'm in my element when I'm entertaining my friends," she says. "I just love preparing for the party, planning the food, getting the house ready, and pulling my dishes out. I love parties and always enjoy my own."

Large parties are Nancy's preference. "It's not that much harder to serve a big crowd," she claims. "It's more cooking, but everything else is the same."

Her keys to entertaining a large number of people include serving buffet style and planning a menu that allows advance preparation. "The main thing is to plan a menu that can be done ahead of time; that's what lets you have fun," Nancy explains.

"I just start early and do a little bit each day. I usually set my table three days ahead because that's the fun part. But I do all the work myself, and then have help at the party to serve food and do cleanup."

For the menu Nancy shares here, she suggests making Tortilla Soup and Bolillos ahead of time and freezing them. "Freeze the soup without the cheese and tortillas," she says. Thaw the soup, then heat when ready to serve, adding cheese and tortillas. "Then thaw and heat the Bolillos before serving."

The turkey casserole involves several preparation steps, but she finds that freezing the sautéed turkey slices saves time later on. The Flan can be made the day before the party, and oranges for Jicama-and-Orange Salad can be sectioned and chopped a day ahead.

Then when David and Nancy greet their guests with a traditional margarita, they join right in and enjoy the fun.

Margaritas   Mixed Nuts
Tortilla Soup
Stuffed Turkey Casserole
Jicama-and-Orange Salad
Baked Zucchini Fans
Stuffed Broiled Avocados
Bolillos   Flan
Mexican Coffee

TORTILLA SOUP

1 cup chopped onion
2 fresh jalapeño peppers, seeded and chopped
4 cloves garlic, minced
¼ cup vegetable oil
2 (14½-ounce) cans stewed tomatoes
2 (10-ounce) cans tomatoes and green chiles
2 (10½-ounce) cans beef bouillon
2 (10¾-ounce) cans chicken broth, undiluted
2 (10¾-ounce) cans tomato soup, undiluted
3 cups water
2 teaspoons ground cumin
½ to 1 teaspoon ground red chiles
2 tablespoons chopped fresh cilantro
12 flour tortillas, cut into ½ inch strips, divided
1 cup (4 ounces) shredded Cheddar cheese

Sauté onion, peppers, and garlic in oil in a large Dutch oven until tender; add next 9 ingredients. Bring to a boil; cover, reduce heat, and simmer 1 hour. Add three-fourths of tortilla strips and shredded cheese. Simmer 5 minutes. Garnish with remaining tortilla strips. Yield: 10 cups.

STUFFED TURKEY CASSEROLE

12 (½- to ¾-inch-thick) slices
    uncooked turkey breast (about
    2½ pounds)
½ cup all-purpose flour
3 tablespoons vegetable oil
Pumpkin Seed Sauce
Rice-and-Onion Stuffing
1½ cups (6 ounces) shredded
    Monterey Jack cheese
Chopped parsley or cilantro

Dredge turkey slices in flour; sauté turkey in oil about 2 minutes on each side or until browned. Set turkey aside. Set skillet and drippings aside for Pumpkin Seed Sauce.

Spoon about 1 cup Pumpkin Seed Sauce into a 13- x 9- x 2-inch casserole. Layer turkey over sauce, overlapping slices slightly. Spoon Rice-and-Onion Stuffing between turkey slices. Top with remaining Pumpkin Seed Sauce. Bake, uncovered, at 350° for 30 minutes. Sprinkle cheese over casserole; bake an additional 5 minutes. Sprinkle with parsley. Yield: 12 servings.

Note: Casserole may be refrigerated several hours or overnight before baking. Allow to come to room temperature before baking.

Pumpkin Seed Sauce

1½ cups chicken broth
2 (4-ounce) cans chopped green
    chiles, drained
¾ cup shelled green pumpkin
    seeds
1 egg, beaten
¼ teaspoon salt
⅛ teaspoon pepper

Combine chicken broth and drippings from sautéed turkey in skillet; bring to a boil, stirring constantly.

Combine chiles and pumpkin seeds in food processor; process until smooth. Add chile mixture to chicken broth mixture, and bring to a boil.

Cover, reduce heat, and simmer 20 minutes. Gradually stir about one-fourth of hot mixture into egg. Add to remaining mixture; stir constantly. Add seasonings. Yield: 2 cups.

Rice-and-Onion Stuffing

2 cups water
¼ teaspoon salt
⅓ cup uncooked long-grain rice
2 medium onions, finely chopped
¼ cup butter or margarine,
    melted
2 cloves garlic, minced
¼ teaspoon salt
¾ teaspoon ground red chiles
Pinch of pepper
Pinch of ground cumin
¼ cup plus 2 tablespoons
    whipping cream

Bring water and ¼ teaspoon salt to a boil; add rice, and bring to a boil. Boil, uncovered, 5 minutes. Drain.

Combine rice and remaining ingredients except whipping cream in a lightly greased 2-quart casserole. Cover and bake at 325° for 45 minutes. Remove from oven; stir in whipping cream. Cover and bake an additional 15 minutes. Yield: about 2½ cups.

JICAMA-AND-ORANGE SALAD

8 cups peeled, cubed jicama
12 oranges, peeled, sectioned,
    and coarsely chopped (about 5
    cups)
1 cup sliced green onions
¾ cup chopped fresh cilantro
3 tablespoons lime juice
3 tablespoons vegetable oil
¼ cup plus 2 tablespoons
    commercial sour cream
⅛ teaspoon salt
Orange slice twist
Fresh cilantro

Combine first 4 ingredients in a large bowl; cover and chill.

Combine lime juice, oil, sour cream, and salt in a jar; cover tightly, and shake vigorously.

Just before serving, drain jicama-orange mixture. Pour dressing over salad; toss gently. Garnish with orange slice and cilantro. Yield: 12 servings.

BAKED ZUCCHINI FANS

3 tablespoons finely chopped
    onion
2 small cloves garlic, crushed
¼ cup olive oil, divided
3 tablespoons soft breadcrumbs
12 small zucchini
¼ cup grated Parmesan cheese

Sauté onion and crushed garlic in 2 tablespoons olive oil until tender. Remove from heat; stir in breadcrumbs. Set aside.

Cut each zucchini into 4 lengthwise slices leaving slices attached on stem end. Fan slices out, and place in 15- x 10- x 1-inch jellyroll pans; brush zucchini fans lightly with remaining 2 tablespoons olive oil.

Sprinkle each zucchini fan lightly with ½ teaspoon breadcrumb mixture and 1 teaspoon Parmesan cheese. Bake at 350° for 15 to 20 minutes or until crisp-tender. Yield: 12 servings.

STUFFED BROILED AVOCADOS

¼ cup sliced green onions
2 tablespoons olive oil
2 (16-ounce) cans whole
    tomatoes, drained and chopped
½ cup soft breadcrumbs, divided
½ cup grated fresh Parmesan
    cheese
6 ripe avocados, unpeeled
2 tablespoons butter or
    margarine, melted
¼ teaspoon salt
¼ teaspoon white pepper

Sauté green onions in olive oil; reduce heat, add tomatoes, and simmer 5 minutes, stirring occasionally. Add ¼ cup breadcrumbs, mixing well. Set mixture aside.

Combine remaining ¼ cup breadcrumbs and Parmesan cheese; set mixture aside.

Cut avocados in half lengthwise; remove seeds. Brush avocado halves with melted butter; sprinkle with salt and pepper. Top avocados with tomato mixture; sprinkle with breadcrumb mixture. Broil stuffed avocados 2 minutes or until cheese melts. Yield: 12 servings.

BOLILLOS

2 cups warm water (105° to 115°)
1 package dry yeast
¼ cup sugar
2 teaspoons salt
4½ to 5 cups unbleached flour, divided
1 tablespoon cornstarch
⅓ cup water
Melted butter

Combine first 4 ingredients in a large mixing bowl; let stand 5 minutes. Add 2 cups unbleached flour, and beat at medium speed of an electric mixer 2 minutes. Gradually stir in enough remaining flour to make a soft dough.

Turn dough out onto a floured surface, and knead until smooth and elastic (about 5 minutes). Place dough in a greased bowl, turning to grease top. Cover and let rise in a warm place (85°), free from drafts, 1½ hours or until doubled in bulk.

Punch dough down, and divide into 12 equal pieces. Shape each piece into a 3½- x 1½-inch roll. Place on a greased baking sheet. Using a sharp knife, make a lengthwise slit 2½ inches long and ½ inch deep in center of each roll.

Combine cornstarch and ⅓ cup water, mixing well; brush on rolls.

Place a pan on lower oven rack; fill pan with boiling water. Place baking sheet with rolls on middle oven rack. Bake at 450° for 10 minutes. Reduce heat to 375°, and bake 20 minutes. Brush rolls with melted butter. Yield: 1 dozen.

FLAN

1 cup sugar
4 eggs, beaten
1 (14-ounce) can sweetened condensed milk
1¾ cups milk
2 teaspoons vanilla extract
½ cup sliced almonds, toasted

Pour sugar into a 10-inch heavy or cast-iron skillet; place over medium heat, stirring constantly with a wooden spoon, until sugar melts and becomes light golden brown. Pour syrup into a 9-inch round cakepan; set aside.

Combine eggs, sweetened condensed milk, milk, and vanilla; beat with a wire whisk. Pour over caramelized sugar; cover pan with aluminum foil, and place in a larger shallow pan. Pour hot water to depth of 1 inch into pan. Bake at 350° for 55 minutes or until a knife inserted near center comes out clean.

Remove pan from water, and uncover; let cool on a wire rack. Cover and chill 4 to 6 hours.

Loosen edges with a spatula. Invert flan onto plate; arrange almonds around top edge. Yield: 8 servings.

MEXICAN COFFEE

12 cups hot brewed coffee
6 ounces piloncillo
1 ounce Mexican chocolate
⅓ cup Kahlúa
Sweetened whipped cream
Grated chocolate

Combine first 3 ingredients, stirring until chocolate melts; add Kahlúa. Pour into cups; top with sweetened whipped cream and grated chocolate. Yield: 12 cups.

Note: ½ cup plus 2 tablespoons sugar, 1½ squares unsweetened chocolate, and ¼ teaspoon ground cinnamon may be substituted for piloncillo (unrefined sugar that is often molded into cones or sticks) and Mexican chocolate.

Beverages Brewed For The Season

When there's a chill in the air, nothing warms the soul or body better than one of these hot brewed beverages. For easy preparation and convenient service, percolator punches, such as Cranberry Percolator Punch, just can't be beat.

HOT BUTTERED RUM

½ cup rum
3 cups apple cider
1 tablespoon plus 1 teaspoon brown sugar
1 tablespoon plus 1 teaspoon butter, divided
4 (3-inch) sticks cinnamon

Combine first 3 ingredients in a saucepan; bring to a boil, stirring until sugar dissolves. Pour into 4 mugs. Add 1 teaspoon butter and 1 cinnamon stick to each mug. Yield: 4 servings.
Marie Horbaly
Springfield, Virginia

STRAWBERRY TEA

2 cups boiling water
4 regular-size tea bags
6 (3-inch) sticks cinnamon,
  broken into pieces
1 teaspoon whole cloves
1 (46-ounce) can pineapple juice
1 (6-ounce) can frozen orange
  juice concentrate, thawed and
  undiluted
1 (6-ounce) can frozen lemonade
  concentrate, thawed and
  undiluted
1 (3-ounce) package
  strawberry-flavored gelatin
2 cups water

Pour 2 cups boiling water over tea bags; cover. Let stand 12 minutes. Remove tea bags.
  Combine cinnamon and cloves in a tea ball or cheesecloth bag.
  Combine tea, spice mixture, and remaining ingredients in a Dutch oven. Bring to a boil. Cover, reduce heat, and simmer 45 minutes. Remove and discard spices. Serve hot. Yield: 10 cups. *Mrs. Carol Seeley*
Burns, Tennessee

HOT SPICED APRICOT TEA

10 whole cloves
2 (2-inch) sticks cinnamon
3 cups water
2 regular-size tea bags
2 (12-ounce) cans apricot nectar
½ to ¾ cup sugar
¼ to ⅓ cup lemon juice

Combine cloves and cinnamon sticks in a cheesecloth bag; set aside.
  Bring water to a boil in a large saucepan; add tea bags. Remove from heat, cover, and steep 5 minutes. Remove tea bags. Add spice mixture and remaining ingredients to tea; bring to a boil. Remove spices, and serve hot. Yield: about 6 cups.
Vickie Lee Black
Arlington, Texas

WASSAIL

1 gallon apple cider, divided
1 teaspoon ground cloves
1 teaspoon ground allspice
1 teaspoon ground nutmeg
1 teaspoon ground cinnamon
1 (6-ounce) can frozen lemonade
  concentrate, thawed and
  undiluted
1 (6-ounce) can frozen orange
  juice concentrate, thawed and
  undiluted
½ cup firmly packed brown
  sugar

Combine 2 cups apple cider and spices in a large Dutch oven; bring to a boil. Reduce heat, and simmer 10 minutes. Add remaining apple cider, lemonade concentrate, orange juice concentrate, and brown sugar. Heat until very hot, but do not boil. Yield: 4½ quarts. *Mrs. Forrest Gilmore*
Lake Placid, Florida

CRANBERRY
PERCOLATOR PUNCH
(pictured om page 306)

2 (32-ounce) bottles cranberry
  juice cocktail
4 (6-ounce) cans frozen lemonade
  concentrate, thawed and
  undiluted
6 cups apple cider
4 (3-inch) sticks cinnamon
2 teaspoons whole cloves
1 teaspoon whole allspice
2 to 3 cups light rum
Lemon wedges (optional)
Whole cloves (optional)

Pour cranberry juice cocktail, lemonade concentrate, and apple cider into a 30-cup percolator; place spices in percolator basket. Perk through complete cycle of electric percolator.
  Remove basket with spices from percolator, and stir in rum. If desired, garnish with lemon wedges studded with whole cloves. Yield: about 20 cups. *Velma P. Kestner*
Berwind, West Virginia

Wild Game
For The Menu

If wild game is an annual treat at your house, you'll enjoy these recipes. Each is delicious enough to serve at any meal for company.

FRUITED STUFFED
WILD GOOSE

1 (3½- to 4-pound) dressed wild
  goose
½ teaspoon salt
⅛ teaspoon pepper
6 slices bacon
1 cup sliced green onions
¼ cup chopped green pepper
1 (8-ounce) package
  herb-seasoned stuffing mix
1¼ cups water
1 cup chopped dried peaches
½ cup chopped pitted dates
1 egg, slightly beaten

Remove giblets and neck from goose; reserve for other uses. Rinse goose thoroughly with cold water; pat dry. Sprinkle salt and pepper inside cavity of goose.

Cook bacon in a large skillet until crisp; remove bacon, reserving drippings in skillet. Crumble bacon, and set aside. Sauté green onions and green pepper in drippings until crisp-tender.

Combine stuffing mix, bacon, green onions, green pepper, 1¼ cups water, peaches, dates, and egg, stirring well. Spoon mixture into goose cavity; close with skewers. Truss goose, and place breast side up on rack in a roasting pan. Insert meat thermometer in thigh, making sure it does not touch bone. Bake, uncovered, at 350° for 1 hour and 45 minutes or until meat thermometer registers 185°.

Spoon any leftover dressing into a lightly greased baking dish. Cover and bake at 350° for 40 minutes or until done. Yield: 2 to 4 servings.
Virginia B. Stalder
Nokesville, Virginia

VENISON TENDERLOIN APPETIZERS

1 (1½- to 2-pound) venison
    tenderloin
½ cup red wine
2 tablespoons olive oil
1½ tablespoons Worcestershire
    sauce
1 teaspoon dried whole thyme
¾ teaspoon onion powder
½ teaspoon cumin seeds
¼ teaspoon pepper
⅛ teaspoon ground cloves
⅛ teaspoon garlic powder

Remove any white membrane surrounding tenderloin. Tie tenderloin with string, if necessary, to hold pieces of meat together. Place tenderloin in a shallow dish.

Combine wine, oil, and Worcestershire sauce; mix well. Add thyme and remaining ingredients, mixing well. Pour over tenderloin, and cover tightly. Refrigerate 8 hours, turning meat occasionally.

Remove tenderloin, reserving marinade. Place on a rack in a roasting pan; insert meat thermometer.

Bake at 425° for 30 minutes or until thermometer registers 160° (medium), basting occasionally with marinade. Allow meat to stand 10 minutes. Slice thinly with an electric knife. Serve with party rolls, mustard, and mayonnaise. Yield: 15 appetizer servings.
Coyet Lowery
Irmo, South Carolina

VENISON KABOBS
(pictured on page 238)

2 pounds boneless venison
    sirloin, cut into 1½-inch cubes
3 cups vegetable oil
¼ cup dry Burgundy
2 tablespoons cider vinegar
1½ tablespoons liquid smoke
2 teaspoons salt
1 teaspoon white pepper
1 teaspoon garlic powder
1 teaspoon onion juice
16 cherry tomatoes
24 small fresh mushrooms
8 small onions
2 large green peppers, cut into
    24 (1-inch) pieces
Hot cooked wild rice

Place meat in a shallow glass container; set aside.

Combine oil and next 7 ingredients; pour over meat. Cover and refrigerate 48 hours, stirring occasionally. Remove meat from marinade, reserving marinade.

Alternate meat and vegetables on skewers; brush with marinade. Grill kabobs over medium-hot coals 15 minutes, turning and basting frequently with marinade. Serve with wild rice. Yield: 8 servings.
R. W. Broome
Houston, Texas

Salads To Make Ahead

Because they add color and texture, salads often occupy a prominent place on Southern menus. During the busy holiday season, salads that can be prepared ahead of time are a real bonus.

CHRISTMAS SALAD
(pictured on page i)

1 (3-ounce) package cream
    cheese, softened
2 tablespoons minced walnuts
2 envelopes unflavored gelatin
3½ cups pineapple juice, divided
2 tablespoons sugar
¼ teaspoon salt
1 tablespoon lemon juice
¾ cup sliced fresh strawberries
½ cup thinly sliced celery
Lettuce leaves
Pineapple slices (optional)
Strawberry fan (optional)

Combine cream cheese and walnuts; stir well. Shape mixture into ½-inch balls. Cover and chill. Sprinkle gelatin over ½ cup pineapple juice in a medium saucepan; let stand 1 minute. Add remaining pineapple juice, sugar, salt, and lemon juice. Cook over medium heat until gelatin dissolves, stirring constantly. Chill until the consistency of unbeaten egg white. Fold in sliced strawberries, celery, and reserved cream cheese balls. Spoon into a lightly oiled 5-cup mold. Cover and chill until firm.

Unmold onto a lettuce-lined serving plate; if desired, garnish with pineapple slices and a strawberry fan. Yield: 10 servings.
Mrs. M. L. Shannon
Fairfield, Alabama

CRANBERRY SALAD

2 (3-ounce) packages cream
   cheese, softened
2 tablespoons mayonnaise
2 tablespoons sugar
1 (16-ounce) can whole-berry
   cranberry sauce
1 (8-ounce) can crushed
   pineapple, drained
½ cup chopped pecans
1 cup whipping cream
½ cup sifted powdered sugar
1 teaspoon vanilla extract

Combine cream cheese, mayonnaise, and sugar, stirring until smooth. Stir in cranberry sauce, pineapple, and chopped pecans.

Beat whipping cream until foamy; gradually add powdered sugar, beating until soft peaks form. Add vanilla. Fold whipped cream into cranberry-cream cheese mixture. Spoon into an 8-inch square dish. Cover and freeze until firm. Yield: 6 to 8 servings.

Mrs. T. J. Compton
Lampasas, Texas

LEMON-CREAM SALAD

1 (10-ounce) bottle lemon-lime
   carbonated beverage
1 cup miniature marshmallows
2 (3-ounce) packages cream
   cheese, cubed
1 (6-ounce) package
   lemon-flavored gelatin
1 (20-ounce) can crushed
   pineapple, undrained
¾ cup chopped pecans
1 cup whipping cream,
   whipped

Combine carbonated beverage, marshmallows, and cream cheese in a heavy saucepan; place over low heat until cream cheese melts, stirring constantly. Remove from heat; add gelatin, stirring until dissolved. Stir in pineapple and chopped pecans. Chill until the consistency of unbeaten egg white. Fold in whipped cream; pour into a lightly oiled 5-cup mold. Cover and chill until firm. Yield: 10 servings. *Mrs. John Sharp*
Jacksonville, Florida

Elegant Preludes To Exciting Meals

Whether your style is elegant or simple and direct, these soups set the stage for sophisticated dining.

Green Pepper Soup, with its pale-green color and rich flavor, is a fine accompaniment to fish or chicken. Tomato Consommé goes well with beef or other red meat.

If you find yourself short of soup bowls and service plates, consider using your favorite plates with clear glass bowls, or mix and match the bowls and plates you have.

GREEN PEPPER SOUP
(pictured on page vii)

4 large green peppers, chopped
2 large onions, chopped
1 tablespoon butter or margarine,
   melted
1 tablespoon vegetable oil
1 tablespoon all-purpose flour
4 cups chicken broth
1 cup half-and-half
¼ teaspoon salt
¼ teaspoon pepper
Sliced scallions (optional)

Sauté green pepper and onion in butter and oil in a Dutch oven. Add flour, and stir until smooth. Cook 1 minute, stirring constantly. Gradually add chicken broth. Bring to a boil; reduce heat, and simmer 5 minutes. Spoon half of mixture into container of an electric blender; process until smooth. Repeat procedure with remaining pepper mixture.

Return mixture to Dutch oven; stir in half-and-half, salt, and pepper. Cook over low heat, stirring constantly, until soup is heated. Garnish with sliced scallions, if desired. Yield: 7 cups. *Deborah Newman*
Raleigh, North Carolina

TOMATO CONSOMMÉ

1 (46-ounce) can vegetable juice
   cocktail or tomato juice
2 beef-flavored bouillon cubes
2 cups water
1 teaspoon prepared horseradish
1 teaspoon Worcestershire sauce
1 teaspoon onion juice
Lemon slices (optional)
Whole cloves (optional)

Combine first 6 ingredients in a Dutch oven. Bring to a boil. If desired, garnish each serving with a slice of lemon studded with whole cloves. Yield: 2 quarts.

Mrs. William L. Clark
Richmond, Kentucky

SWEET POTATO SOUP

1 (17-ounce) can sweet potatoes,
   drained and mashed
1 cup orange juice
½ cup white wine
¼ cup honey
¼ cup commercial sour cream
1 teaspoon pumpkin pie spice
¼ cup flaked coconut, toasted

Combine all ingredients except coconut in container of an electric blender or processor; process until smooth. Refrigerate. Garnish with coconut. Yield: 3⅓ cups. *Mrs. J. A. Allard* *San Antonio, Texas*

CRAB BISQUE

1 (10¾-ounce) can cream of
    mushroom soup, undiluted
1 (10¾-ounce) can cream of
    asparagus soup, undiluted
2 cups milk
1 cup half-and-half
1 (6-ounce) can crabmeat, drained
    and flaked
¼ to ⅓ cup dry white wine or
    sherry

Combine first 4 ingredients in a saucepan; heat thoroughly, stirring occasionally. Add crabmeat and wine; heat thoroughly. Yield: 6 cups.

Judy Archambault Stevenson *Goose Creek, South Carolina*

Winter Fruit Brightens The Meal

Fruit is the natural choice for a simple, yet sweet dessert. It lends flavor and variety to holiday menus and is especially welcome after a filling, heavy meal.

HOLIDAY BROILED GRAPEFRUIT

1 tablespoon plus 1 teaspoon
    grenadine syrup
2 grapefruit, halved
2 maraschino cherries, halved

Spoon 1 teaspoon grenadine syrup over each grapefruit half; top each with a cherry half. Place grapefruit in an 8-inch square pan. Broil 3 inches from heat 3 minutes or until bubbly. Serve warm. Yield: 4 servings.

Marianne Eastland *Doddsville, Mississippi*

WINTER FRUIT WITH CUSTARD SAUCE

1 (12-ounce) package pitted
    prunes
1 (6-ounce) package dried apricots
½ cup firmly packed light brown
    sugar
1 cup water
1 (29-ounce) can peach halves,
    drained
3 pears, cored
3 oranges, peeled and sectioned
1 cup chopped walnuts
3 bananas, sliced
Custard Sauce

Cut prunes and apricots into bite-size pieces. Combine sugar and water in a saucepan; bring to a boil. Add prunes and apricots; remove from heat. Cover and let soak 4 hours. Drain. Place in a large bowl.

Cut peaches and pears into bite-size pieces; add peaches, pears, oranges, and walnuts to prunes and apricots. Chill. Add bananas just before serving. Spoon fruit into serving dishes. Top with Custard Sauce. Yield: 12 servings.

Custard Sauce

¼ cup sugar
1 tablespoon cornstarch
2 cups milk
6 egg yolks, beaten
1 teaspoon almond extract
½ cup whipping cream, whipped

Combine sugar and cornstarch in a small saucepan; gradually stir in milk.

Cook over medium heat, stirring constantly, until mixture comes to a boil. Cook 1 minute, stirring constantly. Remove from heat.

Gradually stir about one-fourth of hot mixture into yolks; add to remaining hot mixture, stirring constantly. Bring mixture to a boil over medium heat, and cook 1 minute, stirring constantly. Remove from heat; stir in almond extract. Pour mixture into bowl, and cover with plastic wrap, gently pressing directly onto custard. Chill. Fold whipped cream into custard. Yield: 3½ cups.

Louise Holmes *Winchester, Tennessee*

BERRY-APPLE PIE

1 (15-ounce) package refrigerated
    piecrusts
4 cups peeled, sliced apples
1 cup frozen blackberries, thawed
    and drained
1 cup fresh cranberries
¾ cup sugar
2 tablespoons cornstarch
2 tablespoons cranberry juice or
    orange juice
2 tablespoons butter or margarine

Line a 9-inch deep-dish pieplate with one piecrust, following package directions; set aside.

Combine apples, blackberries, and cranberries in a large bowl; set aside. Combine sugar and cornstarch; sprinkle over fruit, and drizzle cranberry juice over sugar mixture. Gently toss, and spoon into pieplate; dot with butter, and top with remaining crust. Trim pastry; seal and flute edges. Cut slits in pastry for steam to escape. Bake at 425° for 35 to 40 minutes or until browned. Cool. Yield: one 9-inch pie.

Adelyne Smith *Dunnville, Kentucky*

PINEAPPLE-ORANGE AMBROSIA

6 oranges, peeled and seeded
1 fresh pineapple, peeled and cored
1 cup grated fresh coconut
⅓ cup sugar
2½ tablespoons dry sherry

Cut oranges and pineapple into ½-inch chunks. Combine all ingredients; cover and chill 2 to 4 hours. Yield: 8 servings.
Mary Quesenberry
Dugspur, Virginia

Vary The Vegetables For Your Holiday Menu

The holiday menu typically revolves around turkey and dressing, but don't let that duo upstage the rest of the meal. You'll want to plan appealing side dishes to match the occasion.

FRENCH-STYLE CREAMED GREEN BEANS

1 pound fresh green beans
3 cups water
½ teaspoon salt
1 cup sliced fresh mushrooms
2 tablespoons butter or margarine, melted
½ cup whipping cream
⅛ teaspoon pepper

Wash beans, and remove strings. Cut beans lengthwise into thin strips. Combine beans, water, and salt in a saucepan. Bring to a boil; cover, reduce heat, and simmer 12 minutes or until crisp-tender. Drain.
    Sauté sliced mushrooms in melted butter until tender. Add whipping cream and pepper, stirring well. Stir into beans, and heat thoroughly. Yield: 4 servings.
Maggie Cates
Orlando, Florida

CHRISTMAS POTATOES

3 pounds potatoes
2 large onions, thinly sliced
½ teaspoon salt
¼ cup butter or margarine
3 tablespoons all-purpose flour
2 cups milk
¾ teaspoon salt
¼ teaspoon white pepper
½ cup chopped fresh parsley
1 (2-ounce) jar diced pimiento, drained
Fresh parsley sprigs (optional)
Tomato rose (optional)

Peel and cut enough potatoes into ¼-inch slices to measure 8 cups. Combine potato slices, onion, and ½ teaspoon salt in a large Dutch oven; add water to cover. Bring to a boil; cover, reduce heat, and cook 5 minutes. Drain and set aside.
    Melt butter in a heavy saucepan over low heat; add flour, stirring until smooth. Cook 1 minute, stirring constantly. Gradually add milk; cook over medium heat, stirring constantly, until mixture is thickened and bubbly. Stir in ¾ teaspoon salt and next 3 ingredients.
    Spoon potato mixture into a lightly greased 12- x 8- x 2-inch baking dish; pour sauce over potato mixture. Bake at 375° for 40 to 45 minutes. If desired, garnish with fresh parsley and a tomato rose. Yield: 8 servings.

Clairiece Gilbert Humphrey
Charlottesville, Virginia

SPINACH-ARTICHOKE CASSEROLE

2 (10-ounce) packages frozen chopped spinach
½ cup chopped onion
¼ cup plus 2 tablespoons butter or margarine, melted
½ cup commercial sour cream
¼ cup grated Parmesan cheese
¾ teaspoon salt
¾ teaspoon white pepper
Dash of red pepper
2 (14-ounce) cans artichoke hearts, drained and halved
2 tablespoons grated Parmesan cheese

Cook spinach according to package directions; drain well. Sauté onion in butter in a large skillet until tender. Add spinach, sour cream, and next 4 ingredients, stirring well.
    Place artichokes in a lightly greased 8-inch square baking dish. Spoon spinach mixture over artichokes. Sprinkle with 2 tablespoons Parmesan cheese. Bake at 350° for 25 to 30 minutes. Yield: 8 servings.
Barbara Sherrer
Bay City, Texas

MUSHROOM NEWBURG

1 pound fresh mushrooms, sliced
3 tablespoons butter or margarine, melted
¼ teaspoon salt
¼ teaspoon pepper
3 tablespoons dry sherry
1 tablespoon cognac
1 cup half-and-half
¼ cup whipping cream
2 egg yolks, beaten
Patty shells or toast points

Sauté mushrooms in butter until all liquid evaporates. Add salt and next 3 ingredients; cook, stirring constantly, until all but 1 tablespoon of liquid evaporates. Add half-and-half;

simmer 5 minutes. Blend whipping cream into egg yolks, stirring well. Stir into mushroom mixture; cook over low heat, stirring constantly, until sauce is slightly thickened. Serve over patty shells or toast points. Yield: about 6 servings.

Eleanor K. Brandt
Arlington, Texas

A Turkey With All The Trimmings

What festive season is complete without a kitchen full of friends or relatives, a turkey in the oven, and the aroma of dressing throughout the house? Whether it's your first or fiftieth time to cook the big meal, dependable recipes make the difference between success and failure.

ROAST TURKEY
(pictured on page 307)

1 (12- to 14-pound) turkey
Salt (optional)
Vegetable oil or melted butter
Orange rosettes (optional)
Celery leaves (optional)
Whole almonds (optional)

Remove giblets and neck from turkey; reserve for gravy recipe. Rinse turkey thoroughly with cold water; pat dry. Sprinkle cavity with salt if you are not going to stuff turkey. To stuff, lightly pack dressing into body cavities of turkey. Tuck legs under flap of skin around tail, or close cavity with skewers, and truss. Tie ends of legs to tail with cord. Lift wingtips up and over back, and tuck under turkey.

Place turkey on a roasting rack, breast side up; brush entire bird with oil. Insert meat thermometer in meaty part of thigh, making sure it does not touch bone. Bake at 325° for 4 to 5 hours or until meat thermometer registers 185°. When turkey is two-thirds done, cut the cord or band of skin holding the drumstick ends to the tail; this will ensure that the thighs are cooked internally. Turkey is done when drumsticks are easy to move up and down. Let stand 15 minutes before carving. If desired, garnish with orange rosettes, celery leaves, and almonds. Yield: 20 to 24 servings.

Note: This time is for a stuffed turkey. Unstuffed turkeys require 5 minutes less per pound.

GIBLET GRAVY
(pictured on page 307)

Giblets and neck from 1 turkey
1 small onion, chopped
3 cups water
2 hard-cooked eggs, chopped
2 stalks celery, chopped
¼ teaspoon poultry seasoning
¼ teaspoon marjoram leaves
¼ teaspoon rubbed sage
¼ teaspoon ground thyme
¼ teaspoon pepper
1 teaspoon salt
2 tablespoons cornstarch
¼ cup water

Combine first 3 ingredients in a saucepan. Bring to a boil; cover, reduce heat, and simmer 45 minutes or until giblets are fork-tender. Drain, reserving broth. Remove meat from neck; coarsely chop neck meat and giblets. Set aside.

Add water to reserved broth to equal 3 cups. Combine broth, chopped neck meat and giblets, eggs, and next 7 ingredients. Bring to a boil; reduce heat, and simmer, uncovered, 30 to 45 minutes.

Combine cornstarch and ¼ cup water; stir into broth mixture. Bring to a boil; boil 1 minute. Serve gravy hot over turkey and dressing. Yield: 2⅔ cups.

Helen Dosier
Sparta, North Carolina

Turkey Tips

■ **Thaw the bird carefully.** Leave it in its original wrapper on a tray (to catch the drippings), and refrigerate until completely thawed. A 4- to 12-pound turkey takes 1 to 2 days; a 12- to 20-pound turkey, 2 to 3 days.

■ **If you stuff the turkey, do it just before roasting.** Stuffing the turkey the night before isn't a good idea because bacteria has a chance to grow.

■ **Use a meat thermometer to determine doneness.** The thermometer should be inserted into the thickest part of the thigh muscle, making sure the bulb doesn't touch bone. When the thermometer registers 180° to 185°, the turkey is done.

■ **Store leftovers quickly.** Remove the dressing from the turkey, and refrigerate in a separate container. Refrigerate any leftovers as soon as possible after serving.

CRANBERRY-ORANGE RELISH
(pictured on page 307)

4 cups fresh cranberries
2 cups sugar
½ cup water
½ cup orange juice
1 teaspoon grated orange rind
½ cup slivered almonds
Lettuce leaves (optional)
Orange cups (optional)

Combine first 5 ingredients in a saucepan; bring to a boil. Reduce heat, and simmer, uncovered, 10 minutes or until skins pop, stirring occasionally.

Remove from heat, and stir in almonds. Cool and store in refrigerator. If desired, serve in lettuce-lined orange cups. Yield: 4 cups.
Mrs. Delbert R. Snyder
Williamsburg, Virginia

HARVEST SAUSAGE DRESSING
(pictured on page 307)

1 pound bulk pork sausage
2 cups chopped celery
2 cups sliced mushrooms
1½ cups chopped onion
1 tablespoon plus 1 teaspoon
    chicken-flavored bouillon
    granules
1¾ cups boiling water
2 (8-ounce) packages
    herb-seasoned stuffing mix
1⅓ cups mincemeat
1 (8-ounce) can sliced water
    chestnuts, drained and chopped
2 teaspoons poultry seasoning

Brown sausage in a Dutch oven, stirring to crumble; drain. Return sausage to Dutch oven; add celery, mushrooms, and onion. Cook over low heat until vegetables are crisp-tender. Add bouillon granules and water; bring to a boil.

Add stuffing mix and remaining ingredients to Dutch oven. Stir well, and lightly stuff 2 cups of dressing into body cavity of turkey. Spoon remaining 7 cups of dressing into a lightly greased 12- x 8- x 2-inch baking dish. Cover and bake at 350° for 45 minutes. Yield: 9 cups.
Dorothy L. Akers
Vinton, Virginia

CORNBREAD DRESSING

1 (6-ounce) package cornbread
    mix
1 (5-ounce) can refrigerated
    biscuits
1½ cups chopped onion
1 cup chopped celery
3 tablespoons butter or
    margarine, melted
1 teaspoon salt
1 teaspoon pepper
1 teaspoon rubbed sage
3 cups chicken broth
4 eggs, slightly beaten

Prepare and bake cornbread mix and biscuits according to package directions; cool. Crumble cornbread and biscuits into a large bowl. Set aside.

Sauté onion and celery in butter until crisp-tender; add to cornbread mixture, stirring well. Add salt and remaining ingredients, mixing well. Spoon dressing into a lightly greased 12- x 8- x 2-inch baking dish; bake at 350° for 55 minutes or until golden. Yield: 8 servings.

Note: If desired, substitute 4 or 5 baked biscuits for 1 can refrigerated biscuits.
Wilma Lusk
Gadsden, Alabama

When Dinner's A Duo

When hustle and bustle fill the holidays, it's a rare treat to enjoy a quiet dinner for two, but this simple menu will give you the chance.

For the best timing, we suggest preparing the broccoli first; if time allows, it can be prepared three hours before dinner. Then flatten the chicken breasts (or purchase chicken fillets), and measure the other ingredients for the entrée. Prepare rice; while it cooks, get Hot Fudge Pudding Cake in the oven. Then you're ready to cook the chicken. All that's left is to relax and enjoy a delicious dinner.

Savory Chicken Sauté
Marinated Broccoli
Creamy Parslied Rice
Hot Fudge Pudding Cake

SAVORY CHICKEN SAUTÉ

2 chicken breast halves, skinned
    and boned
¼ teaspoon salt
¼ teaspoon pepper
2 tablespoons all-purpose flour
1 tablespoon butter or margarine
1 tablespoon olive oil
2 tablespoons minced onion
1 cup chicken broth
2 teaspoons tomato paste
1 teaspoon grated orange rind
1 orange, peeled and sliced
    crosswise
Parsley sprigs (optional)

Place each piece of chicken between 2 sheets of wax paper; flatten to ¼-inch thickness. Sprinkle with salt and pepper; dredge chicken in flour.

Heat butter and olive oil in a large skillet. Add chicken, and cook 5 minutes on each side. Remove chicken, and drain on paper towels; keep warm. Add onion to pan drippings in skillet, and cook until soft, but not brown. Stir in chicken broth, tomato paste, and orange rind; cook until heated. Add chicken; cover, reduce heat, and simmer 5 minutes or until chicken is tender. Transfer chicken to warm serving plates. Add orange slices to pan drippings in skillet, and heat. Spoon orange slices and sauce over chicken. Garnish with parsley, if desired. Yield: 2 servings.

Brenda Clark
Phenix City, Alabama

MARINATED BROCCOLI

½ pound fresh broccoli
1 tablespoon rice vinegar
1 tablespoon sesame oil
1 teaspoon soy sauce
1 teaspoon prepared mustard

Trim off large leaves of broccoli; remove tough ends of lower stalks. Wash broccoli, and cut into spears. Place in steaming rack over boiling water. Cover and steam 10 minutes.

Combine vinegar and remaining ingredients. Pour over broccoli, tossing to coat. Cover and chill up to 3 hours. Yield: 2 servings.

Susan Ferguson
New Orleans, Louisiana

CREAMY PARSLIED RICE

¾ cup water
¼ teaspoon salt
⅓ cup uncooked long-grain rice
¼ cup commercial sour cream
¼ cup minced fresh parsley
1½ teaspoons grated onion

Bring water and salt to a boil in a small saucepan; add rice. Cover, reduce heat, and simmer 20 minutes or until rice is tender and water is absorbed. Add sour cream, parsley, and grated onion. Yield: 2 servings.

Jean McIntosh
Spavinaw, Oklahoma

HOT FUDGE PUDDING CAKE

⅓ cup all-purpose flour
¾ teaspoon baking powder
⅛ teaspoon salt
¼ cup sugar
⅓ cup chopped pecans
1 tablespoon cocoa
3 tablespoons milk
1 tablespoon vegetable oil
⅓ cup firmly packed brown sugar
1 tablespoon cocoa
⅔ cup hot water
Ice cream or sweetened whipped cream
Chocolate curls (optional)

Combine first 6 ingredients in a bowl; add milk and oil, stirring well. Spoon batter evenly into an ungreased 1-quart casserole.

Combine brown sugar and 1 tablespoon cocoa; sprinkle over batter. Pour water over top. Bake at 350° for 30 to 35 minutes. Serve with ice cream or sweetened whipped cream. Garnish with chocolate curls, if desired. Yield: 2 to 3 servings.

Pam Shifflett
Bridgeport, West Virginia

Keep The Entrée Easy On The Cook

Put aside the fuss over the menu for Christmas Day, and make sure plans the night before stay simple. You can feed a hungry family of six with these casual entrées, adding little more than a salad on the side.

You can layer the ingredients of Taco Pie ahead of time if you need to; just cover and chill the pie until you're ready to bake it. Remove it from the refrigerator about 20 minutes before baking; otherwise, you'll need to bake it a little longer than the recipe specifies.

SPINACH-STUFFED MANICOTTI

12 manicotti shells
2 (10-ounce) packages frozen chopped spinach, thawed and well drained
2 cups (8 ounces) shredded mozzarella cheese
2 cups cottage cheese
½ cup grated Parmesan cheese
1 small onion, diced
2 tablespoons dried parsley flakes
1 teaspoon dried whole oregano
Dash of hot sauce
Dash of ground nutmeg
1 (32-ounce) jar spaghetti sauce with mushrooms, divided
¼ cup grated Parmesan cheese

Cook manicotti shells according to package directions; rinse, drain, and set aside.

Combine spinach and next 8 ingredients, stirring well. Stuff manicotti shells with spinach mixture.

Spoon 1 cup spaghetti sauce into a lightly greased 13- x 9- x 2-inch baking dish. Arrange stuffed shells over sauce. Spoon remaining sauce over shells; sprinkle with ¼ cup Parmesan cheese.

Cover tightly with aluminum foil, and bake at 350° for 45 minutes or until thoroughly heated. Yield: 6 servings.

Mary Kay Menees
White Pine, Tennessee

TUNA CASSEROLE WITH CHEESE SWIRLS

2 tablespoons diced onion
3 tablespoons diced green pepper
2 tablespoons butter or margarine, melted
3 tablespoons all-purpose flour
1 cup milk
1 (10¾-ounce) can cream of chicken soup, undiluted
1 (9¼-ounce) can white tuna in water, drained and flaked
1 cup all-purpose flour
1 teaspoon baking powder
¼ teaspoon salt
2½ tablespoons shortening
⅓ cup milk
½ cup (2 ounces) shredded Cheddar cheese

Sauté onion and green pepper in butter over medium heat 2 minutes. Add 3 tablespoons flour; cook 1 minute, stirring constantly. Add 1 cup milk, chicken soup, and tuna; stir until smooth. Spoon into a lightly greased 8-inch square baking dish; set aside.

Combine 1 cup flour, baking powder, and salt; cut in shortening until mixture resembles coarse meal. Add ⅓ cup milk; stir with a fork until dry ingredients are moistened. Turn dough out onto a well-floured surface; roll to a 10- x 8-inch rectangle. Sprinkle with cheese. Roll up dough jellyroll fashion, starting at long side; cut into 12 slices. Arrange on top of tuna mixture.

Bake at 400° for 25 minutes or until top is lightly browned. Yield: 6 servings.
Pat Dail
Radford, Virginia

Tip: *To ensure even baking, always lower oven temperature 25° when using heat-proof glass dishes.*

TACO PIE

1 pound ground beef
1 medium onion, chopped
1 (1¼-ounce) package taco seasoning mix
¾ cup water
1 (16-ounce) can refried beans
1 (8-ounce) jar taco sauce, divided
1 baked 9-inch pastry shell
2 cups (8 ounces) shredded Cheddar cheese
1 cup crushed corn chips
Shredded lettuce
Chopped tomato

Cook ground beef and onion in a skillet until meat is browned, stirring to crumble meat. Drain. Add taco seasoning mix and water, stirring well. Bring to a boil; reduce heat, and simmer 20 minutes, stirring occasionally.

Combine refried beans and ⅓ cup taco sauce. Spoon half of bean mixture into bottom of pastry shell. Top with half of meat mixture, half of cheese, and all of corn chips. Repeat layers with remaining bean mixture, meat mixture, and cheese. Bake at 400° for 20 to 25 minutes. Top with lettuce and tomato. Serve with remaining taco sauce. Yield: 6 servings.
Mrs. J. David Stearns
Mobile, Alabama

Tasty Gifts To Make

Folks are always searching for just the right "something" to offer as a holiday remembrance for that thoughtful neighbor, party hostess, understanding teacher, or special friend. A homemade treat created in your kitchen is always appropriate, and is treasured for the gift of your time, as well.

BUTTERSCOTCH RUM FUDGE

1 cup golden raisins
¼ cup light rum
2 cups firmly packed brown sugar
1 cup sugar
½ cup butter or margarine
1 cup evaporated milk
1 (7-ounce) jar marshmallow cream
1 (12-ounce) package butterscotch morsels
½ cup chopped pecans
½ cup chopped walnuts
1 teaspoon rum extract
½ teaspoon vanilla extract

Combine raisins and rum in a small bowl; cover and let stand 8 hours.

Combine brown sugar and next 3 ingredients in a 3-quart saucepan; cook over medium heat, stirring constantly, to soft ball stage (238°). Remove from heat; stir in marshmallow cream and butterscotch morsels. Add raisin mixture, pecans, and remaining ingredients; stir well. Spread mixture in a buttered 8-inch square pan. Cool and cut into squares. Store in an airtight container. Yield: 3½ pounds.
Gayle Nicholas Scott
Chesapeake, Virginia

COFFEE 'N' SPICE PECANS

1 tablespoon instant coffee granules
½ cup sugar
½ teaspoon ground cinnamon
Dash of salt
¼ cup water
3 cups pecan halves, toasted

Combine first 5 ingredients in a medium saucepan, stirring until sugar dissolves. Add pecans, and bring to a boil. Cook 3 minutes, stirring constantly. Spoon onto wax paper, separating pecans with a fork. Store in an airtight container. Yield: 3 cups.
Candice Gardner
Fort Walton Beach, Florida

MINI-MINCEMEAT NUT CAKES

½ cup butter or margarine,
  softened
⅓ cup firmly packed dark brown
  sugar
3 eggs
2½ cups all-purpose flour
1 teaspoon baking powder
½ teaspoon baking soda
1 teaspoon salt
1 (14-ounce) can sweetened
  condensed milk
1 (28-ounce) jar commercial
  mincemeat
2 cups chopped walnuts

Cream butter; gradually add sugar, beating well at medium speed of an electric mixer. Add eggs, one at a time, beating after each addition.

Combine flour, baking powder, soda, and salt; add to creamed mixture alternately with condensed milk, beginning and ending with flour mixture. Mix just until blended after each addition. Stir in mincemeat and walnuts.

Spoon batter into paper-lined miniature (1¾-inch) muffin pans, filling three-fourths full. Bake at 350° for 20 minutes or until a wooden pick inserted in center comes out clean. Remove from pans, and cool completely on wire racks. Yield: 16 dozen.

Note: Nut cakes may be baked and frozen. *Mary Anne M. Woodie*
Mechanicsville, Virginia

BAKED CRANBERRY SAUCE

4 cups fresh cranberries
2 cups sugar
½ teaspoon ground cinnamon
1 (13-ounce) jar orange
  marmalade
3 tablespoons lemon juice
1 cup coarsely chopped walnuts,
  toasted

Wash and drain cranberries; place in a large bowl. Combine sugar and cinnamon; add to cranberries, mixing well. Spoon into a 9-inch square pan; cover with aluminum foil. Bake at 350° for 45 minutes. Add orange marmalade, lemon juice, and walnuts, mixing well. Store in refrigerator. Yield: 4 cups. *Edith Askins*
Greenville, Texas

DELUXE SPICED TEA MIX

2 (26-ounce) jars instant
  orange-flavored breakfast drink
1 (3-ounce) jar instant tea
2 (8½-ounce) packages red
  cinnamon candies
1 (6-ounce) package sweetened
  lemonade-flavored drink mix
1 cup sugar
2 teaspoons ground cinnamon
2 teaspoons ground nutmeg
2 teaspoons ground cloves
2 teaspoons ground allspice

Combine all ingredients, stirring well. Store in an airtight container.

To serve, place 1 tablespoon plus 1 teaspoon mixture in a cup; add 1 cup boiling water, stirring well. Yield: about 14 cups.
Jackie Helen Bergenheier
Wichita Falls, Texas

Delectable
Dinner Rolls

Holiday meals are unique because almost everything is made from scratch—even the bread. If several folks contribute to your family's

menu and it's your turn to bring the bread, this recipe is sure to please.

Extra-Special Rolls lives up to its name. According to Mrs. Ben L. McKinley, Jr., "They're the best I've ever eaten."

EXTRA-SPECIAL ROLLS

2 packages dry yeast
3 tablespoons warm water (105°
  to 115°)
½ cup sugar
½ cup shortening, melted
2 eggs, beaten
1 cup warm water (105° to 115°)
1 teaspoon salt
4 to 4½ cups all-purpose flour,
  divided
¼ cup plus 2 tablespoons butter
  or margarine, softened

Dissolve yeast in 3 tablespoons warm water in a large mixing bowl; let stand 5 minutes. Add sugar, shortening, eggs, 1 cup warm water, salt, and 2 cups flour. Beat at low speed of an electric mixer 1 minute. Gradually stir in enough remaining flour to make a soft dough. Turn dough out onto a lightly floured surface; knead 4 minutes or until smooth and elastic.

Shape dough into a ball, and place in a well-greased bowl, turning to grease top. Cover and let rise in a warm place (85°), free from drafts, 1 hour or until doubled in bulk.

Punch dough down, and divide into fourths. Roll each to a 12-inch circle on a floured surface; spread with butter. Cut each circle into 12 wedges; roll up each wedge, beginning at wide end. Place on lightly greased baking sheets, point side down.

Cover and let rise in a warm place (85°), free from drafts, 1 hour or until doubled in bulk. Bake at 400° for 10 to 12 minutes. Yield: 4 dozen.
Mrs. Ben L. McKinley, Jr.
Dallas, Texas

Calling All Chocolate Lovers

Ted N. Via of Mayfield, Kentucky, fondly refers to his Mocha-Chocolate Cheesecake by another, somewhat different name. He calls it "Ted's Mocha-Chocolate Cheesecake To Die For." A veteran cook, Ted knows it's good. It's the culmination of all that he finds best in the world of chocolate and cheesecake.

MOCHA-CHOCOLATE CHEESECAKE
(pictured on page 239)

1¼ cups chocolate wafer crumbs (about 32 wafers)
¼ cup plus 1 tablespoon unsalted butter or margarine, melted
2 tablespoons slivered almonds, toasted
8 (1-ounce) squares semisweet chocolate
3 (8-ounce) packages cream cheese, softened
1 cup sugar
3 eggs
1½ tablespoons instant coffee granules
2 tablespoons Kahlúa
1 teaspoon vanilla extract
1½ cups commercial sour cream
½ cup whipping cream
1 tablespoon powdered sugar
Chocolate curls (optional)

Combine chocolate wafer crumbs and melted butter; stir well. Press into bottom and 1 inch up sides of a 9-inch springform pan. Sprinkle with slivered almonds. Chill.

Place semisweet chocolate in top of a double boiler; bring water to a boil. Reduce heat to low; cook until chocolate melts.

Beat cream cheese with an electric mixer until light and fluffy. Gradually add 1 cup sugar, beating well. Add eggs, one at a time, beating well after each addition. Add melted chocolate, beating until smooth.

Crush coffee granules with a mortar and pestle or the back of a spoon. Combine coffee granules, Kahlúa, and vanilla; add to chocolate mixture, beating well. Fold in sour cream.

Pour chocolate mixture into crumb crust; place on baking sheet. Bake at 350° for 1 hour. Turn off oven, and let cheesecake stand in oven 30 minutes with door partially open. Remove from oven; cool on wire rack. Cover and chill at least 8 hours.

Beat whipping cream until foamy; gradually add powdered sugar, beating until soft peaks form. Remove sides of springform pan; pipe or dollop whipped cream around edge of cheesecake. Garnish with chocolate curls, if desired. Yield: one 9-inch cheesecake.

CHOCOLATE PUDDING WITH LEMON MERINGUE

1½ cups sugar
¼ cup cocoa
¼ cup cornstarch
3 eggs, separated
2 cups milk
3 tablespoons butter or margarine
1 teaspoon vanilla extract
1 teaspoon lemon juice
¼ teaspoon lemon extract
¼ cup plus 2 tablespoons sugar

Combine 1½ cups sugar, cocoa, and cornstarch in a heavy saucepan; mix well. Stir in egg yolks and milk. Cook over medium heat, stirring constantly, until smooth and thickened. Remove mixture from heat; stir in butter and vanilla. Pour mixture into a 2-quart baking dish.

Beat egg whites (at room temperature) at high speed of an electric mixer 1 minute. Add lemon juice and lemon extract. Gradually add remaining sugar, 1 tablespoon at a time, beating until stiff peaks form and sugar dissolves (2 to 4 minutes). Spread meringue over pudding, sealing to edges of dish. Bake at 350° for 12 to 15 minutes or until golden brown. Yield: 6 servings.

Myradene Elmore
Clanton, Alabama

CHOCOLATE TRIFLE

1 (9-ounce) package devil's food cake mix
¼ to ½ cup rum
1 (21-ounce) can cherry pie filling
Chocolate Custard
1 cup whipping cream
2 tablespoons powdered sugar
¼ cup sliced almonds, toasted

Prepare cake mix according to package directions; cut into ½-inch slices. Line bottom of a 2-quart bowl or trifle dish with half of cake slices; sprinkle with 2 to 4 tablespoons rum. Spoon half of cherry pie filling over cake slices; top with half of Chocolate Custard. Repeat procedure with remaining cake slices, rum, pie filling, and custard. Cover and chill.

Beat whipping cream until foamy; gradually add powdered sugar, beating until soft peaks form. Spread over custard; garnish with almonds. Yield: 6 to 8 servings.

Chocolate Custard

⅔ cup sugar
¼ cup cocoa
⅛ teaspoon salt
3 eggs, beaten
2 cups milk

Combine first 3 ingredients in top of a double boiler. Combine eggs and

milk; gradually stir into dry mixture. Bring water in double boiler to a boil; reduce heat to low, and cook, stirring occasionally, until thickened. Cool. Yield: 3 cups. *Midge Finnerty Washington, Virginia*

ON THE LIGHT SIDE

Try These Low-Cholesterol Desserts

Cutting down on cholesterol and saturated fats doesn't mean having to give up dessert. Many scrumptious holiday desserts fit a low-cholesterol eating plan. The trick is to use egg substitute or egg whites for whole eggs and egg yolks, skim milk products for whole milk products, and margarine or oil for lard and butter.

RASPBERRY TRIFLE

1 cup evaporated skim milk
1 envelope unflavored gelatin
1 cup water
½ cup sugar
2¼ cups unsweetened frozen raspberries, thawed and divided
1 (10½-ounce) loaf angel food cake

Place evaporated milk in a small mixing bowl; freeze until ice crystals form around the edges.

Sprinkle gelatin over water in a heavy saucepan; let stand 1 minute. Add sugar, and cook over low heat, stirring constantly, until gelatin and sugar dissolve.

Remove from heat; chill until mixture is the consistency of unbeaten egg white. Fold 1 cup raspberries into gelatin mixture.

Place remaining 1¼ cups raspberries in container of an electric blender; process until smooth. Fold into gelatin mixture.

Whip evaporated milk at high speed of an electric mixer until stiff peaks form; fold into gelatin mixture.

Cut cake into cubes; fold into gelatin mixture, and pour into a 2½-quart soufflé dish. Cover and chill 8 hours. Yield: 10 servings (166 calories per 1-cup serving).

☐ *4.6 grams protein, 0.3 gram fat, 37 grams carbohydrate, 1 milligram cholesterol, 61 milligrams sodium, and 83 milligrams calcium.*

CHOCOLATE ANGEL FOOD CAKE WITH CUSTARD SAUCE

6 egg whites
½ teaspoon cream of tartar
1 teaspoon vanilla extract
½ cup sugar
⅓ cup sifted cake flour
3 tablespoons unsweetened cocoa
¼ cup sugar
⅛ teaspoon ground cinnamon
Custard Sauce

Beat egg whites (at room temperature) until foamy. Add cream of tartar; beat until soft peaks form. Add vanilla. Add ½ cup sugar, 1 tablespoon at a time, and beat until stiff peaks form.

Sift flour, cocoa, ¼ cup sugar, and cinnamon together; fold gently into egg whites.

Spoon batter into an ungreased 9- x 5- x 3-inch loafpan. Bake at 375° for 25 minutes or until cake springs back when lightly touched. Invert pan; cool 40 minutes. Loosen cake from sides of pan, and remove from pan. Serve cake with Custard Sauce. Yield: 9 servings (94 calories per 1-inch slice).

☐ *2.6 grams protein, 0.2 gram fat, 20.4 grams carbohydrate, 0 milligrams cholesterol, 44 milligrams sodium, and 9 milligrams calcium.*

Custard Sauce

¼ cup sugar
1 teaspoon cornstarch
1 cup skim milk
¼ cup egg substitute
2 tablespoons amaretto

Combine sugar and cornstarch in a heavy saucepan; stir in milk and egg substitute. Cook over medium heat, stirring constantly, until mixture begins to boil. Boil 1 minute, stirring constantly. Remove from heat, and stir in amaretto. Chill before serving. Yield: 1 cup plus 2 tablespoons (24 calories per tablespoon).

☐ *0.8 gram protein, 0 grams fat, 4.5 grams carbohydrate, 0 milligrams cholesterol, 12 milligrams sodium, 18 milligrams calcium.*
Christine McQueen Annville, Kentucky

Tip: *Never add cornstarch to a hot mixture because it will lump. Dilute cornstarch in twice as much cold liquid and stir until smooth. Then gently stir into the hot mixture.*

JEWELED FRUITCAKE

Vegetable cooking spray
¾ cup all-purpose flour
½ cup sugar
½ teaspoon baking powder
¾ cup egg substitute
1½ teaspoons vanilla extract
1 teaspoon grated orange rind
1½ cups chopped pecans
1 cup maraschino cherries
1 cup unsweetened pineapple
 tidbits
1 (8-ounce) package pitted dates,
 diced
1 (8-ounce) package dried
 peaches, diced

Line a 9- x 5- x 3-inch loafpan with aluminum foil; coat with cooking spray, and set loafpan aside.

Combine flour and next 5 ingredients in a large bowl; stir well. Add pecans and remaining ingredients; stir well. Spoon batter into prepared pan. Bake at 300° for 1 hour and 45 minutes or until a wooden pick inserted in center comes out clean. Shield cake the last 30 minutes to prevent overbrowning, if necessary. Remove from oven; let cool 10 minutes on a wire rack. Remove cake from pan; peel aluminum foil from cake, and cool completely on a wire rack. Wrap cake, and store in refrigerator. Yield: 24 servings (153 calories per ⅓-inch slice).

☐ *2.3 grams protein, 5.2 grams fat, 26.4 grams carbohydrate, 0 milligrams cholesterol, 19 milligrams sodium, and 18 milligrams calcium.*
 Teresa Bush-Zurn
 Los Angeles, California

Tip: *For easy chopping of dried fruit, place fruit in freezer 2 hours before chopping. Cut with knife or kitchen shears dipped frequently in hot water to prevent sticking.*

PUMPKIN CHIFFON
(pictured on back cover)

2 envelopes unflavored gelatin
1 cup evaporated skim milk
1 cup canned or mashed cooked
 pumpkin
½ teaspoon pumpkin pie spice
¼ teaspoon lemon rind
¼ teaspoon orange rind
1 (8-ounce) carton plain nonfat
 yogurt
3 egg whites
⅛ teaspoon salt
⅔ cup firmly packed brown
 sugar
½ cup chopped almonds, toasted
 and divided
1 tablespoon plus 1 teaspoon
 graham cracker crumbs

Sprinkle gelatin over evaporated milk in a heavy saucepan; let stand 1 minute. Cook over low heat, stirring constantly, until gelatin dissolves. Add pumpkin and next 3 ingredients; stir well. Chill until consistency of unbeaten egg white. Fold in yogurt (at room temperature).

Combine egg whites (at room temperature) and salt; beat at medium speed of an electric mixer until soft peaks form. Add brown sugar, a little at a time, and beat until stiff peaks form. Fold egg white mixture into pumpkin mixture.

Reserve 2 tablespoons plus 2 teaspoons almonds; set aside. Sprinkle remaining almonds evenly into 8 sherbet dishes; sprinkle each with ¼ teaspoon graham cracker crumbs. Spoon pumpkin mixture into dishes; chill until firm.

Before serving, sprinkle 1 teaspoon toasted chopped almonds and ¼ teaspoon graham cracker crumbs on each dessert. Yield: 8 servings (184 calories per ¾-cup serving).

☐ *8.8 grams protein, 4.6 grams fat, 28.5 grams carbohydrate, 2 milligrams cholesterol, 128 milligrams sodium, and 198 milligrams calcium.*

LIGHT COFFEE DESSERT

¾ cup evaporated skim milk
1 envelope unflavored gelatin
¼ cup water
1 tablespoon instant coffee
 granules
¼ cup sugar
⅓ cup evaporated skim milk
½ teaspoon almond extract

Place ¾ cup evaporated skim milk in a small mixing bowl; freeze until ice crystals form around the edges.

Sprinkle gelatin over water in a small heavy saucepan; let stand 1 minute. Cook over low heat, stirring constantly, until gelatin dissolves. Add coffee granules and sugar; stir until sugar dissolves. Stir in ⅓ cup evaporated skim milk and almond extract. Chill until the consistency of unbeaten egg white.

Beat partially frozen evaporated milk at high speed of an electric mixer until stiff peaks form. Fold into gelatin mixture. Spoon into individual sherbet dishes; chill until firm. Yield: 6 servings (73 calories per ¾-cup serving).

☐ *4.5 grams protein, 0.1 gram fat, 13.5 grams carbohydrate, 2 milligrams cholesterol, 55 milligrams sodium, and 134 milligrams calcium.*

Microwave
The Appetizers

"The ovens are filled with holiday fare, so how can I quickly cook the appetizers?" Sound familiar? It's a frequent challenge during this busy season. Once again, the microwave oven and advance planning can save the situation.

SHRIMP DIP
(pictured on page 238)

1 (8-ounce) package cream
  cheese, softened
1 (11-ounce) can Cheddar cheese
  soup, undiluted
2 (4¼-ounce) cans shrimp,
  drained, rinsed, and chopped
1 clove garlic, minced
⅓ cup white wine
Dash of red pepper
Whole shrimp (optional)

Place softened cream cheese and
Cheddar cheese soup in a 4-cup glass
measure. Microwave at MEDIUM
(50% power) 5 to 6 minutes or until
soup and cheese are smooth, stirring
every 2 minutes. Add canned shrimp,
garlic, wine, and red pepper. Microwave at MEDIUM 4 minutes, stirring after 2 minutes. Garnish with
whole shrimp, if desired.
  Serve with sweet red or green
pepper slices, endive, and breadsticks. Yield: 3¼ cups.

SPINACH-STUFFED MUSHROOMS

1½ pounds medium mushrooms
1 (10-ounce) package frozen
  chopped spinach, thawed
½ (8-ounce) package cream
  cheese, softened
2 teaspoons dried minced onion
¼ teaspoon salt
1 teaspoon lemon juice
2 drops hot sauce
6 slices bacon, cooked, crumbled,
  and divided

Clean mushrooms with damp paper
towels. Remove mushroom stems,
and reserve for other uses.
  Cook spinach according to package
directions; drain and press dry.
  Combine spinach and next 5 ingredients, mixing well. Stir two-thirds of

bacon into spinach mixture. Spoon
spinach mixture into mushroom caps.
  Arrange stuffed mushrooms on a
microwave-safe platter. Cover with
heavy-duty plastic wrap; fold back a
small edge to allow steam to escape.
Microwave at MEDIUM HIGH (70%
power) 7 minutes or until mushrooms
are thoroughly heated, giving dish a
half-turn after 4 minutes. Sprinkle
with remaining bacon. Yield: about 30
appetizer servings.

Note: Spinach-Stuffed Mushrooms
may be made ahead of time and refrigerated until ready to cook.
                    Janet McIntire
                    Marietta, Georgia

Invite Friends For An Appetizer Menu

An appetizer buffet is a refreshing
change from the formal, seated dinner. The foods offered here are a
convenience to entertaining because
most of them can be partially or totally prepared ahead of time.

Fruited Cream Cheese Dip
Shrimp Bayou
Marinated Flank Steak
With Party Rolls, Horseradish,
and Sour Cream
Eggplant Caviar
Crackers
Cucumber-Stuffed Cherry
Tomatoes
Chocolate-Peppermint Brownies

Note: This menu was prepared to
serve 12 to 15 people, but you can
double or triple the recipes.

FRUITED CREAM CHEESE DIP

1 (3-ounce) package cream
  cheese, softened
½ cup commercial sour cream
¼ cup strawberry preserves
1 teaspoon grated lemon rind
1 tablespoon lemon juice
Strawberry fan (optional)

Beat cream cheese at medium speed
of an electric mixer until creamy.
Add sour cream, strawberry preserves, lemon rind, and juice, mixing
until light and fluffy. Spoon into serving dish, and garnish with a strawberry fan, if desired. Serve with
fresh fruit. Yield: 1⅓ cups.
                    Dolly G. Northcutt
                    Fairfield, Alabama

SHRIMP BAYOU
(pictured on pages ii and iii)

3 quarts water
4 pounds unpeeled large fresh
  shrimp
1 cup vegetable oil
⅔ cup finely chopped celery
½ cup chili sauce
3 tablespoons lemon juice
2 tablespoons finely chopped
  chives
2 tablespoons prepared
  horseradish
1 tablespoon prepared mustard
½ teaspoon paprika
½ teaspoon salt
Dash of hot sauce

Bring water to a boil; add shrimp,
and cook 3 to 5 minutes. Drain well;
rinse with cold water. Peel and devein shrimp.
  Combine oil and remaining ingredients; stir well. Add shrimp; toss
gently. Cover and chill 8 hours, tossing occasionally. Yield: 15 appetizer
servings.   *Jerry Ray Barth*
                 Independence, Missouri

MARINATED FLANK STEAK
(pictured on pages ii and iii)

1 (8-ounce) bottle reduced-calorie
  Italian dressing
1 teaspoon Worcestershire sauce
1 teaspoon steak sauce
⅛ teaspoon garlic powder
⅛ teaspoon ground celery seeds
⅛ teaspoon rubbed sage
⅛ teaspoon dried whole oregano
⅛ teaspoon dried whole marjoram
⅛ teaspoon chopped chives
2 bay leaves
1 (1½-pound) flank steak

Combine all ingredients except steak
in a large shallow dish, stirring well.
Place steak in dish; cover and refrigerate 8 hours.

Remove steak from marinade. Grill
steak over hot coals 8 minutes on
each side or to desired degree of
doneness. To serve, thinly slice
steak diagonally across grain. Serve
on party rolls with sour cream and
prepared horseradish. Yield: 12 to 15
appetizer servings.

Note: If desired, broil steak 6 inches
from heat 4 to 5 minutes on each
side or to desired degree of
doneness.   *Mary Frances Donnelly*
Roanoke, Virginia

EGGPLANT CAVIAR
(pictured on pages ii and iii)

1 large eggplant
¾ cup finely chopped green
  pepper
¾ cup finely chopped onion
2 tablespoons olive oil
2 tablespoons butter or
  margarine, melted
1 large tomato, peeled and
  chopped
1 tablespoon catsup
1 teaspoon Worcestershire sauce
¼ teaspoon salt
Dash of pepper
Leaf lettuce

Wash eggplant; cut in half lengthwise. Remove pulp, leaving a ¼-
inch-thick shell, reserving one shell
in which to serve eggplant.

Chop eggplant pulp, and cook in a
small amount of boiling salted water
in a medium saucepan 12 minutes or
until tender. Drain well, and set
cooked eggplant aside.

Sauté chopped green pepper and
chopped onion in hot olive oil and
melted butter in a large skillet until
vegetables are crisp-tender. Add
cooked eggplant pulp, chopped tomato, catsup, Worcestershire sauce,
salt, and pepper. Cook over high
heat until liquid has evaporated. Chill.

Line reserved eggplant shell with
leaf lettuce. Spoon chilled eggplant
mixture into shell. Serve with crackers. Yield: 1¾ cups.
Mrs. Neill Sloan
Lake Village, Arkansas

CUCUMBER-STUFFED
CHERRY TOMATOES
(pictured on pages ii and iii)

2 pints cherry tomatoes
2 (3-ounce) packages cream
  cheese, softened
1 cup shredded cucumber,
  well drained
½ teaspoon curry powder
¼ teaspoon garlic salt
Cucumber wedges (optional)

Cut top off each tomato; scoop out
pulp, reserving for other uses. Invert
tomatoes on paper towels, and let
stand 30 minutes.

Combine cream cheese and next 3
ingredients; beat until blended. Pipe
or spoon mixture into tomato shells.
Garnish each tomato with a cucumber wedge, if desired. Yield: about
2½ dozen.   *Sally Veatch*
Gainesville, Georgia

CHOCOLATE-PEPPERMINT
BROWNIES

4 (1-ounce) squares unsweetened
  chocolate
1 cup butter or margarine
2 cups sugar
1 cup all-purpose flour
Pinch of salt
4 eggs, beaten
1 cup chopped pecans
½ teaspoon peppermint extract
2 cups sifted powdered sugar
¼ cup butter or margarine,
  softened
2 tablespoons evaporated milk or
  half-and-half
1 teaspoon peppermint extract
2 drops red food coloring
3 (1-ounce) squares unsweetened
  chocolate
3 tablespoons butter or margarine

Combine 4 squares chocolate and 1
cup butter in a saucepan; cook over
low heat, stirring until melted.

Combine 2 cups sugar, flour, and
salt; add to chocolate mixture. Add
eggs, pecans, and ½ teaspoon peppermint extract; stir until blended.
Spoon batter into a lightly greased
and floured 13- x 9- x 2-inch pan.
Bake at 350° for 25 minutes or until
a wooden pick inserted in center
comes out clean; let cool in pan.

Combine powdered sugar and next
4 ingredients; beat at medium speed
of an electric mixer until smooth.
Spread frosting over brownies.

Combine 3 squares chocolate and 3
tablespoons butter in a small heavy
saucepan; cook over low heat, stirring constantly, until melted. Spread
over frosting. Cover and store in refrigerator. Cut brownies into bars.
Yield: 4 dozen.   *Barbara Davis*
Lilburn, Georgia

Tip: *Use muffin pans to make extra
large ice cubes for punch.*

Rise And Shine To These Breakfast Breads

Put a little sunshine in your day by starting it with a tasty breakfast bread. Full of fruit, nuts, and spices, these breads are especially good with a tall glass of cold milk or a cup of freshly brewed coffee.

HONEY-WHEAT MUFFINS

1 cup all-purpose flour
½ cup whole wheat flour
2 teaspoons baking powder
½ teaspoon salt
½ teaspoon grated lemon rind
1 egg, beaten
½ cup milk
½ cup honey
¼ cup vegetable oil

Combine first 5 ingredients in a large bowl; make a well in center of mixture. Combine egg, milk, honey, and oil; add to dry ingredients, stirring just until moistened. Spoon into greased muffin pans, filling two-thirds full. Bake at 375° for 20 minutes or until done. Remove from pans immediately. Yield: 1 dozen.

Bunnie George
Birmingham, Alabama

BLUEBERRY COFFEE CAKE

½ cup butter or margarine, softened
1 cup sugar
2 eggs
2 cups all-purpose flour
1 teaspoon baking powder
½ teaspoon baking soda
1 (8-ounce) carton commercial sour cream
1 teaspoon vanilla extract
1 cup frozen or fresh blueberries
1 tablespoon sugar
1 teaspoon ground cinnamon
Powdered sugar (optional)

Cream butter; gradually add 1 cup sugar, beating well at medium speed of an electric mixer. Add eggs, one at a time, beating after each addition.

Combine flour, baking powder, and soda; gradually add to creamed mixture, mixing until blended. Stir in sour cream and vanilla.

Spoon half of batter into a greased and floured 10-inch Bundt pan; sprinkle with blueberries, 1 tablespoon sugar, and cinnamon. Top with remaining batter. Bake at 350° for 45 to 50 minutes. Cool in pan 10 minutes; remove from pan, and let cool completely on a wire rack. Sprinkle with powdered sugar, if desired. Yield: one 10-inch cake.

Mrs. John B. Wright
Greenville, South Carolina

UP-AND-DOWN BISCUITS

2 cups all-purpose flour
1 tablespoon plus 1 teaspoon baking powder
½ teaspoon salt
3 tablespoons sugar
½ teaspoon cream of tartar
½ cup shortening
⅔ cup milk
2 tablespoons butter or margarine, melted
¼ cup sugar
1 tablespoon ground cinnamon

Combine first 5 ingredients; cut in shortening with a pastry blender until mixture resembles coarse meal. Add milk, stirring until dry ingredients are moistened. Turn dough out onto a lightly floured surface, and knead lightly 4 or 5 times.

Roll dough to a 20- x 10-inch rectangle, ¼-inch thick; brush with melted butter. Combine ¼ cup sugar and cinnamon; sprinkle over dough. Cut lengthwise into five 2-inch-wide strips. Stack strips, cinnamon side up, on top of each other. Cut stack into 2-inch sections. Place each stacked section, cut side down, into lightly greased muffin pans. Bake at 425° for 12 minutes or until lightly browned. Yield: 10 biscuits.

Christine Hudson Atwood
Frankfort, Kentucky

FRUIT-AND-CEREAL BRUNCH CAKE

1 cup whole wheat flake cereal
1 cup orange juice
1 egg
¼ cup vegetable oil
¾ cup mashed banana (2 small bananas)
1½ cups all-purpose flour
1 teaspoon baking soda
½ teaspoon salt
½ cup sugar
1 teaspoon ground cinnamon
¼ cup raisins
½ cup firmly packed brown sugar
3 tablespoons all-purpose flour
1 tablespoon ground cinnamon
3 tablespoons butter or margarine
¼ cup chopped pecans

Combine cereal and orange juice in a large bowl; let stand 5 minutes. Combine egg, oil, and banana; add to cereal mixture. Combine 1½ cups flour and next 5 ingredients; add to cereal mixture, stirring just until moistened. Pour batter into a greased 9-inch square pan.

Combine brown sugar, 3 tablespoons flour, and 1 tablespoon cinnamon; cut in butter with a pastry blender until mixture resembles crumbs. Stir in pecans; sprinkle over batter. Bake at 350° for 40 minutes or until a wooden pick inserted in center comes out clean. Yield: 9 servings.

Mrs. Ellie Wells
Lakeland, Florida

Turkey After The Feast

When the holiday feast is over, most of us hope there will be left-over turkey. For some families, the slices disappear quickly in sandwiches. But you'll want to make sure you save some to use in these recipes.

TURKEY-VEGETABLE SOUP

2 baked turkey legs
2 baked turkey wings
8 cups water
1 (46-ounce) can vegetable juice
4 chicken-flavored bouillon cubes
4 medium potatoes, cubed
4 carrots, sliced
3 stalks celery, chopped
3 cups coarsely shredded cabbage
1 large onion, chopped
2 tablespoons sugar
2 tablespoons Worcestershire
    sauce
1 tablespoon lemon juice
½ teaspoon freshly ground pepper
¼ teaspoon hot sauce

Combine all ingredients in a large Dutch oven; bring to a boil over medium heat. Cover, reduce heat, and simmer 2 hours. Remove turkey; let cool. Bone turkey; chop meat, and add to soup. Bring to a boil over medium heat. Yield: about 5½ quarts. *Dorsella Utter*
Louisville, Kentucky

TURKEY FLORENTINE

2 (10-ounce) packages frozen
    spinach
3 tablespoons butter or margarine
3 tablespoons all-purpose flour
1 cup milk
½ cup whipping cream
¼ teaspoon salt
Dash of pepper
¼ teaspoon ground nutmeg
3 cups cooked turkey, cut into
    bite-size pieces
2 tablespoons grated Parmesan
    cheese, divided

Cook spinach according to package directions, omitting salt; drain. Press dry between layers of paper towels.

Melt butter in a heavy saucepan over low heat; add flour, stirring until smooth. Cook 1 minute, stirring constantly. Gradually add milk and whipping cream; cook over medium heat, stirring constantly, until thickened and bubbly. Stir in salt and pepper.

Combine spinach, ½ cup sauce, and nutmeg; spoon into a lightly greased 2-quart shallow casserole. Top evenly with turkey. Stir 1 tablespoon Parmesan cheese into remaining sauce; pour over turkey. Sprinkle with remaining cheese. Bake at 400° for 20 minutes or until browned. Yield: 4 to 6 servings. *Carol Noble*
Burgaw, North Carolina

TURKEY-CHEESE PIE

1 cup all-purpose flour
¼ teaspoon salt
⅓ cup shortening
½ cup (2 ounces) shredded
    Cheddar cheese
2 to 4 tablespoons cold water
2 cups chopped cooked turkey or
    chicken
2 hard-cooked eggs, chopped
1 (2-ounce) jar diced pimiento,
    drained
½ cup chopped celery
½ cup chopped green pepper
½ cup mayonnaise
¼ cup chicken broth
1 tablespoon lemon juice
½ teaspoon salt
1 cup (4 ounces) shredded
    Cheddar cheese
Green pepper slices (optional)

Combine flour and ¼ teaspoon salt; cut in shortening with pastry blender until mixture resembles coarse meal. Stir in ½ cup cheese. Sprinkle cold water (1 tablespoon at a time) evenly over surface; stir with a fork until dry ingredients are moistened. Shape into a ball.

Roll dough to ⅛-inch thickness on a lightly floured surface. Place in a 9-inch pieplate; trim off excess pastry along edges. Fold edges under, and flute.

Prick bottom and sides of pastry generously with a fork. Bake at 450° for 10 minutes.

Combine turkey and next 8 ingredients, stirring well. Spoon mixture into baked pastry shell. Bake at 350° for 15 minutes. Sprinkle 1 cup cheese on pie, and bake an additional 5 minutes. Garnish with green pepper slices, if desired. Let stand 10 minutes before serving. Yield: 6 servings. *Ruth Duke Young*
Montgomery, Alabama

ON THE LIGHT SIDE

Get First-Class Nutrition: Canned, Fresh, Or Frozen

If every vegetable and fruit we ate came right out of the garden, we would be getting the most nutritious produce possible. But not many people these days have fresh produce straight from the garden. Busy schedules and fewer backyard gardens have more people depending on supermarkets for fresh vegetables and fruits and taking advantage of the convenience of canned and frozen versions of these products.

Just how do canned and frozen fruits and vegetables compare with fresh? You may be surprised to learn that canned and frozen produce may, in some cases, be better than fresh. By the time vegetables and fruits are picked, packaged, shipped to a warehouse, transported to a supermarket, purchased, and then placed in the refrigerator or on the counter for several days before being served, they are no longer fresh.

To ensure getting the freshest produce possible at the supermarket, choose produce that is kept on ice, and use it as soon as possible. A quick-cooking method, such as microwaving or steaming, will also help prevent nutrient loss.

And don't feel as though you're serving less nutritious fruits and vegetables when using canned or frozen ones. By the time these versions are cooked and served, the nutritional value is practically the same as cooked fresh vegetables.

ZUCCHINI-AND-TOMATO CASSEROLE

3½ cups sliced zucchini
1 cup sliced onion
1 cup green pepper strips
Vegetable cooking spray
½ teaspoon dried Italian seasoning
¼ teaspoon garlic powder
½ teaspoon pepper
1 (16-ounce) can no-salt-added tomatoes, undrained and chopped

Layer zucchini, sliced onion, and green pepper strips in a 1½-quart casserole coated with cooking spray. Combine seasonings, and sprinkle over layers. Pour tomatoes over casserole. Bake at 350°, uncovered, for 1 hour. Yield: 5 servings (45 calories per ¾-cup serving).

☐ 2.3 grams protein, 0.3 gram fat, 9.9 grams carbohydrate, 0 milligrams cholesterol, 16 milligrams sodium, and 56 milligrams calcium.
Martha T. Leoni
New Bern, North Carolina

BROCCOLI CASSEROLE

½ cup water
1 (10-ounce) package frozen chopped broccoli
½ cup chopped onion
1½ teaspoons cornstarch
¼ teaspoon dried whole thyme
Dash of pepper
½ cup evaporated skim milk
2 tablespoons Neufchâtel cheese
1 tablespoon grated Parmesan cheese

Bring water to a boil in a saucepan; add broccoli, and cook according to package directions. Remove broccoli from saucepan, reserving liquid in pan; add onion, and cook 5 minutes or until tender.

Combine cornstarch, thyme, pepper, and milk; add to onion mixture, and cook over medium heat, stirring constantly, until bubbly. Boil 1 minute, stirring constantly. Remove from heat; stir in Neufchâtel cheese and broccoli. Spoon mixture into serving bowl, and sprinkle with Parmesan cheese. Yield: 4 servings (88 calories per ½-cup serving).

☐ 6.2 grams protein, 3.2 grams fat, 9.9 grams carbohydrate, 10 milligrams cholesterol, 120 milligrams sodium, and 165 milligrams calcium.
Anne M. Grimes
Lexington, Kentucky

SPINACH-TOPPED TOMATOES

8 (½-inch) peeled tomato slices
Vegetable cooking spray
1 (10-ounce) package frozen chopped spinach
¾ cup seasoned, dry breadcrumbs
½ cup thinly sliced green onions
⅓ cup freshly grated Parmesan cheese
½ cup egg substitute
1 tablespoon pimiento strips
¼ teaspoon freshly ground pepper

Arrange tomato slices in a 13- x 9- x 2-inch baking dish coated with cooking spray; set aside.

Cook spinach according to package directions; drain well. Combine spinach and next 4 ingredients; stir well. Spoon 3 tablespoons spinach mixture onto each tomato slice. Garnish with a pimiento strip, and sprinkle with pepper. Bake at 350° for 15 minutes or until lightly browned. Yield: 8 servings (77 calories each).

☐ 5.2 grams protein, 1.7 grams fat, 10.9 grams carbohydrate, 3 milligrams cholesterol, 171 milligrams sodium, and 88 milligrams calcium.

MARINATED BRUSSELS SPROUTS

1 (10-ounce) package frozen baby brussels sprouts
½ cup commercial reduced-calorie Italian dressing
2 tablespoons diced onion
1 clove garlic, minced
1 teaspoon dried parsley flakes
½ teaspoon dried whole dillweed

Cook brussels sprouts according to package directions, omitting salt. Drain thoroughly, and place in a shallow container.

Combine reduced-calorie Italian dressing and remaining ingredients; pour over brussels sprouts. Cover and chill 8 hours; drain. To serve, use wooden picks. Yield: 24 appetizers (35 calories each).

☐ 2.7 grams protein, 0.5 gram fat, 6.7 grams carbohydrate, 0 milligrams cholesterol, 398 milligrams sodium, and 22 milligrams calcium.
Mrs. John Farrell
Elkton, Maryland

INDIAN-STYLE GREEN BEANS

1 teaspoon mustard seeds
1 tablespoon vegetable oil
½ cup chopped onion
¾ cup sliced carrot
1 (16-ounce) package frozen cut green beans
1 teaspoon ground coriander
⅛ teaspoon ground ginger
2 tablespoons lemon juice

Place mustard seeds and oil in a skillet. Sauté over medium heat until seeds begin to pop. Add onion, carrot, and green beans; cook, stirring constantly, 5 minutes. Stir in coriander and ginger; cover, reduce heat, and simmer 8 to 10 minutes. Stir in lemon juice, and serve. Yield: 6 servings (61 calories per ½-cup serving).

☐ 1.9 grams protein, 2.7 grams fat, 9.1 grams carbohydrate, 0 milligrams cholesterol, 9 milligrams sodium, and 49 milligrams calcium.
Melanie Keaton
Richmond, Kentucky

CHILI-CORN CASSEROLE

1 (17-ounce) can cream-style corn
½ cup egg substitute
1 (8-ounce) carton nonfat yogurt
1 (12-ounce) can whole kernel
   corn, drained
1 (4-ounce) can chopped green
   chiles, rinsed and drained
½ cup cornmeal
¾ cup (3 ounces) low-fat process
   Swiss cheese, shredded
¼ cup diced onion
¼ teaspoon white pepper
Vegetable cooking spray

Combine corn and egg substitute in
container of an electric blender; process at high speed until mixture is
smooth. Pour mixture into a medium
bowl. Stir in yogurt (at room temperature) and next 6 ingredients; stir
well. Spoon mixture into a 2-quart
casserole coated with cooking spray.
Cover and bake at 350° for 30 minutes. Stir mixture, and continue to
bake, uncovered, 20 minutes or until
set. Yield: 10 servings (108 calories
per ½-cup serving).

□ *6.3 grams protein, 1 gram fat,
19.4 grams carbohydrate, 3 milligrams cholesterol, 375 milligrams sodium, and 113 milligrams calcium.*

HOMINY-BEAN SALAD

1 (15½-ounce) can yellow
   hominy, drained
1 (16-ounce) can kidney beans,
   rinsed and drained
¼ cup sliced green onions
⅓ cup diced, unpeeled cucumber
¼ cup diced sweet red pepper
2 tablespoons minced fresh
   parsley
3 tablespoons vegetable oil
¼ cup plus 1 tablespoon cider
   vinegar
1 tablespoon water
½ teaspoon dried Italian
   seasoning
1 teaspoon spicy brown mustard
⅛ teaspoon celery seeds
¼ teaspoon chili powder
¼ teaspoon hot sauce
1 cup alfalfa sprouts
Belgian endive (optional)

Combine first 6 ingredients in a shallow dish; set aside.
   Combine oil, vinegar, water, Italian
seasoning, mustard, celery seeds,
chili powder, and hot sauce; pour
mixture over vegetables, tossing
gently. Cover and refrigerate 8
hours, stirring occasionally.
   Remove vegetable mixture from
marinade, using a slotted spoon;
serve on 2 tablespoons alfalfa sprouts
and, if desired, Belgian endive. Yield:
8 servings (102 calories per ½ cup
salad and 2 tablespoons sprouts).

□ *3.7 grams protein, 3.8 grams fat,
14 grams carbohydrate, 0 milligrams
cholesterol, 7 milligrams sodium, and
18 milligrams calcium.*

BLACK BEAN SOUP

1 (15-ounce) can black beans,
   undrained
2 cups water
⅓ cup chopped celery
¼ cup chopped onion
½ teaspoon dry mustard
½ teaspoon olive oil
1 beef-flavored bouillon cube
¼ cup Chablis or other dry white
   wine
Lemon slices (optional)
Parsley (optional)

Reserve 4 black beans; set aside.
Combine remaining beans and next 6
ingredients in a medium saucepan;
simmer over medium heat 20 minutes. Spoon bean mixture into container of an electric blender; blend
until smooth. Reduce speed of
blender; add wine. Divide into bowls.
If desired, garnish each serving with
a lemon slice topped with a sprig of
parsley and a black bean. Yield: 4
servings (162 calories per 1-cup
serving).

□ *9.7 grams protein, 1.3 grams fat,
26.5 grams carbohydrate, 0 milligrams cholesterol, 111 milligrams sodium, and 37 milligrams calcium.*
Dot Smollen Goff
Dickinson, Texas

VEGETABLE SOUP

1 cup sliced carrots
1 cup sliced celery
1½ cups chopped onion
1¾ cups diced potato
¼ teaspoon dried whole thyme
½ teaspoon dried whole basil
2 bay leaves
2 (10½-ounce) cans beef broth,
   undiluted
1¼ cups water
3 (16-ounce) cans no-salt-added
   tomatoes, undrained
1 (10-ounce) package frozen corn
1 (10-ounce) package frozen baby
   lima beans
1 (10-ounce) package frozen cut
   okra
Freshly ground pepper

Combine first 9 ingredients in a large
Dutch oven. Place tomatoes in container of an electric blender; blend
until smooth. Add pureed tomatoes
to Dutch oven; bring to a boil over
high heat. Cover, reduce heat, and
simmer 30 minutes.
   Add corn and lima beans; simmer
20 minutes. Add okra; return mixture to a boil, and cook an additional
5 minutes. Remove bay leaves;
serve in individual soup bowls, and
top with pepper. Yield: 18 cups (210
calories per 1½-cup serving).

□ *27.8 grams protein, 0.7 gram fat,
24.9 grams carbohydrate, 0 milligrams cholesterol, 270 milligrams sodium, and 90 milligrams calcium.*
Julie Feagin
Birmingham, Alabama

PEACHY MELBA ALASKA

1 (7-ounce) loaf angel food cake
Vegetable cooking spray
12 peach halves packed in juice
3 egg whites
¼ teaspoon cream of tartar
¼ cup sugar
1 teaspoon vanilla extract
1 tablespoon sliced almonds
Raspberry Sauce

Cut cake into 12 slices; cut each slice
into a 2½-inch circle with a cookie
cutter. Place on a baking sheet

coated with cooking spray. Drain peaches; pat dry with paper towels. Place a peach half, cut side down, on each cake; set aside.

Beat egg whites (at room temperature) and cream of tartar at high speed of an electric mixer 1 minute. Gradually add sugar, 1 tablespoon at a time, beating until stiff peaks form and sugar dissolves (2 to 4 minutes). Stir in vanilla. Spread meringue over sides and top of each peach and cake, covering completely. Sprinkle almonds on top. Bake at 400° for 8 minutes or until golden brown. Remove from oven, and let cool.

To serve, place 1 tablespoon Raspberry Sauce on each serving plate. Place Peachy Melba Alaska on sauce. Yield: 12 servings (120 calories each with 1 tablespoon Raspberry Sauce).

□ *2.6 grams protein, 0.5 gram fat, 27.7 grams carbohydrate, 0 milligrams cholesterol, 36 milligrams sodium, and 13 milligrams calcium.*

Raspberry Sauce

2 cups fresh or unsweetened frozen raspberries
½ cup grape juice

Thaw raspberries, if necessary. Place raspberries and grape juice in container of an electric blender; blend until smooth. Strain mixture; discard the seeds. Cover and chill; stir before serving. Yield: ¾ cup (14 calories per tablespoon).

□ *0.2 gram protein, 0.1 gram fat, 3.4 grams carbohydrate, 0 milligrams cholesterol, 0 milligrams sodium, and 5 milligrams calcium.*

Theresa Birdner
Birmingham, Alabama

BAKED APRICOT SOUFFLÉ

1 (8-ounce) can unsweetened apricot halves, drained
2 egg whites
Dash of salt
⅓ cup sugar
1 tablespoon lemon juice
Vegetable cooking spray
Golden Sauce

Process apricots in a food mill; set pulp aside.

Beat egg whites (at room temperature) and salt until foamy; gradually add sugar, 1 tablespoon at a time, beating until stiff peaks form. Gently fold in apricot pulp and lemon juice.

Carefully spoon apricot mixture into a 1-quart soufflé dish coated with cooking spray; place in a shallow pan. Pour hot water to depth of 1 inch into pan. Bake at 350° for 35 minutes or until soufflé is puffed and set. Serve with Golden Sauce. Yield: 7 servings (75 calories per ½-cup serving with 1 tablespoon sauce).

□ *1.8 grams protein, 0.8 gram fat, 15.1 grams carbohydrate, 34 milligrams cholesterol, 40 milligrams sodium, and 25 milligrams calcium.*

Golden Sauce

2 egg yolks, beaten
1 cup skim milk
3 tablespoons sugar
1 teaspoon vanilla extract
¼ teaspoon lemon extract

Combine first 3 ingredients in top of a double boiler. Bring water to a boil; reduce heat, and simmer 15 minutes, stirring constantly. Remove from heat; stir in flavorings. Yield: 1 cup (24 calories per tablespoon).

□ *0.9 gram protein, 0.7 gram fat, 3.2 grams carbohydrate, 34 milligrams cholesterol, 9 milligrams sodium, and 22 milligrams calcium.*

Sandra T. Anspach
Rocky Mount, North Carolina

He Has A Way With Cheesecake

John Brady of Vestavia Hills, Alabama, is known for his cheesecake. A member of a gourmet dinner club, John insists that his secret to good cheesecake is starting with the best ingredients he can find.

WHITE CHOCOLATE CHEESECAKE

¾ cup blanched almonds, ground
¾ cup quick-cooking oats, uncooked
¾ cup graham cracker crumbs
¼ cup sugar
¼ cup plus 2 tablespoons butter or margarine, melted
2 (8-ounce) packages cream cheese, softened
1 cup sugar
1 (16-ounce) carton commercial sour cream
1 teaspoon vanilla extract
8 ounces white chocolate, melted
4 egg whites
⅛ teaspoon cream of tartar
1 tablespoon powdered sugar

Combine first 5 ingredients in a medium bowl; blend well. Press into bottom and 2 inches up sides of a 10-inch springform pan. Bake at 350° for 5 minutes. Cool on wire rack.

Combine cream cheese and 1 cup sugar; beat at medium speed of an electric mixer until fluffy. Add sour cream and vanilla; mix well. Stir in melted white chocolate.

Beat egg whites (at room temperature) at high speed of an electric mixer until foamy; add cream of tartar, beating until soft peaks form. Add powdered sugar; beat until stiff peaks form. Fold egg whites into cream cheese mixture; spoon into crust. Bake at 325° for 55 minutes; turn oven off. Leave cheesecake in oven 30 minutes; partially open oven door, and leave cheesecake in oven an additional 30 minutes. Cool. Chill 8 hours. Remove from pan. Yield: 10 to 12 servings.

Note: See Holiday Dessert Tip on page 276 for special presentation of this cheesecake.

Tip: *For a successful cake, measure all the ingredients accurately, follow the recipe without making any substitutions, and use the pan sizes recommended in the recipe.*

Surprise Your Guests With This Special Cake

You'll enjoy the pretty color and delicious flavor that cherry pie filling adds to this cake, but don't pass off the cherries as the main flavoring ingredient. Taste the layers and you'll detect a hint of white chocolate.

WHITE CHOCOLATE-CHERRY CAKE

¼ pound white chocolate, coarsely chopped
½ cup boiling water
1 cup butter or margarine, softened
1¾ cups sugar
4 eggs, separated
½ teaspoon vanilla extract
½ teaspoon almond extract
2½ cups sifted cake flour
1 teaspoon baking soda
1 cup buttermilk
1 (21-ounce) can cherry pie filling
Fluffy Frosting

Combine chocolate and water, stirring until chocolate melts; set aside to cool.

Cream butter; gradually add sugar, beating at medium speed of an electric mixer until light and fluffy. Add egg yolks, one at a time, beating well after each addition. Stir in white chocolate mixture and flavorings.

Combine flour and soda; add flour mixture to chocolate mixture alternately with buttermilk, beginning and ending with flour mixture. Mix well after each addition.

Beat egg whites (at room temperature) until stiff peaks form; gently fold into chocolate mixture. Pour batter into 3 greased and floured 9-inch round cakepans. Bake at 350° for 25 minutes or until a wooden pick inserted in center of each layer comes out clean. Cool in pans 10 minutes; remove layers from pans, and cool completely on wire racks.

Place 1 cake layer on cake platter; spread with ⅔ cup cherry pie filling. Top with second cake layer and pie filling; top with third cake layer. Frost sides and 1 inch of top edge with Fluffy Frosting, leaving an 8-inch circle on top center of cake. Spread remaining pie filling onto center of cake. Yield: one 3-layer cake.

Fluffy Frosting

1 cup light corn syrup
Pinch of salt
2 egg whites
¼ cup sifted powdered sugar
1 teaspoon almond extract

Combine corn syrup and salt in a small saucepan; bring to a boil over medium heat.

Beat egg whites (at room temperature) at high speed of an electric mixer until soft peaks form. Continue beating egg whites, and gradually add hot syrup to egg whites in a slow, steady stream. Gradually add powdered sugar, 1 tablespoon at a time, beating until frosting is thick enough to spread. Beat in almond extract. Yield: enough for one 3-layer cake.

Coffee Complements Desserts

Coffee, a favorite all-occasion beverage, has cooking versatility as well. These desserts don't really taste like coffee as such, but its full, rich flavor enhances the other ingredients.

For convenience and consistency of flavor, we suggest 2 teaspoons instant coffee granules per 1 cup boiling water for strong brewed coffee. Of course, strong, freshly brewed coffee may also be used.

CREAMY COFFEE TORTONI

1 egg white
1 tablespoon instant coffee granules
⅛ teaspoon salt
2 tablespoons sugar
1 cup whipping cream
¼ cup sugar
1 teaspoon vanilla extract
1 tablespoon crème de cacao
½ cup chopped almonds, toasted
Toasted almonds (optional)
Instant coffee granules (optional)

Beat egg white (at room temperature), 1 tablespoon coffee granules, and salt until foamy. Gradually add 2 tablespoons sugar, 1 tablespoon at a time, beating until stiff peaks form.

Beat whipping cream until foamy; gradually add ¼ cup sugar, beating until soft peaks form. Stir in vanilla. Fold whipped cream, crème de cacao, and ½ cup chopped almonds into egg white mixture. Spoon into individual compotes, and freeze. If desired, garnish with toasted almonds and instant coffee granules. Yield: 4 servings.   *Rita W. Cook*
Corpus Christi, Texas

SPICE CAKE WITH CHOCOLATE-COFFEE FROSTING

1 teaspoon baking soda
1 cup buttermilk
1 cup butter or margarine, softened
2 cups firmly packed light brown sugar
3 eggs
2 cups all-purpose flour
2 teaspoons ground cinnamon
1 teaspoon vanilla extract
½ cup golden raisins
½ cup raisins
1 cup chopped pecans
Chocolate-Coffee Frosting

Dissolve soda in buttermilk.

Cream butter; gradually add sugar, beating well at medium speed of an electric mixer. Add eggs, one at a time, beating well after each addition.

Combine flour and cinnamon; add to creamed mixture alternately with buttermilk mixture, beginning and ending with flour mixture. Mix well after each addition. Stir in vanilla, raisins, and pecans.

Pour batter into 3 greased and floured 9-inch round cakepans. Bake at 325° for 25 to 27 minutes or until a wooden pick inserted in center comes out clean. Cool in pans 10 minutes; remove layers from pans, and let cool.

Spread Chocolate-Coffee Frosting between layers and on top and sides of cake. Yield: one 3-layer cake.

Chocolate-Coffee Frosting

1 teaspoon instant coffee
   granules
½ cup boiling water
7 cups sifted powdered sugar
⅔ cup unsweetened cocoa
½ cup butter or margarine,
   softened
1 teaspoon vanilla extract

Dissolve coffee granules in boiling water; set aside.

Combine sugar and cocoa; mix well. Set aside.

Cream butter in a large mixing bowl; add sugar mixture and vanilla. Add coffee mixture gradually, beating constantly at high speed of an electric mixer to desired spreading consistency. Yield: enough for one 3-layer cake.
Toni Rodgers
West Monroe, Louisiana

Capture The Goodness Of Broccoli And Cauliflower

Fresh broccoli and cauliflower are vegetables for all seasons, especially during winter when their flavors are at a peak. Both are good sources of vitamin C and fiber and are naturally low in calories.

ITALIAN CAULIFLOWER-BROCCOLI TOSS

1 cup mayonnaise
½ cup commercial sour cream
1 small onion, chopped
1 (0.7-ounce) envelope Italian
   salad dressing mix
2 tablespoons minced parsley
1½ pounds fresh broccoli, cut
   into flowerets
1 head cauliflower, cut into
   flowerets
1 cup (4 ounces) shredded
   mozzarella cheese

Combine first 5 ingredients; stir well. Combine vegetables and cheese; toss. Add mayonnaise mixture; toss. Chill 3 to 4 hours. Yield: 10 to 12 servings.
Charlene Stultz
Moundsville, West Virginia

BROCCOLI-CAULIFLOWER PASTA SALAD

4 ounces uncooked spaghetti
½ head cauliflower, coarsely
   chopped
½ pound broccoli, coarsely
   chopped
1 small onion, sliced and
   separated into rings
¼ pound fresh mushrooms, sliced
½ sweet red pepper, cut into
   strips
½ green pepper, cut into strips
½ sweet yellow pepper, cut into
   strips
¼ cup sliced ripe olives, drained
¼ cup mayonnaise
3 tablespoons vegetable oil
3 tablespoons apple cider vinegar
2 tablespoons sugar
1 teaspoon pepper
1 teaspoon paprika
¼ teaspoon salt
Lettuce leaves

Cook spaghetti according to package directions; drain. Rinse with cold water; drain.

Combine spaghetti and next 8 ingredients in a large bowl; set aside. Combine mayonnaise and next 6 ingredients; pour over vegetable mixture, and toss gently to coat. Cover

and allow mixture to chill 3 to 4 hours. Toss vegetable mixture again before serving; place mixture in a lettuce-lined salad bowl to serve. Yield: 6 to 8 servings.
Diane I. Gonzalez
Morgantown, West Virginia

BROCCOLI-AND-TURKEY PASTA PIE

6 ounces angel hair pasta
2 eggs, slightly beaten
2 tablespoons butter or
   margarine, melted
⅓ cup grated Parmesan cheese
2 cups broccoli flowerets
2 cloves garlic, minced
1 sweet red pepper, cut into
   julienne strips
1 medium onion, thinly sliced
2 teaspoons dried whole basil
1 tablespoon butter or margarine,
   melted
1½ cups diced cooked turkey
⅓ cup grated Parmesan cheese
2 eggs, slightly beaten
¼ cup half-and-half
¼ teaspoon salt
¼ teaspoon pepper
¼ cup grated Parmesan cheese

Cook pasta according to package directions; drain. Combine 2 eggs and next 2 ingredients; add pasta, and stir well. Spoon into a well-greased 9-inch deep-dish pieplate. Use a spoon to shape pasta into a pie shell. Place weights inside shell; cover and bake at 350° for 10 minutes.

Place broccoli over boiling water in a steaming rack. Cook 10 minutes.

Sauté garlic, red pepper, onion, and basil in 1 tablespoon butter until crisp-tender. Stir in broccoli, turkey, and ⅓ cup Parmesan cheese. Remove from heat.

Combine 2 eggs and next 3 ingredients; stir into vegetable mixture. Spoon into pasta shell. Sprinkle with ¼ cup cheese. Cover with aluminum foil, and bake at 350° for 35 minutes; remove foil, and bake an additional 10 minutes. Let stand 5 minutes. Yield: one 9-inch pie.

CHILLED BROCCOLI WITH LEMON DRESSING

1½ pounds fresh broccoli
¼ cup lemon juice
3 tablespoons olive oil
2 tablespoons thinly sliced green onions
1 teaspoon honey
½ teaspoon paprika
1 clove garlic, crushed

Trim off large leaves of broccoli, and remove tough ends of lower stalks. Wash broccoli thoroughly, and cut into flowerets, reserving stalks for other uses.

Place broccoli, flowerets in vegetable steamer over boiling water; cover and steam 10 to 15 minutes or until broccoli is crisp-tender. Drain broccoli, and chill thoroughly.

Combine lemon juice and remaining ingredients in a small mixing bowl, using a wire whisk; chill thoroughly. Toss with chilled broccoli just before serving. Yield: 6 servings.
Jan Thompson
Highland, Maryland

CAULIFLOWER SCALLOP

1 medium head cauliflower, cut into flowerets
1 (10¾-ounce) can cream of mushroom soup, undiluted
½ cup milk
¾ cup (3 ounces) shredded sharp Cheddar cheese
¼ cup breadcrumbs
1 tablespoon butter or margarine, melted

Cook cauliflower, covered, in a small amount of boiling salted water 8 to 10 minutes or until tender. Drain. Arrange cauliflower in a lightly greased 1½-quart casserole.

Combine mushroom soup, milk, and cheese; spoon over cauliflower. Combine breadcrumbs and butter; sprinkle evenly over cauliflower. Bake at 350° for 30 minutes. Yield: 4 servings.
Mrs. I. W. Hanley
Palm Harbor, Florida

Bake The Catch Of The Day

As more and more Southerners have turned to healthy eating, baked fish has become quite popular. Rich in protein and B vitamins, and low in calories and fat, fish is a natural choice for a healthy meal.

Overcooking is the biggest mistake made when preparing fish. It results in a dry, sometimes tough, piece of fish. To check for doneness, pierce the thickest part with a fork and twist to see if it flakes easily.

TROUT LAURIE

2 pounds trout fillets
1 cup lime juice
1 cup all-purpose flour
1 teaspoon garlic powder
1 teaspoon onion powder
½ cup butter or margarine, melted
⅔ cup water
¼ cup lemon juice
¼ cup sherry
1 (1⅛-ounce) package Hollandaise sauce mix
1 tablespoon chopped chives
1 teaspoon parsley flakes
½ teaspoon garlic powder
1 (6.5-ounce) can claw crabmeat, drained
1 (4-ounce) can sliced mushrooms, drained
¼ cup sliced almonds, toasted
½ teaspoon paprika

Place trout in a large shallow dish; pour lime juice over fish. Cover and marinate 2 hours in refrigerator, turning once. Drain.

Combine flour, 1 teaspoon garlic powder, and onion powder. Dredge fish in flour mixture. Brown fillets in butter in a large heavy skillet on each side, and place in a lightly greased 13- x 9- x 2-inch baking dish.

Add water and next 6 ingredients to drippings in skillet, stirring until blended. Cook over low heat until thickened, stirring constantly.

Stir in crabmeat, mushrooms, and almonds. Spoon mixture over fillets; sprinkle with paprika. Cover and bake at 350° for 30 minutes. Yield: 6 to 8 servings.
Laurie McIntyre
Lake Jackson, Texas

ALMOND BAKED FISH

1½ teaspoons lemon juice
1½ teaspoons butter or margarine, melted
¼ teaspoon salt
4 flounder fillets or other fish fillets (about 1 pound)
⅓ cup mayonnaise
½ cup saltine cracker crumbs
3 tablespoons butter or margarine, melted
2 tablespoons slivered almonds

Combine first 3 ingredients in a 12- x 8- x 2-inch baking dish. Arrange fish in dish; spread mayonnaise over fish.

Combine cracker crumbs, 3 tablespoons melted butter, and almonds; sprinkle over fish. Bake at 400° for 10 to 15 minutes or until fish flakes easily when tested with a fork. Yield: 3 to 4 servings.
Kathleen Stone
Houston, Texas

ITALIAN FISH

1½ pounds flounder fillets or other fish fillets
¼ teaspoon dried whole oregano
⅛ teaspoon pepper
1 (15¼-ounce) jar spaghetti sauce
2 tablespoons minced parsley
1 cup (4 ounces) shredded mozzarella cheese

Arrange flounder fillets in a lightly greased 13- x 9- x 2-inch baking dish; sprinkle with oregano and pepper. Pour spaghetti sauce over fillets; sprinkle with parsley. Bake, uncovered, at 350° for 20 minutes or until fish flakes easily when tested with a fork. Top with cheese, and bake an additional 5 minutes. Yield: 6 servings.
Mary Pappas
Richmond, Virginia

LEMON BARBECUED CATFISH

¼ cup commercial barbecue sauce
¼ teaspoon grated lemon rind
1½ tablespoons lemon juice
¼ teaspoon dried dillweed
1½ pounds catfish fillets

Combine first 4 ingredients; stir well. Brush each side of fillets with sauce, and place in a lightly greased 12- x 8- x 2-inch baking dish. Brush on remaining sauce. Bake at 350° for 25 minutes or until fish flakes easily when tested with a fork. To serve, remove to a serving platter. Yield: 6 servings.
Zelda T. Covey
Birmingham, Alabama

Shape Rice For Show

If you like to surprise dinner guests with something a little out of the ordinary, consider molding rice into attractive shapes. The cohesive texture of rice makes it suitable for different kinds of shaping.

MANDARIN RICE SALAD

2 cups water
½ teaspoon salt
1 cup uncooked regular rice
1 (11-ounce) can mandarin oranges, drained
½ cup thinly sliced celery
½ cup diced green pepper
3 tablespoons chopped green onions
3 tablespoons lemon juice
3 tablespoons olive oil
¼ teaspoon white pepper
Lettuce leaves
4 green onion fans

Combine water and salt in a heavy saucepan; bring to a boil. Gradually add rice, stirring constantly. Cover, reduce heat, and simmer 15 minutes or until rice is tender and water is absorbed. Cover and chill rice.

Set aside 6 orange slices; coarsely chop remaining orange slices.

Combine rice, chopped orange, and next 6 ingredients. Pack rice mixture into an oiled 4-cup mold. Let stand 5 minutes. Invert salad onto a lettuce-lined platter. Garnish with reserved orange slices and green onion fans. Yield: 6 servings.

SPINACH-RICE TIMBALES

2 cups water
½ teaspoon salt
1 cup uncooked regular rice
1 (10-ounce) package frozen chopped spinach
½ cup chopped onion
1 large clove garlic, minced
2 tablespoons butter or margarine, melted
Spinach leaves
Pimiento strips

Combine water and salt in a heavy saucepan; bring to a boil. Gradually add rice, stirring constantly. Cover, reduce heat, and simmer 15 minutes or until rice is tender and water is absorbed. Set aside.

Cook spinach according to package directions; drain well. Sauté onion and garlic in butter until tender. Combine hot rice, cooked spinach, and onion mixture, stirring until blended. Pack rice into 4 oiled 8-ounce pineapple cans. Invert onto spinach-lined serving platter, and garnish with pimiento strips. Yield: 4 servings.

Make Chicken Salad The Entrée

Laced with a variety of vegetables, fruits, and seasonings, chicken salad can serve as the whole meal. And thanks to the versatility of chicken's flavor, you can satisfy your cravings

for spicy Mexican, tangy Oriental, or a fruit-flavored tropical delight.

Most of these recipes call for chopped cooked chicken. Simmering a whole broiler-fryer is the most economical way to obtain it, but you can substitute canned chicken. In our test kitchens, we often simmer chicken breast halves. You can plan on ½ cup of chopped cooked chicken per half. A whole chicken will yield about 2½ to 3 cups of cooked chicken.

ORIENTAL CHICKEN SALAD

2 pounds boned and skinned chicken breasts
¼ cup soy sauce, divided
⅔ cup vegetable oil, divided
1 clove garlic, minced
1 teaspoon grated lemon rind, divided
¼ cup lemon juice
1 pound fresh spinach, washed and drained
½ head iceberg lettuce, torn
3 cups fresh bean sprouts
Salt to taste
¼ cup sesame seeds, toasted

Cut chicken breasts into 1-inch-wide strips; place in a large bowl. Combine 1 tablespoon soy sauce, 2 tablespoons oil, garlic, and ½ teaspoon lemon rind, mixing well. Pour mixture over chicken strips; toss gently. Refrigerate chicken strips 2 to 3 hours. Discard marinade.

Heat 2 tablespoons oil in a skillet. Add one-fourth of chicken; sauté 3 to 5 minutes or until chicken is done. (Do not overcook.) Cook remaining chicken, one fourth at a time, adding oil, if necessary.

Combine chicken with remaining oil, soy sauce, lemon rind, and lemon juice; toss gently.

Combine spinach, lettuce, and bean sprouts in a large bowl; toss gently. Add salt, sesame seeds, and chicken mixture; toss gently. Serve immediately. Yield: 8 servings.
Muriel Joseph
Williston, Florida

POLYNESIAN CHICKEN SALAD

3 cups chopped cooked chicken
1 (15¼-ounce) can pineapple
  chunks, drained
¼ cup plus 2 tablespoons flaked
  coconut
2 stalks celery, thinly sliced
1 teaspoon curry powder
¼ teaspoon salt
⅔ cup mayonnaise
½ cup toasted slivered almonds
1 banana, sliced
Lettuce leaves
1 (11-ounce) can mandarin
  oranges, drained
2 tablespoons flaked coconut,
  toasted

Combine first 7 ingredients in a large bowl; toss lightly. Cover and chill 2 hours. Just before serving, add almonds and banana. Serve on lettuce leaves. Garnish salad with mandarin oranges and toasted coconut. Yield: 4 to 6 servings.   *Iris Brenner*
Ft. McCoy, Florida

MEXICAN CHICKEN SALAD

4 cups chopped cooked chicken
  (about 8 breast halves)
2 cups (8 ounces) shredded sharp
  Cheddar cheese
1 (16-ounce) can red kidney
  beans, drained and rinsed
1 medium onion, chopped
½ cup sliced ripe olives
2 tablespoons chopped sweet red
  pepper
2 tablespoons chopped green
  pepper
1 (4-ounce) can chopped green
  chiles, drained
1 (1¼-ounce) package taco
  seasoning
½ cup commercial sour cream
½ cup mayonnaise
2 medium-size avocados, peeled
  and chopped (optional)
Shredded lettuce
2 medium tomatoes, chopped
Corn chips

Combine first 11 ingredients, stirring well; cover and chill. At serving time, add avocado, if desired.

Arrange lettuce on 8 individual serving plates; spoon about 1 cup chicken mixture onto each. Top with chopped tomato and chips. Yield: 8 servings.   *Laurie McIntyre*
Lake Jackson, Texas

Entrées
With Convenience
In Mind

If you find yourself looking for a fast-to-fix entrée more times than you'd prefer, keep your pantry and freezer stocked with handy convenience items. Ready-to-use products can speed preparation for some tasty main dishes.

STROMBOLI

1 (16-ounce) loaf frozen bread
  dough, thawed
¼ pound thinly sliced ham
¼ pound sliced hard salami
½ teaspoon dried whole basil,
  divided
½ teaspoon dried whole oregano,
  divided
3 ounces sliced provolone cheese
1 cup (4 ounces) shredded
  mozzarella cheese
2 tablespoons butter or
  margarine, melted
1 teaspoon cornmeal

Place bread dough on a lightly greased baking sheet; pat into a 15- x 10-inch rectangle. Arrange ham slices lengthwise down center; place salami on top. Sprinkle with ¼ teaspoon basil and ¼ teaspoon oregano. Arrange provolone cheese over herbs, and top with shredded mozzarella cheese; sprinkle with remaining herbs.
Moisten all edges of dough with water. Bring each long edge of dough to center; press edges together securely to seal. Seal ends.
Brush dough with 1 tablespoon butter. Sprinkle with cornmeal, and

carefully invert. Brush top with remaining butter. Bake at 375° for 20 to 22 minutes. Yield: 4 servings.
Mrs. Robert Nesbit
Augusta, Georgia

HOT TUNA WAFFLE-WICH

1 (8½-ounce) can English peas,
  undrained
1 (10¾-ounce) can cream of
  mushroom soup, undiluted
1 (6½-ounce) can tuna, drained
  and flaked
⅛ teaspoon hot sauce
2 (5-ounce) packages frozen
  waffles
Cheese Sauce

Drain peas, reserving 2 tablespoons liquid. Combine peas, 2 tablespoons liquid, mushroom soup, tuna, and hot sauce in a saucepan. Cook over medium heat, stirring occasionally, until thoroughly heated.
Heat waffles according to package directions. Spoon about ½ cup tuna mixture on half of waffles; place remaining waffles over tuna. Top with Cheese Sauce. Yield: 4 servings.

Cheese Sauce

1 (11-ounce) can cheese soup,
  undiluted
¼ cup milk
1 teaspoon prepared mustard

Combine cheese soup and milk in a small saucepan; stir in mustard. Cook over medium heat until heated. Yield: 1¼ cups.   *Juanita Moye*
West Helena, Arkansas

DOUBLE-CRUST TACO PIE

1 pound ground beef
1 (1¼-ounce) package taco
  seasoning mix
2 (8-ounce) cans refrigerated
  crescent dinner rolls
4 cups (16 ounces) shredded
  Monterey Jack cheese, divided
Commercial sour cream
Commercial salsa
Jalapeño pepper slices

Cook ground beef in a skillet until browned, stirring to crumble meat.

Drain well. Add taco seasoning mix, and prepare according to package directions. Set meat mixture aside.

Unroll one can of crescent rolls into two rectangles; press long sides together to make a 13- x 8-inch rectangle. Repeat process with second can of crescent rolls; set aside. Place one rectangle of dough on an ungreased baking sheet. Sprinkle with 2 cups cheese. Spread ground beef mixture evenly over cheese; sprinkle with remaining 2 cups cheese. Top with second rectangle of dough, pressing all edges to seal.

Bake at 400° for 15 minutes or until browned. Serve with sour cream, salsa, and jalapeño. Yield: 6 servings.
Joe F. Arnold
Birmingham, Alabama

PIZZA CASSEROLE

1 pound lean ground beef
1 large onion, chopped
1 green pepper, chopped
½ teaspoon garlic salt
¼ teaspoon pepper
¼ teaspoon dried whole oregano
¼ teaspoon dried whole basil
1 (14-ounce) jar commercial pizza sauce
1 (8-ounce) package uncooked macaroni
1 (3½-ounce) package sliced pepperoni
1 (4-ounce) package shredded mozzarella cheese

Combine ground beef, onion, and green pepper in a large Dutch oven. Cook until meat is browned, stirring to crumble. Drain well in colander. Return meat mixture to Dutch oven; add garlic salt and next 4 ingredients. Stir well; cover, reduce heat, and simmer 15 minutes.

Cook macaroni according to package directions, omitting salt; drain. Add to meat mixture; stir well. Spoon into a lightly greased 12- x 8- x 2-inch baking dish; top evenly with pepperoni. Cover and bake at 350° for 20 minutes; top with cheese, and bake, uncovered, 5 minutes. Yield: 6 to 8 servings.
Elizabeth M. Haney
Dublin, Virginia

ROAST BEEF TURNOVERS

1 (10-ounce) package frozen patty shells, thawed
2 green onions, sliced
½ cup chopped celery
½ cup sliced mushrooms
2 tablespoons butter or margarine, melted
1¾ cups cubed cooked roast beef
½ cup chopped fresh parsley
¼ cup dry breadcrumbs
¼ teaspoon dried whole basil
⅛ teaspoon salt
¼ teaspoon pepper
1 egg, slightly beaten
1 tablespoon water
1½ teaspoons sesame seeds

Roll each patty shell to a 6-inch circle on a lightly floured surface.

Sauté green onions, celery, and mushrooms in butter until crisp-tender. Stir in roast beef and next 5 ingredients, mixing well. Place ¼ cup beef mixture in center of each pastry circle. Fold circle in half. Press edges of filled pastry firmly together, using a fork dipped in flour. Transfer to an ungreased baking sheet.

Combine egg and water, mixing well. Brush tops of turnovers with egg mixture; sprinkle with sesame seeds. Bake at 400° for 30 minutes or until golden brown. Serve immediately. Yield: 6 servings.
Sue-Sue Hartstern
Louisville, Kentucky

Pork, Party Style

Whether it's time for a gathering of avid sports fans or a casual evening party, Party Pork Sandwiches will be a welcome addition to your menu. Cooking the pork tenderloin in the microwave frees the conventional oven for other appetizers.

If you're short on time, cook the pork the night before. Refrigerate the meat until you're ready to present it on a serving platter.

PARTY PORK SANDWICHES

2 (1- to 1½-pound) pork tenderloins
¼ cup plus 1 tablespoon soy sauce
3 tablespoons vinegar
2 tablespoons lemon juice
1 tablespoon molasses
½ teaspoon crushed red pepper
¼ teaspoon garlic powder
Horseradish Sauce
Commercial party rolls

Place pork tenderloins in a 12- x 8- x 2-inch baking dish. Spear meat in several places. Combine soy sauce vinegar, lemon juice, molasses, red pepper, and garlic, mixing well. Pour marinade over pork tenderloins; cover and refrigerate 3 hours, turning pork occasionally.

Cover pork tightly with heavy-duty plastic wrap; fold back a small edge of wrap to allow steam to escape. Microwave at HIGH 5 minutes. Reduce to MEDIUM (50% power), and microwave 11 to 12 minutes per pound or until thermometer registers 165° internal temperature, rotating dish one half-turn every 6 minutes. Let stand 10 to 15 minutes before slicing.

Serve meat slices with Horseradish Sauce on party rolls. Yield: about 2 dozen appetizers.

Horseradish Sauce

2 tablespoons butter or margarine
2 tablespoons all-purpose flour
1 cup milk
1½ to 2 tablespoons prepared horseradish
¼ teaspoon salt
Dash of white pepper

Place butter in a 1-quart glass measure. Microwave at HIGH 45 seconds or until melted. Add flour, stirring until smooth. Gradually add milk, stirring well. Microwave at HIGH 3 to 4 minutes or until thickened and bubbly, stirring after 2 minutes, then at 1-minute intervals. Stir in horseradish, salt, and pepper. Yield: 1 cup.

Muffins In A Minute

If you like to grab a quick muffin on the way out of the house, then this story is just for you. For these muffin recipes, you can mix up the batter ahead of time, store it in the refrigerator, and bake any number of muffins whenever you want them.

There are several differences in baking muffins in the microwave and baking them conventionally. Because the microwave doesn't use dry heat for cooking, the bread will not form a hard, browned crust.

To simulate the browned appearance, you can sprinkle on spice and nut toppings. For Lemon Muffins, we added a topping of chopped toasted almonds, sugar, and nutmeg. A mixture of paprika and Parmesan cheese gives Cheesy Cornbread Muffins a darker look. And using ingredients such as whole wheat flour, brown sugar, or oats helps give the bread a more traditional appearance.

So that muffins will bake evenly, cups in microwave muffin pans are

arranged in a circle. We suggest using only the outer ones and leaving the center one empty. Or you may use custard cups arranged in a circle. Be sure to use two paper cupcake liners for each muffin.

WHOLE WHEAT BRAN MUFFINS

¾ cup all-purpose flour
¼ cup whole wheat flour
1 tablespoon baking powder
½ teaspoon salt
⅓ cup firmly packed brown sugar
1 cup bran flakes
½ cup chopped dates
1 egg, beaten
¾ cup buttermilk
¼ cup vegetable oil
Vegetable cooking spray
1½ teaspoons sugar
½ teaspoon ground cinnamon

Combine first 7 ingredients in a large bowl; make a well in center of mixture. Combine egg, buttermilk, and oil; add to dry ingredients, stirring just until moistened.

Place 2 paper cupcake liners in each muffin cup in a microwave-safe muffin pan or in 6-ounce custard cups. Spray cupcake liners with cooking spray. Spoon batter into cupcake liners, filling each half-full. Smooth top of batter evenly. Combine sugar and cinnamon; sprinkle on top of batter.

Microwave 6 muffins at a time at HIGH 2½ to 4 minutes or until muffins are no longer doughy, giving pan a half-turn or rearranging custard

cups once. (If using custard cups, arrange in a circle in microwave.) If some muffins seem done before others, remove from oven, and continue baking remaining muffins. Place baked muffins on a cooling rack; let stand 1 minute or until they seem dry on top. Yield: 13 muffins.

CRANBERRY STREUSEL CAKE MUFFINS

½ cup butter or margarine
½ cup sugar
1 egg
1 cup all-purpose flour
¾ teaspoon baking powder
¼ teaspoon grated orange rind
¼ cup milk
¼ cup whole-berry cranberry sauce
Vegetable cooking spray
Streusel Topping

Place butter in a microwave-safe glass measure, and microwave at LOW (30% power) 45 seconds or until softened. Cream butter, beating at medium speed of an electric mixer; gradually add sugar, beating well. Add egg, mixing until blended.

Combine flour, baking powder, and orange rind; add to creamed mixture alternately with milk. Stir in cranberry sauce.

Place 2 paper cupcake liners in each muffin cup in a microwave-safe muffin pan or in 6-ounce custard cups. Spray cupcake liners with cooking spray. Spoon batter into cupcake liners, filling each half-full. Smooth top of batter evenly. Sprinkle Streusel Topping evenly over each muffin.

Microwave 6 muffins at a time at HIGH 2 to 2½ minutes or until muffins are no longer doughy, giving pan a half-turn or rearranging custard cups once. (If using custard cups, arrange in a circle in microwave.) If some muffins seem done before others, remove from oven, and continue baking remaining muffins. Place baked muffins on a cooling rack; let

Muffin Baking Times

It's best to bake six or less muffins at a time. To bake one to four muffins at HIGH, use the following baking times:

- 1 muffin: 30 to 40 seconds
- 2 muffins: 55 seconds to 1 minute and 10 seconds
- 3 muffins: 1 minute and 15 seconds to 1 minute and 30 seconds
- 4 muffins: 1 minute and 30 seconds to 1 minute and 40 seconds

stand 1 minute or until they seem dry on top. Yield: 10 muffins.

Streusel Topping

2 tablespoons butter or margarine
2 tablespoons sugar
2 tablespoons brown sugar
¼ cup all-purpose flour
½ teaspoon ground cinnamon

Place butter in a glass measure; microwave at LOW (30% power) 20 seconds or until softened. Combine butter and remaining ingredients, stirring to form a crumbly mixture. Yield: about ½ cup.

CHEESY CORNBREAD MUFFINS

1 cup yellow cornmeal
1 cup all-purpose flour
1 tablespoon baking powder
½ teaspoon salt
1 egg, beaten
1 cup milk
½ cup vegetable oil
½ cup (2 ounces) shredded
   Cheddar cheese
¼ cup chopped green onions
Vegetable cooking spray
2 tablespoons grated Parmesan
   cheese
½ teaspoon paprika

Combine first 4 ingredients in a mixing bowl; make a well in center. Combine egg, milk, and oil; add to dry ingredients, stirring just until moistened. Stir in Cheddar cheese and green onions. Do not overmix. Place 2 paper cupcake liners in each muffin cup in a microwave-safe muffin pan or in 6-ounce custard cups. Spray cupcake liners with cooking spray. Spoon batter into cupcake liners, filling each two-thirds

full. Smooth top of batter evenly. Combine Parmesan and paprika; sprinkle over muffin batter.

Microwave 6 muffins at a time at HIGH 2¼ to 2½ minutes or until muffins are no longer doughy, giving pan a half-turn or rearranging custard cups once. (If using custard cups, arrange in a circle in microwave.) If some muffins seem done before others, remove from oven, and continue baking remaining muffins. Place baked muffins on a cooling rack; let stand 1 minute or until they seem dry on top. Yield: 1 dozen.

LEMON MUFFINS

3 tablespoons chopped almonds
3 tablespoons sugar
1 teaspoon ground nutmeg
2 cups all-purpose flour
1 tablespoon baking powder
½ teaspoon salt
½ cup sugar
¼ teaspoon grated lemon rind
2 eggs, beaten
½ cup vegetable oil
⅓ cup milk
3 tablespoons lemon juice
Vegetable cooking spray

Place almonds in a microwave-safe pieplate; microwave at HIGH 2½ to 3 minutes, stirring once. Add 3 tablespoons sugar and nutmeg; stir well. Set aside.

Combine flour, baking powder, salt, ½ cup sugar, and lemon rind in a large bowl; make a well in center of mixture. Combine eggs and next 3 ingredients; add to dry ingredients, stirring just until moistened.

Place 2 paper cupcake liners in each muffin cup in a microwave-safe muffin pan or in 6-ounce custard cups. Spray cupcake liners with cooking spray. Spoon batter into cupcake liners, filling each one-third full. Smooth top of batter evenly; sprinkle with almond mixture.

Microwave 6 muffins at a time at HIGH 2 to 2½ minutes or until muffins are no longer doughy, giving pan

a half-turn or rearranging custard cups once. (If using custard cups, arrange in a circle in microwave.) If some muffins seem done before others, remove from oven, and continue baking remaining muffins. Place baked muffins on a cooling rack; let stand 1 minute or until they seem dry on top. Yield: 14 muffins.

Bubbly Beverages

In search of an alternative to soft drinks, Linda Keith of Dallas, Texas, created these refreshing sparkling beverages. She starts with nutritious fruit juice concentrates and accents their fresh flavors with the fizzle of sparkling mineral water.

For children, these beverages are great for celebrations when adults are enjoying champagne. "My son doesn't feel left out because he has his own bubbly drink," Linda says. "I even serve it in a champagne glass."

SPARKLING CRANBERRY JUICE

1 (12-ounce) can frozen cranberry
   juice concentrate, thawed and
   undiluted
1 (23-ounce) bottle sparkling
   mineral water, chilled

Combine cranberry juice concentrate and mineral water, stirring gently. Serve immediately over crushed ice. Yield: 4½ cups.

Tip: *Make ice cubes for a party ahead of time and store them in plastic bags in the freezer. Count on 350 cubes for 50 people or about 7 cubes per person.*

SPARKLING APPLE CIDER

1 (12-ounce) can frozen apple
  juice concentrate, thawed and
  undiluted
1 (23-ounce) bottle sparkling
  mineral water, chilled

Combine apple juice concentrate and
mineral water, stirring gently. Serve
immediately over crushed ice. Yield:
about 4½ cups.

SPARKLING
LEMONADE PUNCH

1 (12-ounce) can frozen lemonade
  concentrate, thawed and
  undiluted
2 cups pineapple juice, chilled
2 (23-ounce) bottles sparkling
  mineral water, chilled

Combine all ingredients, stirring
gently. Serve immediately over
crushed ice. Yield: 9 cups.

From Our Kitchen To Yours

Give the gift of hospitality. Dinner
parties featuring delicious food, con-
genial guests, fresh flowers, and the
soft radiance of candlelight enrich our
lives and build holiday traditions.

The keys to successful entertaining are planning and presentation.
Dinner menus can range from simple
to elegant, but whatever your style,
combine recipes that create a harmo-
nious blend of foods. Planning a special dinner party need not cause

stress. Here are some guidelines to
assist you in serving unforgettable
fare to your guests.

An appetizing and appealing meal
requires thought and imagination.
Give careful consideration to the
color, shape, texture, and flavor of
the food you're planning to serve.
Colors should complement each
other, with some bright and others
muted. Instead of serving foods with
the same color, such as fish, potatoes, and cauliflower, substitute
vivid-colored vegetables. You can
also entice the eye by adding bright
garnishes. Contrasting shapes also
lend interest to a menu. The similar
shapes of flank steak slices, julienne
carrots, and green beans lack excite-
ment. To give more shape variation,
cut vegetables in different ways.

Just as with color and shape, textures should vary. A menu of tenderloin, fluffy rice, and crisp-tender
broccoli spears with hollandaise sauce
mixes a number of different textures,
including crunchy, smooth, creamy,
and chewy. And flavors should not be
repeated; for example, use cheese as
an ingredient in only one dish. To
prevent overpowering the taste
buds, plan only one highly seasoned
or strong-flavored food. Introduce
milder flavors before spicier ones so
your guests enjoy each food's distinctive taste. Alternate flavors that are
spicy and bland or tart and sweet to
please the palate.

Each menu needs a focus, usually
the entrée, with the remaining recipes carefully selected as accompaniments. Repeating specific preparation
of foods, such as stuffed pork chops
and stuffed baked potatoes, limits variety. Include only one recipe with
small pieces, and avoid more than
one mixture, such as marinated bean
salad, Oriental stir-fry, and peas with
pearl onions. If you select a rich,
heavy dish, balance the remaining
menu with lighter foods. Color and
contrast in texture and flavor can be
provided by your salad selection.

The presentation of your food is as
significant as its preparation. As you
envision food on the plate, remember
to keep it simple. Small, enticingly
arranged servings are tempting, so

don't overload the plate. Leave space
between foods. Also hollow out vegetable or fruit containers for relishes,
condiments, or salad dressing.

To avoid a harried cooking schedule, consider oven space and baking
temperatures when you are selecting
recipes. For example, if you have
one oven, it's almost impossible to
prepare a standing rib roast, baked
potatoes, and broccoli casserole all at
the same time.

Foods are best served at their optimum temperatures. Marinated vegetables and chilled salads or soups
create pleasing taste sensations.
Equally important, these make-ahead
recipes will alleviate some of the last-
minute hassles.

Finally, recipes that you select
need to have similar yields. Keep in
mind that when you double or triple a
recipe, pan sizes and cooking times
are not always accurate. Therefore,
it's usually best to prepare the dish
several times.

Holiday Dessert Tip

Create a sensational presentation
by drizzling dessert plates with
light or dark chocolate. For the
dark chocolate drizzle, simply
melt semisweet chocolate baking
pieces, and let cool slightly.
Spoon chocolate into a plastic disposable decorating bag, snip off
the end to make a very small
hole, and drizzle the design on
plates. Refrigerate until the chocolate hardens. For the lighter
chocolate, melt equal amounts of
semisweet chocolate baking
pieces and white chocolate baking
pieces and use the same drizzling
procedure. Refrigerate until chocolate hardens.

Carefully stack decorated
plates, using pieces of wax paper
between each plate, and refrigerate until serving time. Place
White Chocolate Cheesecake
(page 267) on each plate. Garnish
with a strawberry.

DECEMBER

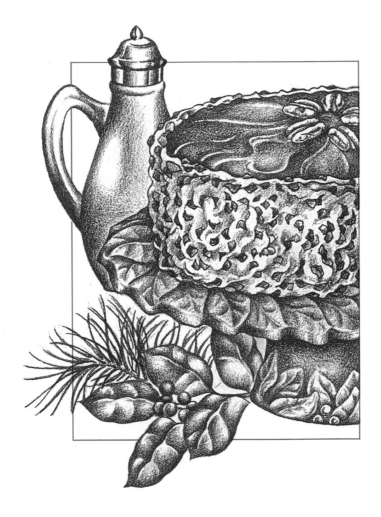

Presenting The Season's Best Desserts

It's the time of year when folks are pulling dog-eared recipes from their files. The family's favorite fruitcake, a special pie, or that traditional cake is a "must" to be served with Christmas dinner. Sometimes the recipe is for the once-a-year occasion, and sometimes, it's such a favorite that it's prepared throughout the year. But always, it's a recipe that's considered impressive by guests and family members alike. It's also one that makes or retains the cook's reputation in the kitchen.

CAROLINA DREAM CAKE
(pictured on cover)

1 cup butter or margarine,
   softened
2 cups sugar
1 teaspoon vanilla extract
3¼ cups sifted all-purpose flour
1 tablespoon plus ½ teaspoon
   baking powder
¾ teaspoon salt
1 cup milk
8 egg whites
Carolina Dream Frosting

Cream butter in a large mixing bowl; gradually add sugar, beating well at medium speed of an electric mixer. Add vanilla, mixing well.

Combine flour, baking powder, and salt; add to creamed mixture alternately with milk, beginning and ending with flour mixture. Mix after each addition.

Beat egg whites (at room temperature) until stiff peaks form; fold into batter.

Grease three 9-inch round cakepans, and line with wax paper; grease wax paper. Pour batter into prepared pans; bake at 350° for 18 to 20 minutes or until a wooden pick inserted in center comes out clean. Cool cake in pans 10 minutes; remove from pans, and let cake cool completely on wire racks. Spread Carolina Dream Frosting between layers and on top and sides of cake. Yield: one 3-layer cake.

Carolina Dream Frosting

12 egg yolks
1¾ cups sugar
½ teaspoon salt
¾ cup butter or margarine
½ cup bourbon
½ cup quartered candied cherries
1½ cups chopped pecans
1½ cups chopped seeded raisins
1½ cups flaked coconut

Combine first 4 ingredients in top of a double boiler; beat at low speed of an electric mixer 30 seconds or just until blended. Bring water to a boil; reduce heat to low, and cook, stirring constantly, until mixture is slightly thickened (about 20 minutes). Remove from heat; add bourbon, and beat at low speed 1 minute. Combine candied cherries and remaining ingredients in a bowl. Pour egg mixture over fruit-nut mixture, mixing well. Cool completely. Yield: 5 cups.

Pat Boschen
Ashland, Virginia

CARAMEL-FILLED BUTTER PECAN CAKE
(pictured on cover)

1 cup shortening
2 cups sugar
4 eggs
3 cups sifted cake flour
2½ teaspoons baking powder
½ teaspoon salt
1 cup milk
1 teaspoon almond extract
1 teaspoon vanilla extract
Caramel Filling
Butter Cream Frosting
1 cup chopped pecans
Pecan halves

Cream shortening in a large mixing bowl; gradually add sugar, beating well at medium speed of an electric mixer. Add eggs, one at a time, beating well after each addition.

Combine flour, baking powder, and salt; add to creamed mixture alternately with milk, beginning and ending with flour mixture. Mix after each addition. Stir in flavorings.

Grease three 9-inch round cakepans, and line with wax paper; grease wax paper. Pour batter into prepared pans; bake at 375° for 22 to 25 minutes or until a wooden pick inserted in center comes out clean. Cool in pans 10 minutes; remove from pans, and let cool completely on wire racks. Spread Caramel Filling between layers and on top of cake. Spread Butter Cream Frosting on sides of cake. Press chopped pecans into frosting on sides of cake. Garnish top with pecan halves. Yield: one 3-layer cake.

Caramel Filling

3 cups sugar, divided
¾ cup milk
1 egg, beaten
Pinch of salt
½ cup butter or margarine,
   cut up

Sprinkle ½ cup sugar in a large heavy saucepan. Place over medium heat, and cook, stirring constantly, until sugar melts and syrup is light golden brown.

Combine remaining 2½ cups sugar, milk, egg, and salt, stirring well; stir in butter. Stir butter mixture into hot caramelized sugar. (The mixture will tend to lump, becoming smooth with further cooking.)

Cook over medium heat, stirring frequently, until a candy thermometer registers 230° (15 to 20 minutes). Cool 5 minutes. Beat with a wooden spoon to almost spreading consistency. Yield: about 2½ cups.

Butter Cream Frosting

⅓ cup butter or margarine, softened
3 cups sifted powdered sugar
2 to 3 tablespoons half-and-half
½ teaspoon vanilla extract

Cream butter at medium speed of an electric mixer; gradually add sugar alternately with half-and-half, beating until light and fluffy. Stir in vanilla. Yield: about 1½ cups. *Bess Feagin Birmingham, Alabama*

BAKED CHRISTMAS PUDDING WITH BRANDY SAUCE
(pictured on cover)

¼ cup butter or margarine, softened
¼ cup sugar
2 eggs
¾ cup molasses
1½ cups finely chopped mixed candied fruit
½ cup finely chopped yellow candied pineapple
½ cup chopped pecans
1½ cups all-purpose flour, divided
1½ teaspoons baking powder
¾ teaspoon baking soda
½ teaspoon salt
1 teaspoon ground cinnamon
½ teaspoon ground allspice
¾ cup milk
Brandy Sauce
10 to 12 sugar cubes (optional)
Lemon extract (optional)

Combine butter and ¼ cup sugar in a large mixing bowl; beat with a wooden spoon until well blended. Add eggs and molasses, mixing well.

Dredge candied fruits and pecans in 2 tablespoons flour; set aside.

Combine remaining flour and next 5 ingredients; add to creamed mixture alternately with milk, beginning and ending with flour mixture. Stir fruit mixture into batter.

Spoon batter into a greased and floured 2-quart ring mold. Cover with aluminum foil. Bake at 350° for 1½ hours. Unmold onto serving platter. Spoon Brandy Sauce over pudding. If desired, soak sugar cubes in lemon extract. Arrange soaked sugar cubes evenly around heat-proof serving platter, and ignite just before serving. Yield: 10 servings.

Brandy Sauce

¼ cup butter or margarine, softened
2 cups sifted powdered sugar
2 to 3 tablespoons milk
½ teaspoon brandy extract

Cream butter, and gradually add powdered sugar. Add enough milk to reach desired consistency. Stir in brandy extract. Yield: ½ cup. *Glenda Marie Stokes Florence, South Carolina*

PUMPKIN CUSTARD

1 cup half-and-half
½ cup whipping cream
2 tablespoons Grand Marnier or other orange-flavored liqueur
¼ teaspoon ground ginger
Pinch of salt
3 eggs
½ cup sugar
1 cup canned mashed pumpkin
1 tablespoon grated lemon rind
Sweetened whipped cream (optional)
Orange rind strips (optional)

Place half-and-half and whipping cream in top of a double boiler; bring water to a boil. Cook until thoroughly heated; set aside.

Combine Grand Marnier, ginger, and salt; set aside.

Beat eggs at medium speed of an electric mixer until frothy; add Grand Marnier mixture, beating until blended. Gradually stir about one-fourth of hot cream into egg mixture; add to remaining hot mixture, beating constantly at low speed of an electric mixer. Add sugar, pumpkin, and lemon rind, beating until mixture is smooth.

Pour custard mixture into six 6-ounce custard cups; cover each with aluminum foil. Set custard cups in a 13- x 9- x 2-inch pan; pour hot water to depth of 1 inch into pan. Bake at 325° for 40 to 45 minutes or until knife inserted in center comes out clean. Remove custard cups from water; cool on a wire rack. Chill 2 hours before serving. If desired, garnish with a dollop of whipped cream and orange rind strips. Yield: 6 servings. *Mrs. C. D. Marshall Boston, Virginia*

CHILLED DEVONSHIRE SOUFFLÉ

2 envelopes unflavored gelatin
½ cup cold water
5 eggs, separated
¾ cup sugar
¼ cup brandy
¼ cup amaretto
2 tablespoons lemon juice
2 cups whipping cream

Sprinkle gelatin over water in a saucepan; let stand 1 minute. Beat egg yolks; stir yolks and sugar into gelatin mixture. Cook over medium heat, stirring constantly, until mixture begins to boil (about 5 minutes). Remove from heat; stir in brandy, amaretto, and lemon juice. Cool.

Beat egg whites (at room temperature) at high speed of an electric mixer until stiff peaks form. Beat whipping cream until soft peaks form. Fold egg whites and whipped cream into gelatin mixture. Spoon mixture into a 2-quart soufflé dish. Chill until firm. Yield: 10 to 12 servings. *Aileen Wright Nashville, Tennessee*

HOLIDAY MERINGUES

3 egg whites
¼ teaspoon cream of tartar
1 teaspoon vanilla extract
1 cup sugar
1 quart lime sherbet
Cranberry sauce (recipe follows)

Beat egg whites (at room temperature) in a small bowl at high speed of an electric mixer until foamy; add cream of tartar and vanilla, beating until soft peaks form. Gradually add sugar, 1 tablespoon at a time, beating until stiff peaks form.

Spoon meringue mixture into 10 mounds on a baking sheet lined with heavy brown paper. Shape meringue mixture into circles, using the back of a spoon and mounding the sides at least ½ inch higher than centers.

Bake at 225° for 1 hour. Turn oven off, and let meringues cool completely before opening oven door. Carefully transfer meringues to serving plates.

Scoop sherbet into shells; top with Cranberry Sauce, and serve immediately. Yield: 10 servings.

Cranberry Sauce

½ cup sugar
2 tablespoons cornstarch
⅛ teaspoon salt
2 cups cranberry juice cocktail
1 tablespoon lemon juice

Combine all ingredients in a heavy saucepan; stir well. Place over medium heat, stirring constantly, until mixture comes to a boil. Boil 1 minute; remove from heat. Cover and chill thoroughly. Yield: 2 cups.

Lorraine Brownell
Salisbury, North Carolina

CRANBERRY SHERBET

3 cups fresh cranberries
2 cups boiling water
1 envelope unflavored gelatin
¼ cup cold water
2 cups sugar
2 cups ginger ale

Combine cranberries and water in a large saucepan; bring to a boil. Reduce heat, and simmer 6 to 8 minutes or until skins pop.

Pour mixture into container of an electric blender or food processor, and process until smooth. Strain mixture into a large saucepan. Bring cranberry mixture to a boil; remove from heat, and set aside.

Sprinkle gelatin over cold water; let stand 1 minute. Add to cranberry puree, stirring until gelatin dissolves. Add sugar, stirring to dissolve. Cool. Stir in ginger ale. Pour into a 13- x 9- x 2-inch pan; freeze until slushy. Spoon mixture into a bowl; beat with an electric mixer until fluffy. Return mixture to pan; freeze until firm. Yield: 5½ cups. *Dorothy Taylor*
Palm City, Florida

CHOCOLATE MOUSSE ROLL

¼ cup plus 2 tablespoons
  all-purpose flour
¾ teaspoon baking powder
¼ teaspoon salt
¼ cup plus 2 tablespoons cocoa
4 eggs, separated
1 teaspoon vanilla extract
¾ cup sugar
1 to 2 tablespoons powdered
  sugar
Chocolate mousse (recipe follows)
White chocolate frosting (recipe
  follows)
Grated chocolate (optional)

Grease a 15- x 10- x 1-inch jellyroll pan, and line with wax paper. Grease and flour wax paper; set aside.

Sift together first 4 ingredients; set aside. Combine egg yolks and vanilla in a large mixing bowl. Stir well, and set aside.

Beat egg whites (at room temperature) at high speed of an electric mixer until foamy. Gradually add sugar, 1 tablespoon at a time, until stiff peaks form. Fold egg whites into yolk mixture. Fold in dry ingredients, stirring well. Spread batter evenly

into prepared pan. Bake at 400° for 8 minutes.

Sift powdered sugar in a 15- x 10-inch rectangle on a towel. When cake is done, immediately loosen from sides of pan, and turn out onto sugared towel. Peel off wax paper. Trim edges; discard. Starting at narrow end, roll up cake and towel together. Place seam side down on a wire rack, and let cool.

Unroll cake, and remove towel. Spread Chocolate Mousse on cake, leaving a 1-inch margin around edges; reroll cake. Place on a serving plate, seam side down. Frost with White Chocolate Frosting. Garnish with grated chocolate, if desired. Yield: 8 to 10 servings.

Chocolate Mousse

1 (6-ounce) package semisweet
  chocolate morsels
1 tablespoon sugar
3 eggs, separated
2 teaspoons vanilla extract
¼ teaspoon cream of tartar
¼ cup sugar

Combine chocolate morsels and 1 tablespoon sugar in top of a double boiler. Cook over boiling water until chocolate melts; let cool.

Combine egg yolks and vanilla; stir into chocolate mixture.

Beat egg whites (at room temperature) and cream of tartar until foamy; gradually add ¼ cup sugar, beating until stiff peaks form. Fold egg white mixture into chocolate mixture; stir well. Cover mousse, and chill 1 hour. Yield: 2⅔ cups.

White Chocolate Frosting

1 cup (4½ ounces) grated white
  chocolate
2 tablespoons butter
2 cups sifted powdered sugar
3 to 4 tablespoons milk

Combine white chocolate and butter in top of a double boiler. Cook over boiling water until chocolate melts; let cool. Add powdered sugar and milk; beat at high speed of an electric mixer until smooth. Yield: 1½ cups.

Mrs. J. O. Branson
Thomasville, North Carolina

CHOCOLATE TRUFFLE DESSERT

1 (8½-ounce) package chocolate wafer cookies, crushed (about 2 cups)
¼ cup plus 2 tablespoons butter or margarine, melted
1 pound semisweet chocolate
½ cup sugar
2 eggs
4 eggs, separated
2 cups whipping cream
¼ cup plus 2 tablespoons sifted powdered sugar
2 cups whipping cream
¼ cup sifted powdered sugar
½ teaspoon vanilla extract
Chocolate Leaves

Combine cookie crumbs and butter in a bowl, mixing well. Press on bottom and 2½ inches up sides of an ungreased 10-inch springform pan. Chill 30 minutes.

Place semisweet chocolate in top of a double boiler; bring water to a boil. Reduce heat to low; cook, stirring occasionally, until chocolate melts. Remove from heat; stir in ½ cup sugar. Cool to lukewarm. Beat 2 eggs and 4 egg yolks slightly. Gradually stir about one-fourth of warm chocolate mixture into beaten eggs; add to remaining warm mixture, stirring constantly.

Beat 2 cups whipping cream in a large mixing bowl until foamy; gradually add ¼ cup plus 2 tablespoons powdered sugar, beating until soft peaks form. Beat 4 egg whites (at room temperature) at high speed of an electric mixer until stiff peaks form. Fold whipped cream and egg whites into chocolate mixture. Spoon mixture into prepared crust. Cover and chill at least 8 hours.

Beat 2 cups whipping cream in a medium mixing bowl until foamy; gradually add ¼ cup powdered sugar, beating until stiff peaks form. Stir in vanilla. Set aside ½ cup whipped cream; spread remaining whipped cream over chocolate filling.

Remove sides of springform pan, and pipe reserved ½ cup whipped cream around edge. Garnish with chocolate leaves. Store in refrigerator. Yield: 10 to 12 servings.

Chocolate Leaves

8 (1-ounce) squares semisweet chocolate
1 tablespoon shortening

Select such nonpoisonous leaves as mint or rose leaves. Wash leaves, and pat dry with paper towels. Melt chocolate and shortening over hot water in a double boiler; let cool slightly.

Using a small spatula, spread a ⅛-inch layer of melted chocolate on the back of each leaf, spreading to the edges. Place chocolate-coated leaves on wax paper-lined baking sheet, chocolate side up; freeze until chocolate is firm, about 10 minutes.

Grasp leaf at stem end, and carefully peel leaf from chocolate. Chill chocolate leaves until ready to use. (Handle carefully since chocolate leaves are thin and will melt quickly from the heat of your hand.)

Lynda A. Wier
Roswell, Georgia

APRICOT TARTS

⅓ cup sugar
2 tablespoons cornstarch
1 cup plus 2 tablespoons apricot nectar
2 tablespoons butter or margarine
1 (17-ounce) can apricot halves, drained and chopped
2 (3-ounce) packages cream cheese, softened
1 teaspoon rum flavoring
12 baked (4-inch) tart shells
Sweetened whipped cream

Combine sugar and cornstarch in a saucepan. Add apricot nectar and butter; bring to a boil, stirring constantly. Boil 1 minute; remove from heat. Stir in chopped apricots. Set mixture aside.

Beat cream cheese at high speed of an electric mixer until creamy; add rum flavoring. Spread 1 tablespoon cream cheese mixture into each tart shell. Spoon apricot mixture over cheese mixture. Chill or serve at room temperature. Garnish with whipped cream. Yield: 12 servings.

Fran Allison
Knoxville, Tennessee

WHITE CHRISTMAS PIE

1 envelope unflavored gelatin
¼ cup cold water
½ cup sugar
¼ cup all-purpose flour
½ teaspoon salt
1½ cups milk
¾ teaspoon vanilla extract
¼ teaspoon almond extract
3 egg whites
¼ teaspoon cream of tartar
¼ cup sugar
½ cup whipping cream, whipped
1 cup flaked coconut
1 baked 9-inch pastry shell
Additional flaked coconut (optional)
Red and green candied cherries

Soften gelatin in cold water; set mixture aside.

Combine ½ cup sugar, flour, and salt in a medium saucepan; gradually add milk, stirring until blended. Cook over medium heat, stirring constantly, until mixture thickens and comes to a boil. Boil 1 minute, stirring constantly. Remove from heat; stir in softened gelatin and vanilla and almond extracts. Cool.

Beat egg whites (at room temperature) and cream of tartar until foamy; gradually add ¼ cup sugar, 1 tablespoon at a time, beating until soft peaks form. Fold egg whites, whipped cream, and 1 cup coconut into gelatin mixture; pour into pastry shell. Sprinkle with additional coconut, if desired. Chill until set. Garnish with candied cherries. Yield: one 9-inch pie.

Dorothy Taylor
Palm City, Florida

CARAMEL-PECAN PIE

1 cup sugar, divided
¼ cup cornstarch
⅛ teaspoon salt
2 cups milk
3 eggs, separated
3 tablespoons butter or margarine
½ teaspoon vanilla extract
½ cup chopped pecans
1 baked 9-inch pastry shell
½ teaspoon cream of tartar
3 tablespoons sugar

Sprinkle ½ cup sugar in a heavy skillet; place over medium heat. Cook, stirring constantly, until sugar melts and syrup is light golden brown.

Combine remaining ½ cup sugar, cornstarch, and salt in a heavy saucepan; gradually stir in milk. Cook over medium heat, stirring constantly, until thickened and bubbly. Beat egg yolks; gradually stir about one-fourth of hot mixture into yolks, and add to remaining hot mixture, stirring constantly. Cook, stirring constantly, until thickened. Stir in caramelized sugar; cook, stirring constantly, until sugar melts. Remove from heat; stir in butter, vanilla, and pecans. Pour into baked pastry shell.

Combine egg whites (at room temperature) and cream of tartar; beat at high speed of an electric mixer until foamy. Gradually add 3 tablespoons sugar, 1 tablespoon at a time, beating until stiff peaks form.

Spread meringue over hot filling, sealing to edge of pastry. Bake at 400° for 8 to 10 minutes or until lightly browned. Cool completely before serving. Yield: one 9-inch pie.

Dora Hancock
Pottsboro, Texas

Tip: *When food boils over in the oven, sprinkle the burned surface with a little salt. This will stop smoke and odor from forming and make the spot easier to clean. Also, rubbing damp salt on dishes in which food has been baked will remove brown spots.*

Ideas For Candied Cherries

Candied cherries belong in more dishes than just fruitcakes as our readers will attest. They're pleasant additions to a variety of recipes, both baked and frozen.

CHRISTMAS FRUIT SQUARES

½ cup butter, softened
1½ cups firmly packed brown sugar
2 eggs
1 cup self-rising flour, divided
2 cups chopped pecans
½ pound red or green candied cherries, chopped
½ pound yellow candied pineapple, chopped
½ cup flaked coconut

Cream butter; gradually add sugar, beating well at medium speed of an electric mixer. Add eggs, one at a time, beating well after each addition. Add ¾ cup flour; stir well.

Combine pecans and remaining ingredients; dredge in ¼ cup flour. Stir fruit mixture into batter. Spoon into a greased and floured 9-inch square pan. Bake at 300° for 1 hour and 10 minutes or until a wooden pick inserted in center comes out clean. Cool in pan on a wire rack. Chill before cutting. Yield: 3 dozen.

Millie Givens
Savannah, Georgia

CHRISTMAS CHERRY COOKIES

1 cup butter or margarine, softened
¼ cup sifted powdered sugar
2 cups all-purpose flour
1 cup chopped pecans
1 teaspoon vanilla extract
36 red or green candied cherries
Powdered sugar

Cream butter and ¼ cup sugar, beating well at medium speed of an electric mixer. Add flour, pecans, and vanilla; mix until well blended.

Shape dough into 1-inch balls; place on ungreased cookie sheets. Press a cherry in center of each cookie. Bake at 325° for 30 minutes. Remove to wire racks to cool slightly. Roll cookies in powdered sugar, and cool completely on wire racks. Yield: 3 dozen.

Edna Solomon
Powell, Tennessee

LADY BALTIMORE TARTS

3 eggs, well beaten
1½ cups firmly packed brown sugar
½ cup light corn syrup
1½ cups chopped pecans
1 cup flaked coconut
½ cup chopped red candied cherries
1 teaspoon vanilla extract
½ teaspoon almond extract
16 (3-inch) unbaked commercial tart shells
Sliced red candied cherries (optional)

Combine first 3 ingredients, stirring until well blended. Stir in pecans, coconut, chopped cherries, and flavorings. Spoon about ¼ cup mixture into each tart shell. Bake at 300° for 40 minutes or until tarts are set. Garnish with sliced cherries, if desired. Yield: 16 (3-inch) tarts.

Aileen Wright
Nashville, Tennessee

HOLIDAY FRUIT FREEZE

½ cup chopped pecans
1 tablespoon butter or margarine,
  melted
2 ripe bananas, mashed
1 cup chopped dates
¼ cup chopped red candied
  cherries
¼ cup chopped green candied
  cherries
2 tablespoons lemon juice
1 quart vanilla ice cream,
  softened
Sliced candied cherries (optional)

Sauté pecans in butter, stirring constantly, about 3 minutes or until toasted. Set aside to cool.

Gently combine pecans, mashed banana, and next 5 ingredients; spread in an 8-inch square pan. Cover and freeze until mixture is firm. Scoop into balls, and serve in compotes. Garnish with sliced cherries, if desired. Yield: 8 servings.

Libby Winstead
Nashville, Tennessee

Stir Up A Quick Bread

Just because you're short of time doesn't mean you have to leave homemade bread off the menu. All these breads take only a few minutes to mix up, and a couple of them bake in 20 minutes or less.

PEPPER-CHEESE BISCUIT FINGERS

2 cups all-purpose flour
1 tablespoon baking powder
½ teaspoon baking soda
1 teaspoon pepper
⅔ cup grated Parmesan cheese
3 tablespoons butter or margarine
1 cup buttermilk
2 tablespoons butter or
  margarine, melted

Combine first 5 ingredients in a medium mixing bowl; cut in 3 tablespoons butter with a pastry blender until mixture resembles coarse meal. Add buttermilk, stirring until dry ingredients are moistened. Turn dough out onto a lighty floured surface, and knead lightly 4 or 5 times.

Roll dough to a 12- x 9-inch rectangle; cut into 3- x 1½-inch rectangles. Place on lightly greased baking sheets; brush with melted butter. Bake at 450° for 10 minutes or until lightly browned. Yield: 2 dozen.

LaJuan Coward
Jasper, Texas

MINI SOUR CREAM MUFFINS

1 cup butter or margarine,
  softened
1 (8-ounce) carton commercial
  sour cream
2 cups self-rising flour

Combine butter and sour cream, mixing until smooth. Gradually stir in flour; stir until blended. Spoon batter into ungreased miniature (1¾-inch) muffin pans, filling each with 1 tablespoon batter. Bake at 350° for 25 to 30 minutes. Yield: 3 dozen.

Juanda Kirchharr
Camden, Alabama

ONION CORNBREAD

2 cups chopped onion
¼ cup butter or margarine,
  melted
1½ cups self-rising
  cornmeal
2 tablespoons sugar
¼ teaspoon dillweed
1 cup (4 ounces) shredded
  Cheddar cheese,
  divided
2 eggs, well beaten
¼ cup milk
¼ cup vegetable oil
1 (8-ounce) carton commercial
  sour cream
1 (8¾-ounce) can cream-style
  corn
Dash of hot sauce

Sauté chopped onion in melted butter in a large skillet until onion is tender; set aside.

Combine cornmeal, sugar, and dillweed in a large bowl; add sautéed onion, ½ cup Cheddar cheese, beaten eggs, milk, vegetable oil, sour cream, cream-style corn, and dash of hot sauce, stirring just until dry ingredients are moistened.

Spoon mixture into a greased 10-inch cast-iron skillet. Bake at 400° for 20 minutes; sprinkle cornbread evenly with remaining ½ cup Cheddar cheese, and bake cornbread an additional 5 minutes. Yield: 8 servings.

Ethel Jernegan
Savannah, Georgia

ORANGE-HONEY MUFFINS

2½ cups all-purpose flour
2 teaspoons baking powder
½ teaspoon baking soda
1 teaspoon salt
⅓ cup wheat germ
¼ cup sugar
1 tablespoon grated orange rind
3 eggs, beaten
¾ cup butter or margarine, melted
½ cup honey
⅓ cup orange juice

Combine first 7 ingredients in a mixing bowl; make a well in center of mixture.

Combine eggs, butter, honey, and orange juice; add to dry ingredients, stirring just until moistened. Spoon into greased muffin pans, filling three-fourths full. Bake at 375° for 15 minutes. Yield: 1½ dozen.

Kathleen L. Hayes
Ballwin, Missouri

CARROT-WALNUT BREAD

1½ cups shredded raw carrot
1 cup boiling water
1 cup firmly packed brown sugar
¼ cup vegetable oil
1 teaspoon grated orange rind
2 eggs, beaten
1⅓ cups all-purpose flour
1 cup whole wheat flour
2½ teaspoons baking powder
1 teaspoon baking soda
½ teaspoon salt
1 cup chopped walnuts

Combine first 5 ingredients in a small bowl, stirring well; cool. Stir in eggs.

Combine flours, baking powder, soda, and salt in a bowl; make a well in center of dry ingredients. Add carrot mixture and walnuts; stir until dry ingredients are moistened.

Spoon batter into a greased and floured 9- x 5- x 3-inch loafpan; bake at 350° for 1 hour or until a wooden pick inserted in center comes out clean. Cool bread in pan 10 minutes; remove from pan, and let bread cool completely on a wire rack. Yield: 1 loaf.

Mary V. Lancaster
Brentwood, Tennessee

Celebrate With Spicy Fruitcakes

Fruitcake is perhaps one of the South's most traditional holiday foods. Store fruitcake wrapped with heavy-duty plastic wrap or bourbon-soaked cheesecloth in airtight containers. The flavor is best if the ingredients can mellow at least two weeks. For easier slicing, store the fruitcake in the refrigerator and cut with an electric knife.

FAMILY FAVORITE FRUITCAKE

2 cups sugar
1½ cups raisins
1 (8-ounce) package pitted dates, chopped
1¾ cups water
⅓ cup shortening
¼ cup apricot brandy
1 pound mixed candied fruit, chopped
¼ pound candied red cherries, chopped
1 cup chopped walnuts
3 cups all-purpose flour, divided
1 teaspoon baking soda
½ teaspoon salt
2 teaspoons ground cinnamon
1 teaspoon ground cloves

Combine first 5 ingredients in a saucepan; simmer, uncovered, 20 minutes, stirring occasionally. Stir in brandy; set aside.

Combine candied fruit, cherries, and walnuts; dredge in ¼ cup flour, stirring to coat evenly. Set aside.

Combine remaining 2¾ cups flour, soda, salt, cinnamon, and cloves, mixing well. Stir in raisin mixture; blend thoroughly. Add candied fruit mixture and stir. Spoon into a greased and floured, brown paper-lined 10-inch tube pan. Bake at 325° for 1 hour and 15 minutes or until a wooden pick inserted in center comes out clean. Cool in pan. Remove cake, and take off paper. Store in an airtight container. Yield: one 10-inch cake.

Sandy R. Stamm
Birmingham, Alabama

ZUCCHINI FRUITCAKE

1 cup mixed candied fruit
1 cup golden raisins
½ cup currants
1 cup chopped walnuts
2 cups shredded zucchini
3 cups all-purpose flour, divided
3 eggs
1 cup vegetable oil
1½ cups sugar
1 teaspoon vanilla extract
1 teaspoon baking soda
½ teaspoon baking powder
½ teaspoon salt
1 tablespoon ground cinnamon
2 teaspoons ground allspice
1½ teaspoons ground nutmeg

Combine first 5 ingredients in a large bowl; add ¼ cup flour, and stir to coat. Set aside.

Combine eggs and oil in a large mixing bowl; beat at medium speed of an electric mixer 1 minute. Add sugar and vanilla; beat at medium speed 30 seconds. Combine remaining 2¾ cups flour, soda, and next 5 ingredients; add to egg mixture. Stir fruit mixture into batter.

Spoon into 2 greased and floured 8- x 5- x 3-inch loafpans; bake at 325° for 1 hour and 15 to 20 minutes or until a wooden pick inserted in center comes out clean. Cool in pans 10 minutes. Remove from pans; cool on wire racks. Yield: 2 loaves.

Trenda Leigh
Richmond, Virginia

Cookies And Candies For Holiday Baking

The creak of the oven door and sighs of delight ring jubilant and familiar as days of feasting and sharing approach. Cookies fill up cookie jars and gift baskets, and tempting tins of candy simply disappear.

Crème de menthe and chocolate are frequently combined in holiday goodies. For example, Dinner Mint Fudge, a candy spiked with crème de menthe, is appropriate for an open house menu or for special gifts.

DINNER MINT FUDGE

2 cups sugar
⅓ cup cocoa
Pinch of salt
⅔ cup milk
2 tablespoons light corn syrup
¼ cup butter or margarine
3 tablespoons crème de menthe

Combine first 5 ingredients in a heavy 3-quart saucepan; cook over medium heat, stirring constantly, until mixture boils. Cover and boil 3 minutes. Remove cover, and cook until mixture reaches soft ball stage (234°). Remove from heat; cool 10 minutes. Add butter and crème de menthe; beat until slightly thickened (about 2 minutes). Pour mixture into a buttered 8-inch square pan. Cool and cut into 2-inch squares. Yield: 16 squares.
Lynda Cable
Hixson, Tennessee

Tip: *During the week, keep a shopping list handy to write down items as you need them. This will eliminate unnecessary trips to the store. Before your weekly shopping trip, make a complete shopping list. If you arrange the list according to the layout of the store, you will save yourself time and steps.*

CHOCOLATE CRÈME DE MENTHE BITES

1¼ cups butter or margarine, melted and divided
½ cup cocoa
3½ cups sifted powdered sugar, divided
1 egg, beaten
1 teaspoon vanilla extract
2 cups graham cracker crumbs
⅓ cup crème de menthe
1½ cups semisweet chocolate morsels

Combine ½ cup melted butter, cocoa, ½ cup powdered sugar, and egg in top of a double boiler, mixing well; bring water to a boil. Reduce heat to low; cook until mixture thickens, stirring constantly. Remove from heat. Add vanilla and cracker crumbs, mixing well. Press mixture into a greased 13- x 9- x 2-inch pan; chill 15 minutes.

Combine ½ cup melted butter, crème de menthe, and remaining 3 cups powdered sugar, beating until blended. Spread over chocolate mixture. Chill 1 hour.

Combine remaining ¼ cup melted butter and chocolate morsels in top of a double boiler. Cook over low heat, stirring until chocolate melts and mixture is smooth. Spread over crème de menthe filling. Cool. Cut into squares. Store in refrigerator. Yield: 8 dozen.
Hyland Justice
Atlanta, Georgia

ALMOND-TOFFEE CRUNCH

½ cup butter
1¼ cups sugar
2 tablespoons water
1 tablespoon light corn syrup
1½ cups finely chopped almonds, toasted and divided
1 teaspoon vanilla extract
½ cup semisweet chocolate morsels

Melt butter in a 3-quart saucepan; stir in sugar, water, and corn syrup. Cook over low heat, stirring gently, until sugar dissolves. Cover and cook over medium heat 2 to 3 minutes to wash down sugar crystals from sides of pan. Uncover and cook to soft crack stage (290°). Remove from heat, and stir in 1 cup almonds and vanilla. Pour onto buttered cookie sheet; quickly spread mixture evenly with spatula. Cool several hours.

Melt chocolate morsels in a double boiler over low heat; keep warm. Loosen edges of toffee, using a sharp knife; invert toffee onto wax paper-lined cookie sheet. Spread melted chocolate over toffee, and sprinkle with remaining ½ cup almonds. Gently press almonds into chocolate. Cool until firm. Break into bite-size pieces; store in refrigerator. Yield: 1½ pounds.
Dina Walker
Garland, Texas

CHOCOLATE-RUM BALLS

1 (8½-ounce) package chocolate wafer cookies, crushed
1 cup chopped pecans
1 cup sifted powdered sugar
¼ cup light corn syrup
¼ cup dark rum
Additional powdered sugar

Combine first 5 ingredients in a large bowl; stir well. Shape into 1-inch balls, and let stand 10 minutes. Sprinkle additional powdered sugar over balls. Yield: 4 dozen.
Audrey Bledsoe
Smyrna, Georgia

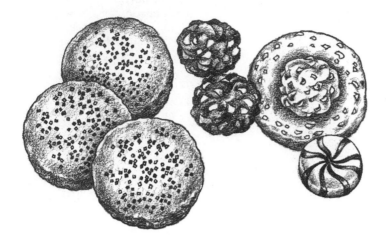

PEPPERMINT CANDY COOKIES

1 cup butter or margarine,
  softened
½ cup sifted powdered sugar
2 cups all-purpose flour
½ cup finely chopped walnuts
1 teaspoon vanilla extract
¼ cup plus 2 tablespoons crushed
  hard peppermint candy
¼ cup plus 2 tablespoons sifted
  powdered sugar
2 tablespoons cream cheese,
  softened
½ cup sifted powdered sugar
1 teaspoon milk

Cream butter; gradually add ½ cup powdered sugar, beating at medium speed of an electric mixer until light and fluffy. Add flour, beating until smooth; stir in walnuts and vanilla. Cover and chill.

Combine peppermint candy and ¼ cup plus 2 tablespoons powdered sugar; mix well. Set aside.

Combine cream cheese and remaining ingredients; stir in 3 tablespoons peppermint candy mixture.

Shape dough into 1-inch balls; press thumb in each cookie leaving an indentation. Spoon about ¼ teaspoon cream cheese mixture in each cookie indentation. Gently pinch edges together to seal; place cookies about 1 inch apart on ungreased cookie sheets.

Bake at 350° for 12 to 15 minutes. Transfer to wire rack to cool slightly. Roll cookies in remaining peppermint candy mixture, and cool completely on wire racks. Yield: 3½ dozen.

Note: These cookies are fragile; do not increase size. *Dorothy L. Akers*
Vinton, Virginia

GOLDEN SUGAR COOKIES

1 cup butter or margarine,
  softened
½ cup sugar
1 egg
1 teaspoon lemon extract
2¼ cups all-purpose flour
1½ teaspoons baking powder
½ teaspoon salt
1 tablespoon whipping cream or
  half-and-half
Red and green decorator sugar
  crystals

Cream butter; gradually add ½ cup sugar, beating at medium speed of an electric mixer until light and fluffy. Add egg to mixture, beating well. Stir in lemon extract.

Combine flour, baking powder, and salt; add to creamed mixture, beating well. Shape dough into two 12-inch rolls; wrap in wax paper, and chill at least 6 hours.

Unwrap rolls, and cut into ¼-inch slices. Place slices on lightly greased cookie sheets. Brush tops of cookies with cream, and sprinkle evenly with sugar crystals. Bake at 400° for 8 minutes. Let cookies cool on wire racks. Yield: 6 dozen.

Note: Cookie dough may be frozen by wrapping securely and freezing up to 1 month. Remove from freezer; slice dough, and bake as directed.
Dorsella Utter
Louisville, Kentucky

FRUITCAKE COOKIES

½ pound yellow candied
  pineapple, chopped
½ pound red candied cherries,
  chopped
½ pound citron, chopped
2½ cups seedless raisins
4 cups chopped pecans
1½ cups all-purpose flour, divided
¼ cup butter or margarine,
  softened
½ cup firmly packed brown sugar
2 eggs
¼ cup strawberry jelly
2 teaspoons baking soda
1½ tablespoons milk
½ teaspoon ground allspice
½ teaspoon ground cinnamon
½ teaspoon ground cloves
½ teaspoon ground nutmeg

Combine first 5 ingredients; dredge in ¾ cup flour, stirring well. Set mixture aside.

Cream butter in a large bowl; gradually add sugar, beating well at medium speed of an electric mixer. Add eggs and jelly, mixing well.

Dissolve soda in milk; add to creamed mixture. Add remaining ¾ cup flour and spices, mixing well.

Fold fruit mixture into batter. Drop by rounded teaspoonfuls onto greased cookie sheets. Bake at 325° for 12 minutes or until done. Cool on wire racks. Yield: 12 dozen.
Carrie Treichel
Johnson City, Tennessee

Tip: *Always measure ingredients accurately. Level dry ingredients in a cup with a knife edge or a spoon handle. Measure liquids in a cup so that the fluid is level with the top of the measuring line. Measure solid shortening by packing it firmly in a graduated measuring cup.*

CHRISTMAS DATE COOKIES

1 teaspoon baking soda
2 teaspoons warm water
½ cup butter or margarine
½ cup shortening
1 (16-ounce) package brown sugar
4 eggs
1 teaspoon salt
1¼ teaspoons ground nutmeg
1 teaspoon ground allspice
1 teaspoon ground cinnamon
2 cups chopped pecans
1 pound pitted dates, chopped
½ cup raisins
1 (10-ounce) jar maraschino
   cherries, drained and chopped
3½ to 4 cups all-purpose flour,
   divided

Dissolve soda in warm water in a small bowl; set aside.

Melt butter and shortening in a saucepan over low heat; cool slightly. Add brown sugar, stirring well. Place butter mixture in a large mixing bowl. Add eggs, one at a time, beating well after each addition. Add soda mixture, salt, and next 3 ingredients, mixing well.

Combine pecans, chopped dates, raisins, and cherries; dredge in ½ cup flour, stirring well. Add to butter mixture, mixing well. Gradually add remaining flour, mixing well until a stiff dough is formed.

Drop dough by rounded teaspoonfuls onto greased cookie sheets. Bake at 350° for 15 minutes or until lightly browned. Cool on wire racks. Yield: 10 dozen. *Madeline Gibbons Little Rock, Arkansas*

New Traditions For Christmas Breakfast

Here we present cherished recipes you shared as evidence of fond holiday memories and the high regard families hold for particular foods.

Best of all, these recipes will save you time on Christmas morning. Some of these dishes may be prepared in advance and frozen; others you may wish to get a head start on the day before Santa's arrival.

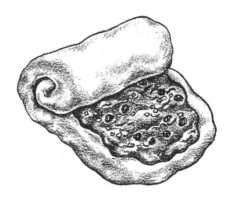

HONEY-CINNAMON SWIRL BREAD

2 packages dry yeast
¼ cup warm water (105° to 115°)
1 cup milk
½ cup shortening
¼ cup sugar
2 teaspoons salt
2 eggs, beaten
4½ to 5 cups all-purpose flour
2 tablespoons butter or
   margarine, melted
Honey Filling
Honey Glaze
Orange rind twist (optional)

Dissolve yeast in warm water in a large mixing bowl; let stand 5 minutes. Combine milk, shortening, sugar, and salt in a heavy saucepan; cook over medium heat, stirring constantly, until shortening melts. Cool to 105° to 115°. Add eggs and milk mixture to yeast mixture, mixing well. Gradually stir in enough flour to make a soft dough.

Turn dough out onto a lightly floured surface, and knead until smooth and elastic (about 8 to 10 minutes). Place in a well-greased bowl, turning to grease top. Cover and let rise in a warm place (85°), free from drafts, 1 hour or until doubled in bulk.

Punch dough down; let rest 10 minutes. Divide dough in half. Roll 1

portion on a lightly floured surface to a 16- x 12-inch rectangle; brush with 1 tablespoon melted butter. Spread dough with half of Honey Filling, leaving a ½-inch border. Starting with short side, roll up jellyroll fashion. Press seam and edges to seal; cut into 1-inch slices. Place slices in a lightly greased 10-inch tube pan, arranging cut sides to bottom and sides of pans. Repeat procedure with remaining dough, staggering layers. Cover and let rise in a warm place, free from drafts, 30 minutes or until doubled in bulk.

Bake at 350° for 40 to 45 minutes or until bread sounds hollow when tapped. Cover with aluminum foil the last 20 minutes of baking, if necessary, to prevent excessive browning.

Invert bread onto a wire rack; let cool. Drizzle with Honey Glaze. Garnish with orange rind twist, if desired. Yield: one 10-inch loaf.

Honey Filling

½ cup honey
¼ cup sugar
⅓ cup raisins
⅓ cup chopped pecans or walnuts
2 tablespoons grated orange rind
1 tablespoon orange juice
1 tablespoon butter or margarine,
   melted
1 teaspoon ground cinnamon

Combine all ingredients; stir well. Yield: about 1¾ cups.

Honey Glaze

⅓ cup honey
⅓ cup sugar
2 teaspoons grated orange rind
2 teaspoons butter or margarine

Combine all ingredients in a saucepan; cook over medium heat, stirring constantly, just until sugar dissolves. Yield: about ⅔ cup.

Note: To freeze, bake bread as directed; cool. Do not glaze. Wrap in aluminum foil. To serve, let come to room temperature; reheat in foil at 300° for 25 minutes. Drizzle with Honey Glaze. *Derrell H. Sears Anderson, South Carolina*

CHRISTMAS JAM

1 (12-ounce) package fresh
    cranberries
2 (10-ounce) packages frozen
    strawberries, thawed
4 cups sugar
1 (3-ounce) package liquid pectin

Position knife blade in food processor
bowl; add cranberries. Top with
cover; process until cranberries are
coarsely chopped. Combine cranberries, strawberries, and sugar in a
Dutch oven; bring to a boil, and cook
1 minute, stirring occasionally. Remove from heat; add pectin to mixture. Return to a full rolling boil; boil
1 minute, stirring constantly. Remove from heat, and skim off foam
with a metal spoon.

Quickly pour jam into hot sterilized
jars, leaving ¼ inch headspace; wipe
jar rims. Cover at once with metal
lids, and screw on bands. Process in
boiling-water bath 5 minutes. Yield: 7
half pints. *Colette Dusold*
Bayonet Point, Florida

FRENCH TOAST AU FROMAGE

3 eggs
½ cup milk
½ cup orange juice
1 (7½-ounce) package soft farmer
    cheese
3 tablespoons honey
1 tablespoon grated orange rind
8 (1½-inch-thick) slices French
    bread
3 tablespoons butter
Sauce Mimosa
Orange sections (optional)
Strawberries (optional)

Combine first 3 ingredients; beat
well. Set aside.

Combine cheese, honey, and orange rind. Make a horizontal pocket
in each bread slice; spoon about 2
tablespoons cheese mixture into each
pocket. Place bread in a 13- x 9- x
2-inch baking dish. Pour egg mixture
over bread slices; turn slices to coat
evenly. Cover and soak 15 minutes
or refrigerate 8 hours.

Melt 1½ tablespoons butter in a
large skillet; arrange 4 slices bread in
skillet, and sauté 4 minutes on each
side or until browned. Repeat procedure with remaining butter and bread
slices. Serve toast with Sauce Mimosa. If desired, garnish toast with
orange sections and strawberries.
Yield: 8 servings.

Sauce Mimosa

1 cup orange juice
1 tablespoon cornstarch
½ cup dry champagne or white
    wine
2 tablespoons honey
1 orange, peeled and sectioned
½ cup strawberries, halved

Combine orange juice and cornstarch
in a medium saucepan; whisk until
blended. Stir in champagne. Bring to
a boil; reduce heat, and cook 1 minute. Stir in honey, orange sections,
and strawberries. Yield: 1⅓ cups.
Lula Bell Hawks
Newport, Arkansas

CHRISTMAS BREAD

1 cup regular oats, uncooked
2 cups boiling water
2 packages dry yeast
⅓ cup warm water (105° to 115°)
½ cup molasses
¼ cup honey
2 tablespoons butter or
    margarine, softened
2½ teaspoons salt
6 to 6½ cups all-purpose flour,
    divided

Combine oats and boiling water, stirring well. Let stand 20 minutes.

Dissolve yeast in warm water in a
large bowl; let stand 5 minutes. Stir

in oats mixture, molasses, honey,
butter, and salt, mixing well. Add 2
cups flour, and stir until smooth.
Gradually add enough remaining flour
to make a soft dough.

Turn dough out onto a lightly
floured surface, and knead until
smooth and elastic (about 5 minutes).
Place in a well-greased bowl, turning
to grease top. Cover and let rise in a
warm place (85°), free from drafts,
1½ hours or until doubled in bulk.

Punch dough down; divide dough
in half, and place on a lightly floured
surface. Knead 2 or 3 times. Shape
each portion into a loaf. Place in 2
greased 9- x 5- x 3-inch loafpans.
Cover and let rise in a warm place
(85°), free from drafts, 1 hour or
until doubled in bulk. Bake at 325°
for 40 minutes or until loaves sound
hollow when tapped; cover with aluminum foil the last 15 minutes of
baking, if necessary, to prevent excessive browning. Remove loaves
from pans, and let cool on wire
racks. Yield: 2 loaves.

Note: To freeze, bake bread as
directed; cool. Wrap in aluminum foil.
To serve, let come to room temperature; reheat in foil at 250° for 10 to
15 minutes. *Scottie Beasley*
Winter Haven, Florida

BREAKFAST PIZZA

1 pound bulk pork sausage
1 (8-ounce) package refrigerated
    crescent dinner rolls
1 cup (4 ounces) shredded sharp
    Cheddar cheese
1 cup (4 ounces) shredded
    mozzarella cheese
6 eggs, beaten
½ cup milk
¾ teaspoon dried whole oregano
⅛ teaspoon pepper
Green and red pepper slices
    (optional)

Cook sausage in a medium skillet
until browned; drain. Set aside.

Separate crescent dough into 8
triangles; place triangles with elon-
gated points toward center in a

greased 12-inch pizza pan. Press bottom and sides to form a crust; seal perforations. Bake at 375° for 5 minutes on lower oven rack. Crust will be puffy when removed from oven. Reduce oven temperature to 350°.

Spoon sausage over dough; sprinkle with cheeses.

Combine eggs and next 3 ingredients; pour over sausage mixture. Bake at 350° on lower oven rack 30 to 35 minutes. Garnish with green and red pepper slices, if desired. Yield: 6 to 8 servings. *Louise Ellis Talbott, Tennessee*

CRANBERRY WASSAIL

1 teaspoon whole cloves
3 (3-inch) sticks cinnamon, broken
1 (48-ounce) jar cranberry juice cocktail
1 (48-ounce) jar apple juice
1 (6-ounce) can frozen lemonade concentrate, thawed and undiluted
⅔ cup water
1 teaspoon ground cinnamon
½ teaspoon ground cloves
½ teaspoon ground ginger
1 (33.8-ounce) bottle ginger ale
Apple wedges (optional)

Tie cloves and cinnamon in a cheesecloth bag; set aside.

Combine cranberry juice cocktail, next 6 ingredients, and spice bag in a Dutch oven; bring to a boil. Cover, reduce heat, and simmer 20 minutes. Uncover and simmer an additional 20 minutes. Discard spice bag. Add ginger ale, and cook until hot. Garnish with apple wedges, if desired. Yield: 17 cups. *Mrs. Ronald D. Smith Houston, Texas*

Tip: *Mix liquid from canned fruit in a jar as you acquire it; use it in a gelatin dessert or as a punch drink.*

Bake A Big Batch Of Rolls

If you're looking for ways to save on holiday baking, one recipe of Big-Batch Rolls may help you bake all the rolls you'll need throughout the season. Sandie Thomas of Cherry Valley, Arkansas, finds that her recipe will yield eight pans of cinnamon rolls or six pans of dinner rolls.

You can bake all the rolls on the same day and freeze them for dinner parties, holiday gifts, or family meals. Because the recipe makes so many pans of rolls, you may want to purchase disposable aluminum pans for baking. The pans make a handy gift-giving container, too.

BIG-BATCH ROLLS

2 packages dry yeast
4 cups warm water (105° to 115°)
1 cup instant nonfat dry milk powder
1 cup sugar
1 cup vegetable oil
1 tablespoon salt
2 teaspoons baking powder
1 teaspoon baking soda
11 to 12 cups all-purpose flour
Melted butter or margarine

Dissolve yeast in warm water in a large mixing bowl; let stand 5 minutes. Add dry milk powder and next 5 ingredients; beat at medium speed of an electric mixer until blended. Gradually stir in enough flour to make a very soft dough. Place dough in a well-greased bowl, turning to grease top. Cover and refrigerate at least 4 hours.

Punch dough down; divide dough in half. Working with one portion of dough at a time, place dough on a lightly floured surface; knead until smooth and elastic, adding more flour, if necessary. Roll dough to ¼-inch thickness. Cut dough with a 2½-inch round cutter. Make a crease with dull edge of knife just off center on each round. Brush lightly with melted butter. Fold larger side over smaller so that edges will meet. Seal. Place 15 rolls in a lightly greased 8-inch square baking pan. Repeat procedure filling two additional 8-inch square pans. Repeat procedure with remaining portion of dough, filling 3 additional 8-inch square pans.

Cover and let rise in a warm place, (85°), free from drafts, 40 minutes or until rolls are doubled in bulk. Bake at 375° for 10 to 15 minutes. Yield: 7½ dozen.

Note: To freeze, prepare and bake rolls as directed; let cool. Wrap in aluminum foil; freeze. To serve, let rolls thaw; then bake in foil at 375° for 5 to 7 minutes or until thoroughly heated.

CINNAMON ROLLS

1 recipe Big-Batch Roll Dough
2 cups sugar
1 to 2 tablespoons ground
  cinnamon
1 cup butter or margarine, melted
4½ cups sifted powdered sugar
⅓ to ½ cup orange juice

Place dough in a well-greased bowl, turning to grease top. Cover and refrigerate at least 4 hours.

Punch dough down; divide into 4 portions. Working with one portion of dough at a time, place dough on a lightly floured surface; knead until smooth and elastic, adding extra flour, if necessary. Roll dough to a 14- x 9-inch rectangle.

Combine 2 cups sugar, cinnamon, and butter, mixing well. Spread one-fourth of cinnamon mixture on dough. Roll dough jellyroll fashion, starting at long side. Pinch seam to seal (do not seal ends). Cut roll into 14 (1-inch) slices; place rolls in 2 greased 8-inch round cakepans (7 rolls in each pan). Repeat process with remaining 3 portions of dough.

Cover and let rise in a warm place, (85°), free from drafts, 40 minutes or until rolls are doubled in bulk. Bake at 375° for 13 to 15 minutes. Cool on wire racks.

Combine powdered sugar and orange juice, stirring until smooth. Drizzle or pipe glaze over warm rolls. Yield: about 4½ dozen.

Note: To freeze, prepare and bake rolls as directed; let cool. Omit glaze. Wrap in aluminum foil; freeze. To serve, let rolls thaw, and bake in foil at 375° for 5 to 10 minutes. Drizzle glaze as directed.

Tip: Sifting flour, with the exception of cake flour, is no longer necessary. Simply stir the flour, gently spoon it into a dry measure, and level the top. Powdered sugar, however, should be sifted to remove the lumps.

Bread Tips

■ Bread made with fruit or nuts should be tested with a straw or wire cake tester in the center. The tester should come out perfectly clean if the bread is done.

■ Clean, dry coffee cans make ideal baking containers to use for baking gift breads.

■ Most recipes for French bread call for placing a pan of hot water in the oven while loaves are baking. This makes the loaves crusty. Brushing the loaves with salt water as they bake thickens and hardens the crust.

■ To prevent fruit or nuts from sinking to the bottom of bread or cake batter, shake them in a bag with a small amount of flour to dust lightly before adding to batter.

■ Heat a knife blade in hot water; dry off quickly for ease in slicing fresh bread. A wet knife does a smooth job cutting fresh cake.

■ To protect the natural flavor of whole wheat flour and ensure a long shelf life, store in a moisture-proof bag in the refrigerator or freezer.

■ The secret of good muffins is in the mixing. Combine all the dry ingredients in a bowl, and form a well in the center of the mixture. Add the liquid all at once and stir only enough to moisten the dry ingredients. The mixture will be lumpy, but further mixing will make the muffins tough.

■ If muffins are done ahead of serving time, loosen them from their cups, tilt slightly, and slide the pan back into the oven to stay warm. This keeps the muffins from steaming on the bottom.

Cake Tips

■ To keep cake layers from sticking in the pan, grease the bottom and sides of the pan and line the bottom with wax paper. (Trace outline of pan on wax paper and cut out.) Pour batter into pan and bake. Invert cake layer on a wire rack to cool; gently peel off wax paper while the cake is still warm.

■ When baking a layer cake, don't let pans touch each other or sides of oven; stagger their placement so that heat can circulate evenly around pans.

■ Make spice cupcakes from a white or yellow cake mix by adding ground spices, such as nutmeg, cinnamon, and cloves.

■ Do not grease pans for angel food and true sponge cakes. These batters need to cling to the side of the pan to reach their full height.

■ When preparing a sheet cake, cut enough servings for one meal; wrap and freeze the remainder. If cake is unfrosted, toppings or frostings can be varied with each serving.

■ Improvise a cake decorator: Fill a plastic sandwich bag with frosting, snip off a tiny corner, and squeeze out icing in swirls.

■ To keep the plate neat while frosting a cake, place three or four strips of wax paper over the edges of the plate. Position the cake on the plate, and fill and frost it; then carefully pull out and discard the wax paper strips.

■ For a fast topping on cakes, place a paper doily on top of cake; dust with powdered sugar. Carefully remove doily, and you'll have a pretty cake design.

Pastry Tips

■ Roll pie pastry on a lightly floured surface, but remember that too much flour toughens the crust. A stockinette rolling pin cover minimizes the amount of flour needed during rolling.

■ To prevent a soggy crust in custard pies or quiche, brush slightly beaten egg white on the uncooked pastry shell to seal it; bake at 425° for 5 to 10 minutes. Add desired filling, and bake according to the recipe directions.

■ Roll pastry lightly; keep in mind that too much handling will result in a tough crust.

■ Pans used for pastry never need greasing because the pastry shell or crumb crust will not stick to the sides of the pan.

■ To give the top crust of a pie a rich brown glaze, brush it lightly with milk before baking.

■ For an attractive pastry shell, brush the top with milk or slightly beaten egg white before baking. Sprinkle top of pastry with sugar for a special glaze.

■ If breads, cakes, or pies are browning too fast, put a piece of aluminum foil over the top and finish baking.

Cookie Tips

■ For perfectly shaped round cookies, pack homemade refrigerator cookie dough into clean 6-ounce juice cans (don't remove bottoms) and freeze dough. Thaw cookie dough about 15 minutes; then open bottom of can and push up, using the top edge as a cutting guide.

■ To shape cookies without rolling and cutting, roll dough into 1-inch balls and place on cookie sheet 2 inches apart; flatten each ball with bottom of glass dipped in sugar.

■ To loosen cake layers or cookies left in the pan too long, return to 350° oven for 2 minutes; remove the food from the pan immediately.

■ Quick-cooking oats, browned in a small amount of butter or margarine, make an economical substitute for chopped nuts in many kinds of cookie recipes.

■ Let cookies cool completely before storing. To keep cookies fresh, store soft and chewy ones in an airtight container, and crisp cookies in a jar with a loose-fitting lid.

Chocolate Tips

■ Use a vegetable peeler to make chocolate curls. Just pull the peeler firmly down the flat surface of a chocolate bar.

■ When melted, semisweet chocolate morsels and semisweet chocolate squares can be used interchangeably.

■ Three tablespoons unsweetened cocoa powder plus 1 tablespoon shortening may be substituted for each 1-ounce square unsweetened chocolate called for in a recipe.

■ Temperature, time, and stirring are important elements when melting chocolate. Chocolate will scorch at too high a temperature; heating too long and stirring too much will cause chocolate to separate into particles that will not melt and blend together.

■ Chocolate must be treated delicately. It should always be stored at a temperature under 75°. If a gray color develops, this is a sign that the cocoa butter has risen to the surface. Flavor and quality will not be lessened, and the gray color will disappear when the chocolate is melted.

Candy Tips

■ To ensure success when using the cold-water test in candy making, always pour the hot syrup into a fresh cup of cold water. Once the water has warmed from having hot syrup added, it's no longer cold enough for an accurate test.

■ Use odd pieces of candy to make a topping for ice cream. Plain chocolate, mints, or cream candies may be placed in top of a double boiler with a little cream and heated until well blended. Serve hot over ice cream or cake, or store in refrigerator and use later cold.

■ Make homemade candy from leftover cake frosting by mixing it with shredded coconut or chopped nuts. Shape into balls and place on wax paper to harden.

■ Avoid doubling a candy recipe. It is better to make a second batch.

■ When using a candy thermometer, make sure the thermometer bulb is in the boiling mixture but not touching the bottom of the pan.

It's Time To Serve Dinner

When many hostesses entertain, the question is not what to serve for dinner, but how to serve it. If you're planning a formal dinner for a small group, you'll probably want a service style more elegant than the family-style approach to which you may be accustomed. And when the crowd is large, arranging the food on plates in the kitchen and presenting them to guests may not be feasible.

So how do you know what type of service to choose? The answer is related to several factors you'll need to analyze. Keep in mind the formality of the menu and the number of courses involved, the number of people you'll be serving, the size and furnishing of your dining area, and whether or not you'll have someone to help you serve. Then pick between these four common types of service.

When the guest list is large, the simplest option is to set the food out for **buffet service** and let guests help themselves. Then they can scatter to the living and dining areas. Try to have a place for everyone to sit, if not on the sofa, then at card tables set up in appropriate places. When it's impossible to seat everyone, make sure the food is simple to eat; plan foods that require only a fork.

Arrange food, plates, napkins, and flatware on the buffet in logical serving order to help guests avoid backtracking. Place plates at the beginning of the line, but put flatware at the end so that your guests won't have to fumble with it as they serve themselves. Place food in logical order, too—main dish, vegetables, salad, bread, and condiments. If the main dish is to be served over rice, place the rice first. Salad dressings and sauces should be placed close to the dish they complement. Set dessert at the end of the buffet or on a serving cart for guests to help themselves after they complete the main meal. Offer beverages from a side table, or serve them from a tray after guests are seated.

The buffet style of serving is a casual and enjoyable way to entertain. Guests usually feel quite at home, and the hostess is freer to visit with guests than with other more complicated styles of service.

When you plan to seat everyone at the dining table, the **family style** of serving is the simplest, most informal approach, and is certainly appropriate for company when the menu is simple and the atmosphere is informal. For this option, the entire meal is placed on the dining table in separate dishes, and the food is served by everyone at the table. The person seated nearest the dish helps himself, and then passes the dish to the right. Offer the dish with the left hand, turning the handle of the dish toward the person receiving it.

The **English style** resembles the family-style method of serving, but is a little more formal. For this option, the food is served at the table by the host and hostess, and is passed by everyone at the table. The host serves the entrée from his seat, and passes each plate to the left toward the hostess, who serves the vegetables. She passes the plate to the left, until it stops at the guest seated to the right of the host. The passing of the plates continues until guests are served counterclockwise; the hostess keeps the last plate for herself. She takes a bite of food to signal for all to eat. If the party is large, however, she may suggest that guests begin eating as soon as they are served.

Another option is for the host to serve the meat as well as the vegetables from his seat, still passing the plates to the left.

The most formal style of serving is **plate service**, which involves all the plates being served in the kitchen and brought to individual diners by the host or hostess. No serving dishes are ever put on the table. The lady of honor on the host's right is always served first, and then others, moving to the left. The plate should always be served from the left, and removed from the right.

Plate service is convenient because there are no serving dishes to wash, and no individual garnishes are needed on serving platters. You might want to put an individual garnish on each plate, however, if the meal itself is not attractive enough to stand alone.

No matter which style of service is chosen, clear the table of all items related to the main meal prior to bringing out the dessert and dessert accessories. The styles for serving dessert are the same as for serving the main meal.

Wintertime Settings

Memories of a white Christmas come to mind when collections of crystal, silver, and gold are combined for a wintertime tablescape. Because collecting holiday ornaments and mementos has become part of the season, it is exciting displaying them as a centerpiece.

Combinations of silver, gold, and crystal establish a formal mood for table settings. Mirrors not only enhance the shine of crystal, the brightness of candlelight, and the sparkle of silver, but here they serve as a background and create a focal point. Shredded mylar adds to the icy, wintertime mood.

An open house for neighborhood friends is Susan Huff's inspiration for her tablescape. Susan and her daughter, Beth Jordan, love mixing their collections of crystal angels with silver Christmas ornaments and candlesticks. White tulips in a glass bubble vase balanced by 30-inch white tapers become the focal point of the table. The translucence of the shredded mylar with a splash of silver mylar ribbon add a wintery look to this tablescape.

Monica Ard, who enjoys having a beautiful table year round, sets up a dazzling gold and crystal tablescape. Guest or no guest, she always has the table beautifully set for the family's enjoyment. She also combines the glitter of gold with the softness of white candles and shredded mylar for a very artistic look.

Entertaining Tips

■ To keep appetizers appealingly hot—and you out of the kitchen—use your chafing dish and warming trays for serving.

■ When preparing finger sandwiches in advance, keep them from drying out by placing them in a shallow container lined with a damp towel and wax paper. Separate sandwich layers with wax paper, and cover with another layer of wax paper and a damp towel; store in refrigerator until ready to use.

■ For an unusual appetizer, wrap melon wedges or fresh figs with prosciutto (thinly sliced Italian ham) and serve with wooden picks.

■ When served as an appetizer course or midway through dinner, a refreshing sherbet cleans the palate so that the food that follows will taste its best.

■ Cut raw turnips into strips and serve as a snack or hors d'ouvre.

■ Keep celery fresh and crisp by wrapping in paper towels; place in a plastic bag in the refrigerator. The towels absorb any excess moisture.

■ Pull a sharp fork down the length of a cucumber before slicing it to give the slices a fancy look.

■ For an interesting change, use fresh pineapple, cantaloupe, or other shells as containers for dips and spreads. Pineapple halves scooped out are beautiful for serving cheese dips or salads. Other fruit shells, such as melon, are nice containers for salads or appetizers.

■ To retain white color of fresh mushrooms, slice just before using or dip in lemon juice.

■ To slice mushrooms quickly and uniformly, use an egg slicer.

■ To serve a congealed salad, invert the mold onto a serving dish; then wrap the mold with a hot towel. The salad will slip out easily.

■ Use canned, not fresh, pineapple in gelatin salads. A natural enzyme in the fresh fruit will prevent the gelatin from setting.

■ For salad success, be sure lettuce is cold, crisp, and dry. Tear, don't cut, lettuce into bite-size pieces. Add the dressing just before serving.

■ Add garlic flavor to salads by rubbing halved garlic cloves around the insides of the salad bowls.

■ Remember that salad greens should never be cut with a knife because it may discolor and bruise the leaves. Gently tearing the leaves is better and makes a prettier salad.

■ Be sure to save your celery leaves. The outer leaves can serve as seasonings in soups, stuffings, and other cooked dishes. The inner leaves add a nice flavor to tossed salads.

■ Add marinated vegetable salads to your next dinner party. They can be prepared in advance and chilled until serving time—an important bonus for the busy cook.

■ If you use a food processor or blender to chop dried fruit, freeze the fruit first. It will be less sticky and easier to chop.

■ Roll lemons, oranges, and grapefruit on a counter before cutting to soften; you will get more juice.

■ Whenever a recipe calls for both the rind and the juice of citrus fruit, wash and grate before juicing.

■ To easily remove the white membrane when peeling an orange, soak the unpeeled orange in boiling water for 5 minutes.

■ Save lemon and orange rinds. Store in the freezer, and grate as needed for pies, cakes, breads, and cookies. Or the rinds can be candied for holiday uses.

■ Bananas that have passed their prime are still useful. Remove and discard any brown portions, and puree the rest to make banana cake or banana bread.

■ Hull strawberries after washing so that they won't become mushy.

■ For a great dessert, pour cream sherry over chilled grapefruit.

■ Sometimes it's a good idea to serve frozen fruit with some ice crystals left in them; the texture will be firmer, more like the texture of fresh fruit.

■ To prepare kiwifruit, first chill the fruit; then peel and thinly slice crosswise for use in recipes or as an eye-catching garnish.

■ To spruce up your punch bowl, add whole fruit and a fruit-filled ice ring made from the same ingredients used in the punch.

■ Try a little calorie-free club soda in grape or apple juice to add a bubbly sparkle and to make the fruit juice calories go further.

■ The key to the best tasting coffee is buying fresh coffee beans and grinding them just before brewing.

Holiday Side Dishes To Save Time

Since turkey, dressing, and rolls usually occupy oven space during the holidays, this is a great time to use the microwave for side dishes. Even if you aren't cooking for company, these recipes are ideal timesavers.

As you cook for the holidays, take advantage of the microwave oven for small cooking tasks. You can use it to melt butter or chocolate, parboil vegetables, thaw packaged frozen foods, and to toast nuts, coconut, and breadcrumbs.

ORANGE-BAKED SWEET POTATOES

2 medium navel oranges
1 tablespoon butter or margarine
1½ tablespoons finely chopped pecans
1 (16-ounce) can cut sweet potatoes, drained and mashed
2 tablespoons brown sugar
3 tablespoons orange juice
½ teaspoon pumpkin pie spice
⅛ teaspoon salt

Cut oranges in half; clip membranes, carefully remove pulp, and chop. Set orange cups and ¼ cup pulp aside.

Place butter in a glass measure. Microwave at HIGH 35 seconds or until melted.

Spread pecans in a pieplate. Microwave at HIGH 2 minutes, stirring after 1 minute.

Combine sweet potatoes, reserved orange pulp, melted butter, pecans, brown sugar, and remaining ingredients; stir well. Spoon mixture into orange cups. Place cups on a pieplate, and cover with wax paper. Microwave at HIGH 5 minutes. Yield: 4 servings.

ASPARAGUS-PEA CASSEROLE

1 (10-ounce) package frozen asparagus, thawed
2 hard-cooked eggs, sliced
1 (17-ounce) can English peas, drained
6 (¾-ounce) slices process American cheese, cut in half diagonally
1 (10¾-ounce) can cream of mushroom soup, undiluted
¼ cup commercial sour cream
¼ teaspoon onion powder
¼ teaspoon white pepper
2 tablespoons butter or margarine
¼ cup dry breadcrumbs

Cut asparagus into 2-inch pieces. If desired, set aside 6 asparagus pieces and 3 egg slices for garnish.

Layer half each of peas and remaining asparagus in a lightly greased 8-inch square dish. Top with remaining egg slices and half of cheese.

Combine mushroom soup, sour cream, onion powder, and pepper, stirring well. Spoon half of soup mixture over cheese. Layer remaining asparagus, peas, and soup mixture.

Place butter in a custard cup, and microwave at HIGH 30 to 45 seconds or until butter melts; add breadcrumbs, stirring well. Sprinkle crumb mixture over asparagus and peas. Microwave at HIGH 10 minutes or until thoroughly heated, giving dish a half-turn after 5 minutes.

Top with remaining cheese slices, and, if desired, garnish with reserved asparagus and egg slices. Cover with aluminum foil, and let stand 5 minutes or until cheese melts. Yield: 6 to 8 servings.

POTATOES WITH HOT BACON DRESSING

4 slices bacon
4 medium potatoes (about 2 pounds)
Vegetable cooking spray
¼ cup red wine vinegar
2 tablespoons olive oil or vegetable oil
2 tablespoons chili sauce
½ teaspoon dry mustard
¼ teaspoon seasoned salt

Place bacon on rack in a 12- x 8- x 2-inch baking dish; cover with paper towels. Microwave at HIGH 3½ to 4 minutes; remove bacon, reserving 2 tablespoons drippings. Crumble bacon, and set aside.

Wash potatoes; pat dry. Cut each potato lengthwise into ¼-inch slices, cutting to 1 inch of end of potato. (The cut potato should resemble a fan.) Place potatoes in a 12- x 8- x 2-inch baking dish, arranging the uncut ends toward the outside; lightly coat potatoes with vegetable cooking spray. Cover with heavy-duty plastic wrap; fold back a small edge of wrap to allow steam to escape. Microwave at HIGH 10 to 12 minutes, turning potatoes once. Let stand 5 minutes.

Combine reserved bacon drippings, vinegar, and remaining ingredients in a 2-cup glass measure, mixing well. Microwave at HIGH 1 to 2 minutes; stir. Pour dressing evenly over potatoes, and sprinkle with crumbled bacon. Yield: 4 servings.

CURRIED PEAS WITH ALMONDS

¼ cup sliced almonds
2 (16-ounce) packages frozen English peas, thawed
3 tablespoons water
½ teaspoon garlic salt
1 tablespoon butter or margarine
1 tablespoon all-purpose flour
½ teaspoon curry powder
½ cup milk
½ teaspoon lemon juice
Dash of salt
Dash of white pepper

Spread almonds evenly in a pieplate; microwave at HIGH 3 minutes, stirring once. Set aside.

Combine peas and water in a 2-quart casserole. Cover tightly with heavy-duty plastic wrap; fold back a small edge of wrap to allow steam to escape. Microwave at HIGH 8 to 10 minutes or until peas are tender, stirring at 4-minute intervals; drain. Add garlic salt, stirring well. Set peas aside.

Place butter in a 2-cup glass measure. Microwave at HIGH 35 seconds or until melted. Add flour and curry powder, stirring until smooth. Gradually add milk, stirring well. Microwave at HIGH 1½ minutes or until thickened and bubbly, stirring once. Stir in lemon juice, salt, and white pepper.

Add curry sauce to peas; stir in almonds. Cover and microwave at HIGH 2 to 3 minutes or until thoroughly heated. Yield: 6 servings.

BEETS WITH SOUR CREAM DRESSING

2½ pounds fresh beets
½ cup water
1 tablespoon butter or margarine
1 tablespoon all-purpose flour
2 tablespoons sugar
⅛ teaspoon salt
1 tablespoon white vinegar
¼ cup commercial sour cream

Trim beets, leaving 1 to 2 inches of tops; scrub well with vegetable brush. Combine beets and water in a 2-quart casserole. Cover and microwave at HIGH 16 to 18 minutes or just until tender. Drain and cool to touch. Trim off beet tops, and rub off skins. Cut beets into ½-inch cubes.

Place butter in a 1-quart casserole; microwave at HIGH 35 seconds. Stir in flour, sugar, salt, and vinegar, mixing well. Add beets, and microwave at HIGH 1 to 2 minutes. Stir in sour cream, and microwave at HIGH 1 minute. Yield: 4 to 6 servings.

Gwen Louer
Roswell, Georgia

FRUIT MÉLANGE

1 (10-ounce) jar orange marmalade
⅓ cup water
¼ cup orange-flavored liqueur
1 (20-ounce) can pineapple chunks, drained
1 (17-ounce) can apricot halves, drained
1 (6-ounce) jar maraschino cherries, drained
1 cup pitted prunes
½ cup flaked coconut

Combine first 3 ingredients in a 2-quart baking dish; stir well. Add pineapple chunks and remaining ingredients, stirring well. Microwave at MEDIUM HIGH (70% power) 8 to 9 minutes or until thoroughly heated, stirring after 4 minutes. Serve immediately. Yield: 8 servings.

Barbara Moore
Tulsa, Oklahoma

Sausage Spices These Dishes

Don't limit sausage to the breakfast menu. Mild or spicy, link or bulk, this popular meat mixture makes tasty offerings for any time of day.

SAUSAGE CRÊPES

1 pound bulk pork sausage
1 (3-ounce) package cream cheese, softened
½ cup (2 ounces) shredded process American cheese
¾ cup commercial sour cream
¼ teaspoon dried whole marjoram, crushed
1 tablespoon milk
Crêpes (recipe follows)
¼ cup commercial sour cream
¼ cup butter or margarine, softened

Cook sausage in a large skillet until browned, stirring to crumble meat; drain. Remove from heat. Stir in next 5 ingredients. Spoon 2 tablespoons sausage mixture down center of each crêpe, and roll up tightly; place crêpes, seam side down, in a lightly greased 13- x 9- x 2-inch baking dish. Cover and bake at 375° for 10 minutes. Combine ¼ cup sour cream and butter. Spread evenly on crêpes. Cover and bake at 375° for 5 minutes or until crêpes are thoroughly heated. Yield: 8 servings.

Crêpes

1 cup all-purpose flour
¼ teaspoon salt
1 cup milk
3 eggs
1 tablespoon vegetable oil

Combine flour, salt, and milk, beating at medium speed of an electric mixer until smooth. Add eggs and 1 tablespoon oil; beat well.

Brush bottom of a 6-inch crêpe pan or heavy skillet with oil; place pan over medium heat just until hot, but not smoking.

Pour 2 tablespoons batter into pan; quickly tilt pan in all directions so that batter covers pan with a thin film. Cook about 1 minute.

Lift edge of crêpe to test for doneness. Crêpe is ready for flipping when it can be shaken loose from pan. Flip crêpe, and cook 30 seconds on other side. (This side is usually spotty brown and is the side on which the filling is placed.)

Place crêpes on a towel, and allow to cool. Repeat until all batter is used. Stack crêpes between layers of wax paper to prevent sticking. Yield: 16 (6-inch) crêpes. *Anna J. Beyer*
Springfield, Virginia

Tip: *Check foods closely as you are shopping to be sure they are not spoiled. Do not buy cans that are badly dented, leaking, or bulging at the ends. Do not select packages which have broken seals.*

HEARTY PINTOS AND SAUSAGE

1 (32-ounce) package dried pinto
  beans
3 smoked ham hocks (about 1.7
  pounds)
1 large onion, chopped
1 clove garlic, minced
3 tablespoons hot Mexican-style
  chili powder
2 teaspoons salt
1 teaspoon ground cumin
½ teaspoon dried whole oregano
3½ quarts water
1 pound fresh chorizo

Sort and wash beans; place in a large
Dutch oven. Cover with water 2
inches above beans; soak 8 hours.
Drain well.

Combine pinto beans and next 8
ingredients in a kettle. Bring mixture
to a boil; cover, reduce heat, and
simmer 2 hours.

Remove casing from sausage, and
cut sausage into small pieces. Stir
sausage into beans; cover and cook 1
hour. Serve with cornbread or tortillas. Yield: 5½ quarts. *Cal Lowry*
Big Spring, Texas

SWEET-AND-SOUR SAUSAGE

1 (12-ounce) package
  brown-and-serve link sausage,
  cut in half crosswise
¾ cup sugar
½ cup vinegar
½ cup water
1 tablespoon chopped green
  pepper
1 tablespoon diced pimiento
1 tablespoon cornstarch
1 tablespoon water
1 teaspoon paprika

Cook sausage in a heavy skillet until
browned, turning often; drain on
paper towels, and set aside.

Combine sugar and next 4 ingredients in a medium saucepan; stir
well. Bring to a boil; reduce heat,
and simmer 5 minutes. Combine
cornstarch and 1 tablespoon water;
stir well. Stir into vinegar mixture;

cook over medium heat, stirring constantly, until smooth and thickened.
Add paprika and sausage; cook over
medium heat, stirring constantly,
until thoroughly heated. Yield: 6 to 8
appetizer servings.

Patricia Andrews
McAlester, Oklahoma

Team Carrots And Potatoes

Who would think of making a pot
roast, vegetable soup, or chicken pot
pie without carrots and potatoes?
These staples are served together in
more than just these traditional favorites as our recipes here reveal.

BEEF ROAST POT PIE

4 medium potatoes, peeled and
  diced
4 carrots, scraped and diced
1 onion, chopped
1 (10½-ounce) can beef broth,
  diluted
3 tablespoons all-purpose flour
½ cup water
3 cups diced cooked roast beef
1 (10-ounce) package frozen
  English peas, thawed
¾ cup all-purpose flour
¾ cup cornmeal
1½ teaspoons baking powder
½ teaspoon salt
1 egg
¾ cup milk
3 tablespoons vegetable oil

Combine first 4 ingredients in a
Dutch oven. Bring to a boil; cover,
reduce heat, and simmer 10 minutes.

Combine 3 tablespoons flour and
water; stir into vegetable mixture,
and cook until thickened (about 2
minutes). Add roast beef and English
peas. Pour mixture into a deep 4-
quart casserole.

Combine ¾ cup flour, cornmeal,
baking powder, and salt. Combine
egg, milk, and oil; add to flour mixture, stirring well. Spoon batter over
vegetable mixture. Bake at 350° for
35 minutes or until cornbread topping
is lightly browned. Yield: 6 to 8
servings. *Mrs. D. S. Wilson*
Tyler, Texas

VEGETABLE-BEEF SOUP

2 beef soup bones
8 cups water
1½ pounds beef for stewing, cut
  into 1-inch cubes
1½ teaspoons salt
1 teaspoon pepper
4 medium potatoes, cubed
4 medium carrots, cubed
2 medium onions, coarsely
  chopped
2 (8-ounce) cans tomato sauce
1 small hot red pepper
½ small cabbage, coarsely
  chopped
1 (17-ounce) can whole kernel
  corn, drained
1 (15-ounce) can English peas,
  drained

Combine soup bones and water in a
large Dutch oven; bring to a boil.
Cover, reduce heat, and simmer 1
hour. Add beef cubes, salt, and pepper; cover and simmer 1 hour. Add
cubed potatoes and next 5 ingredients; cover and simmer 40 minutes. Add corn and peas; simmer,
uncovered, 30 minutes. Yield: about
4½ quarts. *Camilla Dawson*
Madisonville, Kentucky

Tip: *Remember that the darker the
orange color of carrots, the greater
the content of vitamin A.*

PORK CHOPS AND GARDEN VEGETABLES

2 (1-inch-thick) pork chops
1 tablespoon butter or margarine, melted
1 carrot, cut into ½-inch slices
½ cup fresh green beans, cut into 1-inch pieces
1 small potato, peeled and cut into ½-inch cubes
¼ teaspoon dried whole basil
2 (.25-ounce) envelopes instant onion soup mix
⅔ cup water

Brown pork chops on both sides in butter in a large skillet; drain. Add carrot and next 3 ingredients. Combine dry soup mix and water, mixing well. Pour over chops and vegetables. Bring to a boil; cover, reduce heat, and simmer 45 minutes or until chops are tender. Yield: 2 servings.

Mrs. Homer Baxter
Charleston, West Virginia

VEGETABLE PANCAKES

3 tablespoons all-purpose flour
½ teaspoon salt
½ teaspoon poultry seasoning
Dash of red pepper
2 eggs, slightly beaten
⅛ teaspoon Worcestershire sauce
¼ cup diced onion
¼ cup diced sweet red pepper
½ cup shredded carrot
1 cup shredded yellow squash
1 cup shredded potato
½ cup commercial sour cream
1 tablespoon Dijon mustard

Combine first 6 ingredients in a medium bowl; stir well. Stir in onion, diced red pepper, carrot, squash, and potato. For each pancake, spoon about ¼ cup vegetable mixture onto a hot, lightly greased griddle or skillet; turn when edges are browned.

Combine sour cream and mustard in a small bowl; stir well. Serve pancakes immediately with sour cream sauce. Yield: 10 (4-inch) pancakes.

Mary K. B. Quesenberry
Dugspur, Virginia

POTATO-CARROT SOUP

2 medium potatoes, peeled and thinly sliced (about 1 pound)
2 small carrots, scraped and thinly sliced
1 small onion, thinly sliced
3 cups chicken broth
1 cup milk
¼ teaspoon pepper

Combine first 4 ingredients in a Dutch oven; bring to a boil. Cover, reduce heat, and simmer 10 minutes or until vegetables are tender. Spoon mixture into container of an electric blender, and process until smooth.

Return potato mixture to Dutch oven; stir in milk and pepper. Cook over low heat, stirring constantly, until soup is thoroughly heated. Yield: 6 cups.

Miss C. A. Pierce
Greensburg, Kentucky

Tangy Lemon Flavors This Pie

Ruthell Littleton of Devine, Texas, has been making her Buttermilk-Lemon Pie for nearly 30 years. The recipe, which makes two 9-inch pies, is often requested by her friends and family for large get-togethers.

Cornstarch thickens the pie filling; to avoid lumps be sure to mix it with the sugar before adding the buttermilk. Freshly squeezed lemon juice and rind added at the end of cooking give Buttermilk-Lemon Pie a fresh lemon flavor that's hard to beat.

BUTTERMILK-LEMON PIE

2 cups sugar
¼ cup plus 3 tablespoons cornstarch
5 cups buttermilk
1 (3-ounce) package cream cheese, softened
7 eggs, separated
2 teaspoons grated lemon rind
¼ cup lemon juice
2 tablespoons butter or margarine
1 teaspoon lemon extract
2 baked 9-inch pastry shells
¾ teaspoon cream of tartar
¼ cup plus 3 tablespoons powdered sugar
¼ teaspoon lemon extract

Combine 2 cups sugar and cornstarch in a heavy saucepan; gradually add buttermilk, stirring until blended. Add cream cheese and cook over medium heat, stirring constantly, until mixture thickens and comes to a boil. Boil 1 minute.

Beat egg yolks until thick and lemon colored. Gradually stir about one-fourth of hot mixture into yolks; add to remaining hot mixture, stirring constantly. Cook over medium heat, stirring constantly, 2 to 3 minutes. Remove from heat; stir in lemon rind, lemon juice, butter, and 1 teaspoon lemon extract. Spoon into pastry shells.

Beat egg whites (at room temperature) and cream of tartar at high speed of an electric mixer 1 minute. Gradually add powdered sugar, 1 tablespoon at a time, beating until stiff peaks form. Beat in lemon extract. Spread meringue over hot filling, sealing to edge. Bake at 350° for 12 to 15 minutes or until browned. Yield: two 9-inch pies.

Gourmet Chicken Pie

"It's the best chicken pie my wife and I have ever had," boasts Joe Korwin of Macon, Georgia, about the Deluxe Chicken Pie he created. At first glance of the long ingredient list, you may search for an easier recipe, but we promise this pie is worth your time. A blend of eight herbs and spices as well as three cheeses and sour cream distinguish the soup-based sauce.

DELUXE CHICKEN PIE

6 boneless chicken breast halves, skinned and cut into 1-inch pieces
1 medium onion, chopped
2 tablespoons butter or margarine, melted
4 fresh mushrooms, sliced
2 large carrots, cut into thin 1-inch strips
1 stalk celery, chopped
1 cup chicken broth
⅓ cup dry white wine
¼ teaspoon parsley flakes
¼ teaspoon chopped chives
¼ teaspoon dry mustard
⅛ teaspoon garlic powder
⅛ teaspoon chervil leaves
⅛ teaspoon white pepper
⅛ teaspoon freshly ground black pepper
1 tablespoon Worcestershire sauce
1 bay leaf
1 tablespoon plus 1 teaspoon cornstarch
2 tablespoons water
1 (10¾-ounce) can cream of mushroom soup, undiluted
½ cup commercial sour cream
½ cup (2 ounces) shredded Swiss cheese
½ cup (2 ounces) shredded mild or sharp Cheddar cheese
2 tablespoons grated Parmesan cheese
Pastry for double-crust pie

Sauté chicken and onion in butter in a large skillet 5 minutes. Add sliced mushrooms and next 13 ingredients; cover and simmer 10 minutes. Remove bay leaf.

Combine cornstarch and water, stirring until blended; stir into chicken mixture, and cook over medium heat, stirring constantly, until mixture comes to a boil. Remove from heat, and stir in soup, sour cream, and cheeses.

Roll half of pastry to ⅛-inch thickness on a lightly floured surface. Fit into a 2½-quart shallow casserole. Spoon chicken mixture into prepared pastry.

Roll remaining pastry to ⅛-inch thickness on a lightly floured surface. Cut half of pastry into ½-inch strips, using a fluted pastry wheel.

Moisten edge of pastry in pieplate. Arrange strips in lattice design over chicken filling. Trim edges and seal. Make leaf cutouts with remaining pastry. Place leaves on edge of pastry. Bake at 400° for 30 to 40 minutes or until lightly browned. Yield: 6 servings.

Served Like Deli Fare

Knowing how much Mary Peterson of Batesville, Mississippi, loves corned beef, her mother suggested she try Reuben Buns. Mary did, and now she serves these delicious stuffed buns for parties. Guests break them open and spread them with additional mustard.

The buns freeze nicely, making them perfect for a make-ahead meal. A green salad or coleslaw, pickles, and chips make delicious accompaniments. For a fun delicatessen-style supper, set your table with a checked cloth, and serve the meal in individual burger baskets.

REUBEN BUNS

1½ cups all-purpose flour, divided
1 cup rye flour
1 package dry yeast
½ teaspoon caraway seeds
1 cup milk
¼ cup vegetable oil
2 tablespoons sugar
½ teaspoon salt
1 egg, beaten
1 (12-ounce) can corned beef
1 (8-ounce) can chopped sauerkraut, drained well
2 tablespoons horseradish mustard
3 (1-ounce) slices Swiss cheese, cut into 4 triangles each
Additional horseradish mustard (optional)

Combine ½ cup all-purpose flour, rye flour, yeast, and caraway seeds in a large mixing bowl; set aside.

Combine milk, oil, sugar, salt, and egg in a heavy saucepan; stir well. Cook over medium heat, stirring constantly, until warm (115° to 120°). Remove from heat. Pour into dry ingredients; beat at slow speed of electric mixer 3 minutes, scraping sides of bowl as needed. Beat at high speed 3 minutes. Stir in remaining 1 cup flour to make a soft dough. Cover and chill 1 hour.

Combine corned beef, sauerkraut, and 2 tablespoons horseradish mustard; divide into 12 equal portions. Shape each portion into a ball, and set aside.

Divide dough evenly, and spoon into 12 lightly greased muffin cups. With floured fingers, make an indentation in the center of each; place a corned beef ball in each indentation. Cover and let rise in a warm place (85°), free from drafts, 20 minutes. Bake at 375° for 25 to 30 minutes. Top each bun with a cheese triangle; bake 2 to 3 minutes or until cheese melts. Serve buns with additional horseradish mustard, if desired. Yield: 1 dozen.

Note: To freeze, prepare and bake buns as directed; let cool. Wrap in aluminum foil. To serve, let thaw; reheat buns in aluminum foil at 350° for 10 to 15 minutes.

A Menu For Company

When Terry Paulson of Little Rock, Arkansas, has guests for dinner, she often serves Cheesy Lasagna, Spinach Salad, and Easy French Bread. It's a menu that can be prepared ahead and most of the cleanup is done well before guests arrive.

Terry's family especially enjoys leftover Cheesy Lasagna. Four kinds of cheese, artichoke hearts, mushrooms, and ripe olives make it extra special. And its flavor seems to improve with age.

Cheesy Lasagna
Spinach Salad
Easy French Bread

CHEESY LASAGNA

1½ pounds ground beef
1 cup chopped onion
1 cup chopped green pepper
1 (28-ounce) can tomatoes, undrained and chopped
3 (8-ounce) cans tomato sauce
½ teaspoon garlic powder
1 tablespoon dried whole basil
2 tablespoons dried whole oregano
½ teaspoon seasoned salt
4 bay leaves
½ pound fresh mushrooms, sliced
2 tablespoons butter or margarine, melted
9 lasagna noodles
1 egg, beaten
2 cups cottage cheese
2 cups (8 ounces) mozzarella cheese, shredded
1 (14-ounce) can artichoke hearts, drained and quartered
1 (6-ounce) can pitted ripe olives, drained and sliced
1 cup (4 ounces) Swiss cheese, shredded
½ cup grated Parmesan cheese

Cook ground beef, onion, and green pepper in a large Dutch oven until meat is browned, stirring to crumble meat; drain. Stir in tomatoes and next 6 ingredients; reduce heat, and simmer 1 hour or until sauce thickens, stirring occasionally. Remove bay leaves.

Sauté mushrooms in butter; drain. Set aside. Cook lasagna noodles according to package directions; drain. Set aside. Combine egg and cottage cheese, mixing well; set aside.

Spread one-third of sauce in a lightly greased 13- x 9- x 2-inch baking dish. Arrange 3 lasagna noodles on sauce. Layer 1 cup mozzarella cheese and cottage cheese mixture over noodles. Top with 3 lasagna noodles. Spoon one-third of sauce over noodles. Layer mushrooms, artichoke hearts, and ripe olives over sauce. Arrange 3 lasagna noodles over olives, and layer Swiss cheese, remaining mozzarella, and sauce in dish. Cover and bake at 350° for 45 minutes; uncover. Sprinkle with Parmesan cheese, and bake an additional 10 to 15 minutes. Let stand 15 minutes before serving. Yield: 8 to 10 servings.

SPINACH SALAD

1 pound fresh spinach
5 leaves iceberg lettuce
3 green onions, chopped
2 stalks celery, sliced
¼ pound fresh mushrooms, sliced
1 hard-cooked egg, sliced
1 large tomato, cut into wedges
1 cup commercial oil-and-vinegar dressing
1 cup commercial herb-seasoned croutons

Tear spinach and lettuce into bite-size pieces in a large bowl; add green onions and next 4 ingredients. Toss spinach mixture with salad dressing, and sprinkle with croutons before serving. Yield: 8 to 10 servings.

EASY FRENCH BREAD

1 package rapid rise yeast
1 cup warm water (105° to 115°)
4 cups bread flour
1 tablespoon sugar
1 teaspoon salt
⅔ to 1 cup warm water (105° to 115°)
2 tablespoons butter or margarine, melted

Dissolve yeast in 1 cup warm water in a small bowl; let stand 5 minutes.

Combine flour, sugar, and salt in a large mixing bowl. Stir in yeast and enough remaining water to make a soft dough. Cover and let rise in a warm place (85°), free from drafts, 30 minutes or until doubled in bulk.

Turn dough out onto a heavily floured surface; knead until smooth and elastic (about 5 minutes). Divide dough in half. Shape each half into an oval on a heavily floured surface. Fold over lengthwise, and flatten with open hand. Fold it again, and roll with palms of hands to a 15- x 2-inch loaf. Twist and place loaves in greased French bread pans. Brush with butter. Cover and let rise in a warm place (85°), free from drafts, about 30 minutes or until doubled in bulk. Bake at 400° for 40 minutes or until loaves sound hollow when tapped. Yield: 2 loaves.

Garlic Bread: Slice French bread into 1-inch slices. Combine 6 tablespoons softened butter, ¼ to ½ teaspoon garlic salt, and 1½ tablespoons grated Parmesan cheese; spread butter mixture between bread slices. Wrap loaf in aluminum foil, and bake at 350° for 10 minutes or until thoroughly heated. Yield: enough spread for 2 loaves.

From Our Kitchen To Yours

Celebrate the season by setting your table in the tradition of gracious entertaining. Beautiful silver, sparkling crystal, and elegant china create an inviting dining atmosphere. If you follow these simple guidelines, caring for prized possessions will be easier than ever before.

Silver

Whether recently purchased or inherited from a great-grandmother, fine sterling and silverplated tableware and hollowware require particular care. Tarnish is caused by the reaction of silver with oxygen and pollutants in the air. Contact with any form of rubber and the reaction of sulfur in the air with eggs, mayonnaise, and mustard, also tarnish silver. Moist salt causes spots and corrosion.

To properly clean silver, wash or rinse soon after use; soaking silver in water several hours will eventually dull the finish and loosen knife handles. You can wash silver by hand or in the dishwasher. Preferably handwash in hot water using a mild nonabrasive detergent and a soft sponge; rinse the pieces in hot water. (Do not use rubber dishpans.) To avoid spotting and pitting, dry thoroughly; do not place silver on a rubber mat or drainer. If you choose to use an automatic dishwasher, follow the manufacturer's directions, and use the brand of washing and rinsing products specified. Many automatic dishwashing detergents contain bleaching agents, which remove the oxidation that highlights ornate patterns. Load silverware in the dishwasher with handles down and spread pieces out to prevent nesting and scratching. For best results, remove silver from the dishwasher before the drying cycle begins, and hand dry. If the drying cycle has been completed, buffing with a towel is necessary.

Clean tarnished spots as soon as possible. Use a silver cleaner that is nonabrasive and strong enough to remove tarnish but gentle to silver. Chemical dips may leave a dull, flat finish but can be used to clean discolored fork tines. For hard-to-reach areas, a soft bristle brush is helpful. Polish with a clean, soft cloth using long, lengthwise strokes following the silver's contour. Never lacquer or plastic-coat silver; lacquer eventually causes darkening and unattractive flaking and chipping. Be sure to have any damaged silver pieces repaired by an expert.

Proper storage protects silver from scratches and air. To keep silver shiny, use special chests with tarnish-proof linings or line drawers and cabinets with anti-tarnish cloth. Store hollowware in anti-tarnish cloth bags, cotton flannel bags, or flannel-lined cabinets. (Do not use white flannel because sulfur is sometimes used in the bleaching process.) Never wrap silver directly in plastic or use rubberbands as closures. When stacking silver, place something soft between pieces.

Crystal

Careful handling will maintain crystal's value and beauty for generations. When properly washed and stored, crystal is quite durable. Hand-washing is recommended for crystal stemware, particularly gold- or platinum-trimmed crystal. To prevent chipping and breakage, use a plastic dishpan, or line the bottom of the sink with a rubber mat or towel. A rubber nozzle will also help prevent breakage. Remove rings and bracelets to avoid scratching, and wash one piece at a time. Undecorated and thicker crystal may be washed in your dishwasher. When loading, leave adequate room between stemware, and secure pieces between the cushioned prongs in the top rack, making sure the long stems don't interfere with the upper wash arm. Both automatic and hand dishwashing detergents are safe for most crystal. However, etching, a cloudy white film, occurs when dishwasher detergents and softened water come in contact with certain types of glassware. This condition is permanent; therefore, you might choose to wash fine glassware by hand. But whether it's washed by hand or in the dishwasher, dry each piece thoroughly, using a soft, lint-free towel.

Always store crystal stemware right side up to eliminate undue pressure on the rim. Leave a slight space between glasses to prevent rims and edges from scratching each other. For added protection, line shelves with a soft cloth, and check periodically for signs of discoloration or cloudiness. To prevent this hazing condition, keep crystal from moisture and don't store in newspaper, excelsior, or other moisture-absorbing materials. If signs of hazing appear, rub the glass with lemon, or wash immediately in vinegar. If you cannot remove the discoloration, take the crystal to a professional for an acid bath. If your crystal is accidentally chipped on an edge, repair it promptly to prevent further chipping or cracks. If the chip is small, try using an emery board; otherwise, seek professional help for grinding.

Because water temperatures above 130° or drastic temperature changes may cause crystal to crack, never place ice-cold glasses in hot water. Do not burn candles closer than 1 inch from the top of crystal candlesticks because the heat from flames may burst the crystal.

To remove stains from glass bowls, vases, and decanters, soak 8 hours in a solution of ammonia or chlorine bleach and water, or soak 15 minutes in water in which you've dissolved a denture-cleaning tablet. Remove white rings (mineral deposits) inside a vase by adding a water softener to the water. Soak a decanter in a vinegar-and-water solution to dissolve wine sediment; a small amount of sand or uncooked rice swished in the decanter acts as a mild abrasive.

China

Fine china is durable, tremendously versatile, and brings continuous pleasure over the years. Careful handling will not mar its patina or age its looks. Hand-washing is preferred, but many manufacturers agree that most fine china can be washed in the dishwasher. Hand painting and other over-the-glaze decorations cannot withstand intense heat and should be hand-washed. Special china-crystal cycles on automatic dishwashers usually consist of one wash, two rinses, and one dry cycle. If your dishwasher doesn't have a special setting for china, a short or light wash can be substituted. When loading the dishwasher, alternate plates of various sizes to avoid scratching and chipping.

Fine china should be stored as carefully as crystal. Line shelves to provide cushioning, and leave room for easy placement in and out of cabinets. Separate stacked plates with napkins or paper towels, and never stack more than two cups.

When a metal object scrapes across the surface, black or gray marks often appear on dinnerware, and washing usually won't remove it. Try gently rubbing the mark with a mildly abrasive household cleanser.

Entrées That Cook Quick

If the holidays have you scurrying around with only minutes between your arrival home and hunger pangs, try one of these quick entrées. They can be prepared from start to finish in about 30 minutes.

STIR-FRIED BEEF AND VEGETABLES

¾ pound boneless top round steak, trimmed
¼ cup soy sauce
2 tablespoons dry sherry
½ teaspoon ground ginger
⅛ teaspoon garlic powder
1 tablespoon cornstarch
2 tablespoons vegetable oil
2 (10-ounce) packages frozen Chinese-style vegetables
1 (16-ounce) can bean sprouts, drained
Hot cooked rice

Partially freeze steak; slice diagonally across grain into 2- x ½-inch strips.

Combine soy sauce and next 4 ingredients in a bowl; set aside.

Pour oil into wok or heavy skillet; heat at medium high (325°) for 1 minute. Add steak, and stir-fry 5 minutes or until browned; remove from wok. Add vegetables and sauce packet; stir-fry until vegetables are crisp-tender. Add soy sauce mixture, and stir-fry until thickened and bubbly. Add beef and bean sprouts, and stir-fry until thoroughly heated. Serve immediately over rice. Yield: 4 servings.
Thayer Wilson
Augusta, Georgia

CRANBERRY BROILED HAM

1 (8-ounce) can jellied cranberry sauce
2½ tablespoons commercial steak sauce
1½ teaspoons brown sugar
1½ teaspoons vegetable oil
1 teaspoon prepared mustard
1 (1-inch-thick) fully cooked ham slice (about 2 pounds)

Combine first 5 ingredients; stir well. Trim excess fat from ham slice. Place ham in a lightly greased 13- x 9- x 2-inch pan; broil 5 to 6 inches from heat 15 minutes. Turn ham, and spoon cranberry sauce mixture on top. Broil 15 minutes. Yield: 6 to 8 servings.
Velma P. Kestner
Berwind, West Virginia

APRICOT CHICKEN BREASTS

6 chicken breast halves, skinned and boned
¼ cup apricot preserves
¼ cup commercial Russian salad dressing
2 tablespoons white wine
½ teaspoon ground coriander
⅛ teaspoon salt
⅛ teaspoon pepper

Place chicken in a lightly greased 12- x 8- x 2-inch baking dish. Combine preserves and remaining ingredients; pour evenly over chicken. Bake, uncovered, at 350° for 30 minutes or until done. Yield: 6 servings.
Mrs. E. R. Lovell
Jackson, Mississippi

QUICK SCAMPI

1 pound unpeeled medium-size fresh shrimp
¼ cup butter or margarine, melted
1 tablespoon sliced green onions
1 to 2 cloves garlic, minced
1 tablespoon lemon juice
Dash of salt
½ teaspoon grated lemon rind
2 tablespoons minced parsley
¼ teaspoon hot sauce
Lemon slice (optional)
Fresh parsley sprig (optional)

Peel and devein shrimp; set aside. Combine butter and next 4 ingredients in a large skillet; heat until bubbly. Reduce heat to medium; add shrimp. Cook, stirring frequently, about 5 minutes or until shrimp turn pink. Add lemon rind, minced parsley, and hot sauce; toss lightly. If desired, garnish with lemon and parsley; serve immediately. Yield: 2 servings.
Shirley B. Hilliker
Merritt Island, Florida

A Showy Pasta Salad

Fresh seafood and tender pasta—what a winning combination. Make this salad when you're on your final visit to the beach, or simply savor it at home.

SHRIMP-PASTA MEDLEY

5 cups water
1½ pounds unpeeled medium-size fresh shrimp
1 cup rotelle
1 (6-ounce) package frozen snow pea pods, thawed
1 (4-ounce) can button mushrooms, drained
⅓ to ½ cup grated Parmesan cheese
¼ cup sliced celery
¼ cup sliced pimiento-stuffed olives
¼ cup sliced ripe olives
1 teaspoon chopped parsley
1 teaspoon white wine
¼ teaspoon anise flavoring
1 (8-ounce) bottle Italian salad dressing
Lettuce leaves
6 cherry tomatoes, halved
Grated Parmesan cheese (optional)

Bring water to a boil; add shrimp, and cook 3 to 5 minutes. Drain well, and rinse with cold water. Chill. Peel and devein shrimp.

Cook rotelle according to package directions, omitting salt; drain. Rinse with cold water; drain. Combine with snow peas and next 9 ingredients, tossing well; chill at least 1 hour. Spoon onto a lettuce-lined platter. Garnish with tomatoes, and, if desired, sprinkle with Parmesan cheese. Yield: 6 servings.

Marlene M. Rosenkoetter
Wilmington, North Carolina

Tip: *Adding 1 or 2 tablespoons of vegetable oil to the cooking water keeps pasta separated.*

Serve Pasta On The Side

Use only the freshest ingredients—garden ripe tomatoes, a hearty hunk of cheese, and fresh pasta—to make Spinach Tortellini With Tomato Sauce, an appealing side dish. Lisa Grable Wallace of Raleigh, North Carolina, relies on a combination of vibrant flavors to lend Italian zest.

The dish is easy to make and is sure to be a popular addition to many meals. One menu might include the tortellini, grilled chicken or flank steak, a slice of Italian bread, and a green salad.

SPINACH TORTELLINI WITH TOMATO SAUCE

1 (9-ounce) package fresh spinach tortellini
2 cloves garlic, minced
2 tablespoons chopped onion
2 tablespoons olive oil
½ green pepper, chopped
1 hot pepper, seeded and chopped
2 large tomatoes, peeled and chopped
½ teaspoon dried whole oregano
½ teaspoon dried whole basil
½ cup freshly grated Parmesan cheese

Cook spinach tortellini according to package directions; drain. Spoon onto platter.

Sauté garlic and onion in olive oil 3 minutes or until crisp tender. Add peppers, and cook 1 minute. Add tomato, oregano, and basil. Cook 3 minutes, stirring constantly. Spoon mixture over tortellini. Sprinkle with cheese. Serve immediately. Yield: 6 servings.

ON THE LIGHT SIDE

A Traditional, Yet Light Holiday Menu

Christmas dinner calls for a very special menu, one that includes traditional Southern foods and pays attention to light and healthy eating. We've put together a holiday menu that does just that, and one that can be served to everyone. The good news is that it's only about 600 calories per person.

Cream of Crab Soup
Roast Turkey Breast and Gravy
Savory Cornbread Dressing
Holiday Cranberry Relish
Seasoned Green Beans
Glazed Carrots
Layered Ambrosia

CREAM OF CRAB SOUP

½ pound fresh crabmeat
¼ cup diced onion
2 tablespoons reduced-calorie margarine, melted
½ teaspoon Beau Monde seasoning
⅛ teaspoon white pepper
Dash of mace
½ teaspoon hot sauce
1 (12-ounce) can evaporated skim milk
2 tablespoons cornstarch
2 cups skim milk
¼ cup dry sherry
2 teaspoons minced fresh chives

Remove and discard cartilage from crabmeat; set aside.

Sauté onion in margarine in a large saucepan until tender. Stir in Beau Monde seasoning and next 4 ingredients; cook, stirring constantly, until mixture begins to boil. Combine cornstarch and 2 cups skim milk; gradually add to hot mixture. Bring to a boil over medium heat, stirring constantly; cook 1 minute. Reduce heat, and stir in crabmeat and sherry. Garnish with chives. Yield: 5 cups (87 calories per ½-cup serving).

□ *8.7 grams protein, 2 grams fat, 8.5 grams carbohydrate, 14 milligrams cholesterol, 349 milligrams sodium, and 174 milligrams calcium.*

ROAST TURKEY BREAST AND GRAVY
(pictured on page 305)

1 (5- to 5½-pound) turkey breast, skinned
1 medium onion
2 stalks celery, halved
Vegetable cooking spray
1½ tablespoons lemon-pepper seasoning
1½ teaspoons garlic powder
1½ teaspoons onion powder
1 teaspoon poultry seasoning
½ teaspoon paprika
Gravy (recipe follows)
Parsley sprigs (optional)

Rinse turkey breast; pat dry. Place onion and celery in breast cavity; spray breast with cooking spray. Combine lemon-pepper seasoning and next 4 ingredients; sprinkle over breast. Place breast in a browning bag prepared according to package directions; place in a shallow baking pan. Bake at 325° for 1 hour. Cut a slit in top of bag; bake an additional hour or until meat thermometer registers 170°. Transfer to a serving platter. Let stand 15 minutes; carve into thin slices. Reserve onion and pan drippings to make gravy. Garnish with parsley sprigs, if desired. Yield: 14 servings (118 calories per 3-ounce serving turkey).

□ *25.5 grams protein, 0.7 gram fat, 0.9 gram carbohydrate, 70 milligrams cholesterol, 153 milligrams sodium, and 12 milligrams calcium.*

Gravy

3 tablespoons instant nonfat dry milk
1 tablespoon all-purpose flour
½ teaspoon chicken-flavored bouillon granules
½ cup water
½ teaspoon browning-and-seasoning sauce

Pour reserved pan drippings through a gravy skimmer; reserve 1 cup broth, and discard fat. Place broth in container of an electric blender with reserved onion; process until smooth. Pour into a small saucepan; add dry milk and remaining ingredients. Bring to a boil; reduce heat, and simmer 5 minutes, stirring frequently. Yield: 2 cups (18 calories per 3-tablespoon serving).

□ *1.2 grams protein, 0 grams fat, 3 grams carbohydrate, 0 milligrams cholesterol, 57 milligrams sodium, and 30 milligrams calcium.*

SAVORY CORNBREAD DRESSING
(pictured on page 305)

1 cup yellow cornmeal
½ teaspoon baking powder
½ teaspoon baking soda
¼ teaspoon salt
¼ cup egg substitute
1 cup nonfat buttermilk
1 tablespoon reduced-calorie margarine
Butter-flavored vegetable cooking spray
5 slices whole wheat sandwich bread
6 ounces turkey sausage
1½ cups chopped onion
1 cup chopped celery
⅓ cup egg substitute
2 (10½-ounce) cans low-sodium chicken broth
1 cup evaporated skim milk
½ teaspoon poultry seasoning
¼ teaspoon freshly ground pepper
⅛ teaspoon red pepper
2 tablespoons minced fresh parsley
¼ teaspoon paprika

Combine first 4 ingredients in a medium bowl; make a well in center of mixture. Combine ¼ cup egg substitute, buttermilk, and margarine; add to dry ingredients, stirring just until moistened. Spoon into muffin pans coated with cooking spray, filling two-thirds full. Bake at 450° for 10 to 12 minutes, or until lightly browned; cool. Crumble muffins and bread slices into a large bowl.

Cook sausage, onion, and celery in a nonstick skillet coated with cooking spray until sausage is browned. Stir to crumble sausage. Drain and pat dry with paper towels.

Combine ⅓ cup egg substitute, broth, and evaporated milk; add to breadcrumbs, and let stand until liquid is absorbed. Add sausage mixture, poultry seasoning, and next 3 ingredients; stir well.

Spoon dressing into a 12- x 8- x 2-inch baking dish coated with cooking spray. Spray top of unbaked dressing with cooking spray; sprinkle with paprika. Bake at 350° for 1 hour. Yield: 10 servings (184 calories per ⅔-cup serving).

□ *9.2 grams protein, 6.1 grams fat, 22.8 grams carbohydrate, 12 milligrams cholesterol, 405 milligrams sodium, and 170 milligrams calcium.*

Buffet Tips

■ Buffet menus can include late-night desserts after a special gathering of family and friends. A selection of pastries, dessert cheeses, champagne, gourmet coffee, liqueurs, or ice cream is elegantly enticing, yet simple.

■ When planning your menu, choose dishes that are easily served in average portions. They should require only one serving spoon or fork and not need to be cut with a knife.

Cook carrots in a small amount of boiling water 5 to 8 minutes or until crisp-tender; drain. Combine remaining ingredients in a small saucepan; cook over medium heat, stirring constantly, until margarine melts. Add to carrots; toss gently until carrots are glazed. Yield: 10 servings (40 calories per ½-cup serving).

□ *0.6 gram protein, 1.3 grams fat, 7.4 grams carbohydrate, 0 milligrams cholesterol, 96 milligrams sodium, and 17 milligrams calcium.*
Sandra Hensley
San Antonio, Texas

HOLIDAY CRANBERRY RELISH
(pictured on page 305)

1 orange, unpeeled
2 cups fresh cranberries
1 cup diced, unpeeled apple
1 (8-ounce) can crushed
    unsweetened pineapple, drained
⅓ cup sugar

Position knife blade in food processor bowl. Quarter orange, remove seeds, and place fruit in processor bowl. Pulse until coarsely ground. Spoon into a medium bowl; set aside. Place cranberries in processor bowl; pulse until coarsely ground. Add cranberries and remaining ingredients to orange; mix well. Cover and chill 8 hours. Yield: 3 cups (36 calories per 3-tablespoon serving).

□ *0.3 gram protein, 0 grams fat, 10.8 grams carbohydrate, 0 milligrams cholesterol, 0 milligrams sodium, and 12 milligrams calcium.*
Sheryl Shenk
Victoria, Virginia

Tip: *Store food in coolest area of kitchen, away from oven and range.*

SEASONED GREEN BEANS
(pictured on page 305)

2 pounds fresh green beans
¼ cup chopped lean cooked ham
1 beef-flavored bouillon cube
¼ teaspoon freshly ground pepper
1½ cups water

Wash beans, and remove strings; cut beans into 1½-inch pieces. Place in a 5-quart Dutch oven; add remaining ingredients. Bring to a boil; cover, reduce heat, and simmer 20 minutes, stirring occasionally. Yield: 10 servings (37 calories per ½-cup serving).

□ *2.8 grams protein, 0.5 gram fat, 6.5 grams carbohydrate, 4 milligrams cholesterol, 48 milligrams sodium, and 34 milligrams calcium.*

GLAZED CARROTS
(pictured on page 305)

5 cups thinly sliced carrots
2 tablespoons brown sugar
1 teaspoon dry mustard
¼ teaspoon salt
¼ teaspoon hot sauce
1½ tablespoons reduced-calorie
    margarine

LAYERED AMBROSIA
(pictured on page 305)

3 cups orange sections
1 cup pink grapefruit sections
½ cup flaked coconut
1 (8-ounce) can unsweetened
    crushed pineapple, undrained
3 tablespoons honey

Arrange half of orange sections in a glass bowl; top with grapefruit sections, ¼ cup coconut, pineapple, and remaining orange sections. Drizzle with honey, and sprinkle with remaining ¼ cup coconut. Cover and chill 8 hours. Yield: 10 servings (81 calories per ½-cup serving).

□ *0.9 gram protein, 1.3 grams fat, 18.2 grams carbohydrate, 0 milligrams cholesterol, 1 milligram sodium, and 29 milligrams calcium.*

Right: *A Christmas dinner of Cream of Crab Soup, Roast Turkey Breast and Gravy, Savory Cornbread Dressing, Seasoned Green Beans, Glazed Carrots, Holiday Cranberry Relish, and Layered Ambrosia captures Southern tradition while keeping calories and fat low.*
(Recipes begin on page 302.)

Left: *A menu of Roast Turkey,
Giblet Gravy, Cranberry-Orange
Relish, and Harvest Sausage
Dressing is always appropriate for a
holiday gathering. (Recipes begin on
page 253.)*

Far Left: *Celebrate the season with
festive-colored Cranberry Percolator
Punch (page 248).*

Below: *Juicy and golden brown,
Roast Duckling With Wine Jelly (page
243) boasts the sweet flavor of
scuppernong wine.*

Step 1

Step 2

Step 3

Step 4

Step 5

Step 6

Right: *Icing and candy work together to make this Sugarplum Cottage. (The recipe is on the facing page.)*

A House Full Of Sugarplums

Both children and adults will marvel at this Sugarplum Cottage. It's coated with a hard-drying icing that acts like glue to make colorful candies and sugar sprinkles adhere.

The roof is shingled with candy citrus slices, and the door and window boxes are made of chocolate candy bars. The walkway is bricked with chewing gum and lined with gumdrop shrubbery. Ice cream cones form the base of the trees.

Icing-coated, wood-framed candy houses will last for several years if stored properly. Wrap them in a large plastic bag, and keep in a cool, dry place. In addition, the wooden frame is reusable. If you want to change the design of the candies on the house at a later time, wrap it in a plastic bag, and gently tap it all over with a hammer to loosen the icing. Remove the house from the bag, and scrape and chip away the remaining icing and candy, using a putty knife. Remaining bits of icing can be washed away with hot water. Dry the house thoroughly before storing or redecorating.

SUGARPLUM COTTAGE

4 or 5 recipes Royal Icing
About 24 candy citrus slices
Red cinnamon candies
Assorted sugar and candy sprinkles
1 piece ribbon candy
2 (4-ounce) milk chocolate candy bars
About 40 red and green oval-shaped candies
3 red lollipops
Green paste food coloring
About 6 pointed ice cream cones
About 15 sticks red chewing gum
About 40 large green gumdrops

Cut ¼-inch plywood according to dimensions in diagram. Glue pieces of house together using a hot-glue gun, or nail them using short, thin nails. Glue or nail the house to a plywood base *(Step 1)*.

Prepare 1 recipe of Royal Icing at a time. (Icing dries quickly and changes texture as it sits; keep covered at all times when not in use.) Spread icing thinly into gentle swirls on 1 side of roof *(Step 2)*.

Place 8 candy citrus slices on roof, shingle-fashion, adding additional icing to act as glue, if needed. Sprinkle red cinnamon candies on icing up on roof. Tilt house slightly, and sprinkle roof evenly with sugar sprinkles. Repeat to cover other side of roof. Place ribbon candy on roof as the chimney, adding extra icing.

Spread icing thinly in gentle swirls on 1 side of house. Cut several citrus slices into thin strips, and attach to side of house to make a window. Place a citrus slice on opposite sides of the window as shutters. Cut a candy bar to make a 2½- x 1-inch log, and press into icing as a window box. Attach flower-shaped candy sprinkles on window box, using icing. For trim, attach red and green oval candies to house just under roof, alternating colors of candy. Repeat on other side of house.

Spread icing thinly on back of house, and alternate oval candies just under roof. Repeat process on front of house. Trim and attach a candy bar for the front door. Cut away, and discard the stick from 1 lollipop, and attach lollipop as a window above door. Pipe a small amount of icing as windowpanes, using tip No. 3. Using icing, attach small round candy sprinkles around edge of window *(Step 3)*.

Color about 2 cups icing with green food coloring. Pipe leaves on ice cream cones, using tip No. 67, starting at base of cone. Hold cones by the tip as you pipe, and leave tip unfinished so that you'll have something with which to hold the trees. Set trees aside to dry *(Step 4)*.

Working on a small section at a time, spread icing thinly on plywood base, attaching trees and sprinkling with sugar candies and sprinkles as desired before icing dries. Cut chewing gum to make bricks; attach to icing to make walkway. Line walkway and house with green gumdrops as shrubbery. Insert red lollipops into gumdrops on either side of the door; coat stems with green icing *(Step 5)*.

Pipe green icing on tops of trees. To make trees look snowcapped, pipe white icing onto sides and tops of trees, using tip No. 3. Let Sugarplum Cottage dry thoroughly before transporting *(Step 6)*.

Royal Icing

3 egg whites
½ teaspoon cream of tartar
1 (16-ounce) package powdered sugar, sifted

Combine egg whites (at room temperature) and cream of tartar in a large mixing bowl. Beat at medium speed of an electric mixer until frothy. Add half of powdered sugar, mixing well. Add remaining sugar, and beat at high speed 5 to 7 minutes. Yield: about 2 cups.

Note: Icing dries quickly; always keep covered with a damp cloth.

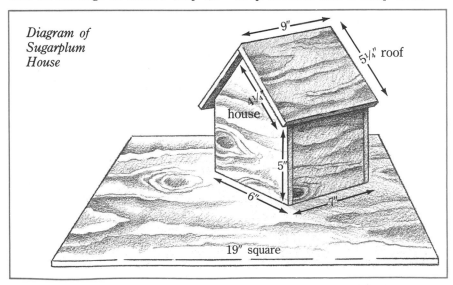

Diagram of Sugarplum House

9"

5¼" roof

4¼" house

5"

6"

7"

19" square

Glossary

à la King—Food prepared in a creamy white sauce containing mushrooms and red and/or green peppers

à la Mode—Food that is served with ice cream

al Dente—The point in the cooking of pasta at which it is still fairly firm to the tooth; that is, very slightly undercooked

Aspic—A jellied meat juice or a liquid held together with gelatin

au Gratin—Food served crusted with breadcrumbs and/or shredded cheese

au Jus—Meat served in its own juice

Bake—To cook any food in an oven by dry heat

Barbecue—To roast meat slowly over coals on a spit or framework, or to roast in an oven, basting intermittently with a special kind of sauce

Batter—A mixture of flour and liquid that is thin enough to pour

Baste—To spoon pan liquid and/or a sauce over meats while they are roasting to prevent surface from drying

Beat—To mix vigorously with a brisk motion with spoon, fork, egg beater, or electric mixer

Béchamel—A white sauce of butter, flour, cream (not milk), and seasonings

Bisque—A thick, creamy soup usually of shellfish, but sometimes made of pureed vegetables

Blanch—To dip food briefly into boiling water

Blend—To stir 2 or more ingredients together until well mixed

Blintz—A cooked crêpe stuffed with cheese or other filling

Boil—To cook food in boiling water or liquid that is mostly water (at 212°F. at sea level) in which bubbles constantly rise to the surface and burst

Boiling-water-bath canning method—Used for processing acid foods, such as fruit, tomatoes, pickled vegetables, and sauerkraut. These acid foods are canned safely at boiling temperatures in a water-bath canner

Borscht—Soup containing beets and other vegetables; it is usually made with a meat stock base

Bouillabaisse—A highly seasoned fish soup or chowder containing two or more kinds of fish

Bouillon—Clear soup made by boiling meat in water

Bouquet Garni—Herbs tied in cheesecloth which are cooked in a mixture and removed before serving

Bourguignon—Name applied to dishes containing Burgundy and often braised onions and mushrooms

Braise—To cook slowly with a small amount of liquid in a covered utensil (less tender cuts of meat may be browned slowly first on all sides in a small amount of shortening; then the meat is seasoned, and water is added)

Bread, to—To coat with crumbs, usually in combination with egg or other binder

Broil—To cook by direct heat, either under the heat of a broiler, over hot coals, or between two hot surfaces

Broth—A thin soup, or a liquid in which meat, fish, or vegetables have been cooked

Brown—To cook in a skillet or oven or under a broiler until brown

Bruise—To partially crush an ingredient, such as herbs, to release flavor for seasoning food

Capers—Buds from a Mediterranean plant, usually packed in brine and used as a condiment in dressings or sauces

Caramelize—To cook white sugar in a skillet over medium heat, stirring constantly, until the sugar forms a golden-brown syrup

Casserole—An ovenproof baking dish, usually with a cover; also the food cooked inside it

Charlotte—A molded dessert containing gelatin, usually formed in a glass dish or a pan that is lined with ladyfingers or pieces of cake

Clarified butter—Butter that has been melted and chilled. The solid is then lifted away from the liquid and discarded. Clarification heightens the smoke point of butter. Clarified butter will stay fresh in the refrigerator for at least 2 months

Coat—To cover completely, as in "coat with flour"

Cocktail—An appetizer; either a beverage or a light, highly seasoned food served before a meal

Coddle—To gently poach in barely simmering water

Compote—Mixed fruit, raw or cooked, usually served in "compote" dishes

Condiments—Seasonings that enhance the flavor of foods with which they are served

Consommé—Clear broth that is made from meat

Cool—To let food stand at room temperature until not warm to the touch

Court Bouillon—A highly seasoned broth made with water and meat, fish or vegetables, and seasonings

Cream, to—To blend together, as sugar and butter, until mixture takes on a smooth, creamy texture

Cream, whipped—Cream that has been whipped until it is stiff

Crème de Cacao—A chocolate-flavored liqueur

Crème de Café—A coffee-flavored liqueur, sometimes used in cooking

Crêpes—Very thin pancakes

Crimp—To seal pastry edges together by pinching

Croquette—Minced food, shaped like a ball, patty, cone, or log, bound with a heavy sauce, breaded, and fried

Croutons—Cubes of bread, toasted or fried, served with soups or salads

Cruller—A doughnut of twisted shape, very light in texture

Cube, to—To cut food into cube-shaped pieces

Curaçao—An orange-flavored liqueur

Cut in, to—To incorporate by cutting or chopping motions, as in cutting shortening into flour for pastry

Demitasse—A small cup of coffee served after dinner

Devil, to—To prepare with spicy seasoning or sauce

Dice—To cut into small cubes

Dissolve—To mix a dry substance with liquid until the dry substance becomes a part of the solution

Dot—To scatter small bits of butter over top of a food

Dust—To lightly sprinkle with a dry ingredient, such as flour

Dredge—To coat with something, usually flour or sugar

Filé—Powder made of sassafras leaves used to season and thicken foods

Fillet—Boneless piece of meat or fish

310

Flambé—To flame, using alcohol as the burning agent; flame causes caramelization, enhancing flavor

Flan—In France, a filled pastry; in Spain, a custard

Florentine—A food containing or placed upon spinach

Flour—To coat with flour

Flute—To make a decorative edge on pastry

Fold—To add a whipped ingredient, such as cream or egg white, to another ingredient by very gentle over-and-under movement

Frappé—A drink whipped with ice to make a thick, frosty consistency

Fricassee—A stew, usually of poultry or veal

Fritter—Vegetable or fruit dipped into, or combined with, batter and fried

Fry—To cook in hot shortening

Garnish—A decoration for a food or a drink

Glaze (To make a shiny surface)—In meat preparation, a jelled broth applied to meat surface; in breads and pastries, a wash of egg or syrup; for doughnuts and cakes, a sugar preparation for coating

Grate—To obtain small particles of food by rubbing on a grater or shredder

Grill—To broil under or over a source of direct heat

Grits—Coarsely ground dried corn, served boiled, or boiled and then fried

Gumbo—Soup or stew made with okra

Herb—Aromatic plant used for seasoning and garnishing foods

Hollandaise—A sauce made of butter, egg, and lemon juice or vinegar

Jardinière—Vegetables in a savory sauce or soup

Julienne—Vegetables cut into strips or a soup containing such vegetables

Kahlúa—A coffee-flavored liqueur

Kirsch—A cherry-flavored brandy

Knead—To work a food (usually dough) by hand, using a folding-back and pressing-forward motion

Marinade—A seasoned liquid in which food is soaked

Marinate, to—To soak food in a seasoned liquid

Meringue—A whole family of egg white-sugar preparations including pie topping, poached meringue used to top custard, crisp meringue dessert shells, and divinity candy

Mince—To chop into very fine pieces

Mornay—White sauce with egg, cream, and cheese added

Mousse—A molded dish based on meat or sweet whipped cream stiffened with egg white and/or gelatin (if mousse contains ice cream, it is called bombe)

Panbroil—To cook over direct heat in an uncovered skillet containing little or no shortening

Panfry—To cook in an uncovered skillet in small amount of shortening

Parboil—To partially cook in boiling water before final cooking

Pare—To shave away the skins of fruits or vegetables

Pasta—A large family of flour paste products, such as spaghetti, macaroni, and noodles

Pâté (French for paste)—A paste made of liver or meat

Petit Four—A small cake, which has been frosted and decorated

Pilau or pilaf—A dish of the Middle East consisting of rice and meat or vegetables in a seasoned stock

Pipe—To squeeze a smooth, shapeable mixture through a decorating bag to make decorative shapes

Poach—To cook in liquid held below the boiling point

Preheat—To turn on oven so that desired temperature will be reached before food is inserted for baking

Puree—A thick sauce or paste made by forcing cooked food through a sieve

Reduce—To boil down, evaporating liquid from a cooked dish

Rémoulade—A rich mayonnaise-based sauce containing anchovy paste, capers, herbs, and mustard

Render—To melt fat away from surrounding meat

Rind—Outer shell or peel of fruit

Roast, to—To cook in oven by dry heat (usually refers to meats)

Roux—A mixture of butter and flour used to thicken gravies and sauces; it may be white or brown, if mixture is browned before liquid is added

Sauté—To fry food lightly over fairly high heat in a small amount of fat in a shallow, open pan

Scald—To heat milk just below the boiling point; to dip certain foods into boiling water before freezing them (procedure is also called blanching)

Scallop—A bivalve mollusk of which only the muscle hinge is eaten; to bake food in a sauce topped with crumbs

Score—To cut shallow gashes on surface of food, as in scoring fat on ham before glazing

Sear—To brown surface of meat over high heat to seal in juices

Set—Term used to describe the consistency of gelatin when it has jelled enough to unmold

Shred—Break into thread-like or stringy pieces, usually by rubbing over the surface of a vegetable shredder

Simmer—To cook gently at a temperature below boiling point

Soufflé—A spongy hot dish, made from a sweet or savory mixture (often milk or cheese), lightened by stiffly beaten egg whites or whipped cream

Steam—To cook food with steam either in a pressure cooker, on a platform in a covered pan, or in a special steamer

Steam-pressure canning method—Used for processing low-acid foods, such as meats, fish, poultry, and most vegetables. A temperature higher than a boiling temperature is required to can these foods safely. The food is processed in a steam-pressure canner at 10 pounds' pressure (240°) to ensure that all of the spoilage micro-organisms are destroyed

Steep—To let food, such as tea, stand in not quite boiling water until the flavor is extracted

Stew—A mixture of meat or fish and vegetables cooked by simmering in its own juices along with other liquid, such as water and/or wine

Stir-fry—To cook quickly in oil over high heat, using light tossing and stirring motions to preserve shape of food

Stock— The broth in which meat, poultry, fish, or vegetables has been cooked

Syrupy—Thickened to about the consistency of egg white

Toast, to—To brown by direct heat, as in a toaster or under broiler

Torte—A round cake, sometimes made with breadcrumbs instead of flour

Tortilla—A Mexican flat bread made of corn or wheat flour

Toss—To mix together with light tossing motions, in order not to bruise delicate food, such as salad greens

Triple Sec—An orange-flavored liqueur

Truss, to—To tie or secure with string or skewers the legs and wings of poultry or game in order to make the bird easier to manage during cooking

Veal—Flesh of milk-fed calf up to 14 weeks of age

Velouté—White sauce made of flour, butter, and a chicken or veal stock, instead of milk

Vinaigrette—A cold sauce of oil and vinegar flavored with parsley, finely chopped onions, and other seasonings; served with cold meats or vegetables or as a dressing with salad greens

Whip—To beat rapidly to increase air and increase volume

Wok—A round bowl-shaped metal cooking utensil of Chinese origin used for stir-frying and steaming (with rack inserted) of various foods

Zest—Gratings of the colored portion of citrus skin

Recipe Title Index

An alphabetical listing of every recipe by exact title
All microwave recipe page numbers are preceded by an "M"

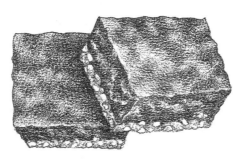

Month-by-Month Index

An alphabetical listing within the month of every food article and accompanying recipes
All microwave recipe page numbers are preceded by an "M"

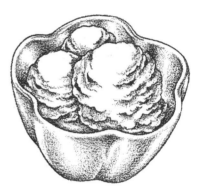

General Recipe Index

A listing of every recipe by food category and/or major ingredient
All microwave recipe page numbers are preceded by an "M"

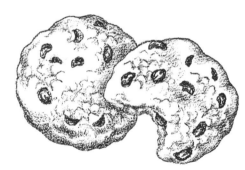

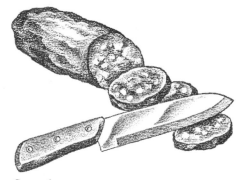

Dates
Brownies, Date-and-Almond, 217
Chocolate Date-Nut Delight, 168
Cookies, Christmas Date, 287

Desserts. *See also* specific types.
Alaska, Peachy Melba, 266
Apple Dumplings with Orange Hard
  Sauce, 224
Apples, Melting, 19
Bananas Foster, 20
Bavarian Cream with Fresh Fruit, 137
Berries with Raspberry Custard Sauce,
  Fresh, 163
Blueberry Dream, 94
Brownie Ice Cream Sandwich Shells, 195
Caramel Surprise, 202
Cherries à la Mode, 202
Cherries Sabayon, 178
Chocolate
  Cream, Heavenly Chocolate, 128
  Date-Nut Delight, Chocolate, 168
  Pots de Crème, Mocha, M45
  Shells with Kahlúa Cream,
    Chocolate, 195
  Trifle, Chocolate, 258
  Truffle Dessert, Chocolate, 281
  Waffles with Strawberry Cream,
    Chocolate, 153
Crème Celeste, 94
Crêpes, Dessert, 134
Éclairs, Minted Miniature, 66
Flan, 247

Frozen
  Chocolate Mint Freeze, 167
  Coffee Dessert, Light, 260
  Coffee Tortoni, Creamy, 268
  Fruit Freeze, Holiday, 283
  Fruit Ice, Mixed, 85
  Fudge-Peanut Ice Cream
    Dessert, 167
  Ice Cream Dessert, Mint, 66
  Ozark Pudding, Frozen, 127
  Peanut Butter Delight, Frozen, 137
  Pumpkin Dessert, Frozen, 167
Fruit
  Compote, Gingered Fruit, 184
  Lemon Curd, Fresh Fruit with, 21
Layered Ambrosia, 304
Lemon Dessert, Layered, 134
Madeleines, 79
Pancakes, Dessert Ginger, 153
Pancakes, Luau Dessert, 154
Parfaits, Chocolate-Peppermint, 65
Pear Fans with Raspberry-Orange Sauce,
  Poached, 22

Pears in Custard, Poached, 20
Pears with Raspberry Sauce,
  Poached, 223
Pineapple 'n' Cream, 202
Pumpkin Chiffon, 260
Pumpkin Chiffon Dessert, 128
Sauces
  Almond-Vanilla Custard Sauce, M177
  Apricot-Walnut Hard Sauce, 153
  Berry Sauce, 135
  Blueberry Sauce, 155
  Brandy Sauce, 279
  Buttered Rum Sauce, Hot, 204
  Caramel-Raisin Sauce, 127
  Chocolate Sauce, Creamy, M177
  Cranberry Sauce, 280
  Custard Sauce, 154, 251, 259
  Golden Sauce, 267
  Hot Cinnamon Sauce, Apple Pie
    with, 210
  Orange Hard Sauce, 225
  Pineapple-Rhubarb Sauce, 94
  Raspberry-Amaretto Sauce, 130
  Raspberry-Orange Sauce, 22
  Raspberry Sauce, 267
  Rhubarb Sauce, Chilled, 94
  Rum Sauce, 32
  Strawberry Sauce, Brandied, 196
Sopaipillas, 112
Soufflé, Chilled Devonshire, 279
Strawberries Marsala, 171
Strawberries Romanoff, 95
Strawberry Coconut Nests, 136
Toffee Dessert, English, 136
Trifle, Easy Strawberry, 201
Trifle, Lemon-Blueberry, 210
Trifle, Raspberry, 259

Dressings. *See* Stuffings and Dressings.
Duck and Duckling
Roast Duckling with Wine Jelly, 243
Dumplings
Apple Dumplings with Orange Hard
  Sauce, 224
Tomato Dumplings, 144

Eggplant
Caviar, Eggplant, 262
Crawfish on Eggplant, Soft-Shell, 222
Fried Eggplant, 111
Eggs
Chile Eggs, 80
Ham and Eggs à la Swiss, 158
Herb Sauce, Eggs in, 80
Omelet, Easy Mexican, 114
Patty Shells, Mushrooms and
  Eggs in, 197
Rancheros, Easy Eggs, 81
Roulade with Mushroom Filling, Egg, 84
Stuffed Eggs, 95
Enchiladas
Bean Enchiladas, Spicy, 18

Fajitas
Beef Fajitas, 233
Chicken Fajitas, 231
Fettuccine
Spinach, Fettuccine and, 90
Spinach Fettuccine, Easy Chicken with, 89
Fillings. *See* Frostings.

Fish. *See also* specific types and Seafood.
Almond Baked Fish, 270
Catfish, Crisp-Fried, 110
Catfish, Lemon Barbecued, 271
Catfish Stew, Cajun-Style, 12
Ceviche, Mexican-Style, 115
Crawfish on Eggplant, Soft-Shell, 222
Fillets, Apple-Carrot Stuffed, M192
Flounder, Broiled, 28
Flounder Stuffed with Shrimp, 51
Grouper with Confetti Vegetables, M189
Haddock Fillets with Zucchini
  Stuffing, M191
Halibut Steaks Italiano, M191
Italian Fish, 270
Mahi Mahi, Macadamia, 164
Orange Roughy with Spinach Pesto, M192
Seasoning Blend, Fish-and-Seafood, 28
Skillet Fish Dinner, 199
Snapper Destin, 222
Snapper, Orangy, 23
Snapper Veracruz, Red, 149
Trout Laurie, 270

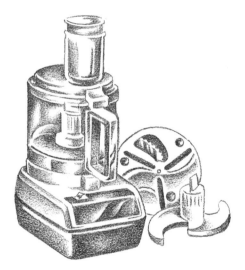

Food Processor
Appetizers
  Dip, Sugar Snap, 91
  Pâté, Chicken Liver, M132
Butter, Green Peppercorn, 60
Crêpes, Basic Processor, 135
Crêpes, Mushroom-Cheese, 135
Desserts
  Crêpes, Dessert, 134
  Crêpes, Strawberry Ice Cream, 135
  Sorbet, Avocado, 117
  Sorbet, Banana-Orange, 117
  Sorbet, Pear-Lemon, 116
  Sorbet, Strawberry, 117
  Tart Shells, 4
Dressing, Creamy Lemon, M193
Sauces and Gravies
  Berry Sauce, 135
  Pumpkin Seed Sauce, 246
Tomatoes, Crab-Stuffed Cherry, 78
Frankfurters
Beans, Stove-Top Franks 'n', 201
Casserole, Hot Doggie, 200
Potluck Dish, Frankaroni, 201
Saucy Franks, 201

Ice Creams and Sherbets
(continued)

Strawberry Sorbet, 117
Tea Granita, Mint, 117
Toffee Ice Cream, 202
Vanilla Ice Cream, Basic, 202

Jams and Jellies
Christmas Jam, 288
Wine Jelly, 243
Jicama
Salad, Jicama-and-Orange, 246

Kabobs
Turkey-and-Fruit Kabobs, 140
Vegetable Kabobs, Tangy
  Marinated, 142
Venison Kabobs, 249
Kiwifruit
Tart, Kiwifruit-Peach, 20

Lamb
Burgers, Mesquite-Grilled
  Lamb, 59
Chops with Shrimp, Lamb, 58
Roasted Lamb Rosemary, 244
Stew, Lamb, 58
Lasagna
Cheesy Lasagna, 299
Chicken Lasagna, 90
Florentine, Lasagna, 196
Leeks
Medley, Carrot-and-Leek, 102
Orange Sauce, Leeks in, 86
Quiche, Cheddar-Leek, 198

Lemon
Beans, Lemon-Mint, 22
Beverages
  Buttered Lemonade, Hot, 208
  Orange-Mint Lemonade, 82
  Punch, Sparkling Lemonade, 276
Broccoli, Lemon, 119
Cabbage, Lemon-Butter, 156
Catfish, Lemon Barbecued, 271
Chicken and Vegetables, Lemon, 118
Chicken, Lemon-Frosted, 170
Chicken Piccata, Herbed, 28
Desserts
  Cake, General Robert E. Lee
    Orange-Lemon, 92
  Cake, Tart Lemon-Cheese, 7
  Curd, Fresh Fruit with Lemon, 21

Filling, Lemon-Cheese, 7
Frosting, Lemony White, 7
Frosting, Orange-Lemon, 92
Ice Cream, Lemonade, 202
Layered Lemon Dessert, 134
Meringue, Chocolate Pudding with
  Lemon, 258
Pie, Buttermilk-Lemon, 297
Pie, Buttermilk-Lemon Cream, 99
Pie, Lemon-Strawberry, 127
Pudding, Old-Fashioned Lemon
  Bread, 95
Sorbet, Pear-Lemon, 116
Soufflés, Quick Lemon Sauce, 43
Soufflé with Raspberry-Amaretto
  Sauce, Frozen Lemon, 130
Tart Shells, Lemon, 195
Trifle, Lemon-Blueberry, 210
Dressing, Chilled Broccoli with
  Lemon, 270
Dressing, Creamy Lemon, M193
Linguine with Garlic and Lemon, 91
Muffins, Lemon, 119, M275
Pork Chops, Lemony, 118
Potato Wedges, Lemon, 21
Sauce, Lemon Meunière, 222
Sauce, Lemony Barbecue, M177
Shrimp, Luscious Lemon, 150
Slaw or Salad Dressing,
  Lemon-Yogurt, 54
Lime
Soup, Lime, 31
Tart, Lime-Pineapple, 6
Linguine
Clam Sauce, Linguine with, 90
Garlic and Lemon, Linguine with, 91

Macaroni
Cheese, Macaroni and, M147, M190
Mangoes
Beef and Rice, Mango-, 138
Pie, Mango-Ginger, 138
Manicotti
Special Manicotti, 50
Stuffed Manicotti, Spinach-, 255
Mayonnaise
Aioli (garlic mayonnaise), 221
Meatballs
Royal Meatballs, 102
Meat Loaf. *See* Beef, Ground/Meat Loaf.
Melons
Balls, Mellowed-Out Melon, 182
Cantaloupe-Cheese Salad, 184
Cantaloupe Meringue Pie, 182
Cantaloupe Sherbet, 183
Cantaloupe Soup, 160
Salad with Dill Dressing,
  Melon, 182
Meringues
Asparagus Meringue, 131
Holiday Meringues, 280
Strawberry Meringue Torte, 136
Microwave
Appetizers
  Brie Appetizer, Bit-of-, M8
  Dip, Chipped Beef, M8
  Dip, Shrimp, M261
  Mushrooms, Spinach-Stuffed, M261
  Pâté, Chicken Liver, M132
  Spread, Chicken Salad Party, M8

Breads
  Chocolate Loaf Bread, M188
  Muffins, Cheesy Cornbread, M275
  Muffins, Cranberry Streusel
    Cake, M274
  Muffins, Lemon, M275
  Muffins, Whole Wheat Bran, M274
Chutney, Autumn Fruit, M230
Desserts
  Cookies, Chocolate-Almond
    Surprise, M45
  Crust, Graham Cracker, M45
  Fudge, Quick-and-Easy, M190
  Ice Cream Cake for
    Grown-Ups, M192
  Pie, Best-Ever Chocolate, M45
  Pie, Quick Pumpkin, M230
  Pots de Crème, Mocha, M45
Fruit Mélange, M295
Macaroni and Cheese, M147, M190
Main Dishes
  Chicken-and-Vegetable Platter, M52
  Chicken Divan Quiche, M125
  Chicken with Noodles, Sesame, M125
  Chili, Turkey-Bean, M213
  Fillets, Apple-Carrot Stuffed, M192
  Grouper with Confetti
    Vegetables, M189
  Haddock Fillets with Zucchini
    Stuffing, M191
  Halibut Steaks Italiano, M191
  Ham, Sweet-and-Sour Glazed, M15
  Meat Loaf, Basic, M14
  Meat Loaf, Easy, M214
  Orange Roughy with Spinach
    Pesto, M192
  Paella, Party, M189
  Peppers, Hearty Stuffed, M214
  Pot Roast, Company, M14
  Pot Roast with Vegetables,
    Marinated, M52
  Tacos, Microwave, M213
Pumpkin, Cooked Fresh, M230
Pumpkin Seeds, Toasted, M230
Salads
  Artichokes with Orzo Salad, M193
  Chicken Salad, Special, M193
  Fruit Salad with Mint Sauce, M96
  Pork-and-Spinach Salad,
    Mandarin, M126
  Potato Salad, German-Style, M194
Sandwiches
  Asparagus-and-Ham Melt
    Sandwiches, M96
  Pork Sandwiches, Party, M273
Sauces and Gravies
  Almond-Vanilla Custard Sauce, M177
  Barbecue Sauce, Lemony, M177
  Chocolate Sauce, Creamy, M177
  Hollandaise Sauce, M177
  Horseradish-Mustard Sauce,
    Creamy, M177
  Horseradish Sauce, M273
  Mint Sauce, M96
Soups and Stews
  Ham Chowder, Creamy, M53
  Pea Soup, Spring, M96
Topping, Streusel, M275
Vegetables
  Asparagus-Pea Casserole, M294
  Beans, Herbed Green, M190

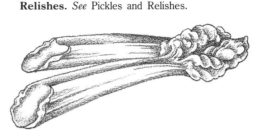

Sauerkraut
  Pork Chops and Sauerkraut, 98
Sausage
  Bake, Creole Sausage-and-Rice, 58
  Bake, Hominy-Sausage, 51
  Bake, Sausage-Cheese, 58
  Basic Sausage, 104
  Brunch for a Bunch, 57
  Casserole, Sausage-Chile Rellenos, 52
  Country Sausage, 104
  Country Sausage, Spiced, 104
  Crêpes, Sausage, 295
  Dressing, Harvest Sausage, 254
  Garlic Sausage, 104
  Italian Sausage, 104
  Italian Sausage Brunch, 57
  Italian Sausage Soup with Tortellini, 46
  Italian Sausage Supper, 164
  Jambalaya, Chicken-and-Sausage, 200
  Loaves, Sausage-Cheese, 235
  Muffins, Sausage, 52
  Pintos and Sausage, Hearty, 296
  Pizza, Breakfast, 288
  Rollups, Sausage-Bacon, 51
  Stuffing, Crown Roast of Pork with
     Cranberry-Sausage, 49
  Sweet-and-Sour Sausage, 296
  Tarts, Sausage 'n' Cheese, 51
  Turnovers, Sausage-Cheese, 231
Scallops
  Sauté, Scallop, 28
Seafood. *See also* specific types and Fish.
  Appetizer, Layered Seafood, 2
  Hot Brown, Seafood, 158
  Paella, Chicken-Seafood, 68
  Paella, Party, M189
  Seasoning Blend, Fish-and-Seafood, 28
Seasonings
  Fish-and-Seafood Seasoning Blend, 28
  Meat Seasoning Blend, 29
  Poultry Seasoning Blend, 28
  Vegetable Seasoning Blend, 29
Sherbets. *See* Ice Creams and Sherbets.
Shrimp
  Appetizer, Layered Seafood, 2
  Bayou, Shrimp, 261
  Chicken Breasts, Stuffed, 50
  Dilled Shrimp, 150
  Dip, Shrimp, M261
  Flounder Stuffed with Shrimp, 51
  Jalapeños, Shrimp-Stuffed, 115
  Lamb Chops with Shrimp, 58
  Lemon Shrimp, Luscious, 150
  Paella, Chicken-Seafood, 68
  Paella, Party, M189
  Pasta Medley, Shrimp-, 302
  Salad, Grapefruit-and-Shrimp, 5
  Salad, Layered Shrimp, 100
  Salad, Shrimp Vermicelli, 139
  Salad with Shrimp, Green, 49
  Scampi, Quick, 301
  Steak and Shrimp, 123
  Stew over Grits, Shrimp, 126
  Sweet-and-Sour Shrimp and
     Chicken, 103
Soufflés
  Apricot Soufflé, Baked, 267
  Blintz Soufflé, 155
  Cheese Soufflé, Cream, 11
  Corn-and-Cheese Soufflé, 122
  Devonshire Soufflé, Chilled, 279

  Lemon Sauce Soufflés, Quick, 43
  Lemon Soufflé with Raspberry-Amaretto
     Sauce, Frozen, 130
Soups. *See also* Chili, Chowders, Stews.
  Avocado Soup, 160
  Bean Soup, Black, 30, 266
  Bisque, Crab, 251
  Broccoli Soup, Cream-of-, 56
  Butternut-and-Apple Soup, Creamed, 228
  Cantaloupe Soup, 160
  Carrot Soup, Cream of, 46
  Cauliflower Soup, Cream of, 12
  Chicken-and-Rice Soup, 236
  Chicken-Noodle Soup, Chunky, 12
  Chicken-Vegetable Soup, 18
  Crab Soup, Cream of, 302
  Fruit Soup, Chilled Fresh, 160
  Green Pepper Soup, 250
  Guadalajara Soup, 30
  Lime Soup, 31
  Mushroom Soup, Chunky, 12
  Pea Soup, Spring, M96
  Potato-Beet Soup, 156
  Potato-Carrot Soup, 297
  Potato-Cucumber Soup, Cold, 160
  Potato Soup, Sweet, 250
  Sausage Soup with Tortellini, Italian, 46
  Split Pea Soup, 235
  Strawberry Soup, 160
  Tomato Consommé, 250
  Tomato Soup, Cold, 160
  Tomato Soup Plus, 170
  Tortilla Soup, 31, 245
  Turkey-Vegetable Soup, 264
  Vegetable-Beef Soup, 296
  Vegetable-Beef Soup, Spicy, 11
  Vegetable Soup, 266
  Watercress Soup, 104
Spaghetti
  Pepperoni Spaghetti, Quick, 40
Spinach
  Bake, Spinach-Cheese, 10
  Bake, Spinach-Ricotta, 97
  Casserole, Spinach-Artichoke, 252
  Chicken Breasts, Fried
     Spinach-Stuffed, 206
  con Queso, Easy Spinach, 101
  Dip, Creamy Spinach, 132
  Fettuccine and Spinach, 90
  Fettuccine, Easy Chicken with Spinach, 89
  Florentine, Lasagna, 196
  Florentine, Turkey, 264
  Manicotti, Spinach-Stuffed, 255
  Mushrooms, Spinach-Stuffed, 131, M261
  Pesto, Orange Roughy with
     Spinach, M192
  Phyllo Triangles, Spinach-Ricotta, 212
  Pie, Spinach, 56
  Pitas, Spinach-Walnut, 43
  Rolls, Spinach-Ham, 78
  Salads
     Citrus Dressing, Spinach Salad
        with, 133
     Pork-and-Spinach Salad,
        Mandarin, M126
     Spinach Salad, 299
  Spread, Spinach, 132
  Squares, Spinach, 131
  Timbales, Spinach-Rice, 271
  Tomatoes, Spinach-Topped, 265
  Tortellini with Tomato Sauce, Spinach, 302

Spreads. *See also* Appetizers/Spreads.
  Broccamoli Curry Spread, 55
  Cheese, Herbed, 152
  Chicken Salad Party Spread, M8
  Spinach Spread, 132
  Watercress Spread, 103

Squash. *See also* Zucchini.
  Apple-and-Pecan-Filled Squash, 228
  Butternut-and-Apple Soup, Creamed, 228
  Cajun Squash, 142
  Pattypan Squash, Stuffed, 142
  Rosemary, Summer Squash with, 143
  Spaghetti Squash with Meat Sauce, M180
  Turban Squash, Stuffed Turks, 228
  Yellow
     Casserole, Yellow Squash, 166
     Country Club Squash, M16
     Croquettes, Squash, 142
     Quiche, Squash-and-Green Chile, 143
Stews. *See also* Chili, Soups.
  Beef Stew, Burgundy, 234
  Burgoo, Kentucky, 235
  Catfish Stew, Cajun-Style, 12
  Lamb Stew, 58
  Pollo en Pipián, Mexican, 31
  Shrimp Stew over Grits, 126
Strawberries
  Banana-Berry Flip, 215
  Cobbler, Strawberry-Rhubarb, 93
  Cream, Strawberry, 153
  Ice Cream Crêpes, Strawberry, 135
  Ice Cream, Strawberry-Banana-Nut, 203
  Jam, Christmas, 288
  Marsala, Strawberries, 171
  Mimosa, Sparkling Strawberry, 169
  Nests, Strawberry Coconut, 136
  Pie, Lemon-Strawberry, 127
  Pie, Strawberry Angel, 136
  Raspberry Custard Sauce, Fresh Berries
     with, 163
  Romanoff, Strawberries, 95
  Sauce, Berry, 135
  Sauce, Brandied Strawberry, 196
  Shortcake, A Favorite Strawberry, 136
  Shortcake, Elegant Strawberry, 37
  Shortcake Jubilee, Strawberry, 209
  Shortcake Shells, Strawberry, 196
  Sorbet, Strawberry, 117
  Soup, Strawberry, 160
  Tea, Strawberry, 248
  Torte, Strawberry Meringue, 136
  Trifle, Easy Strawberry, 201
Stuffings and Dressings
  Cornbread Dressing, 254
  Cornbread Dressing, Savory, 303
  Cranberry-Sausage Stuffing, Crown Roast
     of Pork with, 49